Year 2000

Best Practices for Y2K Millennium Computing

Year 2000

Dick Lefkon

Editor

PRENTICE HALL PTR
UPPER SADDLE RIVER, NEW JERSEY 07458
http://www.phptr.com

ISBN 0-13-646506-4

9 780136 465065

90000

Library of Congress Cataloging-in-Publication Data

```
CIP
Year 2000 : best practices for Y2K millennium computing / Dick
    Lefkon,
  editor.
      p.   cm.
   ISBN 0-13-646506-4
   1. Software maintenance.  2. Year 2000 date conversion (Computer
systems)  I. Lefkon, Dick
QA76.76.S64Y44  1997
005.1'6--dc21                                        97-31257
                                                     CIP
```

Acquisitions Editor: *Bernard M. Goodwin*
Editorial/Production Supervision and Interior Design: *Dit Mosco*
Cover Art & Design Director: *Jerry Votta*
Cover Design: *Anthony Gemmellaro*
Marketing Manager: *Dan Rush*
Manufacturing Manager: *Alexis R. Heydt*

©1998 by Prentice Hall PTR
Prentice-Hall, Inc.
A Simon & Schuster Company
Upper Saddle River, New Jersey 07458

Prentice Hall books are widely used by corporations and government agencies
for training, marketing, and resale.

The publisher offers discounts on this book when ordered in bulk quantities.
For more information, contact Corporate Sales Department, Phone: 800-382-3419; FAX: 201-236-7141;
E-mail: corpsales@prenhall.com
Or write: Prentice Hall PTR, Corporate Sales Dept. One Lake Street, Upper Saddle River, NJ 07458.

Printed in the United States of America
10 9 8 7 6 5 4 3 2 1

ISBN 0-13-646506-4

Prentice-Hall International (UK) Limited, *London*
Prentice-Hall of Australia Pty. Limited, *Sydney*
Prentice-Hall Canada Inc., *Toronto*
Prentice-Hall Hispanoamericana, S.A., *Mexico*
Prentice-Hall of India Private Limited, *New Delhi*
Prentice-Hall of Japan, Inc., *Tokyo*
Simon & Schuster Asia Pte. Ltd., *Singapore*
Editora Prentice-Hall do Brasil, Ltda., *Rio de Janeiro*

Dedicated to Hinda and Irv,

who inspired a people
to
greet each New Year

Contents

Part 8   **Expert: Date Details**   **365**

Part 9   **Expert: Early Testing**   **427**

WILLIAM F. CLINGER, JR., PENNSYLVANIA
CHAIRMAN

BENJAMIN A. GILMAN, NEW YORK
DAN BURTON, INDIANA
J DENNIS HASTERT, ILLINOIS
CONSTANCE A. MORELLA, MARYLAND
CHRISTOPHER SHAYS, CONNECTICUT
STEVEN SCHIFF, NEW MEXICO
ILEANA ROS-LEHTINEN, FLORIDA
WILLIAM H. ZELIFF, JR., NEW HAMPSHIRE
JOHN M. McHUGH, NEW YORK
STEPHEN HORN, CALIFORNIA
JOHN L. MICA, FLORIDA
PETER BLUTE, MASSACHUSETTS
THOMAS M. DAVIS, VIRGINIA
DAVID M. McINTOSH, INDIANA
JON D. FOX, PENNSYLVANIA
RANDY TATE, WASHINGTON
DICK CHRYSLER, MICHIGAN
GIL GUTKNECHT, MINNESOTA
MARK E. SOUDER, INDIANA
WILLIAM J. MARTINI, NEW JERSEY
JOE SCARBOROUGH, FLORIDA
JOHN SHADEGG, ARIZONA
MICHAEL PATRICK FLANAGAN, ILLINOIS
CHARLES F. BASS, NEW HAMPSHIRE
STEVE C. LaTOURETTE, OHIO
MARSHALL "MARK" SANFORD, SOUTH CAROLINA
ROBERT L. EHRLICH, JR., MARYLAND

CARDISS COLLINS, ILLINOIS
RANKING MINORITY MEMBER
HENRY A. WAXMAN, CALIFORNIA
TOM LANTOS, CALIFORNIA
ROBERT E. WISE, JR., WEST VIRGINIA
MAJOR R. OWENS, NEW YORK
EDOLPHUS TOWNS, NEW YORK
JOHN M. SPRATT, JR., SOUTH CAROLINA
LOUISE McINTOSH SLAUGHTER, NEW YORK
PAUL E. KANJORSKI, PENNSYLVANIA
GARY A. CONDIT, CALIFORNIA
COLLIN C. PETERSON, MINNESOTA
KAREN L. THURMAN, FLORIDA
CAROLYN B. MALONEY, NEW YORK
THOMAS M. BARRETT, WISCONSIN
BARBARA-ROSE COLLINS, MICHIGAN
ELEANOR HOLMES NORTON, DC
JAMES P. MORAN, VIRGINIA
GENE GREEN, TEXAS
CARRIE P. MEEK, FLORIDA
CHAKA FATTAH, PENNSYLVANIA
BILL K. BREWSTER, OKLAHOMA
TIM HOLDEN, PENNSYLVANIA

BERNARD SANDERS, VERMONT
INDEPENDENT

MAJORITY—(202) 225-5074
MINORITY—(202) 225-5051

ONE HUNDRED FOURTH CONGRESS

Congress of the United States

House of Representatives

COMMITTEE ON GOVERNMENT REFORM AND OVERSIGHT

2157 RAYBURN HOUSE OFFICE BUILDING

WASHINGTON, DC 20515-6143

Statement of Representative Stephen Horn

Chair, Subcommittee on Government Management, Information and Technology
Congress of the United States, House of Representatives

Year 2000 is a very serious problem and that is what Congress has tried to point out. As you probably know, the Gartner Group said it's a 600 billion dollar worldwide problem, and a 300 billion U.S. problem—and what obviously got our attention in our oversight role was the 30 billion dollars that it might cost the Federal government.

Those figures could be a little high, but I think there's a wakeup call. My interest—and the collective interest of AITP SIG-Mainframe and the groups that testified before us who are dealing with this issue—is that we have to make sure the executives of organizations are well aware of the implications of not moving on this question now.

The clock is ticking, and the resources that are knowledgeable in this area will be gobbled up by the people who are ahead of the curve. The others will come dragging along, sort of like the children's story of who prepares for winter and who doesn't.

So I thank AITP SIG-Mainframe for calling attention to Year 2000. The Congressional committees will continue to call attention to it; our aim has been to send a wake-up call to the Cabinet Secretaries.

As you perhaps know we questioned 24 different major departments and independent agencies in the Federal Government. Since I'm a university professor on leave, I believe in grading on an absolute, not the curve. Some might recall they made it through college "on the curve." Well, I think on this one you either do it or you don't do it!

So when we finished with the hearings we gave 4 As out of the 24, and less than a handful of Bs, and the same with Cs, and one heck of a lot of Ds and Fs— in terms of:

> a lack of planning
> the lack of specifying a person with the responsibility
> the lack of telling us where they're going to get the money
> and if they don't have it, will they ask the President and get his recommendations to the Congress?

On Capitol Hill, I'd say we're very well informed on this due to the work of the House Subcommittee on Government Management, Information and Technology, and the Science Committee's Technology Subcommittee.

Let's not scare people: Let's deal with the situation.

Rep. Steve Horn, subcommittee Chair, receives Grace Hopper Memorial Award for committee's "Year 2000" achievements from Dick Lefkon

Preface

If you are 35 and reading this book at midnight of 1999, you will suddenly qualify for retirement on some pension systems. And if you're 82 or 83 years old at that time, some college selection computers will be eager to bring you in as a standard age first-year student.

In a nutshell, that's the Year 2000/Y2K/Millennium computing crisis: Because most mainframe programs and machines—from Eisenhower through Clinton—stored and used only a two-digit year (97, not 1997), the year after '99 is '00. Take your age, subtract it from 00 and use a sign-free number, and you'll see how the example just described makes sense. If you don't believe me, how do you account for the 104-year-old woman in Minnesota who recently was sent a letter inviting her to join a pre-school there?

Your core Y2K mission is to make your computer systems run right and make their external interfaces conform to (probably) the new FIPS and ANSI date standards reproduced in the first chapter of this book. Your non-IS people will learn to replace non-conformant embedded chips, so that, in March of this "surprise" leap year, your security systems won't automatically seal off the entryways every Friday, thinking it is a Saturday.

Many goofy and amusing stories, often true, can be told about Year 2000 Computing. But it is very serious business. The cost of making the world's information systems work right will rival the cost of the U.S. Savings and Loan debacle—slightly smaller if you consider just the fixes, but larger if you include the damage and displacement costs to those who don't fix.

A single parts factory shutdown recently stopped all General Motors manufacturing for months, so don't suppose that you can fix your systems and ignore whether or not your business partners fix theirs. And offsite code conversion has its savings limits, as you'll expend greater effort setting the inventory, baselining it onsite with confidential data, and retesting.

Can a company change its systems to be Year 2000 conformant? Mostly, yes! I reported on having done this in 1984, and others may have done it earlier and just not reported it. (Having a non-production "time machine" test computer helped.) That company-wide change was in the securities business, and we treated the Y2K need as though it was an inflexible regulatory requirement with noncompliance penalties in both cash and reputation. So should you.

Have organizations known about Y2K for a long time? Most certainly. For instance, attendees at my 1991 Y2K awareness paper presentations at the "Safe Computing" and "National Computer Security" conferences later told me they'd carried the alert back to their own companies, agencies and armed service branches.

Is there a lot of time left? Unfortunately not, and two precedents come to mind. After AIDS was recognized as a general-population threat in 1985, it took eleven years of significant funding to bring forth medicines that can reduce its virus concentrations in the human body. But the U.S. metric conversion—of cost to manufacturing similar to Year 2000 for computing—was never completed, even though given a generous 20 years deadline. Year '00 is approaching much faster, and most suggest you finish before '99.

Should conducting this Millennium war be left entirely to the "soldiers?" Probably not. Programmer/analysts generally reserve highest professional respect for those of greatest expertise, but several of the Y2K gurus gossiping over the Internet don't just want systems to work right and interfaces to carry a four-digit year: They won't rest "until every man, woman and child around the globe" also says "1998" instead of "'98."

Should, then, techies be excluded from the deliberations? Again, no. The CIO sets the strategic course, the Y2K manager devises and executes the plan, but the house expert and soldier programmer/analysts should all also be involved in the planning phases for two reasons: (1) Collectively, they know most skeletons and closets; no outsourcing will as quickly catch dates passed in FILLER fields. And (2) morale must be one of your centerpieces or you'll find skeleton/closet expertise peeling away as each new month adds another dollar or two onto Y2K coder and manager hourly rates.

This book truly represents the state of the art, both for do-it-yourself and for choosing a vendor to help if that's your desire. IBM, GUIDE, SIM, IMF, IMC, ACM, IEEE, AITP/DPMA, and nearly every recognized top professional in this field have permitted their best Y2K work to be reprinted here so that your corporation or agency will have available the knowledge to accomplish this organization-survival mission.

These pages contain at least half the information you'll need to make decisions and take action. Once you absorb respectively the sections for CEO/CIO—expert—manager, you'll know how to obtain any further information needed. You'll also be able to defend yourself from vendors who truly believe they have "the" solution. You'll also be better at separating hard data from fluff at www sites such as dod.mil, gsa.gov, y2klinks.com, and year2000.com—and limiting your (212) 539-3072 Editor's Advice inquiries.

If you had the extra millions or billions, you might be tempted to ignore and outsource the whole issue. Unfortunately, this is not a standard oranges-and-tangerines order, and it won't work just to throw three darts at a vendor list and select the best bid. That's because the solution paths (both outsourced and in-house) differ markedly from each other, and you can't choose if you don't know. For each application, you'll need to decide among date expansion, "smart" century, century "window," date shift in code or data, dropping/replacing the app, or not fixing it this century.

Most technical and management books present one consistent approach. Even where excellent, that viewpoint will work only accidentally for your Y2K effort because of the diversity of distinct cures. The present volume lays out at least three different well-stated solutions to each Y2K issue. To enable this, we ran a four-month public competition for "Year 2000 Best Practices" papers. To publicize its completion, we are presenting a series of two-day Y2K conference free to user organizations, ever since the first edition was published in autumn of 1996.

Even before being revised and expanded, that book was welcomed into the personal libraries of most Year 2000 practitioners; was heavily cited and excerpted in well-known Year 2000-related publications; was the technology resource for expert testimony to joint hearings of the U.S. House of Representatives Subcommittees on Science/Technology and Government Management; and contained material explicitly cited in expert testimony before the U.S. Senate Banking Committee.

With this "final report" in hand, you'll see that Y2K isn't Nobel Prize stuff—just a prohibitively large set of familiar tasks.

The best way to use this compendium is to get people bearing the titles CEO/CIO-expert-manager into a room for a series of meetings. Except for the start-up, all the planning meetings follow your usual format; but at the first meeting, each job title takes on the commitment to absorb a roughly equal slice of this book and at the next meeting to distribute/discuss a typed summary of aspects of our content which are specific to your organization.

For most solutions, running this management-intensive effort under your established successful process will be a good way to proceed: You'll have the ongoing ability to triage nonessential conversions away from critical ones. And, when the inevitable bulge arises, you can divert reliable resources from non-Y2K efforts—not be forced to start inventing the wheel near the scheduled end of your path. Large organizations without an established "funnel" will want to set up a distinct (Y2K) project office.

Remember that AITP used to be named DPMA, Data Processing Management Association. Our task as IS management is—literally—to rescue our organizations. All the co-authors and editors, including the initial project sponsors at AITP's Special Interest Group for Mainframe Computers, want you to succeed!

Dick Lefkon

1
part

CEO/CIO:
The Challenge

Y2K is a worldwide problem, as the Top Ten list by Swiss Bank's Doc Farmer of London points out in a humorous manner. While amusing, all but numbers 5 and 10 still make sense to some in IS or their bosses. Farmer also includes a brief list of non-IS Y2K consequences, potentially resulting in loss of lives.

Whatever the excuses for procrastination, anyone with corporate responsibility should realize that the risk is now personal. Delay any more, writes Dick Lefkon, and your only hope is that Y2K comes as a complete surprise to your competition and the general population.

The Y2K body of knowledge is old and stable—enough so for NYU to award CEU's in it. This book is the first reference to provide everything under one roof; but learning here what you need to fulfill your Y2K commitment doesn't require a Ph. D.

Ernst & Young warn about acquisitions and due diligence—especially SEC Regulation S-K item 303 and Comptroller of the Currency's advisory letter 96-4 demanding Y2K bank compliance. [Ed: For a full legal discussion, see Chapter 7, Y2K Contracts.]

Milt Habeck's six-page winning submission to our paper solicitation gives the whole exposure story in a nutshell, plus a three-page chart listing the Y2K blowup dates for 32 families of software applications!

The dozen "Actionable Caveats" by Ted Fisher and Chris Casey is one of three excerpts from "The Year 2000: Turning Oh-Oh into OK!" The Information Management Forum deserves special thanks for permitting AITP's SIG-Mainframe to show you nearly the entire text of this definitive enterprise-level management approach. See also Parts 3 and 6.

Dick Lefkon's "Seven Methods" tells the CEO/CIO concisely about date expansion, century windowing, intelligent digit, time shifting, and the rest. For an expanded look at each of these, managers and experts are referred to Part 7.

Ascent Logic's brief Compliance piece, along with the 8-digit-date FIPS and ANSI standards, clarifies what form Y2K certification should take; and Lefkon cautions about previous attempts at it.

NIST's CSL Bulletin relates a broad action plan, and Carruthers reminds the CEO of a dozen major exposures the CIO has never considered. Although not explicitly application software-related, some of these exposures can endanger an enterprise just as effectively as those newly 99-year past due accounts.

Lefkon returns to urge your establishment of a Project Management Office (PMO), described further in Part 12.

Finally, Gerhard Adam summarizes the software situation and offers some useful caveats. "First," he says, "review all products for Year 2000 support, especially those which provide automated functions based on data and time (i.e., scheduling systems, storage management, etc.)."

1   *Top Ten List of Excuses Not to Address Year 2000 Issues*

Dale F. (Doc) Farmer
SBC Warburg Corporate Audit

Y2K is a worldwide problem, as shown in the following. While amusing, all but numbers 5 and 10 still make sense to some in IS or their bosses. Also included is a brief list of non-IS Y2K consequences, potentially resulting in loss of lives.

Top Ten List of Excuses Not to Address Year 2000 Issues

1. You've got lots of time, it's only 1998!

2. You bought a magic bullet from a software salesperson.

3. You can afford to be without Accounts Receivables for a year or two.

4. When the time comes, you'll pay someone else to solve it for you.

5. You're getting into real estate anyway.

6. You like midnight phone calls from irate CEOs.

7. You believe maintenance is for wimps. Real managers create new systems.

8. You're not the head of IS, you only work here.

9. You believe that if you ignore the problem it'll go away.

10. You want to surprise your stockholders.

Safety Critical Software Issues

Air traffic control, rail systems, life support control, navigation systems

Will date structure or calculations cause any risk to life & limb?

Could wrong date = wrong location, wrong medication, wrong route?

Could your company be liable if date failure costs lives & property instead of mere cash?

IBM Retention Issues

IBM uses 99/365 to represent permanent retention of files

All permanent files will expire as of that date (31 December 1999)

How this will be addressed by IBM?

What impact to your operating systems and applications?

What impact to your permanent data?

2   _Director's Guide to the Year 2000_

Dick Lefkon
Year 2000 Committee of AITP SIG-Mainframe

As a Director of a major corporation, you are no doubt familiar with the Year 2000 challenge:

> _Left untreated, IS programs and embedded-chip devices will perform as though the new 00-year is 1900, not 2000._

Naturally, informed customers and business partners expect your company to use the coming years wisely to prevent
- time-activated vaults unable to open.
- customer credit accounts suddenly 100 years overdue.
- substantial fines due to electronically misplaced securities.

What Regulators Say

In 1996 the U.S. Controller of the Currency told all National Bank CEOs to complete Year 2000 Compliance by December 31, 1998.

In 1997 the U.S. Senate Banking Committee imposed the December, 1998, requirement on the Federal Reserve Bank and subsidiaries. Quarterly and annual corporate reports to the Securities and Exchange Commission must inform shareholders about the Year 2000 exposure, what you're doing about it, and what it will cost.

What Will Fixing "Y2K" Cost?

The Gartner Group and others have estimated worldwide cost of "Y2K" at approximately two-thirds of a trillion dollars. This figure is about the same as the cost of the U.S. Savings & Loan mishap.

Only a third of that amount will be spent in North America: One and one half 1996 dollars per line of customized code.

> A small brokerage firm with one half million lines of in-house code will need to spend about $750,000 to ready that code for Year 2000.

> A medium-sized bank with 10 million custom code lines can probably hold its in-house migration costs to approximately $15,000,000.

> At least one large Eastern bank and one major securities firm are known to have budgeted more than two hundred million dollars to insulate their information systems and client accounts from Year 2000 vulnerability.

Are Directors and Officers Personally Liable?

Usually not, this time perhaps yes. All Directors are required to exercise *reasonable diligence and care*, making informed decisions.

If "Year 2000" were a surprise to your competitors and the general population, you would not be liable.

Fortunately for our economy, companies like those just cited are well on their way to curing the Year 2000 problem. And this encouraging news is disseminated daily via newspapers and television.

How Can We Stay Within D&O Insurance Coverage?

D&O insurance protects Directors and Officers in instances of normal human fallibility.

Make sure your paper trail shows you took reasonable preventative measures:

> Establish Y2K project leadership and adequate funding.

> Inventory your source code and hardware/software packages.

➤ Perform an analysis and write a plan.

➤ Use automated packages and outside help appropriately.

➤ Track your progress and report it honestly to employees, customers, and regulators.

Your costs per code line will not vary widely from others in your industry. Try to avoid writing budgets with patently unrealistic cost figures.

If you lack the necessary incremental funds, consider following the example of the U.S. Army:

➤ Immediately shut down information systems that are not absolutely mission-critical, and re-deploy their resources to Y2K.

➤ Promptly halt all new development on remaining applications (except for production emergencies) until after they are all Y2K-ready. [Ed: See Chapter 20, *You Might Receive a "C" Grade.*]

Why December 31, 1998?

Ask your IS Director about "Y2K" and you will hear these facts among others:

➤ Every in-house program must be inspected and potential date impacts modified.

➤ The necessary code and/or file changes are fairly simple; but they're pervasive.

➤ Using industry benchmarks, every million lines of code you change will introduce 100 to 1000 undetected errors.

➤ Because of interrelationships, every single program you own **must be re-tested even if it has not been changed.**

December of 1998 is your last chance to "shake down" your modified end-of-year automated processes in a production setting—except for Year 2000 itself!

3   *The Millennium Rollover Is Not a Surprise*

Dick Lefkon
New York University

The Y2K body of knowledge is old and stable—enough so for NYU to award CEUs in it.

> ➤ The Millennium Rollover is not a surprise.
> ➤ The necessary body of knowledge is well defined.
>
> *New York University*
> *School of Continuing Education*
> *Fall Semester, 1996*
> *X53.9807 (SEC 1): Year 2000 Computing Best Practices*
> *1.0 CEU*
> *Instructor: Dick Lefkon*

Description

The course surveys four main components of Year 2000 methods: Strategic issues, needs, solutions, and legal aspects; Technical view of 3GLs, COTS, and custom software; Large scale project management techniques for hardware, software, and testing; Product classes: code converters, version control with capture/replay, test scripters, and clock simulation.

Text

Lefkon (ed.), *Year 2000: Best Practices for Y2K Millennium Computing:* Panic in Year 2000, AITP-SIG Mainframe, 1996

Lessons

1. Needs and Resources: New FIPS and ANSI Standards; project costing; Congressional Final Report on resources; per-line versus per-point cost. Identifying exposures in software and automated processes.
2. Legal and Accounting Issues: FASB and GASB on expensing, Contract wordings from viewpoints of vendor and owner. When one can modify, when demand modification.
3. Awareness and Needs Analysis: Involving the enterprise; needs surveys; HW/SW checklists; formulating a template based on others; success.
4. Five Technical Approaches: Sliding century window, date expansion versus compaction; date code regression beyond the IDD; bridging; interfaces.

5. Four Technical Challenges: Embedded dates; extended-interval aging; isolating production from Millennium work; lost source code.

6. Project Management: The usual seven-step description; models for managing testing; techniques for project coordination/acceleration.

7. Staffing Management: Non-monetary compensation; on-going training for replenishment; staff allocation; determining and managing outsourcing.

8. Present State of Leading, Most-Used Products on PC, Mainframe, UNIX.

9. More on Products: Quiz.

4   *I'm Not Worried...*

Ernst & Young, LLP

I'm Not Worried...

➤ Vendor/Outsourced Software

- Inventory and Review All Formal Agreements

- You May Have to Pay for the Year 2000 Fix if It Is Not Part of Your Maintenance/Outsourcing Agreement

- When Will the Vendor/Outsourcer Be Year 2000 Ready?

➤ It's 1997, Do You Know Where Your Systems and Data Are?

- System and Data Integration Over the Past Decade May Hide Date Problems

- Imbedded Date Fields in Nomenclature May Need to Be Addressed

- Third Party Data Transfers May Contaminate Your 'Fixed' Applications and Databases

I'm Still Not Worried...

- Software License Problems

  - Can You Load Your Package Software on Another CPU Without Incurring Additional Costs?

  - Will It Even Load to Another CPU?

- Due Diligence

  - Be Careful When You Acquire or Merge

  - Reserve the Right to Terminate Any Agreements Due to Year 2000 Reasons

Now I'm Worried...

- U.S. Securities and Exchange Commission

  - Reg. S-K, Item 303, "Management's Discussion and Analysis of Financial Condition and Results of Operations" Must Contain

    - Matters That Would Have Impact on Future Operations and Have Not Had an Impact in the Past

    - Matters That Have Had an Impact on Reported Operations and Are Not Expected to Have Impact on Future Operations

- Shareholder Litigation

  - Likely to Occur If Year 2000 Causes Business Disruption

  - Civil and Criminal Actions May Take Place

Statutory/Regulatory Compliance Requirements

> Department of Defense (DoD)

- Bills H.R. 3230 and S. 1745 Were Introduced to Authorize Appropriations for the DoD to Ensure All 'Information Technology' Acquired and Used Are Year 2000 Compliant

> Office of the Comptroller of the Currency (OCC)

- Advisory Letter 96-4 Advises All National Bank CEOs to Complete Year 2000 Compliance by December 31, 1998

5   # *The Century Date Problem: How Bad Can It Be?*

Milt Habeck
Unbeaten Path International

The short answer to the question posed by this headline to the executive management of today's modern business enterprises is "worse than you can ever imagine." In fact, it is virtually certain that the viability of your business will be severely threatened if your company does not make Year-2000 date compliance of its software systems the top priority of information processing staff right now.

But prudent managers make decisions based on facts, not emotions or fad-driven hysteria. Therefore, as an information processing consultant whose firm has examined first hand the effect the century-date change will have on the major systems applications which drive today's modern businesses, I would like to present a synopsis of our findings.

The Root of the Problem

Most application software operating today's businesses, whether purchased from an outside vendor or created in-house, was designed to accommodate dates only up through calendar year 1999. Though this seems foolish today, the systems in use have evolved over the last 10 to 25 years, from times when the Year 2000 seemed too far away to matter.

Because the software developed in past years stores only the last two digits of the year, if today's system attempts to add one more year to 99 years, there won't be enough room to store the three-digit result and the computer will do what the odometer on your car would do at 99,999 miles. It will turn to zero.

Problems will begin long before the 1999 Christmas season. Many planning lead times based on calendars in various system modules extend for months and sometimes years. As soon as one of those planning horizons or forward-postings reaches January '00, the system will become confused and begin to cause unpredictable problems.

When your company built or acquired its complete, comprehensive, fully integrated software application, the strength of the technology was its ability to use centralized information in many functional ways. Unfortunately, that strength greatly exaggerates the century-date problem. With complex interrelationships, date sequence errors introduced into centralized data, the problem spreads like a deadly plague to many other parts of the system, and erroneous data ends up in places where reliable data is required for daily decisions. At that point, the whole system becomes functionally useless.

In the following pages, we will review how major systems use dates in the processing of vital information and then relate the practical effects on business for a company that fails to make those systems century-date compliant.

Table 5.1 Typical Date Proliferations is a report based on an actual analysis run against the integrated manufacturing system of a major worldwide processed-products manufacturing company. We wanted to know, for a product scheduled for manufacture in January, 2000, what would be the earliest possible occurrence of a date requirement for each module of the integrated system.

Though many modules will be unaffected prior to 2000, the Quality Module, which dictates the ingredients to be used in the bill-of-materials, will be affected starting in October, 1996. The next most serious problem will occur in the Manufacturing Requirements Planning module in October, 1997.

Dates on Screens and Reports

In most large, integrated systems, dates are stored in a standard format which is then translated into whatever format is required by the users of that data. For example, some nations express December 25, 1999 as 12/25/99, and others write 25/12/99. Both of these numbers are derived from the stored format 991225.

Table 5.1   **Century Date Problem for Typical ERP System**   (Page 1 of 3)
Resuscitator 2000 Binoculars™ Report

Appl. ID	Application Description	First Date Problems	Practical Illustration of How Century Change Will Create Issues
AAA	Accounts Payable		System will not allow your company to earn cash discounts if discount period spans 1/2000
BBB	Accounts Receivable	Nov-99	Payments not recognized for cash discount; faulty aging report calculations
CCC	Process Manufacturing	Sep-99	Planned release date for processing orders would be after order completion dates
DDD	Billing	Dec-99	Potential post-shipment invoicing problem if activity spans century; order history sorts inaccurate
EEE	Bill of Materials	Jun-98	Engineering change management functionality diminished by out-of-sequence effectivity dates
FFF	Capacity Planning	Dec-97	Backward scheduling calculations could yield negative values/unpredictable errors
GGG	Data Collection	Jan-00	Transaction records would only have six-digit date information
HHH	Cash Management	Jan-00	Report selections which span the century would be disallowed
III	Cost Accounting	Dec-98	Limited problems except for rolling up costs with out-of-sequence BOM effective dates
JJJ	Foreign Exchange Translation	Jan-00	Exchange rate maintenance will cause calculation faults at change of century
KKK	Help Text	Jan-00	Very little effect...just report heading faults
LLL	Distribution Resources Planning	Jun-99	Resupply orders will have due dates pre-dating order release dates, unpredictable problems

Table 5.1   **Century Date Problem for Typical ERP System**   *(Page 2 of 3)*
Resuscitator 2000 Binoculars™ Report

Appl. ID	*Application Description*	*First Date Problems*	*Practical Illustration of How Century Change Will Create Issues*
MMM	Forecasting	Dec-97	Problems occur when year values are truncated to send data to Master Production Scheduling
NNN	General Ledger	Oct-98	Faulty accounting period definitions; accounting calendar won't allow "00" close to "99" start
OOO	Inventory Management	Jan-00	Inventory transaction history would be mis-sorted; reports spanning century disallowed
PPP	Repetitive Manufacturing	Oct-99	Planned orders from MPS/MRP won't be accurately converted to scheduled releases
QQQ	Quality Scheduling	Sep-99	Quality staff scheduling disrupted when MRP & CRP encounter date discontinuity
RRR	Multiple Factory Management	Jan-00	Should be ok except for selection parameters that include date ranges
SSS	Foreign Exchange Management	Jan-99	Exchange gain/(loss) calculations faulty if recognition date and settlement date span century
TTT	Material Requirements Planning	Dec-97	Horizon date logic disabled across century change; order release date calculation faults
UUU	Customer Order Processing	Nov-99	Orders shipped Dec '99 will immediately look overdue, causing credit hold conditions
VVV	Performance Management	Jan-00	Inaccurate standard readings for date-related measurements spanning century date
WWW	Marketing Planning	Jul-99	Discontinuity in promotion calendar will disrupt definition of start, end dates for deals

Table 5.1   **Century Date Problem for Typical ERP System**   *(Page 3 of 3)*
Resuscitator 2000 Binoculars™ Report

Appl. ID	Application Description	First Date Problems	Practical Illustration of How Century Change Will Create Issues
XXX	Purchasing	Jun-98	PO inquiry spanning century disallowed; faults in measurement of vendor due date performance
YYY	Quality Management	Oct-96	Retest dates for production samples will be sorted to past-due position
ZZZ	Sales Analysis	Jan-00	Sales analysis reports that span century cannot be initiated
ABC	Shop Floor Control	Sep-99	Confusion will result when job completion dates pre-date job release dates
DEF	Menus	Jan-00	Just the date on the menu display would be affected
GHI	System Controls and Parameters		Listing routines, date retrieval, retrieval/validation routines, and job submission routines affected
JKL	Pop-up Information	Jan-00	Any pop-up window that uses dates affected; for example, additional order information
MNO	Reference Routines	Jan-00	Report headings affected, but nothing critical
PQR	Standard Source Library		Some date routines in standard source library would not handle century logic

Totals
RPG & CLP Programs: 2,500
Programs with Dates: 58%
Number of Dates: 39,000

If century information is added to the internal storage number of December 25, 1999, that number would become eight digits long, or 19991225. But if the end-use numbers are not adjusted, they, being six digits long, would be at a loss for how to handle eight digits of information. The net result would be that the reports and displays used to run your business would not work at all or they would be unintelligible.

Dates as Information Drivers

Your software stores and processes millions of transactions for your company, including the payment of invoices, receiving a shipment, booking a collection, scheduling an order, etc.

In all applications, transaction data must be displayed and processed in sequence, using either an ascending or descending order. Examples of this function include order inquiry, inventory transaction history, sales data, manufacturing planning and pegging, capacity planning, general ledger transaction detail, accounts receivable invoices, accounts payable invoices, purchase order inquiry, shop order inquiry and inventory lot allocations, to name a few.

Since dates are stored internally in YYMMDD (YearYear, Month-Month, DayDay) format, the numerical value of the date field determines the sequence. For example, a transaction with a date of 960925 (September 25, 1996) will be processed before a transaction dated 970901 (September 1, 1997) because the former is a lower number than the latter. As you can see, dates in the next century will not be correctly processed relative to dates in the current century because the first two digits of the date field will be zeros. Therefore, even though January 10, 2000 is later on the calendar than December 25, 1999, the numerical processing will put Christmas before New Year's because 991225 will be processed long after 000110. Thus, for all those transaction-based functions listed above, the workload will be turned upside down, resulting in unusable output.

Sorting by dates will be equally futile. Imagine this scenario:

> *It is October '99. Your supply of boric acid is getting low, and your software application calculates that an order should be placed with the supplier in three months, January '00. The computer dutifully stores that information in numerical date order back before World War I.*
>
> *The system then notices that no boric acid is scheduled for future delivery, so it schedules another purchase order for January '00 and proceeds to store that one before World War I as well. Then it does it again, and again, until someone pulls the plug before the system fills the computer with automatically generated boric acid purchase orders that are 99 years overdue.*

Dates in Calculations

In all application areas, dates are used in calculation routines in order to determine other related dates. Here are a few examples:

> If the century date is not fixed, calculations that cross the century mark will require customer payments 99 years before shipment to qualify for a cash discount because in billing and accounts receivable, the due date and discount date are calculated by adding the "customer terms days" to the "invoice date."

> Similarly, orders shipped mid-December on 30-day terms will immediately show up as being overdue by 99 years, which will cause future orders from that customer to be put on credit hold and overdue carrying charges to be vast. This will cause interesting customer relations. One more glitch: the program that prints aging reports won't work.

> If century dates are not fixed in the accounts payable software, calculations that cross the century mark will require your company to make payment 99 years ago to earn a cash discount.

> In manufacturing requirements planning, the century date problem may calculate negative release dates, meaning orders will be released before Joseph and Mary took off for Bethlehem to celebrate the first Christmas.

> In shop floor control, the system will generate complicated circular logic because some jobs would be scheduled for completion before World War I, decades before those same jobs were scheduled to start. That's because "operation start dates" and "end dates" are determined by either backward or forward scheduling.

> In inventory control, many lot dates are calculated by the system based on the transaction date and the "lot expiration days" combined with the "lot reset dates." This means the system will automatically change your inventory policy from FIFO (first in, first out) to OINO (once in, never out).

> In manufacturing planning, where ingredients are changed by "effective dates," the integrity of finished product could be seriously affected by ingredients not being substituted at the specified time or simply not being available at the specified date.

> Sales forecasting dates will cause turmoil when passed to master production scheduling, and forecasted demand for 99 years ago will not be acted on by the system.

> Engineering change management will become challenging because effectivity dates in the new century will be nonsense numbers.

> Sites using multiple currency functionality will learn that applications will be confused as they try to figure out foreign

exchange gains and losses for forward currency obligations that run across the century mark. Multi-national profitability will be reduced to guesswork.

➤ Integrated promotion/order processing/billing systems will become very confused. Companies that have not become century date compliant will probably need to resort to manual customer service systems by late 1999.

➤ Comparing Dates for Information Retrieval

➤ Many applications maintain interrelated calendars for cut-off dates or trigger-dates with associated information. Based on a transaction date, a lookup is performed and corresponding data is retrieved for further processing. Therefore, it is critical for the system to properly determine date sequences. If they do not:

➤ in the General ledger, transactions will end up posted in the wrong accounting periods.

➤ master production scheduling data and material requirements data will be reported in the wrong time periods, completely confusing material planners.

➤ capacity plans relying on the shop calendar to determine work days and holidays as well as the number of hours available for scheduling will plan to have the world end after Christmas 1999, as there will be zero work days available.

➤ Inquiries, reports and transaction processing programs which require "date range" selections as "from" and "to" ranges depend on the ability of the system to determine the relative sequence of the transaction dates. Thus, the system must be able to correctly process transactions selected from 12/07/99 through 010/31/00. If they cannot, general ledger inquiries won't work, sales analyses will generate nonsense data and user-generated inquiries will produce useless reports.

Solving the Problem...The Urgency, the Costs and the Process

I hope, by sharing these findings, that we leave the impression that the century-date conversion challenge is not a simple maintenance task. I also hope we have enlightened various business managers that this is not just a systems problem, it is a business problem, for not only must each individual enterprise prepare itself for the Year 2000; it must ensure its suppliers and customers prepared as well. In case after case, we have found that people underestimate the date conversion task by a factor of five to ten. . . eight man-months typically turn into eighty.

Fixing the problem will cost a considerable amount of money. To some, it will seem like a painful, unnecessary expenditure. Some will consider it "business survival insurance." Others will take funds from the marketing budget, assuming that the competition will not take care of his own problem in time and this business, being well prepared, will gain a significant competitive edge. Whatever the cost today, it will double every six months until January 1999, at which time it will be virtually impossible to perform an adequate century-date conversion project.

In June of 1996, Gartner Group reported that 75 percent of U.K. businesses and 90 percent of U.S. businesses were in a state of total denial on the century-date problem. By the end of 1996, those numbers had shifted in some industries. After witnessing the depth of the problem, I cannot understand why businesses are not actively working to solve it today.

We have summarized the effect of non-century date compliance for each of the modules studied.

Editor's Note: The manufacturing sample showing a dozen dates per program is much too low for the financial industries. The "sub-assemblies" of a typical bond can consist of anywhere from several dates to literally hundreds of dates.

Four Steps to Success

Taking action is a simple four-step process.

1. Make the Year-2000 issue a top priority for your I/S staff.
2. Tell them you want to know the real size of the job at hand.
3. Authorize them to buy whatever Year-2000-specific tools they need to use the computer's own processing power to analyze date fields and automatically rebuild them into century-compliant formats.
4. Ensure that the conversion plan leaves at least a year for testing of converted systems.

I submit that your company's life is at stake; your systems professionals are eager to get this project behind them. The deadline will not move. The detonator is ticking. It's time to take action now.

6   *Actionable Caveats*

Chris Casey
Bytewise Consulting, Inc.

Ted Fisher
Sperduto & Associates, Inc.

This chapter summarizes the *Actionable Caveats*, or important conclusions, which we feel are critical to the success of any compliance project. These statements are at times warnings to help managers be aware of certain pitfalls which could derail or stall their process. Other thoughts are preventive measures which can be implemented to allow the organization to handle the process in a pro-active fashion in order to capture some of the positive opportunities presented by the problem.

1. *The Year 2000 compliance effort is a survival issue.*
   For those who are prone to argue about cost, be prepared to prove that survival is the issue and ask what survival as a firm is worth.

2. *The compliance of others' systems is also a survival issue.*
   The compliance of customers, key suppliers, city, county, state and federal governments, utilities, banks, etc., is also a survival issue for us all. If those with whom you do business fail as a result of their non-compliance, your efforts toward compliance will have been in vain. Enterprise management must realize that they have a real and critical stake in the compliance of their commercial partners.

3. *In most cases, a significant amount of time must pass from the moment when the CEO is informed of the Year 2000 problem to the time when the CEO makes the necessary commitment to address the problem.*
   The amount of time seems to depend upon the CEO's temperament, the general state of the firm and the economic outlook. The range of time required is about three to nine months. With so little time left before January 1, 2000, it is obviously important to complete the awareness-to-commitment process as quickly as possible.

4. *In order to gain the commitment of enterprise management, business and technical managers should assemble a fact-based case for presentation to enterprise management.*
   The first step toward compliance is to convince the CEO and other enterprise management of the scope and potential impact of the Year 2000 problem. An objective case must be prepared and presented to the CEO. This case must convey an appropriate sense of urgency to convince the CEO in a reasonable period of time to make the commitments

necessary to achieve compliance (including testing) within the time available. The presentation must be persuasive and objective, and to the extent possible, should incorporate real data which can be obtained using third-party analysis tools and methods.

5. *Current resources are nowhere near sufficient to deal with the worldwide need.*

   Those organizations which begin the compliance efforts early will have the benefit of best-of-breed technicians. The cream of the crop will be fully committed in a short time. Companies which wait to start their compliance process will face a market of scarce resources.

6. *Competing priorities can derail the compliance process by diverting resources or distracting enterprise management.*

   Competing survival issues can arise (a fire, serious accident, merger. etc.), and attention and commitment to the Year 2000 compliance process can diminish or, at least temporarily, cease. Some form of contingency planning is necessary. So is a means to maintain the involvement and commitment of enterprise management.

7. *There are positive outcomes to compliance that need to be studied for purposes of exploitation.*

   Enhanced customer relations, new customers and prospects, and opportunities for favorable publicity are just a few of the achievable positive outcomes of the Year 2000 compliance process. Cooperative activities with customers, prospects and key suppliers will draw you into closer relationships, will strengthen the trust of the parties involved, and will result in added business and profits.

8. *Exposure to the possibility of lawsuits abounds.*

   Firms must pro-actively manage their legal exposures before, during and after Year 2000 compliance. Intelligent strategies must be developed to minimize such exposures. Some of the exposures include claims against software vendors for failing systems, shareholder actions against board members of non-compliant firms, and customer actions against service organizations, such as banks, brokerage houses and insurance companies.

9. *All stakeholders in the enterprise need to be involved in the compliance process.*

   All parties, including partners, customers, suppliers, media, governmental regulators and shareholders, need to be consulted, kept informed and, to the appropriate extent, involved in the compliance process. Stakeholder involvement is one of the most effective ways of avoiding the erosion of enterprise management's commitment.

10. *A **significant percentage of medium and large sized businesses will not meet the compliance deadline ,and the likelihood of their failure is great.***

If it appears that a particular business is not going to be able to achieve compliance, it may be advisable to pare down the business being done with that enterprise. Eventually, it may be necessary to cease electronic contact with them to avoid the risk of contaminating the data in your system. If their contribution to your business is unique and necessary, identify such businesses early and proactively assist them in their compliance efforts through education, technology transfer or direct involvement.

11. ***Compliance-related activities will continue well beyond January 1, 2000.***
    Many companies will not succeed in achieving full compliance before January 1, 2000, for a variety of reasons. Faced with Year 2000-related system failures, these companies will be forced to revert to manual methods to replace their failed computer information systems. Some companies will successfully tread water with manual systems, while others will drown, discovering too late their dependence on date-sensitive automation. Those that do survive will have to bring their information systems into compliance at some point. As such, January 1, 2000, does not mean an end to compliance efforts. Not all systems and applications will be run on January 1, 2000, or for that matter, in January at all. Special quarterly, semi-quarterly and annual processing may reveal isolated pockets of non-compliance.

12. ***Don't permit your enterprise to become over-reliant on vendors and solution providers during the compliance process.***
    Vendors and solution providers have their limitations, just as you have yours. While you may be able to outsource a significant share of the work, you cannot outsource the responsibility and management of the compliance effort.

7   *Have You Selected These Seven Methods?*

Dick Lefkon
Year 2000 Committee of AITP SIG-Mainframe

There are seven main approaches to the Year 2000 software upgrade task. "Outsource" is not one of them, and if you outsource you'll still need to choose the approach. If you can only list two, you'll have made real decisions about the other five. Deciding not to decide is a decision.

1. **Prune the business.**
2. **Wait.**
3. **Replace the application by a purchase or new build.**

4. **Expand YY year fields to YYYY.**
5. **"Intelligent" digits, other encoding.**
6. **Date "Window(s)."**
7. **Date-shift ("encapsulate") code or data.**

Once your orange systems are made Y2K-compliant by one of these methods, if your green ones aren't yet ok, you'll need to "bridge" from one application to another by using intermediate files or other techniques. When you near completion, bridges between conformant applications are removed. Keep them available, though, for times you want to access your archives.

All seven main approaches are easy to understand, especially number 2. You barely have time to convert 40 percent to 60 percent of your programs fully. Part of your triage approach should be to determine which functions or programs can safely be ignored until next decade because their shortcomings will be cosmetic at worst. For instance, your salespeople won't lynch you for having to scroll past the 12/31 and earlier sales to the 00/04 ones on a "show recent sales first" CICS screen, since this ugliness will only last for days and they'll know their competitors are probably suffering the same inconvenience. Save some cosmetic changes for when there's time.

At the opposite end of "do nothing" are systems which are absolutely critical to the business but have a truly prohibitive Y2K compliance cost. If the company (or line) will become unprofitable due to that outlay, consider shutting it down or selling it. Fast food chains do this frequently with unprofitable stores, and IBM itself has thus far avoided announcing Y2K conformance for the 43xx and 30x1 lines of installed mainframes.

Another "pruning" alternative is to sell that business part to a Y2K-ok competitor—but the SEC won't let you foist it on an unsuspecting party.

Third on the list is a full software replacement. This could modernize your business, but you won't be able to regression-test incrementally. A new build is both costly and deadline-risky, and most business-specific software replacements can't help requiring massive customization efforts.

One smart triage using number 3 might be to toss your low-data store Executive Info system, installing a conformant one to be fed by your revamped apps.

Number 4, full YYYY field expansion, is the most appealing and elegant Y2K date fix approach. You regularly make similar changes to keep up with industry-wide formats. But there aren't time and resources to expand everything to YYYY.

Number 5, "Intelligent digit," is one of three unusual methods. It keeps dates the same length by using the leftmost nibble of the leftmost year byte to hold a century-millennium flag. To use this approach, you have to add various date-encoding and -decoding lines that are anything but obvious. "Seven digit date" is a cross between this method and the one preceding.

```
WWWWWWWWWWWWWWWWWWWWWW
1                    1
9                    9
1                    1
9                    9
1                    1
9                    9
WWWWWWW  1930  WWWWWWW
2                    2
0                    0
2                    2
0                    0
WWWWWWWWWWWWWWWWWWWWWW
```

Sixth of the seven methods is the so-called century window. Pictorially, this looks just like the kitchen window on the TV series *Honeymooners*. The top glass pane represents part of a century of which the YY numbers are above a century "pivot" point. In the diagram, the middle bar of the window is labelled "1930." All years ending with numbers 30 or above are to be interpreted as "19" plus YY. "98" is interpreted as "1998," etc.: IF YY > 30, CC = 19   ELSE CC = 20. Numbers below the bar are future: "20" plus YY.

Coding for a century window probably looks familiar, since much of your legacy code already contains date logic for left-affixing "19" or "20."

A so-called "sliding century window" defines the pivot year as being a certain number of years into the past, starting at the current year. Thus, your 100-year window keeps on advancing, preventing shrinkage of the number of years in your future horizon: IF YY > (now - 50), CC=19.

Last on the list is the quickest—and dirtiest—approach, one which makes no pretense of using the "true" date, as long as the calculations come out right. This date-shift approach downshifts the year by 28. There are seven days to a week and four years to a leap-year cycle; multiplying together and getting 28, you'll find a year shifted this much will have 4th of July and all Sundays in the right place. Taking proper calendar care for new holidays and religious ones, date-related calculations should in theory come out just fine.

Shifting the date requires changing programs (-28/+28 at the start/ exit) or changing the data-store to hold (phony) shifted dates, not true ones. But known-incorrect file data raises a possible need to store duplicate data. And so, a code fix is probably the better means to shift dates.

A single canned program segment can repetitively be used to downshift all relevant dates in a given named copybook. The same holds for upshifts. On the whole, "encapsulation" of programs will probably entail the lowest amount of coding, errors, and testing among the seven approaches.

Nobody wants to use such an artificial approach based on false numbers. However, since it is pretty safe and pretty quick, you might want to put a tab labeled "summer 1998" on this page and read it again when time is short and deadlines are close and "Q&D" is less a dirty word.

(A goofy-sounding but common variation of number 7 is to use the Lilian date, storing untrue dates that are the interval since a certain time in history, not untrue dates measured 28 years backward from the present.)

To summarize: There are seven main approaches to software which isn't yet ready for the Year 2000. Choosing the best mix for you—even if it's executed by a mediocre workforce—will make you look better than selecting the wrong approach and implementing it through a truly outstanding, top-quality outsourcing firm or in-house team.

This decision is yours to make and cannot safely be outsourced.

8   *Four Primary Compliance Criteria*

**Yngvar Tronstad, Jan Peterson, Joe Ramirez,
Jack Ashburner, Grant Robinson**
Ascent Logic Corporation

Although the four criteria as summarized in Table 8.1 fully define century compliance, the essence of compliance implies a balance between cost and risk based on a business perspective, rather than on a technical yardstick. However, such a balance will vary with each enterprise according to its business needs and its technology base. Thus these generic century-compliance criteria need to be decomposed and refined within the context of a particular business case.

The first compliance criterion, General Integrity, is one of several high-level criteria that should guide the effort of making a business century compliant.

General Integrity Criterion

"Desired operations" will continue uninterrupted regardless of value for current date.

Elaboration: As a system date advances normally on a host processor, each date rollover must not lead either the host process or any software executing on the host to erroneous processing. The term "desired operations" is intentionally broad and needs to be interpreted for specific businesses and technologies.

Table 8.1   **The Four Primary Compliance Criteria**

Criterion	Definition
General Integrity	"Desired operations" will continue uninterrupted regardless of value for current date.
Date Integrity	All manipulation of calendar-related data, such as dates, duration, days of week, etc., will produce desired results for all valid date values within the application domain.
Explicit Century	Date elements in the interfaces and data storage permit specifying the century to eliminate date ambiguity.
Implicit Century	For any date element represented without a century, the correct century is unambiguous for all manipulations involving that element.

The technical component of the Year 2000 challenge involves the accurate acceptance, creation, manipulation, and output of calendar-related data. Although the largest concern is whether the system can handle the rollover date to the Year 2000, century compliance is much broader and more diverse. This particular rollover event is a high-risk event that needs to be mitigated; there are several other risk areas. These events can occur not only at rollover to the Year 2000 but well before and well after. It is therefore important to identify and categorize different events and their associated event horizons, which pinpoint the probable timing for the occurrence of a Year 2000 failure.

Date Integrity Criterion

All manipulation of calendar-related data, such as dates, duration, days of week, etc., will produce desired results for all valid date values within the application domain. This century compliance criterion covers correctness of manipulations of date data within manipulation categories such as arithmetic, branching, formatting, storage, and extended semantics. Several examples of these issues are given in Table 8.2. These manipulations need to be made reliable over the range of dates that an application is expected to handle. For example, sales order processing many handle dates from five years in the past to one year into the future.

In contrast, an employee database may store dates of birth from early in the 20th century to planned retirement dates well into the 21st century.

Table 8.2   **Date Integrity Examples**

Category	Examples of manipulation
Arithmetic	Calculate the duration between two dates
	Calculate date based on starting date and duration
	Calculate day of week, day of year, week within year
Branching	Compare two dates
Data Storage	Storing and retrieving
	Sorting and merging
	Searching
	Indexing on disk file or database table
	Moving data within primary memory
Extended Semantics	"99" as a special value for year
	"99.365" as a special value for Julian date
	"00" as a special value for year

Explicit Century Criterion

Date elements in the interfaces and data storage permit specifying the century to eliminate date ambiguity. This criterion essentially requires the capability to store explicit values for century. For example, third-party products that can use a 4-digit year in all date data elements stored and passed across each interface, including the user interface, would satisfy this criteria. A base and offset representation of dates covering all centuries of interest would also satisfy this criterion. Whether this capability should be used to eliminate century ambiguity is part of the last criterion.

Implicit Century Criterion

For any date element represented without century, the correct century is unambiguous for all manipulations involving that element. This last criterion requires that if the century is not explicitly provided, then its value must be correctly inferred from the value of date provided with 100 percent accuracy. For example, the range of values for an "invoice date" would rarely span more than 10 years. Because the century can always be interpreted correctly for an invoice with a 2-digit year, this date element would satisfy this criterion. This criterion permits cost-risk trade-offs that may minimize changes to existing date formats, given that you evaluate the cases for interpretation within the context of your business functions.

9   *FIPS Publication 4–1 Change Notice*

National Institute of Standards and Technology

Following is the text of change 1 to FIPS Publication 4–1, FIPS PUB 4–1, Representation for Calendar Date and Ordinal Date for Information Interchange, dated 25 March, 1996.

Specific Change

Page 2: In reference to paragraph 10, Specifications:

> *For purposes of electronic data interchange in any recorded form among U.S. Government agencies, NIST highly recommends that four-digit year elements be used. The year should encompass a two-digit century that precedes, and is contiguous with, a two-digit year-of-century (e.g., 1999, 2000, etc.). In addition, optional two-digit year time elements specified in ANSI X3.30-1985(R1991) should not be used for the purposes of any data interchange among U.S. Government agencies.*

10   *Proposed Draft Revised American National Standard X3.30, Representation of Date for Information Interchange*

American National Standards Institute

1.   *Scope, purpose, and application*

1.1   The purpose of the American National Standard is to provide a single standard means of representing calendar date for interchange among data systems.

1.2   The scope of this American National Standard is limited to the representation of calendar date for interchange among data systems; it does not describe how the date is determined. This standard was not designed for (nor does it preclude) usage by humans as input to, or output from data systems. This standard does not address how data is converted by data systems to be internally processed and/or stored.

1.3   The representation of calendar date specified in this standard is compatible with other national and international standards. In ISO 8601:1988, the representation specified by this American National Standard is referred to as calendar date-complete representation-basic format.

2.   *Normative references*

The following standard contains provisions that, through reference in this text, constitute provisions of this American National Standard. At the time of publication, the edition indicated was valid. All standards are subject to revision, and parties to agreements based on this American National Standard are encouraged to investigate the possibility of applying the most recent edition of the standard indicated below.

ISO 8601:1988, Data elements and interchange of formats—Information interchange—representation of dates and times.

3.   *Definitions*

For this American National Standard, the following definitions apply:

3.1   Calendar date: A particular year, month, and day of the Gregorian Calendar.

3.2   Calendar day: A particular day within a Gregorian Calendar month.

3.3   Calendar month: A particular month within a Gregorian Calendar year.

3.4   Calendar year: A particular year according to the Gregorian Calendar.

3.5   Gregorian Calendar: A calendar introduced in the year 1582 A.D. and now in general use.

4.   Specifications

4.1   The calendar date shall be represented by eight numeric characters. Calendar date shall be represented in the order of calendar year (YYYY), calendar month (MM), and calendar day (DD). No characters may be added or omitted.

4.2   The allowed values for calendar year are "0001" through "9999". Calendar year is presumed to be anno Domini (A.D.) unless otherwise specified.

4.3   The allowed values for calendar month are "01" through "12", with a leading zero where the number representing the month has only one digit. January is represented by the ordinal number "01", and subsequent months are numbered in ascending sequence from "02" to "12".

4.4   The allowed values for calendar day are "01" through "31", depending on the number of days in a month, with a leading zero where the number representing the day has only one digit. The first day of the month is represented by the ordinal number "01", and subsequent days are numbered in ascending sequence from "02" to the end of the month.

5.   Example

The fourth day of July in the year 1776 is represented as "17760704."

[Editor's Note: The proposed X3.30 revision is related to the combining and revision of time standards X3.43 and X3.51. There will be formal recognition of a leap second. This probably won't affect your applications, but ask your communications providers about it.]

11   *Product Certification and Year 2000 Infrastructure*

Dick Lefkon
Year 2000 Committee of AITP SIG-Mainframe

As of mid-1997, the two Y2K issues of largest financial significance remained unresolved: certification and capitalization.

True Year 200 Conformance certification of software and/or hardware is critical to all user organizations—if perhaps not to the Y2K-pooh-poohing PC houses whose income will slow dramatically as budgets adjust to Y2K.

True certification would collapse many Y2K conversion projects down a purchasing agent sitting at a desk surrounded by vendor catalogues.

GSA, among others, posts an internet list of Y2K product status vendor statements.

But as of late 1997, we had no announcement of real Y2K testing centers paralleling Underwriters Labs "UL" mark for electrical safety, or Corporation for Open Systems' "COS" mark for network interoperability.

Among others, ITAA offered a "registry" or "process survey," depending on the essential honesty of the applicant vendor. Certification is not awarded to individual, tested products. No UL or COS mark yet.

Mitre Corporation does test individual software product Y2K conformance for the U.S. military: specific products but not a service to the public. Comdisco offers a custom offsite testing program for companies' Y2K-modified code: Apparently restricted to programs' main paths, this others' offsite Y2K testing helps consulting houses do Y2K conversions.

Capitalization issues affect neither conformance nor performance, but they may sink many companies and are meaningful, too, for government agencies.

Most of Europe makes no tax distinction between a business expense and a capital outlay. We do: Most office PCs are expensed this year, although originally most were capitalized over several years.

The accounting standards boards (FASB and GASB) treat new software builds or purchases as capitalizable, but today mere modifications (like Y2K) must be expensed in the year incurred.

Taken on its face, expensing Y2K means noticeable drops in corporate (and supplier) income, a $100–$200 million Federal tax shortfall, and a stock market crash as shareholders sell upon learning their favorite companies will be reporting a nickel less profit per share.

One solution proposed by the author (and surely others) consists of Federal legislation offering companies both declaration alternatives for Y2K costs, sufficiently well drawn to exclude IS carpet-cleaning and other irrelevant budgets from that Y2K category sunsetting in 2001.

In a network posting, H Husman offered a silk purse for the 90 percent of Y2K which isn't code change, explaining it "should be rolled out to the rest of the organization to provide ongoing 'infrastructure' advantages." For example:

- ➤ General
    - Standards definition and implementation
    - Mainframe platform and client server platform impact analysis
    - Test environment assessment, operating environment inventory
    - Vendor contact; external interface contact
    - Tool assessment; tool implementation/validation/training
    - Inventory control, impact analysis control
    - Project estimating
    - Facilities management and planning (workspace and access utilization)
    - Capacity planning (system utilization)
- ➤ Configuration management process
    - Change management, issue tracking/prioritization/classification/assignment, change requirement definition (work packet), change request assignment
- ➤ Checkout
    - Work packet assignment, cross reference, impact analysis
- ➤ Quality assurance
    - Migration to test, rebuild, make, test, review of development standards compliance, functional standards compliance, delta versus production version, concurrent maintenance reconciliation, linked component reconciliation
- ➤ Production migration
- ➤ Customer verification
- ➤ Development/maintenance cycle:
    - Track work packet, accept work packet, review metrics, review cross-references, review other impacted work, review change impact analysis, analyze re to change request, change, recompile, review, unit test

CEOs and CIOs may want to make sure the CFO involves the firm's top accounting/audit specialists, since optimal classification of Y2K proportions can materially affect the firm's published financial results.

12   *Millennium Rollover: The Year 2000 Problem*

NIST Computer Systems Laboratory

At one second after January 1, 2000, millions of people will celebrate the beginning of a new year. Many people will also rue the day because of computer hardware and software problems that will create havoc for those who are not prepared. Simply put, many hardware and software systems will cease to work or will produce wrong answers when the Year 2000 arrives. This bulletin provides information that CSL has collected from a variety of sources on the extent of the Year 2000 problem, what organizations are doing about the problem, and where help can be found to deal with the problem.

The Year 2000 Problem

For 30 or 40 years, programmers have stored date information in "MM/DD/YY" format to conserve space in disk storage and computer memory. They adjusted computations to take the two-digit year into consideration when computing time periods, ending dates, and the like. Programmers represented years in the twentieth century as two digits without considering what might happen once the Year 2000 rolled around. At that time, most programmers and project leaders figured that their programs would not last into the twenty-first century. In hindsight, it seems these people should have known better, but they were trying to perform a service to their management by conserving expensive disk and computer memory. Adding two century digits to a date field for a 100-million record file would have added at least 100 megabytes of storage requirement to a disk that cost upwards of $20,000 for 15 to 20 megabytes. It made economic sense to lop off the two century digits.

Now, the industry faces the problem of adding those two century digits back into the date field in order to keep software running and producing correct output. The problem, however, is not isolated to software. Hardware will also cause difficulties for system administrators and chief information officers. System clocks on virtually every personal computer will wind up with corrupted dates on January 1, 2000.

In some cases, the date will appear to roll over to the correct date, but when the machine is turned off and then back on for the next session, an odd date will have taken its place. It may appear as January 1, 1980; January 4, 1980; January 1, %000; or some other combination of characters, all of which will produce erroneous results. The dilemma is not limited to personal computers. Some workstations, minicomputers, mainframes, elevators, and automobile central computers will fall victim to the insidious problem. In most cases, software patches can alleviate the problem to a more-or-less livable extent, but in some cases, the date issue can be resolved only by replacing the hardware.

In software, the problem will be most visible in sorting routines that sort on two-digit year fields. Storing 1999 as 99 and 2000 as 00 will cause the 00 date fields to sort out before the 99 date fields. The consequences of this action can be determined only after the context of its use is understood. Additional difficulties will crop up, and already have.

In one case, a bank's irreplaceable backup tapes were almost used as scratch tapes when a mainframe operator discovered the discrepancy and pulled them from the scratch tape bin. The problem came from the tape management software's use of the date "00/00/00" as the scratch tape indicator in the tape label retention date field. In 1995, tape backups were made with a retention date of December 31, 2000, which was stored in the tape header as "12/31/00." The tape management software looked at only the year portion of the retention date and decided that they had been around long enough. Thank goodness for the observant operator!

Year 2000 horror stories abound, all with the same lesson to be learned. Hopefully, senior executives and chief information officers will realize the severity of the problem and take preventive action. Unfortunately, the solution is expensive and labor-intensive, but there is hope and experience from those who have already taken corrective measures.

What Organizations Can Do About the Problem

William M. Ulrich, in *Application Development Trends'* February 1996 issue, describes the essential elements of a strategy for assisting organizations in solving the Year 2000 problem. These elements include:

> performing an enterprise-wide assessment of the extent of the problem;

> assessing the infrastructure in place and additional requirements to support any new functions associated with the solution;

> deploying strategies for solutions;

> defining validation strategies for testing modifications and assessing the compliance of new software to standards;

> detailing budgeting strategies.

Foremost in deciding what to do is estimating the extent of the problem. For software, the Gartner Group estimated that it will cost between $0.50 and $1 or more per line of executable code to analyze, modify, and test the software. [Editor: Gartner has now approximately doubled this cost-per-line estimate.] Organizations in general have found that 1–2 percent of code will be affected and will have to be modified, but all of the code must be analyzed to make this determination. Estimates translate into one staff-year per 100,000 lines of code! Some organizations, such as banks, may have as many as 10 million lines of code with a higher affected rate than organizations that use information technology to keep accounts, mailing lists, personnel records, etc. This translates into 100 staff-years of effort.

Time Is of the Essence

Once the extent of the problem has been defined, organizations need to formulate a time frame for corrective action and start the process as soon as possible. All of the work should be done before the start of the year 1999 in order to have a sufficient shakedown period for testing changes. With only 220 effective workdays per year (after two weeks of vacation, holidays, and sick leave are factored out), approximately 600 workdays remain until the end of the year 1998. One hundred staff-years over 600 days requires at least 35 persons working on the problem full-time. A large organization may spend between $5 million and $10 million on corrective action. The Gartner Group estimates that Fortune 500 companies will spend between $10 million and $40 million each. Worldwide, the figure is $300–600 billion.

Table 11.1 presents statistics collected over six months from various messages and notices on the World Wide Web (WWW). While not rigorously measured, these figures give an indication of what others have found in trying to deal with the enormity of the problem. The average from this information is that 167,000 lines of code per staff-year can be analyzed, modified, and tested. The scope of the problem for individual organizations can be bounded using a ballpark estimating factor between 100,000 and 167,000 lines of code per staff-year.

A Plan of Action

The most reasonable solution is to attack the problem one step at a time. A suggested means of planning for the work may include the following steps:

Table 12.1 **Size and Effort Estimates**

Comments	Lines of Code	Estimated Staff-hours
Manufacturing system	1,200,000	2,000
Commercial off-the-shelf (source code available)	2,000,000	2,500
2,000 programs	7,000,000	38,000
Retail system	7,500,000	75,000
401K system	1,300,000	9,000
7,000 COBOL programs (83% were affected)	12,000,000	200,000
Total	**31,000,000**	**326,500**

> Select a product to assist in managing the inventory of software and databases involved. Select one or more products to assist in analyzing the software and estimating the extent of the problem. Some of these products will also modify the software and data automatically, but cannot do so for every case. (Some computations are date-related, but cannot be determined from the source code. In such cases, an individual must analyze the source code line by line.)

> Inventory applications, libraries, databases, extraneous files, documentation, and other items that have importance within specific systems. Identify who is responsible for each item.

> Analyze the applications and data. Estimate modifying the source code alone to change those locations that perform date computations and logic operations based on dates. Perform a second estimation that includes modifying databases and all source code that references data fields and all source code affected in the first estimate. If there is an insignificant difference between the two estimates, the recommended course of action is to modify both the databases and the source code. It may be less expensive in the short run to modify only the source code, but more expensive in the long run if maintenance problems crop up over time due to the date processing fixes.

> Assemble a team of programmers, application experts, database designers, and project management based on the overall system requirements. Once estimates are known, the number of personnel required can be determined, particularly in view of the automated tools selected for use.

➤ Modify the system. Three major options are: a) modify the source code to manipulate and perform computations on dates with century digits included; b) use a sliding window time frame to determine date context for computations; and c) incorporate packed date fields and use specialized subroutines for performing the computations. All three of these are expensive and may lead to further maintenance problems in the long run.

➤ Test the modifications. Allow 40–50 percent of the overall project resources for testing, even more if the database is modified. This includes testing documentation to ensure that directions are correct and correspond to the changes made.

Sources of Help for Dealing with the Problem

The major obstacles in succeeding with a Year 2000 problem are:

➤ getting executive management to acknowledge the problem and take serious action;

➤ finding the right suite of tools to assist in the conversion process; and

➤ enlisting the help of knowledgeable professionals.

13   *So You Can't Program Your VCR?*

Harold Carruthers
Edward Jones & Co.

[Editor's Note: As you peruse "Year 2000" magazine articles, books, and even Congressional testimony, you may think you have found a look-alike predecessor to this landmark article by Harold Carruthers. They're look-alikes, all right, but it is Carruthers who spoke first. Congress has had a 1996 version of this book (and Carruthers' chapter) since it first appeared. An expert witness received his permission to use it in widely-reported testimony. Others have expanded his alert. e.g., on "Fire Suppression Systems" into a long list of fire suppression devices—interesting to software specialists but quite superfluous to your Fire Control unit. And so, read this definitive chapter with relish—then **staple it to the chairs of your health manager and major premises officers**![

Some processes are so complex that the most intelligent, highly trained person could not control them due to the reaction speed required, the amount of information to analyze, and the accuracy required in responding to "events" as they occur. If you doubt these facts, then I invite you to control every aspect of a space shuttle launch by using people alone. No automation, no devices, no chance. It isn't possible to maintain safety and still launch a shuttle without automation or automated devices.

Automated devices don't malfunction unless they have a physical defect or the software, microcode, firmware, ROM, PROM, and EPROM program code driving the device malfunctions. Typically, that device encounters a situation that its software was never designed to recognize or act upon. Notice, I didn't say that the situation would never occur. Instead, I said the software was never designed to recognize or act upon the situation. Automated devices must be considered *limited function* computers and subject to the same vulnerabilities as their *full-function* counterparts, such as mainframes, personal computers, or client/server-based systems.

Because automated devices are *limited-function* computers, we can use the same approach for Year 2000 correction processes that we use for *full-function* computers. That process would be:

> Get an inventory of all automated devices. Anything that uses electricity is a candidate.

> Initiate specific Y2K compliance requirements in any RFP devices, include proper language in contracts, and improve device testing procedures to include Y2K compliance.

> Determine every device where date, time, or duration related information is processed, computed, sent, or received.

> Prioritize each device's function to the business's success and customers' well being.

> Determine if any device failure is episodic (one-time occurrence at ultimate midnight) or ongoing (all other times). Many failures can be missed by turning the device *off* and *on* as needed.

> Determine the vendors for each automated device.

> Contact all vendors and request Y2K compliance information for the device and each sub-component. This is much more complex than getting Y2K compliance statements for the more typical business software packages. You'll probably need to send letters to each vendor of each sub-component to get compliance statements. Expect to spend a lot of time here with frustratingly little results.

> Replace, retrofit, or retire the automated device based on failure point, priority, vendor responsiveness, and the time required to accomplish a replacement/retrofit. Retrofit would be an ordeal

requiring disassembly, replacement of the affected components and reassembly.

➤ Test the Y2K compliant devices for proper function and repeat all steps as required.

Some of the following automated devices have either shown Y2K problems or are date, time, or duration dependent. This is just a partial list, and you need to more fully investigate your company's devices.

Critical systems

➤ *Fire suppression systems:* A Y2K failure here will shut down most of your facility.

➤ *Security systems functions included in badge readers, elevators, surveillance systems, parking lot gates for off-hours, vaults of many kinds:* The controlling system may have authorization based on from-to dates and/or from-to times. You still need to get to work.

➤ *Elevator control:* Some elevator systems will go to the bottom floor and stay there if the automation believes maintenance hasn't been performed as required. That decision is based on a comparison of the current date and the date of last maintenance as entered into the systems.

➤ *Time-dependent controls such as parking lot lighting, programmable thermostats controlling HVAC, elevator functions:* Some devices work only during certain times of the day and/or only certain days.

➤ *Power-management functions for HVAC usage and control, UPS backups and related components, off-hour power availability for lighting the building:* These are very complex issues because there are many levels on levels of monitoring. You want to be able to use and monitor devices once you get to the building and do so in relative comfort.

➤ *Environmental-safety systems for detecting changes in humidity, temperature, CO2 levels:* "Extreme" changes are monitored. Some of those changes are based on duration and/or *spike* measurements. You want your employees to be comfortable and safe while you are at work.

➤ *Phone systems including PBX, voicemail, switching, and fax services:* You may need to call your vendors for help.

➤ *Robotics systems:* These include automated assembly processes driven by functions that happen in a certain order for a certain amount of time. Failures in robotics systems have caused products to be wasted for a reason as simple as a container not being at the end of a particular assembly line. The next robotic system continued to visit the area faithfully and on schedule but seeing no product (it was all on the floor) decided there was nothing to do and went back where it came from. Failures of this type are definitely episodic.

> *Any automated device sensitive to the change to and from daylight savings time.*

Non-critical systems

> *Electronic timeclocks:* Do you really want to fight a labor suit (real or imagined) because a timeclock fouled up and didn't record employee time properly?

> *Landscaping systems:* Nothing like lawn sprinklers or water fountains going off in the middle of winter to cause problems. Your corporate sign might not light up at night.

> *Vending machines:* Some machines have direct interfaces with the vendor to indicate low-on-stock and stale-dated items. These systems order more items that will immediately go stale and then order more items that go stale then…Similar failures have already occurred.

> *Miscellaneous times:* Coffee pots and other equipment or timers can be programmed to operate on specific days and at specific times.

Obviously, getting ready for the Year 2000 will require lots of planning and preparation, but the pay-off will be to ensure that your company doesn't experience a millennium meltdown.

14   *The Successful Year 2000 Project Office*

Dick Lefkon
Year 2000 Committee of AITP SIG-Mainframe

During 1997 and 1998, organizations will staff up on legacy application programmers, testers and managers.

Whether stationed in-house or at a consulting workplace, the coders and testers will probably come to do an acceptable job in spite of apparent or discovered experience shortfalls.

Not so the managers. Soon-to-be-anointed Y2K project leaders typically have held the title less than 2.5 years and never themselves ran a huge, tight-timeframe project. They graduated to project leader from being lead technician, and may or may not have received intensive project management training. Also—except for those in brokerage during the 1995 "T+3" implementation[1]—most may never have seen an enterprise-wide upgrade.

A visible structure for Project Management should be in place at each enterprise before doubling its IS budget to accommodate the Year 2000 rollover. Not only will this provide guidelines for newly installed project managers, it also will enable in-house and outsourced resources to be controlled, coordinated and optimized.

Having run a number of general PMOs in years past, the author had set up Y2K-specific PMOs for three multi-billion dollar organizations in the year preceding publication.

Overall, a Project Management Office will usually:

➢ Report to the information executive: CIO, treasurer, etc.
➢ Serve as conduit for outsourcing and purchasing.
➢ Set up and administer the "funnel" to prioritize projects.
➢ Oversee and provide templates for others' project management.
➢ Delineate (sometimes coordinate) system assurance testing.
➢ Coordinate use of Y2K "time machine"/firewall vs. other CPUs.
➢ Provide periodic project progress reports and evaluations.
➢ Manage external contracts—including Y2K conversion progress.
➢ Provide central functions such as
  • Disaster recovery planning & management
  • Central data dictionary and repository
  • Coordination/planning of interplatform/interproject matters.

The Project Management Office may be devoid of specific projects, or it may be assigned management of a sensitive effort such as Y2K. Because there simply aren't enough seasoned managers to go around, it is critical to implement a published structure within which all work.

Having an established successful work intake "funnel" gives the PMO an ongoing ability to triage nonessential conversions away from critical ones. And, when the inevitable bulge arises, organizations can divert resources from non-Y2K/non-production efforts—not be forced to start inventing the wheel near the scheduled end of the Y2K effort.

---

1. Because of a hard-deadline regulatory requirement, stock and bond trading standard "settlement" was shortened from five to three business days. Money payment and securities delivery were required to occur two business days sooner, and legacy code had to be changed enterprise-wide for T+3 instead of T+5. To modify such consequences throughout all systems, parallels much of the logic component of Y2K, albeit not the data component.

15   *Year 2000: The End of IS?*

Gerhard Adam
Syspro, Inc.

The end of IS? How can the Year 2000 possibly be the end of IS? The industry is moving in dozens of directions with newer, better technologies being constantly introduced and exploited. Surely, the Year 2000 problem isn't that serious, or that difficult to fix.

In truth the problem is technically simple to fix. The most serious problem faced by the I/S industry regarding the Year 2000 is the almost uniform lack of concern for fixing it. Make no mistake, this is a significant logistical problem and is extremely labor intensive. For many organizations, it is already too late to easily fix it. So what happened?

What happened is what always happens in I/S; the ability to put off fixing a problem which will occur tomorrow in favor of the one occurring today. This may seem to be sensible, but in reality everyone has known that the Year 2000 would be an issue for years; yet instead of addressing it when it would be easy, most organizations simply ignored the problem. The time is past for which ignoring this problem can be continued without peril. Does this sound too ominous? Too much "doomsday" talk? Well, let's examine the problem and see.

The Problem

The problem of the Year 2000 is actually two separate problems. The first and most difficult involves the current use of two-digit years instead of the full four digits. Since only two digits are used, any operation in which the date is used for comparisons, calculations, sorts, etc., will be in error since the "00" in the Year 2000 will be less than the "99" of 1999. This simple condition causes most instances of date use to be compromised.

The second problem is whether the Year 2000 is a leap year or not. Briefly, it is. The rules governing leap year are normally that the year must be divisible by four. However, at the century mark the requirement is that the year be divisible by 400 as well.

The Consequences

What happens if we don't make these changes? Will systems fail or stop working? Probably not. What will happen is infinitely worse. Systems will continue to operate and simply calculate, sort, and compare every date based only on its numeric value without regard for the results. The ability to corrupt untold volumes of data is truly frightening.

Many articles discuss the Year 2000 with absurd outcomes for date calculations and imply that this is what will be encountered. For example, a baby born in 1999 will be calculated as being –99 years old. In most cases this is unlikely and systems will behave much worse.

For example, an individual born in 1953 will become 53 years old instead of the correct 47 years old. This error is not quite so obvious and could easily become part of a permanent data base without anyone noticing anything wrong. This error would occur because of numerous assumptions made by programmers. First, the subtraction of 53 from 00 would result in an answer of -53. However, most programs do not allow a signed result and so the number is arbitrarily made positive, hence 53 years old.

Imagine how many inventory systems could erroneously calculate shipping times or modify schedules because of the transition between 1999 and 2000. For example, if a business wanted to determine which ordered items were scheduled to arrive within the next sixty days, the calculation would typically take the shipping date and subtract the ordering date from it to determine if it is sixty days or less. If, however, this calculation occurs during the transition between 1999 and 2000, the results will be off probably by several months (see attached Example #1 pg.46). How is such an error going to be detected?

What about loans which involve "aging" an account? How many collection systems are going to be kicked off because of improper aging? How many accounts may be written off as unrecoverable debts because of improper calculations?

Imagine a personnel department attempting to obtain a list of all employees hired after June 1999. If, for example, this query were to occur during June 2000, no employees hired during that year would be included in the query since 00 obviously occurs before 99, and so the data base would not return those results. We would be missing six months worth of data, but the system wouldn't even indicate the loss.

Many people imagine that this problem exists only on large mainframes because of some implicit belief that it is all the fault of "legacy" systems. This is completely wrong. Test your PC[2] using DOS/Windows and see if it can handle the Year 2000 transition. In 70 percent of the sys-

---

2. To test your PC simply set the date to December 31, 1999 11:50 PM. Power off the system and wait about fifteen minutes. Power up the system and check the date. In a large number of cases, the system date reverts to the BIOS date of the machine (Jan 4, 1980).

tems tested by my company, the system reset the date to Jan 4, 1980. How many PC's might be connected to other systems that would take action based on that date? Is it possible that a centralized backup/archival mechanism could take this "1980" data and archive, or simply delete it? The most recent work of an individual would be treated as if it were 20 years old. Is your organization even aware of this exposure? If not, you can begin to understand why this problem is so serious.

The Scope

How can this be fixed? The most straightforward approach is simply to expand the date fields of every program and file which uses them. The requirements of this expansion are not difficult, but they are quite labor intensive.

First, review all vendor products for Year 2000 support, especially those which provide automated functions based on date and time (i.e.: scheduling systems, storage management, tape management, etc.). It is also necessary to ensure that the proper language support is available so that programs can use the four digit year format.

Second, every program will have to be reviewed for date references. Don't be reassured if the program uses it only in a report. The file which the program uses may have to be changed to support a program which maintains it, and consequently the report program will have to be changed as well. The easiest and most effective approach is to assume that all programs will have to be changed.

Third, each program must be changed, and the files it uses will have to be converted as well.

Fourth, programs which display or print the date will have to reviewed to see if the expansion of the date field results in changes to terminal displays, workstations, or reports.

Fifth, a concerted effort to trace all secondary uses of data (i.e., user constructed queries, spreadsheets, personal data bases) to ensure that users understand the consequences of this format change.

The final step is to test these systems and replace faulty existing ones.

There are other technical approaches which may be used, but despite their initial appeal their use may actually make the conversion more difficult and error-prone. The technical alternatives, windowing and date encoding, can be summarized as follows.

Windowing is based on the recognition that the two digits representing a year will only occur once in any 100 year "window" and therefore the application can be coded to exploit this. For example, if a "window" is chosen between 1950 and 2049, the application would simply check whether the date was less than fifty (50) to indicate that it has a century indicator of "20". Conversely, if the date is greater than or equal to fifty (50), then the century indicator is a "19". The major drawback to this technique is that the determination of the century is firmly embedded in the logic of the program and unavailable to anyone else. [Editor's Note: See Part 7 for a possible solution.] If the data were downloaded to a PC spreadsheet, there would be no way to assign a century indicator without knowing explicitly which window the application used.

Date encoding attempts to use the existing date field to indicate the proper century by setting bits or assigning binary codes. This method has numerous caveats which should be carefully reviewed. First, file transfers may become impossible since EBCDIC to ASCII conversions cannot allow binary data to be imbedded in the file. In addition, high level languages can only handle binary data with difficulty so the likelihood of errors in programming logic increases. If the method chosen involves assigning a code, then a file conversion may still be necessary to allow "downward" compatibility with existing data. This system will also fail if the data is already represented in a binary or packed decimal type format.

Summary

It is important to understand that this problem is not technically difficult, nor complicated to correct. What is difficult is getting people interested in fixing it. Everyone has an excuse as to why they have more important things to do, or how there is plenty of time to fix this problem. But let's have a reality check.

Assuming that only programs and files need to be modified and taking about a day to do this for each program, the important question is how many programs need to be changed? Consider that there are fewer than 1000 days until the Year 2000. At one day each,[3] it doesn't leave a lot of time for very many programs. An organization with 10,000 programs would have some serious thinking to do.

Don't think to console yourself with the idea that this is a vendor problem, or that the vendors will develop some magical tool to fix this. While vendors certainly have a role to play, the problem is ultimately yours to deal with. Even if a vendor supports the four digit year, that is

---

3. The assumption of one day per program includes the time necessary to convert the files as well. In most cases, the initial research and coordination effort will take more time than the actual programming changes themselves so the estimate of one day (average) per program is probably conservative.

no guarantee that your organization is actually using it. There is even the possibility that programs written to support a four digit year could be modified within your organization and subsequently lose that support.

Another surprising suggestion which is sometimes made is to convert all existing applications to client/server and thereby derive a technical benefit as well as solving the Year 2000 problem. This recommendation fails on several points:

1. If you don't have time to convert existing applications, you most certainly don't have time to completely rewrite them.
2. Even under the best of circumstances, the attempt to completely replace all systems with client/server would be quite ambitious given the time available.
3. Many applications do not have client/server solutions (i.e., batch jobs), so major redesign and/or business re-engineering efforts would be involved.
4. It is an invalid assumption to suppose that PCs don't have a date problem.

Example 1

An organization wants to plan for ordered items which are scheduled to arrive within the next 60 days so that storage space can be planned for and provided (i.e., warehouse, shelf space, etc.). A COBOL program might consist of the logic shown in Figure 15.1 to perform this function.

Let's assume that on January 3, 2000, a batch application is run to produce a report for the warehouse staff with the following data:

Performing the logic as coded in the program, various intermediate calculation errors will cause negative values to be treated as positive (no sign fields) as well as truncation for large values. This will result in a final calculated answer of 222 days, rather than the correct answer of 8 days.

With this result the program logic indicates that this item should be ignored and not included in the report. The error is not intuitively obvious, and would probably go undetected. What would happen to this company once it is discovered that all the reports and planning are completely wrong?

Note: This example does not account for leap year and is intended only to illustrate the potential integrity exposures rather than be a model for programming techniques.

This article is intended as a "wake-up" call to the I/S people who understand the problem but haven't done anything about it. It is too easy

Figure 15.1   *COBOL Program*

```
Working Storage Section

77      YEAR-NO                                      PIC 9(2).

77      YEAR-DAYS                                    PIC 9(3).

77      NEW-DDD                                      PIC 9(3).

01 ...

        05          CURR-DATE.

                    10          CURR-YY      PIC 9(2).

                    10          CURR-DDD     PIC 9(3).

        05          ORDER-DATE.

                    10          ORDER-YY     PIC 9(2).

                    10          ORDER-DDD    PIC 9(3).

        05          SHIP-DAYS                PIC 9(3).

PROCEDURE DIVISION.

Subtract ORDER-YY from CURR-YY giving YEAR-NO.

Multiply YEAR-NO by 365 giving YEAR-DAYS.

Add CURR_DDD to YEAR-DAYS giving NEW-DDD.

Subtract ORDER-DDD from NEW-DDD giving SHIP-DAYS.

If SHIP-DAYS > 60 go to IGNORE-IT.
```

to find excuses for not handling this problem, or why it isn't as severe as represented, or how there is plenty of time. In fact, the only way to know how bad the problem is, is to look at it. Once it is examined, a course of action can be determined. It has been suggested that the Year 2000 problem is being over-hyped and reminds one of the "Boy Who Cried Wolf." This may be, but it is also useful to remember how that story ends.

CEO/CIO:
Surviving Failure

part

Asked at the autumn 1996 SIG-Mainframe Y2K conference about a publicized CEO survey which concluded there's no Y2K problem, Ken Orr likened the process to surveying a region of lay people on whether they have cancer. He advises us here to perform a real examination. Triage, Orr urges, since tools and time aren't sufficient—and COBOL isn't everything.

Investment analyst John Westergaard says the bear market comes now, as shareholders factor Y2K costs into earnings and decide to sell their stocks and bonds. The stock market will also reflect Y2K uncertainties as 10ks are filed and reviewed by the investment community. Finally, Westergaard adds, the bear market will subside in mid-1999 as the commercial and industrial sectors look to have Y2K under control. Certain federal agencies won't make it.

Co-keynoting that 1996 SIG-Mainframe conference, Westergaard stressed that the stock market crash may have a practical salutary effect: By showing top management that the outside world takes seriously the threat of Year 2000, it will shorten the time which top management wastes [Ed: see Part 6] before accepting the reality of Y2K. Counsellor Greg Cirillo's first recommendation is to get your software agreement out of the file cabinet and read it. He advises you to sidestep "instant" solutions and take the steps which protect your Directors against likely failure. Warren Reid adds that if you don't, the government or shareholders may be able to take away your assets.

"You Might Receive a "C" Grade" adds our Congressional hearings chapter. It summarizes the agency questionnaires referred to by Congressman Horn's book-opening statement, then shows the grizzly grades he awarded. DOD rated only a "C"—and look how that spotlight woke up the Army!

Dick Lefkon then gives two views of Y2K nuclear disaster. The first centers on Y2K consequences of the nuclear instruction, "replace graphite rods after three hours." That's the book's only "awareness" (i.e., scare) piece, and it predates any other known referenced Y2K paper by a few years.

Bill Payne now joins Dick for a nuts and bolts chapter telling how to upgrade your embedded chips devices. Hospitals, etc., should receive upgrade chip packages from the manufacturers, not mail in costly lab equipment for upgrade. Show a copy of this chapter to your equipment sales person if brushed off with the familiar, "Oh, it's very complicated."

Lefkon next argues that successful management methods for your highly coordinated Y2K project are worth teaching to your managers— even though the methods aren't specially minted for this crisis. Most of your managers will find them "new."

Of critical importance, MitreTek's Miro Medek warns of guaranteed failure if you don't test the software before you start to fix it. If you don't baseline test, how do you know whether your wrong results are due to faulty legacy code or to your own faulty cures?

"Are You Testing Enough?" lays out in sequence the additional Year 2000 steps you'll have to perform to avoid failure. These aren't even obvious to most of today's Y2K practitioners, and the ones who fail badly will probably never have taken the time to read this straightforward brief chapter by Dick Lefkon.

16   *Surviving the 21st Century*

Ken Orr
The Ken Orr Institute

Let's outsource

> "To Whom?"

- The IT Industry is at full employment in North America, and will be soon throughout Europe and the Pacific Rim as well. Software Factories will solve only a part of the problem!

Solution 1—Let's automate it!

"We'll just buy a software tool that will scan and replace all of the date fields in our existing code!"

➤ Tools don't exist for all languages.

➤ The tools don't catch everything.

➤ Then there is the question of the "date routines"!

➤ What about Operating Systems?

➤ What about our purchased packages?

What about Operating Systems?

➤ *The Good News*
   • All the Major Vendors have announced they will be Y2000 compliant.

➤ *The Bad News*

   • There is lots of fine print.

   • Operating Systems have to be done first before you can test anything else!

Just finding all the date fields is a major problem, because

➤ Data names aren't clear.

➤ Dates are used everywhere in calculations.

➤ Dates condition calculations.

➤ Programmers have been very inventive!

➤ Nobody's looked at our programs for years!

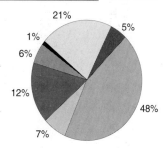

What's involved?

> Nearly 70 percent of Y2000 project activity involves project management and testing!

We can't save all our systems today!

> It is impossible at this late date for any large organization to make all of its systems Y2000 Compliant.

> The competition for resources will get worse and worse.

> We won't even be able to *find* some of our end user developed systems.

> It is poor management to waste scarce resources on "marginal" systems.

> The key is "triage"!

DSS (Data Warehousing)

> One of the major areas that will be hard to save will be Decision Support Systems.

> Solution—Rewrite the top 5–10% of all reports and then develop a Data Warehouse to support the most critical business functions.

Observations

> It is a mistake to assume that if we convert the Mainframe COBOL applications we will be safe.

> It is a mistake to assume that all of our conversion activity will be 100% efficient!

> It is a mistake to assume that we will have enough resources to get the job done!

> Don't take cheap shots if you can avoid it (windowing, code tricks, etc.).

17   *The Y2K Bear Market of 1997–'99*

John Westergaard
Westergaard Online

Beginning mid-February 1997, corporate boardrooms across America will be thrown into shock as directors review audited statements for the year ending December 31, 1996.

The cause of this shock will be the realization that tens and in some cases hundreds of millions of dollars will need to be spent by banks, commercial establishments, industrial corporations and government agencies over the next several years to correct a computer programming glitch that affects virtually every large scale computer system.

The problem will come to a head this spring because the SEC has ruled that the "Management's Discussion and Analysis" segment of 10ks (the annual financial statement submitted to the SEC) for 1996 will be required to include an estimate of the cost of correcting this "glitch" which is known as "The Y2K (Year 2000) Date Compliance Problem."

The problem traces back 40 years to computer languages designed with six digit date fields to save on the cost of computer memory. The digits "19" designating the century were assumed. Thus, the date "December 8, 1971" was entered 12-08-71.

For year 2000, these languages and programs have already in some instances begun recognizing "00" as "1900," which has caused minor dislocations to date. Come the end of 1999, however, the problem will cause computer systems to malfunction throughout the world. Until recently it was assumed that a simple fix to the problem would be uncovered. It hasn't happened.

Correcting the problem requires that computer codes be laboriously analyzed line by line and either passed on, rewritten, or discarded. A company or government agency with 100 million lines of code to be reviewed probably has a $100 million problem, and time is running out as to whether it can be resolved at all in time. The stock market will begin to reflect the uncertainty associated with this problem as 10ks are filed and reviewed by the investment community come February/March and into the summer.

Managements and their boards of directors will be shocked to learn that they will be faced with huge expenditures to correct the Y2K problem, that there will be no certainty that the December 1999 deadline can be met, that the cost of repairing systems will have to be expensed according to a ruling by the Financial Accounting Standards Board, and that even if everything is done right and on time, they may find that customers and vendors are non-compliant and therefore additional large expenditures will be required in years 2001–2002 in cleaning up problems and jury rigging provisional systems.

The bear market will last into mid-1999 when it will become evident that, however large the Y2K problem may be, it will be for the most part resolved in the commercial and industrial sectors. As to government, there will be wide disparities in performance.

Certain federal agencies, notably the IRS, will not be ready. Some state and local governments will also fail to meet compliance standards. But overall, the U.S. will be in o.k. shape and probably well ahead of Europe and Asia.

18   *Prepare for Worse*

Gregory Cirillo
Williams, Mullen, Christian & Dobbins

Ira Kasdan
Galland, Kharasch & Garfinkle, P.C.

The Year 2000 software meltdown has gone prime time: widespread coverage in the media, hearings before Congress—and warnings by tort lawyers that they are preparing to pounce. If you haven't heard by now, many software programs that perform calculations by reference to the calendar year will utter their last meaningful gasp on December 31, 1999; thereafter, these programs will belch out nonsensical results. For example, employees hired in 1996 may be logged in as being employed for negative 96 years as of January 1, 1996 (as the program subtracts 96 from 00).

Even today, you may run into difficulty renting a car if your license expiration date is after 1999. One congressional subcommittee has estimated that the repair cost to the federal government alone is $30 billion. For states and the private sector, the bill could be a multiple of that.

It seems incomprehensible that we allowed a problem of this magnitude to sneak up on us. Doomsday is less than 3.3 years away, but analysts have concluded that it is already too late to fully address the problem. Many will suffer, but some will be impacted more than others. Financial institutions (especially banks), insurance companies, and other industries with intensive date-sensitive computer systems will be the hardest hit, according to many well-respected Year 2000 experts.

Many organizations, both well-established and lesser known, are offering or developing fixes to the problem, and those packages vary significantly in terms of price complexity, efficacy, and guaranteed results. Most of the "Big Six" accounting firms, and all of the major management consulting firms, are hitting the streets with comprehensive solutions. Before you spend, however, consider the following points:

➤ **Principle 1:** *The most important device—and your first line of defense— for protecting yourself from the Year 2000 meltdown is the license agreement in your files. (You did keep it, didn't you?)*

The ultimate fix to your Year 2000 problem may be technical, but the remediation process will begin in your file cabinet. Every piece of software is governed by a license that may have specific provisions critical to addressing the Year 2000 crisis, including warranties, representations as to functionality, and access to the "source code" that's necessary to make fundamental changes to software. Chances are, unless your contract was vigorously negotiated, it probably is subject to broad waivers of warranties and limitations of liability.

Nevertheless, depending on the language of the license, applicable state law, and the skill of legal counsel in deciphering the intent of the parties, the license may have a few precious nuggets that can be used to your advantage. Do not simply jump into a technical solution. Rather, first determine your contractual rights to shift the burden, in whole or in part, to a responsible party. That may affect which technical solution should be selected and how, by whom, and by what means it should be implemented.

➤ **Principle 2:** *The company best able to fix your software (and perhaps the only one capable of doing so lawfully) is the one who developed it, but the window of opportunity for a conciliatory resolution is closing fast.*

Practically, software is modifiable by its source code only; in all likelihood, only the developer of the software has the source code and the right to modify it. Thus, once you know your license rights, your next call should be to the software developer. You may get lucky and find that: (1) the developer already has a patch for the Year 2000 problem; or (2) it is willing to release its source code to permit modification; or (3) if you found useful provisions in your license, the developer itself may feel compelled to undertake the repair.

In all circumstances, the resolution achieved must be carefully documented to ensure that the fix works technically and legally. Keep in mind that conciliatory fixes will become less common as software developers get swamped with calls from, and claims by, frustrated licensees. Settle up amicably, reasonably, and early, and you may achieve a resolution that others may not be afforded. If, however, that avenue is foreclosed, follow the guidelines under the next principle.

> **Principle 3:** _Technology solutions have a religious quality in that (1) there are many variations on the same theme, and (2) you will be told that all of them are absolutely wrong, except for the one being pitched to you._

Nontechnical professionals and managers do not want to learn the inner workings of computer software or hardware. They simply want someone to take control and make the problem go away. But often these nonprofessionals cannot make an informed decision because the fundamental facts and lingo are foreign to them.

On the other hand, technology professionals have a single-minded fervor that often precludes balanced decision making. Ask a Macintosh user what is good about a PC. The answer will be clear, definitive, convincing, and, for the most part, empirically useless.

The bottom line? Year 2000 corrective measures may or may not work, depending on how well you manage each step of the process and how well you have protected the investment you have made in a solution. Remember…there will not be time for you to do it all over again. So, (1) be certain that you are advised of all options, risks, likelihoods, and possible scenarios by technical professionals who have no stake in the outcome; (2) do not rely on the advice and opinions of the solution-seller alone; (3) always seek multiple views, including those of a competent Year 2000 consultant if your technical issues require such expertise; (4) obtain from all service providers the best possible (written) proposals and contractual assurances of a timely and effective fix; and (5) follow Principles 4 and 5, below.

> **Principle 4:** _Do not seek only outside help to implement the solutions; seek qualified help to manage the solutions._

A single adviser/manager should orchestrate the process of assessing and pursuing license rights, selecting and contracting with outside solution providers, and closely managing the implementation of the solution. There will be a multitude of decisions to be made (especially if you need a separate solution provider for each software program you have). Do you replace your system entirely? Contract for a fix? Gear up to sue your vendor? Or do nothing and gear up to defend against the consequences? What will these various options cost? If you do not have diverse in-house capabilities to answer these questions, you should consider hiring an adviser/manager from the outside—no ties to the solution provider(s)—who can act as the company's representative.

➤ **Principle 5:** *Notwithstanding Principles 1 through 4, prepare for the worst (or at least for the next to worst).*

The "worst" means that you will not have taken the necessary steps to fix the problem by January 1, 2000. Since that is unthinkable—and you will have little recourse by then (there is no escaping the turn of the century)—at least prepare for "the next to worst." That means, get ready for the lawsuits against (and perhaps by) you, for they are virtually sure to come—even if you meet that immutable deadline.

Assess the legal issues that must be addressed. For starters, determine what (if any) shareholder disclosures are necessary regarding the problem and the anticipated solutions. This is an especially important issue for publicly traded corporations that are required to identify events or uncertainties that are reasonably likely to result in the corporation's liquidity increasing or decreasing in any material way.

Next, review your existing contracts with customers. What obligations do you have that might be affected by the Year 2000 problem? Do contracts have to be renegotiated or amended? As for future contracts, make sure that the problem is properly addressed. Will a limitation of liability clause do the trick, or are other contractual terms appropriate? These are just a few of the considerations that should be covered.

Finally, directors and officers must be protected. While it may seem unfair to hold directors and top executives responsible for computer glitches, think of it this way: If a bank's computers suddenly cannot handle or accurately make date-sensitive calculations, or if a corporation's computers can't input orders beyond 1999 and revenues are lost, someone will be sued—and you can bet that it won't be the company computer programmer.

The fiduciary duty of due care requires the exercise of reasonable diligence and care, including the obligation to make informed decisions. The standard of care inevitably will be determined by reference to similarly situated boards of directors and officers. If your competitors are getting the necessary advice on Year 2000 issues and are assessing and addressing the problem, you may be in trouble if you do not do likewise.

Following these principles alone may not save you or your company from the millennium meltdown. But at least it should give you a leg up—if nothing more than to stave off the lawsuits against officers and directors, a feat in itself.

19   *You Can Lose Your House and Yacht*

Warren Reid
WSR Consulting Group, LLC

In the past, Directors and Officers (D&Os) used to enjoy an unspoken legal immunity against failed computer systems and related projects within their companies. The typical penalty was firing the project manager, Chief Information Officer (CIO) or CFO. Well, the party's over! With the advent of the ubiquitous Year 2000 problem (caused by the computer storing the Year 2000 as "00" in its bowels), I predict Officers and Directors will be held liable for the impact of this known, predictable, and potentially massive computer failure in their organization.

D&Os are the **fiduciary stewards** of the company and its assets. It is their responsibility to understand the material threats facing the company, enlist appropriate outside expertise if required, investigate alternatives, develop meaningful and reasonable plans, execute such plans expeditiously following the "business judgment rule" to solve problems and minimize risks. After all, with CIOs changing employers every 2.1 years, on average, D&Os can "enjoy" as many as three CIOs between now and the Year 2000—each one with no accountability.

In today's business environment, computers are so key to successful operations that their failure causes catastrophe, not inconvenience! Many organizations, have no backup manual system. Yet, only 30 percent of US companies are even beginning to deal solving the problem. If a company's Year 2000 solution is not available in time and causes the company to lose market share and control over billing, payables, receivables and customer lists, to be unable to schedule manufacturing, or even need to shut down operations for several months, D&Os will share part of the price.

"The Dilbert Dimension"

One of the important legal questions will be to determine the point in time that D&Os will be held liable. Mr. Scott Adams, the developer of Dilbert, syndicated three "Dilbert" comics regarding the Year 2000 in business newspapers nationwide on September 17, 18, and 19, 1996. These comics did not explain why the issue was timely or why the comics were funny. The author correctly assumed that anybody reading the business section of a newspaper would already know about the risks and impact of the Year 2000 problem on their company. The term "The Dilbert Dimension," which I coined with Scott's blessing, I believe marks the latest calendar date from which juries/costs will hold D&Os liable for beginning to address the problem in a diligent and professional manner. Delay, denial, lack of good business judgment, under-budgeting the solution, or worse, hiding from the problem can have serious ramifications beyond hurting the company. Such actions can even be deemed gross negligence or even fraud and violate D&O and E&O insurance policies, allowing shareholders, customers, clients, class action initiators, and allegedly injured parties suits to sue D&Os directly: your house, your housekeeper, and your yacht will be up for grabs!

Audited Financials and Rule 6835

The Dilbert Dimension, however, doesn't excuse the fact that publicly held companies, under a long-standing SEC Release #6835, must include a Management Report (formally known as "Management's Discussion and Analysis of Financial Condition and the Results of Operations") with its filings and audited financial statements. The purpose is to allow investors to look at the "quality" of earnings reported in the audited financials. Those "quantity" figures otherwise reported in financial statements simply tell how the company did in the past, using auditing and accounting rules—telling little about the company's ability to continue to perform at that level.

Under SEC Release #6835, management is required to make known trends, demands, commitments, and events likely to come to fruition, and the *resulting potential impact to the company and its future*. This disclosure is required unless management has determined a material effect is not likely to occur (which I interpret as a position that must be proven). Let me predict that a material effect will occur, and management must address the problems today, or face stiff penalties in court.

The Steps

Addressing the problem involves following certain critical steps. Following a good plan, even if the ultimate solution is not perfect, will probably be enough to enable the D&O defendants to withstand devastating lawsuits that can be expected. Of importance, it is these same steps that will also get your company to a good Year 2000 solution.

With regards to the Year 2000 problem, the steps are: prove you did your homework; assure you have proper project management and backup in place; inventory your software/source code; perform a risk assessment/impact analysis on your organization; adequately communicate the problem, impact, and fix processes within your organization, to your auditors and the SEC, and know how to respond to questions from the press; develop a detailed plan to address the problem and the total resources required on a system-by-system basis; develop a critical path analysis to assure appropriate projects are undertaken first, and develop a sensible budget with contingencies; maintain appropriate documents to prove that the management's plan and commitments to fix the problem were performed on time and professionally; get outside second and even third opinions on progress, use of tools, and alternative solutions to problems; prepare and maintain frank/true status reports that identify progress, problems, options/solutions to problems; maintain documents supporting the investigations/decisions for staffing, surviving CIO turnover and other critical resources (i.e., use of outside consultants, outsourcers, and/or third party Year 2000 solutions providers—the latter which typically addresses only 25%–35% of the problem).

Remember, the Year 2000 problem was caused by human shortsightedness. Some human error will still be allowed by the courts when looking at failed solutions as long as you follow a well-accepted process like the one outlined here. Your solutions must materially work but do not have to be flawless.

20   *You Might Receive a "C" Grade*

Tom Bachman
Mitre

Stephen Horn and Carolyn Maloney
*House Subcommittee on Government Management,
Information and Technology*

Dick Lefkon
New York University

A Beginning

1996 began with Tom Bachman's submission to DOD of the Mitre Assessment of the Effects of Two-Digit Years for the Year 2000.

	Grades	Does the agency have a Year 2000 plan?	Is there a Year 2000 Program Manager?	Does the agency have any cost estimates for Y2K solution?	Did the agency respond to the questions?
International Aid	A	✓	✓	*	✓
Personnel (OPM)	A	✓	✓	✓	✓
Small Business	A	✓	✓	✓	✓
Social Security	A	✓	✓	✓	✓
Education	B	✓	✓	✓	✓
Nuclear Regulatory	B	✓	✓		✓
State	B	✓	✓		✓
Defense	C		✓	✓	✓
Treasury	C	✓	✓		✓
Science Foundation	C	✓			✓
Agriculture	D		✓		✓
Commerce	D		✓		✓
Environmental Protection	D		✓		✓
General Services	D		✓		✓
Health and Human Services	D		✓		✓
Housing (HUD)	D		✓		✓
Interior	D		✓		✓
Justice	D		✓		✓
NASA	D		✓		✓
Veterans Affairs	D		✓		✓
FEMA	F				✓
Labor	F				✓
Energy	F				
Transportation	F				

Figure 20.1   Year 2000 Agency Preparedness

Mitre was asked to scope the Y2K problem and comment of automated tools. Bachman concluded that DOD's "high" per-line cost estimates were conservative; and that tools alone can't solve the problem—and don't even exist for unpopular languages.

He listed what the main problem is, where its found, and why its hard to solve. More than any other in a hundred paper submissions, Bachman's stressed the challenge of system interoperability coordination, analysis and testing.

Legacy systems are often constructed by combining different commercial and government (COTS and GOTS) off-the-shelf code. All tools require a labor investment to operate them, and many of their producers advertise as consultants with a tool.

The Year 2000 problem is unique because of the immovable deadline [Ed: impressed lately by someone who repeated this?] and because faulty systems will fail simultaneously. More work is needed on rating the available tools.

Mitre, too, specified the steps Awareness, Planning, Inventory, Impact analysis, Change, Testing and Implementation.

There were four fairly unique concluding recommendations:

➤ Establish a centralized clearinghouse.
➤ Investigate for security breaches to occur when systems fail.
➤ The problem cannot be resolved by fixing a program at a time.
➤ Identify and mitigate risks where the deadline won't be met.

Worth the Spotlight

House Subcommittee heads Steve Horn and Carolyn Maloney earned SIG-Mainframes' Grace Hopper Memorial Award for Outstanding Achievement in Large Scale Computing, because they were conscientious and alert enough to query Federal Agencies and hold hearings to spotlight Y2K that spring—the same season SIG-Mainframe presented its own Y2K program to AITP/DPMA's full Board of Directors.

You can read Chairman Horn's personal recollections about that process at the beginning of this volume. The "uncurved" grades he describes are shown in Figure 20.1.

Your own internal planning survey can probably borrow some of the two dozen Horn questions shown in Figure 20.3—or this encapsulation:

➤ Have you begun a Y2K effort? When started and what steps? Are you represented on the Interagency working Group on Y2K? [Ed: Now, the Council of CIOs.]

> Risk assessment of vulnerability of programs and applications? If so, show me; if in process, how being performed, when due?

> Have you developed a plan? Does it have timetables, milestones and performance indicators? Do you have a contingency plan? Show me. When invoke it?

> Do you have an inventory of programs, platforms, languages? Users? Lines of code? Lines to be changed? Prioritization? OK, which applications are secondary?

> Who is your project manager—Overall? Day-to-day? Tasks? What's your org chart? Activities of organization components? When were you last given status? Show me the report.

> What resources are/will you devote? Costs by fiscal year, and their components? Can you extract this from existing budget? No?, who much needed? How many person years? Estimated cost per line? Acquisition plans and their status? Proportion of Y2K work to be done in-house vs. outsourced? Have you engaged vendors already? Whom and what dollars?

What Proper Attention Can Do

The Department of Defense did not receive the worst congressional grade, but is was a "C." That was not a matter of pride for the protectors of our liberties, with "conservative" anticipated per-line Y2K costs ranging to $8.50 per line.

By the first quarter of 1997, the Army had turned from laggard to Year 2000 participant, decreeing early shutdown of doomed-anyway systems—and redirecting to Y2K millions of dollars already committed to routine enhancements as shown in Figure 20.2

Department of the Army
Washington, D.C. 20310
March 31, 1997

Memorandum

Subject: Year 2000 Fixes Top Priority

1. Our Army's ability to shoot, move and communicate effectively—both within our Service and in conjunction with Joint and combined forces—has come to rely heavily on automation. The increasing importance of information dominance, with its continual introduction of more sophisticated technological weaponry to the inventory, has made this reliance critical. Consequently, the Year 20000 (Y2K) problem must not be allowed to pose any risk to the warfighter. This is a matter that affects the credibility of the Army with its soldiers and the public that we serve.

2. We must deal with Y2K now so that our soldiers can continue to place well-founded confidence in their weaponry and automation tools through the change in millennium. To this end, each Army organization responsible for system development and maintenance should endure that Y2K is a high systems resource priority. Therefore, effective immediately, all nonessential sustainment and enhancements will be postponed until systems have been analyzed, fixed, tested and certified Y2K compliant using existing resources.

3. As part of this process, *each system will be seriously considered for elimination.* Only those automation systems which truly assist in mission accomplishment should remain in your inventory. Ensure that you are not spending any resources on fixing systems that are no longer essential, or that will not be in use past 1 January 2000.

Denis J. Reimer	**Togo D. West, Jr.**
General, United States Army	*Secretary of the Army*
Chief of Staff	

Figure 20.2   *U.S. Army Policy of Y2K Priority (italics added)*

1. Has your agency begun an effort to ensure that your information systems are year 2000 compliant? If so, when did the effort begin? What steps are they taking to ensure compliance?

2. Has your agency represented on the Interagency Working Group on the Year 2000?

3. Have you performed a risk assessment of the vulnerability of your programs and applications to the year 2000 problem? If one in planned, but has not been completed, indicate when it is expected to be completed and how it is being performed. If it has been completed, please furnish a copy.

4. Have you evaluated the vulnerability of your agency's systems and applications to external organizations, such as states or other entities, that fail to modify their own systems for the year 2000 problem? If one is planned, but has not been completed, indicate when it is expected to be completed and how it is being performed. If such an analysis has been completed, please furnish a copy.

5. Have you developed a plan for the year 2000 problem? If one is planned, but has not been completed, indicate when it is expected to be completed and how it is being developed. If it has been completed, please furnish a copy.

6. Does your year 2000 plan, if completed, contain specific timetables and milestones? What performance indicators are you using for determining whether your computer programs and applications are year 2000 compliant?

7. Do you have contingency plans for your year 2000 project if your agency is unable to complete your year 2000 plan as scheduled? When would you make a decision to implement the plans? If available, provide a copy of the plan.

8. Do you have an inventory of the major computer programs, platforms and languages for your agency? If so, please provide the inventory to the subcommittee.

   a. Does the inventory identify the users for each application?

   b. Does the inventory include the total number of lines of programming code at your agency and the number of lines required to be changed?

Figure 20.3   Subcommittee Questions to Federal Agencies

c. Does the inventory provide an assessment of the likelihood that the application or program may be affected by the year 2000 problem?

9. Have you developed a prioritization of which systems need to be fixed in order to avoid an adverse impact on the public? Have you prioritized your applications and determined which ones can be set aside if all cannot be modified by 2000? Please provide a list of those major applications that have been designated secondary and the activity with which they are used.

10. Who at your agency is your project manager?

a. Who has overall responsibility for the year 2000 issue?

b. Who has day-to-day responsibility?

c. What other responsibilities does the day-to-day manager perform?

11. Provide an organization chart for your year 2000 project, including the reporting arrangements for personnel, including names, titles and grade levels. (Where appropriate, include the activities of constituent components of your agency.)

12. When was the last time you received a status report on the year 2000 project? Please provide a copy of the most recent report.

13. What resources are being devoted or do you project will be devoted to the year 2000 issue?

a. What are your cost estimates, by fiscal year? What are the components of those cost estimates?

b. Have you made or anticipate making any new needs requests for your year 2000 project, as opposed to providing for it through re-programming existing budget? If so, what is the request?

c. How many man years do you estimate will be devoted to the year 2000?

d. What is your estimate of your cost per line of code for your year 2000 project?

e. Do you have any acquisition plans for this project? If so, and what is the status of your plans?

Figure 20.3   Subcommittee Questions to Federal Agencies

f. What proportion of the year 2000 work will be done in-house, and how much will be out-sourced?

g. Have vendors already been engaged? If so, please identify them. What is the scope and dollar value of their contract?

Figure 20.3   Subcommittee Questions to Federal Agencies

21   *Nuclear Disaster and the Millennium Trojan Horse*

Dick Lefkon
New York University

The author has introduced a quarter century of COBOL with this advice: "Shortly after Thanksgiving of 1999, load up your station wagon with canned foods and go on a camping trip for a few months, preferably near caves."

It is easy to forget that the first computers in all countries were used to make more accurate calculations of sines, cosines and tangents for use in plotting projectile trajectories. The projectiles were artillery shells. With explosives. In warfare.

ICBMs and their silos are not the only places where digital servo-mechanisms may avert or precipitate a Y2K thermonuclear conflagration. One need only consider:

"REPLACE GRAPHITE RODS AFTER THREE HOURS."

In the Chernoble disaster humans overrode instructions like these. So can the calendar.

Imagine for a moment you are at the New Year's Eve party in 1999. It is ten o'clock and everyone is consuming champagne and hors d'oeuvres. The microwave stays on for each warm food, and all the lights are turned up festively to power the crystal chandeliers.

Down the highway a bit, the local nuclear plant feels the surge of power consumption, and its software decides to stoke up the oven by withdrawing the graphite suppressors from the nuclear pile. It fully intends to put them back at 1 AM—but 1 AM never comes.

Nuclear installations have peaceful or offensive uses. Given the incentive of legislative oversight, U.S. DOD and DOE related sites are not the problem, even at the estimated $8.50 per line Y2K cost for some applications.

The main danger comes from non-NATO countries which may not have tight enough hold of their nuclear resources and/or may lack the wealth to generate sales calls by the major Y2K vendors. Someone here should phone there.

The author originated this approach at the warfare session of a 1991 NIST/NSA conference. U.S. agencies might not have prioritized staff to "push the channels" then. Now they have more incentive. [Editor: If you don't know Kazakhstan, you don't know nuclear missile silos!]

Here is the first known published "Year 2000" paper. It was initially delivered at the 5th International Computer Virus & Security Conference in March of 1991, then repeated in October at the 14th National Computer Security Conference. The title and author were the same as this chapter's.[1]

THE ORIGINAL ABSTRACT FOLLOWS

As the Millennium is approached, military installations on all sides are targeted to test the date dependencies of internal software in order to identify and address a possible date-related Trojan Horse.

Early Military Computing

In the beginning of the computer age, business applications and home amusements were the farthest thing from the major users' minds. Eniac and its siblings were used primarily for making trigonometric computations. The precise sines, cosines and tangents resulting from their calculating loops went into plotting projectile trajectories.

The projectiles generally were artillery shells, with explosives, in warfare. Some subsequent early use of computers took place for what today are referred to as nuclear missile silos. Movies such as *Dr. Strangelove* may not have been far from the truth in depicting rocketry launches triggered in part by computer decision-making.

---

1. "Nuclear Disaster and the Millennium Trojan Horse" in Holleran, J. (1991), Proceedings from the 14th National Security Conference of the National Institute of Standards and Technology / National Computer Security Center (October 1–4), Washington, D.C.

Historically, most programs did their logical reasoning by arithmetic comparison: Is A greater than B; if so, do such-and-such. Reverse the sign of the numbers, and of course the outcome would change as well.

It is hypothesized that some nuclear missile silos of early construction are present in much their original form today, including the original computer decision-making programs. Further, that at least some of these programs use the current date in part of their reasoning.

Dates and the Millennium Trojan Horse

Many of today's LANs and PCs ask the user to input the date in the form YYMMDD. The conference began on 911001 and ended on 911004. It lasted (B-A) + 1, or 3 + 1, which equals four days. The Thirteenth NCS Conference took place in 1990: 1991–1990 = 1 year.

A surprising computational result occurs between the 23rd and 22nd NCS Conference: 2000–1999 equals 1 year. But using the standard YYMMDD format, 001001–991001 = [negative] 990000. The date difference is negative, and wherever it occurs all the decisions may be backwards—including the decision to arm and launch.

This idea is not so farfetched as it may seem. Recently a financial company's business users discovered to their chagrin that bonds held in 1991 but maturing in 2011 had a profit/loss calculation exactly four times as large—and backwards—the twenty-year span results expected. That even happened using programs written in the 1980s, not the 1950s.

Limitations of Software Quality Assurance

It is a commonplace in commercial programming that the older a system is, the more likely its source code has been lost or otherwise does not match the stored executable binary. Thus, while source code scans and analyses may be helpful, they do not constitute a complete solution.

Ballistics launch software, in either well-known or obscure weapons systems and locations, needs to be exercised judiciously to determine its usage of the calendar date.

Position in Brief

An appeal is made to defense ministries around the world to seek out the full spectrum of computers in their nuclear weapons installations. As each computer is identified, a controlled test of software can be made, such as bringing the date forward in steps, to observe what happens as the Millennium line is crossed.

22   *Replacing Your Embedded Chips*

Bill Payne
Kramer & Kent

Dick Lefkon
Millennium Associates

The design of embedded systems began with the introduction of the microprocessor in the mid 1970s. This preceded the introduction of the Personal Computer by a number of years. Designers found that they could eliminate hundreds of components by replacing the hardware functionality with a microprocessor and a little code. Companies found new markets for products which could be manufactured for lower production costs. This has led to the proliferation of these devices into virtually every area of our daily lives. This in turn, has become a veritable mine field as we approach the year 2000. Even if every mainframe legacy code application were fixed by the year 2000, these embedded systems will wreak havoc with every aspect of our daily lives. There are way too many of them installed to change them all. We must target those areas which have the greatest impact on the safety and security of the nation. The largest problem occurs in that these systems are stand-alone by nature. They are designed to perform only one or two tasks independent of other systems. To fix them will require not only a hardware change but also changes to the embedded software. In a lot of cases, the companies which designed these devices no longer exist. For those which still exist, the company management is too concerned with profitability for the current quarter. They do not and will not spend the money necessary to fix a problem which has not yet occurred. The costs associated with these changes will be enormous if you do them, staggering if you don't.

Hospitals and Process Control

For an overall description of exposures from the seven billion embedded chips sold annually, please see Chapter 13 "So You Can't Program Your VCR" by Harold Carruthers.

Hospitals and more specifically the medical equipment which the staffs have come to rely on, will present one of greatest threats to life. The medical community has become more and more dependent upon technology. Hospital administrations have trimmed their operating costs by eliminating support positions through the use of embedded technology.

Each nurse on a hospital floor can care for a greater number of patients today than at any other time in history. But this is a double-edged sword. The hospital makes more money by having fewer support personnel per patient as long as the technology they rely upon stays operational. This equipment is much more stringent than elevators in regards to periodic maintenance and calibration. Take the simple case of the infusion pump as an example. These devices are designed to administer a specific amount of medicine to a patient over a specific period of time. Today's nurse sets up the medicine and programs the infusion pump with the required parameters and leaves the patient. The nurse knows that if the infusion pump has a failure it will sound an audible alarm. The hospital administration also has come to the conclusion that by relying on the technology of the infusion pump, more patients per nurse can be serviced. When the year 2000 rollover occurs, every infusion pump in the hospital will become inoperable. The embedded controllers will perceive that is has been 100 years since the last maintenance and calibration occurred. It may be assumed that the staff can simply reprogram the infusion pumps with the wrong date to get them operational again. This will not be allowed since the units are already out of calibration. The infusion process will revert back to the setting of a drip rate manually. Every patient receiving an infusion of medicine will have to monitored more closely thereby overloading the patient load on each nurse. As the patient load increases, the quality of care decreases.

Process controls are where the largest amount of embedded systems are found. These can range from simple flow and measurement systems up to the control of an oil refinery or a nuclear power plant. Virtually all manufacturing facilities found throughout the world employ hundreds if not thousands of these devices.

Technical Description of the Problem

One of the best ways to illustrate this problem is to take the reader through the design process for a simple embedded system. For this scenario we'll create a fictitious company called Acme Enterprises. We will assume that we're hired as consultants by Acme Enterprises to design and build a simple door security system. The design criteria from the company is as follows:

1. four entry doors to be monitored
2. four electric door locks (one for each door)
3. normal hours of operation are from 8 a.m. to 5 p.m.
4. no entry on weekends
5. no entry on programmed holidays (set via a Personal Computer)

From this initial criteria, we can see we'll need an embedded system which has four inputs for monitoring the entry doors, four outputs for controlling the electric door locks, a serial interface for communication with a Personal Computer, and a real-time clock chip. The Personal Computer will allow the company personnel to input the dates for the programmed holidays. We will assume that it is Year 2000 compliant. We will also assume that another consultant has already designed the software menu system running on the Personal Computer. All we care about is the serial data stream which will be used to provide a communications channel between the Personal Computer and my embedded system.

Let's begin the design of the embedded system controller. The building blocks of such systems are a microprocessor, Random Access Memory (RAM), Read Only Memory (ROM), a Real-Time Clock (RTC), and various peripheral devices for inputs and outputs.

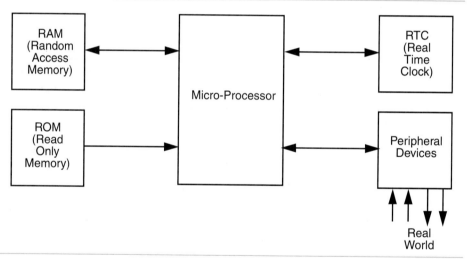

Figure 22.1   Block diagram of a basic embedded controller

The first device to be selected is the microprocessor. There are many different types from various manufacturers to choose from. Suppose you want a low-cost system as far as production costs. This eliminates the PC based systems, the 32-bit embedded processors (such as the Intel 386/486), and most of the 16-bit processors. We are left with 8-bit choices from Intel, Motorola, or Zilog. These are the Intel 8051, the Motorola HC11, and the Zilog Z8 families. The authors prefer the Intel 8051 family of microprocessors. The others are just as capable, but it usually comes down to the whim of the designer. Designing a product which has not existed before taps into the same creativity as any other art form. From the design criteria we know we will also will need RAM and ROM for the system. The RAM will be used for storing data which is variable by nature. Things such as the status of the doors, the number of days of operation, and any variables used by the internal program are located here. The ROM is where the program for the microprocessor itself resides. It tells the microprocessor exactly what to do step by step. It cannot be changed except by replacing the chip in which it resides. By choosing the Intel 8051 you can get both the RAM and the ROM internal to the physical chip. This eliminates two additional components and saves money.

Architecture

The architecture of the Intel 8051 is comprised of three distinct memory areas. These are the internal registers, the program memory (ROM), and the data memory (RAM). Both the program memory (ROM) area and the data memory (RAM) area can access up to 65,536 distinct address locations.

The internal register area is divided into two groups of registers. These are referred to as the scratchpad registers and the special function registers. The 128 scratchpad registers are for general purpose data storage. These registers can be used to hold a small number of temporary variables when high-speed access is needed. The first thirty-two address locations are divided into four eight-byte banks of registers. Each bank of eight registers is referred to as the processor's working registers. These are used as the general purpose registers for the program running in the microprocessor. All instructions referring to registers R0 through R7 will be directed to the selected bank. This allows for a fast context switch by simply changing which register bank the processor is using. The next sixteen address locations are bit-addressable. These locations can be used as software flags by the programmer representing various states and conditions. The microprocessor can distinguish a bit address from a byte address by the instruction being used. The remaining eighty register locations can be used for general purpose data storage. They can also be used as a location for the programmer's stack. The stack is the area where the return address of a calling program is stored when a subroutine is executed. When the call to a subroutine occurs, the address of the calling program is pushed onto the stack. The stack pointer is then decremented to point to the next available storage location. Upon completion of the subroutine a return instruction is executed. The address of the calling program is popped from the stack and inserted into the program counter. The calling program then continues executing the next instruction after the call to the subroutine.

The program and data memory areas of the Intel 8051 each consist of 65,536 separate addressable memory locations. The program memory area is only accessible with read instructions by the microprocessor. The Intel 8051 contains an 8,192 byte program memory on the chip itself. The remaining 57,344 memory location addresses can be used to reference memory locations external to the chip. These can be used to access external Read Only Memory (ROM) chips if needed. The data memory area is external to the Intel 8051. All 65,536 memory address locations can be accessed for both reading and writing. This external area is used to attach memory chips and peripheral chips to the microprocessor.

Design

Let's do a quick check as to where we are in the design process. So far, we have covered the requirements for the microprocessor, the ROM, and the RAM. The Intel 8051 also has four eight-bit general purpose input/output ports. Each port bit is physically connected to an external package pin. This is why the physical package has forty pins. Thirty-two of these are necessary for the four eight-bit ports. The remaining pins are for power and ground, the crystal, and various other control signals. Four of these general purpose port pins will be used as signal inputs from the doors. Each door will have a micro-switch which opens the circuit when the door is physically opened. This action will cause a voltage change on the specific port pin to which it is connected. Four additional general purpose port pins will be used to control the electric locks on the doors. The last two remaining hardware items to be covered are the serial communications port which connects to the Personal Computer and the Real Time Clock (RTC). The serial communications port is already a function which is available in the Intel 8051 chip. We will use this serial port and assume that it is configured properly in the microprocessor. We will however, need another chip which will translate the voltage levels from the microprocessor to the levels required by the Personal Computer. A Maxim MAX232 chip will perform this task quite nicely. So far, our embedded controller for Acme Enterprises is comprised of only two chips.

The Real Time Clock (RTC) will complete our design. This chip will provide the program running in the microprocessor with the ability to know exactly what the time-of-day, day-of-week, and year are. Semiconductor clock chips are available from a variety of vendors. Three of the most popular are the variations available from Motorola, National Semiconductor, and Dallas Semiconductor. In this design, we will use the Dallas Semiconductor DS1287 clock chip. The authors prefer to use this product due to the high level of integration in the device. It uses a derivative of the industry standard Motorola clock and contains its own lithium battery. It is a totally self-contained device. This saves on circuit board space and the cost of additional components such as a battery holder. The Dallas Semiconductor clock chip derives its time base from a 32 KHz crystal running independent of the microprocessor. This crystal is contained within the physical package of the device as is the lithium battery. The information is provided to the system in the form of 0.01 seconds, seconds, minutes, hours, day-of-week, date, month, and a two digit year. The data is always represented in the Binary Coded Decimal (BCD) format except for the hours data. If the mode of operation is selected as 12 hour then one bit of this data byte is used for an AM/PM indicator. If the mode of operation is selected as 24 hour then the first BCD nibble represents the 10-20 hours and the second BCD nibble represents the 0-9 hour. See Figure 22.2. Remember, this device is totally compatible with the industry standard Motorola clock. Therefore, it is NOT year 2000 compliant. It uses a single byte to store the year information. This provides for only two binary coded decimal digits representing the year.

Address	Bit 7	Bit 0
0	0.1 seconds	0.01 seconds
1	10 seconds	seconds
2	10 minutes	minutes
3	10 minutes alarm	minutes alarm
4	10 hours	hours
5	10 hours alarm	hours alarm
6		days
7		days alarm
8	10 date	date
9	10 month	month
A	10 year	year

Figure 22.2   Real Time Clock register organization

Our hardware design is now complete. The embedded controller is comprised of only three chips. The costs associated with manufacturing the hardware have been reduced to the lowest possible level. The only thing remaining is the software which will run on the embedded controller. The simple flow chart in Figure 22.3 depicts the basic operation of the

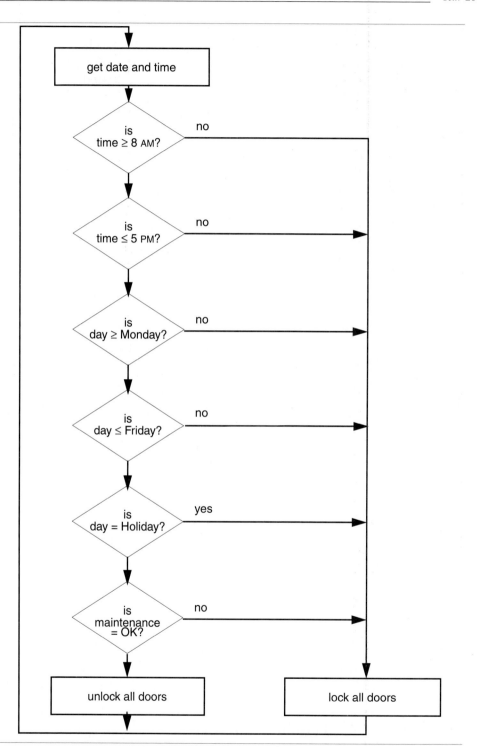

Figure 22.3   *Software flowchart for Acme Enterprises Controller*

software. The system checks the time-of-day and day-of-week to determine the required state of the electric locks. If the time-of-day is between the hours of 8 A.M. and 5 P.M. and the day-of-week is Monday through Friday, the doors are to remain unlocked. If a door is opened at any other time the alarm is to sound. As a safety precaution, let's include a routine which checks to see if the controller has received a yearly maintenance checkup. This will reduce real exposure and legal liability in two specific areas. First, the system is providing security for Acme Enterprises during all off hours. This security will be compromised should the system fail. Second, in normal system operation, it will prevent a system malfunction which could lock the employees out of the building all day on a scheduled work day.

Everything looks great! We have met all of the design criteria as specified by Acme Enterprises. The system is installed and functioning properly. The system becomes taken for granted. As far as upgrading the system over time, the management attitude of Acme Enterprises is a common one. If it ain't broke, don't fix it. Herein lies the problem. The system is working well for the limitations inherent in the design.

Unfortunately, the original designers of the semiconductor clock chips overlooked the potential problem for the year 2000 rollover. At the time these products were designed the cost of silicon wafers was quite high. To have added an additional byte to handle the most significant digits of the year would have affected the cost of the chip. In addition, designers were continually told that the life cycle of a new product was usually three and at best five years. [Editor: So you believed Cold War Era COBOL programmers were the only people who felt this way?]

In the real world, designs are only replaced if they suffer a catastrophic failure. Designs which were based on technologies new in the mid-1970s are still performing their designated functions today. Embedded systems are not like the Personal Computer market, where upgrades every six months are "necessary." As long as the system is performing it's specific task properly, it will remain in place for years.

Two Problems

The problem arises with the two digit year register internal to the clock chip. This year counter will rollover to 00 when the year 2000 arrives. To the embedded system the date will be 1900 instead of the year 2000. Even if the rollover does not initially create a problem, one will still exist with the leap year issue. The year 1900 was NOT a leap year. If the embedded system has anything coded which uses a day-of-week indicator, it will begin to go awry when February 29 shows up. If this system is connected to another system which has been corrected, both could become corrupted.

At press time, Dallas Semiconductor has developed a semiconductor clock chip which is year 2000 compliant. This chip design utilizes a byte wide counter for the upper two binary coded decimal digits representing the hundreds of years. It has also been designed to compensate for the leap year which will occur in the year 2000. This device is the first in the industry to comply with the new ATA specifications from the Personal Computer industry. This chip can be retrofitted into _any existing design_ which utilizes the older Motorola based technology.

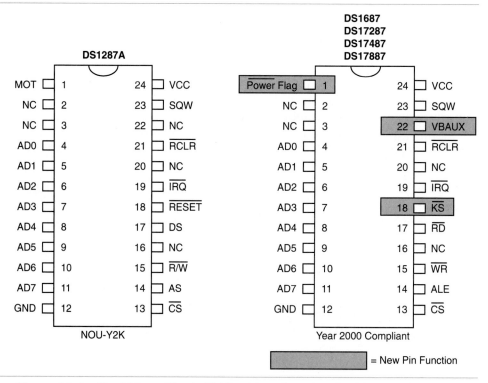

Figure 22.4   Real Time Clock (RTC) : New function for Year 2000

This solution only fixes the hardware side of the embedded systems problem. Unless the software contained in the Read Only Memory (ROM) is changed to access the new data nothing has really changed. Let's go back to the embedded controller which was designed for Acme Enterprises. This system uses a variable to store a date which indicates when the last maintenance check was performed. When the rollover occurs, the system will assume that it has been 100 years since it was last serviced. At this point, the system will pull itself out of service and indicate that a malfunction has occurred. Any embedded controller module which is used to replace this unit will also indicate a malfunction. This will occur as soon as the date is entered into the system.

Let's play with the system designed for Acme Enterprises a little more to bring to light the other problem with the year 2000 rollover. Assume the software for the Acme Enterprises embedded system does not care about the year field in the service variable. When the rollover occurs, nothing happens—yet. When February 29 rolls around the system will be off by one day. This will affect the day-of-week perceived by the system. Wouldn't it be great to have the system assuming that it is Saturday when it is really Friday?

What Embedded Chips to Replace

Figure 22.5 provides an overview as to the general microprocessors used in embedded systems. These three manufacturers represent the core technologies available to a designer. Each of these product families contains derivatives of their basic architectures. The majority of these devices are available as either ROMless or ROMable. The ROMless devices will have an external chip which contains the software code for the embedded system. This can be updated and replaced without removing the existing microprocessor from the system. The ROMable devices contain the embedded software internal to the physical device. These devices will have to be replaced to update a system.

Intel	80x48	80x51	80x52	80x151	80x251	80x96
Motorola	68HC05	8HC08	68HC11	68HC12	68HC16	68300
Zilog	Z86x0x	Z86x6x	Z86x9x	Z80	Z180	Z380

Figure 22.5   *Six types of embedded chips*

How to Replace Embedded Chips for Year 2000

Now that the reader has a good idea as to what an Embedded System is, we can proceed to explaining the processes involved in making an existing system Year 2000 compliant. A few years ago one of the authors designed an Automated fueling Control System for a nationwide corporation. Each system was comprised of a Bar-Code Input unit at the fueling kiosk, a Printer unit for receipts, a Tank Level Monitor unit for measuring the amount of fuel in the underground storage tanks, and a Central Control unit. The Central Control unit was used to coordinate the system and provide and interface to an existing wide area network.

Each of these units is designed as a standalone embedded system. They were networked together using RS-485 Twisted-Pair communications. Each unit was designed using an Intel 8051 microprocessor and a Dallas Semiconductor DS1287 Real-Time-Clock (RTC). As you will remember, the Dallas Semiconductor DS1287 RTC is an enhanced version of the original Motorola RTC. Virtually every clock chip designed is based on the original architecture of the Motorola RTC. Even many Pentium processors use the same basic register layout as this first RTC.

The units are mounted on poles placed at the fueling kiosks. They are exposed to rain, sleet, snow, and extreme temperature variations. The cases which house each unit are NEMA certified for the stated environmental operating conditions. Now that the scene is set, let's proceed to detailing the process required to Y2K-renovate the units.

The first step in making these units Year 2000 compliant, is to go back to the development lab. Each unit will have to be prototyped using the newer Year 2000 clock chip (currently from Dallas Semiconductor). The existing Dallas Semiconductor DS1287 RTCs must be replaced with the newer DS1687 RTC chip. This new device redefines the function of three existing pins on the chip.

Depending on the original design of the circuit board, these new pin functions may require the circuit boards to be cut and jumpered to make the new chips work. The embedded software is the next item to be attacked after the hardware has been updated. Each of the four units has embedded software, specific to the task it is designed to perform. The existing software must be modified to take advantage of the four character year designation in the DS1687 RTC chip. After the new software has been extensively tested, it must be programmed into new Intel 8051 microprocessors.

Beyond the Year 2000 Lab

With this complete, we are now ready to go into the field and begin the update procedure. Our field update component bag will contain four Intel 8051 microprocessors and four Dallas Semiconductor DS1687 RTC chips. Each microprocessor is specific to the unit it is designed for. The RTCs are generic and can be used in any of the units.

The next step involves physically going to each of the units. The NEMA enclosure on each unit will have to be opened. The power supply cabling and all interface cabling must be marked and removed from the circuit board. The circuit board will be removed from the enclosure by removing the retaining screws. The tie-down strap which secures the DS1287 RTC will have to be removed. The DS1287 RTC is one of the fewer socketed devices on the circuit board. This was due to the fact that

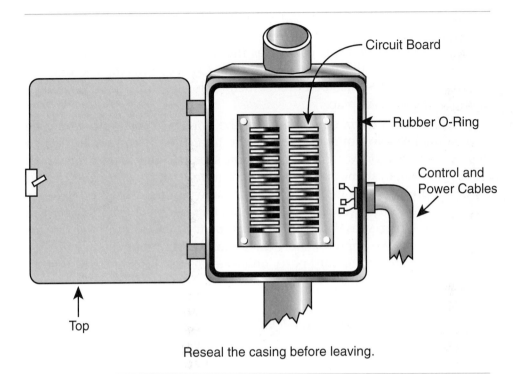

Circuit Board

Rubber O-Ring

Control and
Power Cables

Top

Reseal the casing before leaving.

Figure 22.6   NEMA compliant standalone enclosure

it contains a Lithium energy source internal to the chip package. This makes the replacement a simple task: Removing the older DS1287 RTC and installing the newer DS1687 RTC. A new tie-down strap must be installed to secure the device against vibration.

The replacement of the Intel 8051 microprocessor is next. This will not be so simple as the replacement of the RTC chip. The microprocessor is soldered directly to the circuit board. The use of sockets in a design increases the cost of the product. They are used only when there is no way around it. Each of the forty pins of the microprocessor must be cut to remove the part from the circuit board. Each hole in the circuit board must be desoldered and made clean enough to allow the pin of the replacement microprocessor to be inserted. After the new chip is inserted into the circuit board, each of the forty pins must be individually soldered in place.

Weatherproofing as the Sun Sets

The circuit board can now be reinstalled into the NEMA enclosure. The power cables and other cabling must be reconnected to the circuit board. The rubber O-Ring seal of the NEMA enclosure should probably be replaced at this point. The seal could be damaged after having been exposed to the elements for an extended time. As a precautionary move, it should be replaced. This completes the necessary modifications to just one of the units of the Automated Fueling Control System. The remaining three units must also be updated before this location has a Year-2000-Compliant system in place.

The amount of time necessary for the update of each unit would be approximately two hours. Therefore, the total time necessary to update one simple location would be eight hours or one day. The firm which installed these systems has over three hundred sites across the United States. Some of these installed systems have multiple Bar-Code reader units to service more fueling kiosks. This increases the time required to update the larger sites. With a team of four technicians working on this update, it will take approximately three months to update the overall system. Of concern are the third party units such as the Tank Level Monitor.

23 *Ignore the "New" Y2K Project Management at Your Peril*

Dick Lefkon
Year 2000 Committee of AITP SIG-Mainframe

The project management techniques detailed in this compendium were not specifically invented for Year 2000 migrations. But pretend they were. "Old hat" to you, they are as brand-new and surprising to your candidate Y2K managers as the Three Stooges are brand-new and surprising to your great grandchildren.

As CEO or CIO or CFO, you are used to communicating with subordinates by a single word or question or shrug. If you ask, "What do you suppose we should do about this?" the response may be an immediate "I'll..." or even a two week silence followed by, "Here is how we took care of it."

You are three or more levels up from the coder-supervisor you may once have been, and for over a decade you haven't personally had to corral and direct soldier programmers, whose efforts must coordinate if your Y2K "war" effort is to have any chance at succeeding. Remember, the top of your organization should not only give lip service to Y2K but also promulgate management practices that show respect for the troops while following a discipline.

An example of that discipline is the requirement that all progress be verified via components containing one workweek of effort or less.

It's your neck, and even if you outsource some of the tasks, don't court disaster by forgetting to have less-than-a-week milestones bearing names of individual doers at home or away, and publish them frequently to all concerned: Laissez-faire management is a sure path to Y2K failure.

With an easily visible work horizon, staff have the means to exhibit "team behavior." For instance, you can reward a coder or tester who in timely fashion exercises candor and tells a supervisor that a milestone—or series of milestones—is in trouble. When the braggart sharpshooter is diverted to help bring it in, the milestone accomplishment should nonetheless be attributed to the slowpoke: Without his or her candid notification, that whole coordinated subsystem goal could have gone down the drain. That forthright tester has enabled the gray box in Figure 23.1 to be filled in—and saved your published subsystem rollout date from failure!

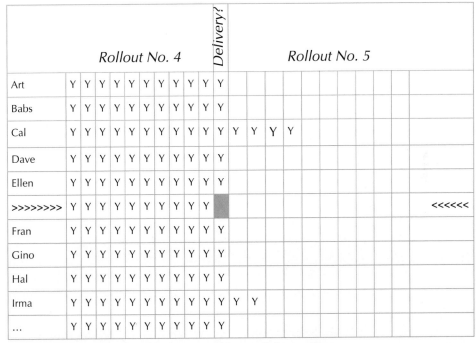

Figure 23.1   *Tight coordination in large deliverables*

Now consider the other side of the coin. For whatever reason, suppose some coders or testers can't see lateness or admit it to themselves. If management allocates the time and effort to break down tasks to two-day milestones, at least you'll get an early flag to spur you to action when complex tasks are in danger of failure. Bite-sized milestones (or inchstones) are easy to spot-check and publish on a done/not-done basis.

When an individual programming or coding task is large enough to report that it is "80 percent done," you have a problem. You have no idea how much really *is* done, and it's your own fault if the "late" gray box above threatens to make Rollout number 4 six weeks late instead of two days late!

Make no mistake: It is hard work and unpleasant for a supervisor to sit down with a programmer for two hours to negotiate that six-week "atomic" task down into fifteen bite-sized ones. The programmer—who must be treated with respect—will at first consider the supervisor's insistence unprecedented (it is!) and unreasonable (based on accustomed methods). The supervisor needs to be steeled to be disliked by the programmer during the two hours it will take for the six-week large goal to be reworked into fifteen trackable ones. The manager won't cause lasting damage by managing: Their normal personal relationship will resume tomorrow.

The Compleat Manager Part later in the book contains article reprints concerning project acceleration, project control, and coding standards. Most Y2K managers and project leaders have been on the job less than three years. Unlike the top officers, they may never have received training in "obvious" close-supervision techniques. They can learn them by reading, or formal training, or higher management's clear example.

24   *How Do You Know Without Testing?*

Miro Medek
Mitretek Systems

The "how much testing we need" discussion just highlights some of the behavior I see around when omitting some basic steps and approaches that will cost us time and resources in the testing and implementation phases.

You have to decide how much risk you can take by not testing a system thoroughly before putting it back into production. But before you even touch the system, you had better establish your baseline, Y2K compliance criteria, test scenarios, data, and expected test results for Y2K compliance testing. Establishing the baseline requires you to recompile your programs, build the system, and run your compliance tests to see how the system behaves— before you change even one line of code!

I am sure that every shop has a "few" programs that you have not touched in a long time—never mind tested. Now, if you do not establish your Y2K baseline, how do you know

> - that the current system will fail and how it will fail?
> - what are you supposed to "fix"?
> - that your modifications worked and fixed the system behavior?
> - that the wrong results you are getting are due to your needing to modify a few more lines of code, not to your having introduced a new problem through your code modification?

I am amazed to see people chasing after date references in the code and changing them before even knowing how the system fails and how it is supposed to behave. I can guarantee that you will have a heck of a time distinguishing between what you fixed and what you broke through your Y2K conversion!

Do not fool yourself. Statistical data from software maintenance show that when you "fix" dates and associated logic in systems containing 10 million lines of code (assuming that about 3–5 percent of code is "impacted"), you WILL introduce more than 1,000 new functional errors! Don't believe that a Y2K project will be any different from projects in the past—just worse because of shorter and shorter deadlines.

I once headed the technical operation for a software vendor which published a new software release at least once a year. Despite extensive testing based on regression tests, some bugs never failed to make it through.

If you do not establish your baseline, and if you do not test, please explain to me how you can guarantee that the system works and has the same base functionality?!

Thus, it's not only "how much" but also "when" to test.

25   *Are You Testing Enough?*

Dick Lefkon
Millennium Associates

The previous chapter represents *essential understanding*. Baseline testing—from unequivocal production source code—is your *necessary* starting point. Don't republish Figure 25.1 but you're certainly authorized to blow it up as large as you can, pin it up inside every Y2K cubicle, and tape it to every vertical wall in your Year 2000 testing Area!

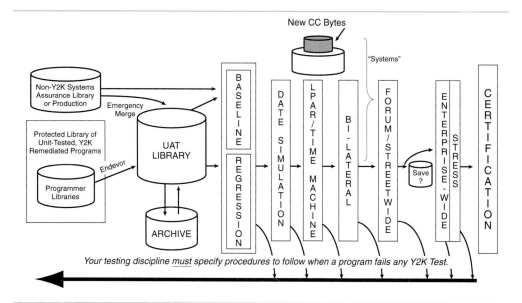

Figure 25.1   Editor's preferred sequence of Y2K UAT testing © 1997 Dick Lefkon

In the upper left, notice that you'll have to accommodate emergency production changes—generated either through malfunction or via unequivocal new regulatory requirements. Look along the bottom arrow and be reminded that when your testing process detects a program flaw you had better have—*in advance*—an efficient way to recycle the flawed remediated code into testable re-remediated. Otherwise, coders and testers will spend all their time pointing their fingers, not applying them to keyboards!

Parts 9 and 10 will explain the testing jargon and Y2K specifics you've heard concerning date-specific testing, as well as the more standard testing phases. However, since 1996 this is the only book we know of, which explicitly deals with large-scale Bilateral and Forum Testing.

You have, no doubt, experienced bilateral testing before: At the end of testing a remote transaction feature, you've contacted the distant company or agency and arranged to run "real" transactions against a phony account or product type which they set up for you. This must be coordinated between the *two sides*, hence the name *bi-lateral*.

Rarely (if at all) have you seen *many* distinct business partners all required to make their data dance at exactly the same time. It's a full-dress rehearsal, in which all business people in town go down to the

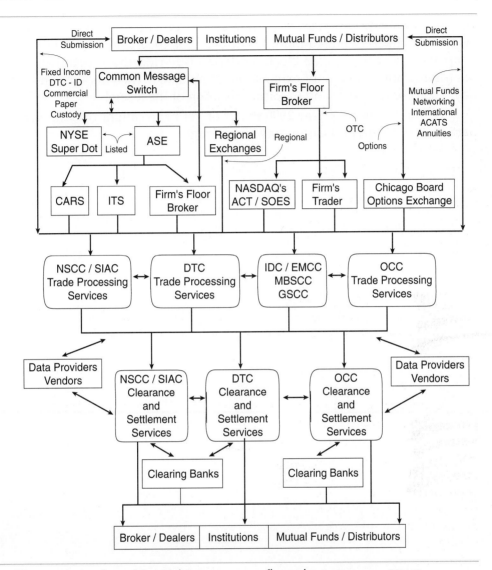

Figure 25.2   Securities industry process flow chart (Courtesy of SIAC)

Town Forum and carry on business ("in" Year 2000, etc.) in its full diversity. Hence the name, Forum Testing.

If you're in that 84 percent of our economy which *isn't* financial, the complexity of Figure 25.2 might look frightening! But if you're in a bank, brokerage, etc., you'll readily recognize the names of your many "neighbor" trading partners.

Do a single security trade[2] and your electronic impulses become a little steel ball bouncing and ricocheting across the pinball paths of this Financial Entities Forum diagram prepared by the Securities Industry

Automation Corporation (SIAC). At one time, on one day, *everyone* residing on this diagram must mount his or her Year 2000 Time Machine, start it up with a synchronized clock, and ride-ride-ride those planned test securities transactions until exhaustion. Then batch. Then another on-line day. Then comparisons and excommunication of the losers!

Forum Testing for Year 2000 may not yet have caught up with your particular segment of the economy. But it might.

---

2. Few industries can boast/grieve a Forum diagram as complex as SIAC's. Investment companies are definitely the Y2K leaders in this regard. That's why, if you talk about Forum testing "on the [Wall] Street" folks will refer to it as *Streetwide Testing*.

CEO/CIO:
Getting Started

Now you know what the problem is (Part 1) and how bad it can be (Part 2). ITAA begins Part 3 by urging against piecemeal approaches. Viasoft then scopes out the specific Y2K need and cost for a dozen industries and mentions outsourcing. It is interesting that 40 percent of their clients plan to implement date expansion to eight digits.

Dan Miech describes seven suggested meetings and assessment points, then lists nine key vulnerabilities—beginning with noncompliant customers and suppliers. Besides a 10 percent/80 percent rule for customer revenue, he points out that one tenth of your suppliers are critical to your product. Also, to the extent that Y2K failures will shut down businesses, financial institutions should watch the business-loan 80 percent of their loan portfolios.

Fisher and Casey now return to describe the four main phases they feel a Y2K effort should contain: information gathering, planning, implementation and testing. And Micro Focus helps your first step by furnishing two dozen specific metrics for possible use in your assessment: size of databases with stored date information; number of copybooks with date references, etc.

After Jim Zetwick's assurance that development need not cease, there is a Cap Gemini introduction to alternatives—including a score of warnings on contractors used for outsourcing: no tools, just methodology; no methodology, just tools; a "one size fits all" approach; a fully freeform, custom approach; little discussion of testing; no lifecycle; etc.

Next, Platinum walks you step by step through major project tasks: plan the project, determine all date formats, locate the data, determine components, change systems/programs/utilities/ databases, convert stored data, test changes (further detailed), and manage the change control process.

Both Platinum and Judy Brand describe a variety of test types. Brand stresses the need for a testing firewall, and she suggests the use of low-cost "pygmy" S/390 computers by IBM and CDS for this purpose (or to replace whatever old iron Big Blue may not support come the Millennium). She discusses practical testing issues—such as capacity, availability, partitioning, and safety—and concludes with economies due to post-2000 usage.

Finally, Gerhard Adam returns to start your preliminary assessment process with his 18-question (per application!) survey accompanied by explanatory instructions. It is one of many special-purpose surveys and checklists found throughout this book. We urge you to synthesize and customize to create your uniquely applicable forms, not start from ground zero and either leave out important data or follow the lead of a vendor with a good boardroom presentation.

26   *Software Conversion: Issues and Observations*

Information Technology Association of America

The Year 2000 software conversion is not limited to the data center. On the contrary, client/server and workstation implementations are just as likely to have two-digit year references in their code. Managing the conversion in a geographically distributed, technologically diverse client/ server environment is apt to add to total costs. Organizations need to "step back" from the immediate concerns and get a clear view of the total problem set. With the advent of electronic benefits transfer, electronic data interchange, electronic funds transfer and other forms of electronic commerce, many computer systems interconnect multiple firms or government agencies. The Year 2000 software conversion must be considered from all points in a trading community.

While not every application and system needs to be converted at once, companies and agencies need to adopt a systematic approach to the conversion process. A "head in the sand" attitude, a piecemeal process— or a decision to simply pass the conversion challenge on to a newcomer— exacerbates the situation by reducing the amount of time to manage the situation effectively, leads to configuration management problems, and increases the urgency of conducting the conversion. Conversely, early attention to the situation can allow time to address the extensive parallel testing requirements, system-wide impact analysis and changes, and ramifications such as necessary changes to archival tape libraries.

27 *Metrics and Findings*

Viasoft

Findings

Still Early in the Year 2000 Game

It is startling to note how few of the organizations surveyed have begun to fix the Year 2000 problem (see Figure 27.1). Fifty percent of the organizations were either in the "no money down" awareness phase, in search of a sponsor, or had assigned a sponsor but have not undertaken any substantial work. This loss of ground will be difficult to make up as the number of resources available becomes increasingly limited. The longer an organization waits, the more expensive and complex the conversion effort.

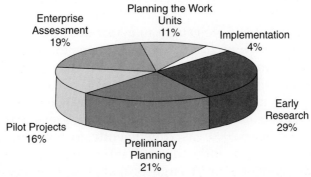

*Figure 27.1 **Still early in the game** (Source: VIASOFT 1996 User Conference Survey)*

Until now, Information System (IS) organizations had the luxury of time to either start with an enterprise assessment (19 percent) or get their feet wet with a pilot Year 2000 project that analyzes a representative application suspected of having significant date problems. The pilot project then goes through the entire conversion life-cycle, from assessment to completion, in order to assess the effort, uncover potential pitfalls, and fine tune process and project management activities. However, as time passes, there are fewer technical options and the nature of the problem shifts from a technical challenge to a business-critical threat. The Gartner Group states: *"by the end of 1999, less than 50 percent of IS organizations will have 100 percent Y2K compliance in their application portfolio."* To minimize business disruption, IS organizations must identify applications and prioritize their conversion in accordance with their strategic value and time horizon to failure. This effort will require the involvement of the business units in order to single out critical applications, all of which may further delay the whole endeavor.

Costly but Mandatory

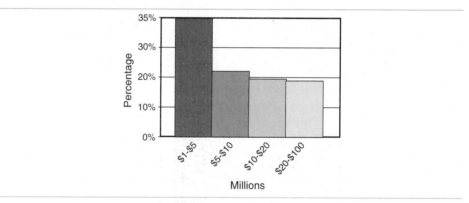

Figure 27.2 Year 2000 spending

Many IS organizations are caught in a Year 2000 dilemma. They have no past experience to draw from, and there seems to be very little return on investment. Furthermore, they are juggling many top-priority projects and are continually challenged to meet end user deadlines. Yet, if the year 2000 problem is not addressed, it may cause major disruption to the business, and even result in business failure. IS executives are scrambling to present the Year 2000 case intelligently to top management. These executives have very little internal information readily accessible to estimate the cost of such a large project, and industry estimates look costly, though realistic (about $1.15/line of code [LOC] according to Gartner Group). Today many IS departments still do not have a clear idea of how much they will spend on the year 2000 problem and seem hesitant to find out. This lack of knowledge is shown by the limited number (34 percent) of survey respondents able to estimate the cost of their year 2000 conversion.

Of those who have assessed the total cost of a Year 2000 project, 35 percent expect to spend $1–$5 million, 21 percent $5–$10 million, 19 percent $10–$20 million, including two organizations which each expect to spend over $100 million (see Figure 27.2). When comparing the distribution of these costs to the size of the application portfolios, there is a direct correlation between number of programs and LOC impacted and projected cost (see Figure 27.3).

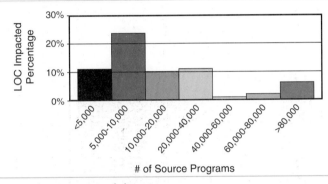

Figure 27.3 *Application portfolio size*

The data gathered from year 2000 engagements helps to substantiate the findings from the User Conference Survey. The metrics show that on average and across industries, 78 percent of an enterprise's application portfolio is impacted by the year 2000 virus, with variations from as low as 44 percent to as high as 100 percent. The greatest fluctuation was found within a single industry sector, finance (see Figure 27.4).

This discovery exemplifies how pervasive dates are within applications and the degree to which critical applications might be at risk. The year 2000 metrics also reveal that, on average, a mere 3 percent of the total LOC are impacted by the year 2000 virus. Since the majority of applications are impacted (78 percent), an organization will need to analyze each application to find the impacted LOC.

Based on our findings, the average cost of conversion per LOC (see Figure 27.5) substantiated the year 2000 project estimations by the Gartner Group. Cost estimates vary depending upon organizational readiness including project/process management skills and experience, architecture and framework, and availability of hardware, software and human resources. The total cost of the conversion per LOC ranges from a low of

Figure 27.4   *Application portfolios impacted per enterprise*

Industry	Total Programs	% Programs Impacted	%Programs Impacted (Min)	% Programs Impacted (Max)	Total LOC	% LOC Impacted	% LOC Impacted (Min)	% LOC Impacted (Max)
Computer, Software	5,313.00	89.35			10,612,724.00	4.06		
Finance	3,854.75	76.44	44.67	100.00	5,564,947.50	1.78	1.37	2.75
Government, Local	2,483.67	85.02	71.65	93.18	5,348,362.00	8.44	1.30	20.18
Government, State	109.00	88.99			191,409.00	5.54		
Health Care	3,501.00	78,63	70.87	86.38	3,687,173.50	3.14	3.04	3.23
Insurance	7,841.50	82.02	65.83	90.43	9,141,698.00	4.99	2.50	7.15
Manufacturing	5,836,00	73.73	55.63	93.37	5,585,203.67	2.65	1.97	3.66
Retail	1,295.00	93.75			2,024,127.00	1.72		
Telecommunications	10,776.50	67.70	52.07	80.65	13,897,797.50	1.47	0.92	1.97
Transportation	11,087.40	76.11	63.04	83.92	15,615,196.40	2.53	1.74	2.01
Utility	8,316.00	79.26	69.51	89.00	9,409,592.00	1.51	0.99	2.04
Totals	216,057.00				286,576,032.00			
Industry Averages	6,354.62	78.00			8,428,706.82	3.00		

$.95 to a high of $1.45 as of July 1996. (However, it should be noted that this average cost is likely to climb dramatically as resources become increasingly limited.) We also expect that the costs of testing and managing the overall conversion effort will continue to rise.

Rise of Outsourcing

Although most User Conference attendees indicated that they did not have an estimate of their year 2000 conversion costs, many did indicate a need for additional computing and human resources. As seen by the service industry at large and Solution Providers specifically, outsourcing of partial or complete year 2000 projects is on the rise and will continue to rise until solution provider resources are completely booked. The survey data shows that 47 percent of respondents are planning to supplement their conversion effort with external providers (see Figure 27.6).

Program-Level Metrics

	Average
Cost per Program	$1,229.00
Cost per Impacted Program	$1,645.00
Hours per Program	2.77
Hour per Impacted Program	3.31
Cost per LOC	$1.02
Cost per Impacted LOC	53.40

Figure 27.5   *Average cost per logical LOC*

Our experience shows that the average IS organization is balancing outsourcing activities with internal efforts to minimize the risk of disrupting critical applications and ongoing maintenance. This is a reasonable option at this time, as most central IS organizations have neither the project/process management expertise nor the resources to carry out such a massive project to completion.

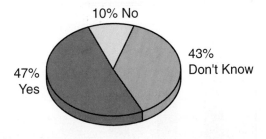

10% No

43%
Don't Know

47%
Yes

Figure 27.6   *Is your company planning to hire outside staff to support your conversion effort?*

When considering application outsourcing options for the year 2000, organizations may choose one of the following conversion strategies:

- Fix/maintain a company's specific set of applications (e.g., human resources) in a "factory"
- Perform application testing activities from integration to system testing in a specialized testing center (e.g., COMDISCO Millennium Testing Services)

> Bring people in to run the project and/or the tools
> Transitional: move to client/server, package, components.

Even though a company may outsource varying portions of their Year 2000 conversion project, the central IS organization will still play the dominant role in sponsorship and coordination, and ultimately will be accountable for results.

Problem Shifting

As stated earlier, the procrastination of IS organizations has now elevated the problem from a technical challenge to a threatening, business-critical issue. There is not enough time left to make every application year 2000 compliant before systems begin to fail. Aligning IS strategies with business priorities is a critical objective for all year 2000 projects. Applications must be converted based on business criticality and time horizon of failure. IS organizations must relinquish the desire to try to convert every single application written in any "language du jour." When User Conference attendees were asked which languages beyond COBOL were perceived as critical, they listed a vast array of conventional, exotic, and antique languages. Given this list, organizations may be setting themselves up for failure in trying to tackle too much in the little time remaining (see Figure 27.7).

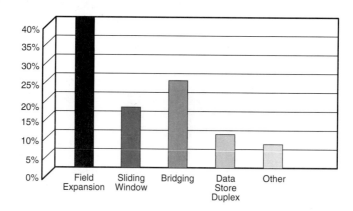

Figure 27.7 Conversion strategy

IS organizations must identify the business-critical applications that will fail first, and this created the need for thorough planning. Likewise, technical conversion strategies are evolving from total field expansion to a range of more flexible and less hazardous techniques such as bridging.

28   *Surround Yourself with Solutions*

Daniel Miech
Terasys[SM], Inc.

The key to surviving the Year 2000 (Y2K) issue is to surround your business with solutions. This means assessing the Y2K problem from a business perspective and uncovering as many vulnerabilities as possible, over and above your internal computer software and hardware issues. To accomplish this, a high level strategic assessment should be conducted. This article describes the necessary steps to uncovering Y2K vulnerabilities and provides some example exposures.

An effective Y2K strategic assessment process includes the following steps:

➤ The Initial Meeting

Conduct an open dialogue with Executive Management to discuss Y2K, the level of awareness, and the probable implications to your organization. If a person has not been designated as the Y2K manager or sponsor for your organization, do so now.

➤ Current Business Model Review

Review with your Business Analyst the key strategic business issues impacting your organization, the strategic processes which drive your business, and the information applications deployed which support your current business model.

➤ Future Business Plans

Take a look ahead at your strategic business plan and identify any key elements or information technology changes critical to reaching your desired business state. Generally, this is a complete review of your three to five year business plan.

➤ Information Infrastructure Review

Meet with IS Management to review the major hardware components which comprise your information infrastructure, and define key relationships and dependencies between business processes and information infrastructure.

➤ Business Applications

Take an initial look at the Y2K compliance of the major software applications that support your business. Define key relationships and dependencies between business processes and information infrastructure.

➤ Communicating With and Within Your Business

With IS Management and a Business Analyst, look at the communication systems in place, how the organization communicates, and determine the entities which are vital inflows and outflows to your business.

➤ Strategic Assessment Results

Using the results from the previous steps, prepare a document that identifies the strategic areas of vulnerability concerning Y2K and the impact on strategic business issues. Include recommendations as to how the risk associated with the vulnerability can be minimized.

Take the time to hold one or more mediated Y2K strategic assessment sessions, and you will uncover ignored Year 2000 exposures such as these:

➤ _Vulnerability 1:_ **10 percent of your customer base generates 80 percent of your revenue.**

What assurance do you have that your key customers are effectively addressing Y2K issues and will not cause any disruption to your business? Will their ineffectiveness in dealing with Y2K issues change their ability to buy? How large is a customer's Y2K exposure, can they afford to resolve it, and are they planning to survive beyond 1999?

Determine what they are doing to resolve their Y2K issues. Share your Y2K plans and assure them of no future disruption to their business due to date transition issues on your part. Review your service level agreement with your customers and include such assurances.

➤ _Vulnerability 2:_ **80 percent of your expenditures for supplies/ services/materials go to 20 percent of all suppliers/vendors; 50 percent of these are key suppliers critical to producing product.**

How large is each supplier's Y2K exposure? What assurance has been obtained that each supplier is effectively addressing Y2K issues and will not cause any disruption to your business?

Engage your supplier in Y2K resolution with you, especially those which are key to producing your product. Determine what each supplier is doing to resolve his Y2K issues. Obtain assurances in writing.

➤ _Vulnerability 3:_ **Security Systems**

Will you be able to enter your facility on January 3, 2000? Will the system behave properly?

Obtain written assurance that security systems will not cause disruption to the business.

➤ _Vulnerability 4:_ **Telephone Services**

How vital is phone communication to your organization? Voice mail? Faxing? Other transmissions of data over phone lines? EDI?

➤ *Vulnerability 5:* **Payroll functions are out-sourced.**

What assurance is there that your people will not experience disruption in compensation? automatic deposit? the calculating, recording, and transmittal of employee wage information?

Thoroughly assess your payroll provider and obtain written assurance from them that no disruption to your business will occur due to year 2000 date transition issues.

➤ *Vulnerability 6:* **Acquisition of other companies**

What is the level of Y2K exposure within the company you are considering of acquiring? Are they effectively dealing with Y2K issues? How is the exposure expense being funded? What impact will this acquisition have on your long term revenue and profitability goals?

Include a Y2K strategic assessment as part of your acquisition review process to aid your decision and negotiations.

➤ *Vulnerability 7:* **80 percent of outstanding loans are to businesses.**

What assurance has the lending institution obtained that the business customer is effectively addressing Y2K issues? What level of risk to the financial institution is associated with outstanding business loans?

Obtain clear direction from examiners and regulators as to the level of assurance which is needed to minimize business loan risk associated with Y2K vulnerabilities. Consider obtaining that assurance from major business customers through audit or assessment.

➤ *Vulnerability 8:* **Engineering and Manufacturing Systems**

What is the mix between in-house engineering and manufacturing versus out-sourced? What assurance has been obtained indicating such systems will not cause disruption to business?

Obtain written assurances that such systems will not disrupt engineering and manufacturing business processes.

➤ *Vulnerability 9:* **Process Control**

How much date, time, and calendar functions are imbedded within your process control systems? Dates are very pervasive throughout such systems. What safety and regulatory issues are involved? Professor Lefkon's example "replace graphite rods after three hours" is very applicable here.

Obtain written assurances that such systems will not cause disruption to the business due to date transition issues and will not introduce increased safety and regulatory risk.

The vulnerabilities discovered from a Y2K strategic assessment emphasize that Y2K is not just a computer problem, it is a full-scale business problem. The key to success or survival is surrounding yourself with solutions in addition to addressing internal computing issues. We all have Y2K problems. We all need to focus on solving them together, at the same time, and before the same deadline.

29 *Technical Solution Overview*

Chris Casey
Bytewise Consulting, Inc.

Ted Fisher
Sperduto & Associates, Inc.

Copyright © 1996 The Information Management Forum

Although a myriad of methodologies for bringing companies into compliance with the Year 2000 have emerged from various solution providers, the process itself can be generalized and divided into a few essential phases. These phases are described below, along with some of the key activities which should take place during the phase. This technical overview is written with the non-technical manager in mind.

Step 1: Information Gathering

The purpose of this phase is to answer the following questions:
- How much (roughly) is the solution going to cost?
- What happens if the company does nothing?
- How will the company pay for it?
- In general, what are the options?

Primary Activities

1. **Impact Analysis** to determine the extent of date-sensitive processing as well as the potential failures which could result from incorrect date handling. Impact analysis involves scanning existing source code (if available) to find date references. The outcome of the analysis is a rough estimate of a measurement (e.g., lines of code, incidence of date reference, and number of modules). These statistics can be used to determine a rough cost of the project using any of several commonly cited cost estimates.

2. ***Business Risk Assessment*** to identify potential impacts outside of the traditional technology areas of the business. The assessment looks to uncover risks such as legal exposures, impact on stock price and shareholders, public relations impacts, production, accounting or financial impacts. The purpose of this assessment is to provide a broader picture of the scope by demonstrating that it impacts the business as a whole, not only the data center.

3. ***Application Inventory*** to itemize what applications and systems software (computer programs) exist on the company's information systems. This inventory should include those programs which are currently in use, as well as those which are old, dead, or were used only one time. This latter group of unused programs can be examined to determine if they can be cleaned out at some point in the process. Having an accurate inventory of applications is important for several reasons: (a) to confirm that all applications have been converted, by checking the converted list with the starting inventory; (b) to identify dead or old code which can be deleted; (c) to document the information processing assets of the corporation; (d) to identify critical programs where no source code is available.

4. ***Collect vendor and tool information*** to begin the screening process. By examining the competencies of vendors, enterprise management will be better prepared to request and evaluate proposals from those vendors who are qualified to address the needs of the specific situation. It may be helpful to prepare a matrix of solution vendors, plotting them based on whatever criteria are deemed important, such as tool set, experience with platform/languages, experience in the industry, etc.

5. ***Identify available resources*** (internal and external) that can be deployed as a part of the compliance process. Enterprise management must keep in mind, however, that every resource allocated to the compliance process is one that is not available to work on the day-to-day activities and maintenance of systems. This activity should target the project management and higher-level personnel who can be given responsibility during the process.

6. ***Form Year 2000 Project Committee*** to oversee and coordinate the compliance process. This committee should include representation from corporate lines of business and functional areas such as I/T, legal, marketing, production and risk management. It must have the direct involvement of enterprise management. A key activity of the committee will be to facilitate continuous communication.

Primary Outcomes / Deliverables

1. Cost and Budget Estimates
2. Business Risk Assessment Report
3. Resource Lists
4. RFP/RFI (where appropriate)
5. Committee Roster
6. Pilot Project

Step 2: Planning

Step one should have produced a reasonable estimate of the size of the problem for the enterprise in terms of cost, as well as the potential impact on various areas of the business. Additionally, the company should have a general idea regarding vendors, tools and solution alternatives available in the market. The objective of step two, then, is to establish a plan or schedule for bringing the company's systems into compliance. This project schedule, like any other, should identify priorities and dependencies, estimated activity times, and resource requirements throughout the process.

A difficult aspect of the compliance process is deciding where to start. With most (if not all) of today's complicated information systems, applications are interrelated, exchanging data back and forth. This tight coupling of systems presents a scheduling challenge for the compliance process. If one application is "fixed" and put back into operation, will it fail when it receives non-compliant data from other programs? Will it cause other systems to fail by sending compliant data to non-compliant applications?

For small to medium-sized projects, it may be feasible to convert all systems at one time (excluding testing). For larger systems, however, the sheer volume of work required makes it difficult, if not impossible, to handle all applications at one time. Even if such an effort is possible, it is most likely not the best approach. There is valuable experience to be gained during the incremental steps of bringing systems into compliance. As one system is completed successfully, subsequent conversion phases can learn from the previous experience.

It should be clear then, that planning (i.e., project scheduling and management) is one of the most critical phases of the technical conversion. It will be during this process that problems and obstacles can have their most damaging impacts—delaying schedules, diverting resources, etc. With a known deadline that will not move (01/01/00), the compliance process cannot afford to be derailed.

Specifically, the planning phase should include the following primary activities:

1. Project scheduling, including:
    > Prioritizing of application conversions
    > Resource assignment (money, staff, consultants, etc.)
    > Identification of most appropriate pilot projects
2. Receive and review vendor proposals and quotes

Primary Outcomes / Deliverables

1. Pert Charts, or other project management schedules
2. Resource allocation lists
3. Cost estimates (both in-house and vendor proposals)

Step 3: Implementation

When beginning Step 3, the company should have a firm grasp on what work needs to be done, according to a certain time schedule, and at a determined cost. Implementation, simply stated, involves putting plans into action. For the most part, implementation will involve converting existing systems to allow them to handle the Year 2000. The specific approach for conversion may differ, depending on the specifics of each situation. In short, during the implementation step, you will fix existing code, replace existing code or retire existing code.

Although this phase is primarily technical, the involvement of enterprise management is crucial to ensure that schedules are met, resources are available and appropriately allocated, disruptions are minimized, and all stakeholders are kept informed of the steps being taken by the corporation.

Primary Activities

1. Use pilot projects initially, rather than a full-scale implementation, to gain valuable experience about the compliance process, and to work with various solution vendors, if appropriate, to discover the strengths and weaknesses of each.
2. Convert non-compliant code into code which can correctly process dates beyond the Year 2000.
3. Replace existing code with newly developed application code, either because the original source code is not available, or if it is feasible (and not too risky) to update the code at this point.
4. Build the interface bridges between systems where appropriate to achieve interaction.

5. Eliminate dead, old, or unnecessary programs that are otherwise taking up storage space, draining processing time or increasing maintenance costs.

6. Document the process and all changes made during the compliance process.

7. Use high-level meetings to maintain communication and focus during the compliance process. Enterprise managers, as well as technicians, should participate in these meetings.

8. Develop a contingency plan to create viable alternatives in the event any mission- critical systems fail or are not completed on time. Year 2000 contingency plans, like disaster recovery plans, could include redundant systems, outsourcing agreements, additional insurance or other options.

Primary Outcomes / Deliverables

1. Year 2000 compliant systems (already unit tested)
2. Process documentation, including a summary of all changes, replacements, retirements made during the process
3. Progress meeting minutes
4. Contingency plans

Step 4: Systems Testing

It is of critical importance that newly compliant systems be thoroughly tested before being put into live operation. Unit testing will have been done, so this testing is directed to ensure that the vendors' parts work together without causing any of these to fail.

Testing can involve the following activities:

1. Simulations, using sample data, to test the functional compliance of systems both in forward and backward processing. Forward processing is a transaction that spans forward into the next millennium, such as a five-year auto loan processed in 1996. Backward processing, on the other hand, involves retroactive date handling, such as calculating someone's age, or determining expiration of inventory or backup tapes based on creation date.

2. Concurrent processing, using live transactions input into both the old and new systems. Requires separate hardware and software systems, but allows the company to verify that the new systems perform functionally the same as before the compliance process.

Primary Outcomes / Deliverables

1. Fully tested, Year 2000 compliant systems.

30   Assessment Metrics Checklist

Micro Focus Limited

In order to plan the time and resources you will need to conduct your Softfactory/2000 Assessment, you will want to make an initial assessment of the magnitude of software that should be assessed to determine the extent and severity of your century date handling exposure. Supplement this checklist with metrics for other sources of date information and date handling. Determine which of these metrics you will need to use to estimate your assessment's scope:

> number of applications with date-handling routines
> size of databases that have stored date information
> number of reports and screen displays with date information
> number of copybooks with date references
> number of JCL statements with date parameters
> number of purchased programs that could have date handling problems
> *<metrics for your unique assessment needs>*

Using these metrics and others you identify, identify the metrics you will use to determine the scope of your assessment.

> number of potentially-affected applications to be analyzed during assessment (percentage of total)
> number of database records to be examined (percentage of total)
> number of other software components (copybooks, JCL, etc.) to be analyzed during assessment (percentage of total)
> average assessment time per application
> average assessment time per database record
> average assessment time per other software component

Use these estimates to compute an estimated investment in your Softfactory/2000 Assessment.

Candidate Assessment Metrics Checklist

Use only the metrics that will give you the data you need to meet your assessment objectives. Consider metrics in the checklist below, as well as standard metrics you may already be using for other maintenance or reengineering projects.

Direct metrics include those you can measure directly from the analysis. Consider estimating totals based on analysis of a representative sample of software applications, etc.

> ➤ Total Number of Affected Source Statements
> ➤ Total Number of Affected Database Date Fields
> ➤ Total Number of Affected Date Fields in Reports
> ➤ Total Number of Affected Date Fields in Screen Displays
> ➤ Total Number of Date References in Copybooks
> ➤ Total Number of JCL Statements with Affected Date Parameters
> ➤ Vendor's Estimate of Time and Cost to Make Purchased Software Century Date Safe
> ➤ Number and Cost of Software Packages That Will Need to Be Fully Replaced

Qualitative Information Gathering: Not all metrics produce quantitative data. Some metrics may be in the form of questions to experts, for their opinions on the business implications for your century date exposure. Depending on what questions you must answer to meet your assessment objectives, you may find these questions useful in consulting with your end users, application maintenance staff, and others with special knowledge about your organization's software.

> ➤ When are we likely to feel a business impact if we don't address our century date problem?
> ➤ What is the severity (Critical, Serious, etc.) of the century date handling defects in our software?
> ➤ Are there defects that could cause loss of business or loss of end user good will? (Be sure to get the end users' view of this!)
> ➤ Is there a realistic scenario whereby software currently targeted to be replaced before it causes century date problems would still be in use when the problem strikes? (Capture that scenario and an estimate of its likelihood.)

31   *New Development Initiatives*

Jim Zetwick
Borden Foods Corporation

The Year 2000 project can successfully be implemented without compromising an organization's new development initiatives. As a development manager responsible for my organization's Year 2000 project, I feel the following factors are important considerations when striving to keep new development schedules on time while not compromising the Year 2000 project. I believe that the key to achieving parallel development requirements depends upon three major factors:

1. A "Year 2000 Literate" organization
2. A disciplined project management style
3. An investment in technical staff and their interests.

A more detailed explanation of each factor follows.

Year 2000 Literate Organization

The definition of a Year 2000 literate organization can be debated among software and business personnel around the world. An organization is year 2000 literate if its employee base understands the totality of the Y2K problem as it affects their organization and directly relates to their business objectives and strategy. You can infer from this definition that a year 2000 literate organization's senior management (CEO, CIO, CFO) must be informed and understand the problem from a strategic perspective. This is the single most important component to successfully achieve a year 2000 literate organization. The degree to which these senior managers place importance on the year 2000 project will dictate how seriously the project is taken by managers and workers in their organization. Once top level support is committed to and promoted to managers and associates, the level of competence surrounding the problem will begin to rise.

Without each functional business unit understanding the importance of fixing this problem as it relates to their objectives and strategy as outlined by senior management, a compromise of the information technology staff's development strategies will ultimately begin. This compromise will result in a Year 2000 project drifting aimlessly without regard to the consequences of non-compliance. The end result will be systems intended to support business objectives that cannot be met due to Year 2000 related complications. These complications are the result of ignoring the Year 2000 project as a result of compromising a business strategy with no Year 2000 priorities. The Year 2000 literate organization, however, does not compromise the Year 2000 project for new application development to meet short term business objectives. The managers of functional units who initiate new development requests are cognizant of the overall organization's Year 2000 initiative. As a result, their requests are properly aligned with meeting the overall business strategy and objectives.

A Disciplined Project Management Style

Organizations that have employed strong management methods are positioned well to meet the requirements of a Year 2000 project without compromising new development initiatives. Strong project management is a requisite to success. Although obvious to most, the project manager selected to manage the Year 2000 project corresponds directly to the importance senior management places on the project. If a "light," inexperienced manager is in place, the organization should ask themselves if they truly have integrated the Year 2000 problem into its overall strategy and objectives. The selected manager's ability to negotiate new development initiatives without compromising the Y2K project is lessened if the functional managers view the manager as light or inexperience. The manager selected should have strong authority and affiliation with an organization's senior management. Immediately, the project is viewed with more credibility and as directly correlated with the organization's strategy and objectives.

An Investment in Technical Staff and Their Interests

As has been widely reported, the Year 2000 problem will place a premium on scarce technical resources. Technical resources will jump jobs for higher pay and increased benefits as the bidding war between firms to staff their Year 2000 project begins. In order to meet the Year 2000 project demands without compromising new development initiatives, resources must be available. Organizations must look to new compensation packages to retain technical staff to keep them content. The traditional methods of base salary and annual merit increases will not suffice. Performance incentive bonuses based on meeting Year 2000 project schedules is one method an organization can implement to help retain technical staff. Employing this method provides incentive for completing tasks on time, thus enabling resources to focus their work on the Year 2000 project and new development initiatives. If turnover persists on the Year 2000 project due to increased competition, damaging results will be incurred. Resources originally assigned to new development initiatives will be recruited to the Year 2000 project, thus impacting the new development schedule. The functional managers who makes the new development request will become frustrated and begin to polarize their requests with the Year 2000 initiative. The importance of retaining all of SD staff is critical to an organization's ability to successfully meet the requirements of the Year 2000 project and new development initiatives.

Conclusion

New development initiatives will not be compromised for the Year 2000 project if an organization educates its employees on Y2K from the top down, assigns strong project management to the project, and implements a creative, performance-based incentive package for their technical resources. Implementing these factors is the key to success for any organization that intends to meet the challenges of a dynamic business environment and solve the Year 2000 problem.

32   *Catastrophe or Opportunity?*

Cap Gemini America
1-888-Y2K Today
www.usa.capgemini.com/y2K

Programs to Fix per Week		Years Left to Fix When You Want to be Done – When You Can Start Renovating Aggressively								
		4 1/2	4	3 1/2	3	2 1/2	2	1 1/2	1	1/2
Number of Programs	2,000	9	10	11	13	16	20	27	40	80
	5,000	22	25	29	33	40	50	67	100	200
	10,000	44	50	57	67	80	100	133	200	400
	15,000	67	75	86	100	120	150	200	300	600
	25,000	111	125	143	167	200	250	333	500	1,000
	50,000	222	250	286	333	400	500	667	1,000	2,000
	75,000	333	375	429	500	600	750	1,000	1,500	3,000
	100,000	444	500	571	667	800	1,000	1,333	2,000	4,000

Time to Get Started

On a per-program basis this is not a complex problem. There are simply a lot of programs with date fields and date-related calculations all over the place.

Two additional conditions make matters even worse:

1. In many programming tools, including the ever-pervasive COBOL and Assembler, date fields are not labeled as such. To identify all date fields, and therefore to quantify your millennium exposure, you need to craft and apply some rapid, intelligent and detailed assessment techniques.

2. Every program and job stream (and copybook and data file if expansion is chosen as your technical strategy) will need to come off line, get fixed and tested, and brought be back on-line. Doing this all at once would put you out of business for an unacceptably long stretch. Therefore, implementation of your renovated inventory will inevitably need to be phased. If your technical strategy is expansion, you have the additional complexity of renovated programs trying to read unrenovated files. And vice versa. Without careful up-front strategic planning designed to minimize the incidences of old-communicating-to-new, and the availability of bridging tools to temporarily patch the necessary incidences, bridging would become your biggest headache and number one hour-burner.

You're facing tens of thousands of hours of coding and testing, none of which can even begin until you've first assessed your exposure and then determined an enterprise-wide rollout/bridging strategy. And since your company has probably not faced anything similar before, that, too, will take a lot of time.

This is shaping up as a war-footing, "guns or butter" choice: With your talent tied up here, how can you continue to develop new applications and maintain your service level? But when will that choice be made?

Unfortunately, until something blows up, the organizational sense of urgency will remain with the traditional development, maintenance and enhancement work. Well, at least there are three or four years left to solve the millennium thing, right? Wrong.

Beware of this kind of thinking. The Gartner Group estimates that 20 percent of a company's systems are already affected by corrupted data, which will result not only in ABENDs but also in soft failures that may well go undetected. Yet another important reason to get started now.

Analysis Paralysis

Anticipate that your customers, and your own company, will need to be shaken into action. It won't come easy. Why such resistance? As serious as this is, it's also a very bizarre situation. Rational responses are not typical. The full emotional cycle of denial, anger, bargaining, depression, and acceptance must be traversed. As a champion of change, you'll need to recognize and try to accelerate this.

In addition to emotional resistance, the myth of the "magic bullet" is as comforting as it is misguided. Misunderstanding or misinterpreting the facts also counters rationality: The scope and urgency are far beyond the capacities of most managers' radar screens.

The more accurate information you have about the size and scope of your problem and the alternatives to a solution, the easier it will be to get others on board and get the project funded.

Your Solution Alternatives

As you face the millennium change problem, you may adapt a mixed bag of solutions. You might renovate some of your existing applications, replace others with custom-built systems, or replace yet others with pre-packaged software. Of course, for the third option to be viable, the package software itself needs to be Year 2000 ready. In many ways, companies in the software and computer services businesses are just like everyone else, only they'll be more significantly affected and sooner.

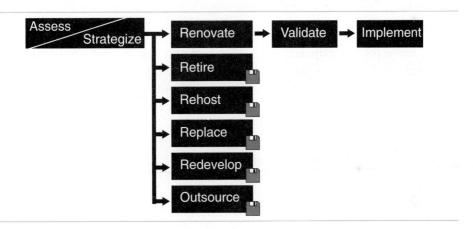

Renovation will inevitably be a major part of everyone's solution. Here are some potential approaches:

- Renovate each program when it's opened for routine maintenance;
- Do the fix as a major project initiative;
- Outsource the entire maintenance function, including the Year 2000 fix;
- Partner with a full service vendor specializing in the millennium issue.

The best solution probably entails a combination of the latter three, while the first approach is dangerously naive.

Routine Maintenance

The idea of quietly fixing the problem in the background is very tempting. Chipping away at it as each program is opened up for routine maintenance over many years would seem to be a way to get the project done while keeping it low profile. Piggy-back it with the introduction of a few workbench style maintenance tools and a data repository, and you can have your cake and eat it too.

What's wrong with this? First, a typical shop will routinely open up less than 20 percent of its legacy programs during a five year period. Second, the catch-as-catch-can approach is inherently inefficient, difficult to standardize and track, and prone to oversight and error. Third, sharing old and new format files will be a nightmare. Finally, having never done anything quite like this before, you'll need to invent a process, chewing up and defocusing valuable management time.

Ultimately, this approach is a futile attempt to hide 60,000 plus hours of effort. Experienced teachers know that biting the bullet is preferable to taking one through the heart.

Major Project Initiative

If you have the appropriate resources and can devote the time and focus required, or if it's too late to sign up with a credible services provider, you may want to address the problem in-house. Other good reasons to pursue this strategy are if you want to have control over your project or if your data requires the highest security.

An in-house approach requires creating a (very) large project, budgeting for it, winning management team backing, searching out or custom-building appropriate tools, developing methods and standards, marshalling the human resources, and then going for it.

Since this is one project you can't let slip, there are a number of ways to increase your chances of success:

> Seek out a proven methodology that has been specifically developed for the Year 2000 issue and incorporates lessons learned over numerous Year 2000 projects. A number of services vendors offer their proprietary methodologies for your in-house use. This approach will allow you to take advantage of the learning curve that they've been through and, hopefully, incorporated into their processes.

> Acquire highly automated tools. The more automated the tools, the more rapid and consistent your solution, and the less stress will be placed on your organization in terms of resources and morale issues. Tools that are interwoven with methodologies will allow you to achieve a more seamless approach. You may also be able to get utility beyond 2000 from automated tools that allow you to use the data gathered to build a repository.

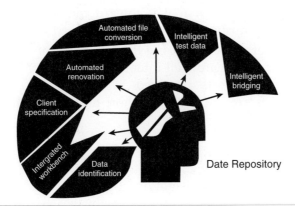

- ➤ Develop a factory approach. This has been proven to increase productivity and allow for the focus and knowledge-sharing important to a successful project.
- ➤ Protect your resources. Spirits may be assuaged by big salary increases: Industry pundits have forecast a doubling of programmer salaries each year through the end of the century to meet Year 2000-crisis supply requirements! In parts of the Midwest, its reported that COBOL programmers can jump to another company with a $10,000 increase.

Approaching your in-house project by adopting proven tools, methodologies and processes from experienced Year 2000 vendors will increase your chances of being done on time. You should also be able to get the vendor's support through training, documentation and help desk access. If this is your approach, you may want to be sure that the vendor has a core competence in skills transfer.

Outsource

Some companies will use the millennium issue as the final straw of rationalization to outsource IT services. The more evidence that "analysis paralysis" is at work, that their IT team is incapable of solving the problem that it (arguably) created, the more likely this course.

No value judgments here. There are many solid business reasons for taking such a step. But it is a big step. Since the Year 2000 solution will be an important deliverable of the outsourcing contract, be sure that the vendor's capabilities are equivalent to those you would require if you were to pick them as a partner to solve the problem yourself.

Partnership

A synergistic partnership with a vendor is always a "best buy." Ideally, the contributions the vendor makes toward the solution are optimally blended with your contributions.

Strengths offset weaknesses, but there are a lot of vendors out there. Some are excellent. Some are well-intentioned, but naive. Some are char-latans. Since the skill sets involved in a Year 2000 fix are highly specialized, chances are your normal short list of consultants will come up, well, short.

Expansion vs. Interpretation

Whether you choose to renovate in-house or with a partner, your technical strategy, interpretation or expansion is very important to the overall renovation budget, schedule, and risk.

Expansion of date fields involves modifying source code, job control and data files to expand the 2-digit year field to a 4-digit field that includes the century. Interpretation, on the other hand, involves adjust-ing program logic to "interpret" the 2-digit year field as a century and year field. The most simple interpretation algorithm treats years before a defined "cutoff" date as 20xx and years after as 19xx. Job control and data files are not affected.

Experience shows that expansion involves changing 75–90 percent of program source. Record alignment must be carefully handled for all expanded data files and, for every expanded data file, potential batch and on-line bridging is required to maintain compatibility between unrenovated and renovated data files—a large implementation effort. However, the benefits of expansion include its applicability for all dates and reduced future maintenance.

Interpretation is a safer solution since it requires changing only pro-grams, not files or JCL. It also requires fewer overall changes to source code (maybe up to 60 percent less changes to programs) because only cal-culations and comparisons require change. Some data files are not changed, there is little or no bridging, no data conversion, no alignment problems and, therefore, lower immediate cost and risk. Providing an interpretation solution for dates in keys and sorting involves planning. Sorting often requires alternative sort sequences or the use of third party sort tools that also support interpretation. Years in VSAM and database keys is the trickiest complexity in an interpretation. Proper key order must be preserved and support existing data. When performing I/Os encode and decode routines have to be invoked. However, only Year 2000 plus dates need to be coded.

Interpretation does have limited applicability—if dates span more than 99 years, they cannot be interpreted easily, whereas expansion works in all cases. Code maintenance is more complex, and interfacing with outside systems is complicated.

After considering the benefits and concerns of both strategies, many companies are choosing a mixed bag: interpreting wherever possible and expanding only when necessary.

Your choice of expansion or interpretation must take into consideration your systems and business requirements. It will affect your renovation today in terms of your cost, schedule and risk, as well as your future course.

How to Find a Partner?

The RFP Pilot Trap

While it is good practice to float an RFP for a Pilot with most new IT development work, Year 2000 is "different." What are the costs of delaying? For every month you spend on the project's front end with an RFP process, you add one to the back end when, experts warn, costs will be significantly higher. You also increase your risk of not being done on time.

If you still want an RFP, it's easy to get into apples-and-oranges confusion with a good vendor if your RFP and their process are based on different paradigms. For example, you may have a mix of COBOL, Assembler, and FOCUS. Should you issue an RFP for a "Proof of Concept" Pilot covering all of these technologies? How relevant to a good choice is file bridging in your Pilot sample? How can testing be factored in? How does the small scale of the Pilot relate to the high volume requirements which follow? What is the relative importance of a vendor being able to talk the talk in several programming languages versus another vendor's ability to walk the talk in one or two?

Is it sensible to bundle a COBOL-to-COBOL370 conversion into the Year 2000 RFP, or is it naive to add complexity?

Before choosing "the RFP for a Pilot" route, ask yourself: Do I know enough to ask the right questions and to properly judge the results?

Find the Right Partner

To find the right partner, you must first know yourself and the nature of the help you'll need.

> What help will you need to effectively communicate scope and urgency to executive management?

Vendor "Red Flags"

Here are some things to watch out for in a vendor's millennium "solution"
✗ Little discussion of testing
✗ Little discussion of bridging
✗ Little appreciation that the problem is "now"
✗ Little time set aside for planning or strategy
✗ A lifecycle heavy on making the changes and light on testing them
✗ No lifecycle
✗ No methodology, just tools
✗ No tools, just methodology
✗ Tool = "magic" bullet
✗ A "one size fits all" approach
✗ A fully freeform, custom approach
✗ No track record
✗ Small company, questionable financial stamina
✗ Questionable commitment to Year 2000 fix
✗ Only approach is expansion or "date routine"
✗ Approach is entirely dependent on their people
✗ Approach is dependent on third party and/or off-shore resources

> Can your company weave through decisions to "replace, rehost, renovate," or do you need a vendor with the strategic depth to help you through this?

> How close are your applications to failure? Do you know which systems will fail early and how this failure relates to other systems up- and downstream? What are the business consequences of systems failure?

> Do you know the relationship between development initiatives and system failure dates? Which initiatives should be accelerated,

and which have no chance of being ready in time? How will you align priorities to minimize Year 2000 risk?

➢ What is your package software risk? How affected is data you receive from, or send to, the outside world?

➢ Does your inventory have other problems that must be solved, possibly in conjunction with a Year 2000 fix?

➢ Are your people prepared to share the burden? (Skills? Manpower? Morale?)

➢ Do you have a handle on where your dates are, and the complexity of your date-related calculations and compares?

➢ Do you have an established test environment and test methods? Are large amounts of DASD available for testing?

➢ Is your source code well inventoried, or will it be an adventure just to find it?

When you understand what you need, you must then judge vendor claims.

Vendor Selection

No Year 2000 vendor can yet offer a plethora of specific experience. This is a new field. However, a legitimate vendor won't need to invent the wheel on your dime, either.

The best solutions to the millennium problem will offer major economies of scale. Committed vendors will have invested in tools and processes sufficient to generate factory efficiencies.

Once you've eliminated the "never wastes" and understand the nature of your company's needs, you're ready to zero in on the right vendor. Given the newness of everyone's Year 2000 offering, it'll be necessary to judge a vendor by its track record in related services. Some of the more traditional IT services which could reasonably be expected to provide the basis for a robust Year 2000 service are:

➢ Reengineering/platform migration;

➢ Database migration;

➢ Language reengineering;

➢ IT Strategy;

➢ Client/Server migration;

➢ Project management.

Find a vendor with a solid track record in the above who has made a significant incremental investment in Year 2000 tools and solutions, and you could have a winner!

33 *Project Tasks*

Platinum Technology, Inc.

If existing software has captured or processed only the last two digits of the year in a date, then resulting calculations, comparisons and sorting of data will be in error when the century portion of a date changes from 1999 to 2000. Costs associated with problems caused by inaccurate processing are hard to estimate; recovery may be difficult or even impossible in some systems. The Year 2000 Challenge will likely have a major impact on systems critical to the success of every enterprise dependent upon date-based data and processing.

The cost to any organization faced with Year 2000 will, undoubtedly, be high. A major manual effort is required to ensure legacy systems reliability. A manual effort of this magnitude may take hundreds, even thousands of hours. While information workers are dedicated to this project, other high-priority projects in the pipeline must wait on resource availability.

Without expanding the effort, the MIS organization risks miscalculations, incorrect sorts, and wrong comparisons. When data processing problems are discovered, systems are down while the problem is diagnosed and fixed. System outages represent the most costly part of the problem because of the lost productivity of workers during the down time. Productivity losses, and the associated costs, expand at an exponential rate over time.

Further complicating the challenge is the fact that after nearly three decades of development, today's MVS environment is highly integrated. The interrelationships of systems, programs, utilities and databases create thousands, even millions of connections. If a change is made in one application program, then every system component integrated within the application's job stream or interactive processing needs to be reviewed for possible errors introduced by the change.

Year 2000 is intimidating to even the most sophisticated MIS organization, because virtually every system component processes date data. What could be a simple problem, theoretically, if it were isolated to a few instances, becomes quite complex because there are so many changes to be made, and so many relationships are potentially affected. And, of course, since any change can introduce the possibility of error, many changes imply the near probability of errors.

Additionally, a maintenance project of this type places a difficult burden on even the most conscientious information worker. The worker can use a 3270 terminal or workstation and various utilities such as ISPF/ PDF as tools to assist in the various tasks, but most of the individual tasks are essentially simple and repetitious in nature. Even though an information worker wants to do excellent work, it is very difficult to remain focused on redundant tasks, and error is often introduced because a bored person is easily distracted.

Information management professionals are faced with a potentially giant project, critical to the future of the organization, with very little immediate payback. It will consume a large portion of system resources, in terms of people, processing power and storage requirements. It will postpone other vital, high priority projects which upper management is demanding, with a rapidly approaching deadline. And, if this project is not completed, it carries high risks with unknown but greatly feared impact on the information needs of the entire enterprise!

Plan the Project: The first task for the Year 2000 Project Team is to determine the scope and impact of the problem. Sampling techniques may be used to determine how many different date formats have been used. Program modules in applications known to be date-intensive, such as scheduling applications, should be examined, as well as applications thought to be independent of date processing. Mission critical applications deserve the most intense scrutiny, while systems that are seldom used probably deserve the least. The only exception would be the processes which are used for disaster recovery. Although probably, the least used system components, obviously they must be included in the conversion effort. Once the scope of the project has been defined, then task plans and resource estimates may be completed.

Determine All Date Formats: The next phase of the project will be to do a thorough analysis to determine all of the different formats for dates which are used in program logic and control card type input to utilities and processes. Then, the formats which will be used in the future must be defined. Each previous format should then be examined to determine if a conversion is required, and if so, associated with a new format.

Locate the Data: Next, the project team must locate and record each occurrence of a date in all system components, and determine whether or not it requires conversion. The large number of components that must be reviewed for all of the potentially different representations of dates dictates that these tasks will be repetitive and very time consuming. To be thorough, each occurrence must be checked individually. Every sort, comparison and calculation that is performed using dates must be examined for accuracy and reliability. Even five date formats in a thousand library entries creates 5,000 individual tasks to be completed.

Determine Component Relationships: Next are the tasks of establishing the interrelationship of system components. Each system, program, utility and database that contains or processes dates must be examined to determine the links to other components. Then the other components must be reviewed to determine the impact of the change. Again, more highly repetitive tasks to be completed.

Change Systems, Programs, Utilities and Databases: Once date-based data and processing have been located, each occurrence must be modified to conform to new standards. Many organizations will require audit procedures to ensure that the new data standards have been applied. The entire change process must be controlled and managed to ensure component synchronization and system integrity. These tasks are time consuming and repetitive, and are critical to the success of the implementation.

Convert Stored Data: Once processing logic changes have been completed, stored data must be reformatted. A typical process for reformatting files to expand the space for year data will involve three steps. The first is writing a program to read each record in a file; the second is to insert the new data format; and the third is to rewrite the new record to a file. Each unique type of record definition may require a different program to properly reformat the record. COBOL or other high-level language programs could be developed to accomplish this reformatting process. The time required for developing and testing of these one-time-use conversion programs could be significant, but at least this is one phase of the project which is fairly easy to estimate and implement.

Test Changes: Planned changes to systems, programs, utilities and databases obviously must be tested to ensure the coded changes are working as designed and are producing the desired results and that production processing failures are prevented. The barriers to information processing perfection are many: logic problems, poor coding techniques, hardware or software constraints, errors from the processing of bad data, incorrect calculation algorithms, or lack of resource availability because of inadequate capacity planning, to name just a few. Processing failures may be minimized by performing thorough testing of all system components involved with a change to simulate real-world processing conditions wherever possible.

➢ *Test and Result Data Management:* Once a test plan has been completed, data to test and to verify the results of each case should be collected for each case. This data may come from existing test data bases, production data bases, system's journals, or created manually based on the test plans. The data must be restored and synchronized at the beginning of each test cycle.

This is necessary to provide consistent results in order to compare the output of each test cycle.

> *Unit and Function Testing:* Even small programs, ones with only a few hundred lines of code, could have hundreds, if not thousands, of different branching or processing conditions. Ideally, every possible variation that invokes a different branching or processing condition should be checked and verified for accuracy. Each variation should have a corresponding test case which is executed each time any change to the processing logic takes place. Once a unit has been tested with an exhaustive and inclusive series of test cases and has successfully executed each test case after the last change to the program has been made, it is appropriate to perform concurrency testing.

> *Concurrency Testing:* Concurrency tests can identify problems resulting from insufficient system resources. A component's use of memory, buffers, data locations, and processing cycles should be tested to ensure that the component can handle simultaneous actions and perform with integrity.

Additionally, poor design of the sequence of events used when multiple file or data base accesses are required within a single logical unit of work (LUW), can create data contention conditions, known as "deadlocks" or a "deadly embrace." This can occur when two or more LUWs are trying to reserve a unit of data for exclusive use. When one LUW is waiting on a resource locked out by another, and the second LUW is waiting on a resource locked by the first, an infinite wait state can be created. This type of processing problem in data base technology is often very difficult or even impossible to detect with manual test procedures prior to production implementation.

Concurrency testing typically involves running the same unit (system, program or utility) in different Task Control Blocks (TCBs) at the same time against the same data base. Concurrency testing may be designed for multiple concurrent batch jobs, multiple concurrent online system transactions and batch and online systems running against the same data base concurrently.

> *Integration Testing:* This type of test verifies that data flows smoothly through each integration point within and across application systems. While the dependencies of processing units within business application areas are often obvious, integration points between and among different application areas may not be well documented. Integration testing usually involves the creation of various sets or cycles of test cases by bringing together

all of the test cases used in testing the individual units, then executing more encompassing tests of application systems against this composite of test cases.

➤ *Stress Testing:* Stress testing models how systems will perform under maximum resource demand conditions and may help anticipate answers to questions such as: Will software failures occur? Will unexpected bottlenecks develop? Will system performance degrade significantly after changes are made to the system? How may performance be improved by varying the priorities and resources committed to processing units?

Service agreements are now modeled for compliance within performance benchmarks. Stress testing performed with a variety of loads and situations can protect the organization from system failure and subsequent processing outages during peak demand periods.

Unfortunately, this type of testing can be very costly and difficult to perform if not automated, and, ultimately, even more costly if not done at all.

➤ *Regression Testing:* Regression testing attempts to ensure that a change to one part of a system does not introduce an unwanted or unanticipated change elsewhere. Some regression testing occurs naturally while conducting other types of tests. Planned regression testing involves creating baselines of data and processing modules as of a particular point in time, then implementing changes and executing the system again. Then the output from the baseline cycle must be compared with the output from the system after the changes were implemented.

Regression testing is also an excellent tool for a MVS shop to test current production system components, even when changes have not been implemented. Regression testing can verify that mission-critical components continue to function correctly. This can be particularly valuable when a maintenance release is applied to system level software.

➤ *Acceptance Testing:* Once a unit has been certified by the previous testing conducted from the information processing organization, representatives of the users of the system should examine the processing results of the changed unit to ensure that it meets their specifications. Users usually conduct their own tests based on their own test cases to ensure that the changed system is functioning properly according to their requirements, and that performance attributes, such as response time, are acceptable.

Manage the Change Control Process: Even the smallest EDP shop has a complex change control process environment to manage. At the minimum there are source libraries for programs; copy libraries for file or database formats (copy members); libraries for commonly used utilities and subroutines; and load libraries which contain compiled programs that have been link-edited. These exist for both on-line and batch systems. On-line systems also have control tables for programs, transactions, files, terminals and other resources. Many systems have control parameters which are passed by mechanisms such as JCL and external tables. For each type of listed system component, every shop has at least one test version and one production version.

Implementation of changes as comprehensive as the Year 2000 project requires that any migration of system components such as source libraries, copy libraries, subroutine libraries, load libraries and control tables must be synchronized. As a critical safeguard, backup copies of current versions of all appropriate system resources should be made available for recovery processes if system failures should occur.

The process of production roll out is a very critical point in the change control process. Even after all the tests and changing of system components have been coordinated and completed, failures do happen at the time the modified system is placed into production. When this happens, the system must be restored to its original status prior to the roll out, with as little delay as possible.

34   *Year 2000 Firewall: Using an Inexpensive Time Machine*

Judy Brand
JBG Pygmy Mainframes

Most analysts discussing the Year 2000 effort are agreed that half or more of the labor used will be expended in various phases of testing. [Editor: See Figure 25.1.] Including their time-specific components (e.g., Time Machine Testing), the main test types are Baseline Testing, Programmer Unit Testing, Regression Testing, System Integration Testing, Bilateral Testing, Forum Testing, Enterprise-Wide Stress Testing, and Pre-Production Full System Testing.

One almost never hears of an instance where a hardware solution is less effective than the software solution it replaces—as long as the hardware works correctly and is affordable. Two pygmy mainframes—IBM's

R390 mainframe and CDSI's CDS-2000—cost about one-fifth the price of the least expensive old-line IBM/Fujitsu/Amdahl mainframe. And their Entry System Level (ESL) classification means that standard software used upon it costs anywhere from one-third to one-thirtieth as much as the same software licenses on older, often weaker, mainframes. But why spend any testing money on hardware, rather than software solutions?

Employing an inexpensive, separate time machine can serve two distinct purposes simultaneously: First, to act as a firewall, protecting the production mainframe(s) from the inevitable system abends associated with software testing; and second, to make the testing itself more genuine and dependable.

Protective Walls

The firewall aspect of using an inexpensive test-only mainframe—versus a testing region or VM guest or MVS LPAR on an existing production computer—has several aspects; e.g., performance degradation, MTBF, etc. [Editor: For example, a testing operator who enters the commands "V OFF, DASD / INIT DASD" from an LPAR can cause production data corruption far beyond that LPAR.]

Testing constitutes by far the largest group of Y2K project components, whether to verify an outside software vendor's claim a package will survive the 2000 rollover if teamed with your in-house software, or to certify your fixes of that legacy software.

In seven of the eight major kinds of application testing (i.e., all but the last run of stress testing), it is unnecessary to run against the complete applications database at full speed. Tests that are automatically scripted—or otherwise at least planned—can be quite effective using a finite but self-consistent set of live or masked data. (The terabyte capacity of the R390 or CDS-2000 is certainly adequate for at least seven of the eight named testing modes.)

In fact, the emerging IEEE 2000.2 Standard for Year 2000 Testing explicitly encourages doing your comparison stress testing entirely on a non-production machine, as long as you re-run the Baseline Test on that machine to see the difference.

For typical installations, the terabyte capacity of an R390 or CDS-2000 is certainly adequate for at least seven of the eight common testing modes, and usually full Pre-Production as well.

In all eight major cases of testing, it is safer to have a physically separate testing machine than to try to execute essentially risky tests against an LPAR in a main production machine. That is what firewalls are for: A major purpose of testing software before installing it is to elicit errors—

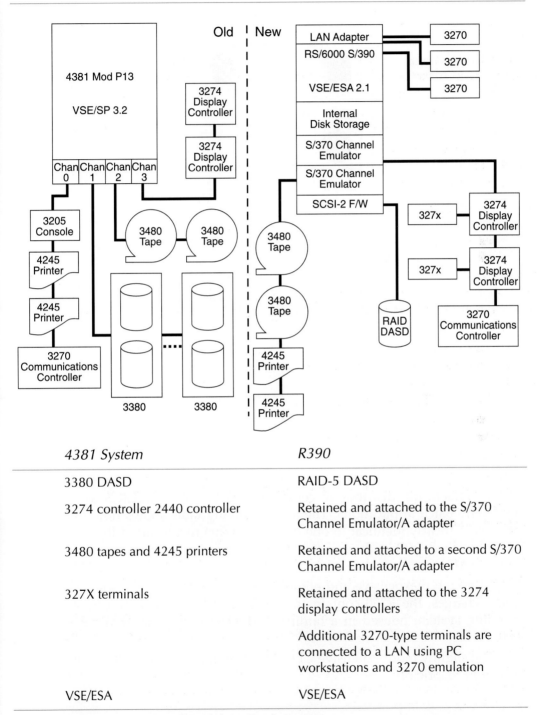

4381 System	R390
3380 DASD	RAID-5 DASD
3274 controller 2440 controller	Retained and attached to the S/370 Channel Emulator/A adapter
3480 tapes and 4245 printers	Retained and attached to a second S/370 Channel Emulator/A adapter
327X terminals	Retained and attached to the 3274 display controllers
	Additional 3270-type terminals are connected to a LAN using PC workstations and 3270 emulation
VSE/ESA	VSE/ESA

Figure 34.1 **4381 Model 13 Replacement**

Reprinted by permission from GC28-1619 *IBM RISC System/390 and System/390 Server-on-Board: Is It Right for You?* Copyright © 1995, 1996 by International Business Machines Corporation

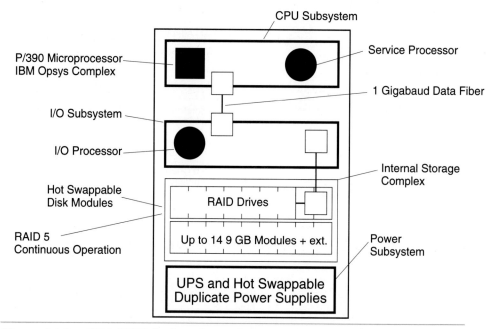

Figure 34.2   CDS 2000 fault resistant features (Courtesy of CDS)

including those that produce abends—before it goes into live production. Better now than then.

R390's and CDS-2000's Year 2000 conformance certification assist is not limited to software. As Figure 34.1 demonstrates, the R390 can be of use in responding to inadequate or missing Y2K firmware/hardware upgrades.

Figure 34.1, the 4381 Replacement diagram furnished by IBM, refers to a manufacturing distribution center with over 100 VSE/CICS users, plus many batch applications. The accompanying table shows how that conversion (nearly identical to one done this year) retains all of the non-DASD-attached I/O and provides expansion for additional terminals using a LAN.

Although inexpensive and eligible for the low IBM "ESL" software license charges, the R390 contains a full-fledged hardcoded IBM S/390 operating system, housed in a familiar industry workhorse, IBM's RS/6000.

The slightly more expensive CDS-2000 contains the same IBM S/390 card and ESL pricing.

Delineating Walls

Even restricted to Year 2000 *software* testing, broadening your pygmy mainframe use to an inexpensive group of R390s and CDS-2000s, can provide cycles in burst when needed, and improve overall productivity through an unambiguous division of labor. Figure 34.3 shows such an arrangement schematically: In physical terms, each pygmy computer can be placed at whatever site is most appropriate for its use.

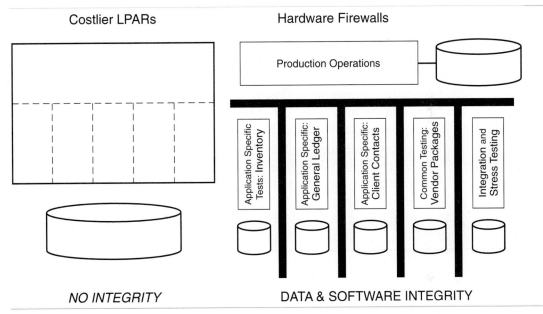

Figure 34.3   Y2K test environments

Thanks to IBM's ESL pricing, the total one-time IBM software cost for the full cluster shown is only 21 percent of the software license cost for a "Group 35" machine of equivalent MIPS. Software savings alone may be enough to pay for the R390 or CDS-2000 hardware.

As depicted, each major application workgroup within an enterprise ("Inventory," etc.) can schedule and test its own portion of the Year 2000 remediation and validation. Reducing contention and cross-scheduling among application-related groups means enhancing accountability and productivity. Moreover, the ill effects of testing any one major Y2K application "clump" are stopped by its firewall—kept not only from the main production computer(s), but also from the other Year 2000 application groups.

Besides physically partitioning the testing of logically distinct applications, this arrangement provides dedicated environments for the central Y2K test functions of Integration/Stress/Pre-Production, as well as the aging of vendor software packages.

Survivability Past 2000

IBM-based pygmy mainframes have a use and survivability well past the turn of the century.

There are six easily understandable post-2000 uses.

1. An unspecialized but real ongoing pygmy use is to provide incremental cycles and processing for the main production computer. From file transmissions to report printing, offloading of main batch tasks can help preserve the batch window in the face of a steadily increasing IT workload.

2. Potentially enormous software license savings can be captured by moving an archive query or other 6-to-8 MIPS production application off the main machine onto the pygmy's generous storage.

3. The aging of incoming vendor packages is a real need. Just as your PC/LAN unit has probably done since the early 1990s, a quarantining machine can help probe the safety of newly acquired software, in an environment that inexpensively mimics production. [Editor: Don't ignore this point, since the Y2K problem is like malaria; once you have applied the cure, look for it to occur in the backwards direction facing 1999 and earlier.]

4. Another kind of incoming software, trusted but sometimes misunderstood, is the constant lineup of system upgrades. While quarantining these may have value, too, your clearest gain here is a dedicated pygmy on which to parameterize and tune the new version or release. This infrastructure improvement clearly increases availability: Production no longer has to shut down regularly between 6:00 and 8:00 PM for the Software Support group; and programmers need not be expelled from the Data Center every fifth weekend.

5. Intensive testing of new system upgrades can be carried out in a pre-certified environment. There may be less software to test at one time, but your systematic test procedures are now well-developed and worth continuing.

6. Finally, remember that each application-designated R390 or CDS-2000 is a transferable resource: All the techniques and efficiencies physically present on it stay intact as it passes to the owner of the next IT crisis. Year 2000 won't be your enterprise's last mission-critical software need.

35   *Starting the Assessment Process*

Gerhard Adam
Syspro, Inc.

The survey provided in this section is intended to assist in starting the process of evaluation necessary to determine the exposure to Year 2000 problems. The use of surveys has many advantages and disadvantages. It is not intended that surveys replace comprehensive review or study, but rather that they be used to raise the necessary questions and build consensus to the formation of a year 2000 project team.

Advantages:

The primary advantage of surveys is to articulate the necessary questions to begin the assessment process. While more questions might be added, it should be remembered that the information gained from surveys is only preliminary and should not require extensive research to be completed. It should only take a few minutes to complete the questionnaires since the results should be a reflection of the present state of knowledge rather than that which could be obtained through more research.

Another benefit of a survey is that it marks the beginning of the year 2000 effort, by starting to raise the awareness of the problem to management. Once the survey results have been returned, it is possible to begin more detailed examinations to determine reliability as well as to understand the nature of the issues which need to be resolved.

Disadvantages:

There are shortcomings within the survey process which should be considered

- There may be a lack of explicit knowledge regarding the application systems.
- There may be a desire to gloss over the scope of the problem with reasons like "the system will be replaced anyway" or "it will be no problem to change."

It is entirely possible that many of the results returned will be in error. While this isn't immediately useful in assessing the year 2000 exposure, it is useful in gauging the degree to which assumptions are being made with potentially negative results. An answer of "I don't know" is equally important as the detailed knowledge of the system being reviewed.

Conclusions:

Reviewing the results of questionnaires may raise as many questions as it answers. Once obtained, this information can be used to guide the assessment process by pointing out areas which need to be examined more closely, management approvals which may need to be expressly obtained, and uncertainties in the directions being taken by vendors supplying software.

Surveys are not comprehensive enough to answer all the questions raised by the year 2000, but with judicious and honest usage, the process by which an assessment can be conducted will have begun.

Figure 35.1 **Year 2000 Applications Survey**

1. Application name: _____

2. Do current plans call for replacement or rewrite of this system?

    Yes ☐   No ☐   Don't Know ☐

    a. If yes, specify timeframe: 1 Yr. ☐   2 Yrs. ☐   3 Yrs. ☐   4 Yrs. ☐   Unknown ☐

    b. Has project been approved? Yes ☐   No ☐   Don't Know ☐

3. Is this a vendor maintained software package? Yes ☐   No ☐   Don't Know ☐

    a. If yes, when will it be year 2000 compliant? _____

4. Are YEARS used in this system expressed in the full four digits?

    Yes ☐   No ☐   Don't Know ☐

5. What is the status of achieving year 2000 compliance for this system?

    ☐ Implemented   ☐ Subroutine to manipulate date

    ☐ Plan to implement   ☐ Date encoding

    ☐ Plan to convert to 4-digit year   ☐ Windowing

    ☐ End-user approved plan   ☐ Other _____

    ☐ No plans

6. Approximately how many programs exist within this system? _____

7. Are any programs missing source code? Yes ☐   No ☐   Don't Know ☐

8. Approximately how many files exist within this system? _____

9. List the different file types which exist in this system (i.e.: VSAM, DB2, etc.).

_____

_____

10. Are dates used as indexes within files? Yes ☐   No ☐   Don't Know ☐

11. Is the system documentation accurate and up to date? Yes ☐   No ☐   Don't Know ☐

12. Has system been tested using Year 2000 dates in files? Yes ☐   No ☐   Don't Know ☐

13. Has a date standard been developed for future changes to this system?

    Yes ☐   No ☐   Don't Know ☐

14. Is any of the data in this system subject to file transfers to other systems (i.e., PC's, data warehouse, external companies/sources, etc.)?

    Yes ☐   No ☐   Don't Know ☐

    If external company, who owns (or establishes) the date standard?

    _____

15. Does this system exchange data with other application systems?

    Yes ☐   No ☐   Don't Know ☐

16. Was system tested with other application systems using Year 2000 data?

    Yes ☐   No ☐   Don't Know ☐

17. Are there currently problems being experienced in regards to year 2000 issues?

    Yes ☐   No ☐   Don't Know ☐

    If yes, please describe _____

    _____

18. Please add any additional comments which may be useful in evaluating the readiness of this system for year 2000 compliance.

    _____

    _____

    _____

Year 2000 Applications Survey Directions

The purpose of this survey is to provide a high level view of the activities currently occurring within the applications development area regarding the year 2000. This survey should be completed by the applications development managers to include all systems for which they are responsible.

   Note: This survey should be completed in a few minutes and require no research. Since it is designed to assess the current state of year 2000 compliance, it is necessary to reflect all of the uncertainties and doubts which may exist for a particular system. This is not intended to be a comprehensive review or "sizing" document.

Question 1:

This entry should simply contain the name and/or acronym by which the system is commonly known and recognized.

Question 2:

The response to this question indicates whether the system being reviewed is a candidate for replacement and/or major revision. If it is, the follow-up questions assess the time-frame and whether the project have management/end-user approval.

   Note: If a system is a candidate for replacement, the survey should still be filled out, since an appreciation of the work required over the next three years (regarding year 2000 compliance) must include any assumptions of this sort.

Question 3:

This question will determine whether the system is a vendor supplied/ maintained product or whether the software was developed in-house. If the answer to this question is YES, then the Vendor Product Survey should be completed instead of this one.

Question 4:

This question is simply assessing whether the system is already using four-digit years or not.

Question 5:

The answer to this question should include all the appropriate blocks. For example, there may be a plan to implement a windowing technique using a subroutine which has NOT been approved by the end-users. In this case the "Plan to Implement," "Subroutine to manipulate date," and "Windowing" blocks should be checked.

Question 6:

Indicate the approximate number of programs (including subroutines) which exist in this system.

Question 7:

If program source code is missing, this should be indicated in this block.

Question 8:

Indicate the approximate number of files which are part of this system. This number should include all files used regardless of whether they are part of other systems as well.

Question 9:

Indicate the different types of files and/or data bases which are used by this system. The different types should indicate logical organization (i.e., SYBASE, DB2, VSAM).

Question 10:

Indicate whether dates are used as keys to access information within the files indicated in question 9. It is not necessary to indicate whether they are four-digit or whatever their use is.

Question 11:

Indicate whether system documentation is accurate regarding program/ file relationships, usage (i.e., update or read-only), output, etc. In short, is the documentation accurate enough to use for analyzing the work required for a year 2000 project?

Question 12:

Indicate whether the system has been tested using year 2000 dates in the files themselves. If no test data exists (or the test can't be confirmed), then respond NO to this question.

Question 13:

Indicate whether the system has a date standard or been certified in any way to ensure that future changes are consistent with year 2000 compliance.

Question 14:

Indicate whether data from this system is used in Electronic Data Interchange (EDI) or with other physically separate systems. This would include file transfers to PCs, etc.

Question 15:

Indicate whether data from this system is used by other applications on the same physical system (or environment, in the case of multiple CPUs).

Question 16:

If the system interacts with other application systems, were these environments tested using year 2000 data? If test data is unavailable or the test can't be confirmed, respond with a NO.

Question 17:

Indicate whether year 2000 or date related problems are already occurring (and being circumvented). If such problems are occurring, give a brief description as to their nature.

Question 18:

Indicate any additional information which may be useful in assessing this system's compliance for the year 2000. Special considerations and/or requirements which have not been addressed previously should be listed here.

Summary:

It should be remembered that this document is not a substitute for comprehensive analysis and sizing, but rather a vehicle for providing a high-level assessment as to an organization's potential exposure. By reviewing the answers to these questions, it should be more apparent to senior management how ready the applications really are and when to begin to generate an appropriate level of urgency to resolve it.

part 4

CEO/CIO: The Cost

Costing procedures are always subject to negotiation. This part recounts six distinct viewpoints.

Dick Lefkon starts us off with a reminder to budget all Y2K activities. In three examples, Congress has caught up with agencies that failed to track replacement of critical systems, remediation of non-critical ones, and embedded-chip device fixes in general.

Michael Gerner presents five more reasons why it made sense heretofore not to expand the date.

John Trewolla urges exploding objectives as finely as possible and assessing the workers before applying your fudge factor. He shows how to be nonplussed if an outside bid is solicited, and suggests not getting pinned down to a single figure—or to last week's figure!

The public domain DOD/Mitre "ESTIM8R" article is half algorithm, half cataloguing of cost points.

Sanford Feld furnishes an IBM costing survey to justify spending a little less on consultants and a little more on increased hardware capacity.

Capers Jones concludes with what has become the most-quoted statistical estimates in Y2Kdom.

Analyzing programs by function points instead of linecounts, Jones builds table after table:

➤ function point density by language
➤ U.S. software portfolio size by industry
➤ U.S. billions in repair cost by industry

➤ U.S. billions in repair costs by state

➤ Billions of Y2K dollars required per country

[Ed: Where will Italy get the $13 billion?]

Jones also tells you the greatest litigation exposures. He, too, furnishes questions to ask Y2K vendors. He estimates that 80 percent of Y2K software fix costs will precede 1/1/00, but 73 percent of related hardware costs will follow it!

Banks, brokers, insurers and healthcare all stand a 2 percent chance of going out of business that day. Next to this, S&L was puny.

36 *Budget All Activities*

Dick Lefkon
Year 2000 Committee of AITP SIG-Mainframe

A recent Congressional report shows the U.S. Defense Department is now 7 years ahead of the Department of Energy: DOD will be able to finish its own Y2K conversion by the year 2012.

Most eighth graders can predict how long it will take to fill a fifty gallon tank when you have two consecutive fullness readings taken a fixed time period apart from each other. Congressman Steve Horn taught college before chairing the House Government Reform, Information and Technology Subcommittee, and his post-eighth-grade staffers did exactly that math using May, August, and November quarterly reports they required from every U.S. Agency.

Departments of Energy and Labor have calculated Y2K completion dates in 2019, DOD in 2012, Transportation and Personnel Management 2010, and Agriculture, Treasury, and GSA respectively 2005, 2004, and 2002. Other U.S. agencies whose steady progress won't succeed this decade are NASA, FEMA, AID, Education, Justice, and HHS—also, probably, HUD, Commerce, and State. The State Department tracks its 12 Mission-Critical systems being repaired, but not the larger workload of 30 Mission-Critical ones slotted for replacement.

After twenty months of Horn's Y2K spotlight hearings, only three of the two dozen agencies listed in Figure 36.1 were at least one third implemented by November 15, 1997: Social Security (80%), Small Business (59%), and Environmental Protection (40%). Although most reported doing 100% of their Assessment phases, not a single one is expected to finish Y2K by this New Year's Eve. Agency-reported completion percents for Renovation and Testing phases are also shown.

The statuses and predictions may be overly optimistic. For instance, Horn criticized HHS for reporting 100% Assessment when 53% of external Medicare systems were unassessed; DOT for excluding 153 mission-critical FAA systems from the Renovation queue; and DOD for its silence on 21,911 Business-Important and Business-Critical systems, "any one of which could bring down a computer [running some of DOD's 3,143] Mission-Critical systems."

Besides making more accurate reports that show workload data for second-tier systems and the mission-critical ones scheduled for replacement instead of repair, agencies were strongly urged to start reporting separate workloads for Noncompletion Contingency Planning and the Embedded Chip Renovation category. Chips are real work that must be accomplished, reported Horn.

Agency Name	Assessment	Remediation*	Testing	Implementation	Comply in Year
SSA	ALL	80	74	80	NEXT
NSF	ALL	50	42	NONE	NEXT
SBA	ALL	63	60	59	NEXT
EPA	ALL	50	40	40	NEXT
Interior	96%	41	37	29	NEXT
VA	90%	61	38	25	NEXT
NRC	ALL	25	23	29	NEXT
HUD	ALL	45	27	22	NEXT?
State	ALL	25*	25	NONE	NEXT?
Commerce	ALL	30	23	22	NEXT?
FEMA	ALL	29	29	21	2K
NASA	ALL	14	11	11	2K
AID	95%	8	8	8	2K

Figure 36.1   U.S. Agencies self-reported Y2K percent completions, with computed compliance years.

Agency Name	Assessment	Remediation*	Testing	Implementation	Comply in Year
Education	ALL	20	NONE	NONE	2K
HHS	ALL?	35	20	15	2001
Justice	ALL	18	11	6	2001
GSA	ALL	25	18	17	2002
Treasury	80%	44	8	8	2004
Agriculture	ALL	12	6	7	2005
OPM	ALL	9	NONE	NONE	2010
DOT	80%	9	5	2	2010
DOD	92%	44*	18	2	2012
Labor	ALL	16	12	7	2019
DOE	ALL	13	11	4	2019

Source: House Subcommittee on Management, Information and Technology
Notes: ? May be overly optimistic
        * Omits non-mission-critical systems and all replacements. See story.

Figure 36.1   U.S. Agencies self-reported Y2K percent completions, with computed compliance years.

37   *Five More Reasons Many Delayed*

Michael Gerner
Unibol, Ltd.

Code Re-use

It has always made sound economic sense not to redevelop the wheel. Virtually all new applications have algorithms and even code incorporated from previous systems. This speeds up development and results (usually) in more reliable systems.

The re-use of algorithms which have a hidden date processing fault is one reason why the year 2000 problem is so huge and why some people have likened it to an immense virus. As the algorithms are used and reused, so their deadly payload is spread through more and more systems. Finding and dealing with each problem is rather like tracking down a particular strand in a bowl of spaghetti. Even worse, every strand touching this strand has to be examined for contamination. As most of us know to our cost, dealing with spaghetti can be a messy business. It would take a huge problem on a corporation-threatening scale to force us down that route!

Historical Data

The information built up painstakingly over an organization's history has been likened by some to the "corporate crown jewels." Companies make profits mining though this heap of data looking for the nuggets that yield competitive edge. Successive applications are built on this asset to further improve performance for the future.

Which means that successive applications are being built on the basis of what may be faulty data. Not that it was faulty at the time of writing. It may not even be faulty now. But it sure could be when the century rolls over.

The problem is, changing the data means changing the applications accessing that data. And this has ramifications outside the scope of the MIS department. With the PC revolution, development and control of many applications has typically passed out of the control of the IT professionals into the hands of the end users. So changing the core corporation data means immense inconvenience and cost to all those end users. Who wants to grasp that particular nettle?

Even the best and most modern code in the world can be hamstrung by historical data that is faulty. And nobody has relished the thought of sifting through the family jewels looking for paste. Especially when, so far, it has tasted, smelled and looked like the real thing.

Other Business Priorities

With the increasing pace of change in IT, MIS have been hard pushed enough to keep up with the pack, let alone look over their shoulder at what might be creeping up on them. The urgent has taken priority over the essential, in order to meet the user community's demands. As the old saying goes, "We were too busy fighting to worry about tactics."

MIS departments who took pride in their responsiveness to user demands are probably the worst hit in this case. When the department is measured by metrics built on their speed of response to user demands, there is little incentive to devote resources into pro-actively looking for new problems.

This doesn't say a lot for the long term forecasting and management of MIS workload. That may be a bitter pill for MIS managers to swallow, but for many it is the harsh truth. Sometimes the truth hurts, but it must be faced up to and dealt with sooner or later. Otherwise, the accumulated small oversights of decades can band together into an almighty ambush by the end of the century.

Business Process Re-engineering

No matter what the consultants say, the net result of BPR is reduced head count and less "fat" in the company, which is fine until a crisis outside the requirements foreseen by the BPR analysis hits. Like the Year 2000 software problem.

When MIS have been downsized to simply provide the required business functions of the company, that is precisely what MIS will do: no less and certainly no more. The "slack time" that could have been devoted to addressing the year 2000 issue before it became urgent has been deliberately cut out of the system in the search for leaner and meaner business processes. Furthermore, because they now lack the internal resources to handle the year 2000 problem, companies who have been through BPR downsizing will be forced to outsource the Year 2000 fix project. Ironically, this contract could end up in the hands of the very consultant who advocated their BPR process in the first place.

Whereas MIS infrastructure has been totally outsourced, the situation is possibly even worse. Typically an outsourcing contract does NOT include Year 2000 work. In fact, at least one outsourcing firm has publicly stated that if their clients try to get them to cover Year 2000 conversion within the maintenance contract, they will terminate the contract. So outsourced MIS will not handle the Year 2000 problem unless they are asked to do it and are paid for doing it. And who is going to ask them, if the non-MIS management in the corporation are unaware of the problem? Shedding expensive MIS expertise from the corporation may have cut costs in the short term, but it exposes the corporation to any IT related problems which fall outside the domain of the outsourcing contract. Such as the Year 2000.

Accounting Conventions

Typically, accounting conventions have treated expenditure on software to be an expense in the period incurred. The capitalization of software as an asset is still a thorny issue yet to be tackled to the satisfaction of the accountants.

This means that spending money on maintaining software has been treated like a telephone bill. It gets paid regularly for the use of the service, but at the end of the day does not increase a corporation's net worth.

In other words, if a medium sized company spends US$5,000,000 to solve their year 2000 problem, that money comes straight off the bottom line with no increase in assets in the balance sheet to reflect the fact that the corporation will now (probably) survive past 1/1/2000. It is the difficulty of convincing a CEO that a $5 million hit on the Profit & Loss Account is "A Good Thing To Do" that has largely contributed to the inertia on this issue. It would take an exceptionally brave MIS manager to spoil a CEO's day with THAT news.

Hindsight Is 20-20, Foresight Is Normally Less Effective!

Looking back on it all, of course we can see the faults and where decisions could have been better made. A four-year-old child can understand the 2 digit year problem, but four-year-old children don't usually write applications, let alone run corporations.

38   *Project Cost Estimating: Simple to Sophisticated*

John Trewolla
Trewolla Technology Taskforce

The simplest "rule of thumb" project, estimating rule I've found is from Gustavo Pedemonte. He discusses using the 1 man-day per program (module) rule. Frankly, from my *very limited* experience with my clients (only one is actually coding as I write this!), this rule seems pretty safe. I thought it would overstate the level of effort substantially, but I'm observing that by the time a programmer chases down all of the "gotchas," a day per program module is probably a pretty good average for COBOL-based applications with average segmentation and copybook calls.

The most sophisticated "rule of thumb" project, estimating idea I've seen recently is discussed in Bob Coble's summary of the metrics discussed in the Murray & Murray book. I've read parts of this book (copies are hard to find!) and found it to be of very narrow use—at least to me. But, if your management is bedazzled by esoteric exponentiated algorithms, this posting will be of real value to you.

Between these two extremes, I believe that there is no better tool for predicting project costs than experience. What I mean is, until you actually roll up your sleeves and get started on the project, all estimating tools suffer from the same lack of basis in the facts of your specific application. So, the approach I use is:

1. Using Capers-Jones's "Function Points" model of functional decomposition, divide the project into as many individual steps/modules/tasks as possible. The more the better! Make each step/module/task as small as you possibly can. For "average" projects, I keep dividing the project steps until my list has at least 50 to 150 individual steps/modules/tasks.

2. Based upon any estimating module you wish, predict the level of effort required to complete each task—and then multiply your prediction by 1.5 to 2.0, depending upon how optimistic your team has been. (If they're typically optimistic, use 2.0 as a factor. If they are all young bucks with less than 5 years of experience, use 2.5!)

3. Add up the numbers and then add as much again for testing/integration and debugging. (Multiply by 2.0)

4. Take that total and add 25 percent for meetings, administration and paperwork. (Multiply by 1.25)

5. Multiply this level of effort by your company's "magic number" for labor costs. (This number, in my experience, has so little relation to what programmers and managers are actually paid that I've never figured out whether reality is a component of the equation!)

6. Present this cost to management as a *range!* I like to take the cost as predicted above and present the range as −10 percent and +25 percent. Management usually complains about not having a "hard" cost figure—but I remind them that the purpose of a budget number is to make an intelligent management decision about the allocation of company resources. The project will cost whatever it costs! The purpose of my preparing a projection of costs is to allow management to be prepared to pay for what is always an uncertain and never-done-before-so-we-don't-really-know-what-it-will-take project.

A benefit of presenting a project's cost as a range is that it gets you off the hook when the numbers don't come out on the money—and we both know that they never will!

7. When management complains about the cost and tries to argue you down to some number they find more comfortable, ***stand your ground!*** Instead,

   a. remind them that you did not come up with these numbers arbitrarily and they cannot be adjusted arbitrarily.

   b. Suggest that they consider abandoning parts of the project to re-duce the scope and cost.

   c. If your project is large enough, suggest that they consider shipping some of the work overseas to a software factory (which may or may not make sense, depending upon the "magic numbers" you assign for your internal labor costs!).
If they still don't like your numbers and think that they can afford the delay of having some outside consultant prepare new numbers for them,

   d. stand aside and let someone else prepare a budget without your in-put. Then compare the answers.

If you've done what I've suggested above, I predict that their numbers and your numbers will be within 20 percent of each other. (I'm speaking as an independent software project management consultant with 20+ years of experience.)

Your company's "magic numbers" may make the outside guy's numbers more attractive to your management. If so, hire the outside guy and his company to do the work. This gets you off the hotseat of a thankless project. If not, at least you've gotten credibility with your own management at the cost of the delay introduced by the time required by the outside guy to prepare his cost projections.

8. Finally, ***and most important***, revise your project budget numbers as you actually undertake and complete the project! There is no better estimating tool than experience with the project itself.

I've managed over 300 projects for more than 200 clients during the last 20 years, and I've learned something: it's a really good idea to get management used to the idea early in a project that projects are dynamic and budgets have to be flexible—both up and down. I've learned that the worst mistake I can make is to allow a project budget which is prepared in optimistic ignorance early in a project to remain unchanged in the face of actual experience!

39 *E-S-T-I-M-8-R*

U. S. Department of Defense

Year 2000 Cost Estimating

The purpose of this guidance is to develop a rough order of magnitude cost to find, fix, and test systems for the Year 2000 problem. This estimate does not include costs to make the systems' hardware and systems' software (commercial hardware and software associated with the system) Year 2000 compliant. These are additional costs which can be significant, especially if there is a requirement to produce a microchip (piece of firmware).

Completing this estimate requires knowing the number of Source Lines of Code (SLOC).

STEP 1: Multiply SLOC times 0.8 = number of executable Lines of Code (LOC). This approximates the number of executable lines of code (LOC). The 0.8 is a "rule of thumb" constant based on experience.

STEP 2: Multiply LOC times $1.70 = Cost to find & fix problems and test solutions. The $1.70 is a very rough estimate (made by the Gartner Group) of the average cost for finding and fixing Year 2000 problems and testing Year 2000 solutions. There are many factors which affect the estimate. These factors are enumerated on the attached pages along with other factors to consider in determining total costs. Your estimate should be adjusted based on knowledge of the system(s) and the relevance of the factors.

A labor rate of $10K/Staff Month (contract services support) is a reasonable planning estimate for equating dollars to staff months of work effort.

10 staff years/ 1 Million LOC

Preliminary Year 2000 Cost Factors Checklist

Note: Year 2000 "compliancy" includes proper processing of leap years [The Year 2000 is a leap year.]

Application Software:

- Size: Number of executable lines of code (LOC)
- Age: Older code tends to be less structured and thus harder to understand
- Complexity: Relative intricateness/understandability of business rules
- Documentation: Degree of documentation available and its understandability
- Programmer: Familiarity with the program code; level of skill/ competency/expertise
- Source Code: Availability
- Date-"Intensiveness": Relative number of date related calculations/comparisons

➢ Embedded Dates: Frequency of date use as part of data element or in data element codes

➢ Date Formats Used: Consistency within the system of a standard date format

➢ Year 2000 Strategy (field expansion/procedural code/sliding window): Different strategies to achieve Year 2000 "compliancy" have different costs.

➢ Language: Some languages (e.g., COBOL 68) are unable to properly process the Year 2000, so the software will have to be upgraded/changed. [Additionally, the language relates to the availability of Year 2000 COTS tools, programmers to work on the system, and availability of Year 2000 compliant COTS.]

Hardware and System Software:

➢ Year 2000 Compliancy of Each of the Components of the Technical Environment is Required. [Often only a current version of a product will be Year 2000 compliant.]

➢ Operating System

➢ Major Subsystems: Sometimes subsystems have different technical environment components.

➢ Database Management System (DBMS)

➢ Compilers/Cross-Assemblers (available—sometimes they don't exist)

➢ Teleprocessing (TP) Monitors

➢ Homegrown/Locally Developed Software: Software used in conjunction with the system

➢ Workstation Software: Consider the quantity needed.

➢ Workstation BIOS (handles the "system clock function"): 60 to 80 percent of PC BIOSs are not Year 2000 compliant—most are soldered to the "motherboard," some are reprogrammable, some are "socketed" and can be replaced.

➢ Programmer: Familiarity with the hardware and operating system; level of skill/competency/expertise

➢ Programmer System Software (utilities and development tools): To support making changes to the software

➢ Capacity/Usage Level: Making a systems Year 2000 compliant may increase storage (DASD) requirements or even CPU requirements and cause a need to purchase a larger computer or more DASD.

➤ Embedded Software (microchips/circuit cards; e.g., PABXs, security system (access control), cash registers): They may be directly or indirectly related to a system and may not be Year 2000 compliant. The availability of compliant hardware or the cost of developing it and the quantity required, must be considered.

➤ Communications: Telecommunications hardware and software upon which the system depends must be considered.

➤ Network Timestamps (LAN/WAN network clock time) upon which the system is dependent

Databases/Files:

➤ Number of Date-Related Data Elements

➤ Amount of Available DASD (storage space)

Year 2000 Tool Support:

➤ Availability: Many languages and/or technical environments do not have Year 2000 COTS tools, so tools must be developed in-house or specifically contracted for development.

➤ Quality

External Interfaces/Middleware

➤ Data Sources: Must be evaluated and "bridges" planned as required

➤ Data Outputs: Must be evaluated and "bridges" planned as required

➤ EDI Transaction Sets: System may generate some EDI transactions or get input from EDI transactions, which may require bridges

➤ Reports: Systems may generate paper reports which need to be modified

➤ Screens: Systems may have screens used by users, which require modification

System Plans:

➤ Planned Major Upgrade: May be used to do Year 2000 compliance work at the same time to reduce costs

➤ Termination: System may be eliminated before a Year 2000 problem occurs

➤ Replacement: System is planned for COTS replacement or reengineering before a Year 2000 problem

Miscellaneous System-Related Information:

➤ Sort Routine Year 2000 Compliancy

➤ Backup Routine Year 2000 Compliancy

➤ Archival Routine Year 2000 Compliancy

➤ System Criticality/Priority: Really not required for cost estimate, but a good time to record this critical planning information

➤ Risk Analysis If System Fails: Really not required for estimating cost, but a good time to collect this critical planning information. Consequences of system failure must be considered

➤ Risk Analysis (if system not made Year 2000 compliant): Many systems have only a small "window of vulnerability" during which not being able to process Year 2000 properly occurs. Consideration must be given if this "window" is acceptable; i.e., the system won't be used during that period, or a "workaround" will be established for that period; e.g., manual processing

➤ Contingency and Continuity of Operations Planning

Year 2000 Management:

➤ Project Management

➤ Configuration Management

➤ Change Management

➤ Contract(or) Management

➤ Year 2000 Emergency Reaction Team

Year 2000 Testing:

➤ Establishing Test Environment

➤ Unit Testing

➤ Integrated Testing

➤ Year 2000 Simulation Testing: Can sometimes require mirror of production environment. Might not be possible until technical environment is made Year 2000 compliant?

40   *Capacity? Swap Consultant, Mainframe*

Sanford Keith Feld
Bestbuilt Systems

My contributions to this compendium are based on interaction with many colleagues and approximately 400 potential S/390 hardware clients in the three calendar years leading to publication. It strikes me that no matter how expert the technicians, no matter how brilliant the managers, lack of freely usable computer capacity and availability is the single largest cause for cost and timeline overruns of anywhere from 15 percent upward.

Whether the true world cost of Year 2000 upgrades will meet the Gartner Group's estimate of six hundred billion U.S. dollars or not, saving 15 percent of it—or even a few percent of it—can be significant. Recent reports about the U.S. economy as a whole point out that our productivity has not risen this decade as it did in the previous one. Perhaps that is because we have slowed down on automation and then demanded increased workarounds as government agencies and major corporations have right-sized personnel away.

For most organizations, the Year 2000 effort will move in the opposite direction, with systems workforces that are temporarily larger, although not necessarily used with more efficiency than before. My suggestion for organizations planning temporary expansion of 20 or 40 chairs is simple: Instead add only 19 or 39 bodies, and at that vacant desk place an IBM S390, CDS-2000, or other inexpensive mainframe, making your Year 2000 unit both self-contained and self-sufficient. Then other departments cannot ruin your schedule by removing the CPU.

Every programmer who has worked on the original legacy code will recall the times that programming development ceased or ground to a halt as end-of-month processing began—or the daily 3:00 PM sort took place—or the main computers were down over the weekend so Software Support could upgrade versions—or the main computers were just down, period.

Every enterprise has to stay functional, and it has to stay competitive—even if it is a state or U.S. agency. The main business of the enterprise rightly should take precedence over Year 2000 development—or any other kind of development! It should be obvious what rules the Head of Operations will institute immediately after the first date-modified program crashes the primary mainframe. If not, just think back and recall why the most recent two firings/demotions of CICS coders took place.

Inexpensive pygmy mainframes by IBM and others use the same cables to existing Glass House printers, tape drives, networks and other devices. The one current exception is a need to dump/restore from 33XX disk farms onto RAID storage devices with a nonstop recovery redundancy feature. A pygmy costs about the same as one year of a contract consultant; when the furloughed consultant returns, she will see 15 percent better efficiency and availability, too.

Software savings due to IBM's (and others) ESL pricing will probably pay for the hardware anyway and systems staff maintenance costs are exactly the same for an LPAR. One more benefit stems from R390 pygmies with AIX. If mainframe needs really do subside after 1999, the non-

390 component is a full-fledged industry standard UNIX computer and can help implement decade-old plans to move everything off the mainframe onto UNIX.

MVS/TSO Performance

IBM

Reprinted by permission from GC28-1619 *IBM RISC System/390 and System/390 Server-on-Board: Is It Right for You?* copyright © 1995, 1996 by International Business Machines Corporation

The R390 provides 32MB and 128MB of storage. For an MVS/TSO environment, only a few users can be supported at 32MB, and therefore 32MB is not recommended. At 128MB, approximately 50 users can be supported, based on an internal IBM MVS/TSO workload. This TSO workload is designed to represent the work done by a TSO end-user community developing and testing programs interactively using ISPF/PDF. Workload activities include editing and browsing source data, compilation, execution, program testing, graphics, and information management transactions. There are 25 different scripts, each consisting of a related set of activities in the form of TSO commands. CLISTs are implicitly and explicitly invoked. The think time is exponentially distributed with an average of 15 seconds between scripts, and the internal response time limit is 2 seconds. Compile and assembly operations comprise about 5 percent of the IBM TSO workload. When workloads with a higher percentage of these operations are encountered, fewer users can be supported.

While the internal response times achieved by the R390 are within the specified limits, other S/390 processors, due to their standard I/O design point, typically yield lower response times. Since internal response time is one of several factors that contribute to end-user response time, there may be some instances where end-user times are longer than those achieved by other S/390 processors. There are many instances, particularly in remote applications, where use of the R390 can eliminate or reduce other time components to yield net improvement in overall response time.

The capacity of the R390 is determined by the characteristics of the work that is run on the processor. One of the key parameters of the work is the I/O content. For the MVS/TSO workload, paging can become a significant component of I/O as the number of users is increased for a given storage size. When significant paging occurs, the total I/O demand can exceed the capability of the R390 and cause the response time to exceed the specified limit. The maximum number of users supported for a given

storage size and think time is related to the working set size for the average user, which is approximately 1MB. Larger working set sizes will
generally support fewer users, and a smaller working set size will allow
a greater number of users.

The users supported is based on projections for RS/6000 Model 591
using a 7137 configured for RAID-5 disk arrays. A customer's actual performance will vary depending on many factors such as I/O content, system
configuration, available storage, and the specific workload being processed.

Other MVS Workloads

The performance data in Figure 40.1 provides guidance to help you
determine if your dedicated MVS production on-line workloads will fit
on the R/390. It includes several on-line environments and their key
characteristics. Due to the inherent I/O content of these workloads, the
disk I/O rate becomes a key factor to consider as you evaluate the
potential use of the R/390 in your business.

The data in the table is based on a RS/6000 Model 591 system that
has 128MB of S/390 storage and two 7137 RAID-5 disk arrays. The drives
are configured into two arrays with one logical drive each. Each logical
drive contains ten 3380 (various densities) equivalents loaded with the
workload components so that the I/O rates to either logical drive was no
more than 60 percent of the total average I/O rate. A smaller system with
a single array on a single channel will handle about half the I/Os and
users shown.

Workload Type	Users/ Terminals	Think Time (seconds)	Response Time (seconds)	I/O per Second	Number of Disk Arrays
IMS/DL1	120	11	1	50	2
IMS/DB2	30	4	1	50	2
CICS	140	12	1	40	2

Figure 40.1   Other MVS Workloads

While the internal response times typically achieved by the R390 are
within the specified limits, other S/390 processors, due to their standard
I/O design point, typically yield lower response times. Since internal
response time is one of several factors that contribute to end-user
response time, there may be some instances where end-user times are
longer than those achieved by other S/390 processors. There are many

instances, particularly in remote applications, where use of the R390 can eliminate or reduce other time components to yield net improvement in overall response time.

The IBM internal IMS workload consists of light to moderate transactions covering diverse business functions, including order entry, stock control, inventory tracking, production specification, hotel reservations, banking, and teller systems. These applications are similar to the CICS applications but contain IMS functions, such as logging and recovery. The IMS workload contains sets of 17 unique transactions, each using a different database. The workload uses both VSAM and OSAM databases with VSAM primary and secondary indexes.

The DB2 workload consists of light to moderate transactions from two defined and well-structured applications, inventory tracking and stock control. IMS/DC is used as the transaction manager. The applications are functionally similar, but not identical to, two of the IMS/DL1 and CICS applications. The DB2 work contains seven unique transactions. Conversational and wait-for-input transactions are not included in the DB2 workload.

CICS work consists of light to moderate transactions from many of the same applications mentioned for the IMS work. The CICS applications are written in COBOL or assembler and are functionally similar, but not identical, to the applications used in the IMS workload and uses VSAM data sets only. There are six sets of 17 unique transactions, and five of these are run above the 16 megabyte line.

The data shown here is based on a configuration that has 128MB of storage, a RS/6000 Model 591 with 256MB of storage, and two 7137 RAID-5 disk arrays. Actual performance a customer will experience will vary depending on many factors, such as I/O content, system configuration, available storage, and the specific workload being processed.

Figure 40.2 shows the number of users that can be handled for the two possible memory sizes based on an internal IBM VM/CMS program development workload. This workload is designed to represent the VM/CMS end-user community. Workload activities include program input and editing, compilation, execution, and program test. Each user runs in a separate virtual machine and enters a variety of CMS and CP commands related to the activities called scripts. There are 17 such scripts containing these command sets. The number of users is based on an average think time of approximately 26 seconds between commands and an end-user average response time of one second or less.

VM/CMS Performance

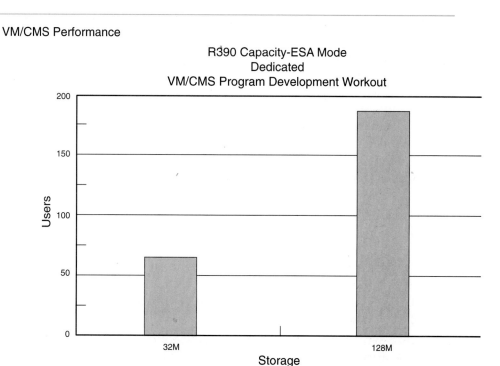

Figure 40.2   *R390 Capacity—ESA Mode*

Planning Worksheet

The following questions will help you determine whether the R/390 is right for your business. At the end of the worksheet, you will know (1) if it is right for you, (2) if it is not right for you, or (3) if you need to contact Bestbuilt Systems for further analysis.

1. Specify the amount of disk storage (GB) you need for your planned environment.
    a. The disk storage required is able to be configured on the RISC/6000 (Terabytes).
    b. Not applicable
    c. The disk storage required is not able to be configured on the RS/6000
    d. Not applicable

2. What is the total number of lines per minute required for printing?
    a. Fewer than 800
    b. Between 801 and 2000
    c. Between 2001 and 20000
    d. More than 20000

3. MVS: How many MVS/TSO application development users are supported?

   a. Fewer than 50 (See *MVS/TSO Performance*)
   b. Not applicable
   c. More than 50
   d. Not applicable

4. VM: How many VM application development users are supported?

   a. Fewer than 50
   b. Between 51 and 150
   c. More than 150
   d. Not applicable

5. If you are running an interactive database workload, what is the expected number of disk I/O operations per second?

   a. Fewer than 20
   b. Between 21 and 60
   c. Between 61 and 150
   d. More than 150

6. How many communication lines do you require?

   a. 16 or fewer
   b. More than 16

7. If you plan to replace an existing 43xx or 937x machine, what are you replacing?

   a. A 4331, 4341, 4361, 4381-11, 9373, 9375, or 9377
   b. A 4381-21 or larger capacity model that is underutilized
   c. A 4381-21 or larger capacity model that is near or fully utilized
   d. Not applicable

8. Do you have a critical time requirement for your batch window?

   a. No
   b. Not applicable
   c. Yes

9. Does your planned workload fit with anticipated growth over your investment period? Refer to *Performance* titles for more information.

   a. Yes
   b. Not applicable
   c. No
   d. Not applicable

If you answered (a) to all the above questions after reading all the pertinent information, a single R/390 looks like a good fit for your business. Call Bestbuilt Systems (888) 588-1999. [Editor: The regular IBM sales force doesn't sell the pygmy computers.]

If you answered (b) to any of the above questions, please refer to the specified section to determine if your workload can be run on the R/390. If the workload can run, consider it an (a) answer, if not consider it a (d) answer. If you are still not able to determine the feasibility of your workload with the additional information provided, consider it a (c) answer.

If you answered (c) to any of the above questions, further analysis is required to determine if workloads and data can be logically divided between two R/390s or between an existing machine and an R/390. For more information contact Bestbuilt Systems.

If you answered (d) to any of the above questions, the R/390 is not a fit due to the complexity involved in managing the required number of systems and maintenance of the platform.

Planning for a New Environment

The following questionnaire outlines the S/370 or S/390 environment that you want to move to the R390. This information guides you through the worksheet analysis and planning guide in the next sections. In addition, this information is important if you need to call for further help with analysis. Answer the questions based on the workload you plan to run on the R390. Complete a separate questionnaire for each machine type you plan to replace or application you plan to move.

1. Current system, if applicable:

Machine Type	Model	Memory	CPU Utilization	S/370 Mode S/390 Mode
_____	_____	_____	_____	_____

2. Type of DASD installed or connected:

Type	Quantity	GB
0671 3310 3370 9332 9335 9336 (FBA)	_____	_____
3375 3380 (CKD)	_____	_____
Other _____	_____	_____
	Total	_____

3. What operating system are you currently running and planning to run?

Current: VM/HPO   VM/SP   VM/XA   VM/ESA   DOS/VSE   VSE/SP   VSE/ESA   MVS/SP   MVS/XA   MVS/ESA
Planned: VM/ESA   VSE/ESA   MVS/ESA

4. What type of workload are you planning on running?

Planned: CMS   CICS   DB2   IMS   BATCH   TSO

5. Performance:

You can find disk I/O information by using the following programs:

VM: VMPRF or VM RTM

VSE: Explore

MVS: RMF

Current number of disk I/Os per second   _____

Projected number of disk I/O per second
(based on adding/removing workloads)   _____

6. Types of I/O devices that are currently attached on the system. The Host Attachment column defines attachment method currently used to connect the devices to your system.

I/O Device	Machine Type	Host Attachment (Chn/LAN/ Coax/TP)	Performance	Other
Printers:			Lines/Minute	
	_____	_____	_____	_____	_____
	_____	_____	_____	_____	_____
	_____	_____	_____	_____	_____
	_____	_____	_____	_____	_____

Tapes:			Tape Performance (KB/sec)	Block Size
	_____	_____	_____	_____
	_____	_____	_____	_____
	_____	_____	_____	_____
	_____	_____	_____	_____

Display Controllers:			# of Users	
	_____	_____	_____	
	_____	_____	_____	
	_____	_____	_____	
	_____	_____	_____	

Communication Controllers:			Speed (bps)	# of Lines	Devices/Line
	_____	_____	_____	_____	_____
	_____	_____	_____	_____	_____
	_____	_____	_____	_____	_____
	_____	_____	_____	_____	_____

7. User Network Information:

	Local	Remote	No. Users
HARDWARE:			
Token Ring Network (16MB/4MB)			
Ethernet 802.3	_____	_____	_____
Channel Attach (VTAM/BTAM)	_____	_____	_____
	_____	_____	_____
SOFTWARE:			
HP/UX			
UNIXWARE	_____	_____	_____
Banyan Vines	_____	_____	_____
via SNA/VTAM	_____	_____	_____
via TCP/IP (host/LAN)	_____	_____	_____
OS/2 LAN Server	_____	_____	_____
Novell	_____	_____	_____
	_____	_____	_____
Others:			
	_____	_____	_____
	_____	_____	_____
	_____	_____	_____
	_____	_____	_____

Payback

Budget Items	Current Monthly Budget		R/390 3-Year Cost	
• Environmentals				
- Power	• _____		• _____	$.10/kw in US
- Cooling	• _____		• _____ 0	n/a
- Floor Space	• _____		• _____ 0	small!
• Maintenance				
- DASD	• _____		• _____ 0	internal
- Processor	• _____		• _____ 0	1 year warranty
• S/390 Software	• _____	MLC	• _____	OTC
• Hardware Cost	• _____ 0	paid	• _____	R/390 hardware
• TOTALS	• _____		• _____	

Note: If you have monthly connectivity costs, such as dedicated or switched lines cost that you are eliminating or reducing by using the R/390, add those to your current monthly costs before doing the following calculation.

Return on Investment

Total Cost of R/390

$$\frac{\text{Total Cost of R/390}}{\text{Total Current Monthly Budget}} = \underline{} = \underline{} \quad \text{Break-Even Period (months)}$$

Total Current Monthly Budget

---

41   *Global Economic Impact*

Capers Jones
Software Productivity Research, Inc.

Abstract

From the start of the computing era until the early 1990's, magnetic storage of information was expensive and storage capacities were limited. As a result, software applications routinely conserved space by using only two digits for recording calendar years; i.e., the year 1990 would be stored as 90. When the 20th century ends, many software applications will stop or produce erroneous results since their logic cannot deal with the transition from 1999 to 2000 when the dates are stored in two-digit form and their calendars change from 99 to 00. Because this problem is embedded in millions of aging software applications, the costs of fixing the "year 2000 problem" appear to constitute the most expensive single problem in human history.

If the problem is not fixed, then the errors in software associated with finance, taxation, insurance, and even operation of aircraft can lead to the most expensive litigation in human history. However, once the problem is fixed, enterprises will have much better knowledge of their software portfolios and application structures than ever before. A strong caution is indicated: failure to repair year 2000 problems carefully with full testing and performance optimization can degrade software performance and data entry throughput by more than 20 percent. Approximately October of 1997 is the last point at which year 2000 repairs can start with a reasonable probability of finishing before 2000.

Function Points Versus Lines of Code Metrics for the Year 2000 Problem

The first step in exploring the economic consequences of the year 2000 problem is to construct an approximate inventory of the total volume of software installed and operational in the United States, and then utilize the U.S. data as a jumping off place for evaluating the hazards of other countries.

This is not an easy task and probably cannot be done with high precision. But by making some reasonable assumptions, it is possible to put together a picture of U.S. software that can serve as a jumping off place for exploring the magnitude of the year 2000 problem on a global or at least multi-national basis.

Although some research organizations such as the Gartner Group have attempted to enumerate the costs of the year 2000 problem using the "lines of code" or LOC metric, that metric is not accurate enough for serious economic analysis of software problems.

Function Points and Programming Languages

As of 1996, the Software Productivity Research catalog of programming languages (Table of programming Languages and Levels, Version 8, SPR 1996) identifies almost 500 programming languages in current usage.

For some of the languages that are impacted by the year 2000 problem, there is no accurate definition of what a "line of code" is in that language. For example, it is very difficult to enumerate lines of code for languages such as query-by-example (QBE), the control functions of Visual Basic, spreadsheets such as Lotus and Excel, data base languages, and a host of others.

Even for procedural languages such as COBOL and FORTRAN, there are wide variations in how lines of code are counted. A survey of software journals carried out by the author found that about one third of the software literature used physical lines as the basis for determining lines of code, one third used logical statements, and the remaining third did not identify which method was used.

Since the difference between the number of physical lines and logical statements in a COBOL program can amount to more than 300 percent, it can be seen that the ambiguity associated with using lines of code is far too great for serious economic study.

In this study, the well-known function point metric will be utilized. Function point metric originated in the 1970s within IBM, and has become the most widely used metric in the software world. The International Function Point Users Group (IFPUG) is the largest software measurement association in the United States, and there are affiliated associations in some 20 countries.

It is now late 1996. The only applications that could be built and deployed between now and the end of 1999 are those that are less than 2000 function points in size:

Table 41.1 **Average Software Development Schedules in Terms of Calendar Months**

Size	End-User	MIS	Outsource	Commercial	System	Military	Average
1FP	0.05	0.10	0.10	0.20	0.20	.0.30	0.16
10FP	0.50	0.75	0.90	1.00	1.25	2.00	1.07
100FP	3.50	9.00	9.50	11.00	12.00	15.00	10.00
1000FP	0.00	24.00	22.00	24.00	28.00	38.00	27.20
10000FP	0.00	48.00	44.00	46.00	47.00	64.00	49.80
100000FP	0.00	72.00	68.00	66.00	78.00	85.00	73.80
Average	0.68	25.64	24.08	24.70	27.74	34.05	27.00

Table 41.1 is taken from the second edition of my recent book *Applied Software Measurement* (McGraw Hill, 1996). It shows the U.S. averages for six software subindustries and for six size plateaus, each an order of magnitude apart. The size is expressed in terms of function points and ranges from 1 function point to 100,000 function points. The subindustries are those of end-user development, management information systems (MIS), outsource or contract development, systems software, commercial software, and military software.

Note that any software development project larger than about 2000 function points that starts in 1997 will not be completed until some time after the year 2000 problem has already occurred.

Numerically software applications less than 2000 function points in size comprise about 65 percent of the applications with year 2000 problems, while the other 45 percent are larger than 2000 function points. However, in terms of the work effort needed, the situation is reversed: about 65 percent of the effort for year 2000 repairs will be expended on larger systems in excess of 2000 function points. Indeed, some applications with year 2000 problems are in the size range of 100,000 function points and would take more than 10 years to redevelop.

(A simple rule of thumb for determining approximate software development schedules is to raise the size of the application in function points to the 0.45 power. That rule of thumb gives the number of calendar months from the start of deployment until delivery.)

In other words, none of the major software applications in either the United States or the rest of the world can be replaced between now and the end of the century. You have to fix the year 2000 problem in your current applications, like it or not.

The function point count of a software application is based on enumerating five external attributes of the application:

> Inputs
> Outputs
> Inquiries
> Logical files
> Interfaces

These five attributes are assigned various weighting factors, and there are also adjustments for complexity. The actual counting rules assumed in this study are based on the Version 4.0 counting practices manual published by International Function Point Users Group (*IFPUG Counting Practices Manual*, 1995).

Because some readers may be unfamiliar with the function point metric, it is useful to show the relationship between function points and lines of code for various languages, using the rules for logical statement counts, defined in *Applied Software Measurement*.

Table 41.2   **Ratios of Logical Source Code Statements to Function Points for Selected Programming Languages**   *(Page 1 of 2)*

Language	Nominal Level	Source Statements per Function Point		
		Low	Mean	High
1st Generation	1.00	220	320	500
Basic assembly	1.00	200	320	450
Macro assembly	1.50	130	213	300
C	2.50	60	128	170
BASIC (interpreted)	2.50	70	128	165

Table 41.2 **Ratios of Logical Source Code Statements to Function Points for Selected Programming Languages** *(Page 2 of 2)*

Language	Nominal Level	Source Statements per Function Point		
		Low	Mean	High
2ND Generation	3.00	55	107	165
FORTRAN	3.00	75	107	160
ALGOL	3.00	68	107	165
COBOL	3.00	65	107	150
CMS2	3.00	70	107	135
JOVIAL	3.00	70	107	165
PASCAL	3.50	50	91	125
3rd Generation	4.00	45	80	125
PL/I	4.00	65	80	95
MODULA 2	4.00	70	80	90
Ada83	4.50	60	71	80
LISP	5.00	25	64	80
FORTH	5.00	27	64	85
QUICK BASIC	5.50	38	58	90
C++	6.00	30	53	125
Ada 95	6.50	28	49	110
Data base	8.00	25	40	75
Visual Basic (Windows)	10.00	20	32	37
APL (default value)	10.00	10	32	45
SMALLTALK	15.00	15	21	40
Generators	20.00	10	16	20
Screen painters	20.00	8	16	30
SQL	27.00	7	12	15
Spreadsheets	50.00	3	6	9

Table 41.2 merely illustrates why "lines of code" metrics are difficult to apply to general software economic issues that span multiple programming languages. There are hundreds of programming languages and they vary in power over an enormous range. Moreover, for a significant number of modern programming languages such as the "visual" languages, the concept of a line of code is not truly relevant.

The Volume of United States Software Expressed in Terms of Function Points

By interesting coincidence each reference to a calendar date in a software application seems to require approximately one function point to encode in quite a large variety of programming languages. This coincidence makes expressing the effort and costs in terms of work hours per function point, function points per staff month, and cost per function point comparatively straight-forward.

In terms of languages that are affected by the year 2000 problem, these languages are probably the top of the heap in year 2000 impact, listed in order of the numbers of applications in U.S. software portfolios as of 1996:

Note that Table 41.3 reveals a hidden aspect of the year 2000 problem. There are only about 1,920,000 professional software personnel in the United States, but Table 41.3 shows a total of 3,450,000 programmers. The reason that the total for programmers is so large is that it includes applications developed by non-professional programmers such as accountants, managers, and engineers.

Computer literacy is very common in the United States, and end-user applications constitute a large but invisible component of the year 2000 problem. For software that was done by professional software personnel, the software usually resides in a formal corporate portfolio, often under formal configuration control.

End-user applications, on the other hand, typically reside on the C drives of personal computers in someone's office and are under no configuration control at all. Other than the originator of the application, it may be that no one in the company even knows of the existence of the software. Yet some of these privately developed end-user applications are used for important business purposes within the enterprise.

Support for finding and fixing the year 2000 problem will be much tougher for some languages than for others. Assembly language applications will probably be the toughest, because many date calculations are hard to find since they are performed using register manipulation.

Table 41.3   **Impact of the Year 2000 Problem for Selected Languages**

Language	Programmers	Applications	Function Points
COBOL	550,000	12,100,000	605,000,000
Spreadsheets	600,000	3,600,000	54,000,000
C	200,000	2,600,000	156,000,000
Basic	250,000	2,250,000	45,000,000
Query	150,000	1,950,000	29,250,000
Data Base	200,000	1,600,000	120,000,000
C++	175,000	1,400,000	105,000,000
PASCAL	90,000	1,080,000	54,000,000
Assembly	50,000	750,000	93,750,000
Ada83	90,000	720,000	54,000,000
FORTRAN	50,000	575,000	28,750,000
PL/I	30,000	270,000	13,500,000
Jovial	15,000	105,000	7,875,000
Other	1,000,000	7,000,000	336,000,000
TOTAL	3,450,000	36,000,000	1,702,125,000

Another language that may be difficult in year 2000 terms is PL/I. IBM was pushing the PL/I language very hard as a business tool in the early 1970s, and several industries such as oil and energy began to adopt PL/I. As of 1996, however, there is a shortage of both tools for analyzing PL/I programs and also a shortage of trained PL/I programmers.

However, as this report was written, several vendors had announced expanded year 2000 support that includes PL/I among other languages. This support is welcome, but of course still does not compensate for the lack of experienced PL/I programmers on a global basis.

Other programming languages that manifest the year 2000 problem but have a current shortage of available tools or available trained programmers 2 include ALGOL, APL, Basic, CHILL, CMS2, CORAL, Forth, Lisp, MODULA, MUMPS, PASCAL, Prolog, Ratfor, RPG, and the host of proprietary languages which companies have built for their own use, such as ITT's ESPL/I and IBM's PLS.

The language that probably has the highest incidence of year 2000 calculations is COBOL since that is a very old language dating back to the 1960s and is also widely used for business applications. However, COBOL has the most plentiful supply of year 2000 tools and services of any language. Indeed, from a scan of the advertisements in software journals, it appears that COBOL may have more year 2000 support than all other languages put together.

Mixed Language Applications and the Year 2000 Problem

One other aspect of the Year 2000 problem that has not yet received adequate attention is that of dealing with applications that contain multiple programming languages. Among SPR's data base of information covering about 7,000 software projects, roughly 2,000 of them contain more than one programming language. Mixed language applications are very common among all classes of software: systems, military, information systems, and commercial. Some of the more common programming language combinations include:

- Ada and CMS2
- Ada and Jovial
- Basic and assembly
- C and assembly
- C and C++
- C++ and assembly
- COBOL and data base languages
- COBOL and PL/I
- COBOL and RPG
- COBOL and SQL
- COBOL and SQL and data base languages

About 30 percent of U.S. software applications contain at least two languages. The maximum number of programming languages which we have observed in a single system is 12. It is hard enough to find and fix year 2000 problems for applications containing only one language, and those containing multiple languages will be even harder.

Although the data is preliminary, rough rules of thumb can be hypothesized for the additional effort of finding and fixing year 2000 problems in mixed language applications:

Hopefully, the vendors and service bureaus that are now gearing up to perform year 2000 repairs will be able to handle mixed-language applications for at least the more common combinations, such as COBOL and SQL.

Table 41.4 **Impact of Multiple Programming Languages on Year 2000 Repair Effort**

Number of Languages in Application	Percent Increase in Year 2000 Repair Efforts
1	0%
2	15%
3	20%
4	25%
5	30%
6	35%

The Size of the Year 2000 Problem for the United States

So far as can be determined by the author, there has never been an accurate or even approximate inventory of the total volume of software deployed within any country. The data presented here is known to be imperfect and to have a high margin of error. However, for studying problems such as the year 2000 issue, it is better to have partly speculative data with a high margin of error than no data at all. Hopefully, future research can correct any errors and improve the accuracy of the results. But if the information were not published at all, there might be no incentive to carry out research that will eliminate any errors shown here.

The Volume of Software Installed in the United States

Using the assumptions for portfolios, sites, and software staffs discussed earlier, Table 41.5 shows the approximate size of the installed software portfolios in the United States. The data in Table 41.5 is derived from multiple sources, and can be assumed to have a large but unknown margin of error.

Regardless of the margin of error in Table 41.5, one fact is painfully obvious. The United States is the world's largest producer and largest consumer of software, so the costs of the year 2000 problem is one of those comparatively rare problems that affects industrialized and computerized nations much more severely than those that are not yet fully automated.

This same statement is true of industries and governments as well as countries. Industries such as banking and insurance that are highly

Table 41.5 **U.S. Software Applications, Sites, Staff, and Software Portfolios (Portfolio Volumes Expressed in Function Points)**

Industries	Applications	Software Sites	Software Staff	Portfolio Size: Function Points
Military	6,000,000	1,000	200,000	300,000,000
Manufacturing	1,800,000	8,500	250,000	200,000,000
Finance	2,454,545	2,500	150,000	135,000,000
Services	2,222,222	1,500	125,000	100,000,000
Communications	1,800,000	1,000	100,000	90,000,000
Insurance	1,800,000	1,500	90,000	81,000,000
Defense	1,600,000	2,000	100,000	80,000,000
Wholesale	1,777,778	1,500	100,000	80,000,000
Federal	1,333,333	500	75,000	60,000,000
Retail	1,200,000	3,500	75,000	60,000,000
Software	1,050,000	1,000	75,000	52,500,000
Health care	510,000	1,500	30,000	25,500,000
Municipal	533,333	1,500	30,000	24,000,000
Energy	500,000	1,000	25,000	20,000,000
Transportation	416,667	1,000	25,000	18,750,000
States	355,556	150	20,000	16,000,000
Other	8,002,668	15,000	450,000	360,000,000
TOTAL	36,000,546	44,650	1,920,000	1,702,750,000

automated will have much higher costs associated with the year 2000 problem than less automated groups such as publishing.

Also, the potential liabilities associated with litigation also seem to correlate with the volumes of software used by an industry. However, the litigation potential is also affected by the probability that not fixing the year 2000 problem will cause economic damage.

In considering the impact of the year 2000 problem, it is obvious that the expenses will be large primarily because the problem is found throughout the entire portfolio of legacy applications. Changing any single application might not be too difficult, but when *every* application, or at least a high percentage of applications, owned by a large company is affected, the cumulative effort will be enormous.

Table 41.6 provides rough approximations of the percentage of port-folios that are likely to be modified, and the anticipated productivity rates for finding and repairing the year 2000 problem:

Table 41.6   **Productivity Assumptions for Year 2000 Repairs (Productivity Rates Expressed in Function Points per Person Month)**

Industries	Portfolio Size: Function Points	Year 2000 Impact	Portfolio Changes	Productivity FP per PM	Effort in Person Months
Military	300,000,000	7.00%	21,000,000	11.00	1,909,091
Finance	135,000,000	6.00%	8,100,000	18.00	450,000
Manufacturing	200,000,000	5.00%	10,000,000	18.00	555,556
Communications	90,000,000	8.00%	7,200,000	17.00	423,529
Services	100,000,000	10.00%	10,000,000	18.00	555,556
Insurance	81,000,000	10.00%	8,100,000	18.00	450,000
Wholesale	80,000,000	11.00%	8,800,000	17.00	517,647
Federal	60,000,000	10.00%	6,000,000	15.00	400,000
Defense	80,000,000	4.00%	3,200,000	12.00	266,667
Retail	60,000,000	11.00%	6,600,000	16.00	412,500
Software	52,500,000	7.00%	3,675,000	19.00	193,421
Municipal	24,000,000	10.00%	2,400,000	16.00	150,000
Health care	25,500,000	7.00%	1,785,000	16.00	111,563
States	16,000,000	10.00%	1,600,000	16.00	100,000
Energy	20,000,000	7.00%	1,400,000	16.00	87,500
Transportation	18,750,000	7.00%	1,312,500	16.00	82,031
Other	360,000,000	8.00%	28,800,000	16.00	1,800,000
TOTAL	1,702,750,000	8.12%	138,223,235	16.18	8,465,060

The technical work associated with finding and fixing the year 2000 problem can be broken down into four discrete activities:

1. Finding and isolating the year 2000 sections of applications
2. Modifying the applications to repair the problem
3. Testing the repairs to ensure that they work
4. Regression testing the application to ensure no secondary damage has occurred.

Table 41.6 assumes that all four of these activities will be performed. However, from preliminary observations of companies that have already begun their year 2000 work, steps 3 and 4 (testing and regression testing) are sometimes performed in a very careless fashion. Carelessness in regression testing and validating Year 2000 repairs will have three damaging impacts later that can run well into the 21st century:

> Missed year 2000 instances will be plentiful and troublesome.
> Bad fixes or fresh bugs accidentally injected will be common and troublesome.
> The performance or execution speeds of applications will be seriously degraded.

The approximate distribution of effort over the four aspects of the year 2000 problem will vary significantly by language, due to the presence or absence of available tools.

Finding and isolating the year 2000 problem should be easiest for object-oriented languages (i.e., Objective C, Smalltalk, etc.) where dates are handled in well-formed class libraries. Next would be COBOL, since there are several specialized tools that can seek out date references in COBOL applications. Such tools also exist for other common languages such as C and FORTRAN. The toughest language will probably be assembly, followed by languages that have tool shortages such as PL/I, LISP, FORTH and the like.

Here are the major Year 2000 activities and their percent range of total costs:

>	Finding the year 2000 instances	10% to 50%
>	Fixing the year 2000 instances	15% to 30%
>	Testing the year 2000 repairs	10% to 30%
>	Regression testing the portfolio	20% to 50%

The next aspect of the study of the year 2000 problem is to assign approximate costs for the overall repairs that must be performed. Here there is quite a bit of uncertainty, since there are large variances in cost structure by industry and by geography. For example, the costs of updating financial applications in New York City or San Francisco will be much greater than the costs of updating retail applications in the rural South because urban areas have higher compensation rates than rural and because financial institutions have higher compensation rates than retail.

Table 41.7 shows the approximate United States costs for finding and fixing the year 2000 problem.

The platform on which the application resides will also affect the costs. Common platforms such as IBM mainframes and AS400 machines will be comparatively straightforward, as will standard IBM compatible personal computers. UNIX, OS/2, DOS, Macintosh, and various Windows versions will need repairs, but all are marketed by vendors that are actively moving toward year 2000 compliance. Tougher will be software that runs on "orphan" platforms or on specialized computers such as military on-board ANYUK computers.

Hardware and Performance Implications of the Year 2000 Problem

Fixing the year 2000 problem in software will have some possible implications for the performance of the applications, which may necessitate hardware upgrades to more powerful computers.

The performance and hardware implications of the year 2000 problem are underreported in the literature and at conferences. Many mainframe software applications have been optimized to reduce machine utilization and maximize throughput. Any year 2000 repairs that are made in a hasty or perfunctory manner without adequate testing and reoptimization can result in several major problems:

- ➤ Introduction of bad fixes or new bugs as a by-product of year 2000 repairs.
- ➤ Major degradation of application throughput and data center efficiency levels.

The author estimates that sloppy year 2000 repairs are likely to affect mainframe data centers the most, since the bulk of aging U.S. legacy applications were originally built for IBM mainframe computers.

It is difficult to estimate precisely, but I suspect that the minimum degradation from the year 2000 problem will be a de facto 10 percent loss in data center throughput. This is the most conservative estimate. The most probable estimate is about 20 percent or higher. The worst-case scenario might cause a 30 percent slowdown in data center efficiency and throughput, which could trigger a set of catastrophic secondary problems in things like delayed billings, slow processing of tax returns, and a host of other speed-related issues.

Table 41.7   **United States Repair Costs for the Year 2000 Problem**

Industries	Effort PM	Burdened $/PM	Costs	Costs per Changed FP	Costs per Total FP
Military	1,909,091	$7,500	$14,318,181,818	$682	$48
Finance	450,000	$11,000	$4,950,000,000	$611	$37
Manufacturing	555,556	$8,400	$4,666,666,667	$467	$23
Communications	423,529	$10,000	$4,235,294,118	$558	$47
Services	555,556	$8,000	$4,444,444,444	$444	$44
Insurance	450,000	$9,200	$4,140,000,000	$511	$51
Wholesale	517,647	$7,500	$3,882,352,941	$441	$49
Federal	400,000	$7,900	$3,160,000,000	$527	$53
Defense	266,667	$11,000	$2,933,333,333	$917	$37
Retail	412,500	$7,500	$3,093,750,000	$469	$52
Software	193,421	$9,000	$1,740,789,474	$474	$33
Municipal	150,000	$7,000	$1,050,000,000	$438	$44
Health care	111,563	$8,000	$892,500,000	$500	$35
States	100,000	$7,700	$770,000,000	$481	$48
Energy	87,500	$8,000	$700,000,000	$500	$35
Transportation	82,031	$8,000	$656,250,000	$500	$35
Other	1,800,000	$8,400	$15,120,000,000	$525	$42
TOTAL	8,465,060	$8,476	$70,753,562,795	$512	$42

An independent model of performance degradation in response to sloppy year 2000 repairs has also been reported by Dr. Howard Rubin. His model reaches a similar conclusion, and places the performance loss at something over 20 percent.

The normal response to a major degradation of throughput is either expensive optimization of software applications, major increases in hardware capacity, or both. I would predict that performance tuning of applications degraded by careless year 2000 testing might add $5,000,000 to the U.S. Year 2000 costs, while hardware upgrades to service the demand could add $10,000,000 to $20,000,000 in the years 1999 through about 2005 to U.S. Year 2000 costs.

Table 41.8   ***Per Capita Effort and Costs for the Year 2000 Problem***

Industries	Months per Staff Member	Costs per Capita
Military	9.55	$71,591
Insurance	5.00	$46,000
Communications	4.24	$42,353
Federal	5.33	$42,133
Retail	5.50	$41,250
Wholesale	5.18	$38,824
States	5.00	$38,500
Services	4.44	$35,556
Municipal	5.00	$35,000
Other	4.00	$33,600
Finance	3.00	$33,000
Health care	3.72	$29,750
Defense	2.67	$29,333
Energy	3.50	$28,000
Transportation	3.28	$26,250
Software	2.58	$23,211
Manufacturing	2.22	$18,667
TOTAL	4.41	$36,851

Note that hardware and data center costs are not measured using function points, so these costs are over and above the software costs discussed later in this report.

In round numbers, preliminary analysis suggests that about $40 will be expended for every function point in existing portfolios. Since most corporations own more than 100,000 function points and major corporations own more than 1,000,000 function points, the cumulative costs will be major indeed.

Year 2000 Repairs by Industry

Another interesting aspect of the year 2000 problem is to consider how much effort must be expended between now and the year 2000 by the software community. It appears that the problem is large enough so that essentially every technical worker in the software domain will become engaged for more than four months between now and 1999! If this hypothesis is true, then the year 2000 problem may well be one of the largest and most expensive technical problems in all of human history.

Table 41.8 shows the approximate effort in terms of expended person months and costs between now and the end of the century on a per capita basis. That is, the effort and costs are expressed in terms of the impact on every software technical worker in the United States, ranked in descending order.

In general, the human race is not very good in preventing disasters and tends to wait until the last minute (or beyond) before taking action. That tendency is already visible in the context of the year 2000 problem.

The time to start fixing this problem was 1995. It is now 1996 as this report is written, and time is already beginning to run short. Approximately October of the year 1997 is the last year that mid-sized corporations can commence their year 2000 repairs with any hope of finishing before the end of the century even with an automated year 2000 search engine, as can be seen in Table 41.9:

Table 41.9 **Percentage of Year 2000 Repairs Completed Based on Start Year and Use of Manual or Automated Search Procedures**

Year When 2000 Repairs Start	Percent of Applications Corrected by 1999 (Manual Search)	Percent of Applications Corrected by 1999 (Automated Search)
1994	100%	100%
1995	!00%	100%
1996	99%	100%
1997	80%	99%
1998	70%	85%
1999	30%	60%

It should be noted that the year 2000 problem is one where automated search engines are going to be highly beneficial. However, the accuracy of these search engines is still something of an unknown value.

Right now no one is sure if automated year 2000 search engines will find 100 percent of the year 2000 instances. On the other hand, no one is sure if manual searches will find 100 percent of the year 2000 instances either. (There is also an opposite problem of reporting false year 2000 instances, but this is less serious than missing real year 2000 hits.)

An interesting question as this report is written in late 1996 is, "What percent of Year 2000 repairs have already been accomplished, and what percent remain to be done?" This is a hard question to answer.

Unfortunately, the great majority of companies and government groups are still in preliminary fact-finding mode and have not yet begun the tougher work of actually seeking out the year 2000 hits and making corrections. The result of this lag time in getting started means that a significant number of companies will still be working on year 2000 repairs when the clock runs out at midnight on December 31, 1999.

Further, repairs made during calendar year 1999 and especially during the last half of 1999 are probably going to be rushed and careless, so there will be a high probability of missed year 2000 hits, performance degradation, bad fixes, and the other problems associated with excessive haste and poor quality control.

From queries and surveys among our clients, the following expenditure pattern seems to be a rough approximation:

If the year 2000 problem follows the pattern just illustrated, software repairs will peak during calendar year 1999. However, hardware upgrades and legal expenses will not peak until 2000 and 2001, respectively. In other words, the year 2000 problem will leave a trail of major expenses until well into the 21st century.

Year 2000 Repairs by Company Size

To chief information officers (CIOs), chief executives (CEOs) and other managers concerned with enterprise software, the most important topic is not what the problem is going to cost the country or their industry, but rather what the problem is going to cost their particular enterprise.

Unfortunately, it would require an on-site study of each enterprise to quantify the exact costs. Indeed, as this report is written many enterprises have already commissioned site studies to begin to quantify the expenses of the year 2000 problem.

However, by using some of the general assumptions shown earlier, it is possible to state the approximate overall costs of fixing the year 2000

Table 41.10   Trail of Year 2000 Expenses for Software, Hardware, and Litigation From 1994 Through 2005 AD

Year When 2000 Repairs Start	Software Expense Percent	Hardware Expense Percent	Litigation Expense Percent
1994	1%	0%	0%
1995	3%	0%	0%
1996	10%	1%	1%
1997	15%	1%	2%
1998	20%	5%	5%
1999	30%	20%	10%
2000	15%	25%	20%
2001	4%	20%	30%
2002	2%	15%	15%
2003	0%	10%	10%
2004	0%	2%	5%
2005	0%	1%	2%

problem for enterprises of various sizes. Table 41.11 is based on the total number of technical software staff employed, and shows approximate costs for enterprises with as few as five technical personnel, up to enterprises with as many as 10,000 technical personnel.

Some of the background assumptions going into Table 41.11 include:

➤ A generic burdened cost per staff month of $8,400 is assumed.

➤ Large enterprises are geographically dispersed, and this raises repair costs.

➤ Large enterprises have more large systems, and they are harder to fix.

Table 41.11 has a significant margin of error and is not a substitute for a thorough on-site analysis of an enterprise's actual portfolio.

In order to refine the information shown in Table 41.11, readers are urged to carry out the following six-step analysis either on their own or aided by consultants who are specializing in the year 2000 problem:

1. Quantify the size of your portfolio of legacy applications.
2. Quantify the size of your software data bases and repositories.

Table 41.11   **Effort and Costs of the Year 2000 Problem by Size of Software Staff**

Software Staff	Number of Sites	Portfolio Size in FP	Effort in Months	Total Costs	Cost per FP
5	1	6,000	23	$197,784	$33
10	1	11,500	45	$379,087	$33
25	1	27,500	107	$906,511	$33
50	1	50,000	194	$1,648,203	$33
100	1	95,000	416	$3,523,033	$37
500	2	450,000	1,969	$16,688,051	$37
1000	3	900,000	4,200	$35,601,176	$40
5000	5	4,500,000	21,000	$178,005,882	$40
10000	10	9,000,00	42,000	$356,011,765	$40
20000	15	18,000,000	84,000	$712,023,529	$40

3. Explore the incidence of year 2000 references in your legacy applications.
4. Explore the incidence of year 2000 references in your current data bases.
5. Estimate the effort to repair each year 2000 reference.
6. Estimate the effort to test and validate each year 2000 reference.

It should be obvious but unfortunately it is not, that a seventh step must also be included:

7. Stop using two-digit date fields in your new applications!

As stated earlier, by interesting coincidence each reference to a calendar date in a software application seems to require approximately one function point to encode in quite a large variety of programming languages. This coincidence makes expressing the effort and costs in terms of work hours per function point, function points per staff month, and cost per function point comparatively straight-forward.

Year 2000 Repairs by Programming Language

It is also interesting to consider the approximate costs of the year 2000 problem for selected programming languages. Table 41.12 gives the cost per language, although with a high margin of error.

Table 41.12 **Approximate Costs for the Year 2000 Problem by Language**

Language	Function Points	$ per FP	Total Cost
COBOL	605,000,000	$28	$16,940,000,000
Spreadsheets	54,000,000	$35	$1,890,000,000
C	156,000,000	$35	$5,460,000,000
V-Basic	45,000,000	$30	$1,350,000,000
Query	29,250,000	$40	$1,170,000,000
Data Base	120,000,000	$45	$5,400,000,000
C++	105,000,000	$35	$3,675,000,000
PASCAL	54,000,000	$40	$2,160,000,000
Assembly	93,750,000	$80	$7,500,000,000
Ada 83	54,00,000	$35	$1,890,000,000
FORTRAN	28,750,000	$35	$1,006,250,000
PL/I	13,500,000	$65	$877,500,000
Jovial	7,875,000	$60	$472,500,000
Other	336,000,000	$60	$20,160,000,000
TOTAL	1,702,120,000	$45	$69,951,250,000

Although COBOL is the language with the greatest number of year 2000 "hits," it will probably be among the least expensive to modify due to the large numbers of specialized tools and consulting groups in the COBOL domain.

Dr. Tom Love of the Worldstreet Journal software company and a well-known expert on OO topics reports that object-oriented languages such as Objective C, Smalltalk, Eiffel, etc., should be among the *least* expensive if the applications are well formed and the date calculations are handled by formal class libraries. Indeed, since object-oriented business applications are comparatively recent, many may already use adequate space for all date digits and hence the year 2000 problem may not be present in some OO applications.

On the other hand, the OO paradigm has a steep learning curve, and there may also be OO applications with incorrect date calculations "hard coded" into the applications just as they would be in procedural languages.

The most expensive languages will probably be assembly language and PL/I, both of which have shortages of tools and trained personnel. Table 41.12 shows the approximate overall expenses by language:

Although this data has a high margin of error, it appears that the repair costs for the year 2000 problem may be one of the largest single technology expenses in human history.

It is of interest to consider the relative proportion of expense among the four major activities associated with the year 2000 problem for selected programming languages as shown in Table 41.13

Note that Table 41.13 includes CHILL, CMS2, Jovial, and ALGOL which are not in Table 41.12. Table 41.13 is only approximate and has a high margin of error. However, it is obvious that there will be significant differences from language to language based on the presence or absence of available year 2000 tools, and on the structure of the language itself.

Repairing Data Bases, Repositories, and Data Warehouses

Software costs and economic studies can be expressed by means of function point metrics. Unfortunately, there is no equivalent metric for dealing with the volume of information stored in data bases, repositories, and data warehouses. In other words, the industry lacks a "data point" metric. As a result, there are no published statistics on the volumes of data and information owned by corporations and government agencies. Also as a result there is no easy way to perform an economic analysis of the data impact of the year 2000 problem.

Thus as this report is written, the impact of the year 2000 problem on data bases, repositories, and data warehouses is still uncertain. However, preliminary indications of relative costs lead to the following hypothesis:

For every dollar spent on changing software applications, it will probably be necessary to spend another dollar on changing data bases. However for data-intensive industries such as insurance and finance, and for data-intensive government agencies such as Social Security, the data-repair costs will perhaps be twice those of fixing the software itself!

Due to the lack of data metrics, the volume of on-line information can only be approximated. Table 41.14 shows the approximate amount of data maintained by large corporations such as IBM and AT&T with perhaps 250,000 total employees:

Since the example shown here is a corporation stated to have 250,000 employees, it is interesting to note that the volume of corporate information stored by the case study corporation amounts to more than

Table 41.13 **Distribution of Year 2000 Expense by Programming Language (Results shown in terms of Cost per Function Points)**

Language	Finding Year 2000 Instances	Repairing Year 2000 Instances	Testing Year 2000 Instances	Portfolio Regression Test	TOTAL
Assembly	$25	$20	$20	$15	$80
PL/I	$25	$10	$15	$15	$65
Jovial	$20	$12	$13	$15	$60
CMS2	$20	$12	$13	$15	$60
CHILL	$20	$15	$15	$10	$60
ALGOL	$15	$12	$13	$10	$50
Data Base	$7	$13	$15	$10	$45
Query	$10	$12	$12	$6	$40
PASCAL	$5	$10	$15	$10	$40
C++	$8	$6	$13	$8	$35
Spreadsheets	$5	$7	$20	$3	$35
C	$15	$7	$5	$8	$35
Ada83	$5	$7	$8	$15	$35
FORTRAN	$5	$7	$13	$10	$35
4-GLs	$5	$10	$10	$10	$35
V-Basic	$5	$5	$15	$5	$30
COBOL	$5	$6	$7	$10	$28
SMALLTALK	$3	$3	$5	$7	$18
Average	$11	$10	$13	$10	$44

1,000 pages per employee. How much of this information will require year 2000 changes is an important but currently unanswered question.

Table 41.15 shows the hypothetical costs of data repairs with a very large but unknown margin of error:

Table 41.14   **Relative Volumes of Stored Information in Major Corporations**

Kind of Information	Pages Stored	Percent Stored On-Line	Year 2000 Impact?
Customer information	90,000,000	50%	Yes
Product information	50,000,000	50%	Yes
Software applications	40,000,000	75%	Yes
Email messages	30,000,000	95%	No
Reference information	15,000,000	20%	No
Personnel information	12,500,000	50%	Yes
Graphics/images	10,000,000	50%	No
Correspondence	5,000,000	10%	No
Defect information	2,500,000	50%	Yes
Supplier information	1,500,000	25%	Yes
Tutorial/training material	1,000,000	50%	No
Litigation/legal information	1,000,000	25%	Yes
Total Volume	272,000,000		

Unfortunately, because data base repair productivity rates are essentially a topic with no citations in the literature, the information presented here for the costs of data repairs is largely speculative.

Litigation Potential for the Year 2000 Problem

The costs of repairing the year 2000 problem can be quantified with acceptable precision for software itself, and guessed at for data base repairs. The last and most alarming component of the year 2000 problem is the potential expenses for litigation and possible damages for *not* fixing the year 2000 problem.

As stated earlier, six kinds of litigation can be envisioned in the context of the year 2000 problems:

1. Litigation filed by clients whose finances or investments have been damaged.

Table 41.15   **Hypothetical Data Base Repair Costs for Year 2000**

Industries	Software Cost	Data Base Cost	Total Cost
Military	$13,363,636,364	$12,027,272,727	$25,390,909.901
Finance	$4,950,000,000	$5,445,000,000	$10,395,000,000
Manufacturing	$4,444,444,444	$3,111,111,111	$7,555,555,556
Communications	$4,235,294,118	$2,964,705,882	$7,200,000,000
Services	$4,166,666,667	$3,333,333,333	$7,500,000,000
Insurance	$4,050,000,000	$5,062,500,000	$9,112,500,000
Wholesale	$3,882,352,941	$2,911,764,706	$6,794,117,647
Federal	$3,400,000,000	$3,060,000,000	$6,460,000,000
Defense	$2,933,333,333	$2,640,000,000	$5,573,333,333
Retail	$3,093,750,000	$2,010,937,500	$5,104,687,500
Software	$1,740,789,474	$1,392,631,579	$3,133,421,053
Municipal	$1,020,000,000	$765,000,000	$1,785,000,000
Health care	$892,500,000	$624,750,000	$1,517,250,000
States	$770,000,000	$616,000,000	$1,386,000,000
Energy	$700,000,000	$525,000,000	$1,225,000,000
Transportation	$656,250,000	$459,375,000	$1,115,625,000
Other	$14,400,000,000	$10,800,000,000	$25,200,000,000
TOTAL	$68,699,017,341	$57,749,381,839	$126,448,399,179

2. Litigation filed by shareholders of companies whose software does not safely make the year 2000 transition.
3. Litigation associated with any deaths or injuries derived from the year 2000 problem.
4. Class-action litigation filed by various affected customers of computers or software packages.
5. Litigation filed by companies who utilized outsource vendors, contractors, consultants, or commercial year 2000 tools but where Year 2000 problems still slipped through and caused damage.

6. Litigation against hardware manufacturers such as computer companies and defense contractors if the year 2000 problem resides in hardware or embedded microcode as well as software.

Potential litigation is not easy to predict. Further, when litigation does occur the outcome is not easy to predict. However, the United States is a very litigious country, and damage awards are often set at astronomical values. It is possible that the litigation expenses (and any damages if suits are lost) for the year 2000 problem can exceed the direct costs of repairs by as much as 20 to 1 in cases where negligence and violation of fiduciary duty are proven or at least confirmed by jury decisions.

Table 41.16 shows the litigation potential for the industries discussed thus far for four of the six kinds of litigation. Suits against vendors are subsumed under "client suits" rather than being shown separately. Suits against hardware vendors would be distributed across the other categories.

The senior executives of corporations have what is called a fiduciary responsibility to act in the best interests of the shareholders of the companies they serve. Failure to take action to repair the year 2000 problem has at least the potential to damage or even end the careers of about half of the senior executives in the United States.

Attorneys' fees and damage awards for the year 2000 problem are difficult to estimate using any kind of historical data, since a problem of this magnitude has not occurred before. For the U.S. as a whole, I suspect that legal fees associated with year 2000 lawsuits will come to close to $2,000,000,000 between about 1997 and 2005, which is the window of major year 2000 litigation.

Damages and punitive damages are even harder to assess, but possibly $100,000,000,000 is a likely number for the United States as a whole.

Expressed another way, a major bank, insurance company, or Fortune 500 company in general might expect to pay about $750,000 a year in year 2000 legal fees between 1997 and 2005.

Since more companies are very likely to end up suing each other, the potential of damages paid out might be offset by damages payments that come in. However, it would be surprising if less than $100,000,000 per company ends up being paid out for year 2000 damages among the Fortune 500 class of enterprises.

Risk of Business Failure Due to the Year 2000 Problem

One of the most serious potential problems associated with the year 2000 crisis is that some companies may go bankrupt or fail either as a direct

Table 41.16   **Litigation Potential for Failure to Repair the Year 2000 Problem**

Industry	Client Suits	Shareholder Suits	Injury Suits	Class Action Suits
Military	Low	Low	Very High	Low
Finance	High	High	Low	High
Manufacturing	High	High	High	High
Communications	High	High	Low	High
Services	High	High	Low	High
Insurance	High	High	Low	High
Wholesale	High	High	Low	Low
Federal	High	None	High	High
Defense	High	High	High	High
Retail	High	High	Low	High
Software	High	High	Low	High
Municipal	High	None	Low	High
Health care	High	High	High	High
States	High	None	High	High
Energy	High	High	Low	High
Transportation	High	High	Very High	High

result of the year 2000 problem, or as a possible defensive measure to stave off massive damages due to year 2000 litigation.

There is insufficient data to predict the probable number of business failures that might be attributed to the year 2000 problem with any degree of accuracy, but from observing the recent history of business failures for other causes, it is possible to form some preliminary hypotheses.

There are four ways of examining the business failure potential associated with the year 2000 crisis:

1. Failure potentials based on the size of the company.
2. Failure potentials based on the industry in which the company resides.

3. Failure potentials based on the financial health of the company.

4. Failure potentials based on probable year 2000 litigation against the company.

Following are some preliminary observations on failure potentials based on these four criteria.

Business Failure Potentials Based on Company Size

In evaluating the potential for business failure based on company size, the preliminary conclusion is that mid-sized corporations with from 1,000 to 10,000 total employees are probably at greater risk than either larger or smaller enterprises.

Very large companies in the Fortune 500 class will be heavily impacted by year 2000 repairs, but many are already engaged in making those repairs, and most have adequate financial resources to complete the task either on their own or with the assistance of specialized year 2000 tool and service vendors.

My estimate is that the chance of a business failure among the Fortune 500 class is only about 1 percent, unless some of them declare bankruptcy as an emergency measure to avoid damages due to litigation.

Very small companies with less than 100 total employees will be impacted by the year 2000 problem, and sometimes severely, but these companies usually do not own very much software, so they can probably deal with the situation. My estimate is that the chance of failure for small companies as a direct impact of the year 2000 problem is about 3 percent, unless they are a direct target of year 2000 litigation for some reason. (Of course small companies fail all the time for a variety of reasons, so my 3 percent estimate is a delta on top of the already notable failure rate of small enterprises that exceeds 50 percent in the first two years after incorporation.)

Mid-sized corporations with from about 1,000 to 10,000 total employees have historically shown a distressing tendency to utilize quite a lot of software, but to be only marginally competent in how they build and maintain this software.

In a year 2000 context, mid-sized corporations will probably be late in getting started on their year 2000 repairs, will underestimate and underbudget for their year 2000 work, will not bring in the appropriate tools and specialists, and will probably not have any contingency plans in place on what to do with applications that don't make the changes in time. I place the failure probability of mid-sized U.D. corporations at about 5 percent to 7 percent.

There are about 30,000 companies in the "mid sized" range in the United States, and a 5 percent to 7 percent business failure rate would mean that from 1500 to perhaps 2100 companies might close or file for bankruptcy as a result of the year 2000 problem. This is a significant number and it is an open question, whether the impact of the year 2000 problem is severe enough to trigger a recession.

Business Failure Potentials Based on Industry

In considering the probability of year 2000 problems causing failures by industry, the industries that are most likely to be affected are those that utilize software for key business operations: banks, brokers, credit unions, health care, insurance, manufacturing, retail, wholesale. All of these probably have at least a 2 percent chance of going out of business or declaring bankruptcy to stave off damages and litigation.

Somewhat more ominous are the possibilities that industries not always recognized as software-intensive will fail due to the year 2000 problem: city governments, county and provincial governments, public utilities, and telephone companies may also fail.

Perhaps the most hazardous of any of these is not an industry at all, but the effect of the year 2000 problem on state, provincial, country, and city government operations may well cause a rash of bankrupt government organizations or at least drastic reductions in the services they provide.

In the United States many local government agencies use computers and software for a variety of revenue and disbursement purposes. Unfortunately governments as a class are often not very sophisticated about building or maintaining their software. They are typically under funded, and many can't even afford to bring in year 2000 consultants.

The probable result will be a rash of lawsuits against a wide variety of government organizations. In any case, the impact of the year 2000 problem will no doubt reduce many government services because the money to fix the year 2000 problem has got to come from somewhere.

Public utilities for water and electricity, and all telephone companies, utilize software for both technical and administrative purposes. Some of these organizations are large and sophisticated in how they build software, but others have been somewhat careless. The year 2000 problem may cause some of these utility companies to fail, and in any case will probably raise the costs of their services to consumers.

Business Failure Potentials Based on Financial Health

The year 2000 problem is going to be very expensive no matter how the repairs are accomplished. This obvious fact means that companies whose cash flow and finances are already marginal will have a significant probability of failing under the added expenses of the year 2000 problem. Since perhaps 10 percent of small to mid-sized companies in the United States are already in some kind of financial distress, the added burden of the year 2000 problem may put many of them out of business.

What is not so obvious is that the venture capital community will be seriously impacted by the year 2000 problem. Right now venture capital is pouring into new year 2000 startups, and into many other kinds of software startups as well.

The venture capital community should have included year 2000 compliance as part of the due diligence process starting in about 1994, but hardly any venture group even thought about the problem. When the costs of year 2000 repairs to venture-backed companies is factored in to business plans, the anticipated 10 to 1 yield which VC's expect will shrink to nothing. This means that 2nd, 3rd, or additional rounds of financing may evaporate.

Business Failure Potentials Based on Litigation

Readers of John Grisham's book *The Rainmaker* are aware of how a lawsuit against an insurance company triggered a deliberate bankruptcy filing in order to stave off having to pay damages.

The year 2000 problem will obviously cause a lot of litigation, and hence many organizations will consider filing for bankruptcy rather than face having to pay year 2000 damage claims.

The year 2000 crisis is likely to focus legal attention on three topics that have not been significant to software professionals and software companies in the past, but that may well become major topics as the year 2000 problem manifests itself:

1. Professional malpractice
2. Violation of fiduciary duty
3. Consequential damages

The topic of professional malpractice has long been a major source of litigation for medical practitioners, and a significant source of litigation against attorneys and some forms of engineers such as civil engineers.

The claim of professional malpractice has not been levied against software personnel very often, but the year 2000 problem may cause this to change. In particular, year 2000 vendors themselves who contract to make repairs but fail may find this charge brought against them.

The concept of professional malpractice is that a knowledge worker failed to perform duties in a way that matched the standard level of acceptable behavior for the topic in question.

One likely target of professional malpractice claims may be some of the year 2000 tool and service providers. It often happens when problems of a significant nature occur that a great many marginal organizations and even outright frauds move into the arena in order to make a quick profit. Companies seeking year 2000 assistance are cautioned to be alert to this fact, and to use due diligence when seeking year 2000 service providers.

It is somewhat ironic that the very insurance companies that offer malpractice insurance for physicians may find the same charges brought against them if they fail to repair the year 2000 problem in time.

Executives and boards of directors of corporations have what is called a fiduciary duty to act in the best interests of their corporations. Since the onrushing year 2000 problem is a very obvious one, the boards and top executives of companies that do not take effective and rapid action to solve the problem may well find themselves sued by shareholders.

The software industry has not yet encountered the risk of consequential damages for the bugs and errors that are common in software. The idea of consequential damages is that in addition to paying for repairs or replacement of a defective product, the vendor may have to pay for any lost business or secondary damages that result.

For example, suppose you use a $200 spreadsheet to calculate a bid for a $1,000,000 contract. If there is an error in the spreadsheet that causes you not to get the contract, then under the concept of consequential damages, the vendor might be ordered to pay you not only for your out of pocket $200 for the defective spreadsheet but an additional $1,000,00 for the business you lost due to using the spreadsheet.

Since the year 2000 problem permeates almost every piece of financial and long-range planning software ever written, the year 2000 problem is likely to elevate the topic of consequential damages to a very significant place in software litigation.

Aggregation of All Year 2000 Software Related Costs for the United States

Because hardware upgrades, data base repairs, and litigation expenses are not normalized using function point metrics, the only kind of convenient overall aggregation of year 2000 expenses is a simple summation of the various components. Table 41.17 gives a rough approximation of all major year 2000 cost elements:

Table 41.17   **Overall Total of United States Year 2000 Expense Elements**

Year 2000 Topic	U.S. Year 2000 Costs
Software Repairs	$70,000,000,000
Data base Repairs	$60,000,000,000
Hardware Chip Replacements	$10,000,000,000
Hardware Performance Upgrades	$20,000,000,000
Litigation and Damages	$100,000,000,000
U.S. TOTAL	$260,000,000,000

It is an interesting "sanity check" to see the year 2000 costs per capita for United States citizens. Assuming a AD 2000 population for the United States of about 280,000,000 citizens, then the per capita year 2000 costs for the United States amounts to about $928 for every citizen.

Assuming a U.S. working population at the end of the century of roughly 120,000,000 workers, then about $2,167 would be the cost for every working person in the United States.

Assuming only software workers, with a century-end total of about 1,920,000 technical software staff plus managers, the overall costs would amount to about $135,417 for everyone in the U.S. software business at the end of the century. This is a very significant expense that is likely to cause a number of software-intensive companies to file for bankruptcy prior to the end of the 20th century.

If we back out of litigation and hardware costs, or course, the per capita expenses drop by more than 50 percent. They are still a rather significant amount and may well have a disrupting affect on the U.S. economy and will certainly disrupt the cash flow and profitability of a large number of enterprises.

Although function points are not normally used for dealing with hardware costs or litigation, it is a simple calculation to divide estimated total U.S. expenses of $260,000,000,000 by the anticipated U.S. software portfolio of 1,702,750,000 function points. This results in a per function point cost of about $152.69 for every function point deployed in the United States.

Here, too, backing out litigation and hardware costs would lower the amount by more than 50 percent. Even with this reduction, the overall total is quite an alarming figure for the United States.

International Year 2000 Repair Effort for Thirty Countries

The year 2000 problem is an interesting one because it affects industrialized nations more severely than those which are less dependent upon computers and software for business and government operations.

Although the year 2000 problem is of global concern, it is starting to appear that the most heavily industrialized and computer-intensive countries are going to bear the brunt of the expenses. The United States, Japan, Germany, France, the United Kingdom, and Brazil will probably be the most heavily impacted.

Conversely, countries such as India and the Ukraine may find themselves in an advantageous position as a result of the year 2000 problem, since they will probably have a surplus of skill programming personnel available during a period that the heavy software countries are mired in year 2000 repair work.

Year 2000 Repairs by Country

The first topic of interest is the year 2000 repair costs in the countries that have the most software personnel employed and the largest volumes of software in production. Table 41.18 gives a rough approximation of year 2000 software repair effort in some 30 countries. There is a high margin of error with Table 41.18. It should be noted that some of the data in the table is simply derived from the previous U.S. data and extrapolated for other countries. The demographic data for software personnel is limited to professionals and ignores end-user programming.

The portfolio sizes are based on ratios of U.S. portfolios, and the volume of Year 2000 software changes is artificially held constant at 9.5 percent which means that just under 10 percent of the code in global applications are assumed to require year 2000 updates. This is a questionable assumption, but a reasonable starting place.

The effort to make the Year 2000 changes is also held constant at 16 function points per staff month. Here too, the assumption is questionable, but is at least a starting place for more detailed analysis.

It should be noted once again that Table 41.18 is built upon a series of assumptions and hypotheses which may be incorrect. There are possible errors in every column, and the data is suitable only for discussions and for preliminary economic analysis. However, the importance of the year 2000 problem is such that publishing preliminary data with a high

Table 41.18   **Estimated Year 2000 Software Repair Effort for Thirty Countries**   *(Page 1 of 2)*

Country	Software Staff (Professional)	Portfolio in Funct. Pts.	Year 2000 Hits in Funct. Pts.	Year 2000 Repairs (Months)	% of U.S. Effort
United States	1,920,000	1,570,560,000	149,203,200	9,325,200	100.00%
Japan	900,000	738,000,000	70,100,000	4,381,875	46.99%
Russia	770,000	539,000,000	51,205,000	3,200,313	34.32%
Germany	550,000	440,000,000	41,800,000	2,612,500	28.02%
United Kingdom	390,000	312,000,000	29,640,000	1,852,500	19.87%
Brazil	475,000	308,750,000	29,331,250	1,833,203	19.66%
France	385,000	308,000,000	29,260,000	1,828,750	19.61%
China	990,000	297,000,000	28,215,000	1,763,438	18.91%
Italy	375,000	290,625,000	27,609,375	1,725,586	18.50%
India	750,000	225,000,000	21,375,000	1,335,938	14.33%
South Korea	300,000	210,000,000	19,950,000	1,246,875	13.37%
Ukraine	260,000	195,000,000	18,525,000	1,157,813	12.42%
Mexico	275,000	178,750,000	16,981,250	1,061,328	11.38%
Spain	235,000	170,375,000	16,185,625	1,011,602	10.85%
Canada	185,000	144,300,000	13,708,500	856,781	9.19%
Turkey	210,000	141,750,000	13,466,250	841,641	9.03%
Thailand	175,000	105,000,000	9,975,000	623,438	6.69%
Poland	190,000	104,500,000	9,927,500	620,469	6.65%
Taiwan	125,000	93,750,000	8,906,250	556,641	5.97%
Australia	110,000	85,250,000	8,098,750	506,172	5.43%
Netherlands	100,000	77,500,000	7,362,500	460,156	4.93%
Argentina	110,000	77,000,000	7,315,000	457,188	4.90%
Indonesia	175,000	74,375,000	7,065,625	441,602	4.74%
Egypt	145,000	68,875,000	6,543,125	408,945	4.39%
Philippines	145,000	66,700,000	6,336,500	396,031	4.25%

Table 41.18   **Estimated Year 2000 Software Repair Effort for Thirty Countries**   *(Page 2 of 2)*

Country	Software Staff (Professional)	Portfolio in Funct. Pts.	Year 2000 Hits in Funct. Pts.	Year 2000 Repairs (Months)	% of U.S. Effort
Pakistan	135,000	57,375,000	5,450,625	340,664	3.65%
South Africa	75,000	56,250,000	5,343,750	333,984	3.58%
Belgium	65,000	50,375,000	4,785,625	299,102	3.21%
Portugal	65,000	45,500,000	4,322,500	270,156	2.90%
Sweden	60,000	45,000,000	4,275,000	267,188	2.87%
SUM	7,087,205,000	7,076,560,000	672,273,200	42,017,075	

margin of error may be better than waiting for corrected data, since the end of the 20th century is approaching very rapidly.

The data in Tables 17 and 18 reveals a potential problem for the U.S. software industry. Since the U.S. is the country with the largest software portfolio, it will be the most heavily impacted by year 2000 repairs. This fact may give other countries a chance to make significant headway in global software markets in several fashions:

➤ By offshore outsourcing year 2000 repairs.
➤ By offshore outsourcing of other development and maintenance projects while U.S. software personnel are entangled in the Year 2000 morass.

A possible business outcome of the year 2000 problem is that the United States will lose its dominant market position in the software industry, while countries such as India, China, Russia and the Ukraine gain market shares since they are not as heavily impacted by year 2000 work and will have a substantial surplus of software technical personnel while the U.S. enters a period of shortage.

Table 41.19 shows approximate costs for repairing software in 30 countries. This table uses a number of simplifying assumptions, such as basing all salary and burden rates on percentages of U.S. norms. This means that the costs are rough and only approximate, but should be within the "ball park" for the countries in question.

Because Table 41.18 uses generic data and rounded values, the overall results are slightly different from the more detailed data shown earlier by language and industry. Given the overall uncertainty of year 2000 costs, this difference, while noticeable, is not significant. The costs should be alarmingly high no matter how precisely they are stated.

Table 41.19 **Estimated Expenses for Year 2000 Software Repairs in 30 Countries**

Country	Monthly Salary and Burden	Effort in Staff Months	Year 2000 Repair Costs
United States	$8,000	9,325,200	$74,601,600,000
Japan	$9,600	4,381,875	$42,066,000,000
Russia	$4,000	3,200,313	$12,801,250,000
Germany	$9,200	2,612,500	$24,035,000,000
United Kingdom	$9,200	1,852,500	$17,043,000,000
Brazil	$7,760	1,833,203	$14,225,656,250
France	$9,200	1,828,750	$16,824,500,000
China	$1,000	1,763,438	$1,763,437,500
Italy	$7,760	1,725,586	$13,390,546,875
India	$1,200	1,335,938	$1,603,125,000
South Korea	$7,200	1,246,875	$8,977,500,000
Ukraine	$3,600	1,157,813	$4,168,125,000
Mexico	$7,200	1,061,328	$7,641,562,500
Spain	$6,800	1,011,602	$6,878,890,625
Canada	$8,400	856,781	$7,196,962,500
Turkey	$7,400	841,641	$6,228,140,625
Thailand	$5,200	623,438	$3,241,875,000
Poland	$6,000	620,469	$3,722,812,500
Taiwan	$7,520	556,641	$4,185,937,500
Australia	$7,760	506,172	$3,927,893,750
Netherlands	$8,800	460,156	$4,049,375,000
Argentina	$7,200	457,188	$3,291,750,000
Indonesia	$3,600	441,602	$1,589,765,625

Table 41.19   **Estimated Expenses for Year 2000 Software Repairs in 30 Countries**

Country	Monthly Salary and Burden	Effort in Staff Months	Year 2000 Repair Costs
Egypt	$6,000	408,945	$2,453,671,875
Philippines	$3,200	396,031	$4,267,300,000
Pakistan	$1,000	340,664	$340,664,063
South Africa	$7,600	333,984	$2,538,281,250
Belgium	$9,600	299,102	$2,871,375,000
Portugal	$7,200	270,156	$1,945,125,000
Sweden	$9,200	267,188	$2,458,125,000
SUM/AVG.	$6,580	42,017,075	$297,329,248,438

Note that Table 41.18 shows only software repair costs. Over and above software repairs will be found several other expense elements:

➤ Data base repairs

➤ Hardware upgrades and retuning of applications

➤ Litigation costs

➤ Damages awarded from litigation

Another important factor not dealt with in this study, nor in the similar Gartner Group study, is the long-range impact of inflation on year 2000 repair costs. Note that the financial data shown in this report assumes current 1996 dollars. By 2000 inflation will no doubt raise the dollar and other currency amounts significantly, and perhaps alarmingly.

Table 41.20 shows the year 2000 repair costs in descending order of magnitude, starting with the United States. Although year 2000 repairs will be troublesome everywhere, it can be hypothesized that the top half of Table 41.20 will have a much greater set of problems than the lower half.

Indeed, it is possible for the countries with the lowest year 2000 repairs to expand their software markets significantly by outsourcing surplus software engineering capacity to the countries whose software personnel are likely to be preempted by emergency year 2000 upgrades.

The future is hard to predict, but the economic consequences of the year 2000 problem are likely to be severe for the industrialized nations and potentially advantageous for countries that lagged in early automation and computerization.

Table 41.20 ranks the overall software costs for the year 2000 problem, and shows the percentage of U.S. costs on a country by country basis. This table ranks the countries in descending order, and also shows the percentage of United States costs that are likely to be expended.

Note that Table 41.20 deals only with software repair costs and does not include hardware upgrades, data base repairs, or litigation expenses.

Table 41.20 **Ranking of Relative Year 2000 Software Repairs for 30 Countries** (Page 1 of 2)

Country	Year 2000 Repair Costs	Percent of U.S. Year 2000 Cost
United States	$74,601,600,000	100.00%
Japan	$42,066,000,000	56.39%
Germany	$24,035,000,000	32.22%
United Kingdom	$17,043,000,000	22.85%
France	$16,824,500,000	22.55%
Brazil	$14,225,656,250	19.07%
Italy	$13,390,546,875	17.95%
Russia	$12,801,250,000	17.16%
South Korea	$8,977,500,000	12.03%
Mexico	$7,641,562,500	10.24%
Canada	$7,196,962,500	9.65%
Spain	$6,878,890,625	9.22%
Turkey	$6,228,140,625	8.35%
Taiwan	$4,185,937,500	5.61%
Ukraine	$4,168,125,000	5.59%
Netherlands	$4,049,375,000	5.43%
Australia	$3,927,893,750	5.27%

Table 41.20 **Ranking of Relative Year 2000 Software Repairs for
30 Countries** (Page 2 of 2)

Country	Year 2000 Repair Costs	Percent of U.S. Year 2000 Cost
Poland	$3,722,812,500	4.99%
Argentina	$3,291,750,000	4.41%
Thailand	$3,241,875,000	4.35%
Belgium	$2,871,375,000	3.85%
South Africa	$2,538,281,250	3.40%
Sweden	$2,458,125,000	3.30%
Egypt	$2,453,671,875	3.29%
Portugal	$1,945,125,000	2.61%
China	$1,763,437,500	2.36%
India	$1,603,125,000	2.15%
Indonesia	$1,589,765,625	2.13%
Philippines	$4,267,300,000	1.70%
Pakistan	$340,664,063	0.46%
SUM/AVG.	$297,329,248,438	

For litigation, the United States is assumed to have a much higher total of global costs than for the other year 2000 expense elements. For the litigation amount I estimated that U.S. litigation would amount to about 33 percent of world totals.

The rationale for this assumption is that the United States is a much more litigious country than the other major industrial powers, such as Japan, Germany, France, the United Kingdom, and many others. My assumption on litigation percentages may well be wrong, but I'm not aware of any other data on this topic.

Aggregation of Global Year 2000 Repair Expenses

Tables 17 through 24 show only the 30 largest countries in terms of their software populations and hence anticipated software expenses. Since there are roughly 200 countries in the Untied Nations, an interesting

Table 41.21   **Overall Total of Global Year 2000 Expense Elements**

Year 2000 Topic	Global Year 2000 Costs
Software Repairs	$530,000,000,000
Data base Repairs	$454,000,000,000
Hardware Chip Replacements	$75,000,000,000
Hardware Performance Upgrades	$150,000,000,000
Litigation and Damages	$300,000,000,000
WORLD TOTAL	$1,510,000,000,000

question is that of the magnitude of effort and costs for the 170 or so countries that are not shown separately.

My overall global demographic data indicates that the world population of software professionals circa 1996 totals to about 12,500,000 (with a high margin of error). The 30 countries enumerated here had a total professional population of just over 7,000,000. Assuming both sets of assumptions are true, the absent 170 countries would have a combined software population of about 5,500,000.

It is interesting that the average software population for the 30 countries that are enumerated here is about 233,000 per country. The average software population for the 170 countries that are not shown separately averages about 32,000 per country.

Assuming that the ratio of year 2000 expenses is similar to the ratio of software personnel (a questionable assumption but at least a starting point) then the year 2000 expenses for the missing 170 countries would total to about $233,000,000,000. This amounts to about $1,371,000,000 per country.

By contrast, the average cost for the 30 countries that are shown separately is about $9,900,00,000 per country. Of course "averages" are not very meaningful when whole countries are considered, but the results do give a sanity check to the approximate costs on a global basis.

Adding the invisible costs for the missing countries to the visible costs for the 30 countries shown here yields an approximate global cost of $530,000,000,000 for year 2000 software repairs.

For year 2000 software repairs, the U.S. total of roughly $70,000,000,000 amounts to about 13.2 percent of the global total of $530,000,000,000. This raises an interesting question as to the entire total of all year 2000 repairs on a global basis when software, hardware, data bases, and litigation are all considered.

Table 41.21 is an attempt to assemble a global picture of all major year 2000 cost elements simply to judge the rough magnitude of costs. For every cost element except litigation, the U.S. ratio of 13.2 percent of global totals was used. Note that unlike tables 15 through 17, which showed only 30 countries, Table 19 is based on the assumption that all of the approximately 200 countries constituting the United Nations will have Year 2000 expenses.

No matter how things turn out, it is certain that the software industry in every country will be undergoing a major transformation between the years 1996 and 2005 in reaction to the Year 2000 problem.

One of the problems faced by the software industry is sociological. We have not been regarded by the older professions such as electrical and mechanical engineers as being true engineers or even true professionals. The fact that the software industry, collectively, has brought about one of the most expensive and hazardous problems in human history when it could easily have been avoided is going to lower our status even more.

Not only is the year 2000 problem one of the most expensive problems in human history, it is also one of the most embarrassing. This problem has been theoretically discussed for more than 25 years, and its significance has been hypothesized with increasing alarm for more than 10 years. It is not a credit to the human race nor to the software industry that such an obvious problem with such a straight-forward technical solution should have reached the magnitude that is likely to occur.

On the other hand, the year 2000 problem is symptomatic of a general human tendency to avoid trying to solve problems until the evidence is overwhelming. The historical difficulties which medical researchers such as Lister and Semmelweis had in introducing sterile surgical procedures, and the earlier resistance to Jenner's concept of vaccination, illustrates that software is not the only learned profession that does not move swiftly to minimize potential risks.

Benefits of Solving the Year 2000 Problem

It is no secret that software is the most troubling technology of the 20th century. A surprising aspect of the year 2000 problem is that the companies that solve this problem are going to end up knowing much more about their software than ever before. Even better, their software will be in much more stable and reliable condition than it is right now.

Recall that the year 2000 problem is only one instance of a large class of similar problems where storage limitations caused insufficient space to be reserved. The same tools that attack or solve the year 2000 problem can also be applied to the other instances so the software that is repaired should be more robust than now. Further, the detailed inventory of software portfolios and corporate data bases and repositories needed for year 2000 repairs will give corporations and government agencies a much improved ability to match their software projects to the needs of their operating units.

It would be premature and highly optimistic to say that solving the year 2000 problem will have positive return on investment. However, there will certainly be significant positive value to solving the year 2000 problem.

If aspects of game theory are applied to the year 2000 problem, the results indicate that a rapid and thorough attack on the year 2000 problem is the minimax solution; i.e. the solution that will give the best return for the lowest expense.

Consider the following hypothesis: For every dollar spent on repairing the year 2000 problem, the value in terms of greater reliability and stability of software will probably return fifty cents in reduced maintenance costs for the applications in question.

For every dollar *not* spent on repairing the year 2000 problem, the anticipated costs of litigation and potential damages will probably amount to more than ten dollars.

The expenses of repairing the year 2000 problem are going to occur, like it or not. Since delays in attacking the year 2000 problem lower the probability of successful repairs and raise the probability of litigation, the overall conclusion is that a rapid attack on the year 2000 problem is the best economic solution.

Summary and Conclusions

The year 2000 problem is rapidly approaching, and is one of the most critical issues ever faced by the software industry or by any industry for that matter. Because the year 2000 problem has been developing for 25 years and affects many aging legacy applications, the one-time costs for year 2000 repairs are going to be alarmingly high.

However, the year 2000 problem cannot be ignored and will not go away by itself. The best response to the year 2000 problem is a rapid and energetic attack as early as possible. The worst response is to ignore the problem or to understate its importance.

The information presented in this report is preliminary and is believed by the author to have a large but unknown margin of error. However, even preliminary data is better than none when it comes to dealing with a problem as severe as the year 2000 problem.

CEO/CIO: Senior Management Approaches

part 5

"Doing nothing is not an option," explain Casey and Fisher in this unique, thorough and straightforward guide to the information officer about to knock on the door of top management to discuss the Year 2000. They begin by tracing the history of 2-digit years, "a technical problem that requires a management response."

It is imperative to surmount resistance on the part of senior management, to commit resources and funds to allow the IS department to begin to assess the exposure and to develop explicit plans.

Senior management is likely to resist—through ignorance, avoidance and disbelief. But don't permit the mistake of letting Year 2000 compliance be classified as a mere maintenance task. Nebraska raised its sales tax to pay for Y2K; how will you? If you do, your company's compliance can be put to competitive advantage.

To risk what are possibly years of profits to fix Y2K, top management must perceive it as a life-or-death issue. But this, in turn, involves Elisabeth Kübler-Ross's five phases of moving from awareness to acceptance: denial, anger, bargaining, depression and acceptance. Only at the fifth phase can constructive work begin. It's the I/S manager's task to help top management make that trip.

At the beginning, shocked by the size of Y2K, top managers may express denial by shopping around for better news.

You might avoid shoot-the-messenger by bringing in unbiased facilitators to break the news. Using some overwhelming facts can help get you out of the denial pan and into the anger fire.

Faced with omnidirectional anger, hide behind the facilitator and try to wait it out, rather than you or your staff feeling guilty and reacting. Then, when top management starts to negotiate for a truncated solution as a means to postpone the inevitable, realize that you're getting close to acceptance.

As depression sets in upstairs, carefully assess resources and identify who helped your case. Once the inactivity and boredom subside, then status meetings, press releases and commitment of resources evidence a together, pro-active team moving forward.

Keeping your focus on a management (not just technical) plane can help capture ancillary benefits like continued insurability, vestigial application elimination, better staff morale, and expanded/new customer relationships.

The paper contains a phase-by-phase description of what leadership should be doing while managers and programmers are accomplishing and cleaning up after the technical task. At project end, be sure to take a post-compliance audit and publicize the "silver lining."

42   *Enterprise Management Approach*

Chris Casey
Bytewise Consulting, Inc.

Ted Fisher
Sperduto & Associates, Inc.

After years of providing timely and accurate information, a problem is creeping up on many of our computer systems and applications. This problem has to be resolved by the time it becomes necessary to process data using the Year 2000. In fact, some of the impact has already been felt in those companies which deal with long-term transactions, such as insurance policies, mortgages and contracts which extend beyond December 31, 1999.

Until recently, it has been accepted as standard practice within the Information Technology community to drop the century when storing and processing dates. Thus the year *1996* would be recorded and used as 96. The problem relates to what happens when the computer works with the year *00*. Many mission-critical computer systems, from mainframes to PCs, may generate volumes of inaccurate data and reports, or may cease to function all together. Invoicing, inventory control, purchasing, check processing, interest calculation, and a wide variety of other critical business functions are potentially affected.

From a technical perspective, correcting this problem is fairly straightforward. Find the date references in the program code or data files, and take one of several available options to change them so they can handle the Year 2000. In a company with a small portfolio of systems, this most likely does not present a significant challenge. However, with the average medium-to large-size business maintaining several thousand separate computer programs and millions of lines of code, the sheer volume of work to be completed and the business risks of not fixing the problem make the Year 2000 an expensive and critical project—in many cases, an issue of survival.

Failure to address the Year 2000 problem puts the company in jeopardy. It exposes customers, prospects, suppliers, and other stakeholders to significant risks because of their electronic interactions with corporate systems. Additionally, companies face legal exposures resulting from system failures, contractual non-performance, or shareholder dissatisfaction as a result of the Year 2000.

This report is directed at senior enterprise management, Information Systems management, and functional and departmental management. While the Year 2000 problem may be technical in nature, solving it requires a strong management response; too much is at stake, too many resources are required, and too many areas of the business *outside of technology* are impacted. This report examines how the dialogue among enterprise, business, and I/S management should change to facilitate communication and collaboration to solve the Year 2000 problem. Business impacts are analyzed, as well as the many opportunities for capturing a positive competitive advantage as a result of the solution process.

Some of the positive outcomes identified include:

- ➤ Increased market share through stronger relationships with customers and prospects;
- ➤ Learning and experience gained by going through the conversion process, including comprehensive documentation of information processing assets;
- ➤ Continued insurability;
- ➤ Creative and powerful advertising opportunities.

43   *Year 2000 Scope and Impact*

For many organizations, the next millennium presents the largest and most encompassing challenge ever undertaken by information systems departments. The "Year 2000 problem," as it is known, will force organizations to make enterprise-wide modifications and enhancements to information systems, both in the data center and on the desktops. According to widely cited estimates, the problem could cost large companies from $5 to $25 million each, and up to $600 billion worldwide. Companies that do not bring their systems into compliance with the next millennium could face costly system failures. Worse than system shut-downs, however, some companies may realize too late that their systems have continued to operate while producing grossly and perhaps negligently erroneous data.

The scope of the Year 2000 problem extends far beyond the Information Systems department. There are several technical approaches available, any of which can be employed given enough time and money (chapter 29 *Technical Solution Overview* in Part 3 on page 98). But which resources can be applied and the timing and the effects that will have on other business initiatives is beyond the scope of the Information Systems department. Also beyond its scope is the ability to put into place the coordination that must occur where organizational lines are crossed between divisions, business units, functions and departments. Lack of compliance of any unit of the enterprise will cause processing and data problems in any of the others that either send or receive data from it.

The problem impacts the Information Technology department itself by creating a significant resource requirement, and by imposing a project deadline which cannot be extended. Also, the Year 2000 problem affects end users, both on the desktop and at the departmental information server level. Those systems (especially PC-based systems) which draw upon the resources of larger departmental servers and mainframe systems for spreadsheets, etc., are likewise vulnerable. Additionally, the Year 2000 problem will impact key suppliers, customers, and others with whom you do business.

Who can be impacted?

➢   Internally: Business units, functional and staff areas.

➢   Externally: Customers, business partners, and suppliers.

Although businesses frequently refer to the Year 2000 as a "problem," we believe that the rules of business and law will ultimately make Year 2000 compliance a requirement. Doing nothing is not a viable option. Generally, the technologists assert that the requirement for compliance must be accepted for what it is, without other benefits, save survival of the business. We say, instead, that there is an opportunity for organizations to update their knowledge of the information systems during the compliance process *and capture significant competitive advantages along the way.*

44   *Requirements, in Business Terms*

What is the Year 2000 problem from a business perspective? Stated another way, why is it a problem for *businesses*?

Many systems today rely on only two digits to represent the year—1996 would be stored as *96*. As a result, these computers will interpret the Year 2000 (represented as *00*) as 1900. Any date-sensitive transaction, such as billing, payroll, automatic expiration of inventory, calculation of interest payments and receipts and loan schedules would be handled incorrectly (Figure 44.1). Erroneous bills could be sent to customers. Expensive inventory could be designated as expired, and destroyed. Automatic debits of interest could be reversed into automatic credits. Electronic data interchange systems could crash. All of these scenarios and more could occur, at a cost of millions of dollars to correct. Without the ability to process information and day-to-day transactions, the ultimate cost, however, could be the failure of the business.

Many managers, at any level, would question why systems in which the organization has already invested millions of dollars would suddenly require such an extensive and expensive overhaul. As a society, we have come to have high expectations of technology, despite its relative youth. This typically is not the case of other, more mechanical "technologies."

Early systems were developed using then state-of-the-art methods (Figure 44.2). Given the limitations of storage and processing power, programmers were forced to conserve wherever possible. One of the methods accepted as the conventional wisdom of the time was to truncate the four-digit year to two digits, omitting the century. This practice started when computers had severe internal processing restrictions, and it was continued to avoid upgrades when the cost of adding internal memory and disk storage was calculated in the millions of dollars. It was the relatively recent advent of cheap processing power and storage that did away with the common practice of using the two-digit date.

Many argue that the Year 2000 problem is a mainframe problem, and that other systems such as mid-range or personal computers will not be affected. It is true that PCs are inherently easier to fix, due to the

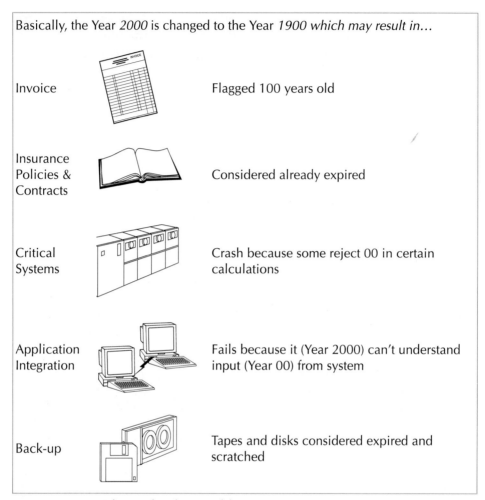

Basically, the Year *2000* is changed to the Year *1900 which may result in…*

Invoice — Flagged 100 years old

Insurance Policies & Contracts — Considered already expired

Critical Systems — Crash because some reject 00 in certain calculations

Application Integration — Fails because it (Year 2000) can't understand input (Year 00) from system

Back-up — Tapes and disks considered expired and scratched

Figure 44.1   **What is the date problem?**

shorter life cycle of most desktop systems and the relative ease of upgrading the system and application-level programs. It is not true, however, that PCs will not be affected. Desktop applications such as spreadsheets, complex word processing documents and user-level analytical tools all may draw key information from larger, more vulnerable systems.

Also, many "home-grown" applications are in use throughout the organization. These programs typically are created by end users, or by departmental staff, outside the purview of enterprise technology management. These applications (often spreadsheets or database access programs) exchange information across departmental lines, with the enterprise data center, or even outside of the business with customers and suppliers.

A Journey in the Evolution of Computing	
1960s	Capacity limitations force conservation of internal memory and disk storage CHOICE—Truncate dates and automate, or don't automate
1970s–1980s	Capacity limitations removed, but memory and disk storage still very expensive CHOICE—Stop truncating dates and spend millions on upgrades, or continue truncating
1990s	The era when computing capacity becomes a commodity CHOICE—Stop truncating dates

Figure 44.2   *Why did it happen?*

Finally, there are many date-sensitive machines, devices and other business appliances which may be impacted adversely by the problem. Elevators, security systems, postage meters, ATM machines and other date-encoded devices may not be equipped to handle '00' properly.

Thus, in "solving" the Year 2000 problem, the entire enterprise must be considered—not just the traditional data center.

While solving the problem may seem technical and tedious, managers must be aware of the cost of the solution in order to decide how best to proceed. Estimates on the size of the Year 2000 requirement range from $5 million to $100 million for the largest U.S. corporations, up to $300 billion to $600 billion worldwide. As a specific example, in Michigan, *Consumers Power Co.* expects to spend $20 million to $45 million to fix 350 vulnerable computer systems. At electric utility company *Con Ed*, becoming compliant could require 100 work-years and cost upwards of $5 million, according to their Year 2000 project manager.

Ask information system managers today if they know about the problem, and the answer will most likely be *Yes*. Ask the same managers where they are in addressing the problem, and the response sounds less confident. The fact is that while most organizations are superficially aware of the existence of the problem, they are doing little about it or are in the very early stages of a remedial program. In fact, some individuals have estimated that as many as half of all companies are doing nothing.

For a variety of reasons, there seems to be a general reluctance on the part of senior management to commit resources and funds to allow I/S departments to begin to assess their exposure and develop plans to bring their organization into compliance. This situation exists, despite strong arguments by computer industry experts who favor commitment to action. For example, one informal survey of I/S managers conducted by *InformationWeek* found that not a single U.S. company is completely 2000-ready. In another survey conducted by The *Information Management Forum*, only 12 percent of the I/S managers surveyed said they had a formal plan to deal with it.

Geoffrey H. Wold, partner for MIS consulting with St. Paul, Minn.-based accounting and consulting firm McGladney & Pullen, noted that "large companies will need up to five years to identify the parts of their computer programs that need changing, make the changes and then test all of the programs. At big corporations," Wold said, "such a project will take staff years measured in decades of labor-intensive hours."

Thus, the average Year 2000 compliance project for large corporations could require up to 100 or more of programmer-years! If the widely cited industry standard is true that 25 percent of all projects that require more than 25 programmer years of effort are never delivered, senior managers must become involved in the compliance process to ensure that an appropriate solution is achieved.

How can it be that organizations are not fully involved in the process of solving what for many will likely be the largest project ever undertaken by I/S departments? The answer is complex, but goes to the heart of the Year 2000 beast—*The Year 2000 problem is a technical problem that requires a management response.*

The decisions about updating strategic technologies, whether in manufacturing or information systems, are the responsibility of senior enterprise management. The mere fact that more businesses are not currently addressing the Year 2000 problem is evidence of a managerial and leadership problem. Nonetheless, technology management, departmental leaders, and others in the organization must face the challenge of convincing enterprise management that the problem is real, and that it must be addressed at the highest levels.

Although superficially a technical problem, the response to the Year 2000 must involve all levels of management for a variety of reasons, including:

> *The possibility that systems failure or, more likely, corrupted data could affect internal operations, customer service fulfillment and business transactions with external partners, suppliers and other organizations.*

> *The solution can be very expensive.* However, it isn't a case of all or nothing. A system's benefits need to be weighed against the cost of failure. This also provides the opportunity to weed out systems that are of marginal or no value.

> ➤ *The solution may require coordination between divisions and business units*. Where data flows across division or business unit lines, decisions need to be made on which technical solution to apply and when compliance will occur. Divisional and business unit management (technical and non-technical) should coordinate with peers, under the guidance of senior corporate executives, to ensure that priorities are recognized and addressed, resources are handled efficiently, and conflicts are resolved as quickly as possible to minimize disruptions to the solution process (Figure 44.3).

Six Reasons Why it Isn't

1. Needs enterprise-wide solution
   Solution choice—Coordination of Integration and Implementation

2. Corrupt data or non-performance will result in potential ill-will and liability

3. Cost of cure

4. Reordering of priorities and business initiatives

5. Heavy and, perhaps, sensitive coordination with business partners and suppliers

6. Policy guidance

Figure 44.3   Isn't senior management involvement overkill?

> ➤ *A part of the Year 2000 problem exists in departmental systems and on desktops*, either of which may be outside the normal purview of the corporate or divisional I/T unit.
>
> ➤ *The solution will require coordination with business partners and suppliers to reach a common understanding of what each defines as compliance*, and to set up the necessary mechanism to follow progress. There is also the consideration of what to do if they won't be compliant within the requisite time frame.
>
> ➤ *There are significant legal and regulatory exposures for many corporations* which must be identified and addressed in appropriate manners.
>
> ➤ *Corporate I/S management may not have sufficient authority to respond to the problem itself*. Enterprise management should take an active role to provide enterprise-wide leadership for the project and to ensure that the solution follows strategic goals and objectives.
>
> ➤ *Outsourced applications and other third-party software may not be compliant*. Vendors may be reluctant to commit to definite action plans for bringing their systems into compliance. Vendors may have a legal obligation to maintain some applications. Enterprise

management should recognize that software vendors are faced with the same scenario of weighing the costs and benefits of compliance. Enterprise management may be able to apply pressure to influence and help determine the position of the vendor on Year 2000 compliance.

The first and perhaps greatest challenge is in convincing senior enterprise management that while the problem seems technical, it is broad enough in scope and infrastructure that it can (and must) be handled using business tools and techniques in the hands of enterprise and departmental managers. The solution should involve strategic planning, skillful public relations, internal and external communications (with staff, customers, suppliers, prospects), legal and financial interventions, and other traditionally non-technology tools.

45   *Board Room: Legal, Accounting, Marketing, Risk*

As the expression goes, "If it walks like a duck and talks like a duck, it must be a duck." So how can a problem which involves computer software, computer hardware platforms, reprogramming requirements and the like be anything but a technical issue?

What makes the Year 2000 problem unique is the scope of its impact, touching virtually all functional areas of a business, including legal, accounting, production, marketing and, of course, management (Figure 45.1). The implications of non-compliance for the organization are significant and also extend beyond the entire business to harmful effects on customers and suppliers.

Much of the effort is in finding where the problems are. It might seem that a date or date field would be immediately obvious. Not so, as many of the programming techniques used to store dates and use them in calculations make them very obtuse. Arguably, finding where the problems occur is a job for technologists. This assumes that the systems are under the control of I/S. Those systems outside the data center, such as specific departmental systems, third-party software, etc., may be difficult to analyze.

Enterprise managers may be inclined to delegate the compliance process to I/S management and staff exclusively. Such an approach risks ignoring (to the detriment of the company) the many significant, non-technical impacts of the Year 2000 problem. These include legal, finance and accounting, marketing and public relations, production, risk management and human resources implications.

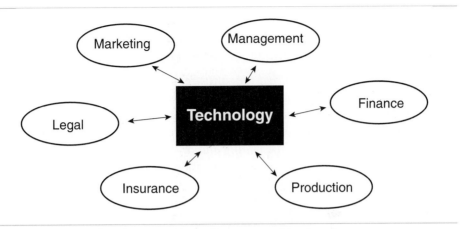

Figure 45.1   Technology touches all aspects of business

Legal

The legal implications for non-compliance involve issues of liability, negligence and responsibility. A major underwriter of business insurance (e.g., errors and omissions, or business interruption) may find itself liable for tens of billions of dollars in claims if it fails to perform adequate due diligence to determine insurability. Simply asking the question "What are you doing with regard to Year 2000 compliance?" and verifying that the client has an appropriate plan to bring itself into compliance may garner enough information to make a rational and justifiable decision (read: *defensible*) concerning that client's insurability. Failing in this regard may leave the insurer liable for crippling levels of claims.

In the area of contracts, there are a myriad of legal issues surrounding the Year 2000. Do existing vendor software maintenance contracts contain provisions to handle century-related software failures? On the vendor side, what are the responsibilities for future releases of software (Figure 45.2)? How long should a company be responsible for the proper functioning of software and hardware products, especially if newer versions of the products have been released? Only the courts will determine what *statute of limitations* exists, if any, on the warranties of information systems, software and hardware.

Would an appliance manufacturing company whose products include third-party supplied computer circuit chips be held responsible for the failure of those chips in the Year 2000? What about a national supplier of point-of-sale retail devices? Would this company be legally responsible if its machines cannot accept credit cards bearing an expiration date of *01/00*?

One method of addressing contractual issues for the Year 2000 problem is to insert compliance language in software maintenance agreements. An example of one such compliance clause reads:

> *The licenser warrants that the software, which is licensed to license hereunder and used by licensee prior to, during or after the calendar year 2000, includes or shall include, at no added cost to licensee, design and performance so the licensee shall not experience software abnormally ending and/or invalid and/or incorrect results from the software in the operation of the business of the licensee. The software design to ensure Year 2000 compatibility shall include, but not be limited to, date data century recognition, calculations that accommodate some century and multi-century formulas and date values, and date data interface values that reflect the century.*

> *[Source: Gartner Group]*

Obviously, each business should develop contractual language based on the specific needs of the business after consulting with legal professionals.

Figure 45.2   Contracts in the Year 2000

Modern production facilities which rely on just-in-time inventory and scheduling control methods may come to a halt in the event of a computer failure in a component supplier's systems. Would the board of directors of a major automotive corporation be held responsible in a shareholder action after the production lines come to a halt in the Year 2000? Enterprise management should examine their legal responsibilities to employees, including union contracts, to suppliers, shareholders and customers to determine the possible repercussions of a system failure.

Corporate officers will be unable to avoid the responsibility for compliance. In the U.S., SEC Rule #6835 requires corporations to disclose in audited annual reports known trends, demands, commitments and events that are likely to come to fruition, and the resulting impact to the company and its future. The certainty of the Year 2000 and its potential impact on the corporation will force enterprise management to disclose to their stakeholders, customers and competition its exposure to the Year 2000.

This disclosure requirement will bring to light the preparedness of corporations to deal with this issue. Only then can responsible, informed, and legally defensible decisions be made about:

> mergers, acquisitions and buyouts;

> partnerships, joint ventures and sub-contractor selection;

> financial investments made by the corporation; and
> other situations where the integrity of the information systems is vital to the success of a business venture.

The bottom line is that a Year 2000 compliant organization must make a conscious decision whether to continue to do business with companies whose systems are not compliant and where their data could corrupt that of others. The flaws of their systems could become tragic flaws for their electronic partners. The Year 2000 represents the possibility of business-related failures on many fronts, some of which may pose serious legal exposures for the organization. Only by being aware of these implications and proactively managing them can the organization protect itself. While ignorance may be bliss, it may be taken for negligence in the Year 2000.

Finance and Accounting

With millions of dollars to be spent by companies in bringing their systems into Year 2000 compliance, the question is *how to finance it?*

In the U.S., there has been little discussion at the government level regarding how this expenditure should or will be handled for taxation purposes. The state of Nebraska, for example, recently approved an additional sales tax to cover part of the estimated $30 million cost of fixing their Year 2000 problem.

For private firms, though, can the costs be capitalized and depreciated over time, or should the costs be expensed as incurred?

Corporations must consider the financial impact of solving the immediate problem, and they must also incorporate their future plans into their analysis. The investment required to become compliant may force enterprise management to forego other previously planned technology purchases and upgrades, such as a move to client/server or SAP.

So, where will businesses find the money to solve the problem (Figure 45.3)? For projects of this financial magnitude, there are a variety of budgeting and resource allocation options, all of which must be evaluated and weighed according to the practices, objectives, strategic plans and risk position of the business. Most companies have and should use their established procedures to handle a financial analysis of this scale.

Marketing and Public Relations

Handled incorrectly, the Year 2000 crisis will be a public relations nightmare. Handled properly, however, it could be a PR coup. Imagine the negative impact of news stories bringing attention to the fact that a specific industry or a specific company was facing a business-threatening

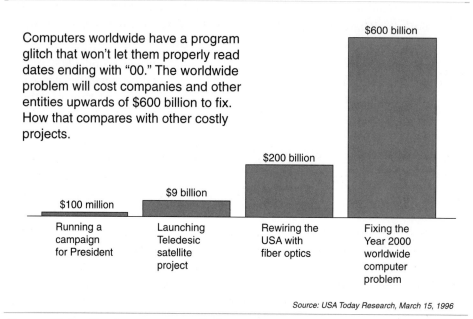

Computers worldwide have a program glitch that won't let them properly read dates ending with "00." The worldwide problem will cost companies and other entities upwards of $600 billion to fix. How that compares with other costly projects.

$600 billion

$200 billion

$9 billion

$100 million

| Running a campaign for President | Launching Teledesic satellite project | Rewiring the USA with fiber optics | Fixing the Year 2000 worldwide computer problem |

Source: USA Today Research, March 15, 1996

Figure 45.3   Costly computer glitch

situation because of the Year 2000 problem. How much damage would such a media uproar cause?

Imagine, on the other hand, that a company already working toward Year 2000 compliance begins to proactively acknowledge that there is a problem, and that they are hard at work to ensure the ongoing quality of their products or services, and better yet, that they offer some form of assistance to their customers and prospects to help them become compliant. With this aggressive approach, the company would be able to position itself as proactive (rather than reactive) and concerned enough about its business relationships to "go public" with the story.

Such a PR strategy would immediately put competitors on the defensive. And, for those companies fortunate enough to complete their compliance efforts early (first, second, third, etc., in an industry and/or community), they would be able to distinguish themselves further from the competition based on Year 2000 compliance. For many industries, compliance can become a powerful positioning tool. In banking and financial services, for instance, the perception that investments are safer with a Year 2000 compliant company may be enough to win new customers. In manufacturing, how can a company sell a product that it cannot produce as a result of system failures?

Thus, from a marketing perspective, compliance is a reliability issue, one to be proudly paraded before customers, suppliers, prospects and competitors. The positive gains, even if maintainable only until others come into compliance, could generate gains in market share, public image and credibility.

Production

Production and manufacturing systems are clearly impacted by Year 2000 non-compliance. Automated materials requirements planning (MRP) systems, which rely on date-sensitive schedules for both production and inventory scheduling, are vulnerable. Their inability to produce accurate or timely production schedules could result in expensive production slow-downs (or shut-downs) or create bottlenecks as key components are not available when needed.

Specifically in inventory control, many companies deal with stock with a specific shelf-life. Such inventory may be automatically flagged for disposal based on messages from control systems. Impacted by the Year 2000, systems may incorrectly interpret the expiration dates on key, expensive inventory (such as groceries, pharmaceuticals, genetic materials, etc.) and order the disposal of the inventory items prematurely.

Purchase order and invoicing systems which are integrated with production systems may fail to generate correct orders and invoices, creating an administrative burden for the company. Supplies may not be received when needed, and receivables payments may be delayed, presenting a cash flow crunch for the organization.

Risk Management

Companies that have active, formal risk management and insurance businesses will be acutely aware of the impact of the Year 2000 on such operations. There are a variety of risks which can be identified, measured and managed by the company.

Supplier reliability is perhaps the most important, yet unrecognized risk. While companies may spend millions to bring their own systems into compliance, their suppliers may not be acting as diligently. The compliant company may become an island surrounded by an essential but unreachable network of suppliers because of their non-compliance.

In light of the fact that other companies may not succeed in their compliance efforts, managing investments or equity holdings in other companies becomes a risky proposition. Should a company completely divest its positions held in other companies if these companies fail to provide sufficient evidence of their progress toward Year 2000 compliance? Or should a company seek to leverage its investment position to force others into compliance? This latter course may be necessary in vertically integrated industries, where relationships with external suppliers are essential to the success and survival of the business.

IT executives can help form persuasive arguments for senior management based on risk avoidance and the Year 2000. Overall, however, the risks of non-compliance must be shown to far outweigh the costs of compliance.

Human Resources

The human resource issues raised by the Year 2000 problem are challenging. Ultimately, a company's ability to manage its human resource assets during and after the Year 2000 compliance process may be the essential ingredient to success. The compliance process will be a long and tedious project, with highly stressful demands placed on both the managers of the process as well as the technicians and programmers. Continuity of staff during the process will significantly enhance overall productivity. Conversely, turnover, either internally generated or resulting from corporate pirating, will greatly reduce the effectiveness of the process, increase delays and magnify project costs.

One of the significant costs of turnover is the loss of that person's knowledge and experience. The compliance process will force businesses to examine in great detail their business and technical processes. Thus, those involved in the compliance process, as a part of the business, will acquire valuable insight into how the business works.

The learning possibilities of the Year 2000 project is one of its major opportunities. Even given a conscientious attempt to generate documentation, to a large extent this learning will reside in the project participants themselves. Thus, in order to leverage the learning advantages of the compliance process, companies must do whatever they can to retain the personnel who participated.

It is widely believed that as we move into 1997 and beyond and the number of companies working on compliance increases, the supply of skilled staff will not meet the demand. Companies will be competing for staff with other companies as well as with Year 2000 solution vendors. Based on experience in similar situations, the solution providers (vendors and consultants) will offer seemingly extravagant salaries, making it difficult for companies to retain skilled technical staff.

Large companies and government agencies may face an additional challenge: - fixed wage agreements, either through union contracts or preset budgets. Many companies will find that although the prevailing salaries for legacy programmers are rising sharply, fixed contracts which cover one or more years will prevent companies from competing for their own technical staff. As more and more private companies become aware of the scope of the problem in their own organizations, enterprise managers will begin recruiting any and all competent legacy programmers with open checkbooks.

Obviously, the Year 2000 impacts many areas of the organization, not only the data center. In presenting its case for action, either prior to commitment or during the compliance process, CIOs and other senior management must remain aware of the many potential impacts of non-compliance across the organization. Carefully defining and subsequently managing the non-compliance impacts on each functional area within each organization and its industry will be the key to a successful project.

46   *Getting from Awareness to Acceptance*

Mid-level managers (both technical and business) are in a difficult position in the Year 2000 compliance process. Typically, these managers will have a greater initial awareness, and in the case of technical managers, will have a better understanding of the issues surrounding the Year 2000 problem. They must always remember that there are several real opportunities to be gained as a result of the Year 2000 compliance process. The challenge, however, in capturing the rewards is to bring awareness and understanding to senior management so that management can provide the support and sustain the commitment necessary to bring the organization into compliance.

For a variety of reasons, senior management may resist accepting the need to act (Figure 46.1). Ignorance, avoidance and disbelief all contribute to a perception on the part of senior management that the problem does not warrant their attention. Thus, the first priority must be to change this perception and replace it with a perspective which is conducive to positive action.

Where awareness does exist among top enterprise managers, dread of the immediate consequences of the high cost of remedial action on the part of some executives can cost delays of six to 12 months. Where and when this dread is perceived, professional assistance should be brought in immediately to deal with the situation. Corporate psychologists capable and experienced in coaching and counseling executives can function effectively in these circumstances as facilitators.

10. You want to surprise your stockholders.

9. You've got time—it's only 1997.

8. You never liked using computers in the first place.

7. Your "mission-critical" systems aren't.

6. You've made a large investment in an abacus company.

5. It's not a problem...it's a "challenge."

4. You can afford to be without your account receivables for a year or two.

3. You believe this is all a plot by consultants to create a problem where none exists.

2. You like paying COBOL programmers $240K to implement 10-year projects in an afternoon.

And the number one reason...
1. **You're moving all your applications to Nintendo!**

Figure 46.1   _Top 10 reasons you're ignoring the Year 2000 problem (Source: Peter de Jager)_

Year 2000 Problem Affects All of the Organization's Stakeholders

What is the correct perspective that will enable top management to see the problem for what it is, and to do what is necessary to address the problem? Top decision-makers must be able to accept the Year 2000 effort as primarily a management problem and secondarily a technical one. Senior managers must be made to understand the enterprise-wide impacts, as well as recognize the ubiquitous nature of date-sensitive data not only throughout the organization but also throughout the business and government communities.

Year 2000 Compliance Not a Maintenance Issue

Perhaps from a technologist's perspective, the Year 2000 can be viewed as a maintenance problem. In many ways, it is one—albeit an extremely expensive and risky one that could impact the entire organization, key customers and suppliers.

So what can be done to capture the attention and involvement of enterprise and non-technical business management? Initially, the Year 2000 problem must be distinguished from _just being a maintenance issue_ in the minds of enterprise management if it is to be given sufficient priority and resources. The usual maintenance perspective views a project as simply something that needs fixing. Further, such problems are perceived as not involving integrated solutions or strategic implications. In short, the implication to applying a maintenance approach to the Year 2000 problem is that senior management really does not need to be involved and all decision making for the solution is delegated to lower-level staff.

Even though, in its narrowest sense, a maintenance perspective is appropriate on a system-by-system basis, the overall implications and potential impacts are simply too broad for a delegated, tactical solution. Consider, for example, a mortgage company which identified Year 2000 impacts in its fixed 30-year mortgage system in the 1970s. It "fixed" that system, only to face the same problem again in 1985 with their 15-year systems. After patching the 15-year system, they were forced to deal with the 10-year system in 1990. Each patch was completed ad hoc and in isolation, resulting in three fragmented systems which do not interoperate efficiently. Now, the mortgage company has to go back and fix all the fixes! It is apparent that what is discouraged is a narrow, short-sighted, and "quick fix" orientation. Isolated, unintegrated solutions may be appropriate in certain situations; fire-fighting the Year 2000 will leave behind only a scorched landscape.

Technical management must prepare itself with strong arguments against adopting the maintenance paradigm. Examples of how non-compliance impacts non-technical areas of the business, as well as how the Year 2000 will affect the entire industry, will add credibility to the proposition to top management that this problem warrants their attention, commitment and continued involvement. One way to do this is to bring line and functional management into the process early to explore the risks of non-compliance and to describe them in business terms.

Psychological Factors at Play

After awareness sets in, the next step is for top management to convert awareness into acceptance, and acceptance into commitment. I/T executives must recognize that though the magnitude of the Year 2000 requirement has the attention of enterprise management, the battle is not won. Enterprise management must ultimately commit the resources of the organization to the compliance effort. Being aware of a problem and acting on it are two completely different things.

Unfortunately, acceptance may be far more difficult to achieve than awareness. The key for I/T executives during this phase is their own awareness and understanding of the psychological process taking place as enterprise management struggles to accept the need to move forward.

By knowing the psychological obstacles management will face, they can provide the support and information necessary to assist management in coming to grips with the situation.

One must ask why managers are not dealing more aggressively with the situation. The manager is beset with the possible loss of a year or several years of profit and a suspicion that he or she is understaffed to cope with the size and complexity of the requirement.

When dealing with issues of survival or tragedy, individuals typically pass through five distinct phases, according to Dr. Elisabeth Kübler-Ross, M.D.[1] As individual CEOs and their staffs attempt to deal with the difficult issues of Year 2000 compliance, it is important to remember that these phases are psychological defense mechanisms.

The process of moving from awareness to acceptance is marked by the passage through five distinct phases of *denial, anger, bargaining, depression and acceptance* . In the beginning, at initial awareness, top management's resistance to change is at its highest. Systems have been working well, no problems have been encountered, and there has been no need to change anything. Upon awareness of the problem, the manager's subconscious resistance to change is weakened, but only slightly. The earlier defenses are strongest at maintaining status quo. In other words, top management will strive to avoid acceptance of the situation at all costs. At each successive level, however, that resolve diminishes. Ultimately all resistance is removed and acceptance is unavoidable. It is at this point, and not before, that constructive work can begin on the Year 2000 problem.

The phases shown in Figure 46.2 are described below, with suggestions on how to support enterprise management during each phase. It is important to note that the awareness-to-acceptance process will vary considerably from organization to organization. Some organizations may take six to 12 months before acceptance sets in, while for others, acceptance may be almost immediate. The difference will probably be due to past experience with technology issues and relations with the technologists within the organization.

There are ways enterprise management can be supported during the awareness-to-acceptance process, ways which will begin forging the relationships necessary to enable an effective compliance solution that captures the competitive advantages compliance can provide.

Phase 1: Denial—Perhaps the very size of the Year 2000 problem begs disbelief on the part of senior management, or for that matter, many I/T managers. Denial functions as a buffer after unexpected shocking

---

1. Dr. Elisabeth Kübler-Ross, M.D. is the author of *On Death and Dying*, 1969.

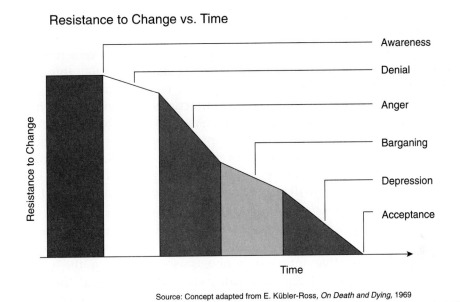

Source: Concept adapted from E. Kübler-Ross, *On Death and Dying*, 1969

Figure 46.2   *Awareness to acceptance*

news, allows the individual to collect himself and, with time, mobilize other, less radical defenses. Although short-lived as a defense mechanism, denial can be characterized by *shopping around* in order to get other, hopefully more positive, opinions or alternatives than those offered.

No one enjoys being the bearer of bad news, in personal or professional life. The size, scope and potential impact of the Year 2000 problem make it difficult to accept and may be met with hostility, fear and other unpleasant responses. Facilitators can be brought in to deliver the message and to promote constructive, pro-active discussion, answer questions, and educate management on the psychological issues. Such facilitators bring with them the benefit of an external perspective, which should be objective and unbiased in terms of the history and politics of the organization. Additionally, they should bring to the table interpersonal skills, broad knowledge and experience of other companies and industries. As in other situations, facilitators can provide a valuable service in delivering an unpopular message and may be able to deal successfully with some of the initial fallout of denial and anger.

A little bit of information can go a long way in dealing with denial. In the face of overwhelming data (both internal and external in focus), top management will find it difficult to remain in denial. Although denial is a non-productive stage, the next stage can be even more dangerous for the organization and must be handled with care.

Phase 2: Anger—Denial is generally replaced with anger and rage. The question of enterprise management changes from "This can't be happening, can it?" to "Why my company?!"

It takes seasoned facilitators to cope with the anger which abounds under these circumstances. In contrast to the stage of denial, this stage is very difficult to cope with from the point of view of staff. The reason is the fact that anger is displaced in all directions and projected onto the environment at times almost at random. As with a family of terminally ill patients, managers and staff need to place themselves in top management's position to understand the origin of the anger. Upon seeing how the comfort level of the manager has been completely disrupted by this event, perhaps the staff will appreciate the position of management.

This phase has several unfortunate and counter-productive consequences. Staff react with guilt or shame, and avoid confrontations and dealings with management—in effect, cutting off communication and hindering the effective interaction necessary for solving the problem. Those below senior management must seek to understand the reasons for the anger and not take it personally. Most likely, the origins of the problem have little or nothing to do with the people who become the target of the anger. A seasoned manager can endure the temporary discomfort, knowing that *this too shall pass.*

Phase 3: Bargaining—With terminally ill patients, bargaining is really an attempt to postpone the inevitable. With terminally ill companies, there is no difference. This phase represents yet another attempt on the part of senior management to avoid acceptance of the situation. The stronger, aggressive defenses of denial and anger have given way to the beginnings of compromise. For top management, this is not a truthful examination of alternative solutions; that would indicate an acceptance of the problem. Rather, enterprise managers may seek other explanations for the situation, which may possibly require less disruptive or less expensive solutions. Some of these seemingly feasible alternatives could range from minor software modifications (too small in scope) to major system or platform migrations or reengineering efforts (too large and risky).

The key at this point is to recognize that the defenses against acceptance are weakening as a result of efforts to guide enterprise management from awareness to acceptance.

Phase 4: Depression—Depression is a physiologically necessary stage prior to acceptance of reality. One's anger has turned inward against oneself. One becomes inactive until boredom and/or intellect forces one to become active again.

Depression is the final precursor to acceptance of the possible implications of non-compliance. While there are several potentially positive opportunities to be captured during the compliance process, during this phase the beginnings of a sense of purpose are forged. Management should take stock of available resources and identify those who have assisted in bringing to light the reality of the Year 2000 problem.

When all resistance has been removed and depression has worn itself out, leaving all defenses torn down, top management can finally accept the challenge before it.

Phase 5: Acceptance—Although it is the ultimate goal, acceptance may be a difficult stage. Part of the difficulty lies in recognizing acceptance. How will I/T executives know that senior executives have accepted the scope of the Year 2000 problem?

Kübler-Ross defines acceptance as being "marked by neither depression nor anger. Feelings of not being able to fight it any longer. Acceptance of reality and the need to move on. It is determined resignation." At this point, top management will have been presented with sufficient, overwhelming and ultimately irrefutable information which defies denial.

Acceptance will be recognized by the commitment of resources, reassignment of personnel, status meetings, and press releases, all activities which outwardly indicate pro-active movement on the Year 2000 problem.

Having gone through the process together, IT executives and staff will have a closer relationship with top management, at least with respect to the Year 2000 problem. Together, with mutual respect and understanding of the task ahead, constructive progress can begin.

47   *Perspective, Conflict, Commitment, Scope Creep*

At the outset of solving the Year 2000 problem, both top management and the entire organization must be aware of two things. First, there is no magical solution to the problem. Secondly, there are identifiable and achievable advantages to the process, some of which are available immediately (Figure 47.1).

No Silver Bullet

The solution is not on some psychic solutions hotline. Nor is the solution in the writings of high-profile consultants and pundits. Equally, the solution isn't on the shelves of the IS shop. According to Frederick Brooks, a noted author and educator on software development, "because

> ➤ There is no silver bullet—requires planning, resources and perfect execution
>
> ➤ There are opportunities for benefits—but only if actively pursued
>
> ➤ Critical Success Factors for management
>   • Communications need to be informative, frequent, and widespread
>   • Let business objectives guide the technical response
>   • Conflicts will surely arise—and need to be quickly resolved
>   • Maintaining commitment will be difficult—but mandatory

Figure 47.1   Management considerations

of inherent complexities in large software systems such as those affected by the Year 2000, there can be no silver bullet." If it can be assumed, as Brooks does, that software development and maintenance is a technical endeavor as opposed to wishful thinking, then "that very step, the beginning of hope, in itself dashes all hopes of magical solutions."

There are some automated solutions on the market today. Unfortunately, they only address about 30 percent of the project. While it can be anticipated that there will be some additional automation, it has to be recognized that much of the effort involved is painstaking human review of actual contents of files and programs already identified as possibly containing a date. Also, testing and integration tasks may consume as much as 60 percent to 70 percent of the overall effort, much of which has to be reviewed manually.

Achieving compliance will be a laborious and difficult process. However, the rewards for success can be greater than just the survival of the corporation. Companies which demand a greater return on their investment, but have yet to see such possibilities, need to be aware that with the proper management perspective and commitment, there are significant competitive advantages to be gained.

Capture Benefits Now!

There are several significant benefits to be gained during the Year 2000 compliance process. And, yes, some of these benefits are attainable from the beginning of the project. It requires only awareness and managerial action to realize these benefits. *Treating the compliance process as a technical project, however, will eliminate the possibility of the organization ever seeing most of the advantages.*

At the beginning of the solution process, it is important to have in mind that there are activities which can be taking place on the management side of the business which can generate significant advantages by

> garnering new customers and solidifying existing relationships,

> cleaning out system inventory (little used applications, dead/old code, etc.),

> increasing the project's overall effectiveness and return,

> decreasing project costs and overruns,

> minimizing disruptions to business during the compliance process,

> enhancing morale and productivity among staff, and producing several other competitive benefits of the compliance process.

Critical Success Factors for Management

IT executives will find themselves in the challenging position of being the focal point of attention from not only technical staff but also enterprise management. Technicians and non-technical personnel alike will be brought together to work on an enterprise-wide problem. The challenge for IT executives then is to keep the effort focused on the objective (compliance) and to facilitate creative thinking. The possibilities for unique and dynamic solutions are tremendous. Fostering an environment conducive to such creative work (and maintaining it) will be the foremost trial for management.

In meeting the managerial challenges of the Year 2000, the business must remain aware of the following factors which can greatly impact the success of the compliance process.

Communication—A frequently stated problem in IS development is poor communication between technologists and users. The latter group can include both staff and all levels of business enterprise management. I/S has been criticized for making assumptions about the needs of the business, without consulting users or management.

To achieve compliance, the methods and processes of the business need to be carefully scrutinized. Many of the core activities of the business could be affected. As a result, there must be managerial involvement in the decisions about these processes.

A failure on the part of either side (technical and non-technical) of the business to maintain open and active lines of communication during the compliance process will result in systems which may not perform as desired, or which simply are not in synch with the views of top management or the needs of users.

In order to facilitate such communication, businesses should consider the use of cross-functional business teams. Such teams, representing all pertinent areas of the business, should meet regularly to discuss progress and report back to their respective managers, including top management.

Solution Must Reflect Business Perspective—Whatever solution path is chosen for the Year 2000 problem, it must be derived from the business perspective. Top management must work to see that, given its size and scope, the solution is aligned with business objectives and vision. The compliance process has the potential to radically change the technological direction of a corporation. If for no other reason, many companies will be forced to set aside other major systems upgrades or projects. As such, the investment made now in this project must not contradict the strategic plans of the corporation.

To achieve this end, top management, including CIOs, should ensure that selected solution vendors have the necessary business acumen, and not only technical expertise. Many solution providers, recognizing their own lack of business skills, are supplementing their offerings with the assistance of management consultants/facilitators to round out the solution package.

While the solution vendors will play a large and visible role in the compliance process, enterprise management must remain involved to maintain control over the project. If a vendor is allowed to manage and implement the overwhelming majority of the compliance process, many of the potential advantages of the process will leave with the vendor. Enterprise management cannot outsource accountability and responsibility for a project of this scope and magnitude.

Solving the Year 2000 problem is straightforward from a technical perspective. Given adequate resources, money and time, the process of identifying non-compliant code, converting it, testing it and putting it into production should be readily achievable. What makes the process so complex is its size and scope throughout the entire organization, as well as the risks associated with failure. Managing the resources, staff, schedules, vendors, customers, media, regulators, and all other stakeholders of the business is the strongest challenge of the Year 2000 problem.

In short, we can resolve the technical issues. The more difficult question is _Can enterprise management effectively implement the solution and manage the compliance process?_

Conflict Resolution—Conflicts are bound to arise during the course of the Year 2000 solution. Political infighting, different divisions vying for scarce resources, specific individuals grasping credit, others throwing blame, all are dark possibilities during the compliance process. The key to dealing with such conflicts will be creative thinking on the part of top management.

Managers, or outside consultants/facilitators, if utilized, must work quickly in resolving conflicts to ensure that the conflict does not divert attention, time or resources away from the ultimate goal of compliance. Parties involved in the conflict must be informed of the priorities of the business. Their personal conflicts have arisen because their personal priorities have superseded those of the business. When all parties can understand that their dispute is disruptive and counterproductive to the goals of the organization, then a creative solution to the dispute can emerge. Getting to a win-win situation, in the absence of threats and blame, should be the objective of conflict resolution.

Maintaining Commitment—The most important factor which will impact the success of the project will be the commitment of top management. It is imperative that top management remain committed and informed throughout the process, or else the process may fall apart.

A common phenomenon in many individuals is the gradual decline of commitment. At the beginning of new projects, participants are excited and willing to give their full attention. Over time, however, that commitment lessens as other priorities arise or attention is diverted to other, more immediately gratifying activities.

This weakening of commitment, as depicted in Figure 47.2, can cripple the Year 2000 process. This project will be long, with few high points along the way. There will be many obstacles to overcome and many hard battles fought. The opportunities for diversion of commitment will abound.

To combat such a decline of commitment, top management must be kept involved and informed of significant events relating to the process. Information will be the key weapon in this fight. As the expression goes, *out of sight, out of mind*. The company must make sure that the Year 2000 process never goes out of sight of top management.

Scope Creep—A common frustration with technology projects is their tendency to grow with time, adding functionality (and costs) not originally intended at the outset. This phenomenon is referred to as *scope creep*. After becoming involved in a large technology project, businesses often begin to add elements which are only superficially related to the original scope of the project. These seemingly justifiable "functional enhancements" inevitably drive up project costs, cause significant schedule delays and increase the overall risk of failure of technology projects.

Managers may be tempted to use the Year 2000 compliance project as an excuse to make changes or enhancements to existing systems, or to undertake a significant renovation or redevelopment. A final factor

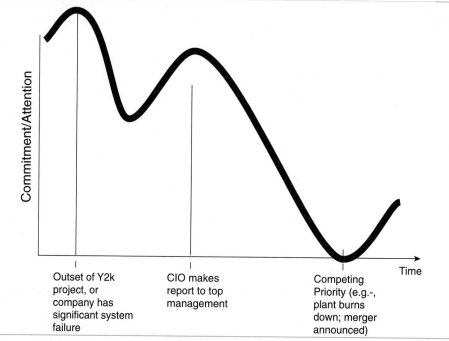

Figure 47.2   Attenuation of commitment

which will greatly impact the success of the Year 2000 compliance effort will be enterprise management's ability to control scope creep. The risks associated with non-compliance are great enough without being compounded by additional variables. Scope creep must be avoided at all costs.

48   *Solution: Time, Cost, Risk*

There are three principal factors to be considered in dealing with the Year 2000 problem—time, cost and risk.

Time—Many companies, especially in financial services, are already being impacted by the Year 2000. Thirty-year mortgages were impacted in 1970. Expense budgets, capital budgets, pension plans and sales forecasts will all be impacted long before January 1, 2000. Companies that believe they can wait until 1999 to begin addressing the problem will most likely be affected before then, and will not have enough time left to implement the solution.

Cost—To some extent, costs have already been discussed. There are other relevant costs, aside from the millions of dollars spent on the actual conversion efforts. There are opportunity costs, which must also be factored into the equation. What will the organization have to give up to become Year 2000 compliant? New plants or equipment? Planned acquisitions? Reengineering hopes? These are strategic issues which must be answered by top management.

While estimating the cost of the project is necessary, there is perhaps a more appropriate question to ask regarding costs. What will it cost if the organization does nothing or does too little? Will the business be able to wait one or two years before starting the process, in hopes of a silver bullet emerging?

Several individuals have commented that if all Year 2000 vendors were able to double their capacity, they would still be able to serve only one-quarter of the total business need for conversion services. There is certainly a looming shortage of COBOL programmers, which is already starting to be felt. Average wages have risen sharply recently, almost doubling in some cases. Thus, qualified programmers and technical managers are in short supply. It has been estimated that the cost of the Year 2000 will increase after 1996 at 20 percent to 50 percent per year, while the skills to address the crisis will diminish due to supply and demand (Figure 48.1).

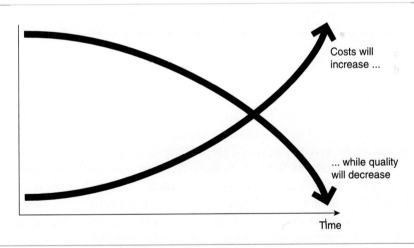

Figure 48.1   *Laws of supply and demand*

Risk—What are the consequences of failure? What are the risks associated with various solution alternatives? Risk is inherent in any venture, and it must be managed according to the risk tolerance levels of the corporation.

The Year 2000 presents opportunities for some reward, great reward and colossal reward. Each level carries different levels of risk. That risk may be in terms of more money or more resources—more bells and whistles and time. It may also involve taking the opportunity to develop entirely new systems rather than fix existing ones. As previously mentioned, scope creep can hinder or cripple the success of Year 2000 compliance efforts. The risks of delay or failure must be weighed against any possible gains achievable from expanding the project scope.

The Make-or-Buy Decision

In general, management has four strategic choices to resolving the Year 2000 problem. The term "strategic" implies that these options concern actions and results that transcend a technical solution. From the manager's perspective, how should the project be handled?

First, the company could do nothing. This is not a viable option, given the probability of system failures and their potentially catastrophic impact.

Second, the company could handle the compliance effort with internal resources only. This would require diverting existing staff and resources away from current and planned initiatives and could create problems in handling day-to-day maintenance needs. Given the size and nature of the Year 2000 process, this option is not viable for most corporations.

The third managerial option for handling the Year 2000 project is to outsource it completely. To do this, the vendors will have to learn the company's business, its processes and its systems. This option is very costly in terms of dollars paid and in the amount of time consumed in transferring knowledge to outside technicians. It will be extremely risky for the company not to have active participation at the working level in integration and systems testing phases. The company will still have to be involved, and should at a minimum have an internal project team to work with the vendor and report back to management. Completely outsourcing the project also prevents the company from being able to capture several potential advantages during the process.

The fourth strategic option would be a *partnering* combination of outsourcing and internal resources. Using a *solution vendor* to provide as much of the technical labor considered appropriate, while using existing staff to manage as much of the process as possible, will allow the company to gain the benefits of technology transfer. In other words, the company could learn from the efforts of the solution vendor, and retain that learning in the company rather than have it leave with the vendor.

49   *Methodology Phase I: Non-Compliance Risks, Positives*

Herbert Lovelace, columnist for *InformationWeek*, recently wrote: "Methodology is a fancy word. It costs you a lot of money when a consultant uses it—even more than when they use 'paradigm shift.'" At this point, it is appropriate to offer some form of prescriptive process, a methodology, to help senior I/S executives and other technical managers, enterprise management and the entire organization deal with the difficulties discussed above, and to enable them to reap some benefits from the Year 2000 compliance process beyond survival.

As shown in Figure 49.1, there is a logical division in the process of addressing the problem. The most obvious section, and that typically discussed by most consultants and vendors, is the technical solution phase. A general overview of the major phases of the technical solution is provided earlier in this book (chapter 29 *Technical Solution Overview* in Part 3 on page 98).

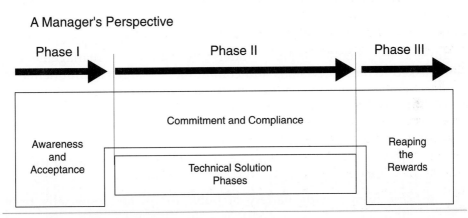

A Manager's Perspective

Phase I   Phase II   Phase III

Commitment and Compliance

Awareness and Acceptance

Technical Solution Phases

Reaping the Rewards

Figure 49.1   The Year 2000 solution process

There are, however, three additional and important phases which surround the technical phase and which make the business solution complete.

Phase 1: Front End Piece—Awareness to Acceptance

In the first phase of the Year 2000 compliance effort, the primary objective is to get the involvement and commitment of enterprise management. This phase is characterized by the psychological process of going from initial awareness, through all of the defensive coping mechanisms of denial, anger, bargaining and depression. Finally, senior management will accept the situation for what it is, realizing the truth of what lies ahead. It will be at this time, and not before, that senior management will be able to commit not only themselves but also the resources of the organization to solving the Year 2000 problem.

A difficult question for I/T executives and other managers will be *How can commitment be recognized?* Given that achieving commitment is largely an internal, psychological process of the individual (in this case, top managers), commitment can be judged only by the external actions of the managers. In other words, when top management gives the green light and signs the contracts to proceed with the solution, commitment is there.

The next important question is *What can be done to bring enterprise management to commitment?* There are at least four primary activities that functional and technical managers can perform which will greatly assist enterprise management in first recognizing the Year 2000 requirement, and ultimately conquering the psychological defenses which precede acceptance and commitment.

Education—The most effective tool available in gaining commitment from senior management is education. Enterprise management should be educated about the nature of the compliance requirement, its origin and its potential impact. Understand that senior management is being asked to make decisions and commitments, large commitments, in a subject matter about which they most likely have little in-depth knowledge. Yet, to comprehend the scope and severity of the Year 2000 problem, senior management has to increase their awareness of at least some of the technical issues and their enterprise-wide ramifications.

An effective education campaign should include as many of the following as possible (or tolerable):

Articles, from a wide variety of publications, and especially from non-technical journals which discuss the business aspect of non-compliance.

Conference materials (collected at seminars and workshops) where appropriate and not too technically oriented. These materials usually contain a wealth of statistical and other expert information about the problem.

Examples of other companies, especially in similar industries, with information about their assessed impact, progress and estimated costs.

Internal Data—While general information about the problem, possible impacts and other information are extremely valuable in addressing the barriers which stand before commitment, external information should be complemented with internal data to bring the Year 2000 problem into perspective. A preliminary technical impact analysis, performed internally, can provide a rough estimate of the size and scope of the task ahead.

The preliminary impact analysis need not be perfect, just reasonably close. There are several rules-of-thumb which can be used as a basis for estimating the project. On a cost per line of code basis, estimates have ranged from as low as 50¢ to as high as $1.50 per line of code. These amounts do not include testing, which some have speculated to be the largest and most expensive aspect of the conversion project. Another estimating method would be to thoroughly examine a sample application(s) to determine the extent of work to be done, and then generate an estimate based on the size and function of other applications relative to the sample. There are other quick-and-dirty methods as well. In general, though, the purpose of these methods is to arrive at a very rough estimate. Spending too much time and energy at this stage is not fruitful. The goal is to win a commitment of funds to conduct a larger, more precise impact analysis.

When presenting initial figures for the purpose of gaining commitment from top management, one must guard against offering figures which are too low in an attempt to minimize the problem for top management. This will only do a disservice to the technical operation, and to the business as a whole. In fact, should the numbers have to be adjusted upward significantly, it may be difficult to justify the increase and gain commitment a second time because the credibility of the messenger may have been damaged.

Identify and Articulate Risks of Non-Compliance—Third, but not necessarily final, all levels of management should be made aware of the probabilities of being impacted by the risks associated with non-compliance. In particular, senior I/T executives and departmental managers should bring these risks to the attention of those in the organization who have the appropriate scope and authority to assess and act on the potential risks. Risks include not only technical risks of system failure but also the business risks associated with failures. Such risks include:

> *Legal, financial, strategic, production or other risks* impacting key functional areas of the business.

> *Customer or supplier risks.* What would be the cost to the organization in terms of lost revenue from customers or interruption of services from suppliers in the event their systems experience Year 2000-related failures?

In order to identify the non-technical risks, the organization may want to develop a *business risk assessment*. This assessment should candidly lay out the likely repercussions of Year 2000-related system failures on various strategic and functional areas of the business. The assessment should also include estimates of the probability of such outcomes, as well as the costs to the business should the identified impact come to fruition.

In the end, however, the principal objective of articulating the risks of non-compliance is to make senior management aware that the Year 2000 problem extends beyond the confines of the data center and deserves their attention, involvement and commitment. By associating risks with bottom-line dollars, the Year 2000 requirement becomes more realistic and believable.

Talk-up the Positives—Why have so many businesses stalled or resisted accepting the reality of the Year 2000 problem? Why does the smoker who acknowledges the dangers of smoking continue to smoke? Overcoming the initial resistance to change, of moving from a point of familiarity to one of uncertainty, requires a shift in the balance of positives and negatives. While negative arguments, such as high cost, risk of business failure, etc., can be stacked up, some individuals, like smokers, may acknowledge the risks, yet still not commit to change. In such instances, what may be required is some positive justification for change.

There are numerous positive outcomes that are possible as a result of compliance efforts.

- Increased market share through stronger relationships with customers and prospects;
- Profitable partnerships;
- Learning gained during the compliance process;
- Continued insurability;
- Creditworthiness and cash flow;
- Human resource advantages;
- Favorable publicity;
- Creative and powerful advertising (e.g., customer testimonials, etc.).

Some of these competitive opportunities are available now, others later. Some positive opportunities are tangible, while others are not. In the end, however, it can be said that considerable benefits can be gained from an otherwise grim situation. By making themselves aware of these positive possibilities, I/T executives can stack the scale in favor of pro-active change, starting now!

Through information, both positive and negative, senior management can be provided with the necessary data to overcome their own psychological barriers to acceptance, and ultimately commit to addressing the Year 2000 problem.

50   *Phase II: Teams, Impact Analysis, Contingency*

This phase is characterized primarily by the technical solution. After enterprise management has emerged from phase one with an acceptance of the need to move forward with the compliance process, the technical staff can go to work solving the problem. There is, however, a significant and essential continuing role for senior management while the technical solution unfolds. There must be an awareness that it is during this outwardly technical phase that the attention and commitment of top management is most likely to attenuate. In addition to managing the technical process, I/T executives must also proactively ensure enterprise management's continued involvement.

From both a technical and business perspective, the overall objective of this phase is Year 2000 compliance. This phase is the nuts-and-bolts phase of the compliance effort. Responsibilities will be delegated and work will be carried out along the way to producing Year 2000 compliant systems.

From a business perspective, however, there are several key activities which should take place, some of which are reactive, to deal with difficulties during the process.

Project Team Development—Before any work can be done, a senior management team must be assembled which will organize and coordinate the compliance efforts. This team must have representation from all major areas of the business impacted by the Year 2000 problem. In many organizations, assembling such a team, and only one team, to handle the Year 2000 conversion may be difficult due to a large number of distinct lines of business or business units, each with their own I/S function and reporting structure.

Figure 50.1 shows an organization which has separate business units and departments, each with their own key functional areas, such as production, marketing, financial and information systems. These business units often develop and maintain separate hardware and software systems, apart from Corporate I/S.

In such a structure, there may be a need for multiple Year 2000 project committees, including an enterprise committee representing corporate-wide interests. Additional committees from other lines of business or divisions may be necessary, depending on the organizational structure of the company.

It will be essential for the project team to have input from key functional areas. Senior level involvement, either in person or via an immediate direct report, is an essential ingredient if the compliance process is to be successful. Senior management must ensure that the

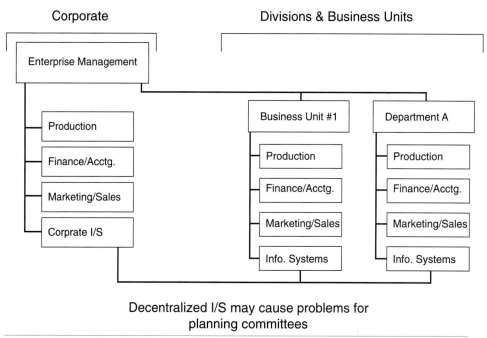

Corporate   Divisions & Business Units

Figure 50.1   Organization

corporate project team is constantly provided the authority to carry out its responsibilities.

Further, each project team must have a full-time leader. The number one reason this project is likely to fail will be ineffective or inconsistent leadership. Top management cannot afford to change project leadership from time to time. This will waste valuable time and destroy the relationships developed. There are different management and oversight demands of the Year 2000 project leader which may compromise the manager's effectiveness or place him/her in a conflict situation. In either event, the manager's ability to focus on Year 2000 issues will be significantly hindered by competing concerns and responsibilities outside the scope of the Year 2000 compliance project.

In short, appointing a part-time leader sends a message to staff that senior management is not fully committed to fixing the problem, or that they do not perceive it as being sufficiently serious to warrant senior management attention.

Once assembled, the team(s) will have enterprise-spanning knowledge and perspective, and will be able to draw on its depth to develop the most effective and appropriate options for addressing the Year 2000 challenge.

Impact Analysis—A preliminary impact analysis may have been performed during phase one to be used to convince top management of the need for action. In fact, it is quite possible that in order to gain the full commitment and acceptance of senior management, some preliminary research and analysis may be required during phase one. This impact analysis should consider the scope of the problem, its potential costs (both tangible and intangible), and associated risks of non-compliance. There are a variety of tools to assist technical managers in performing this initial impact analysis. Also, for some organizations, bringing in outside consultants may be an effective option.

During phase two, this impact analysis must be honed and clarified. Whether this is the first attempt at assessing the potential impact of non-compliance or the second effort, this impact analysis should be as detailed as possible with respect to expected costs, project scheduling requirements (dependencies and event horizons) and failure risks (for prioritizing). From a business perspective, though, there are other considerations beyond the purely technical.

In addition to performing a technical impact analysis, technical managers should participate along with others on the Year 2000 project team in performing a business impact audit (sometimes called a *business risk assessment*) to identify as many of the potential exposures to various business areas as possible. This business audit will determine, in large part, the makeup of the Year 2000 project committee based on the major functional areas identified as impacted by non-compliant systems.

The business audit will serve as a road map for management as it plots its course through the next few years. Strategic planning efforts, both short- and long-term, will be affected by the information in the business impact audit.

One aspect of impact analysis which is frequently overlooked is how the project will be funded and how costs will be allocated across the enterprise. Early on during the compliance process, senior management must determine how resources will be allocated (and charged) to the various divisions within the company. This allocation can be based on existing business rules (e.g., as a percent of revenue or use of I/S services). Alternatively, the costs of compliance can be paid by the I/S department and charged back to various units based on some pre-determined formula. Whatever method is ultimately used, determining how the costs are to be borne by the organization is an integral part of assessing the impact of the Year 2000 problem.

Contingency Planning (for Non-Compliance)—As with any other project, the business must plan for some degree of failure. While 100 percent Year 2000 compliance is the ultimate goal, because of the volume and nature of the work, such a goal is unrealistic. Businesses must, therefore, create contingency plans to deal with the most likely impacts of non-compliance, such as system failures, legal actions, lost business and customer complaints.

Armed with a business impact audit, managers can begin the process of developing contingency plans to avoid or mitigate the impact of the various identified business risks. Depending on the nature of the risk and the nature of the industries involved, businesses may face windfall gains in consumer demand for goods and services should a major competitor's systems fail. Can the compliant business capitalize on this opportunity? Probably not if the opportunity was unexpected. With forewarning and contingency planning, however, the business will be able to react quickly and capture the opportunity.

Manage Political Climate—Unfortunately, any project of the size and scope of the Year 2000 compliance effort is vulnerable to political problems. No organization is immune. As such, it is best to be prepared for political flare-ups, and to be able to resolve them quickly and fairly. The key, however, is to insulate the compliance process from the detrimental effects of political posturing, diversion of resources (staff, funds, etc.), distraction of top management attention, and the obfuscation of the objectives of the compliance process.

Manage Competing Priorities—Like political confrontations, competing priorities are bound to arise during the course of the Year 2000 compliance process. Competing priorities are events or situations which are large enough, important enough, or simply surprising enough to warrant the attention of the organization and possibly result in the temporary diversion of resources.

For example, until recently, ValuJet Airlines has been focused on positioning itself as the low-cost, no frills carrier to many cities across the United States. The achievement of this strategic objective was of paramount importance to the organization. The devastating and tragic crash of a flight in Florida justifiably diverted the full attention and resources of ValuJet, its top management and staff, away from the strategic objective and on the immediate situation.

Certainly, there may be potential survival issues which arise during the course of the Year 2000 compliance effort. Some may be more immediate in nature, such as the example described above. How can the organization cope with such a situation and get back on track with the compliance process?

There is no denying that such competing priorities can potentially derail Year 2000 compliance efforts. Such crises must be addressed, or the business may enter a period of internal or external turmoil. The only consideration in such an event is to restart the compliance process as soon as possible and to prevent the organization from being diverted for so long that its commitment wanes. Competing priorities are particularly dangerous in that they could be used as an avoidance mechanism for top management.

The Year 2000 problem will not go away by itself. This is one deadline that cannot be extended.

Intermediate Progress Checkpoint Meetings—Communication will be a key factor in the success of Year 2000 compliance projects. One method of facilitating constant communication is to hold regular monthly intermediate progress checkpoint meetings (Figure 50.2). They are an absolute necessity to avoid a dilution of top management's commitment to Year 2000 compliance. These meetings should be officially sanctioned and attended by senior management (or direct reports) to convey the importance of the meeting.

Their purpose should be to share information about the experiences (positive and negative) to date of the various Year 2000 efforts. Such sharing will hopefully reduce redundant work and foster creative solutions. The synergy possible from such meetings will greatly enhance the effectiveness of the compliance process by transferring the learning gained by each individual to the group.

Organizations could consider having an outside facilitator manage these meetings. Such an arrangement could produce several benefits:

- reduced administrative burden on internal staff
- increased participation and formality
- enhanced discussion, with objective perspective
- unbiased reporting to top management of compliance progress.

One of the problems associated with scope creep is that it often goes unnoticed by enterprise management until far into the project. By then, schedules are already behind, and budgets are overrun. Regular progress meetings can facilitate the communication necessary to control scope creep by ensuring that enterprise management is involved in the decision process during the Year 2000 compliance project.

These meetings will prove invaluable in keeping top management informed and involved in the process. Additionally, the meetings will foster an environment of cooperation and team-centered problem solving. At a minimum, these meetings and the reports generated from each meeting can begin the process of institutionalizing the knowledge and experience gained during the compliance process.

Intermediate Checkpoint Progress Report Meeting

Note: Should be attended by six to 10 top ranking, voting members of the Year 2000 Standing Committee. Fifty percent of these should be composed of IS leadership, always to include the CIO. The other 50 percent should be composed of enterprise management leadership, of whom the CEO (or COO) should attend every other meeting and the CFO should attend the alternate meetings. Others may be asked to attend to supply information or to observe.

I. Call Meeting to Order

II. Old Business

    A. Ask for reports on each major category or activity. Those reporting should provide comparison with previous reports, new problems being encountered, remedial plans or proposals where the current status is behind schedule.

    B. Ask for report on the status of morale and the adequacy of the staff to deal with the current needs. This report should include staff work hours spent on the major categories of the project, as well as other special projects and a comparison with budgeted work hours.

    C. Discuss the state of relations with service providers and key vendors. This discussion should cover the status of activities assigned to them and comparisons with the schedules for accomplishment of objectives.

III. New Business

List new developments since previous meeting to include but not be limited to the following:

    A. Any new developments occurring with respect to major concerns. These would include important matters affecting the firm as a whole as well as the Year 2000 compliance project;

    B. New developments regarding corporate concerns;

    C. New technology that has become available (hardware, software, new methodologies and procedures, etc.);

    D. New legislation affecting the Year 2000 project;

    E. New tax considerations;

    F. Other.

IV. Other Matters Requiring Attention

For example, competing survival issues, new projects not related to the Year 2000, etc.

V. Schedule Next Meeting

Set the date and time of the next meeting and require that minutes of this meeting be distributed a full week prior to the next meeting, along with a proposed agenda and a request for suggestions for other items to be discussed.

Figure 50.2 **Sample agenda**

Marketing and PR—It should be evident by now that during the course of the compliance process, information will play a key role in how successful the process will be. By utilizing various channels of communication, the organization can disseminate information both internally and externally. In general, however, the goal of all public relations efforts should be to educate all stakeholders and constituents, including employees, stockholders, customers, prospects, suppliers, general public, media and regulators (if they are involved).

Internal communications, such as brochures, newsletters, electronic messaging, and the like, can be valuable tools to keep the entire organization informed and involved in the compliance effort. They can be useful in sharing knowledge and experience during the process. They can be focused on specific needs. Senior management could sponsor and keynote an internal (or external, for outside stakeholders) seminar series to update the company on its progress. Such involvement on the part of top management may be inspiring to staff, and sends a clear signal that the project has the continuing support of senior management.

External communications serve to educate clients, prospects, shareholders, suppliers and even competition about management's pro-active efforts to resolve the Year 2000 problem. Such marketing efforts can be leveraged to position the organization as a leader in Year 2000 compliance or used to distinguish the company based on its response to the crisis. External communications could be in the form of press releases, published articles, advertisements and home pages on the Internet.

At the end of Phase II, the organization should emerge Year 2000 compliant! Systems have been replaced or fixed. From a business perspective, however, there is one additional, yet extremely important, phase.

51   *Phase III: Reaping the Rewards*

After achieving compliance, what more could there be? The objective of this third phase is to quantify and bring home many of the positive outcomes of the compliance process. This phase is essentially a debriefing, to discover two primary items:

> What happened?
> What did the company get for it?

Post-Compliance Audit—To answer these questions, and to realize the benefits of the answers, enterprise management should take inventory of the process to discover what was learned). This can be accomplished with a post-compliance audit:

> The rewards will be there!
> Do a post-compliance audit to find them.
> Once found, communicate them widely.
> Use them as leverage for future endeavors.

This audit should be conducted by a disinterested party to ensure that the reports are not biased. The audit should carefully examine the organizational effectiveness during the compliance process, looking for:

> unresolved issues,
> human resource conflicts,
> unique and effective collaborations,
> process bottlenecks,
> staff stars (those who performed exceptionally well), and
> other occurrences of interest, which indicate areas of positive or negative organizational behavior.

This audit, a learning audit of sorts, serves to remember and record the learning that occurred in the organization during the process. This learning can be applied in the future as other large projects present themselves.

More Marketing and PR—Once the process has been successfully completed, top management should waste no time in letting others know about the success. Doing so can mitigate any damage to the company's image that may have occurred during the compliance process. Furthermore, being Year 2000 compliant may give the corporation a competitive advantage over some or all of its rivals, for varying lengths of time.

The morale of the organization may have taken a beating during the process. Communicating positive information about the success of the process and the returns gained will convey a sense of accomplishment and pride throughout the organization.

Enhance New and Existing Customer Relations—The final activity of Phase III is to enhance the relationships forged during the compliance process. The process brought together customers, suppliers, shareholders and other interested parties, all of whom were involved to some degree (even if only as passive spectators), to solve a mutual problem. The organization can now capitalize on these new bonds. This third phase may seem to be a formality. However, it is essential if the organization is to capture the silver lining of the Year 2000 problem.

The Silver Lining

Throughout this book, we have referred to "positive outcomes," "silver lining," "opportunities," all related to the Year 2000 problem. Many people feel that other than survival, there is no return on investment for Year 2000 compliance efforts. To the contrary, as should be evident by this point, there are several definite opportunities for reaping a positive return on the investment in Year 2000 compliance.

By articulating these attainable positive outcomes as the organization prepares to tackle the Year 2000 problem, I/T executives and senior management will be better able to convey to staff the specifics of the benefits to be gained during the compliance process.

Increased Market Share through Stronger Relations with Customers and Prospects—Sharing awareness with customers and key suppliers and especially being the first in an industry to bring the problem to the attention of customers and prospects tends to bring these valuable constituents closer to the organization. By going one step further and assisting customers and prospects by sharing information and actual experiences to help them in their own compliance process, a company can forge an even stronger relationship. A closer relationship, and one with deepened trust, typically results in a more profitable and longer-lasting relationship.

Top management, from the beginning of the process, can proactively inform and assist customers and vendors in their Year 2000 solutions. It is a win-win situation. If customers and vendors are not compliant, the company cannot do business with them. Top management must understand that the company can lose business if customers and vendors are not compliant. For example, an automotive manufacturer sole-sources gas tanks. That vendor is not Year 2000 compliant and its automated production scheduling system fails, resulting in no gas tanks shipped to the manufacturer in the middle of a long production run. The auto company's production run is interrupted at a cost of millions of dollars a day.

Chubb Insurance hopes to educate its business partners on the issue. "We're going to take an aggressive stance to educate our clients, as well as those we do business with, such as banks or other insurers," says John Jung, vice president and Year 2000 project manager for Chubb.[2] Chubb sees the Year 2000 as an opportunity to add value to the businesses of customers and vendors by sharing information and experiences about the compliance process.

> Potential for increased market share
> Possible new partnerships
> Cleaning up the systems and applications inventory

2. *A Focus on Strategies & Early Experiences—Year 2000 Date Issues*, 1996, The Information Forum.

➤ A learning experience

➤ Continued insurability

➤ Potential favorable publicity and advertising material

A company cannot rely on vendors and customers to become compliant on their own. In fact, their compliance may be as large a survival issue as your own compliance. At a minimum, your organization must obtain some kind of commitment and monitor vendor and customer progress. "We're requesting that vendors certify that their products will work to the Year 2100," says John F. Burns, vice president at Canadian Imperial Bank of Commerce (CIBC). If it appears that compliance is not proceeding on schedule, your company may be forced to seek out other vendors. If customers are not proceeding on schedule, maybe they need more assistance, which your organization may be able to provide.

Possible Partnerships

In many cases, businesses may find themselves collaborating with customers, vendors or even competitors during the Year 2000 compliance process. The benefits of shared knowledge and distributed costs can often bring about more creative and effective solutions. This collaborative environment may create opportunities for new partnerships and joint ventures beyond the Year 2000, which will further cement existing relationships.

Learning Gained during Compliance Process

Although top management may not realize it, there is a tremendous advantage in the learning gained from the process itself. The compliance process will force organizations to examine their present systems—the result of this examination will be a detailed inventory of what systems they presently have and what state those systems are in. The in-depth knowledge of key information systems will allow organizations to transfer that knowledge gained to future projects to handle them more effectively and productively. This information transfer can be accomplished only if the knowledge is captured and documented. Management should make sure that this opportunity is not lost and that comprehensive documentation is maintained.

During the initial phases of the effort, several other opportunities relating to systems inventory will be available.

➤ Examining which systems are no longer being used and no longer required. As in other parts of the business, dead or very slow moving inventory still accrue costs.

> Determining whether the results obtained from an application system are worth the cost of keeping it in production. It may be that the best option is to discontinue use of the system.
> Providing a double check on business resumption/disaster recovery information and procedures.

In summary, as a result of the compliance process, the organization will have, finally, an inventory of all systems. Old and unused programs and dead code will have been removed from the systems, improving the performance and reducing the maintenance requirements of systems. A new rapport between IS and the business staff will have been formed. I/S will be able to integrate future changes and upgrades more efficiently, aided by well-maintained documentation of systems, source code and modifications.

When similar large crises happen again—maybe the adoption of the metric system?—the company will be better equipped to handle the conversion process.

Continued Insurability

Many corporations may be unable to qualify for certain types of insurance, such as errors and omissions or business interruption, should they fail to provide underwriters with adequate evidence of Year 2000 compliance. Major insurers are already adding questions about Year 2000 compliance to their periodic reviews and due diligence efforts. If insurance coverage is available for the non-compliant, rates may be astronomical, giving a cost advantage to compliant companies.

Human Resource Advantages

The attention paid to personnel in the company during the compliance process, to listening to their input, to involving them in the process will create a positive attitude throughout the organization. Benefits such as reduced turnover, increased loyalty, increased productivity, and decreased resistance to change are all within the realm of possibilities.

Almost all projects deliver these kinds of advantages. The unprecedented enterprise-wide scope of the Year 2000 requirement will generate a significantly greater positive impact on the organization's staff.

Additionally, the teams used during the compliance process should not be simply discarded. The organization now has, and should foster, an experienced "fire fighting team." This cross-functional team has worked through the largest IS project ever, and has succeeded. The rapport developed among team members is valuable. This team, in whole or in part, can be used to deal with future business crises which would considerably reduce the interpersonal relationship building, role definition and organizational learning curve aspects of the new endeavors.

Favorable Publicity

The pro-active steps undertaken by enterprise management during the compliance process make for newsworthy press releases, which can result in favorable publicity for the organization. These releases tend to generate favorable word-of-mouth comments among newspapers, business journals, news trade press, etc. Press releases citing your efforts to address the Year 2000 requirements, to assist customers and vendors with their efforts, and other proactive behaviors by enterprise management are bound to result in good publicity.

Creative and Powerful Advertising

Becoming compliant early gives the organization the opportunity to advertise that achievement. In fact, the compliance process does not need to be completed to do so. Being well into the process is a positive position and can be advertised accordingly. Companies can incorporate customer testimonials into advertising and marketing campaigns. Seminars demonstrating a pro-active approach to achieving compliance can become a powerful means for attracting new customers.

Conclusion

Our intention with this work was to present a case for enterprise level action on solving the Year 2000 problem by providing a tool for managers, at any level, to raise awareness, gain commitment and motivate action on the problem in their organizations. While the solution will be costly, time-consuming and risky for the businesses, we hope we have laid a foundation of proactive steps to capture what we feel are real, significant competitive opportunities presented by the compliance process.

A summary of the major recommendations and concerns which managers should be aware of when dealing with Year 2000 issues can be found earlier in this book (chapter 6 *Actionable Caveats* in Part 1 on page 19). While the Year 2000 is several years away, the time for action is now.

One positive note, perhaps: January 1, 2000, happens to be a Saturday. Have a nice weekend!

6

part

CEO/CIO:
Y2K Contracts

Assign this chapter to your Legal Department and external counsel, and they will be stars the next day. Or read it yourself and negotiate well. Don't overlook the three contract forms, either.

Jeff Jinnett's corporate issues summary has a good bibliography and also cites Internet web sites. He warns you to inventory your software and corresponding licenses and maintenance agreements, as well as outsourcing contracts. Write the request for a free Y2K upgrade or you may lose those rights. Jinnett also furnishes a form to help plot your entire data flow to find out what's where and determine potential contamination points.

A software copyright or maintenance contract might stop you from working or contracting a cure for Y2K at the source code level, even while "force majeure" may let the vendor off the hook. If as author you don't want your P.R. to haunt you as an implied or explicit warranty, devise a good disclaimer.

Auditors are required to be picky, so anticipate some sort of Y2K uncertainty note on your financial statements, including the annual report and any security registration. Delaware's Business Judgment Rule and other facets of due diligence are detailed. Obviously, you should involve your chief counsel deeply in Y2K issues.

Courtney H. Bailey tackles vendor liability, primarily in programming services. Since software written after 1978 still belongs to the individual corporate author—along with all derivative works such as your upgrade—you want to hire counsel unless you're sure the client owns the copyright or has clear permission to change the software. The concept of "fair use" may loosen even this restriction if the software will die because the author won't perform a Y2K upgrade.

Sale of a turnkey system or to address a business need, puts you into jurisdiction of the Universal Commercial Code (UCC). The sections here on fraud and misrepresentation are worth reading. Some useful caveats: Counsel can help you by drafting a disclaimer or reasonable estimate of liquidated damages for contract breach. If you're the customer, try getting warranty of future performance.

Immediately following is GAO's suggested Y2K warranty language, trailed by Timothy Feathers' compliance wording and sample warranty.

For the customer side of remediation contracts, turn to Greg Cirillo's "Negotiating Your Remediation Contract" on page 639 of *Outsource Management*. He says to look for vendor deep pockets and adequate staffing. In case of slippage or glitch, specify a workout, not a war.

Warren Reid's article mixes law and a variety of other aspects, and Ira Kasdan concludes by specifying what has to be done to protect the executive chamber.

52   *Corporate Legal Issues*

Jeff Jinnett, Of Counsel,
LeBoeuf , Lamb, Greene & MacRae, L.L.P.

A serious computer problem, variously known as the "Year 2000," "Y2K," "Century Date Change" or "Millennium Bug" problem, faces many companies. Although computer experts have done much to promote awareness of some of the technical issues surrounding the Year 2000 problem, little has been published concerning the related legal issues. This article is intended to provide a summary discussion of some of the major legal issues which may arise due to the Year 2000 problem and is written with non-lawyers as well as lawyers in mind.

Many Companies Will Not Become Year 2000 Compliant in Time

According to Gartner Group, 30% of all companies and governments have not started on their Year 2000 projects.[1] Gartner Group, Inc., has also estimated (with a probability of 0.7) that approximately 50 percent of the companies with this software problem may not become Year 2000 compliant in time and will have all or part of their computer systems shut down (or start producing incorrect data) on or after January 1,

2000.[2] Major software vendors such as IBM are in the process of issuing Year 2000 upgrades to existing software products (see, e.g., the URL of http://www.software.ibm.com/year2000/perspect.html). For major companies with heavily customized software systems, however, much of the corrective work will have to be done by the companies themselves.

Technical/Legal Inventory

Software Inventory/Data Processing Flow Chart

The first step a company should take to become Year 2000 compliant is to prepare an inventory of the hardware and software being utilized in its business. Although the Year 2000 problem is primarily a mainframe software problem, it can also exist in computer hardware (e.g., clocks in the BIOS code located on the PC (Rom) chips), in client/server environments and in PC software. In addition to utilizing scanning software (which searches a networked system to locate and identity software packages on the system), the company should prepare a data processing flow chart with supporting documentation showing specific processing steps being performed by the company's computer system in order to accomplish the required business functions.

All software programs known to be owned or licensed by the company should then be identified to the flow chart in order to determine if any processing steps are revealed which have no software programs identified to them, thus revealing previously unknown, undocumented software in use (see Form at the end of this article). In some cases, undocumented software can enter a computer system if staff computer technicians use third party applications, tools and utilities to solve pressing processing problems and neglect to notify higher management that new software has been inserted into the system.

Some companies reportedly are foregoing the inventory step, proceeding directly to corrective Year 2000 work on their computer systems. In the final testing phase, however, this may result in the computer system refusing to test as Year 2000 compliant due to undocumented software applications, tools or utilities which have not been fully corrected. As noted below, moreover, a failure to conduct the initial inventory phase in conjunction with a legal audit may lead to problems in preserving the company's legal rights against software vendors.

Legal Audit

Once all software packages are identified, the company's general counsel and/or outside counsel should locate and review the license agreements and long-term maintenance agreements relating to all third party licensed software. The company will then be able to identify the appropriate vendor to contact in order to request information as to the availability of Year 2000 software upgrades. (See also Year 2000 upgrade informational sources such as the URL of http://www.auditserve.com/yr2000/yr2ktrk.html.)

It has been reported in the press that companies have begun sending letters to all of their software vendors requesting information as to when their software will become Year 2000 compliant.[3] In some instances the software licensed has undergone a product name change during the years, or the owner/licensor of the software has changed its name or been the subject of an acquisition. In that case, a search of various computer databases such as Lexis®-Nexis® [4] may be necessary in order to determine the correct current vendor and product name.

Potential Obligation of Maintenance Vendors to Fix Year 2000 Problems

A further purpose is served by locating the relevant license agreements and maintenance agreements for all third party licensed software. If the third party license agreement is accompanied by a long-term maintenance agreement surviving past January 1, 2000, the vendor may have an obligation to make its software Year 2000 compliant at the vendor's expense. Counsel will need to review the relevant license and maintenance agreements in this regard, but until recently, many such agreements were silent as to the Year 2000 problem.

Some vendors may disclaim liability for providing Year 2000 upgrades at no additional cost under the maintenance agreements, arguing that the year 2000 problem was well-known to the computer industry and constitutes an "assumed risk" of the customer. The failure to at least request a vendor in writing to make its software Year 2000 compliant at its own cost under the long-term maintenance agreement may constitute a waiver by the customer of its right later to seek reimbursement for the costs it incurs in making the changes itself. It would also, in that event, deprive the customer's insurer of subrogation rights against the vendor.

Potential Obligation of Outsourcing Vendors to Fix Year 2000 Problems

Companies should also review all their data processing outsourcing agreements in order to determine if the outsourcing vendors may have an obligation to undertake the Year 2000 compliance work at their cost. It has been suggested that key provisions in the typical outsourcing agreement which may be relevant to this analysis are the sections dealing with the scope of facilities management and the size of anticipated workload.[5]

Company counsel should also examine any provisions in the out-sourcing agreement whereby the outsourcing vendor agrees as part of its fixed fee to cure any "defects," "bugs" or "viruses" found within the soft-ware programs used in processing the company's data. The "Millennium Bug" might not technically be viewed to be a virus, since a virus is typi-cally understood to be a software program that can "infect" other programs by modifying them to include a version, possibly evolved, of itself.[6] The Year 2000 problem might, however, be viewed to constitute a "defect" or "bug" within the program, which interferes with the pro-gram's intended operation.

The obligation for an outsourcing vendor to cure software defects in the system sometimes is found in a systems software maintenance provision in the data processing outsourcing agreement. A typical provision of that type might read essentially as follows:

> *Systems Software Maintenance. As part of the Base Services, Ven-dor shall provide Customer with Systems Software maintenance and Systems Software production support services as described in Exhibit ____, including but not limited to (1) preventive and cor-rective maintenance to correct defects and failures in the Systems Software and any third party systems software, (2) installing, testing and maintaining upgrades to the Systems Software and any third party systems software and (3) changes, enhancements and replacements of the Systems Software or additional Systems Software, as Vendor deems necessary, in order to perform the Ser-vices in accordance with the Performance Standard. . .*

As in the case of long term maintenance providers, outsourcing ven-dors may strongly resist the suggestion that year 2000 corrective costs be absorbed as part of their fixed fee. Companies in this situation still may decide to make the demand of their outsourcing vendor in writing rather than waive it. The company then would proceed to correct the Year 2000 problem at its expense while expressly preserving its right at a later date to seek reimbursement of its costs from the outsourcing vendor.

Product Switches

Some software vendors may abandon hardware and/or software products rather than incur the cost of creating Year 2000 upgrades. Hardware vendors may also decide to abandon products in order to kill off a second-user market and force customers to upgrade to more expensive equipment. A careful review of the relevant agreements with the vendor will then be necessary in order to determine the vendor's legal ability to force such a product switch.

Contaminated Third Party Data

A company's computer system, even if Year 2000 compliant, may fail to process, and may produce error messages or generate incorrect data if the company receives contaminated programs and/or data from third party suppliers which are not Year 2000 compliant. In this respect, the Year 2000 "Millennium Bug," even though not created with malicious intent and possibly not technically constituting a "virus," may still be thought of as acting in the manner of a "virus" that can re-infect a computer system even after it has been made Year 2000 compliant.

A complete data processing flow chart of the company's computer systems would help to resolve this difficulty by identifying where third party software programs and/or data is input and processed. Companies which are vulnerable to non-Year 2000 compliant software or data from outside suppliers should (a) contact their suppliers at an early date in order to determine their suppliers' Year 2000 compliance plans and (b) monitor their suppliers' progress in actually becoming Year 2000 compliant. Company counsel should also analyze what legal recourse may be available in the form of indemnification provisions and similar provisions in the company's contracts with the suppliers which could serve to protect the company in the event the suppliers do not become Year 2000 compliant in time.

General Contract Issues

Year 2000 Compliance Warranties

Various companies and governmental agencies have reportedly revised their standard contract forms to require that any new software proposed to be sold or licensed to them be Year 2000 compliant.[7] The following are a few sources for examples of Year 2000 compliance warranty language: (a) GSA Year 2000 contract language presented to the Year 2000 Interagency Committee, at the URL of http://www.itpolicy.gsa.gov/mks/yr2000/y2kfnl.htm; (b) "Year 2000 Warranty," located at the URL of http://www.year2000.com/archive/warranty.html; (c) Michael Krieger, "Drafting Tip: The Threat of 2000: Calendar Clause Protection," in the May 1996 issue of *Cyberspace Lawyer,* Vol. 1, No. 2; (d) National Institute of Standards and Technology, Department of Commerce: FIPS PUB 4-1, "Representation for Calendar Date and Ordinal Date for Information Interchange," located at the URL of http://www.nist.gov/itl/div879/yr2000.htm; and (e) APT Data Services, "Pain or Gain in the Year 2000?," *Computer Business Review,* March 1, 1996, No. 36, vol. 4.

It should be noted that the vendor should be required to both "represent" and "warrant" as to its product being Year 2000 compliant so that the customer is legally entitled to both equitable remedies (such as rescission of the contract) for a breach of the "representation" and remedies at law (such as money damages) for breach of the "warranty."

"Millennium Bug" as an Event of "Force Majeure"

Many contracts contain a "force majeure" clause which protects a contract party from a claim of default when it fails to perform due to an Act of God or other event beyond the party's reasonable control. It is unlikely that the Year 2000 problem would be viewed as an Act of God, since it is a known problem which can be corrected with enough planning and resources. However, depending on the particular language used in each force majeure clause and the facts and circumstances surrounding the failure to perform, the Year 2000 problem may be claimed to constitute an event of "force majeure" in some contract disputes. Some companies may wish to alter their standard force majeure language to rule out the Year 2000 problem specifically.

Software License/Copyright Restrictions

As the time remaining for corrective work becomes short, some companies may decide to simply provide an off-line copy of all of their computer applications, tools and utilities to a Year 2000 service provider. The service provider would then load the software onto its computer system in order to perform the Year 2000 corrective work. One legal issue which should be kept in mind is that many software licenses contain confidentiality restrictions barring the licensee from disclosing, or providing a copy of, the software to any third party without the consent of the licensor.

Even if the service provider were to copy the company's software onto an off-line computer system at the licensee's premises, the vendor may argue that the creation of this maintenance copy, despite its retention on the licensee's premises, constitutes a breach of the license agreement and an infringement of the vendor's copyright in the software program.

Further, if the Year 2000 service provider were to decompile, disassemble or otherwise reverse engineer a software application where it had been given only an "object code" version of the software (i.e., software in a format readable only by the computer and not by a human programmer), this would also violate a related software license agreement which prohibited such reverse engineering. Although Section 117 of the U.S. Copyright act arguably permits the purchaser of a copy of software to modify the copy in order to be able to correct the Year 2000 problem, a licensee of software who is prohibited from modifying the licensed software would be expected to honor the license restrictions.[8] The licensee in that instance would normally contact the vendor for a Year 2000 upgrade or modification or obtain the vendor's consent to make the modification itself.

In addition, some maintenance agreements provide that warranties as to system performance automatically become void if any party other than the software maintenance vendor modifies the system. Care should be taken to avoid this result, where possible.

A difficult legal issue arises if the licensor indicates that it will issue a Year 2000 upgrade in mid-1999 and the "object code only" licensee doubts that the licensor will meet even that late deadline. It is conceivable that in cases where the licensee cannot replace the defective software, the licensee may decide to reverse engineer the software in order to obtain access to source code and modify it, taking the risk of a breach of license agreement lawsuit from the vendor, rather than the risk of not receiving a Year 2000 upgrade in time. In such a case, the licensee's breach of the agreement might appear less egregious if the licensee made the modifications itself, rather than have an unaffiliated third party service provider make the modifications.

In light of the above issues, service providers offering Year 2000 corrective services may attempt to provide their services on an "as is" basis and may require indemnifications from their customers against third party licensor suits for infringement.

Export Restrictions on Encryption Software

Companies may decide to retain the services of an overseas Year 2000 service provider, such as a programming facility in India, the Philippines or South Africa, in order to obtain the services of less expensive programmers. Also, programmers experienced in COBOL ("COmmon Business Oriented Language") and other relevant programming languages may become scarce in the next few years as their services are booked up for Year 2000 corrective work by individual companies and Year 2000 service providers. Companies starting their Year 2000 corrective work late may be forced to retain programmers outside the U.S. in order to gain access to the quantity of personnel needed.

In that event, the company should be careful to examine any cryptographic software applications in its software system portfolio prior to export. Encrypted applications might include wire transfer systems, communications systems or any other software application where the processed data is encrypted to make it secure. (For additional information on cryptography and encryption software, see RSA's "FAQ 3.0 on Cryptography," at the URL of http://www.rsa.com/rsalabs/newfaq.)

Under the Arms Export Control Act, certain encryption software is listed on a U.S. Munitions List and is prohibited from being exported. The prohibition is enforced by the Office of Defense Trade Controls ("DTC") in the U.S. Department of State pursuant to its International Traffic in Arms Regulations ("ITAR"). Under certain circumstances, the DTC may decide pursuant to a "commodity jurisdiction" procedure that the software proposed to be exported has both a commercial and military potential use and is governed by the less restrictive Export Administration Regulations ("EAR"). The exporting company then may apply for a license to export the encryption software from the U.S. Department of Commerce. If jurisdiction remains with the State Department, however, the export request might also have to be reviewed and approved by the National Security Agency.

Due Diligence on Acquisitions

In connection with all due diligence investigations of target companies, the acquiring company should investigate the target company's Year 2000 compliance status. Some companies may decide to sell divisions or subsidiaries before the Year 2000 because it would cost more to make the division or subsidiary Year 2000 compliant than its net revenues justified. The acquiring company should make this same analysis and either reserve the right to adjust the purchase price to reflect this Year 2000 compliance cost or reserve the right to "walk" in the event the acquiring company's post-due diligence estimate of the Year 2000 compliance cost exceeds a pre-agreed maximum.

Disclosure Issues

The *Wall Street Journal,* in an article entitled "The Year 2000 and the CEOs' Big Secret,"[9] reported that companies with significant Year 2000 problems were reluctant to talk about the magnitude of their Year 2000 corrective work, for fear of providing damaging information to future plaintiffs in the event the Year 2000 problems were not corrected in time. As is discussed in more detail below, companies may not be able to safely hide their Year 2000 problems because disclosure may be required under various accounting standards, securities laws and bank examination policies.

Accounting Standards Which May Mandate Disclosure

The guiding principles for the preparation by a company of its financial statements are "generally accepted accounting principles" (GAAP). The standards are promulgated by FASB and the American Institute of

Certified Public Accountants (AICPA). One of the GAAP principles promulgated by FASB is Statement of Financial Accounting Standards No. 5 (SFAS 5) ("Accounting for Contingencies"), which provides that contingencies which are reasonably possible, whether or not the amount can be calculated or estimated, must be disclosed in a note to the financial statements.

Statement of Financial Auditing Standards

SFAS 5 defines a "contingency" as an existing condition, situation, or set of circumstances involving uncertainty as to possible gain or loss to an enterprise that will ultimately be resolved when one or more future events occur or fail to occur. SFAS 5 uses three classifications:

1. Probable—the future contingent event is likely to occur.
2. Remote—there is only a slight chance that the future event will occur.
3. Reasonably possible—the chance of the event occurring is more than remote, but less than probable.

SFAS 5 gives as an example of a "loss contingency" the "risk of loss or damage to enterprise property by fire, explosion or other hazards," which definition arguably could include the crippling of an enterprise's computer system by the "Millennium Bug." If it is reasonably possible that the company will not become Year 2000 compliant in time, SFAS 5 appears to require the company to disclose this fact in a note to the audited financials.

Moreover, if (a) it is "probable" that the company will not become Year 2000 compliant in time, (b) an asset has been impaired or a liability incurred as of the date of the financial statements, and (c) the amount of the loss can be reasonably estimated, then a charge against earnings for the estimated loss may be required under SFAS 5 and the liability would be reported in the body of the financial statements.

Statements on Auditing Standards

At some time prior to January 1, 2000, a company's independent public accounts ("auditors") may feel obliged in their audit of the company's financial statements to examine the likelihood of the company's failing to become Year 2000 compliant in time. Auditors may wish to document their assessment of the Year 2000 disclosures by their clients in order to show compliance with applicable Statements on Auditing Standards (SAS), promulgated pursuant to the AICPA's Generally Accepted Auditing Standards (GAAS), the guiding standards for the audit of financial statements. SAS No. 53 ("The Auditor's Responsibilities to Detect and Report Errors and Irregularities") imposes on auditors the duty to plan each audit to provide reasonable assurance of detecting "errors," defined as unintentional misstatements and omissions, and "irregularities," defined as intentionally false or misleading statements, that reach a "financial statement" level of materiality. SAS No. 59 ("The Auditor's Consideration of an Entity's Ability to Continue as a Going Concern"), which relates to a company's ability to remain a going concern for a "reasonable period" not to exceed one year, may also force the auditor (commencing in 1999) to consider the effect on the company of a failure to become Year 2000 compliant.

The auditors therefore may be obligated, in order to demonstrate compliance with SAS Nos. 53 and 59, to review the company's Year 2000 compliance plan and the status of its implementation. Other Statements of Auditing Standards, such as SAS No. 54 ("Illegal Acts By Clients"), may also raise significant issues with respect to the impact of a failure to become Year 2000 compliant on a company's financial reporting.

Pressure to Disclose Due to Potential Securities Law Liability of Auditors

An auditor is considered to be an "expert" under Section 11(b) of the Securities Act of 1993 ("1933 Act") for purposes of the financial statements reported on by the auditor and included, together with the auditor's opinion, as the "expertised" portion of the issuer's registration statement in connection with the sale of securities. As is discussed in more detail below, auditors have securities law liability for material misstatements or omissions in the company's financial statements.

In particular, auditors are held to a higher obligation to exercise "due diligence" with respect to their portion of the registration statement than non-experts, such as the issuer and the underwriter, are held to with respect to the entire registration statement. With respect to the "expertised" financial statement portion of the registration statement, the issuer and underwriter are not required to have made an investigation but must establish that they had no reasonable grounds to believe and did not believe that there was a material misrepresentation or omission in the "expertised" financial statement portion.

As a result of the auditors' higher "due diligence" obligation (and in light of the potentially disastrous impact on a company's business operations if it failed to become Year 2000 compliant in time), auditors are likely to become more cautious in the next few years in dealing with a company's Year 2000 compliance problem in the course of auditing the company's financial statements.

Disclosure in Auditors' Opinions

In a standard unqualified opinion, the auditors would typically state, among other things, that (1) the financial statements are the responsibility of the company's management, (2) the auditors' responsibility is to express an opinion on these financial statements based on their audit, which audit was conducted in accordance with GAAS, (3) GAAS requires the auditors to plan and perform the audit to obtain reasonable assurance about whether the financial statements are free of material misstatement, and (4) in the auditors' opinion, the financial statements present fairly, in all material respects, the financial position of the company as of a particular date, and the results of its operations and its cash flows for the year then ended in conformity with GAAP.

If a note were added to the company's financial statements concerning the Year 2000 problem and the auditors were to decide that a departure from the standard unqualified opinion is required due to uncertainty concerning the company's Year 2000 problem, the auditors might add an additional explanatory paragraph to their standard unqualified opinion that reads something like the following:

> "As discussed in Note ____ to the financial statements, a material portion of the Company's hardware and software computer system used in the conduct of its operations requires correction with respect to the so-called 'Year 2000' problem, as is more fully described in Note ____. The Company has adopted a Year 2000 corrective plan and is in the process of implementing that corrective plan. The ultimate success or failure of the corrective plan and the extent of such success or failure cannot presently be determined. Accordingly, no provision for any liability that may result from the failure of the Company to implement fully its Year 2000 corrective plan has been made in the accompanying financial statements."

If the financial statements were to fail to include a note with respect to the Year 2000 problem and the potential liability arising with respect to the problem, despite the auditors' recommendation to the company that such a note be added, the auditors may decide to issue a qualified opinion which states that the financial statements present fairly, in all material respects, the financial position of the company, "with the exception of" the effects of the Year 2000 matter, as described in an explanatory paragraph preceding the opinion paragraph of the report.[10]

Securities Laws Which May Mandate Disclosure

Public companies are required to file an annual report on Form 10-K and quarterly reports on Form 10-Q with the U.S. Securities and Exchange Commission (SEC). Pursuant to Reg. S-K, Item 303, each such annual report and quarterly report must include a section entitled "Management's Discussion and Analysis of Financial Condition and Results of Operations" (MD&A). Instruction 3 to Item 303(a) provides that:

> *The discussion and analysis shall focus specifically on material events and uncertainties known to management that would cause reported financial information not to be necessarily indicative of future operating results or of future financial condition. This would include descriptions and amounts of (A) matter that would have an impact on future operations and have not had an impact in the past, and (B) matters that have had an impact on reported operations and are not expected to have an impact upon future operations.*

On May 12, 1997, the SEC issued a statement as part of a "Current Issues and Rulemaking Projects" release confirming the obligation of public companies to disclose information in their annual reports and quarterly reports about their Year 2000 problems if deemed material under Reg. S-K. This statement has been included in subsequent revisions of the release. The SEC issued Staff Legal Bulletin No. 5 on October 8, 1997, which further emphasized this existing disclosure obligation (see the URL of "http://www.sec.gov/rules/othrindx.htm").

Illustrative of this is the SEC's Securities Act Release No. 6385, implemented in Financial Reporting Release No. 36 (May 18, 1989), which provides that a disclosure duty exists when "a[n]... uncertainty is both presently known to management and reasonably likely to have material effects on the registrant's financial condition or results of operations." Essentially, disclosure would be required in the MD&A unless management decided that "a material effect on the registrant's financial condition or results of operations is not reasonably likely to occur."

Potential Liability of Officers and Directors of a Public Company Which Fails to Disclose a Year 2000 Problem and Then Fails to Become Year 2000 Compliant in Time

As noted above, under certain circumstances, a public company would be required to disclose its Year 2000 problem in the MD&A section of its annual report, quarterly reports and in the company's financial statements. If the company were to fail to disclose a Year 2000 problem when required to do so, the securities law consequences could be significant.

The annual report is often incorporated by reference into a company's registration statement pursuant to the SEC's "Integrated Disclosure System," for purposes of registering stock for issuance to the public. Section 6(a) of the 1933 Act requires that every registration statement (which includes the prospectus) be signed by the issuing corporations's principal executive officers, its principal accounting officer and a majority of the board of directors.

Section 11(a) of the 1933 Act makes every signatory to the registration statement (and every director of the issuer, whether a signatory or not) liable for material misstatements and omissions to any person who acquires securities issued under it. Underwriters, auditors and lawyers involved in the issuer's stock offering may also be held liable under Section 11. Evidence of "due diligence," however, can provide a defense against a Section 11 action. (See, e.g., Rule 176 ("Reasonable Investigation and Reasonable Grounds for Belief Under Section 11"), promulgated by the SEC under Securities Act Release No. 6335.)

Further, under Section 12(2) of the 1933 Act, an issuer may be held liable to a shareholder in a private action for any untrue statement in a prospectus of a material fact or failure to state a material fact necessary to make the statements made in the prospectus not misleading. Section 12(2) applies to any public offer or sale of a security (whether registered or not) "by means of a prospectus or oral communication." The issuer is afforded a "due diligence" defense if it "did not know, and in the exercise of reasonable care could not have known" of the falsity.

In addition, Section 10(b) of the Securities Exchange Act of 1934 (Exchange Act), as interpreted by Rule 10b-5 of the SEC, essentially makes it unlawful for any person (which may include the issuer, underwriter, auditors and attorneys) to sell any security in interstate commerce while employing a "manipulative or deceptive device," which term includes making any untrue statement or omitting any statement of a material fact.

A private action by a purchaser under Section 10(b) and Rule 10b-5 must allege a material and false representation or omission by the issuer in connection with the purchase and sale of securities, the use of means and instrumentalities of interstate commerce, scienter (intent to deceive, manipulate or defraud, or in certain cases, recklessness), reliance by plaintiff and damages suffered by plaintiff. A private action under Section 11 of the 1933 Act need not allege intent to deceive.

The SEC itself may institute enforcement actions with respect to registration statements which contain material and false representations or omissions under Section 17(a) of the 1933 Act (which covers any fraudulent scheme in an offer or sale of securities, whether in the course of an initial distribution or in the course of ordinary market trading) and under Rule 10b-5 under the Exchange Act. Section 24 of the 1933 Act provides for criminal penalties for securities law violations.

Purchasers of securities may also avail themselves of the protection afforded by the disclosure and liability provisions of the securities laws ("Blue Sky" laws) enacted by the various states.

Standards of Care of a Director

The laws of the state of a company's incorporation typically impose standards of care on the company's directors, which could be breached if the directors are grossly negligent in dealing with the Year 2000 problem, resulting in potential personal liability for the directors. The Model Business Corporation Act (Section 8.30(a)), adopted by some of the states, defines the director's duty of care as the duty to act in good faith with the care an ordinarily prudent person in a like position would exercise under similar circumstances and in a manner the director reasonably believes to be in the best interests of the company.

Some states, like Delaware, have not codified the duty of care, but Delaware courts have held that directors should act with the care of an ordinarily prudent person.[11] Some state due care codifications add a requirement that the director use "reasonable inquiry." Section 209(1) of the California Corporation Code sets forth an example of such a provision, providing that:

> *"A director shall perform the duties of a director, including duties as a member of any committee of the board upon which the director may serve, in good faith, in a manner such director believes to be in the best interests of the corporation and its shareholders and with such care, including reasonable inquiry, as an ordinarily prudent person in a like position would use under similar circumstances."*

Shareholder Suits

If a public company fails to adequately disclose its Year 2000 problem in its annual report on Form 10-K, quarterly reports on Form 10-Q and in its registration statements and subsequently has to substantially curtail or shut down its business on or after January 1, 2000 due to the problem, produces incorrect data commencing on that date, or otherwise experiences substantial operational difficulties resulting in damage to its business, the company's stock price is likely to drop. Shareholder suits based on one or more of the above federal and/or state securities laws are likely to follow. Civil and/or criminal enforcement action by federal and/or state securities authorities might also occur.

In addition, irrespective of whether adequate disclosure of the year 2000 problem was made or not, in the event a public or private company fails to become Year 2000 compliant in time, the shareholders may institute individual suits, or derivative suits in the name of the company, against the directors alleging breach of their duty of care under state law.

Documentation of Year 2000 Compliance Program to Establish Due Diligence Defense and Protection Under the Business Judgment Rule

Directors are permitted to rely on the reports of the company's officers, counsel and third party experts in the course of making corporate decisions. In the event a company's board of directors adopted a Year 2000 corrective plan, but the company unexpectedly failed to become Year 2000 compliant in time and the directors were sued by the company's shareholders, the directors would likely find it useful to be able to produce detailed documentation as to the company's Year 2000 corrective plan and the diligence with which it was pursued.

The "Business Judgment Rule" essentially protects directors from court review and liability for an honest mistake of business judgment so long as the challenged board decision was intended to serve the business purposes of the corporation and did not involve fraud, illegality or conflict of interest. The exact formulation of the Business Judgment Rule varies from state to state, and some courts require the directors to show that they performed appropriate "due diligence" in informing themselves of the merits of the business issue before reaching a decision.

As an example of a codification of the Business Judgment Rule, Section 141(e) of the Delaware general Corporation Law provides that:

> *A member of the board of directors, or a member of any committee designated by the board of directors, shall, in the performance of his duties, be fully protected in relying in good faith upon the records of the corporation and upon such information, opinions, reports or statements presented to the corporation by any of the corporation's officers or employees, or committees of the board of directors, or by any other person as to matters the member reasonably believes are within such other person's professional or expert competence and who has been selected with reasonable care by or on behalf of the corporation.*

In some states such as Delaware, director liability for breach of the duty of care, under the Business Judgment Rule, has been held by courts to require a showing that the directors acted with gross negligence.[12]

However, the Business Judgment Rule has been held by some courts not to apply to protect the directors where they abdicated their functions and failed to act. In that instance, the directors could be held liable against a showing of simple negligence.[13]

Thus, in order to avail themselves of the protection of the Business Judgment Rule to deflect shareholder suits seeking court review of the company's adoption and implementation of its Year 2000 corrective plan, the directors may need to show that they had consulted with Year 2000 experts and responsible corporate officials in a timely manner prior to adopting the corporation's Year 2000 corrective plan. This documentation also could serve to establish a "due diligence" defense in the event the directors become the subject of a lawsuit under Sections 11 or 12(2) of the 1933 Act or Section 10(b) of the Exchange Act and Rule 10b-5.

Statutory Limitations on Liability, Corporate Indemnification and D & O Insurance Coverage

Under the corporation laws of some states such as Delaware, companies (1) are permitted (with the approval of their shareholders) to limit or eliminate their directors' (and in some instances officers') monetary liability for breaches of their fiduciary duties, and (2) may indemnify their directors against expenses, judgments, fines and settlement payments in third-party actions and derivative actions, provided the directors acted in good faith and in a manner they reasonably believed to be in the best interests of the company.[14]

However, although many state laws permit companies to adopt the above limitation of liability and liberal indemnification policies, not all companies have adopted such limitation of liability and indemnification policies and incorporated them into their charter documents. Some corporations also have no D&O liability insurance or have policies with low policy limits.

Since the potential liability of officers and directors of a company which fails to become Year 2000 compliant in time could be considerable, company counsel should review with the company's directors and officers the company's D&O insurance policies, limitation of liability provisions and indemnification provisions so that they may be revised and updated appropriately. Officers and directors who have received personal indemnification agreements from their companies may wish to have their personal counsel re-review the agreements with the Year 2000 problem in mind.

Disclosure Due to Bank Examinations

Regulated banks with significant loan portfolios are likely to be reviewing their exposure to major debtors that have serious Year 2000 compliance problems.[15] This is in part because bank examiners are likely to be reviewing loan portfolios of banks in the next few years to determine if adequate allowances have been made for possible loan defaults due to Year 2000 compliance problems. (See, e.g., the Federal Financial Institutions Examination Council (FFIEC) Interagency Policy Statement on the Allowance for Loan and Lease Losses (ALLL).)

For companies with major lines of credit or outstanding bank loans , the Year 2000 compliance problem, if not handled correctly, may seriously cripple the company's finances even prior to the Year 2000. For example, if a company's line of credit is callable in the event the auditor's letter is qualified in any respect, the delivery of an audit letter in 1999 which is qualified as to the Year 2000 compliance issue might trigger a loss of the bank line of credit at the very time when funds are needed to finish the Year 2000 corrective work.

Statutory/Regulatory Compliance Mandates

At the present time, it does not appear that the federal government has enacted any statues or promulgated any regulations requiring any private sector companies to become Year 2000 compliant as a matter of law. However, bills have been introduced in both the U.S. House of Representatives and the U.S. Senate, authorizing appropriations for the Department of Defense (DoD), including a mandate on the Secretary of Defense to ensure that all "information technology" acquired and used by the DOD be Year 2000 compliant.

The Office of the Comptroller of the Currency (OCC) has recognized that this computer problem could wreak havoc in the banking industry. On June 17, 1996, the OCC issued Advisory Letters (jointly with the FFIEC) to the CEOs of all national banks, advising them that their banks should correct the Year 2000 problem by the end of 1998, leaving one full year for testing (see the URL of http://www.occ.ustreas.gov/ftp/advisory/96-4att.txt).

The U.S. House of Representatives and the U.S. Senate have held extensive public hearings on the year 2000 problem (see, e.g., the URLs of "http://www.itpolicy.gsa.gov/mks/yr2000/y210cong.htm" and "http://www.senate.gov/~banking/hearings.htm").

It is possible, due to heightened public concern in the future, that federal and/or state mandates for companies in the private sector to become Year 2000 compliant may be issued. If statutory or regulatory mandates are enacted, the Private Securities Litigation Reform Act of 1995 (Pub.L. 104-67) may become of considerable importance to the disclosure issue. This act amends the Exchange Act by adding a new Section 10A (codified at 15 USCA 78j-1(a)), which requires auditors to include in their audits of public companies "procedures designed to provide reasonable assurance of detecting illegal acts that would have a direct and material effect on the determination of financial statement amounts." Section 10A (15 USCA 78j-1(f)) defines "illegal acts" as "an act or omission that violates any law, or any rule or regulation having the force of law."

Thus, if statutory or regulatory Year 2000 mandates are passed at any point in the future, the new Section 10A obligations will come fully into play. The auditors must inform management and the board of directors of the occurrence of an "illegal act" (whether or not it is perceived to have a material effect on the company). If, after doing this, the auditors determine that timely and appropriate remedial action is not being taken by management with respect to the illegal act (i.e., complying with the statutory or regulatory Year 2000 compliance mandate) and the auditors reasonably expect the failure to take remedial action to result in the issuance of a non-standard audit report, or resignation from the audit engagement, the auditors must report the situation to the board of directors.

The board then must report the auditors' conclusions to the SEC within one business day thereafter. The auditors are immune from private action for the findings in their report to the board of directors, but are subject to SEC civil penalties if the report is not issued as required.

Insurance Issues

Business Interruption Insurance

Insurance policies which cover "business interruption" claims (such as property insurance policies) usually require that the business interruption result from a "fortuitous event." A "fortuitous" event has been interpreted by some courts, based on Restatement of Contracts 291, comment [a], to be "an event which so far as the parties to the contract are aware, is dependent on chance." It can be easily argued that since the Year 2000 problem has been well known for years and is totally within the control of the insured to correct, it does not qualify as a "fortuitous" event. Insurance carriers issuing business interruption insurance may decide to highlight the Year 2000 problem in an insert or letter to their insureds in the next year in order to be able to establish conclusively that their insureds were aware of the issue.

Directors & Officers Liability Insurance

If a public company were to fail to become Year 2000 compliant in time and shareholder suits against the directors and officers were to result, the company's D & O policy would become of critical importance. Generally, D & O policies will not make any payment, to cite some of the typical exclusions, for any loss arising from any claims made against any director or officer:

1. for any fines or penalties imposed in a criminal suit action or proceeding;
2. where the loss represents a personal profit or advantage illegally taken by the officer or director;
3. where the loss was brought about by the fraudulent, dishonest or criminal acts of the director or officer, provided that the acts brought about or contributed to the claim adjudicated;
4. for bodily injury, sickness, disease or death of any person, assault, battery, mental anguish, or emotional distress;
5. for damage to or destruction or loss of use of tangible property; or
6. for injury based on invasion of privacy, wrongful entry, eviction, false arrest, false imprisonment, malicious prosecution, libel or slander.

It therefore appears that so long as the insured company is making some effort to correct its Year 2000 problem, even if it is grossly negligent in the process, it still may be covered by its D & O insurance.

However, if a director or officer knew of a fact or circumstance which was likely to give rise to a claim (e.g., a material Year 2000 compliance problem) and failed to disclose or misrepresented the fact or circumstance in the application for D & O insurance, the insurance company may refuse to make payment for any loss arising from a claim against such officer or director.

Although D & O insurance is usually renewed every year, the renewal application usually requests little information and usually does not request any confirmation that no material change has occurred with respect to the representations of the company contained in the original D & O insurance application. Thus, unless a company is applying for D & O insurance for the first time or is switching insurers, its Year 2000 problem may not come up in the renewal process. In light of this, companies with significant Year 2000 problems and a short-form renewal application may hesitate to switch D & O insurers prior to the Year 2000.

Some D & O insurance renewal applications, however, do attempt to ascertain the insured's risk of potential loss, asking, for example, for information about material changes in the insured's financial statements or audit committee procedures. Accordingly, counsel for the insured should review the D & O insurance policy renewal application with the Year 2000 problem in mind to see if any disclosure is required.

Collateral Litigation Damage

There may be any number of instances in which the failure to become Year 2000 compliant can cause collateral litigation damage. As an example of how a company may be adversely affected in a collateral respect due to its failure to become Year 2000 compliant, consider the following hypothetical. Assume that the Federal Aviation Administration (FAA) issues a regulation in 1998 mandating that all air carriers become Year 2000 compliant by December 31, 1999. A plane crashes in February of the year 2000, and the air carrier is sued.

At trial, plaintiff's counsel introduces into evidence the fact that certain parts in the plane were supposed to have been replaced pursuant to a pre-set maintenance schedule in January of 2000. The parts were not replaced, however, due to the failure of the carrier's maintenance computers to be made Year 2000 compliant, resulting in an incorrect calculation of each part's "time in service." Although it is unclear as to whether the parts involved were the proximate cause of the crash, the jury takes the new testimony as evidence of the carrier's reckless attitude toward safety, discounts the carrier's testimony as to lack of culpability with respect to the crash, gives the plaintiff the benefit of the doubt as to "proximate cause" and imposes punitive damages in addition to compensatory damages in order to "send a message."

Conclusion

Computer experts and chief information officers of corporations have long known of the Year 2000 problem from a technical point of view. As is evident from the above discussion, the legal issues surrounding the Year 2000 problem can be equally as thorny and merit serious attention. Failure to address the legal issues surrounding the Year 2000 problem can lead to (a) delays from third party vendor lawsuits, (b) loss of claims against vendors who otherwise might be required to pay for Year 2000 corrective costs, (c) legal liabilities for the company and (d) personal monetary liability for the company's officers and directors.

It is recommended, therefore, that any company facing a serious Year 2000 problem involve its general counsel and/or outside counsel, together with its CIO and Year 2000 experts, in the preparation, review and implementation of the company's Year 2000 corrective plan. The final Year 2000 corrective plan should be formally reviewed and approved by the company's key officers and its board of directors so as to lay the groundwork for the officers and directors to be able to establish a "due diligence" defense under securities laws and under the "Business Judgment Rule." Finally, the company's charter limitation of liability and indemnification provisions and D & O insurance policy should be reviewed and amended as appropriate.

> ***Author's Note:*** *This article is intended to provide general information and is not intended to provide legal advice regarding specific transactions or matters.*

Figure 52.1   **Software Questionnaire**

Software Application Description:

Software Application Name:

Software Acronym:

Number On Data Processing Flow Chart:
[For Example, "No. 62"]

Major Business Functions:

Application Receives Data From:
[Identify Software Applications Which Feed Data To The Subject Software Application—For Example, Application 63]

Processes Data And Distributes It To Following Software Applications For Further Processing: [Identify Software Applications—For Example, Applications 59 And 61]

Is Software Application Owned: ☐ Yes   ☐ No
If Yes, Identify Vendor And Identify License Agreement:

Is Source Code Available: ☐ Yes   ☐ No

Is Application The Subject Of A Maintenance Agreement: ☐ Yes   ☐ No
If Yes, Identify Maintenance Agreement

References

1. See the URL of "http://www.gartner4.gartnerweb.com/gg/static/itjournal/gspecial1.htm".
2. See *"Year 2000 Problem" Gains National Attention* at the URL of http://www.gartner.com/aboutgg/pressrel/pry2000.html.
3. See Paul Barker, "Consultant Warns IS: Economic Chaos Looms," *Computing Canada*, June 20, 1996.
4. Lexis® and Nexis® are registered trademarks of Reed Elsevier Properties, Inc.

5. See John Xenakis, "The Fin de Siecle Computer Virus," *CFO,* July 1995, Vol. 11, No. 7, p. 67.

6. See Dr. F. Cohen, *A Short Course on Computer Viruses* (2d Ed.) (Wiley Professional Computing, 1994) at p. 2.

7. See, e.g., Thomas Hoffman and Julia King, "Small Vendors Pressed for Year 2000 Remedy," *Computerworld* , May 6, 1996, at p. 1.

8. See, e.g., R. Nimmer, *The Law of Computer Technology* (Warren, Gorham & Lamont, 1996) at p. 1–109. Record companies and book publishers typically sell copies of their records and books to the public. Some vendors similarly sell their software or multimedia works in diskette or CD-ROM form to their buying public. Most software today, however, is licensed to the customer, rather than sold, because it allows the vendor greater control of the use and further disposition of the software. For further information on the distinction between the sale and license of software, see e.g., S. Fishman, *Copyright Your Software* (Nolo Press, 1994) at p. 12/5-12/9.

9. See Roger Lowenstein, "The Year 2000 and the CEO's Big Secret," *The Wall Street Journal* , July 25, 1996, at p. C1, col. 3.

10. See Terry Lloyd and Dan Goldwasser, "The Work of the Outside Accountant" in *Practicing Law Institute, Accounting for Lawyers* (1995) at p. 169.

11. See E. Brodsky and M. Adamski, *Law of Corporate Officers and Directors* (Clark Boardman Callaghan, 1995), Section 2:04, at p. 2-11 and 2-12.

12. Id., at Section 2:07, p. 2-29.

13. Id., at Section 2:12, p. 2-51 through 2-56.

14. Id., at Section 2:05, p. 2-16 through 2-24, Section 19:03, p. 19-4 through 19-17.

15. See Grant Buckler, "Financial Sector Grapples With 2000 Bug," *Newsbytes* , July 11, 1996.

53 *Vendor Liability*

Courtney H. Bailey, Esq.
Finnegan, Henderson, Farabow, Garrett & Dunner, L.L.P.

A detailed look at the potential liability vendors face from the Year 2000 problem is valuable since, as January 1, 2000 comes closer, an excess of litigation will spring up focusing on who is responsible for the problem and, more importantly, who is responsible for shouldering the cost of fixing it.

Legal views expressed here are those of the author, and are provided as an overview only. Specific legal questions regarding your company's precise liability should be discussed with a qualified attorney.

Let's consider some of the legal pitfalls vendors face in traversing these uncharted "liability" waters and how you can recognize and avoid them.

Copyright Considerations When Performing Modification Services

In addition to counseling and advising clients who face the Y2000 Problem, the IT markets for Y2000 services will consist primarily of programming services geared to upgrading and maintaining existing computer systems so as to make these systems Y2000 compliant.

If you, as an information technology provider, choose to compete in this software upgrade and system maintenance market, always have your clients provide you with all information they have regarding the circumstances under which their systems were acquired, including development contracts, transfer documents, assignments and licenses. Review of this information is crucial because you must have a clear picture of the ownership/licensing status of the software you'll be working on before entering into an agreement to perform modifications.

Ownership status of computer software is vital in determining whether you or your client has the right to make modifications to a particular piece of software in order to achieve Y2000 compliance. Furthermore, you must determine whether your client has the right to hire someone other than the original software developer to perform the modifications.

Under United States copyright laws, computer software is considered a literary work. Therefore, the author of the software acquires a copyright for the software for either the life of the author plus fifty (50) years or, in the case of corporate authors, for seventy-five (75) years. (These periods of copyright ownership apply to computer software authored after January 1, 1978.)

One of the exclusive rights afforded to authors under our copyright laws is the "right to prepare derivative works." A derivative work is a work based on one or more preexisting copyrighted works. Although the current case law is not clear, some believe that any modification which affects the functioning of a computer program will constitute the creation of a derivative work. The derivative work, of course, is the post-modification software program.

A corporation can be the author of a computer software program if the software was originally created as a "work for hire." A work for hire arises when the software is created by an employee of the corporation within the course and scope of his regular employment. In this instance, the company itself would be considered the author of the software.

If your Y2000 client has developed its own software "in-house," it is likely that the individuals who wrote the software were employees of your client at the time they wrote the software. In that case, as a "work for hire," the copyright in the software would belong to your client. As the owner of the copyright, your client has the ability and freedom to hire a third party to make whatever changes it chooses to the software.

If your client has licensed the software from the copyright owner, its ability to make (or hire you to make) modifications to the software will be controlled by the license agreement. It is likely that such a license will prohibit third-party modifications of the software. A thorough review of all licensing documents is advised prior to beginning any work.

In the event that your client is subject to a license which restricts its ability to modify the software, you or your client should first contact the original software developer to determine whether Y2000-compliant upgrades are available. In the event that the original developer fails to offer Y2000-compliant upgrades, your client should seek to obtain that developer's permission to perform the necessary modifications. In the event such permission is not forthcoming, your client should consider some of the available legal remedies which are discussed below. If the original developer does not provide upgrades and is unwilling to grant permission to your client to perform the modifications, seek advice from competent copyright counsel prior to embarking on a modification contract. This may help shield you from potentially enhanced liability for willful copyright infringement.

If the materials provided by your client show that your client neither developed the software at issue itself nor holds a license from the original developer, but actually owns the software outright, it is important to remember that even though your client may own the software it still does not own the copyright unless a valid copyright assignment has been made. If your client owns the software, but not the copyright, it may still have the right to perform limited Y2000 modifications under the copyright laws.

The Copyright Act grants "owners" of software programs the right to make or authorize the making of an adaptation of the computer program provided that such adaptation is created as an "essential step" in using the computer program in conjunction with a machine. In the event of Y2000 compliance, a very strong argument can be made that modifications relating to the Y2000 Problem are "an essential step" in using the program. This is especially true if the program will become inoperative after December 31, 1999. However, further modification, which is not related to or necessary for the continued operation of the computer software, is not likely authorized under this statute and would be considered to be the creation of an unauthorized derivative work.

Other possible arguments a software owner might make to defend a claim of copyright infringement on the basis of modifications to ensure Y2000 compliance include fair use, the first sale doctrine, and a "private use" defense.

The Copyright Act provides that "fair use" can be made of copyrighted works. This means that an individual can engage in acts which are infringing under the statute, but that such acts are excused because of the circumstances of use. The statute requires that four factors be considered in assessing whether a use is fair:

1. the purpose and character of the defendant's use of the copyrighted work;
2. the nature of the work;
3. the substantiality of the taking from the work; and
4. the effect of the defendant's use upon the market for the work.

In the Y2000 compliance context, if the original developer refuses to provide an upgrade or perform ongoing maintenance to cause software to become Y2000 compliant, a very strong argument can be made that modifications in order to achieve Y2000 compliance are "fair." However, if the original developer provides upgrades or is providing maintenance services and you would be performing the modifications in competition with the original developer's business activities, it is much less likely that a court would find such use fair. Although the cases are somewhat unsettled on this topic, it would be advisable to get advice from counsel on a particular situation or to ask your client to indemnify you for possible copyright infringement claims.

The "first sale doctrine" provides that once an author of a work makes the first sale of a copy of that work, that author's rights are exhausted with regards to that particular copy. In the Y2000 compliance context, an argument can be made that a software developer has received the rewards of its work through payment for the original copy of the software purchased. This prevents a copyright owner from controlling the use to which the software is put after it has left his hands. However, the application of the first sale doctrine in the instance of substantial modifications of the program is likely to be limited. Additionally, similar to the "essential step modification" discussed above, the first sale doctrine applies only to "owners" of copies of the software, not to mere licensees.

A third possible argument which could be made to defend a claim of copyright infringement is that of a "private use" defense. This is essentially an equitable defense that allows purchasers of software the right to use the software to satisfy the needs for which it was originally purchased; however, such a defense would exclude any commercial aspects to modifications which were made. It is likely that this type of argument would protect the client, but not the entity who is trying to market services related to Y2000 compliance.

Unfortunately, at this time, the copyright laws may not adequately address some of the unique problems associated with the protection of computer software. Different schemes have been proposed and discussed by commentators, but the law does not reflect many computer program-specific provisions. Consider the issues outlined above carefully before entering into any contract to provide modification services. Protect yourself and your client by fully considering the intellectual property ramifications of the work that you do. If the owner of the copyright in the software determines that your Y2000 compliance activities are infringing, the time and expense of potential litigation can negate any benefits you may receive from entering the burgeoning Y2000 market for modification services.

Other Legal Aspects You Should Consider Prior to Entering the Y2000 Market for Services

Most of the remaining legal issues which arise in connection with the Y2000 Problem in computer software concern general issues of contract and tort liability and are relevant in any transaction involving the sale of software.

Contractual Liability:

> Express Warranties

Contractual liability is based on breach of warranty. Warranties may be either expressed or implied. An express warranty is a statement presented as fact, a product description or a promise made concerning the software product. If these representations become part of the "basis of the bargain" between the parties to the contract, then these representations will be treated as an express warranty that the product will perform as represented. In order to determine the scope of the warranties which accompany a software transaction, it is important to look at all transaction documents, product manuals or sales/marketing materials which may have accompanied the sale of the software. In this event, a sales piece which states that "This product will take you into the next century and beyond" may very well be treated as an express warranty that the product at issue is Y2000 compliant.

Whether or not these types of representations are considered to be part of a contract between the vendor and the ultimate software user depends on the terms of the contract between the parties. An effective disclaimer can usually be devised which will make clear that such statements are not assurances regarding the quality of the product and are not part of the sales contract. In the instance of a shrink wrap license, it is unlikely that a disclaimer as to these types of warranties would be effective as courts are electing to prevent vendors from "giving with one hand and taking away with the other." However, if the contract consists of a sales document or license which was negotiated and executed by the parties as equal bargaining partners, courts are much more likely to allow disclaimers of warranties to stand. It is important to continually review all advertisements and marketing pieces as well as to instruct your sales staff regarding the legal effect of the statements they make to your customers.

➢ Implied Warranties

If your software transaction is governed by the Uniform Commercial Code (U.C.C.), which does not strictly apply to software programming services per se, but does apply to "goods" such as a computer system sold with software installed, two types of implied warranties may arise. These warranties are the warranty of merchantability and the warranty of fitness for a particular purpose. These warranties are not triggered by representations on the part of the software vendor but arise by operation of law. The warranty of merchantability provides that in every sale of goods there is a promise that the software is suited for the ordinary purposes for which such software would be used. That is, if a certain type of software would be expected to have a ten-year life span or would be used to calculate dates beyond the year 2000 in ordinary circumstances, failure to provide a Y2000-compliant product would constitute a breach of that warranty. An investigation must be made to determine the ordinary expectations of a user of this type of software prior to determining whether a breach has actually occurred.

The implied warranty of fitness for a particular purpose arises when the vendor has knowledge that the purchaser is buying the product in order to fulfill a particular need and that the purchaser is relying on the superior skill or knowledge of the vendor to provide the appropriate product. This warranty is especially significant in instances in which the vendor is also serving as a software developer or as a consultant to the purchaser of the software. In the situation where a customer comes to a developer and asks for a particular type of system which would need to operate beyond the year 2000, failure of that developer to cause the system to be Y2000 compliant would constitute a breach of this warranty. Both of these implied warranties may be disclaimed in a contract for the sale of the software if such disclaimer conforms to the requirements of the U.C.C. Otherwise, the disclaimer will be considered to be ineffective and liability can arise for breach.

Tort (Wrongful Act or Damage) Liability:

Possible non-contract claims which might arise in a software transaction concerning a non-Y2000 compliant software product include fraud and misrepresentation, fraud in the inducement, negligent misrepresentation, professional malpractice, negligent design, and strict liability.

> Fraud and Misrepresentation

Tangentially connected to a claim for breach of express warranty, a claim for fraud and misrepresentation requires the purchaser to prove that the software vendor had intent to deceive and that the customer detrimentally relied on the deceptive representation. This type of claim is very difficult to prove and is many times precluded by a claim for breach of contract under express warranty if an intent to deceive cannot be shown. Additionally, as discussed above, a properly drafted contract disclaimer can greatly limit the potential liability stemming from express representations. Liability for fraud arises just as it sounds: if you intentionally represent a system to be Y2000 compliant (when you know that it's not) in order to induce a purchaser to buy, liability for fraud can arise.

> Fraud in the Inducement

A claim of fraud in the inducement can be made when a plaintiff believes that it was led to enter into a contract due to the fraudulent misrepresentations of the vendor. In instances where statements outside the contract are effectively disclaimed with regards to the performance of the software, a fraud in the inducement claim could still be made to seek recovery outside the contract altogether if the vendor intentionally misleads the customer regarding the contents of the contract. For example, a vendor could represent that the contract protects the customer (or provides a remedy against the vendor) from Y2000 problems when it really doesn't.

> Negligent Misrepresentation

This cause of action is not available in all states, but in those states that do recognize it, a buyer is able to recover for a misrepresentation without being required to prove deceptive intent on the part of the vendor. Liability under this theory might arise if a vendor were to assure a customer that a particular system was Y2000 compliant without knowing whether this was true. If a plaintiff can show that the statement was, in fact, not true and the vendor should have reasonably known this, liability under this theory may arise. However, liability under this theory may be limited because states which allow this cause of action usually require proof of a special relationship between the parties which gives rise to a duty on the part of the vendor to provide accurate and non-misleading information.

➤ Professional Malpractice

Although this particular claim has not been fully litigated in the courts yet, it remains a viable claim in the instance of non-Y2000 compliant software, especially in the instance of custom designed software which is developed by specialized software firms. Under this theory, "professionals" are held to a higher standard of care than ordinary vendors. A vendor who holds itself out as having special expertise or training in Y2000 issues may run into trouble if it fails to live up to its billing.

➤ Negligent Design and Strict Liability

These two theories arise under a products liability theory of recovery. Accordingly, courts are usually reluctant to allow recovery under a negligent design or strict liability standard if only economic damage is alleged. However, in the instance where non-Y2000 compliance leads to the personal injury of an individual, design flaws inherent in the product could lead to a viable claim for negligent design or strict liability. The potential exposure for such claims in the event of an avionics software program or a medical equipment software program can be astronomical if Y2000 compliance is not immediately reviewed and remedied, if necessary.

How You Can Limit Your Potential Liability:

➤ Vendors

As discussed above, vendors can limit their potential contractual liability by disclaiming warranties. Express representations outside the contract can be limited by including appropriate integration and merger clauses. These clauses would state clearly that the terms of the contract control and that representations not contained in the contract are inoperative. However, such clauses do not bar the tort claims of fraud and misrepresentation as discussed above, so additional assurances must be sought from the customer to the effect that the customer did not rely on any representations outside of the contract when deciding to make the software purchase.

A liquidated damages provision can be included in all contracts provided that the estimate of damages stated in the contract is a reasonable estimate of damage incurred due to breach of contract. Recovery can also be limited to the repair or replacement of the software, in this case the upgrade or modification of the current software version to a Y2000 compliant version. As long as these types of provisions are negotiated between the parties and are made explicit in the contract, courts are likely to let them stand. However, before entering into such an agreement you should have the agreement reviewed by competent legal counsel. Placing similar limitations on product liability claims is much more difficult than the contract disclaimers for fraud and misrepresentation discussed above. However, these claims are also much more difficult for the plaintiff to prove and, hence, recovery is difficult.

If you believe that you are facing exposure for potential tort liability, it is best to take immediate remedial measures in order to correct any perceived defects in the software due to non-Y2000 compliance. For vendors, the road to the year 2000 is fraught with danger and potential liability. Attention to the niceties of copyright ownership and appropriate contracting and sales activities can make the transition much smoother. There is a tremendous business opportunity presented by the Y2000 problem. However, the potential for liability, if not addressed early, looms just as large.

Buyers

For software purchasers, you may be wondering now what you can do to protect your rights if you have made non-Y2000 compliant software purchases. There are effective ways in which customers can protect themselves from the above limitations of liability and recover damages which may result from defective software. Many of the problems faced by computer software purchasers can be avoided by diligent negotiation and attention to contract drafting. Remember, you are the customer. In many instances a vendor will be willing to modify their standard contract (even if it is on a pre-printed form) in order to get your business. If you are paying for a software system which should reasonably take you beyond the year 2000, you are entitled to assurance that you get what you pay for. In the event that the software vendor attempts to limit all warranties express or implied in the contract, it is advisable to require the software vendor to provide some warranties stating that the software will meet some objectively determined performance criteria. Therefore, before entering into a software purchase contract, it is helpful to determine exactly what your expectations of the software's performance will be and make every attempt possible to include these terms in the contract.

Furthermore, if you are relying on any particular representations outside of the contract as the basis for your purchase, you should have those included by reference in the contract as well. For example, if you are relying on a copy of the user's manual to determine whether the software will perform in accordance with your needs, a reference in the contract incorporating the manual will serve as a warranty from the vendor that the software will perform as depicted in the manual.

Reference to external representations and documents can also serve as the basis for a claim for fraud, misrepresentation, or negligent design. The purchaser of software should also make some provision for warranting future performance. This means that a purchaser of software should ensure it has a reasonable period in which to test and review the software in order to determine that such software conforms to the user's expectations and the representations provided in the contract. A test period should be provided to determine whether the software is Y2000 compliant. This is necessary because, even though the vendor may warrant that the system is Y2000 compliant and would therefore be liable under the contract if the system failed with the turn of the century, you can protect yourself from the disruption of your business if you are able to assess any deficiencies prior to that date.

54   *Recommended Contract Language*

General Services Administration

Commercial Supply Products Warranty

This clause is recommended for voluntary use by Federal agencies in their solicitations and contracts for Year 2000 compliant software, hardware, and systems comprised of commercial information technology products with the following exceptions: (1) the requirement will not continue to exist after December 31, 1999, or (2) the agency has decided to accept offers from vendors that do not have the needed Year 2000 compliant products, but will be required under the contract to upgrade the information technology items to be Year 2000 compliant by a suitable date in advance of the year 2000. The clause may be used when some but not all of the products being acquired are required to be Year 2000 compliant.

The words "listed below" in the clause refer to products that the offeror has identified as being Year 2000 compliant in response to the procuring agency's specifications. For unlisted products, contracting officers are reminded to adhere to the provisions of Federal Acquisition Regulations (FAR) Part 12, and to obtain an express warranty that includes repair and replacement of any such defective unlisted products discovered within a reasonable period of time after acceptance if merchantability and fitness for use are waived and not included in the offeror's commercial warranty for those unlisted products.

Year 2000 Warranty—Commercial Supply Items

The contractor warrants that each hardware, software, and firmware product delivered under this contract and listed below shall be able to accurately process date data (including, but not limited to, calculating, comparing, and sequencing) from, into, and between the twentieth and twenty-first centuries, including leap year calculations, when used in accordance with the product documentation provided by the contractor, provided that all listed or unlisted products (e.g., hardware, software, firmware) used in combination with such listed product properly exchange date data with it. If the contract requires that specific listed products must perform as a system in accordance with the foregoing warranty, then that warranty shall apply to those listed products as a system. The duration of this warranty and the remedies available to the Government for breach of this warranty shall be defined in, and subject to, the terms and limitations of the contractor's standard commercial warranty or warranties contained in this contract, provided that notwithstanding any provision to the contrary in such commercial warranty or warranties, the remedies available to the Government under this warranty shall include repair or replacement of any listed product whose non-compliance is discovered and made known to the contractor in writing within ninety (90) days after acceptance. Nothing is this warranty shall be construed to limit any rights or remedies the Government may otherwise have under this contract with respect to defects other than Year 2000 performance.

Note for solicitations and new contracts: The solicitation should describe the existing computer system or the products (i.e., firmware, middleware, etc.) that will be used with the commercial products and systems being acquired, and as appropriate, whether those existing systems and products are Year 2000 compliant, and any efforts currently underway to provide this capability.

Note for existing contracts: It is recommended that agencies negotiate modifications to existing contracts for acquisition of new products using the above clause as a guide. Prior to modifying the contract, the project team must ensure (1) that performance is possible considering the characteristics of the existing products, (2) the suppliers' agreements with the integrator will allow this work to be performed, (3) cost of performance will not be prohibitive, and (4) that the contractor will agree to the modification (should be a bilateral modification). The Government may elect to acquire versions of those products that warrant accurate performance in the processing of date and date related data.

Non-Commercial Supply Items Warranty

This clause is recommended for voluntary use by agencies for their solicitations and contracts for custom computer items (e.g., hardware, software, and systems) with the following exceptions: (1) the requirement will not continue to exist after December 31, 1999, or (2) the agency has decided to accept offers from vendors that do not have the needed Year 2000 compliant items, but will be required under the contract to upgrade those items to be Year 2000 compliant by a suitable date in advance of the Year 2000. The clause may be used when some but not all of the items being acquired are required to be Year 2000 compliant. The words "listed below" in the clause refer to items that the offeror has identified as being Year 2000 compliant in response to the procuring agency's specifications.

> _The contractor warrants that each non-commercial item of hardware, software, and firmware delivered or developed under this contract and listed below shall be able to accurately process date data (including, but not limited to, calculating, comparing, and sequencing) from, into, and between the twentieth and twenty-first centuries, including leap year calculations, when used in accordance with the item documentation provided by the contractor, provided that all listed or unlisted items (e.g., hardware, software, firmware) used in combination with such listed item properly exchange date data with it. If the contract requires that specific listed items must perform as a system in accordance with the foregoing_

warranty, then that warranty shall apply to those listed items as a system. The duration of this warranty and the remedies available to the Government for breach of this warranty shall be as defined in, and subject to, the terms and limitations of any general warranty provisions of this contract, provided that notwithstanding any provision to the contrary in such warranty provision(s), or in the absence of any such warranty provision(s), the remedies available to the Government under this warranty shall include repair or replacement of any listed item whose non-compliance is discovered and made known to the contractor in writing within ninety (90) days after acceptance. Nothing in this warranty shall be construed to limit any rights or remedies the Government may otherwise have under this contract with respect to defects other than Year 2000 performance.

Note for solicitations and new contracts: The solicitation should describe the existing computer system or the items (i.e., firmware, middleware, etc.) that will be used with the software and systems being acquired, and as appropriate, whether those existing systems, items, and software are Year 2000 compliant, any efforts currently underway to provide this capability.

Note for existing contracts: It is recommended that agencies negotiate modifications to existing contracts for acquisition of new items using the above clause as a guide. Prior to modifying the contract, the project team must ensure (1) that performance is possible considering the characteristics of the existing items, (2) the suppliers' agreements with the integrator will allow this work to be performed, (3) cost of performance will not be prohibitive, and (4) that the contractor will agree to the modification (should be a bilateral modification). The Government may elect to acquire versions of those items that warrant accurate performance in the processing of date and date related data.

55   *Warranty and Compliance Agreements*

Timothy Feathers
Hillix, Brewer, Hoffhaus, Whittaker & Wright, L.L.C.

> **Note:** *NOBODY takes responsibility for how you use this document. You are strongly advised to consult with your own legal counsel in all legal matters. This is provided only to serve as an example of what might be included in a Y2K Warranty.*

1. Licensor represents and warrants that the Software is designed to be used prior to, during, and after the calendar year 2000 A.D., and that the Software will operate during each such time period without error relating to date data, specifically including any error relating to, or the product of, date data which represents or references different centuries or more than one century.

2. Without limiting the generality of the foregoing, Licensor further represents and warrants:

   a. That the Software will not abnormally end or provide invalid or incorrect results as a result of date data, specifically including date data which represents or references different centuries or more than one century;

   b. That the Software has been designed to ensure year 2000 compatibility, including, but not limited to, date data century recognition, calculations which accommodate same century and multi-century formulas and date values, and date data interface values that reflect the century;

   c. That the software includes "year 2000 capabilities." For the purposes of this Agreement, "year 2000 capabilities" means the Software:

      • (i) will manage and manipulate data involving dates, including single century formulas and multi-century formulas, and will not cause an abnormally ending scenario within the application or generate incorrect values or invalid results involving such dates; and

      • (ii) provides that all date-related user interface functionalities and data fields include the indication of century; and

      • (iii) provides that all date-related data interface functionalities include the indication of century.

3. Definitions

   ➤ Four Digit Year Format

      shall mean a format that allows entry or processing of a four digit year date: the first two digits will designate the century and the second two digits shall designate the year within the century. As an example, 1996 shall mean the 96th year of the 20th century.

> Leap Year

shall mean the year during which an extra day is added in February (February 29th). Leap Year occurs in all years divisible by 400 or evenly divisible by 4 and not evenly divisible by 100. For example, 1996 is a Leap Year since it is divisible by 4 and not evenly divisible by 100. 2000 is a Leap Year since it is divisible by 400.

> Year 2000 Compliant

shall mean that the data outside of the range 1990-1999 will be correctly processed in any level of computer hardware or software including, but not limited to, microcode, firmware, application programs, files and databases.

4. Year 2000 Compliance Performance Warranty Licensor further warrants and represents that the Product is and will continue to be Year 2000 Compliant. All date processing by Product will include Four Digit Year Format and recognize and correctly process dates for Leap Year. Additionally, all date sorting by Product that includes a "year category" shall be done based on the Four Digit Year Format code.

5. Remedies for Non-Compliance of Warranty Licensor agrees to pay liquidated damages in the amount of $per day for each day the Product fails to maintain and uphold the Year 2000 Compliance Performance Warranty described in Section of this Agreement.

Year 2000 Warranties

Licensor represents and warrants that:

A. The Software will function without error or interruption related to Date Data, specifically including errors or interruptions from functions which may involve Date Data from more than one century;

B. The Software requires that all Date Data (whether received from users, systems, applications or other sources) include an indication of century in each instance;

C. All date output and results, in any form, shall include an indication of century in each instance.

When used in this Section _, the term "Date Data" shall mean any data or input which includes an indication of or reference to date. The foregoing is in addition to the other representations and warranties set forth herein.

Year 2000 Compliance Agreement

THIS COMPLIANCE AGREEMENT is made by and between _____("Licensee") and _____ ("Licensor") effective as of the _____ day of_____ 199__

Recitals

WHEREAS, Licensor and Licensee are parties to that certain Software License Agreement dated 19___ (the "License Agreement"); and

WHEREAS, Licensee has requested that Licensor provide additional warranties regarding the Software, particularly regarding Year 2000 Compliance (as hereafter defined); and

WHEREAS, Licensor is willing to provide the requested warranties on the terms and conditions set forth in this Agreement.

NOW, THEREFORE, in consideration of the Recitals, the continuation of the relationship between Licensor and Licensee, the mutual promises and agreements set forth in the License Agreement, and herein, and for the sum of One Hundred Dollars and other good and valuable consideration, the receipt and sufficiency of which are acknowledged, the parties hereto agree as follows:

1. Year 2000 Compliance.

    1.1 Licensor represents and warrants that the Software is designed to be used prior to, during, and after the calendar year 2000 A.D., and that the Software will operate during each such time period without error relating to date data, specifically including any error relating to, or the product of, date data which represents or references different centuries or more than one century.

    1.2 Without limiting the generality of the foregoing, Licensor further represents and warrants:

    - 1.2.1 That the Software will not abnormally end or provide invalid or incorrect results as a result of date data, specifically including date data which represents or references different centuries or more than one century;

    - 1.2.2 That the Software has been designed to ensure year 2000 compatibility, including, but not limited to, date data century recognition, calculations which accommodate same century and multi-century formulas and date values, and date data interface values that reflect the century;

- 1.2.3 That the software includes "year 2000 capabilities." For the purposes of this Agreement, "year 2000 capabilities" means the Software:
  - (i) will manage and manipulate data involving dates, including single century formulas and multi-century formulas, and will not cause an abnormally ending scenario within the application or generate incorrect values or invalid results involving such dates; and
  - (ii) provides that all date-related user interface functionalities and data fields include the indication of century; and
  - (iii) provides that all date-related data interface functionalities include the indication of century.

1.3 The term "Year 2000 Compliance Warranty" shall mean, collectively, the warranties set forth in this Section 1.

2. Term. The Year 2000 Compliance Warranty set forth herein shall begin as of the date of the License Agreement and end on the date after January 1, 2000, subsequent to which the Software has operated without a breach of the Year 2000 Compliance Warranty for a consecutive six month period.

3. Waiver of Limitation of Liability. Any provisions of the License Agreement which tend to limit or eliminate the liability of either party shall have no application with respect to the Year 2000 Compliance Warranty set forth herein.

4. Limitation on Use/Limitation on Liability. In the event that Licensee is entitled to modify the software pursuant to the License Agreement, Licensee agrees that it shall not modify the Software in any manner which would affect the performance of the Software in such a manner as to cause it to fail to meet the Year 2000 Compliance Warranty set forth herein. There shall be no liability on the part of Licensor for any failure of the Software to conform to the Year 2000 Compliance Warranty to the extent that any such failure is attributable to a modification of the Software by Licensee

5. Provisions of Compliance Agreement Controlling. In the event of any conflict or apparent conflict between the terms and conditions of the License Agreement and the terms and conditions of this Compliance Agreement, the terms and conditions of this Compliance Agreement shall control. Except to the extent otherwise set forth herein, the terms and conditions of the License Agreement shall remain in full force and effect.

6. Entire Agreement. This Compliance Agreement, together with the License Agreement, constitutes the entire agreement between the parties

with respect to the subject matter hereof. This Compliance Agreement shall not be modified except by later written agreement signed by both parties

IN WITNESS WHEREOF the parties have executed this Agreement the day and date first set forth above.

---

56   *Challenges and Legal Aspects*

Warren Reid
WSR Consulting Group, LLC

The Legal Trend

There is an increasing trend toward litigation as a solution to failed systems and failed systems projects. In fact, the future of your success as a user, developer, or an executive may not depend on the brilliance of your technical staff, the speed of taking your product idea to market or your global strategic alliances. In today's ever complex society, Silicon Valley and business users are finding the newest high-tech growth industry to be—litigation! And I believe the Year 2000 Millennium Bug will move the law *over the top!*

Up until now, when there have been serious systems failures such as the Denver Airport Baggage Handling System, Domino's Pizza Delivery System, or Adidas International's Shoe Distribution system, the solution typically was to terminate the Chief Information Officer or the project manager responsible for the project. However, because of the sure impact of the Year 2000 Millennium Bug, new laws and interpretations will be created to motivate and punish the today's real culprits for the Year 2000 Bug—that is, management and their reluctance to do anything about it!

First, a Word from Our Sponsor—The Millennium Bug

When our clocks ring in the new millennium, they will also tighten the noose around many computer systems and the companies that rely upon them. This is because hundreds of thousands of companies and sites have legacy systems that include hard-coded date fields that allow only two bytes to express the "year" field—so, 1999 is stored as "99," and 2000 is stored as "00." Subtracting 1999 from 2000 results in "-99" (i.e., "00 minus 99"), which will cause calculations that rely on that result later in the programs to surely go awry in inexplicable ways, create errors and/ or crash!

In addition to that, most of today's chips used in PCs and microcomputers that keep track of time will fail (especially if the computer is turned off, then back on again) as a result of the 12/31/99 to 1/1/00 (sic) crossing. They will automatically reset to 1/1/80. This problem can easily be addressed by chip manufacturers by the Year 2000, but you must get those chips into your machines.

Just think of this scenario which can be even worse than the Bank Holiday mandated by President Roosevelt, whereby the President closed banks until they could be audited for stability and control before re-opening weeks and weeks later. If you had no money in your pocket, you had to barter or somehow muddle along.

While approximately 75 percent of all banks and insurance companies are beginning to develop plans to address the Year 2000 Millennium problem, virtually no one else is. Today, some favorite magazines won't let one subscribe for five years (i.e., past the Year 2000) because their systems won't allow it. Others will, but are keeping all of the paperwork around so that they can re-enter my subscription for an additional year after they address the problem (twice the work)! Also, once we fix, and test, and re-compile, and re-document and implement all of the fixes, how will we run our archive files—which operate under the two digit restriction of the old systems?

Worse Than You Think

Many problems typically not associated with the millennium change will occur on January 1, 1999. The same programmers, designers, and developers who didn't think their system would still be in use in the Year 2000 also did not believe those same systems would still be in use in the year 1999. Therefore, they coded the two-digit year field with the characters "99" to have a special logic. For instance if someone was entering the dates of legal documents into a database and no year was specified in that document, the coders would enter a "99" as a default. Third party tape library management systems use the "99" code to activate special instructions for destroying or archiving tape libraries. In other applications, programmers may use the "99" to mean end of file. In each instance, the year 1999, as stored simply as "99," will cause errors as the special logic takes over.

Accordingly, it is smart to have your millennium solution implemented and tested by December 31, 1998. *Since it is wise to leave a full year for necessary testing and surprises, companies with large, sophisticated systems should target December 31, 1997 as the critical date.* Given the track record for systems developers as being too-overly-optimistic or unskilled in estimating complex and massive systems maintenance projects, this targeted date will be missed in most cases. One targeted date that cannot be missed, and cannot be negotiated away, is January 1, 2000!

It will come, but your technology staff may not come with it! Due to the shortage of programmers to address this problem, many of your key and talented technology staff-persons, who could develop and implement a solution within your company, will be hired away for far greater "consulting fees" than their current salaries—leaving you and your company in a most precarious position. The Wall Street Journal recently indicated that executive search firms are beginning to specialize in the "Year 2000 Solutions Executives." Where do you think these executives will come from? Whom will they steal from you?

Peter de Jager, in recent testimony to the Science Committee of the House of Representatives stated, "Computer practitioners are the most optimistic people in the world. Despite all evidence to the contrary, we believe that the next application we write will be bug-free. We believe the bug we just found is the last one. We believe the next release of a software product will solve all the errors in the prior release and introduce no new ones. Sadly, these beliefs are totally without foundation..."

It is time to specify your problem, identify the impact, develop a plan given your corporate constraints and liabilities, and proceed with your solutions at full speed. And for goodness sakes, *leave time to fix the new errors that are introduced during the fix process!*

Look Before You Leap

To make matters worse, the Year 2000 is a leap year, which most developers have forgotten. But in the modern business world, losing one day can have major ramifications, especially in terms of payrolls, interest calculations, due dates, comparative financials, employee benefits, welfare checks and so on.

I must share a most interesting story about my current Mexican holiday at this point. On a recent trip to Puerto Vallarta, I found myself on a "booze cruise"—where the drinks flowed readily. As I rarely drink, I stayed aside from most of the other people and engaged myself in conversation with a couple standing near the railing at the far side of the ship. The gentleman I was talking to was a mid-level information systems manager for a large regional transportation company. After talking for awhile, I asked whether he had heard of the Year 2000 problem and how he and his company were preparing for it. A broad smile covered his face. "We fixed it already!" he replied. I was impressed to say the least—but also a little bit skeptical.

I followed with, "Did you know that the year 2000 was a 'leap year?'"

"Heck" he responded. "it's not only a leap year—it's a 'super leap year!'—it has thirty days!"

I asked myself in disbelief, "Where do otherwise sane folks get these crazy ideas?" After more discussion, we finally tracked down this erroneous conception to something that he had heard on a famous television quiz show—probably its first wrong answer in years. Well, it's back to the drawing boards for this company—otherwise paychecks will be delayed albeit perhaps a bit larger, and schedules will be messed up.

Directors

Fortune 500 companies can expect $20–$40 million each on average to address the problem. The painful truth is that you do not even get anything for your effort (like new reports, more capability, improved performance, more detail, etc.)—except the ability to open your doors on the first or second of January, 2000.

Examine what might happen to an organization's management elite—the Board of Directors. It is the legal obligation of Directors of US companies to act as the "stewards of the company's assets." It is their job to plan and perform strategically. Thirty years ago, in the area of corporate systems, the failure of internal computers would have been an inconvenience to US companies. By contrast today, a failure today would cripple most businesses!

Because the Year 2000 Millennium Bug is certain and material, and because it will continue to be discussed more openly in daily press and magazines, officers will not be able to hide behind the fact that this was beyond their control or knowledge. In fact, even the "excusable delay" clauses typically found in contracts, which hold that corporations shall not be responsible for failure or delay in performance of their obligations under an agreement because of Acts of God and due to causes beyond their reasonable control, *will provide no succor for directors* . The Year 2000 Millennium Bug is known and *will come* , and doing nothing about it will not be a defense, even if the argument is "we were unable to predict or didn't know how bad it was going to be." In addition, Directors will need to have some insight into the health of the corporation's key suppliers so that even if their own company is ready and Year 2000 Compliant, it won't be affected materially by second-hand bugs.

Outsourcers

In addition, I think outsourcing and/or software maintenance companies will also have an extra responsibility (almost a fiduciary responsibility) to ensure that the information assets of its customers are protected and will continue to perform without interruption. In fact, outsourcers today are marketing to potential customers the promise that they will address the Year 2000 for their customers as part of the Outsourcing deal—a truly tempting offer.

An outsourcer or maintenance company that fails to adequately address the Year 2000 problem will be hit hard. They will find little or no sympathy from the legal system and juries will judge such companies as negligent or grossly negligent. In such situations, in addition to the losses, punitive damages may even be assessed. Some lawyer colleagues believe that the closer the Outsourcing contract is signed to the Year 2000, the more likely the Outsourcer will be held liable for such problems— even if the issue is not specifically addressed in the contract at all.

Other Parties

Lastly, venture capitalists, vendors, bankers, investment companies, and others that directly or indirectly invest or make loans to companies, will need to know the compliance of the systems of the company regarding the year 2000 standards. If you recommend that your clients invest in companies that cannot ship or receive goods, pay their payrolls, or provide promised or mandated employee benefits because of Year 2000 defects, you may be liable for not performing due diligence, meeting industry standards, malpractice or much worse. Obviously, the same will be true for insurance companies and reinsurers. If you insure a company that is doing nothing about the Year 2000 Bug, how can you say you did your due diligence in writing insurance for that party?

While it is possible for some organizations and consultants to limit their liability through specific disclaimers and limitations of damages, and express warranties, it really behooves executives, legislators, and industries as a whole to work together to solve this problem. If you think it isn't going to be pretty the way you understand it now, just think about trying to work this out in a courtroom environment!

Another Word of Caution

Many legacy systems are written in languages where the supply of programmers is very limited indeed—language such as Pascal, PL/1, JOVIAL, BAL, etc., and where structured and modular coding techniques and documentation were oftentimes ignored. In addition, some of these programs are of systems software complexity, adding yet another dimension for failure.

Secondly, people often think they will simply be able to search their source code (if it exists) for "YY" (i.e., the data mask for a two-digit year). According to Human Resource Systems expert Timothy S. Laundrie, where security is foremost, variable names encoded into human indecipherable codes won't be found looking for "YY" dates:

- hire date
- date in job
- date in department
- adjusted service date
- birth date
- date next salary review
- date next performance review
- benefit enrollment date
- benefit eligibility date
- date last record change
- date last salary change
- date last physical exam
- family member birth dates
- company property expiration dates
- license/certification expiration dates
- earnings date
- deductions start date
- deductions end date
- I-9 verification date
- leave of absence start
- leave of absence end
- termination date
- education/membership dates
- skills dates
- on-the-job industry dates

In mid 1996, the Assistant Secretary of the Navy issued a memo on the Internet regarding the Year 2000 problem survey, and enclosed formal worksheets entitled "Department of the Navy Year 2000 Problem Survey." In the cover sheet, the Secretary states:

It is imperative we assure the reliability and dependability of De-partmentoftheNavysystems,whetherautomatedinformationsys-tems,commandandcontrolapplications,orweaponssystems. We areactivelyengagedinanawarenesscampaigntoensurethatevery Department of the Navy system is assessed for potential impact of the Year 2000 problem. The awareness campaign includes a world wide web page located at url http://www.nismc.navy.mil. Further, we are assisting with the Department of Defense in a proactive dia-loguewithindustryassociationsforYear2000compliantproducts.

I request your assistance to assess the **entire inventory of systems under your purview** *(emphasis provided) for potential Year 2000 problems. Enclosure (1) includes two worksheets, the first for data gathering,and the second for reporting cumulative status to my ac-tion officer by 10 July 1996 and semi-annually thereafter until all cited problems have been fixed, tested, and successfully fielded...*

What is of importance is not only that to do business with the Navy, and later the entire Department of Defense, you will have to be Year 2000 compliant in the systems that you sell and deliver, but also that all of your systems, including those internal systems that you use to manage your business, do your accounting, plan your production scheduling, develop your distribution schedules, etc. *must also be Year 2000 compliant.* The implication is that the Government cannot afford to do business with an organization that supplies and maintains Year 2000 compliant soft-ware to the Government, if that organization will not be able to stay in business because of Year 2000 problems in its own internal systems. What good is a five year maintenance contract spanning the millennium, if the organization providing such support is unable to cut paychecks for its employees or invoices for its customers and thus goes into bankruptcy or out of business anyway?

What to Do

If in fact you do find yourself in court five years from now, in front of a jury that the opposing side picked because it had no understanding of computers, what can you do to appropriately defend yourself—now? It turns out that the same tasks you need to perform to defend yourself are also the same ones you need to solve the Year 2000 problem for your organization. So, in this sense, doing the right thing, in fact, will work for your systems, for your organization, as well as in court!

During a court appearance your Chief Information, Financial, Oper-ations, and Executive Officers, along with the Chairman of your Board, will likely receive a subpoena to produce the following, upon which they will be deposed and eventually cross examined:

1. *Homework:*

   Proof that you did your homework. Put together a Steering Committee consisting of Management, Users, Technical Staff, and an outside Consultant, if necessary, to plan and oversee the project—and to make tough decisions regarding how to balance quality, cost, resources, and the drop-dead date. Make sure staffers are afforded the proper and necessary resources such as:

   ➤ Time to attend significant conferences such as the USPDI "Year 2000 Solutions Conference" and others

   ➤ Subscriptions to appropriate magazines such as *Tick, Tick, Tick...* and others

   ➤ Join a regional Solutions 2000 Group so that you can share problems and solutions with others dealing the same challenges

   ➤ Attend software tools vendor demonstrations, so that your company and team can be afforded the "best" tools for your needs

   ➤ Attend appropriate chat sessions and other Internet resources

2. *Project Management and Tools:*

   Assurances that you had proper Project Management in place. When all is said and done, remember that for most CIOs this may well be the largest and most difficult project that they have ever had to manage. There will most likely be multiple operating systems and hardware platforms involved, multiple applications, multiple applications, and multiple internal and external organizations to manage.

   To make matters worse, the project team will be modifying productions systems in pieces. Mistakes can impact current operations, profits, and market share. There are special and unique risks associated with making your mainframe think it's operating in the year 2000 for testing if you are concurrently running today's production. Some software will even begin to destroy itself if it recognizes that you are trying to operate it after the license data expires (which can very well be in 1998 or 1999).

   Testing specialists, selected configuration management and change control tools, and interactive testing tools and methodologies must be in place to assure that production is not inadvertently impacted. Special testbeds will be required to allow for operating current production systems concurrently with simulated future-dated environments.

3. *Software Inventory:*

   An inventory of software at your company (beginning today) including:

➤ Source Code
➤ Object Code (Where Source Doesn't Exist)
➤ Required Compilers
➤ Operating Systems
➤ Utilities
➤ Files
➤ Archives
➤ Third Party Software Applications
➤ Third Party Software Tools

Remember: you have such software on your mainframes, mini-computers, client server networks, and PCs. And with up to 40 percent of all PC applications run without the knowledge of the Information Systems Group, inventorying the latter group is important indeed!

4. *Risk Analysis*:

A Risk Assessment and Statement Of Impact the Year 2000 problem will have on the organization. Risk is the product of "probability of occurrence" and "impact when it does occur." Choose from among your alternative solutions carefully and based upon risk. With adaptation, here are the alternatives as described by UNISYS Team2000:

➤ RE-tire systems or eliminate application functions no longer used or needed
➤ RE-engineer applications to accomplish millennium compliance and perhaps a few critical new functions
➤ RE-source, i.e., outsource your applications
➤ RE-place your applications with commercial applications packages
➤ RE-do your current applications with field expansion or procedure/program modifications (i.e., where possible have your application interpret the two year date fields as 19XX if the two year digits are 50-99, and interpret the data as 20xx if the digits are between 00-49)
➤ RE-format your data base to convert the year fields appropriately
➤ RE-lax, i.e., leave the application as is
➤ RE-sign, especially if management won't commit to supporting the Millennium project.

There is one more "RE" you should also consider as it relates to your archived files: "RE-visit." That is, with all the work required to get 2000 compliant for your production applications, it probably makes sense to not worry about your archives until you really need to access them (unless you are aware of the need for such information for an upcoming merger, acquisition, tax audit, etc.). You can always RE-visit the archive situation later.

5. *Adequate Communications:*

Appropriate communications regarding the problem, impact, and fix process within and across all levels in the organization

6. *A Project Plan:*

A detailed plan of how the problem will be addressed and the required resources in total and on an application basis (software tools, space and time, training, dollars, staff, hardware, special testing software, etc.) needed to fix the problem.

Don't forget to include time and resources for developing interfaces between your systems and outside applications.

7. *Critical Path Analysis:*

A budget and critical path analysis to ensure the "appropriate" projects are undertaken first, typically a combination of: (1) simple and fast projects to allow the software team to get into a "success mentality" and (2) the programs with the most negative impact on the organization.

8. *Suitable Documentation:*

Appropriate documents to show that the plan was executed and that the commitments made by management to fix the problem were, in fact, executed on a timely and professional basis. Defect tracking/analysis tools, complexity analyzers, test path coverage analyzers, debuggers, and test execution monitors are also helpful in proving this area.

9. *Reliable Status Reports:*

Frank and true status reports indicating the:
- Work plan for the period
- Work completed during the period
- Problems that arose
- Solutions that were implemented
- Work plan for next period
- Summary of Good and Bad News

10. *Documentation of Alternatives:*

Documents supporting the investigation of the following alternatives to help address the Year 2000 problem:
- Use of outside consultants

> Use of part-time employees or special tiger tech team
> Specialized training
> Deferring of implementation of new systems to correct the current systems
> Advancing the implementation of new systems to eliminate the current systems
> Use of special tools of all kinds to enhance the productivity of the Year 2000 fix team, and the quality of all the fixes.

Example of a "Millennium Compliance" Provision

With all the risk associated with the Millennium change, it is probably smart to try to memorialize your company's policy into a "millennium compliance" contract provision. This is important not only for dealings with your external vendors of hardware, software, and firmware components, but also appropriate for a company's own internal focus on in-house developed software. Note this is not a substitute for specific standards to be used by developers when constructing new software.

Conclusion

Failing to fix your upcoming Year 2000 problem can not only cause disruption and loss of market share, productivity, and profitability in your company, but will expose the company and you to class action law suits, possible loss of coverage from insurance companies, malpractice for professionals, and director and officer liability.

The good news is that if you address the problem in a planned and professional manner, and execute and implement reliable solutions, you will most likely be in fine shape in a court of law. Note that there is no requirement that all your solutions be perfect and complete. The Year 2000 problem was caused by short-sightedness and human error. Some human error will still be allowed for by the courts when looking at failed solutions—as long as you follow a well accepted process like that outlined above. Your solutions must materially work—but do not have to be perfect!

57 *Ten Action Items*

Ira Kasdan
Galland, Kharasch & Garfinkle, P.C.

By now you've heard all about the Year 2000 problem. From all the hype in the press you know that as things stand today, on Saturday January 1, 2000, your corporation's computers and data bases will "think" that it is Monday, January 1, 1900—if they "think" at all. You have yet to hear from your CEO or CFO, but you know that sooner rather than later they will be seeking your opinion on the legal ramifications stemming from the problem. Are you prepared? Do you have a game plan? Do you even know what the legal issues are? Ready or not, you ought to be considering the following action items.

There are at least five legal areas of concern, some of which cut across each other: (1) D&O liability; (2) licensing, copyright, warranty, and related questions; (3) employment/personnel matters; (4) issues of insurance coverage; and (5) lawsuits by and against your company.

D&O Liability

One, if not a major, responsibility of in-house counsel is to advise directors and officers of their susceptibility to legal exposure. While in-house counsel, in their representation of the corporation, may be conflicted from representation of board members and company personnel in their individual capacity, corporate lawyers must protect directors and officers when the corporation's interests coincide with the interests of the corporation's business people. The Year 2000 problem represents such an instance.

Most states require directors and officers to exercise a duty of care consistent with that of an ordinary prudent person in similar circumstances. That means (at the very least) that, if your competitor is addressing the Year 2000 problem and your company is not, there will be D&O exposure. Simply stated, if a corporation does not take appropriate steps to assess and rectify the Year 2000 problem and the corporation suffers financially as a result, blame will be laid squarely at the doorstep of directors and officers.

Thus, **action item no. 1** for in-house counsel is to make sure that your board and officers are aware of the Year 2000 problem. With that awareness, the corporation should designate appropriate people and/or committees to analyze the scope of the Year 2000 problem and begin implementing remedial steps to fix it.

For their own and the corporation's protection, the actions taken by management to identify and rectify the Year 2000 problem should be documented and preserved. Although a *paper trail* could contain (at best) embarrassing and (at worst) *damaging* information that can be discovered in litigation later on, this risk is outweighed by the risk of not being able to establish the diligence with which the corporation pursued corrective action. Of course, this does not mean that one should not exercise care before committing something to writing. Nonetheless, the "Business Judgment Rule," under which courts will not impose liability for honest mistakes of business judgment, should shield the corporation and its helmsmen from the perils normally associated with a paper trail—provided that there is no fraud, illegality, or conflict of interest, which, in any case, the "Business Judgment Rule" obviously does not protect.

Action Item no. 2 is to analyze what (if any) disclosures must be made to shareholders. Matters to be considered for disclosure include, but are not necessarily limited to, the degree of the company's Year 2000 problem, the projected costs of remediation and whether such costs will materially affect the company's bottom line. In making this latter determination, a critical issue will be whether the costs will be treated as capital expenditures that can be spread over a number of years or will be considered business expenses that can be charged immediately. It is highly advisable for in-house counsel, the company's CFO, and its outside auditors to coordinate the company's stance on these issues.

Licensing, Copyright, Warranty, and Related Issues

It will be up to management to decide whether to replace or repair computer systems affected by the Year 2000 problem. In order to make an informed decision, management will need to know, through its in-house staff or outside experts, the flexibility it may have to modify existing code. This, in turn, will depend on how restrictive the agreements and licenses that govern those systems are.

Consequently, **action item no. 3** is for corporate counsel to initiate an audit of all software agreements and licenses to determine what contractual provisions will come into play if the company chooses remediation over replacement. The company's rights to remediate will require a careful review of such clauses in the original agreements with outside vendors that cover the use of the program, ownership of the technology, copyright grants, warranties, and remedies for system failures. At the same time, the legal auditors should look out for contractual provisions, such as limitations on liability clauses, that may figure prominently in potential future litigation against the original software providers.

Even if management decides to replace rather than to repair software, there is an important role for counsel. The last thing a company needs is to spend millions and later discover that its newly installed systems are not Year 2000 compliant. **Action item no. 4**, therefore, is for company attorneys to ensure that contracts for the purchase or installation of replacement components precisely define what Year 2000 "compliance" is and how it will be demonstrated well in advance of the turn of the century. In this regard, the parties may agree upon the need for third party certification that a system is Year 2000 compliant. Appropriate provisions must be negotiated and drafted to cover these and related matters, such as the remedies available to the company should a newly installed system fail.

Employment/Personnel Matters

The current consensus is that there are not enough adequately trained programmers available to complete the remediation process in the government and private sectors by 2000. And the predictions are that it only will get worse.

It is worth bearing in mind that much of the Year 2000 problem lies in so-called "legacy systems" in which today's programmers are not necessarily well versed. The upshot is that a company which has qualified programmers to fix the problem will need to hold on to them, while companies without the necessary talent pool will seek to hire them away. **Action item no. 5** for in-house counsel is to craft contract terms that will safeguard against company employees being spirited away. It will be the responsibility of counsel to insert into employment agreements reasonable non-compete clauses and appropriate provisions to enable a company to obtain necessary injunctive relief to preserve its workforce. But, more important, management inevitably will be required to offer incentives—bonuses, stock options, extended employment beyond the turn of the century (assuming the Year 2000 software problems are solved by then), and/or lucrative buy-outs and severance terms—to keep employees crucial to the remediation process. These employment contract clauses, too, will need to be drafted by counsel.

Insurance Coverage

Whatever a company does to remedy its Year 2000 problems will cost money—substantial amounts of it. J.P. Morgan & Company has estimated *conservatively* that the total expenditures in the private and public sectors will be in the $200 billion range. Others estimate that the remediation costs will reach $600 billion. Who will be liable for these enormous sums? **Action item no. 6** is for corporate counsel to examine the company's own, and the company's D&O, insurance policies to determine whether there is coverage under general liability and/or errors and omissions provisions, or whether coverage is excluded by other provisions. At the same time, if there is coverage, it is important to ascertain whether the coverage is on an "occurrence" or "claims made" basis (which, in turn, may govern which year's insurance applies).

In addition, **action item no. 7** for in-house counsel is to advise management on new insurance policies that are intended to address Year 2000 issues specifically. As of this writing, it appears that some insurance carriers will cover Year 2000 system failures. However, these policies must be scrutinized carefully by company lawyers to ensure the fullest possible coverage. By the same token, exclusionary provisions must be reviewed just as carefully and, to the extent possible, limited or negotiated out in order to maximize the company's rights.

Finally, as part of **action item no. 8**, counsel should advise company officers that outside remediation services provided to the company must be backed by appropriate insurance, which at a minimum should name your company as an additional insured, and extend at least through the year 2001. It will be counsel's task to request and review those insurance contracts and provide guidance to the company on whether the coverage is adequate from a legal perspective.

Litigation

Is now the time to be thinking about litigation—so far in advance of the turn of the millennium? You better believe it, especially if, when push comes to shove, by December 31, 1999, your company or your suppliers will not be fully Year 2000 compliant.

What preparations should you be taking now? At the very least, **action item no. 9** is to identify the potential parties whom your company may wish to sue and the parties who would sue your company.

The to-sue list will begin to emerge upon your review of the agreements and licenses of vendors who supplied the ineffective software. In addition, you may add to that list companies upon whom your company relies but which themselves do not meet Year 2000 compliance standards. None of this is to say that your company actually will, or will even want to, sue anyone. Indeed, once the lists are readied, the advisable course will be to open lines of communication in order to avoid disputes and lawsuits (provided, of course, that you are not creating a statutes of limitations problem by merely talking instead of litigating). Certainly, the earlier a company initiates negotiations with software and other service providers, the better the chances it will be able to elude a litigious end. On the other hand, you should be ready to draft the appropriate demand letters when and if it becomes appropriate to do so.

As to the list of potential parties who may sue you—such as shareholders or other parties who rely on your company's services and who would be damaged by your company's Year 2000 non-compliance—it will never be too early to prepare. With regard to shareholder suits, the precautionary steps to be taken, as outlined above in connection with director and shareholder liability, obviously should be followed. With regard to those relying on your company's services, it obviously is most prudent for counsel to be able to monitor developments along the way and offer appropriate advice in order to posture the case in the most favorable light for your company.

Finally, you and your company should also keep in mind that pursuing available means of alternative dispute resolution ("ADR"), such as arbitration or mediation, may be a better course of action than courtroom litigation to resolve Year 2000 dispute. Indeed, ADR may be dictated by contract in certain instances.

And so we come to **action item no. 10:** Prayer. Pray that your company listens to those who are warning of the perils of inaction; pray that management heeds those warnings and takes action; and pray that management allows you to implement action items 1 through 9.

7
part

Expert: Seven Methods

Take a moment to review Chapter 7 on code revision, which introduces (and is also named) Seven Methods. This part (Part 7) fleshes out the seven alternatives from many angles—with useful and time-trimming examples.

Larry Baltezore re-introduces "Date Windowing." He gives straight-for-ward explanations of fixed and sliding century windows. Baltezore (among many others) especially likes century windows for applications nearing their sunset. However, with typical code fixes twice as fast as expanding YY to YYYY, century windows have much wider benefits. For instance, "bridging" software can be implemented without coding!

Long ago you paid for IBM's DFSORT or SyncSort's SyncSort. Today, both of them have a Y2K fix that allows you to implement a variety of century window choices. This lets you convert between YY and YYYY. You can also set up a sort leaving the YY as-is, but interpreted. Interestingly, both SORT-sellers represent the stored YY in the same four formats, with identical names.

In DFSORT, using new data type Y2C in "SORT FIELDS (7,2,Y2C,A...)" will sequence against a century window with pivot year at JCL parm Y2PAST=1968 or 30 (if run in 1998). To expand the record, use "OPTION COPY, Y2PAST=1930" along with output file card, "OUTREC=(1,1,Y2D,...)".

With parameter CENTWIN=1968, SyncSort does much the same thing. It has a "sliding window" option: With CENTWIN=30, the pivot year is set at sixty years before whatever today's year is.

It is beneficial immediately to work through Chapters 59 (DFSORT) or 60 (SyncSort). The exercise will cement your understanding of fixed and sliding windows, stirring your imagination concerning cost-free mid-project bridges between non-conformant and Y2K-conformant program groups and data stores.

Dick Lefkon's brief entry suggests you core-store a full list of century window "pivot years" in a table side-by-side with their date application names. [Since the Editor coined that term in 1996, it has become the standard name for the dividing line in a century window.] These parameterized turning points remain external to all code and can be updated annually. They're even useful with source code missing.

Next, Robert Louton compares "Procedural and Data Change:" His GTE diagram provides a logical decision tree for choosing a procedural (century inference) versus data (YYYY) approach. Andrew Eldridge's matching text names code complication as the main drawback for century, while date expansion's sins are of bigness: impact, disk space, cost and project size. Imagine an example for each bullet point and you'll finish wiser than many self-proclaimed Y2K experts.

Gerhard Adam enumerates these two "Change Strategies" and adds a third approach, date encoding. (Show your coders his COBOL examples.) He critiques all three methods and points out the impossibility of a single cross-platform enterprise date standard.

To these, Viasoft adds the option of twinned databases—one Y2K conformant, one not—and opts instead for impregnating programs with "Dynamic Bridging" code that knows whether the record read has format YY or YYYY.

In "Time Shifting," Don Estes remarks that a 28-year downshift keeps most dates in the 1900s while not disturbing the pattern of Sundays etc. Either downshift the stored data or time-shift the years after/before input/output. Estes then continues on, recounting the common types of Y2K code fix and discussing their relative risks.

Last, IBM classifies Y2K "Reformatting" with a full recounting of good and bad points for YYYY, windowing and encoding. IBM emphasizes bridges and urges you use a common date routine enterprise-wide. And only IBM can have you switch to ICF catalogs, ducking VSAM's 991231 deletions: Recent vintage VSAM files already use it; for the efficient ones, use the familiar new/load/erase/rename tactic.

58   *Date Windowing*

Larry Baltezore
State of California

Date windowing is one of many solutions needed to effectively address Year 2000 compliance requirements for any business or agency that develops or maintains custom software applications. Typically, these applications support vital business processes within an enterprise, and regardless of the overall approach chosen to ensure compliance, date windowing is almost certain to be part of the solution.

What Is a Date Window?

A date window is nothing more than computer code used to convert date data from one form to another for internal storage or further manipulation. The most common use of date windowing in this context (Year 2000 compliance) is to convert dates from a 2-digit year field to a 4-digit field that includes the century. The concept is relatively simple. Programmers create logic that establishes a date window of so many years before and after a given year. Additional logic is provided that determines which part of the window the year fits and then the appropriate century digits are added to create a fully specified year field CCYY or YYYY. An example of this window logic borrowed from a California State Agency is as follows.

Fixed Window Century Calculation

```
02 prefix-CENTURY-BREAK-YEAR-LIT          PIC 99   VALUE 40.

02 prefix-20th-CENTURY LIT                PIC 99   VALUE 19.

02 prefix-21st-CENTURY-LIT                PIC 99   VALUE 20.

IF field-YY>prefix-CENTURY-BREAK-YEAR-LIT
     MOVE prefix-20th-CENTURY TO field-CC

ELSE
     MOVE prefix-21st-CENTURY TO field-CC
```

Note: If the CENTURY-BREAK-YEAR-LIT is set at 40 then the program can handle processing until 2039, when it could be adjusted.

There are generally two types of date windows, sliding and fixed. An example of a fixed window is shown above. Fixed windows employ a pivot value that dates will be compared to. In this example the programmer has determined that all two digit years less than 40 need a century value of 20 and greater than 40 need a century value of 19. Correspondingly the programmer sets the CENTURY-BREAK-YEAR value to 40. This creates a *fixed* window (1940 to 2039) that returns valid results until 2039 at which time it begins to fail by returning invalid century values (e.g. 19 instead of 20). However, at some time prior to 2039 the programmer can adjust logic and the CENTURY-BREAK-YEAR value to extend the life of the fixed window or make a new one.

A sliding window once established returns valid century results indefinitely. Sliding window logic uses arguments to specify the year to be converted while other arguments determine the range for a given window. The window also obtains the system date as part of the logic needed to make necessary calculations. The State of Texas' Standards Review and Recommendation Publication discusses Year 2000 sliding window support established by the ANSI COBOL Committee (X3J4). Logic based on sliding window algorithms is provided as COBOL compiler functions for mapping 2-digit years (YY) into 4-digit years (YYYY); 6-digit Gregorian dates (YYMMDD) into 8-digit dates (YYYYMMDD); and 5-digit Julian dates (YYDDD) into 7-digit Julian dates (YYYYDDD). These functions are listed below along with some results that show results for a YEAR function.

ANSI COBOL Sliding Window Functions

FUNCTION YEAR-TO-YYYY (arg-1, [arg-2])
FUNCTION DAY-TO-YYYYDDD (arg-1, [arg-2])
FUNCTION DATE-TO-YYYYMMDD (arg-1, [arg-2])
Note: Arg-1 is the two digit year to be converted while arg-2, when added to the year at the time of execution, defines the ending year of a 100-year interval (sliding window), into which the year of arg-1 falls.

Example: Sliding Window Results for FUNCTION YEAR-TO-YYYY (52,40)

Year Executed	Window	Result
1998	1939-2038	1952
2001	1942-2041	1952
2015	1956-2055	2052

When Should You Consider Using a Date Window?

Using a date window depends on project approach. There are two fundamental approaches used for achieving Year 2000 compliance, data and procedural. The data approach focuses on expanding date fields and storing them internally with 4-digit years for subsequent manipulation and transfer. The procedural approach uses procedures to manipulate dates with 2-digit years but only to the extent necessary to meet immediate processing requirements. This approach tries to avoid the costs associated with expanding dates by minimizing the number of changes needed in data definition and file/database structure. Both approaches have merit, and determining factors will be based on near term business survival and long term information mission area economic considerations. Many organizations will end up using a combination of these two approaches.

The procedural approach uses windowing for a variety of reasons. Some applications have a very limited period of time remaining in their life cycle which makes a procedure driven solution based on windowing more cost effective than date expansion. Other applications may be so close to a critical event horizon (system failure) that they don't have the time or resources required to expand dates. In these cases, windowing can be used effectively to prevent a disaster.

When date expansion is utilized, some windowing is still required. Windows are needed as part of an external bridge program that allows a Year 2000 compliant application to interface effectively with other applications that are not yet compliant. Once the enterprise's total portfolio of applications is made Year 2000 compliant, these external bridges can be removed. Internal bridges, those that map inputs from within an application (user input screens, key entry, batch processing, etc.) to internal storage are required and normally must remain in place until they are no longer needed by the business function or user.

Windowing thus becomes a primary means of implementing a procedural approach. With this approach dates are stored in files and databases as 2-digit years, and every time a 4-digit year is needed, the stored date year field must be expanded by windowing or some other means. If packed date fields are employed, additional procedural steps are required to prepare dates for use with windowing. Although near term costs are perceived to be lower when using the procedural approach, the overall life cycle cost to maintain the application is expected to be higher due to the larger size (in terms of LOC), greater complexity, and more programmer resources required for modifying these applications later on.

Guidelines for Implementing Date Windows

Guidelines for implementing date windows are essentially the same for either the fixed or sliding approach. Keep the number of different windowing routines to the minimum by standardizing on a few. Remember that sliding windows remain valid indefinitely and will require less maintenance. A single sliding window routine is variable (via arguments) and can be used to meet a wide variety of needs. Fixed windows tend to _break_ over time and may require extensive logic changes. I recommend using sliding windows whenever possible. Also when establishing a set of standard sliding window routines, consider using those that may be supplied as an integral part of your organization's technical support environment. The sliding window example discussed previously mentions three functions that can be found in a COBOL development environment.

Conclusion

Use discernment when implementing date windows. Their use must be integrated into an enterprise's comprehensive Year 2000 solution set. Remember, date windows (fixed or sliding) will be needed to help make most applications Year 2000 compliant regardless of the overall technical approach selected. Finally, date windowing can help reduce the cost of making application software portfolios compliant.

59   _Bridging: Fixed and Sliding Windows—DFSORT_

IBM

Reprinted by permission from GC28-1251 _The Year 2000 and 2-Digit Dates: A Guide for Planning and Implementation_ copyright © 1995, 1996 by International Business Machines Corporation

DFSORT V1R13 (with PTF UN90139) provides Year 2000 capabilities by providing the ability to sort, merge, and transform 2-digit years according to a specified sliding or fixed 100-year window. New Y2C, Y2Z, Y2P, and Y2D formats, in conjunction with a new Y2PAST installation and run-time option, allow you to handle 2-digit year data in the following ways:

> Set the appropriate 100-year window for your applications. For example, set a 100-year window of 1915-2014 or 1950-2049.

> Order 2-digit character, zoned decimal, packed decimal, or decimal year data, according to the 100-year window, using DFSORT's SORT and MERGE control statements. For example, order 96 (representing 1996) before 00 (representing 2000) in ascending sequence, or order 00 before 96 in descending sequence.

> Transform 2-digit character, zoned decimal, packed decimal, or decimal year data to 4-digit character year data, according to the 100-year window, using DFSORT's OUTFIL control statement. For example, transform 99 to 1999 and 04 to 2004.

These DFSORT enhancements allow you to continue to use 2-digit years for sorting and merging, and assist those situations when you want to change 2-digit-year data to 4-digit-year data.

Sliding and Fixed 100-Year Windows

A new installation and run-time option allows you to specify a sliding or fixed 100-year window to be used with 2-digit years. Y2PAST=s (two digits) specifies a SLIDING 100-year window starting s years before the current year. For example, if the current year is 1996, Y2PAST=80 starts the 100-year window at 1996 - 80 = 1916, providing a 100-year window of 1916 through 2015. In 1997, this 100-year window automatically slides to 1917 through 2016.

Y2PAST=f (four-digit year) specifies a FIXED 100-year window starting at f. For example, Y2PAST=1950 starts the 100-year window at 1950, providing a 100-year window of 1950 through 2049. Thus, Y2PAST allows you to control how DFSORT interprets the 2-digit years 00-99 on a site-wide or application-specific basis.

As an example, both Y2PAST=1915 and Y2PAST=83 used in 1998 give a 100-year window of 1915 through 2014, and result in the following interpretation of 2-digit year formatted data by DFSORT:

YY	Interpreted As:
00	2000
14	2014
15	1915
61	1961
62	1962
99	1999

2-Digit Data Year Formats

New formats allow you to identify 2-digit character, zoned decimal, packed decimal and decimal year data for special DFSORT processing as follows (yy represents 2-digit year data in the examples below):

Format	Meaning
Y2C	identifies 2-digit, 2-byte character year data such as C'yy,' C'mm/dd/yy', or C'yy.mm.dd'
Y2Z	identifies 2-digit, 2-byte zoned decimal year data such as Z'yy,' Z'mmddyy,' or Z'yymmdd'
Y2P	identifies 2-digit, 2-byte packed decimal year data such as P'yy,' P'dddyy,' or P'yymmdd'
Y2D	identifies 2-digit, 1-byte decimal year data such as D'yy' or P'yyddd'

Sorting and Merging 2-Digit Years

You can use the new Y2C, Y2Z, Y2P, and Y2D formats in DFSORT's SORT and MERGE statements to identify specific 2-digit year data to be ordered according to the 100-year window.

A simple example of the control statements to sort a C'mm/dd/yy' field (assume the current year is 1998) follows:

```
* Set the 100-year window to 1962 through 2061
 OPTION Y2PAST=36
* Sort C 'mm/dd/yy' as C'yymmdd'
 SORT FIELDS=(7,2,Y2C,A,  * sort yy using 100-year window
             1,2,CH,A,   * sort mm
             4,2,CH,A)   * sort dd
```

These control statements provide the following sort results:

Input Data (CH)	Sorted Output Data (CH)
06/22/15	03/18/62
10/03/00	09/01/99
11/14/61	10/03/00
08/16/14	08/16/14
09/01/99	08/17/14
03/18/62	06/22/15
08/17/14	11/14/61

Transforming 2-Digit Years to 4-Digit Years

You can use the new Y2C, Y2Z, Y2P, and Y2D formats in the OUTREC operand of DFSORT's OUTFIL statement to identify 2-digit year data to be changed to 4-digit year data according to the 100-year window.

A simple example of the control statements to transform a P'yyddd' field follows:

```
* Set the 100-year fixed window to 1970 through 2069
  OPTION COPY,Y2PAST=1970
* Change P'yyddd' to C'yyyy/ddd'
  OUTFIL FNAMES=Y4,
  OUTREC=(1,1,Y2D,     * change X'yy' to C'yyyy' using
*                      *    100-year window
         C'/',         * insert C'/'
         2,2,PD,M11)   * change P'ddd' to C'ddd'
```

This code provides the following transformation results:

Input Data (HEX)	Transformed Output Data (CH)
92012F	1992/012
70225C	1970/225
69153F	2069/153
00001F	2000/001
99321F	1999/321
12054C	2012/054

60 *Bridging: Fixed and Sliding Windows— SyncSort MVS*

SyncSort Incorporated

$$\text{CENTWIN} = \begin{Bmatrix} s \\ f \end{Bmatrix}$$

The CENTWIN PARM option defines a sliding or fixed 100-year window that determines the century to which 2-digit year data belongs when processed by SORT, MERGE, OUTREC, or OUTREC OUTFIL control statements.

Date data formats (Y2C, Y2D, Y2P, and Y2Z) work with CENTWIN to treat a 2-digit year value as a 4-digit year. The date data formats can be specified on SORT or MERGE control statements to correctly collate 2-digit years that span century boundaries, or they can be specified on an OUTREC or OUTFIL OUTREC control statement to convert 2-digit years (yy) to displayable 4-digit output (yyyy). In addition, two date data formats are provided for the OUTREC and OUTFIL OUTREC year conversion facility. These formats (Y2ID and Y2IP), used with CENTWIN processing, expand a 2-digit year in packed decimal format to a 4-digit year. The packed decimal format is maintained in the output field.

CENTWIN ensures that year data spanning centuries will be sequenced correctly. Without CENTWIN processing, an ascending sort/merge would sequence the year '01' before the year '98.' With CENTWIN processing, the '01' field could be recognized as a twenty-first century date (2001) and would thus be sequenced after '98' (1998) for an ascending sort.

The CENTWIN option generates either a sliding or fixed century window, depending on which form of CENTWIN is used: CENTWIN=s or CENTWIN=f.

> CENTWIN=s specifies a sliding century window, which automatically advances as the current year changes.

The variable s is a number 0 through 100. This value is subtracted from the current year to set a century-window starting point. For example, in 1996 CENTWIN=20 would create the century window 1976 through 2075. Ten years later in 2006, the century starting year would slide to 1986 (2006 minus 20 = 1986) and the century window would be 1986 through 2085.

The CENTWIN default is s=0, which means the current year is the starting year of a century window.

> CENTWIN=f specifies a fixed century window. The variable f is a four digit year (yyyy) between 1000 and 3000.

For example, CENTWIN=1976 establishes a fixed starting year 1976 for the century window 1976 through 2075. This window will not change as the current year changes.

The century window defined by CENTWIN controls processing of year-data. If a 2-digit year field (indicated by Y2C, Y2D, Y2P, Y2Z, Y2ID or Y2IP) has a value less than the last 2 digits of the century window start year, the year field will be treated as a year in the century following the year of the century window. All other 2-digit years will be treated as in the same century as the century window start year.

For example, consider the century window 1950 through 2049. The 2-digit year fields would be processed as follows:

Two digit Field	Processed as Year
01	2001
49	2049
50	1950
99	1999

An ascending sort of the above sample data would produce output data in the following sequence:

Two-digit Field	Processed as Year
50	1950
99	1999
01	2001
49	2049

CENTWIN (Century Window) Sort/Merge Processing

The CENTWIN run-time or installation option acts on 2-digit year data that spans centuries. CENTWIN treats 2-digit year data as a 4-digit year and sequences the data according to the 4-digit representation.

CENTWIN generates a century window (for example, 1950 through 2049) that determines what century a two-digit year field belongs to. CENTWIN ensures that year data spanning centuries will be sequenced correctly. Without CENTWIN processing, an ascending sort/merge would sequence the year '01' before the year '98.' With CENTWIN processing, the '01' field could be recognized as a twenty-first century date (2001) and would thus be sequenced after '98' (1998).

CENTWIN processing only applies to data defined as date data formats: Y2C, Y2D, Y2P, and Y2Z. These data formats enable SyncSort to process 2-digit year fields as 4-digit years. A related data format, PD0, can be used to process the month and day portions of packed decimal date fields. To correctly specify date fields for CENTWIN SORT/MERGE processing, you should be familiar with the CENTWIN-related data formats.

The following describes each of the date formats and provides example SORT control statements:

Note: For simplicity, the sample date fields in the example SORT statements below begin at byte 20. Also note that date data is always sorted in the following order: year (yy), month (mm), day (dd).

> Y2C and Y2Z

These formats represent 2-digit, 2-byte year data in either character (Y2C) or zoned decimal (Y2Z) format. Either Y2C and Y2Z
formats can be used with data of the form

Y'xyxy'

where y is a hexadecimal year digit 0-9 and x is hexadecimal 0
through F. Y2C and Y2Z ignore the x digits, leaving yy, the 2-digit
unsigned year representation.

Suppose you have a character or zoned decimal date field mmddyy that begins at byte 20. You can use either Y2C or Y2Z to
depict the yy field. As the following example indicates, you could
specify three sort keys to correctly sort this date:

```
SORT FIELDS=(24,2,Y2C,A,  * sort yy field as 4-digit year
            20,2,CH,A,  * sort mm field
            22,2,CH,A) * sort dd field
```

The yy field (24,2) will be processed according to the century window setting. For example, if CENTWIN=1945, the field yy=45 will
be sequenced as if it were 1945, and yy=44 would be sequenced as
if it were 2044. Thus for an ascending sort, '44' would **follow** '45.'

> Y2D

This format is used to sort 2-digit, 1-byte packed decimal year
data with CENTWIN processing. Use Y2D to extract the year data
(yy) from packed date fields.

For example, consider a 3-byte packed decimal data field defined as

yyddds

This field has the year (yy) in the first byte and the day (ddd) in
bytes 2 and 3. The packed decimal sign (s) would be in the last
digit (half byte) of the third byte. To sort this date field, which
begins at byte 20, with 4-digit years processing, use the following
SORT control statement:

```
SORT FIELDS=(20,1,Y2D,A,  * sorts 2-digit year (yy) as 4-digit year
            (21,2,PD,A) * sorts ddds as 3 digits (ddd)
```

> Y2P

This format is used to sort or merge 2-digit, **2-byte** packed decimal year data with CENTWIN processing. Use Y2D to extract the
year data (yy) from packed decimal date fields spanning two

bytes. For example, a packed decimal date of the form yymmdd would be stored as four bytes:

yymmdd = X'0yydmmddC'

where the trailing C (sometimes F) is a positive sign and the leading 0 pads the field on the left to make an even number of digits.

Notice that the components of the date, span the bytes:

0y ym md dC

Y2P handles this condition by ignoring the first and last half bytes of the 2-byte field specification. Thus, Y2P Processes 0yym as yy, ignoring the leading digit (0) and the trailing digit (m) that is part of the month.

the following example uses Y2P to sort the year portion of the date field, which begins at byte 20:

```
SORT FIELDS=(20,2,Y2P,A) * sorts yy field as 4-digit year
```

The field specification 20,2,Y2P treats X'0yym' as X'yy', and CEN-TWIN processing sorts yy as a 4-digit year yyyy.

➤ PD0

This format is used to sort or merge 2-8 byte packed decimal data. PD0 ignores the first digit and trailing sign during processing. PD0 is normally used in conjunction with the Y2P data format. The Y2P format is used to process the 2-digit year portion of a packed decimal date field, while the PD0 format is used to process the month and day portion of the field.

Although PD0 is typically used with Y2P, the PD0 format itself is not affected by CENTWIN processing.

Consider the packed decimal date field used in the example above:

yymmdd = X'0yymmddC'

where the trailing C (sometimes F) is a positive sign and the leading 0 pads the field on the left to make an even number of digits.

Notice that the components of the date span bytes:

0y ym md dC

The date can be processed as follows:

* Y2P processes the year component X'0yym' as X'yy'.
* PD0 processes the month and day components X'ymmddC' as X'mmdd.'

The following SORT control statement can be used to sort the entire date with CENTWIN processing:

```
SORT FIELDS=(20,2,Y2P,A,* Treats X'0yym' as X'yy'; sorts yy as
                        * yyyy
              (21,3,PD0,A) * Treats X'ymmddC' as X'mmdd'
```

Converting Year Data with Century Window Processing on OUTREC or OUTFIL OUTREC

A two-digit year field, as specified by the Y2C, Y2D, Y2P, Y2Z, Y2ID and Y2IP formats, can be converted on output to a four-digit year.

The Y2C and Y2Z formats specify 2-digit year data that is in display format. The 2-digit data will be expanded to a 4-digit field containing the appropriate Century value.

The Y2D and Y2P formats specify 2-digit year values in packed decimal format. The processing applied to these fields will create a 4-digit year value converted to a displayable character format.

The Y2ID and Y2IP formats take as input the same 2-digit packed decimal year data as defined by Y2D and Y2P, but produce 4-digit year output that remains in packed decimal format.

Sample OUTREC Control Statements with CENTWIN Processing

For century window processing, data conversion is determined by the century window defined by the CENTWIN parameter. For example, a two-digit year field in character format at position 20 in the input record could be expanded with the following specification:

```
OUTREC FIELDS=(1,19      * Copies first 19 bytes of record.
               20,2,Y2C, * Converts 2-digit year to 4-digit year.
               22,59)    * Copies remaining 59 bytes.
```

Note that the expansion of the year data from 2 to 4 digits increases the output record length by 2 bytes compared to the input record length.

The CENTWIN setting determines the century of the 2-digit year field.

If CENTWIN=1980, then a year field in the input record would be converted as follows:

SORTIN Input	OUTREC Output
13	2013
49	2049
80	1980
92	1992

As a second example, consider the following packed decimal date field:

yymdd = X'0yymmddC'

Suppose you want to output a displayable four-digit year in character format in the form

mm/dd/yyyy

To accomplish this, specify the following OUTREC control statement:

```
OUTREC FIELDS=(1,19,          * copy first portion of record
           21,2,PD0,EDIT=(TT), * convert X'ymmd' to X'mm' then C'mm'
           C'/',              * insert slash
           22,2,PD0,EDIT=(TT) * convert X'mddC' to X'dd' then C'dd'
           C'/'               * insert slash
           20,2,Y2P           * convert X'0yym' to X'yy' then C'yyyy'
           24,76)             * copy rest of record
```

The 4-digit year output from the input year field (20,2,Y2P) depends on the CENTWIN setting. The following sample input and output data shows the case for CENTWIN=80:

SORTIN Input Date Field	OUTREC Output Date Field
0800329C	03/29/1980
0790603C	06/03/2079

To expand a 3-byte packed decimal date field of the form X'yyddds' to a 4-byte packed field of the form X'yyyyddds' that contains a prefixed century value, specify an OUTREC control statement such as the following:

```
OUTREC FIELDS=(1,19,     * copy first portion of record
           20,1,Y2ID,    * convert X'yy' to X'yyyy'
           21,60)        * copy rest of record starting with
                         * the X'ddds' of the date field
```

Note that in the above example the output record length will be 1 byte larger than the input record length.

To expand a 4-byte packed decimal date field of the form X'0yymmdds' to a 5-byte packed field of the form x'0yyyymmdds' that contains a prefixed century value, specify an OUTREC control statement such as the following:

```
OUTREC FIELDS=(1,19,      * copy first portion of record
              20,1,Y2ID,  * convert X'0yym' to X'0yyyym'
              21,60)      * copy rest of record starting with
                          * the X'mdds' of the date field
```

As with Y2ID conversion, the output record length will be 1 byte larger than the input length.

61   _New Windowing Method_

Dick Lefkon
Year 2000 Committee of AITP SIG-Mainframe

To some, "Year 2000 compliance" requires that interfaces (e.g., stored files and transmissions) in general use the new FIPS/ANSI date format.

Expanding current output records of 185 bytes having 7 2-digit years, into 199-byte records is simple and unintrusive: Copy/modify programs or sorts are still among the fastest in any system; and if production time seems threatened, even this rapid task can be off-loaded via shared DASD, etc.

Legacy programs commonly have either of two kinds of century simulation:

> uniformly appending the prefix "19" to the value of a two-byte year

> prefixing with "20" or "19" depending on YY being respectively less or greater than a hard-coded number; e.g., a comparison such as "< 30" opens up a 100-year-long "window" which will end in 2029.

How decide the breakpoint of the "century window"? Is 1950/2049 better? Why choose permanently? Parameterize the window's pivot year, this way:

Instead of updating "IF YY < 30 . . ." into "IF YY < 50 . . .",

Simply change it to "IF YY < LINKAGE-PIVOT . . ."

One thing nearly every data center provides for its programs, is central access to common parameters: Next business day's date, overnight interest rate, etc. These might be available from a one-record DASD file, operating system storage area, or LOAD/HOLD table. The century-window's pivot point(s) can fit there just as easily as the holiday schedule.

For example, a three column table in core, can contain a list of date application mnemonics and the corresponding pivot years: 50 for DELivery date, 96 for TRAding date, etc. Sliding (relative) window pivots such as -7 for PURge date, can also fit. The parameterized turning points remain external to all code and can be updated annually and table reassembled:

Mnemonic	Value	Fix/Sli Flag	Other [col not assembled]
DEL	50	F	verbiage; e.g., last mod date & who pushdown history, description of date type
TRA	96	F	
PUR	-7	S	

In certain applications, progressive date-reset tests may show the *only* change needed is to wrap the interfaces using bridges. Here, only the STEP0 (incoming) or STEP99 (outgoing) file fixer needs the retrievable pivot parameter.

When only "19/20" prefixing code is detected internally by scanners, the programmer (or tool) can parameterize it, perhaps flagging contextually out-of-range cases. In fact, even load modules with missing/wrong source may be reverse-engineered by replacing ALC's DC of (19) "30" with a pointer to the parameterized pivot date, and adding communication trappings to receive it.

62   *Procedural and Data Change*

Andrew Eldridge
Complete Business Solutions, Inc.

Robert Louton
GTE

Many data processing organizations are beginning to deal with the issue of the Year 2000 challenge within their business applications. It has become clear that "millennium compliance" (sometimes called "millennium conversion," "century compliance," or "the Year 2000 Problem") is one of the largest maintenance tasks ever faced by an IS group. Every program, application, database, and line of code is potentially affected. Since it is a critical issue in the survival of computer-dependent businesses and

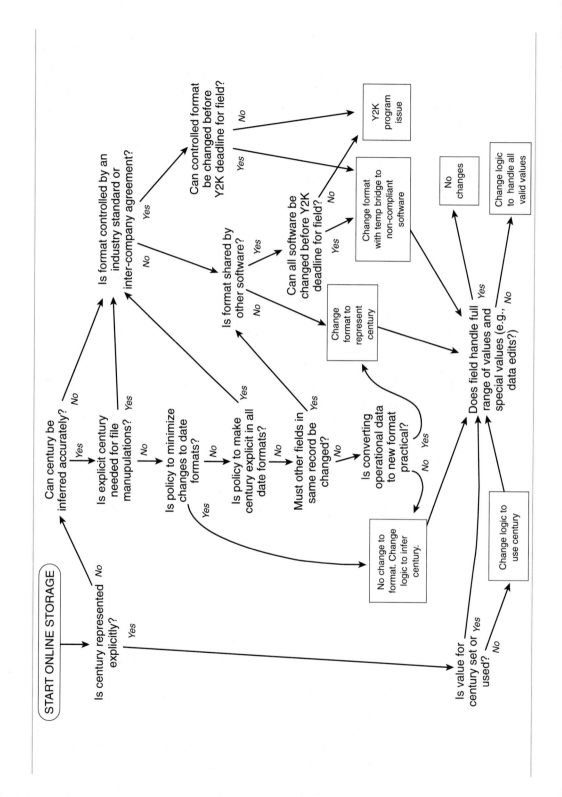

organizations, it is also one that must be managed rather than simply delegated.

At the technical level, there are fundamentally two options for changing software to prepare it for the new millennium. These are the "procedural" solution, and the "data" solution. For those organizations still analyzing the problem, the choice of the approach is an important decision which will impact every aspect of the process, from the impact analysis, through to the conversion. Each approach has its strengths, and the chosen approach will differ for each organization and possibly each application. This article sets out to examine the issues, and evaluate the strengths and weaknesses of each approach.

Defining The Issues

Firstly, it is necessary to define the Year 2000 issue. (Those of you familiar with the basic issues may wish to skip the next two paragraphs) Software applications frequently manipulate dates represented by only 2 digit year values e.g. 97 for 1997. When working with dates only from the 20th century, year arithmetic and comparisons yield correct results e.g. 20 years before the current year, 1997, can be calculated by subtracting 20 from 97, yielding 77. Similarly, in a comparison, 77 (representing 1977) is less than 97 (representing 1997), as we would expect.

Now let's say the current year is 2003. If we perform the same arithmetic, subtracting 20 from the 2 digit year produces –17, not 83 as it should. Also, although we know 83 (representing 1983) is an earlier year than 03 (representing 2003), in our comparison 83 is NOT less than 03. Programs with these kinds of logic and calculations will malfunction as systems begin processing dates for years beyond 1999. Strictly speaking, this mathematical limitation is the extent of the Year 2000 issue. It relates to the fact that data has "rolled over" into the next century.

Data May Become Ambiguous

A secondary issue which arises with 2 digit years is that the data may ultimately become ambiguous. For example, let's take a license expiry date, and assume that the license expiry can never be more than 10 years in the future. If the current year is 96, then an expiry year of 01 could only be interpreted as 2001, and the century has therefore been inferred without ambiguity. If we kept a history of these expiry dates however, and we kept the history for more than 100 years, ultimately we wouldn't be able to tell the difference between 01 representing 2001 and 01 representing 2101. With historical data this may become an issue, and in these cases there is no choice but to record the additional information i.e. the century digits, in order to make the data meaningful. The loss of mean-ing in the data occurs when newly stored historical data contains the same values as dates 100 years before or after. If the application's earliest historical 2 digit year is 65 (for 1965), this won't be a problem until the year 2065 needs to be stored in the same database i.e. it does not have the same urgency as the Year 2000 problem. It is necessary to distinguish the issue of ambiguity caused by 2 digit years from the Year 2000 rollover effect caused by 2 digit years.

The terms "century compliant" and "millennium compliant" have been used to describe applications which do not suffer processing errors when years from the 21st century are processed within the application. The important observation is that it is possible to permanently correct an existing application either by changing the data to include century digits in the years (the "data" approach), or by changing the processing to deal with the century rollover complexities of 2 digit years (the "procedural" approach). In other words, century compliance does not mean necessar-ily that century digits must be explicit or that dates should follow a specific format. For practical reasons, century compliance means simply that Y2K events will not occur, however, the software is designed or changed to achieve this. Naturally, a 4 digit year is one means toward this end. Yet many applications can operate successfully across the cen-tury change by inferring the century from 2 digit years. When performed correctly, either approach results in the desired century compliance, and the argument about whether the data was wrong or the code was wrong is a moot point. Thus a definition of compliance should permit both the "data" and "procedural" approaches.

Arguments supporting each approach typically presume that only one can be the right answer. Supporters of the data solution will argue that the mathematics was always correct, but the data was incomplete. Supporters of the procedural solution will counter that the century is usu-ally inferable and that the code should have been written better. It matters little whether you determine that the bridge was too low, or the load was too high, when altering either or both will get you past the obstacle.

The choice between the data and procedural approaches should be a cost-benefit trade-off rather than dogmatic adherence to either. Each offers advantages and disadvantages. Rarely would either be categori-cally favorable for all of an organization's software. Addressing the Year 2000 challenge is fundamentally a software maintenance activity of worldwide proportions, and the optimal approach for each application must take into account the condition of that specific software and its role in the business process.

Triage: Priorities For Compliance

As the year 2000 approaches, companies will experience increasing pressure to ensure that their systems will operate across the century change. Priorities may change, and a more expedient approach to century compliance may become the only solution. An IS department should have the following priorities in decreasing order of importance:

1. Keep the company in business
2. Keep mission critical computing resources functioning and producing correct results
3. Make all computing resources century compliant
4. Ensure that new computing resources are century compliant
5. Make all computing resources compliant with industry standards

This priority list suggests that if your organization has the time and money, the computing resources should be made compliant with standards such as (revised) ANSI X3.30 or ISO 8601. Other organizations might only be able to perform selective century compliance on mission critical systems.

Myths About the Data Approach

1. *If you change the data, you won't need to change the source code.*
   At the very least you will need to change data declarations and recompile. If the compiler or other horizontal software such as the DBMS or CICS is now at a higher version than when the software was last compiled, the software may operate differently from before. In addition, you will need to remove special logic to deal with century rollover of 2 digit years. By far the largest impact is reworking all the special year manipulation logic which moves 4 digit years to 2 digit data items and vice versa. Furthermore, new logic will be required to improve the functionality of the user interface on screens.
2. *There will be no messy code required to infer the century from a 2 digit year.*
   OS/VS COBOL and VS COBOL II do not support 4 digit years in the system date, and applications accessing this date will still need to infer the century. (This is a special case of internal bridge logic). Bridge programs accepting input from external systems may need to infer the century. If users are allowed to enter 2 digit years, the century needs to be inferred here also.
3. *Changing to 4 digit years will eliminate all logic errors.*
   Applications can contain date arithmetic, such as subtracting 1 from the year portion of a Gregorian date. Changing to 4 digit years cor-

rects the problem of a negative result in the year 2000, but will not address the more subtle condition caused by subtracting 1 from the year when the date is 29 February in a leap year.

4. *Changing the data means fixing the problem once, whereas fixing the code means fixing every program that accesses the data.*

   Unfortunately, the data is key, and changing its structure has a large ripple effect. When the data changes, so too must its copybooks. If the record is referenced in a sort, the control statements may need to change. If the record is stored in a VSAM file, the DEFINE must change, and so on.

Arguments For the Data Approach

> Easier code upgrade effort required, and results in simpler date logic in programs.

> Eliminates 2 digit year ambiguity and the year 2000 rollover issue simultaneously.

> Eliminates overload of documenting complex date logic, and hardcoded century values.

> As more and more interfacing systems carry 4 digit years, bridging requirements decrease. Data is more portable when the majority of other applications use 4 digit years.

> Enables a consistency of approach with newly developed century compliant systems.

Arguments Against the Data Approach

> Changing data structures impacts the whole system: programs, copybooks, SYSINs, jobs, DCBs, sorts, VSAM defines. Portions of the system with no direct date functionality are also impacted requiring recompiling and testing.

> Flow-on effect to data warehouses and other duplicated data.

> Every recompiled program must be tested, or the whole system must be tested.

> Data conversion process can be costly. Archived data may require conversion or support by special logic. The cut-over is complex, potentially needing to support both the new and old data formats simultaneously.

> Increases space required and may impact processing volumes and speeds.

- Exposes the system to a significant change with associated risk. The look and feel of the system is changed.
- Increases the complexity of configuration management with parallel production enhancements.
- During system testing and/or cut-over, disk requirements may peak at twice the production data volume.
- Test requirements are as for a major system change, and may require special considerations such as dedicated test regions. Testing with future system dates may necessitate an isolated or virtual host.
- Project is large. Management is critical.
- The commonality of copybooks creates data dependencies which make it difficult to isolate program changes. Each conversion event is likely to impact a sizable portion of an application or a whole application, or will require intra-application bridging software.

Myths About the Procedural Approach

1. The sorting of date fields will be a serious problem

   It is possible to change the collating sequence using sort utilities if that is necessary. IBM has recently provided 2 digit year sorting functionality within DFSORT, enabling applications to retain 2 digit years even in sort fields. [Ed: SyncSort, too; see Chapters 59 and 60.] Some sorts are to group related items, and may not need to sort 00 after 99 in any case.

2. The procedural approach simply defers the problem to a later date

   The procedural approach to century compliance can be completely effective. A sliding window technique guarantees correct inference of the century. If 2 digit years will become ambiguous over time, they need to be converted to 4 digits independently, and they will not be affected by the century change event per se. The argument that the procedural solution is "quick and dirty" is naive.

3. The user interface will not need to change

   While it is not essential, it makes sense to enhance the user interface to use 4 digit years where possible (on display, not input), because there is insufficient contextual information in a date such as 01/02/03 to determine which number represents the year.

Arguments For the Procedural Approach

- Program changes can be made and tested in isolation from other interdependent systems.

> The exposure to change is limited to parts of programs where program logic is modified. The look and feel of the system is preserved. This reduces risk.

> Testing can be targeted, reducing testing cost. Testing is as for incremental maintenance.

> Existing test data and archive data remains unexpanded.

> Configuration management is simplified.

> Project is smaller.

Arguments Against the Procedural Approach

> Date logic may be complex due to the need in some processing to cater for century rollover explicitly. Ongoing maintenance is more expensive.

> Century inference requires context-specific year range criteria to enable years to be interpreted i.e. each date element may require a different pivot year.

> As more and more interfacing systems carry 4 digit years, bridging requirements will increase.

> Procedural logic for century rollover may have greater processing impact than extending the data items.

> Sort complexity may be increased. Additional processes may be required for other ordered constructs such as VSAM files. Some dates in key fields may need to be expanded selectively.

Having identified the strengths and weaknesses of each approach, an organization should weigh the benefits to the organization as it relates to their special circumstances, on an application by application basis. Factors that should influence this decision are software lifecycle, date intensity and manipulations, and degree of interdependence.

Many decisions will hinge on the age of the application and its projected lifespan. If the system is very stable and likely to be retired in the next 5 years, the procedural approach leaves data untouched and tends to simplify the testing and cut-over. Changing the data in an existing system tears at the very fabric which ties the system together and consequently, the data approach should not be considered lightly. In contrast, if the system is the flagship of the organization, and it is likely to be maintained for another 10 or 20 years, changing all the date data to 4 digit years may enhance its life expectancy at a justifiable cost of conversion.

If an application has very few date variables or negligible date arithmetic, the procedural approach may be cheaper and simpler to implement.

With large numbers of date variables or higher frequency of date comparisons, arithmetic and other manipulations, the benefits of the procedural approach are diminished. Because the procedural approach expands the dates on the fly, the added complexity may become unacceptable. In some cases, dates must be expanded to guarantee the correct sort sequence or VSAM record sequence.

Applications which share interfaces with other systems must coordinate any decision to follow the data approach. Any change to shared data will affect all software producing, updating, or reading it. For application data with a high fan-in or fan-out, the data approach involves far more complexity in testing and implementation. The use of bridges is an option to decouple somewhat the cut-over of one system or sub-system from another. Eventually bridges are removed, and this constitutes a software change which must be tested. The degree that applications are interdependent, must be factored into the decision.

The use of third-party tools and services in Year 2000 conversions is an option to consider. It is unclear that this option offers a cost or schedule advantage. Instead, tools offer more exhaustive analysis of the code than manual methods, and the services an opportunity to free existing staff for continuing maintenance and enhancement. These tools and services are geared primarily toward the data approach, though a date arithmetic subroutine can be used effectively to reduce the complexity in a procedural approach. Thus, going with Year 2000 solution providers for an application generally defines the approach for that application.

GTE has developed an example of a decision chart which guides the analyst toward the best solution based on a number of organizational and data related factors.

63   *Change Strategies*

Gerhard Adam
Syspro, Inc.

In coping with the year 2000 problem, there are numerous suggestions and circumventions which have appeared. Many of these proposed techniques are overly simplistic and tend to overlook significant problems in implementation. The strategies for programming methods can be broadly classified into three primary areas: two to four digit conversion, windowing, and date encoding. This article will explore these techniques and point out some of the pitfalls they represent.

Before we examine the year 2000 change strategies it should be understood that the primary focus of this article pertains to enterprise-wide systems where the sharing of data and/or processes exists. If a program and its data exist in complete isolation with no possibility of interaction with other elements within the enterprise, then any solution may be a legitimate strategy for solving the year 2000 problem.[1]

Two-to-Four Digit Conversion

The conversion of two-digit dates into four-digit dates is the most straightforward approach to the year 2000 problem. Since the year is formally designated as a four-digit expression, any solution must ultimately provide this result regardless of any "shortcuts."

The conversion to a four-digit format is technically simple, although it may be quite labor intensive. The primary objection to this approach is the need to convert every file to use the expanded number of digits. Before we write off this approach as being too idealistic, let's examine what is actually involved.

In this, as in *all* solutions, the first step is to identify all date references within programs. Once this has been accomplished these references must be correlated to the files and a "model" must be constructed which shows the relationships of programs and files to each other. The set of programs and files which are related represents the smallest programming "unit" [Editor: "clump"] which must be changed simultaneously to accommodate the year 2000.

A test environment must then be constructed where the programs are changed and the files will be converted to include four-digit years in every record. While this seems to be quite a bit of work, there are some significant advantages to this approach, as well as some disadvantages.

One of the primary advantages in this method is the process of testing changes for year 2000 compliance. The following steps would take place within the test environment:

1. Convert all file definitions to four-digit years.
2. Convert all files to accommodate four-digit years. This will include writing conversion programs to "fill-in" the missing century indicators.

---

1. An example of this might be SMF data within the MVS environment. While programs may reference SMF data, there is no external interaction in which SMF participates that would require a broader application of change strategies. If the programs referencing the SMF data understand how a year 2000 strategy was implemented they will function correctly as long as they follow the same rules.

3. Test changes with new files.

Note that in this example, there is no need to change the application's logic since it is only the length of the year which is changing. As long as the operand name is unchanged, the logic portion of a program will continue to operate as before except that four-digits instead of two will now be used. This has a tremendous advantage because application logic does not have to be tested since it is unchanged. Consider the following examples of calculating a person's age.

Two-digit year		Four-digit year	
COBOL Program.		COBOL Program.	
Working Storage Section.		Working Storage Section.	
77 AGE	PIC 9(2).	77 AGE	PIC 9(2).
01		01	
05 CURR-YEAR	PIC 9(2).	05 CURR-YEAR	PIC 9(4).
05 CURR-MON	PIC 9(2).	05 CURR-MON	PIC 9(2).
05 CURR-DAY	PIC 9(2).	05 CURR-DAY	PIC 9(2).
01		01	
05 BIRTH-YEAR	PIC 9(2).	05 BIRTH-YEAR	PIC 9(4).
05 BIRTH-MON	PIC 9(2).	05 BIRTH-MON	PIC 9(2).
05 BIRTH-DAY	PIC 9(2).	05 BIRTH-DAY	PIC 9(2).
PROCEDURE DIVISION.		PROCEDURE DIVISION.	
Subtract BIRTH-YEAR from CURR-YEAR giving AGE.		Subtract BIRTH-YEAR from CURR-YEAR giving AGE.	

In the examples, it is easy to see how the logic within the Procedure Division is unchanged despite the changes in the field lengths being used. This greatly reduces the requirements of testing for year 2000 compliance using this method.

In practice the requirements of testing can be accomplished by executing a parallel jobstream between production and the test environment. If the results are identical then the logic within the applications is at least as sound as it was prior to conversion.

While there may be a need to add application logic in some instances, in most cases this will be unnecessary and the greatest possibility for errors to be introduced is allowing two-digit fields to be introduced into four-digit definitions. This particular problem can be addressed by ensuring proper editing of fields.

The disadvantages of this method rest primarily on the extra DASD space which will be consumed by the expansion of records to accommodate four-digit years.[2] Additional concerns might include changes in blocksizes, buffer pool sizes, etc. While these points may present some slight concern, they have generally been overstated.

Date Windowing

Windowing techniques are based on the knowledge that any two digit representation of the date only occurs once within any 100 year period. It is possible to identify a 100 year "window" which can be readily exploited by the application. For example, if the window chosen ranges from 1950 to 2049, it is easily seen how an application can determine the century by simply examining the last two digits. If the last two digits are greater than or equal to 50, the century must be 19, likewise if the last two digits are less than fifty the century must be 20.

The initial appeal of this technique is based on avoiding the need to expand files, but the problems in this method can be quite severe.

The biggest failing of this technique is that there is no external way to interpret the date. The only true definition of the year is hidden in the application logic. If the data is passed to another application, or transferred to another system, it is impossible for that system to interpret the date properly without a CORPORATE-WIDE standard.

In the absence of a standard this technique can have disastrous consequences. A system could exchange information with another system using a different window. It would be impossible to determine how the last two digits are being used without explicitly understanding the logic in each. Any differences would result in errors.

As in the previous strategy, the first step must be to identify all date references within programs and the files with which they are used. Once a windowing standard has been selected, then each date reference must be changed as well as providing a four-digit area in which the date can be used.

Using the same example as previously for calculating ages we see that a new work area had to be defined to hold a four-digit year as well as

---

2. The primary DASD increase will be to accommodate files being converted during the period where production and test must coexist.

the amount of programming logic which had to be added to accommodate the decisions necessary to interpret the windowing standard employed.

Another point to consider when contemplating windowing techniques is whether it is even possible to establish a corporate-wide standard. This is especially important if data may be moved to PCs or other environments where the program logic will no longer be available to interpret the information being transferred.

Windowing technique

COBOL Program.

Working Storage Section.

```
77 AGE                    PIC 9(2).

01 WK-CURR-YR.

    05 WK-CURR-CI         PIC 9(2).

    05 WK-CURR-YEAR       PIC 9(2).

01 WK-BIRTH-YR.

    05 WK-BIRTH-CI        PIC 9(2).

    05 WK-BIRTH-YEAR      PIC 9(2).

01 .....

    05 CURR-YEAR          PIC 9(2).

    05 CURR-MON           PIC 9(2).

    05 CURR-DAY           PIC 9(2).

01 .....

    05 BIRTH-YEAR         PIC 9(2).

    05 BIRTH-MON          PIC 9(2).

    05 BIRTH-DAY          PIC 9(2).

PROCEDURE DIVISION.

If CURR-YEAR < 50 MOVE '20' TO WK-CURR-CI
        ELSE MOVE '19' to WK-CURR-CI.

MOVE CURR-YEAR TO WK-CURR-YEAR.
```

Windowing technique

If BIRTH-YEAR < 50 Move '20' To WK-BIRTH-CI
      ELSE MOVE '19' to WK-BIRTH-CI.

MOVE BIRTH-YEAR TO WK-BIRTH-YEAR.

SUBTRACT WK-BIRTH-YR FROM WK-CURR-YR GIVING AGE.

Date Encoding

This programming technique is intended to provide a code to accommodate the change of century. In some cases this may be a digit such as "0" or "1" to indicate 1900 or 2000 respectively. In other instances a "bit" may be set to provide the same information. Other variations establish a base year to which binary values are added, for example using a base year of 1900, by adding a single binary byte (up to X'FF' or 255) support could be generated for years ranging from 1900 to 2155.[3]

On the surface this technique appears to provide a programming solution which can avoid conversion of files or increased space usage. The negative aspects of this solution are significant and need to be carefully examined.

It has been suggested that adding a one byte century indicator of "0" or "1" would solve the problem, but this also requires that the files be expanded, so if this effort is going to be made, there is no reason why the date shouldn't be represented by the full four-digits. The justification for using a 0 or 1 is that there would be no reason to change all the current dates since they would by default contain a zero and represent a century indicator of '19.' This argument is flawed because a zero must still be added and there is no greater difficulty in expanding the file with a default of 19 versus a zero. An alternative solution proposes that a "bit" may be set providing a century indicator. Much of the viability of this technique depends on how the date is currently represented. If the date is a packed decimal field, then it can only be used if there are unused portions of the field already. If expansion is required, then the argument reverts to that used previously; namely why not simply convert to the full four digits.

---

3. In fact this has been done by many systems software vendors. It should be recognized that most of these systems are assumed to operate in isolation (i.e.: don't directly interface to other applications), and also that this approach requires that the problem be addressed again at some future date.

A bit cannot be arbitrarily added to a packed decimal field if its use would result in the date no longer being in a packed decimal formal (IE: X'99365F' becomes X'A9365F'). In addition, the date represented by X'99365F' has no room for easily definable bits. It is possible to select a bit which is never used (i.e.: the second-order bit in the byte filled with the X'36'). When this is used the date might be expressed as X'99765F'[4] where the second-order bit setting indicates the year 2000, but this becomes a very complex and arbitrary way of coding dates and is probably unworkable to any significant extent.

Another problem presented by binary data is that it cannot be transferred to PC's in any ordinary way. Since file transfers typically convert data from EBCDIC to ASCII, there can be no binary data imbedded in the file since this couldn't be translated. This is a significant concern in cases where data may be downloaded and used in spreadsheets or databases.

Even if data can be successfully transferred, the problem of interpreting it comes up. Since most high-level languages don't handle binary very well, this problem could be quite severe on other platforms where subroutines and machine languages are not readily used.

An additional concern is the complicated application logic which must be added and specifically tested. As already indicated, high-level languages do not handle binary data very well so the potential for introducing errors increases dramatically. Even though it is possible to provide assembler language subroutines which would handle the problem, the application which calls the subroutine would still have to be changed to accommodate the translation of the field to its four-digit representation.

Testing requires that databases and files must specifically include year 2000 data to exercise the logic which has been added. This may require a considerable amount of extra work. In addition, it is also possible for errors to be introduced after the conversion is completed by future maintenance changes. The greater the complexity in the application logic, the greater the likelihood that future changes may compromise the initial conversion.

---

4. The binary representation of the X'36' is 0011 0110 and since the second leftmost zero is never used, it could be used by an assembler program to indicate the century. When this bit is used, the binary expression would be 0111 0110 or X'76'. Note also that this is the only bit which can be set and retain the packed decimal format.

Summary

Obviously not all of the problems and pitfalls have been described in this article, and my bias for four-digit conversion may be apparent. Examination of the issues raised within the context of each individual environment should provide some insight as to the problems which may be encountered.

It is possible (in fact, quite likely) that some of these techniques may be implemented by vendors, introducing all the problems previously discussed. In many cases, these modifications will be exceedingly restrictive on how data managed by these systems can be used in the future.

Still, it may be necessary to employ some of these alternate methods in unusual circumstances. This is especially true in environments where physical DASD constraints may preclude coexistence of test and production files. While such circumstances may exist, the conversion to four-digits must still be eventually undertaken. The ability to circumvent this problem indefinitely is unrealistic. It would be exceedingly foolish to do all this work and discover five years from now that the conversion must be done again because of changing business objectives or technology.

It is by no means certain that alternatives to four-digit conversion are faster or cheaper, so any claims to the contrary should be carefully examined for applicability to your circumstances. If an alternative technique is to be explored ensure that proper planning occurs for future maintenance and standards compliance.

As unpleasant as the alternatives may appear, the problem is most readily solved by converting the dates to their true formats, which are four-digits. Once this occurs, the problem has been truly solved.

Note: The programming examples used in this article are not intended to illustrate programming techniques, nor serve as models for good programming. They are intended only to show the scope of activity associated with various year 2000 strategies.

64   _Dynamic Bridging_

Viasoft

What Conversion Options Are Available?

Organizations are quickly realizing that they have fewer conversion options than were available just a few years ago. Strategies such as proactively re-engineering application systems, replacing systems with third-party application packages, or converting systems to client/server platforms are becoming more difficult to implement. Time constraints and the high degree of risk in adopting these strategies, are causing companies to evaluate more pragmatic approaches to solving their year 2000 problem.

Companies that are unable to adopt one of the strategies mentioned above will be faced with making some kind of programmatic change to their applications in order to achieve year 2000 compliance. These programmatic changes can be classified into two categories:

> *Date Field Expansion* —expand the existing two-digit-year date fields to accommodate four-digit-year date fields.
> *Date Field Interpretation* —incorporate workaround logic into programs to convert two-digit year date fields to four-digit year date fields.

There are six general conversion strategies that incorporate these two approaches:

1. Date Field Expansion Strategy
2. Smart Century Digit Date Field Strategy
3. Century Window Strategy
4. Datastore Duplexing Strategy
5. Standard Date Routine Strategy
6. Bridging Strategy

Date Field Expansion Strategy

The Date Field Expansion Strategy involves expanding an existing date field that does not contain a century indicator (e.g., MMDDYY) to one that supports multi-century date values (e.g., MMDDCCYY). Clearly, from a programming perspective, expanding the date fields is the most straightforward approach, as well as the easiest to test. However, it is also the hardest to implement. Because all application components related to a specific date field must be modified at the same time as the field is expanded to accommodate the expanded definition (see Figure 64.1).

Benefits

> Eliminates exposure to the year 2000 century date change (i.e., dates past December 31, 1999) in current files/databases and programs.
> Supports any date value can be supported having millennium-century digits ranging from 00 through 99.

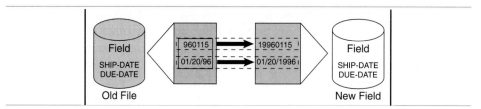

Figure 64.1   *Data field expansion example*

➤ Enables compliance with ISO and ANSI date format standards.

➤ Eliminates the need for users who directly access datastores containing expanded date fields to interpret the date value.

Drawbacks

➤ Requires that all application components (i.e., programs, copybooks, JCL, files, etc.) that reference the date field can be taken out of production, converted, tested and put into production at the same time.

➤ Increases physical record sizes, which could then exceed the physical limit of access methods.

The massive synchronization of changes to programs and files required to implement the Date Field Expansion strategy is extremely difficult. It introduces project management problems such as requiring all source code to be frozen for long periods of time (preventing any further maintenance activities until these changes are complete). It also introduces difficulties associated with managing parallel development functions.

Smart Century Digit Date Field Strategy

This smart century digit approach, also known as "date value encoding," uses an encoding scheme to represent the century value, usually as a one-byte indicator.

Although any unique character can be assigned to represent a specific century value, the most common scheme is shown below in Figure 64.2.

Code	Century	Value
0	19th century	18
1	20th century	19
2	21st century	20

Figure 64.2   *Smart century digit example*

Organizations should select the code value that ensures proper sort sequencing (i.e., 1 is less than 2). This date field conversion technique is most appropriate when the existing date format has an unused digit that can be used to indicate the century code (e.g., 1="1900", 2="2000"). This situation occurs when a six-digit date field is stored in packed storage format—(i.e., PIC S9(6) COMP-3). The Smart Century Digit approach requires that the physical data and all logic based components that access the date fields be converted in a single effort (e.g., this approach requires both data and program changes).

Benefits

> Eliminates additional space in data files if the date fields are in packed storage format.
> Offers a viable upgrade solution where a small percentage of programs are date sensitive.

Drawbacks

> Requires programming of additional procedural logic to interpret the century codes.
> Dictates that all application components (i.e., programs, copybooks, JCL, files, etc.) referencing the date field be taken out of production, converted, tested and put into production at the same time.
> May increase physical record sizes, which could then exceed the physical limit of access methods.
> Requires users who access the data file with end-user tools, to interpret the date field.

The introduction of processing logic to interpret the century codes adds to the program maintenance burden. If the date fields in the file are subsequently expanded, then all of this processing logic must be removed, and the program retested. This strategy is best implemented as a temporary or short-term solution due to the increased overhead in processing.

Century Window Strategy

The century window strategy establishes a base year as the "pivot" between two centuries. Date years that are greater than or equal to the base year are considered to be within the current century. Date years that are less than the base year are considered to be within the next century. Thus, if the base year is 1930, then a two-digit date year value of 31 would be considered to be the year '1931' and a two-digit date year value of 29 would be considered to be the year '2029'. A two-digit year value of 30 would be interpreted as the year '1930' given that the rule is "greater than or equal to" the base year (see Figure 64.3). Note, the interpretation rules *must be consistent* in all programs for a specific date field within the organization, as well as externally if the data is shared with other organizations.

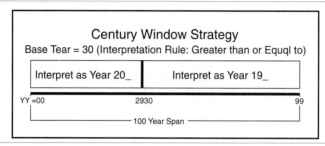

Figure 64.3   *Century windowing technique*

Typically an organization can use the century windowing technique to avoid or postpone physical field expansion while supporting dual-century date processing past Dec. 31, 1999.

Organizations whose applications use date fields that contain year values spanning more than one hundred years cannot use the century window technique. For example, birth dates and insurance policy start/end dates may touch three centuries (i.e., 18_, 19_ and 20_).

Benefits

> Eliminates the need to expand files/databases for existing two-digit year dates.
> Provides a "window" of time past the year 2000, either to perform a physical file/database expansion accommodating four-digit year dates or to replace the existing system with a system that is already year 2000 compliant.
> Supports reading of archived files that do not have four-digit year date fields.

Drawbacks

> Dictates that all programs having access (read or write) to the file/database containing a century-windowed date field have the appropriate interpretation logic.
> Requires users who access the data file with end-user toolsets, to interpret the date field.

> Poses problems for sorting and query tools (e.g., using SQL to access records with dates greater than 1999).

Datastore Duplexing Strategy

The datastore duplexing strategy involves the creation of a "duplicate" file/database so that one datastore contains un-expanded records (with two-digit year date fields) and the second contains expanded records (four-digit year date fields—see Figure 64.4).

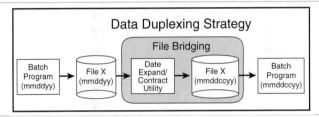

Figure 64.4   **Data duplexing**

This technique uses an external process to copy an existing file and creates a year 2000 compliant format of the same data. Both year 2000 compliant and non-compliant programs can then process the data without any code modifications. The duplicated datastore can be deleted following completion of the last processing job, provided that it is recreated in each processing cycle.

Datastore duplexing is most applicable to batch processing—this technique is not easily deployed for files/databases that are maintained via on-line transaction processing. [Editor: Not necessarily true. Those who routinely work with online systems will recognize a parallel to the morning Start-up File. As transactions occur throughout the day, snapshots are written to a transfile for eventual application to the master database during the batch cycle. Knowing this, we were able to schedule online testing at a current Y2K client, several weeks prior to the multi-feed batch Y2K testing.]

Depending on the type, size, and usage of the data store, data duplexing may provide a more controlled conversion. The data duplication (date expand/contract) utility step can be migrated down the batch processing stream as each subsequent program is converted to read the new expanded date file. Typically, this is a temporary solution, and is usually coupled with field expansion and/or century-window strategies.

Very large files/databases are not good candidates for data duplexing as their duplication may require too much disk (DASD) and CPU resources. Their duplication may also adversely impact batch processing timeframes/windows.

Benefits

> Enables a phased conversion of large/complex batch processing streams by establishing an external conversion process between year 2000 compliant and non-compliant programs—this process can be migrated up or down the batch processing stream as each program is upgraded.
> Supports electronic data interchange (EDI) files with external organizations.
> Supports upload/download of data between the mainframe and end-user systems.

Drawbacks

> Requires significant additional disk (DASD) storage to save the second copy of the data.
> Supports batch processing only. [Ed.: Depending on where you focus)
> Provides only a short-term solution for the year 2000 problem.

Standard Date Routine Strategy

One or more standard date routine may be used in conjunction with the primary year 2000 conversion strategies. The standard (common) date routines can be developed in-house or commercially purchased. If an existing in-house date routine is not year 2000 compliant, the conversion effort involves the modification of or replacement of the current program logic (i.e., call logic) to call a new date routine at the appropriate points within the program logic flow. The degree of code change depends on the structure of the program logic and date routine call parameters.

Benefits

> Ready-access to standard date routines.
> Easily and quickly modify existing in-house noncompliant routines.

Drawbacks

> Dictates that both old and new (year 2000 compliant) versions of the common date routine are active in the production environment until all calls to the old routine have been replaced.
> Requires implementation of one or more of the primary conversion strategies.

Bridging Strategy

A Bridging strategy is a combination of the date field expansion and century window techniques that enables date field definitions within programs to be expanded without requiring the simultaneous expansion of their related files/databases.

This strategy involves the same modifications of the program logic to accommodate expanded (year 2000 compliant) date fields as in the Date Field Expansion strategy. Additionally however, interpretive logic is incorporated within the program to check whether or not the program requires the bridging technique. The bridging routine determines if input or output records contain compliant (four-digit year) or non-compliant (two-digit year) date fields, immediately after a datastore read or before a datastore write. The "I/O bridge" logic then expands or contracts the date fields appropriately based on the current status of each specific datastore being accessed (see Figure 64.5).

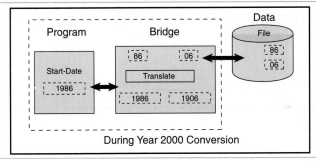

Figure 64.5   *Dynamic bridging*

The key advantage of this dynamic bridging strategy is that individual programs can be upgraded to support expanded date fields, validated, and then put back into the production environment "ready" for the future conversion of the physical datastores.

This approach is best suited for critical on-line transaction processing environments as it enables large numbers of programs to be upgraded over a period of time in preparation for the conversion of the master file/database over a weekend window.

Benefits

➢ Eliminates exposure to the year 2000 century date change (i.e., dates past December 31, 1999) in current files/databases and programs.

> Supports any date value having millennium-century digits ranging from 00 through 99.

> Enables compliance with ISO and ANSI date format standards.

> Supports a phased field expansion that does not require all impacted components to be converted and migrated at the same time.

> Requires minimal code changes, except "bridging" logic required to convert the date from a two-digit year representation to a four-digit one and vice versa.

Drawbacks

> Requires that both field expansion and I/O bridging logic be incorporated into existing programs.

> Potentially impacts high volume transaction processing service levels that incorporate I/O calls to the bridging routine.

> Poses problems for sorting and query tools (e.g., using SQL to access records with dates greater than 1999).

65   *Time Shifting*

Don Estes
Don Estes & Associates

Abstract

Well known Year 2000 technical strategies include replacement, date expansion, and various forms of windowing. This Chapter discusses what was learned from two proof of concept pilot projects exploring two different implementations of time shifting strategies, one in process as this was written. Benefits may include shorter time to implement, easier deployment, lower cost, reduced testing burdens, and minimal risk profiles. Offsetting these benefits is the absence of any added value in the application other than extending its time horizon into the 21st century.

Introduction

Time shifting strategies are similar to windowing in that a 6 position date is maintained, but differ in that the programs effectively execute in the past. There are two variations of time shifting:

1. Data encapsulation, in which modified programs execute in the past against unchanged data

2. Program encapsulation, in which unmodified programs execute in the past against data which has been turned back in time

Date expansion strategies change the data, the data descriptions within the programs, and change logic throughout the programs. Windowing schemes allowing maintenance of a 6 position date will usually localize the changes to procedural logic, thus markedly reducing the scope as compared to date expansion; but the changes are still pervasive throughout the programs.

Data encapsulation in most cases will localize changes to the input and output logic sections of the program, which shift the data back in time on input and forward on output. Thus, we add a new layer which is logically isolated from the rest of the program. Program encapsulation in most cases changes no code at all, which makes it a perfect solution for cases where the source library is seriously lacking in integrity. In this strategy, firewalls are constructed at the points where data enter and leave the system, which shift the data back in time on input and forward on output. Thus, the only architectural difference between the two strategies is that data encapsulation does the time shift internally to the program and program encapsulation does the time shift externally to the program.

Pilot Project —Data Encapsulation

The data encapsulation pilot required changes to several dozen programs, mostly batch but some on-line CICS. All the programs were IBM MVS environment COBOL programs executing against VSAM and flat files. Date fields in files were identified manually and were stored in a database keyed on file name and containing the offset and format of the year. In a full scale project, we expect to use data analysis to identify date fields. The following manual program modifications were required:

> SORT ... USING ... GIVING ... had to be replaced with SORT ... INPUT PROCEDURE ... OUTPUT PROCEDURE ...

> External JCL sorts were replaced with COBOL SORTs

> Where a date field was sorted, a century field had to be added to the sort SD and to the SORT statement; the century was populated in the INPUT PROCEDURE and otherwise ignored.
[Editor: For this and the next point, consider Chapters 59 or 60.]

> Group level moves to SD record areas containing dates had to be replaced with elementary item moves or an intermediate group level to allow addition of the century field for sorting

➤ Program logic testing against a constant date (IF A > 910101 PER-FORM A ELSE PERFORM B) had to be changed to a date field containing the constant date

➤ If a date were contained in the VSAM index, then the record and index had to be expanded by the century field, which was automatically populated on writes; group level moves were replaced with elementary item moves

➤ Output painted into a buffer or record area with STRING had to be replaced with elementary item moves

➤ Each READ or WRITE statement, including functional equivalents such as CALLs to retrieve or send messages or data and variants such as ACCEPT and DISPLAY, was replaced by a PER-FORMed paragraph containing only the READ and WRITE statements

Note: The critical characteristic of these changes is that no knowledge of the program logic is required to fulfill them. This constitutes the first major benefit and one of two significant time reducers. Otherwise, standardized subroutine CALLs were added as follows:

➤ Program initialization referencing each date constant

➤ READ or equivalent paragraph executed a CALL after each input

➤ WRITE or equivalent paragraph executed a CALL before each output

Each CALL shifted the data by the constant number of years chosen at planning time, 28 years in this case. Although the list above is moderately long, in practice very few programs required changes beyond the initialization, READ and WRITE CALLs.

At the conclusion, this system had been "time warped" from allowing data to range from 1900 to 1999, to allowing data to range from 1928 to 2027. However, the subroutines contain a switch to turn on or off the time shift, so that once all the data are in the 21st century the shift can be turned off, immediately changing the range to 2000 to 2099.

As we refine our methods, we expect to put exceptional date offset logic into the date offset subroutines for data encapsulation, so we can simulate 1997, 1998, and later years simply by changing a global parameter at run time. However, we find the methodology to be so robust as a result of the minimally invasive nature of the modifications, and so few faults were found in practice, that we may elect to reduce the testing burden even further as we and our customers gain further confidence in the methodology.

Pilot Project—Program Encapsulation

The program encapsulation pilot is not complete as of this writing. The proof of concept design involves a small number of programs, including a single on-line program. We are linking an OS/2 microcomputer in front of the mainframe to process all the transaction traffic, using our date database derived from code analysis to shift the dates by four years down on input and by four years up on output. We have no IF tests against date constants, so there will be no program changes at all. We have to pass one transaction file in and out, which requires writing a simple COBOL program to read and write the file, adding or subtracting on a parameter switch. We shift the dates in the body of the reports (but not the date/time stamp in the heading) by writing a simple program to pass the report files and synchronize the print lines for time shifting. Finally, we have to convert the data files by subtracting four from every stored year field.

What We Learned

Most importantly, we learned that the data encapsulation strategy demonstrably works and, based on progress to date, we expect the program encapsulation to work as well. Both approaches save significant time over either date expansion or windowing, mostly due to reduced analysis, reduced number of lines to change, and reduced testing burden.

The only restriction we found was that the range of data stored was limited to 100 less the time shift constant, restricting us to a range of 72 years for our data encapsulation pilot and 96 years for our program encapsulation pilot. Less obviously, whereas a standard windowing strategy can define different ranges for different date types within a system, both of these mandate a constant date offset for all dates. There is a bit of additional system overhead, but this is expected to be minor. For program encapsulation where the data are turned back in time, there is a point of potential confusion with ad hoc report query tools.

With regard to metrics for the data encapsulation, we found less than two hours were required per program for analysis and modification. Testing consisted of production parallel from the outset, and the few faults introduced were found quickly. Although the total testing time averaged to less than one hour per program, we feel that on a large scale project the total testing time per program will go up, so that the planning should be based on two programs per day per programmer for analysis, modification and testing. More extensive testing, including shifting dates forward one year at a time, must be added to this total, so that if you plan five runs of parallel rather than one then the metric should perhaps be closer to one program per day per programmer, all included. This does not include opportunities for further automation of modifications and testing.

The program encapsulation design bypasses the minor problems with sorting and index ordering affecting data encapsulation. Had there been an IF test against a date constant, we would have had to recompile the affected program or, if we were missing the source, disassemble or patch the object code. Other than this, we have found nothing that requires us to change the programs.

On the other hand, writing the report modification routines could become very tedious in a full scale project, so in that case we may elect a hybrid of the two designs and recompile the reports (where we have the source) to add the offset to the year while creating the print line.

We anticipate the following metrics for the program encapsulation project to be confirmed on completion. We shift from a per program metric to a per transaction and per report metric. Once we have built the OS/2 transaction processing system, it is a matter of a few minutes per transaction to define the transformation, and roughly an hour per simple report. We could have provided the preprocessing and postprocessing on the mainframe rather than on a separate platform, but we felt it was better to relieve the mainframe of any burden possible. On the other hand, the logic on the OS/2 platform could be ported to the mainframe relatively easily if required in a particular case.

Program encapsulation has the additional burden of converting the data, which we anticipate will run roughly an hour per file plus operational run time. This leaves testing. Like data encapsulation, program encapsulation testing will start with production parallel testing, and we expect it to require only a brief time to find the few faults introduced into the system. We figure one hour per program for testing, multiplied times the number of runs required and the number of times we had to reconvert the data with different date offsets for testing.

Summary

The program encapsulation method was found to be somewhat quicker than data encapsulation and is expected to become substantially more so with larger and larger projects, but both were substantially faster than date expansion or windowing strategies. As a result, our anticipated use of this method for buying time to complete the reengineering of a system or for a life preserver for projects in trouble seems to hold merit. However, it does need to be proved on a much larger scale in case of problems not contained within our small sample of programs. Finally, the criterion for choosing between the two methods would be time available before the event horizon, and the number of interfaces (for program encapsulation) versus number of programs (for data encapsulation).

66   *Migration Strategies*

Don Estes
Don Estes & Associates

Copyright © 1996 Logica, Inc.

Abstract

Year 2000 projects are inherently of substantial risk. Faulty or late delivery may place many organizations at risk of disproportionate expenditure or even bankruptcy. These issues may be magnified as many organizations are late in grappling with the Year 2000 problem. Rough estimates put the likelihood of project failure as high as one in three. This paper explores some of the elements that enter into Year 2000 risk analysis, a sample of the risk mitigation strategies which can reduce that failure rate to an acceptable level, and some financial considerations to guide decisions.

Introduction

Year 2000 is not a technical problem. It is primarily a business problem and secondarily a logistical problem. The implications of failing to be ready to conduct business in the Year 2000 will vary depending on the industry and the business area. As such, it should be organized and managed as any other business challenge. One must start by reviewing the elements of risk and then evaluating the mitigation strategies in order to develop a plan. Although the issue originates in the technology, a technical solution may not always be the best solution. One must evaluate the strategic objectives, financial investments, and priorities of the business. When a technical solution will support the business plan, project management becomes key to reducing further risk during solution implementation and testing. If the problem is managed solely as a technical challenge, additional risk is introduced when the business implications are not understood and addressed.

Technical Risk Elements

Year 2000 projects are a special case of system conversion projects, and draw on the extensive history and experience of some organizations with these failure-prone projects. That experience shows that small elements frequently overlooked in the early stages of an effort can have substantial, even profound effects on the success or the failure of a project. Since many sites manage these projects as technical projects and few sites have experience with project management on the scale of most Year 2000 projects, project design tends to overlook the logistical issues until late in the process. For example, the logistical complexity of testing and deploying system fixes in multiple interacting programs in multiple locations precludes changing courses late in the game. At that point, if there is an issue that could have been solved by an alternative technical strategy, it is too late.

System conversion projects in trouble typically flounder on deployment or testing. Consider a project where the reorganization time for the database would force the organization off-line for days or even weeks to meet the schedule, or where insufficient computer resources are available and additional resources are unavailable due to demand.

Testing, and the problems revealed by testing, constitute the largest source of project failure. Conversion projects frequently start out well and may well get into the 90% completion range before stalling. This happens because errors identified late in the process cause ripple effects back to other programs previously thought to be completed, and the process of rework and re-rework can cause a project to bog down interminably.

Finally, the issues of economies of scale have to be considered. The risk and the mitigation strategies that can be considered vary as the projects scale up. A project design for 1,000 programs can be perfectly adequate but wholly inadequate for 100,00 programs. Conversely, strategies to automate the process of conversion, testing and deployment may be too expensive with 1,000 programs, but when applied to a 100,000 program project they can reduce the overall cost while decreasing the risk.

There is a second business risk associated with testing. Outsourcing organizations may naively sign up to assure "Year 2000 Compliance," but not rigorously define exactly what that means. Consider the starting point—that the organization cannot prove "Year 1996 Compliance"— which is another way of saying that it is easier to prove the presence of faults, rather than their absence. The vendor and client organizations, whether they be internal or external, must define to the most minute detail what defines successful compliance testing before the project starts. In most cases, the definition will be equivalence of results, not correctness of results. This assures the organization that the required testing will be performed satisfactorily, and that the vendor's motivations are aligned with the organization's real requirements.

Project Management Risk

It can be stated that Year 2000 projects will succeed or fail based on the strength of the project management. An organization or third party supplier should be reviewed against the following critical success factors:

> History of consistent on-time delivery of highly technical projects,

> Formal project management methodology,

> Proven integrity of source code library,

> Rigorous programming standards, and

> Proven effective software maintenance methodology and technology.

Unless the score is a perfect 100 percent, the organization is at risk. Mitigation of this risk requires engaging the services of a proven vendor who can provide project design and object management services to complement internal staff (if an internal project) or to subcontractors (if an offshore agency will be handling the bulk work). [Editor: As a possibly easier alternative, have your managers read Part 12 of this book.]

Financial Risk

Despite the obvious risk of a large cash expenditure to any organization, there are other, more subtle financial risks to an organization from Year 2000 issues. The next most obvious one is the effect of organizational disruption resulting from undetected faults in repaired programs, which in the extreme case may result in lawsuits from customers whose contracts could not be fulfilled. Then, one must consider the ripple effects of disruption of suppliers and customers. Finally, one must consider how the sum of all the small scale disruptions across multiple organizations in many industries at the same time could have macroeconomic effects, that is, lead to what is commonly known as a recession. Is your organization positioned to survive these financial risks, and are you positioned to potentially profit from the effects on your competitors?

There is a second category of financial risk for publicly traded businesses: substantial stock price reductions. Unless the decision is reversed, FASB has ruled (in the USA, at least) that Year 2000 repair costs must be expensed in the year incurred and cannot be capitalized over many years. This could result in substantial reductions in earnings for those years, and a proportional fall in price.

This risk can be mitigated by adopting a replacement strategy, described below, rather than a repair strategy, since replacement systems can be capitalized over their expected lifetime. This leads to a technical risk of missing the delivery time, so that a replacement strategy adopted to allow capitalization may have to include a time shifting project (see below) as a technical fall-back or as a precursor.

Technical Strategies

For the purposes of discussion, we divide the primary technical strategies in the following six categories. Risk, cost, time, and residual value to the organization decrease from the top of the list to the bottom. The corollary to this rule is that as time horizons shorten, strategies toward the bottom will become the only choices available.

Replacement strategies

1. Redevelopment of a new system
2. Licensing of a package solution

General Repair strategies

3. Field expansion to an 8 position date
4. Windowing to maintain a 6 position date

Time shifting strategies

5. Data encapsulation, in which the program executes in the past against current data
6. Program encapsulation, in which the programs are not changed at all, but the data is turned back in time on input and forward on output

The level of code modification for these alterations is related to the level of risk. The more code is changed and the more widely dispersed the changes throughout the program, the greater the risk. Replacement with a wholly new system replaces all the code, so the risk is greatest.

Replacement with a package is arguably much lower risk, since the code has been proven at other user sites. Although not free from risk, package replacement where the package is not to be modified is probably the fastest and least risky option. However, this is so provided that the business needs can be met, and provided that the business can adapt its procedures to the needs of the package. Modifying a package to meet the business needs, on the other hand, will greatly increase the risk to successful completion, and is a strategy that should not be considered at this late date unless there is a fall-back plan in place in case of failure.

Field expansion changes code throughout the data definitions as well as procedural logic, so that this constitutes the most risky of the repair strategies on coverage grounds. In addition, experience from platform migration projects indicates that data definition changes introduce a higher fault rate than logic changes, so that field expansion is doubly the most risky, despite being the most intellectually satisfying technical strategy.

Windowing schemes allowing maintenance of a 6 position date will usually localize the changes to procedural logic, thus markedly reducing the risk as compared to a field expansion project.

The two time shifting strategies, data encapsulation and program encapsulation, change the least amount of code, and therefore constitute the lowest risk projects on code coverage grounds. Data encapsulation localizes changes to the input and output logic sections of the program, and to any logic which contains a constant date for comparison purposes. Program encapsulation in most cases changes no code at all, at most changing logic comparing against a constant date, which makes it a perfect solution for cases where the source library is seriously lacking in integrity. In this strategy, firewalls are constructed at the points where data enter and leave the system which shift the data back in time on input and forward on output.

Looking at the technical strategies purely from the point of view of risk, the two time shifting strategies are by far the most attractive. Secondarily, they offer lower cost and faster time to completion, the latter consideration coming to dominate decisions as we enter into 1998. Depending on the technical details, a time shifting project may cost one-half to one-quarter of a field expansion project, both because of less effort expended and because of reduced testing requirements. However, these approaches provide the least residual value to the organization, and offer the least elegant technical solution, albeit ones which may save more than one organization from extinction.

Business Strategies

Considered as a business problem, at least four alternatives are available for review depending on the initial assessment and the business priorities:

> Outsource the activity or business area to a service provider who has already solved the problem, which can be viewed as a variation on licensing a package solution;

> Liquidate the business unit(s) affected, particularly where marginally performing units will require substantial investment to remain operational;

> Live with the failures, which can be viable for many businesses which are not wholly dependent on the computer;

> Go to manual processing.

Of course, none of these are as intellectually satisfying as fixing the problem, but when one considers the far reaching implications that may occur with a failed technical project, they may take on a new luster if they allow the business to declare victory.

Risk Mitigation Strategies

At a high-level, risk mitigation falls into three categories:

> Evaluate the need to do the project—does it really need to be done?

> Evaluate the alternatives and select the one lowest in risk (e.g., time-shifting versus replacement);

> And finally, ensure your plan incorporates a backup plan at each step with triggers to initiate its implementation.

It should be understood, that if a business solution is adopted over a technical solution, then the risk has been minimized. For example, if a business unit is sold or the work is outsourced, then the problem will be addressed and the project will by definition be a success.

The most intellectually satisfying solutions to a significant Year 2000 problem are likely to be replacement with a new system or date expansion in an existing system, both of which constitute the most ambitious projects available (and both of which arguably deliver the greatest residual benefits to the organization). However, both are high on the list of risk-prone strategies. Unless there is an acceptable package solution available, the organization should choose a mitigation strategy that develops a more modest project in order to assure success.

If an ambitious strategy is to be adopted, and the level of risk is quantified and understood, the mitigation strategy is to buy an insurance policy in the form of a fall back plan. If Plan A is risky, then hire a vendor on retainer to develop a low risk Plan B and stand ready to swing into action with it the moment any critical dates are missed in Plan A.

This is the old strategy of set a thief to catch a thief. By having a vendor with a vested interest in exposing problems by constantly auditing the Plan A project, management has the best situation possible with regard to insurance. This has an additional benefit for the officers of any publicly traded corporation.

Summary

In summary, Year 2000 projects are exactly the type of project that will bog down at the 11th hour, and many organizations will suffer from a failure to expose risks early in the process and mitigate them. Some mitigation strategies will add expense to the cost of Year 2000 repair, while others may reduce costs. With an expectation for a high rate of failure, either by missing the deadline or delivering faulty repair work, organizations can protect themselves and their officers in a variety of ways. The ways to do so boils down to doing the least rather than the most ambitious project, defining a fall-back plan, and externally auditing progress during the process.

67   *Reformatting Year-Date Notation*

IBM

Reprinted by permission from GC28-1251 *The Year 2000 and 2-Digit Dates: A Guide for Planning and Implementation* copyright © 1995, 1996 by International Business Machines Corporation

This chapter provides a number of techniques that you can employ to correct improper date notation and use. Because some techniques are appropriate only to unique situations, this section also lists the advantages, disadvantages, and IBM recommendations for their use; however, IBM is not aware of particulars regarding your unique system environment or external influences.

IBM is not responsible for your results or consequences of your implementation.

When selecting a proposed Year 2000 solution, evaluate the following factors:

1. What is the external impact due to incompatible date format changes?

   That is, what other programs or what output will be affected and to what extent will those programs require change if this solution is implemented for this particular program?

2. How current are the program modules that reference the date formats externalized by the exposures?

   That is, are there any plans to either eliminate or replace this particular program or routine, the programs that input to it, or those that receive or use its output?

3. What functions will be impaired due to Year 2000 exposures?

   That is, will any mission-critical function within your company be compromised due to not reworking or replacing a particular program?

Solutions and Techniques

As you identify Year 2000 exposures, your next step is to rework the current program and data exposures to make your applications Year 2000-ready. You can apply the following solutions to remove potential Year 2000 exposures. Each solution is presented with an example technique to change the potential exposure. These suggested techniques might require both program and data changes. Several solutions and techniques and their associated pros and cons follow:

Solution #1: Conversion to Full 4-Digit-Year Format

This solution is a 4-digit solution that externalizes a 4-digit-year format. This approach requires changes to both the data and the programs by _converting all references and/or uses_   of 2-digit-year format (YY) to 4-digit-year format (YYYY). It also requires that you convert all software programs that reference or use the updated data simultaneously, or use a 'bridging' mechanism to perform the conversion between old and new data and programs. You should accomplish this program and data conversion in steps. Otherwise, you will likely encounter immediate data integrity problems caused by the inconsistency of date/time data formats.

To ease your migration, you might consider ignoring any non-impact (cosmetic) data fields in the YY format. A cosmetic date is one, that if externalized, is only interpreted by humans and is otherwise of little functional value. Such occurrences might include the date on an output separator page or a display-only date on a screen in a panel-driven application.

Note: Be careful when selecting those situations that you decide to ignore and call cosmetic only. Be certain that they will not cause any data integrity exposures or ambiguity or are not accessed by any other program. Such instances of non-problem YY formats appear in a report header that shows the printing date of the report. The date is meant for human understanding only, not computer program manipulation. Consider the potential for future change. For example:

> ➤ Today's reports might be written to a data set tomorrow
> ➤ Display-only dates today might prove useful as a collating value when reachieving that output tomorrow to meet a new business or government standard.
> ➤ Even when viewed by a human, 2-digit dates can prove ambiguous if the data spans 100 years.

If you allow the end user to continue to input 2-digit dates for compatibility and ease of data entry, then the responsibility to translate that data into a full 4-digit date falls to you, the application or systems programmer. One possible solution is to apply a context-sensitive prompt to allow the user to select a century indicator. For example, allow all date to be entered as 2-digit dates and automatically prefix those with the current century unless the date is a future date or historical date. What constitutes "future" or "historical" is your decision but could be any date other than today's current day, week, month, year, and so on. Using this scheme, a future date in context of a loan maturity date could be set to 20yy, or a historical date automatically forces the user to select a century from a 'choose a century' (...16, 17, 18) prompt list.

Pros and Cons

Pros

1. Can provide 4-digit-year format. It is currently considered to be the *only* complete, permanent, and obvious solution.
2. Provides increased security against potential inappropriate decisions today if you do not selectively ignore 'cosmetic-only' situations.
3. Can ease your migration if you selectively ignore 'cosmetic-only' situations.

Cons

1. Need to convert the year data from 2-digit format to 4-digit format in all cases.
2. Requires that you relocate adjacent fields in the date field layout, and usually requires that you increase record lengths.
3. Inherent future risk in initial assessment that determined a particularly situation can be ignored as 'cosmetic only'.
4. Increased DASD space usage required due to data field expansion of data (consider including not only active but also archive data) and duplicate DASD space during conversion.
5. Might experience a performance impact due to increased time in processing and date access.
6. Some programming languages allow integer dates that are offset from a base date to be stored in files, data bases or passed as parameters between programs. Such integer dates provided by COBOL intrinsic functions, Language Environment callable services, the CICS FORMATTIME command DAYCOUNT option, and other similar functions in the description for "integer date" can potentially produce ambiguous data and errors. This can occur because each integer-date scheme employs a unique starting date. Therefore, avoid mixing incompatible integer dates.

Solution #2: Windowing Techniques

This is a 2-digit solution that externalizes either 2-digit or 4-digit-year formats. This approach requires changes to your programs only; no data changes are required.

Caution: These approaches can be applied only to dates within a maximum 100-year period at any one time. This solution is considered temporary because there is no guarantee that in the future, your applications will not expand to process dates that are more than 100 years apart. Therefore, this approach always carries with it a potential future exposure. (For example, humans are living longer. therefore data bases that include birthdays (medical, civil, insurance, and so on) and the applications that access that data are already at risk with many dates spanning 100+ years.)

Two types of *windowing* techniques have been defined: the fixed window technique and the sliding (rolling) window technique.

Fixed Window Technique

The *fixed window* technique uses a static 100-year interval that generally crosses a century boundary. This technique determines the century of a 2-digit year by comparing the 2-digit year against a window of 100 years. The user specifies the number of years in the past and future relative to a specific year within the 100-year interval.

Consider this specific example: if the years of date-related data of your application fall in the range of 1960-January-01 to 2059-December-31, you can use a 2-digit year to distinguish dates prior to the year 2000 from the year 2000 and beyond. If using the current system year of 1996, the number of years in the past and future are specified as 35 and 64, respectively. Program logic determines the century based on the following data checking. If the 2-digit year representation of a specific year is "xy" then if:

> "xy"≥61, then it is a 20th century date (19 "xy")

> Otherwise (that is, "xy"≤60), it is a 21st century date (20 "xy").

If, for example, you need to maintain a window of 35 past years and 64 future years, such that in 1997 your application can successfully deal with dates in the range 1962 through 2061, you need to adjust this program checking every year. The inherent future risk when employing this technique should be obvious, and when compared to the sliding window technique is far less desirable.

Furthermore, you will likely need to use a different 100-year window for each application because the date context varies among them. In so doing, you are adding one more level of complicity to your overall programming environment—that of potentially losing track of when each application must be adjusted or which applications require yearly window adjustment.

Pros and Cons

Pros

1. No need to expand the 2-digit-year data to a 4-digit format.
2. Can provide 4-digit-year format for data reference.

3. Can distinguish years from different centuries using only 2-digit-year format (provided the years being processed are in a range of 100 years at any one time).

4. Can be useful if the particular program is being phased out, and a temporary solution is appropriate.

Cons

1. Potential exposures exist when/if the function of the software application needs to process years beyond the range of 100 years.

2. Expect a performance impact in direct proportion to the quantity of date processing the particular application handles due to the overhead of 2- to 4-digit-year conversion.

3. All programs that use the fixed window technique might need to be manually updated on a yearly basis depending on how your date routine is packaged.

4. All programs that accept output from the fixed window technique must use the same assumptions (current date, past and future windows).

5. Retaining a 2-digit year representation does not provide collating sequence support. Nor does the use of a fixed window technique provide indexing sequence support when 2-digit years are used as index keys in indexed files. You will need to provide additional processing to obtain correct collating and indexing sequence output.

Sliding Window Technique

The *sliding window* technique uses a self-advancing 100-year interval that generally crosses a century boundary. This technique determines the century of a 2-digit year by comparing the 2-digit year against a window of 100 years. The user specifies the number of years in the past and future relative to the system year (generally the current year) that the system sets and maintains. Your applications can access the date that the system sets and automatically advances. This is the main advantage of using a sliding window over the fixed window (where the window is immovable without manually revising the programs each year).

As appropriate to your application environment, you can maintain more than one window. For example, you could set one window to process historical dates, one for mortgage dates, one for birth dates, and so on; and the program adjusts the system date and past and future windows to meet the specific application's needs.

Consider this specific example. If the dates in your application fall into a range of 35 years in the past and 64 years into the future, based on the year of writing, 1995, your program can accept and accurately deal with dates of 1960 through 2059. Next year, 1996, the window advances and your application accurately deals with dates of 1961 through 2060.

Graphically, Figure 67.1 illustrates this example using the current (1995) 100-year window and that same window when the current system date has progressed to the year 2024.

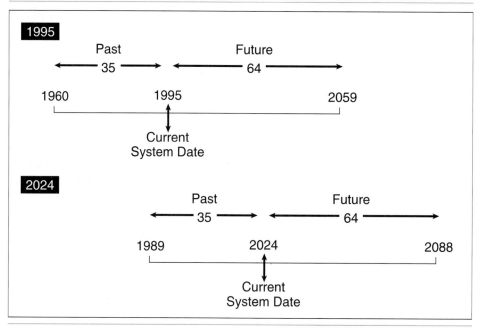

Figure 67.1   Graphical representation of the sliding window technique. (Using two current system dates, 1995 and 2024, as an example.)

A sliding window approach requires programming logic to interpret the meaning of all 2-digit year data. Such additional programming logic could be packaged into a common data/time service routine, callable from a 2-digit year data exploiter. This would reduce the programming overhead and impact to the calling programs. IBM's product, Language Environment, provides common date/time service routines with sliding window features. By default, Language Environment uses a window of 80 years in the past and 20 years into the future that automatically adjusts based on the current year date.

Pros and Cons

Pros
1. No need to expand the 2-digit-year format to a 4-digit format.
2. Can provide 4-digit-year format for data reference.

3. Can distinguish years from different centuries using only 2-digit-year format (provided the years being processed are in the range of 100 years at any one time).

4. No need to convert the date data to a new date representation scheme.

Cons

1. Potential exposures exist when/if the function of the software application needs to process years beyond the range of 100 years

2. Potential performance impact in direct proportion to the quantity of date processing the particular application handles

3. All programs that accept output from the sliding window technique must use the same assumptions (current date, past and future windows)

4. Retaining a 2-digit year representation does not provide collating sequence support. Nor does the use of a sliding window technique provide indexing sequence support when 2-digit years are used as index keys in indexed files. You will need to provide additional processing to obtain correct collating and indexing sequence output.

Solution #3: A 2-Digit Encoding/Compression Scheme

This is a 2-digit solution that externalizes only a 2-digit-year format. It requires changes to both your data and your programs. It also requires that you convert, simultaneously, all applications that reference or use the updated data.

Example techniques that are useful when using this solution include *encoding* or *compressing* 4-digit-year data into 2-digit existing space. This section presents several specific examples, many others exist and might prove more applicable to your specific needs.

Caution: Apply this approach with caution. It is generally considered to be the least desirable approach. Be certain that the new encoding or numbering scheme does not affect the proper functioning of your programs after all the data changes are implemented.

This solution is considered temporary because there is no guarantee that in the future, your applications will not expand to process dates that are outside the encoding limits.

Some examples include:

> **Example 1**: Convert the numbering scheme from two decimal digits to two hexadecimal digits. Two hexadecimal digits allow the ability to represent numbers up to 255; therefore, providing the ability to represent dates between 1900 and 2155, for example:

```
1900 + X 'FF' = 1900 + 255 = 2155
```

Specific date conversions might be:

- Convert the year 1900 represented by D '00' to X '00'
- Convert the year 1999 represented by D '99' to X '63'
- Convert the year 2000 represented by D '00' to X '64'

➤ **Example 2**: Convert the data type from the 2-byte character representation of the 2-digit year to a 1-byte *unsigned packed decimal* (two digit) representation, and use the freed byte to append two *unsigned packed decimal* digits to represent a 4-digit year. For example:

- Convert the year 1900 (represented by character string '00' (= EBCDIC   X 'F0F0')) to unsigned packed decimal X '00' and prefix unsigned   packed decimal X '19' in front of X '00' to yield X '1900' in unsigned   packed decimal.
- Convert the year 1999 (represented by character string '99' (= EBCDIC   X 'F9F9 ')) to unsigned packed decimal X '99' and prefix unsigned   packed decimal X '19' in front of X '99' to yield X '1999' in unsigned   packed decimal.
- Convert the year 2000 (represented by character string '00' (= EBCDIC   X 'F0F0')) to unsigned packed decimal X '00' and prefix unsigned   packed decimal X '20' in front of X '00' to yield X '2000' in unsigned   packed decimal.

➤ **Example 3**: Convert the numbering scheme from decimal to a user-defined numbering scheme. The mapping between the new and old schemes can be defined by a table or mapping function; and the conversion between the two numbering schemes can be done by table lookup or functional mapping. Figure 67.2 presents one such possible user-defined table that provides for values up to 1295 within a 2-digit field. This scheme uses the characters 0-9 and A-Z to represent decimal values 0-35, respectively. This base 36 notation is thereby capable of extending the hexadecimal example on page 5-7 by 1040 more years. For example:

```
D '1900' + base[36] 'ZZ' = 1900 + 1295 = 3195
```

2-Character Year (Encoded) Value	Converted Data/Year Value	Year (When Using 1900 as the Base Year)
00 – 0Z	00 –35	1900 – 1935
10 – 1Z	36 – 71	1936 – 1971
20 – 2Z	72 – 107	1972 – 2007

Figure 67.2   Example user-defined date/year conversion table

2-Character Year (Encoded) Value	Converted Data/Year Value	Year (When Using 1900 as the Base Year)
30 – 3Z	108 – 143	2008 – 2043
40 – 4Z	144 – 179	2044 – 2079
...		
R0 – RZ	972 – 1007	2872 – 2907
...		
Z0 – ZZ	1260 – 1295	3160 – 3195

Figure 67.2   Example user-defined date/year conversion table

> **Example 4**: Pack a 3-digit date field with a 4-digit year date by the use of the "CYY" format. Using a conversion table or offset, you can indicate, for example, that C=0, 1, or 2 represents 19, 20, or 21, respectively. When your application appends the "C" to the "YY" field, your system produces full, 4-digit year dates, the range of which depends on the conversion mechanism. Using decimals 0-9 to represent 19-28, this scheme provides a solution from 1900 through 2899, but it is likely to require end-user procedural changes, education, and typical learning curve time and errors.

One advantage to setting C=0 to represent 19 and so on is that it might provide a compatible, non-disruptive change to some existing application routines if such a field is currently prefixed to your "YY" data field and set to 0.

A variation on this same scheme would include the use of the "CCYY" format where the "CC" can be used to represent the actual century indicator, 18, 19, 20 and so on, or an encoded value for example, "00," "01," and "02," to represent 19, 20, 21, respectively.

When adding either the "C" or "CC" prefix to the "YY" field for "CYY" or "CCYY" representation, "C" or "CC" can be extracted from a separate field, one that is not necessarily adjacent to or preceding the "YY" field. This then can relieve any restrictions you might currently have due to your date field length. It does, however, require further programming logic and data manipulation.

Pros and Cons

Pros

1. No need to expand the 2-digit-year data format to 4-digit data format. (For example, there is no need to increase the fields in data bases and tables to accommodate dates above 99 which would increase DASD

usage.) Further, this saves the effort that would be required to rebuild your database(s).

2. Can distinguish years from different centuries using the 2-character-year format.

3. If you use a COBOL COMP-3 format, you can pack a CCYYMMDD date into an existing 6-byte field (with one byte left over). This technique allows you to retain the original field size and eliminates your need to relocate adjacent fields. Applications that use the data for calculations run faster because the data is already packed.

4. If you use a flagged Julian format (CYYDDD) where "C" is used as the 'century indicator, the format does not require expansion of the date field.

Cons

1. Depending upon the choice of data representation you implement, this scheme can be applied only to a limited date range. For example, you are limited to 255 years when using hexadecimal representation.

2. All programs that use this scheme and need to access the output of the 2-character conversion must change simultaneously.

3. Due to data conversion (calls and processing) you might experience a performance impact in direct proportion to the quantity of date processing the particular application handles.

4. Depending upon the choice of data representation you implement, you might experience incorrect data sequencing if you do not add further programming logic.

5. Encoded dates require conversion whenever you work with that data. Therefore, the presence of encoded dates will add another layer of complexity to such tasks as problem determination.

6. You must convert the data before it can be displayed in Gregorian format, and some encoded data can only be viewed in hexadecimal format. This is both impractical for human reading and also impractical or impossible to print.

Using a Common Date/Time Service Routine

In large system applications it is common to find that more than one date/time service is in use. However, some date/time service routines might have Year 2000 exposures of their own: for example, the routine(s) might only provide a 2-digit-year format. Fixing the exposed date/time routine(s) is one possible solution. Selecting a vendor date/time routine that is Year 2000-ready for consolidation and/or replacement of your 'in-house' date/time service routines is another alternative.

While fixing your current date/time routine(s) exposures, you might find it worth your effort to consolidate all your date/time service routines into one *common date/time service routine* . If you then detect any Year 2000 exposures during or following the consolidation, you can reformat your program and data and decide on the appropriate solution(s) you will use. That is, you can package any new code, encoding and conversion routines, windowing-specific data, and so on into the common date/time service routine. This common date/time service routine package might then be considered a 4-digit solution that externalizes both 2-digit and 4-digit-year formats. The benefit of using such a common date/time service routine is lower future maintenance because all services are consolidated rather than replicated throughout your applications.

Considerations When Selecting Solutions

Potential 2-digit-year exposures can be classified into two categories (low impact and high impact). When selecting an appropriate solution(s) for the 'impact' categories, be certain to consider not only the applicability of the solution(s) on the module itself but also the potential impact and adjustments on the external modules that receive data from this module. You have three basic choices when assessing how to address each application. You can:

> Change the application,
> Change the application and the data, or
> Invest in a new application (which could also require some date data changes).

Certainly, most IS organizations will build their Year-2000-ready system on a combination of these choices. When more than one solution appears feasible, weigh its appropriateness based on:

> Time available
> Resources available (personnel and hardware)
> Project cost (individual application conversions and overall)

As today's IS environment becomes increasingly more complex and sophisticated, the instances of program and data isolation decreases. Networking, open and distributed computing allow data to flow from site to site, system program to application program (or application program to system program), and so on. You must ensure that these layers of software 'speak the same language.' As you add in-house code and Solution-Developer-written code, and migrate your operating system, be certain to review that software for date format compatibility.

Solution Applicability

Different combinations of solutions are applicable to different situations. Evaluate solutions based on a 'best-solution combination' basis when considering both a module itself and other related modules. For example, when applying:

> **Solution #1** (full 4-digit solution) to a certain module, another module that receives data from this module could receive:

  • 2-digit-year data as before, provided there is no exposure for itself or

  • 2-digit-year data as before and apply Solution #2 (windowing techniques) for its own exposures or

  • 4-digit-year data and apply Solution #1 (full 4-digit solution) for its own exposure removal.

> **Solution #2** (windowing techniques) to a certain module, another module that receives data from this module might either receive 2-digit-year data as before and apply Solution #2 itself or receive 4-digit-year data and apply Solution #1 (full 4-digit solution) for its own exposure removal.

> **Solution #3** (the encoding or compression technique) to a certain module, another module that receives data from this module might need to apply Solution #3 as well to maintain data consistency with the data representation scheme. Another alternative is to apply Solution #3 to the impacted module, and then convert that 2-digit-year format to 4-digit-year format before externalizing that data to another module. This receiving module can then proceed with 4-digit data, and if necessary, apply Solution #1 (full 4-digit solution) to adopt the 4-digit-year data for its own exposure removal.

Bridge Programs Help Stage Format Conversions

Bridge programs are often used to convert data from one record format to another. If you use such a program, it should define the:

> Input date format and encoding method

> Output date format and encoding method

> Logic that converts the data from input format to output format based on their encoding methods.

You can apply bridge programs during program execution or file and/or database conversion. For application during program execution, the conversion occurs each time data is passed between programs or between program and source data using different record formats. For application during file and/or database conversion, the bridge program reads one record at a time from the source, transparently converts the record format, and writes out the data in the new format to the destination. The process is incremental and can continue until all the records in the source are converted.

Bridge programs for data format conversion provide the following benefits:

> Granularity when changing the code and/or data

With the scope of the Year 2000 project, it is not practical (if possible) to change all the code and data at once. Bridge programs allow the gradual conversion of the programs and/or data and still maintain the compatibility between different data formats. For example, you can change some of your programs to adopt a new data format and still be able to communicate to programs using the old format (after conversion by the bridge programs). Therefore, changes to the remainder of your programs can be performed in an incremental manner as convenient.

> Flexibility when choosing appropriate solutions

Bridge programs allow you to select the appropriate mix of different solutions to best meet your specific circumstances while maintaining the compatibility between different data formats. For example, you can design your programs so that they can process data in different formats. You can then have active data in a 4-digit-year format and archive the same type of data in 2-digit-year format. The bridge program distinguishes the data in these various formats by reading the records and, when necessary, converting the data to the appropriate format.

Other Programming Situations

Other programming situations you should consider might include:

> The possibility that a data format has become outdated and will not function correctly beyond 1999-December-31 (or earlier) Such data formats might be outdated even earlier and have already been superseded by another method by the Solution Developer. For example, The MVS platform will no longer support VSAM catalogs for processing when the system date is beyond 1999. To support data sets which need to have explicit expiration dates beyond the end of 1999, or to create cataloged data sets after 1999 on MVS systems, you must use ICF catalogs. Using VSAM catalogs on the MVS platform (including OS/390) will no longer

function, this requires a programming change to take advantage of the alternative solution.

> When migrating to Year 2000 support, your applications (operations) might support only 2-digit-year format, only 4-digit-year format, or both formats. It is possible that the 2-digit values are assumed to be 19xx dates. Therefore, be aware that all these must be eventually updated or the functions will likely fail or give unpredictable results after 1999-December-31.

> Changes to operations procedures

Be certain to educate your operators about command changes so that they know when they must use a full 4-digit date (for example, 2000, to avoid implying 1900 if they only enter 00).

> When erroneous data would be produced for a limited and known timeframe and changes are not justified

You might have a situation that is best handled manually to meet a short time period where programming changes simply aren't justified. Consider using 2-digit-year data if a timeframe such as a single 24-hour period (1999-December-31 to 2000-January-01) or a single week (1999-December-25 through 2000-January-01) would be the only time your application will not provide correct results. For example, a program that looks at a sales report to compare the current day's merchandise movement with the previous 7 days. Because there would only be 8 reports containing both 1999 dates and 2000 dates, you might decide to handle the problem manually rather than changing the code.

Note: Don't fail to use a certain amount of common sense when deciding what applications to change, which to replace, and which to ignore. Do not lose your perspective of your institution's business needs and priorities and the impact and cost a particular application's change might have on attaining those goals.

Guidelines

While retaining a perspective of any external impact, module currency, and what functions are impaired due to Year 2000 exposures, use the following guidelines when applying Year 2000 solutions.

Note: This is not intended to be an exhaustive guideline, but rather a foundation upon which to start your specific Year 2000 date-data resolution.

1. Establish an in-house 'date standard.' Conformance to currently published standards such as those listed below would be a valuable starting point. The earlier such a standard is in place, the sooner your IS

organization will avoid creating new date issues and propagating current ones. You can refer to:

> ANSI X3.30-1985 (R1991) Representation for Calendar Date and Ordinal Date for Information Interchange

> ANSI X3.51-1994 Information Systems—Representations of Universal Time, Local Time Differentials, and United States Time Zone References for Information Interchange

> ISO 8601:1988 Data elements and interchange formats—Information interchange—Representation of dates and times

2. Minimize potential impact to external references due to incompatible date format changes. For example,

> Maintain the 2-digit-year format as an option when 4-digit format is required for an application program interface (API) that provides 2-digit-year data references.

3. *Avoid* any ad-hoc solutions; such solutions inevitably require a future problem investigation and removal, and should be considered temporary solutions only. For example [Editor: albeit far-fetched]:

> Do not fix the leap year calculation formula by adding logic to check if the current year is the year 2000. This solution will temporarily fix the leap year calculation problem by singling out the year 2000, but it does not fix the leap year calculation problem for all other years that are a multiple of 400.

4. A 2-digit-year format might be acceptable for human-only viewing purposes, for example, screen panels, hardcopy reports, and so on. However, any such data can be, and often is, added to a data set and then read by another program. A 'log' that can be used as input to any program should *not* be considered in this (low-impact, for human viewing only) category.

5. When changing the date format of any 'log,' ensure that all the contributing programs adopt the new date format as well.

6. Consider the Year 2000 solutions listed in this document for applicability in the following order.

> Using a common date/time service routine (a 4-digit 'solution' - that can support both 2- and 4-digit formats). This is:

- Considered a long-term solution.

- *The recommended solution* for its ability to recognize and correctly manipulate both 2- and 4-digit-year formats, thereby providing a long-term solution and no impact to 2-digit-year data references.

➤ Solution #1 (conversion to a full 4-digit-year format that externalizes 4-digit formats)

  • Considered a long-term solution.

  • Only supports 4-digit-year formats that will have impact on 2-digit year data reference.

➤ Solution #2 (windowing techniques that externalize both 2- and 4-digit formats)

  • Considered a temporary solution and **should only be used when solution #1 is not practical**. (This is a debatable issue, because there are applications that deal only with years in the range of 100 years. However, there is no guarantee that the functions of the applications will never change in the future and then require 4-digit-year formats.)

  • Has potential exposures when the function of the program needs to process years beyond the range of 100 years.

  Use this solution only when:

  • Processing is always limited to the current date data; for example, at the time of IPL or time of job creation.

  • Expanding the date-data field is costly, and the function of the program will be phased out before any exposure occurs.

➤ Solution #3 (2-digit encoding/compression scheme that externalizes 2-digit formats)

  • Has potential exposures when the function of the program needs to process years beyond the range that can be covered by the encoding or compression scheme.

  • Should be used only when expanding the date-data field is too costly and the function of the software program will be phased out before any exposure occurs.

8

part

Expert: Date Details

Now that you've reviewed the overall code change methods, start your deeper look with IBM's "Exposures" piece. It gives dozens of sample date names, where to seek them, and levels of exposure. Data and control sharing between modules—especially in COBOL LINKAGE, FORTRAN COMMON and PL/I EXTERNAL—escalates your exposure and must be verified in the receiving module.

Mike Lips follows IBM with ten technical points. Since many programs will mistakenly skip 2/29/00, its transactions may be dropped or else posted to an adjacent day. Watch out for interchanging "serial dates," the byte-saving offsets from 1/1/1900 (CICS), 1/1/1601 (COBOL/370), 10/15/ 1582 (LE), 1/1/0001 (DB2), etc. Finance [see Chapter 14] and Real Estate (e.g., Year 2121) are especially vulnerable to normal left truncation.

Under Miscellaneous, Lips's lead entry is the appearance of dates in keys. [Editor: If you are about to discard a diskpack anyway, get a stopwatch and measure the MTBF of a date-bounded loop which never ends and in each pass updates the same-key disk record.] Richard Bergeron's Embedded Dates article follows up with further instances such as LIFO, expiration, and policy numbers.

Next is Patrick Hagan's description of the newest set of COBOL routines from IBM. Once you learn them you can ignore them, he states: IBM would like you to convert all your COBOL II systems to COBOL 85, also known as COBOL for VM and MVS. You don't have to.

Hagan notes the personal experience of using Cobol II and COBOL 85 programs in tandem with no apparent ill effects. Cobol 85 has two types of new functions available. The first includes callable LE routines such as trigonometric functions. The second is a new set of intrinsic COBOL functions which sound the same but must be preceded by the word, FUNCTION. The new date format is YYYMMDDhhmmsscc+hhmm.

Hagan says, make the obvious changes for Y2K and your current COBOL II systems will run just fine come the Millennium. The new date-related functions are uniquely useful if your installation never composed date routines of its own, or is unable/unwilling to upgrade them to YYYY, or unaware of commercial COBOL date routine sets or Harold Zbiegien's generously furnished date algorithms immediately after Hagan.

It is well worth the time to comb through some of these date routine sets for possible enterprise-wide adoption.

Jerome and Marilyn Murray give an in-depth treatment of date differences in Extended Interval Aging. They discuss which March date is exactly one month after February 29th. The Murrays include examples of BAL and matching pseudocode. [Editor: BAL is widespread—including YOUR site—and even if your own specialization is otherwise, it's a good idea to spend some time seeing how dates are handled in Mainframe Assember.]

Finally, Bill Brew gives a five-step sequence for each subsystem: Define it; find too-narrow dates; fix fields, bytes, screens, reports; fix data as stored (possibly making bridges) or use; severally test. Software's ability to find or fix dates usually stems from pattern "seeds" (name strings and P/Cs) or negative "filters" naming fields to bypass, e.g., the filter MMMY limits the fields highlighted by seeds MY and MM. Yield can be increased and false positives reduced by revising and repeating.

For one person to plow meticulously through this entire Part, might slow your Impact Analysis and/or result in headaches. Nothing prevents the designated Expert from farming out chapter sections to subordinates, then working through everything in a follow-up meeting.

As Expert, you need to have command of the technical side to emphasize for top management both the key exposures and the recommended solutions, respectively this and the preceding chapter. Special Y2K testing is next.

68   *Identifying 2-Digit-Year Exposures*

IBM

Reprinted by permission from GC28-1251 *The Year 2000 and 2-Digit Dates: A Guide for Planning and Implementation* copyright © 1995, 1996 by International Business Machines Corporation

To identify the potential exposures caused by using 2-digit-year representations of dates, you first need to locate references to all date-related data.

Locating References

Locating date-related data and code is itself a major piece of the work effort that you must address. The most complete method starts with an inventory of every programming entity used in your IS center. Once compiled, you can review each program individually. Alternatively, use the following, more systematic, approaches to locate 2-digit-year data and date-related code. (Solution Developer products are available to assist this effort.)

1. Review the following documents for direct or indirect references to date-related data and formats. Then trace these references back to the application source code to locate references in that code as well.

   - Requests for proposal
   - Statements of work
   - Planning documents that describe future IS needs
   - Existing studies about the current system
   - Software development standards and process documents
   - Software quality assurance requirements
   - System requirements specifications
   - System design specifications
   - Program specifications
   - User instructions and procedures
   - Data dictionaries

2. Review program information for date references to include, for example, date variables, date functions or routines, and character strings. Character strings might include the following in either your code or its comments:

   - AS-OF, ASOF
   - BEGIN, BEG, BGN
   - MDY, MMDDYY, MMYY
   - MONTH, MON, MO, MMM

> CCYY
> CYYDDD, CYYDDMM, CYYMMDD
> CURR, CURRENT
> DATE, DAT, DTE, DT
> DAY, DA, DD
> DDMMYY, DDDYY
> DIFFDATE
> DOB
> DOH
> END
> EXPIRE, EXP
> JULIAN

> START
> TERM

> TIME
> TIMESTAMP, TIME-STAMP
> TIMEDATE
> THISDATE
> TOD, T-O-D
> WEEK
> WEEKDAY
> YEAR, YR, YY
> YMD, YYMMDD, YYDDD
> and so on.

> Data entry forms, screen display formats, report formats

> Definitions of data fields, records, structures, files, and databases

> Source code, computer program listings, cross-reference reports

> Command languages, for example, JCL, REXX, CLIST, EXEC, and CL

> Data indexes and catalogs, table sizes

> Data dictionaries

> Date/time service routines

> Sort routines

3. Use a test system.

Install an isolated, non-production system with a duplicated image of your system and application software. In large systems, this could be an LPAR (logical partition) of the mainframe, or for other platforms consider dedicating a separate machine, segregated (in either time or place) from any other system(s). This segregation is crucial to guarantee that you will avoid contamination due to system clock advancement or untested, and yet imperfect, modified code.

> With a changed date/time setting

Set the system date and time to a future date and time value after 2000-January-01. During such testing, be certain to use compatible data that is synchronized with the revised application software, that data crosses a 100-year boundary, and be certain to update your current operating procedures to reflect this new data requirement as well. For example, the 100-year window could be 1900-1999 or 1995-2094, or you could use both range types. The more you vary your window type(s), the more incorrect code you will uncover. This testing will help you identify many (but not all) Year 2000 exposures.

➢ With changed data

If you only change date fields in a routine, you are not introducing new logic into that routine. Although the fields are increased from 2-digit to 4-digit fields, you only need to recompile the routine to generate those new field lengths. If you didn't change the logic, you needn't test that logic. [Editor:…saving you part of a Unit Test as long as you've never made a typo.] Typical testing is appropriate in a separate test system using new data, but Year-2000-specific testing is generally unnecessary. In this testing, ensure that the changes in the operand lengths produce the expected results. If the results match those produced prior to your changes, then the application is successfully performing data calculations using the new 4-digit data rather than the previous 2-digit data, and you have met your migration criteria.

4. Use a combination of the above approaches.

Tracing References Back to their Source

For any potential exposure identified, identify all direct and indirect references of this exposure. You can do so by tracing the flow of the data to identify its immediate source and destination and then repeating the tracing process until all sources and destinations of all potential data exposures are identified.

Determining the Impact of 2-Digit-Year Data Fields

Once you have located date-related data fields by one or more of the above approaches, you can classify the use or reference of those fields into one of the following categories:

➢ Low Impact

- The program uses a 4-digit-year representation in all occurrences.

- The program uses a 2-digit-year representation within itself, but does not have any internal exposures, nor does it externalize the 2-digit year in any way.

- The program uses a 2-digit-year representation within itself, but does not have internal exposures. The 2-digit year IS externalized, but cannot be referenced (for example, for display-only) by any other program.

Note: Such output might be labelled as 'cosmetic only' and for interpretation by a human only, but this too might have its own set of ramifications.

* A municipality that tracks school-age children will more frequently begin 'inviting' centenarians to enroll in kindergarten. If a printout of residents reads: "Birthdate: 10/14/92," what would the clerk compiling a list of 6-year-old children in 1998 assume?

* Another type of exposure is externalized by 'display-only' dates that have been coordinated with a hard-coded '19' for the century. Such 2-digit exposures might exist for terminal display or special forms where the '19' is pre-printed. Therefore, be aware of, and consider, potential impact of date fields in all situations; these might not always be obvious exposures.

➤ High Impact

* The program uses a 2-digit-year representation within a program. It does not have internal exposures, but the 2-digit year is externalized and could be referenced by another program.

* The program uses a 2-digit-year representation and has internal exposures.

Investigating How Other Software Entities Use the Data

You also need to investigate the ways data is shared among software entities. The greater the degree and scope of data sharing, the more global is your task and the more critical is the need to prevent the further propagation of and data 'contamination' by 2-digit-year data. Except possibly in a rather small IS environment, you cannot know how output is used by all other programs that might access it. Several factors that affect how data is shared or used among software entities which follow. These factors and the types of data sharing provide some of the links making up this data 'web.'

Data Sharing

Three factors affect the sharing of data between modules:

1. The number of data items passed between modules. (The more data passed, the tighter the relationship.)

2. The amount of control data passed between modules. (The more control data passed, the tighter the relationship.)

3. The amount of global data elements shared between modules. (The more global data elements shared, the tighter the relationship.)

Several types of data sharing can occur between two modules in a system: Two modules can communicate:

> Through a variable or data structure (for example, array, table, or record) that is passed directly as a parameter between the two modules. The data is used for problem-related data processing not for program control purposes.

> Through a variable or data structure (for example, array, table, or record) that is passed directly as a parameter between the two modules. However, only part of the data in these composite data elements is needed in the call, that is, more data is passed than needed. A change in one of the data structures to accommodate a change in either the calling or called module can affect other modules as well.

> By passing data from one module to another to control the order of instruction execution. (For example, a control flag is set in one module and tested in a CASE or WHEN statement in another module).

> By passing data between modules through some mutually agreed upon location in a global data area (for example, FORTRAN COMMON and PL/I EXTERNAL features). A change in one module might then require changes in other modules sharing the same data area.

> By one module reaching into the internals of another module to get or deposit data or control its function. (For example, a branch from one module's code into another module. A change in either module might require a thorough analysis of the internals of both modules to determine how to deal with the consequences of the change.)

If contaminated data (2-digit-year data) is shared among modules, you must identify the exposure caused by the data sharing on the receiving side of the transaction.

Once you have identified Year2000 exposures, apply the appropriate techniques to reformat these date and time representations.

69   *Technical Solutions*

Michael Lips
Platinum Technology, Inc.

As the year 2000 draws closer, an increasing number of companies will begin to convert their date-defective systems. Although it has been argued that date logic is not exactly "rocket science," and without trying to distinguish today's rocket science from what we actually used to send men to the moon and back, it is nevertheless safe to say that date logic is not trivial, and in some cases it can be quite complex. In this chapter, we will explore some of the intricacies of calendar date processing that companies will discover as they dig into their programs and files.

Leap-Year Logic

Let's start with the basics of leap-year logic. Most people (including current and past programmers) do not realize that the year 2000 is a leap year. As it turns out, there are three leap-year rules, as defined in 1582 by Pope Gregory XIII: (1) If the year is divisible by four, it's a leap year. (2) If it's divisible by 100, it's not a leap year. (3) If it's divisible by 400, however, it is a leap year. Thus 1900 was not a leap year, 2000 will be a leap year, and 2100 will not be a leap year.

Because there is such confusion in this area, it is not surprising to find program logic that performs tests for yearly values of 88, 92, and 96 but avoids the "year" 00 entirely. Nor is it surprising to find programs that treat February 2000 as a special month in the leap year with 30 days rather than the normal 29. Nor again is it surprising to find logic that includes the first two leap-year rules but not the third. The consequences of using defective leap-year logic on February 29, 2000, include but are not limited to:

➤ Transactions that may abend

➤ Transactions that may disappear entirely

➤ Transactions that will mistakenly double-post to February 28 or March 1

Leap-year logic is only one area of vulnerability and a relatively limited one at that. As we proceed, we'll discover issues that represent even greater risk.

Inversion Consequences

The year-2000 problem with which most of us are familiar is the so-called inversion or wraparound phenomenon. This is caused by programs that will interpret "00" as "1900" rather than "2000" and will mistakenly perform calculations 99 years into the past rather than 1 year into the future. This problem is essentially the remnant of a bad habit that began in the early days of data processing. During the 1960s, disk space and memory were limited. To conserve these resources, dates were stored without a century value, because it was "understood" to be 19. Under such circumstances, there was not only no need to store the century, there was actually an incentive not to. Unfortunately, the habit has continued, and today it possesses a momentum that may not necessarily be reversible. Although many of us are responsible, none of us is really to blame. After all, six-digit dates were the de facto standard, and prior to 1988, six-digit dates were even officially sanctioned by the Federal Information Processing Standard (FIPS). Regardless of origin and accountability, we have nevertheless inherited a sizable legacy of defective data (i.e., files and records) and defective logic (i.e., programs, subroutines). Let's start by exploring some of the issues surrounding the storage of dates as data.

Nonstandardized Date Storage

Lack of standardization may be nowhere more evident than in the multitude of date formats found throughout our records, files, tables, and databases. Among these formats are the common Gregorian representations, which include the day, month, and year (with or without century), and Julian formats, which include the day within year and the year (with or without the century value). Within our files, there are also examples of edited dates with dashes, slashes, spelled-out months, and so on. Furthermore, there are even nines-complement dates wherein every digit has been subtracted from nine so the massaged date will sort in a sequence opposite to that of the original date. Oftentimes this is done when the date is part of a larger key and there is a desire to sort the date and the rest of the key in opposite sequences.

In addition to these formats are the so-called "serial dates," which are counts of the number of days from a particular base date. Some IT shops use a base date that is not necessarily the same as the base date of other shops. And to add to the confusion, there are situations in which vendors and vendor products don't even share a common base date. For example, consider the following IBM products: the reference date for DB2 is January 1, 0001; the reference date for LE370 is October 15, 1582; the reference date for COBOL 370 is January 1, 1601; and the reference date for CICS is January 1, 1900. Obviously, date formats have not evolved in a very standardized fashion. But possibly worse yet are examples of nonstandardized date logic. Now let's explore some of the serious issues surrounding date calculations that are neither rigorous nor necessarily correct.

Nonstandardized Date Logic

General Considerations

As we delve into the realm of date logic, we quickly begin to see just how varied such logic can be. It can be as complex as pages of program code, or it can be as simple as a single sort key. Most of the time, however, date logic is found in the form of highly specialized date routines. For some shops, there may be one highly specialized routine that converts a date from a Gregorian format to a Julian format, while a different but equally specialized routine may convert a date from a Julian format to a Gregorian format. In such a shop, there are likely to be even more routines that, for example, test for holiday status or determine the day of the week.

The difficulty with highly specialized routines is that it's often difficult for programmers to find examples of the desired routine and subsequently to train themselves in the required protocol. In some shops, date routines were written in a quick-and-dirty fashion to support business functionality that was needed on the spur of the moment. Other times, date logic was written inline, as paragraphs of hard-coded logic, simply because no one could find a date routine with the required functionality. And finally, although most date logic is performed as part of an externally invoked date routine or executed internally as hard-coded logic, there are instances where logic is performed by means of a COBOL copybook that is brought into the program at compilation time.

Current Date Retrieval

Another issue surrounding nonstandardized date logic is that of current-date retrieval itself. One of the most important distinctions to make is between a current date that is retrieved from a predetermined source, such as a file or table or SYSIN, and a current date that is retrieved from the computer's clock. The former example is usually a run-date or "parm-date" and is typically used in a batch cycle to keep the aging the same whether the program is executed before or after midnight. The latter example, however, is a date that is retrieved from the system through special registers or intrinsic functions.

Depending on the environment and/or language dialect, the century value may or may not be available for return to the calling application program. For example, ANSI 85, OS/VS, and COBOL II do not provide the century. The century is available, however, in ANSI 89 and COBOL 370. In a CICS environment, the century is not available in EIBDATE, but it is available by using ABSTIME and FORMATTIME. The danger in not having the century value supplied is that some programs are remiss in how they handle the missing century. Sometimes the century value is ignored, and therefore it remains uninitialized as spaces, zeros, low values, or high values. Other times the century value is assigned a hard-coded "19," which is the classic "patch-it" approach. This "solution" works fine through December 31, 1999, after which time it will be immediately wrong. Current date retrieval is a serious form of date logic and as such merits special attention.

Bizarre Example

Some date logic may be difficult to follow because a certain "clever" technique was used. For example, sometime during the history of data processing someone discovered that if a six-digit date is multiplied by 1,000,001, a string will result wherein the date lies next to itself. From this superstring, substrings, containing dates of various alternate formats can be extracted. Thus, there are programs that will convert a MMDDYY format to YYMMDD format by multiplying a six-digit number by a seven-digit number. This is not only cryptic and difficult to maintain, it's also highly inefficient. But it is there.

High-Order Truncation

Probably one of the greatest risks associated with the year-2000 problem is the potential for high-order truncation. This can easily occur when computations go totally awry and the intermediate variables are too small to hold the results. In such a case, the sign and/or the most significant digits could be lost. Let's consider an example. We start by observing that the correct answer for the number of days between January 1, 2000, and December 31, 1999, is +1. However, if the date calculation thinks 00 is 1900, then the computed answer will be 99 years backward. Since the number of days in −99 years is −36,525, that becomes the nominal answer. With any luck at all, such an answer would stand out.

However, let's suppose the program was using an unsigned intermediate working storage variable with only two digits. Under such conditions, the program could compute an answer of +25 (due to the loss of the sign and the three most significant digits). Since +25 is somewhat close to the correct answer of +1, the corrupted answer could go undetected for days, weeks, or months. From such an example it should be clear that over the next few years we run the serious risk of contaminating our databases without even realizing it. Furthermore, by the time the problems are discovered, if ever, it may be too late to recover, particularly if certain critical files are no longer available.

Not Limited to the 1900s and 2000s

We should not assume that the year-2000 issue is limited to just the 1900s and the 2000s. Granted, most applications use a century value of 19 or 20, but there are commercial examples of century values other than 19 or 20. One example is a county government in Florida that allows property holders to reserve mineral rights 125 years into the future. Therefore, county residents who apply for such real estate protection in 1996 will have a century value of 2121 posted to their record.

Another commercial example (and a common one at that) is birth dates. Although many birth dates go back to 1800s, some go back further still. There are well-established insurance companies that store birth dates for original life insurance policy-holders who were born in the 1700s, and these companies process those dates as part of their life expectancy actuarial analyses. But the primary reason birth dates are such a challenging commercial application is that their range is greater than 100 years. Thus it can be very difficult to determine the century value just by looking at the value of the year. For example, it is mathematically impossible to look at 94 and know if it means 1894 or 1994. What is required is another piece of application knowledge so that the century value can be deduced, (e.g., the individual is a veteran of World War I, or the individual has come into the clinic to be treated for colic). As we implement solutions for the year 2000 and begin to use century windowing techniques, it is important to apply such solutions carefully and with enough power to span several centuries.

Miscellaneous Issues

Although the year-2000 focus tends to be on mainstream COBOL systems, other areas of data processing are at equally serious risk. For example, whenever a date is part of a key, there is the risk that dates with 00 year values will be retrieved before dates with year values of 99, even though "2000" comes after "1999." A few examples where a date may be part of a key are: SORTs, SQL Where Clauses, IMS Segment Search Arguments, and VSAM KSDS files.

Other areas in data processing where we may find dates and date logic (including semiannual processes) are macros, TSO Clists, ROSPROCS, WYLBUR EXECS, CMS EXECS, REXX EXECS. There are also examples of dates that are embedded in data set names (e.g., SYS-

LIB.TXNMAY95.FISCAL) or dates that are embedded within data structures (e.g., a policy identification created by concatenating a person's birthdate to the initials of his or her name).

Regrettably, one of the more subtle dangers to date usage results from impact analyses that are conducted without a complete understanding of the corporate architecture. For example, many studies "conclude" that screens do not have to be changed because they are merely displayed, and, therefore, the operator will be able to figure them out. However, in some shops, with a hybrid client-server system (where the mainframe is the data server and legacy programs are wrapped to make them appear as objects), the CICS screen may not simply be displayed but may in fact be transmitted to a PC client that screen-scrapes information from the BMS map and processes the bases further. Thus what had been thought to be an optional change upon the BMS map as a display may become mandatory change upon the BMS map as a file.

As we dig even deeper into our systems, we see that dates are also used heavily in the user community, not just within the information systems department. In such situations, it is common to discover examples of production jobs written in EASYTRIEVE or DYL280 that are maintained and submitted by the users themselves. These jobs are just as vulnerable to the year-2000 problem and just as demanding of proper attention.

As we explore further still, we see that the year-2000 problem is not even limited to in-house custom code. Software that is purchased from outside vendors is also susceptible to the year 2000. In such circumstances, the software may have been modified by your company, and your company may or may not be under maintenance. Since your company is vulnerable to the whims of the vendor, it is crucial to begin dialog now! Find out if the vendor is addressing the year-2000 problem and when it plans to have the new version ready. Determine if the proposed delivery date will allow your company enough time to install the new version and decide if there are other areas, such as in-house systems, that will have to interface with the new version of the product.

Beyond all this is the recognition that one of the most serious risks to the year 2000 is not even technical. It has more to do with the year 2000 as a source management quality-assurance issue. Your company may be missing source code, or the source code you have may not necessarily be current. [Editor: If you've never recompiled all source at once, seven percent of your binaries are without matching source.] Likewise, there may be multiple versions to resolve.

Finally, and with a sense or irony, remember that even if your shop becomes 100 percent year-2000-compliant, unless there are standards, and they are enforced, it is likely that your systems will become corrupted again by someone who, lapsing back into old habits, reintroduces six-digit dates. In other words, date certification is an ongoing process that requires discipline and commitment.

Conclusion

So what does this all mean? In a sense, it means that we are fortunate. The year 2000 is actually providing the impetus to clean up 30 years of poorly defined dates and date logic. Taken in this light, we can view the next few years as a wonderful opportunity to set things right, potentially once and for all.

70   *Embedded Dates*

Richard Bergeon
Data Dimensions, Inc.

Copyright © 1996 Data Dimensions, Inc.

An *embedded* date is one which is used as a component of a longer alphanumeric character string to identify uniquely a particular item or event. Embedded dates are commonly found in invoice numbers, such as 94090013 where 9409 is the year and month of issue. Embedded dates also appear as components of policy numbers, license numbers, storage bin tags, merchandise sales tags, transaction numbers and date stamps. Embedded dates typically appear in four formats:

Type	Format	Common Application
Prefix	YYMMXXXX	Invoice #
Suffix	XXXXYYMM	Policy #
Encapsulated	XXYYMMXX	License #
Date/Time Stamp	XXX-YYMMDD-HHMMSS.SS or YYMMDD-HHMMSS.SS-XXX	Transaction Identification

When dates appear at the beginning or end of the field they are often used for *intelligence*—providing the observer with status information. Encapsulated dates are rarely significant.

Embedded dates can cause serious problems, some problems have a humorous side. Systems with embedded dates may misclassify or select 105-year olds along with 5-year olds; this happened recently in one state, where an elderly woman was sent a notice to appear for her first day of kindergarten.

Other problems may appear in the near future. Birth dates used in drivers' licenses and personal identification cards may cause problems. While it is rare to find a centenarian driving a vehicle today, this will change as people live, and remain physically active, longer.

Application Intelligence

When a field contains an embedded date, the following questions must be answered:

> Is it used to determine item aging or age?
> Is it used to sort the item into sequence?
> Is there a calculation being made?

If the answer to any of these questions is "Yes," then decisions have to be made about whether to include century in the identifier. This is where the serious problems begin.

Impact

Embedded dates create several problems for Millennium analysts. The major impact of the use of embedded dates is that it increases the number of programs that must be searched for, located, analyzed and converted. If included in a policy number, all programs which reference policy number (whether as POLNO, POLNUM, POL_NO, POLICY etc.) must be assessed.

The second issue encountered is the familiar one of file expansion. The decision must be made to expand the file or leave it as is. Expanding the field impacts reports and screen formats. Some organizations have attempted to squeeze the century in by substituting alphabetic or symbolic characters for year or month forgetting that system users employ the date for inspiring action.

The application client is usually involved in resolving the third common issue—what to do about embedded dates. The business reasons most often associated with embedded dates are inventory accounting (LIFO, FIFO); prioritization, expiration or accessibility. How the client uses them determines whether century is significant. If century is required, the support staff must be prepared to answer questions about the number, nature and complexity of revisions of date processing routines required. Unfortunately, involving the application client often opens the door to requests for other changes that may have been dormant for years. Now that the application requires modification those changes may appear justified.

Case Histories

Encryption—At least one government organization has a problem because the date is part of their encryption algorithm. Failure to resolve this problem will result in all data encrypted prior to 12/31/1999 becoming inaccessible on 1/1/2000.

Physical Limitations —One apparel retailer uses dates as a prefix to their stock item number. The retailer spent several million dollars on encoding and scanning equipment that could read the garment number. The scanners have a physical limitation on the length of the scan, so the date field cannot simply be lengthened. The other characters and digits are equally significant and cannot be dropped or truncated. Yet, if the century field is not added all inventory dated "99" or earlier will not be tracked correctly (e.g., they won't be aged for distribution, disposition or mark down).

The company's only options appear to be to either acquire new coders and scanners which can handle the longer field length, or _interpret_ dates to save space. The first solution means that some items will have to be dual tagged for some period as the current equipment is duplicated, and then replaced, at all sites. There may be problems with facility requirements. The second solution requires significant software analysis, conversion and redevelopment.

Date Stamping

Date stamping is another intelligent use of embedded dates in records. Date stamps are automatically placed on the record by the system for such things as transaction tracing and backup recovery. Date stamps often create problems as the formats change, e.g. old data is not recognized by the new recovery routines. If changes are not made, the transactions or records may be processed out of sequence.

Some relational database management systems employ standardized date stamp formats which include century. Organizations have, for example, overridden the standard date stamp and substituted a truncated (century-less) format. They do this for different reasons. One frequently given is that organization standard routines were built for IMS to query the date stamp. These were continued because not all applications have moved from IMS. When such a situation occurs there are usually new legacy requirements which require conversions before the vendor standard format is reinstated. Other organizations have created special date stamp requirements, such as, tagging records with the date of creation and date of expiration. This method is used by a brokerage firm to track stock purchases. The expiration date is calculated from the purchase execution date. This calculation will result in an execution date earlier than the purchase date at the end of 1999.

Special Situations

Space Saving—Some organizations have gone to great lengths to minimize the space used to store dates. Some dates may actually look encrypted. A year may be arbitrarily assigned the value of "A," and the next given "B," etc. We refer to these date formats as *interpreted* . The format of the field may appear as YDDD, where Y has an alphanumeric, or even symbolic, value. We have also seen formats of YMDD where both year and month appear with values of 1 – 9, 0, A or B.

Zero Prefix Suppression —In situations where dates appear at the beginning of the identifier, we encounter a new difficulty. Some application software automatically suppresses leading zeros in numeric fields. This can create data misinterpretation when significant digits are left off reports. It can also cause miscalculations. "00" can be treated as null data and be rejected, cause a calculation error, or cause a zero divide error.

71   *COBOL*

Patrick Hagan
Project One Computer Consultants

The current representation of dates in the IBM mainframe COBOL environment uses a two-digit field to hold the year. In the year 2000 this limited year representation will create numerous failures which will impair business operations. Before giving the LE COBOL/370 elements for fixing the Year 2000 problem let me clear up some of the misconceptions about solving the problem.

1. Companies do not need extra tools or software to solve the Year 2000 problem. If they have the programming resources to fix it, they do not need any new software. But due to the lack of resources and the severe time constraint some tools will be needed to analyze, fix, and test the

software inventory. LE COBOL 370 provides some functions and callable routines to fix the problem, but it is only one method and a company does not have to upgrade to LE COBOL/370 in order to become
Year 2000 compliant.

2. Not all the programs with dates need to be changed. Only those programs which send or receive files which are EXTERNAL to the company often must be changed to FOUR (4) digit years. Internal files and
programs can use any method as long as it is consistent between departments, but the four digit year is the best way to solve the problem.
This is the recommendation of all the standards organizations including NIST, ISO, and ANSI. If a company does not use four digit years
when required for EXTERNAL files, they better have real good lawyers
or prepare to go out of business before the year 2000.

3. The problem is technically easy to fix: A) find the programs with dates,
B) decide what method to use to fix a particular program, C) fix it, D)
test it, E) put it into production. The difficulty is caused by the huge
number of programs that potentially need to be fixed and the level of
project management needed to fix them. Decisions need to be made
quickly and the actual work must be started as soon as possible. Most
large organizations operate like elephants while a Year 2000 project
must be handled by mice—i.e., get in and get out.

I have used COBOL II and COBOL/370 (aka COBOL for VM and
MVS) cooperatively within the same application with no apparent ill
effects. The COBOL II compile does not hit COBOL/370's special libraries. The LE/370 callable routines (date conversion, etc.) can be called
from COBOL/370 but not from COBOL II, so you would need LE/370 if
you had never developed standard date routines or were unable or
unwilling to upgrade them for Y2K.

Most major organizations routinely upgrade to the current versions
of VM and MVS. That upgrade does not entail a COBOL/370 upgrade.
COBOL II is still going to be supported by IBM, at least into 2001.

The current representation of dates in the IBM mainframe COBOL
environment uses a two-digit field to represent the year. In the year 2000
this limited year representation will create numerous failures which will
impair business operations. The method presented here involves converting to Language Environment/370 and COBOL/370 in order to make the
necessary programming changes. By upgrading to COBOL/370 a company might get the extra benefit of avoiding expensing all the Year 2000
expenses in the year incurred as required by the FASB. COBOL/370 uses
intrinsic functions while Language Environment/370 (LE/370) provides
CALLable services to provide date routines.

COBOL/370's Intrinsic Functions

1. The CURRENT-DATE function returns a 21-character alphanumeric value that represents the calendar date, time of day, and time differential from Greenwich Mean Time provided by the system on which the function is evaluated.

   The format is:

Bytes	Description
1-4	Year
5-6	Month
7-8	Day
9-10	Number of hours past midnight (00 to 23)
11-12	Number of minutes past the hour (00 to 59)
13-14	Number of seconds past the minute (00 to 59)
15-16	Number of hundredths of second past the second (00 to 99)
17	Either '+'or '-' for time behind Greenwich(–) or ahead(+).
18-19	Number of hours that the time is behind or ahead of Greenwich time.
20-21	Number of additional minutes that the time is behind or ahead of Greenwich time.

   Syntax:

   FUNCTION CURRENT-DATE

2. The DATE-OF-INTEGER function returns a numeric value that represents a date in the Gregorian format (YYYYMMDD). It requires one argument which is a number in integer format which is the number of days since December 31, 1800.

   Syntax:

   FUNCTION DATE-OF-INTEGER (integer-argument)

3. The DAY-OF-INTEGER function returns a numeric value that represents a date in the Julian format (YYYYDDD). It requires one argument which is a number in integer format.

   Syntax:

   FUNCTION DAY-OF-INTEGER (integer-argument)

4. The INTEGER-OF-DATE function returns an integer date format that represents a date in the Gregorian format YYYYMMDD). It requires one argument which is a number in form YYYYMMDD.

   Syntax:

   FUNCTION INTEGER-OF-DATE (YYYYMMDD-argument)

5. The INTEGER-OF-DAY function returns an integer date format that represents a date in the Julian date (YYYYDDD). It requires one argument which is a number in form YYYYDDD.

   Syntax:

   FUNCTION INTEGER-OF-DAY (YYYYDDD-argument)

6. Here is an example to get just the date using the CURRENT-DATE function:

   MOVE FUNCTION CURRENT-DATE (1:8) TO receiving field

The Language Environment/370 Date and Time CALLable services use the Lilian integer date format which is a number representing the number of days since October 14, 1582. The advantage of using these services is they allow the year to be two digits while the COBOL/370 intrinsic functions require the year to be four digits. Since these CALLable services have an extensive parameter call setup they will only be listed here. If you want to use them properly you should refer to the explanations and examples in the IBM LE/370 Programming Guide.

1.	CEEDAYS	- Convert Date to Lilian
2.	CEEDATE	- Convert Lilian Date to Character
3.	CEEDATM	- Convert Seconds to Character Timestamp
4.	CEEDYWK	- Calculate Day of Week from Lilian Date
5.	CEEGMT	- Get Greenwich Mean Time (same as CEEUTC)
6.	CEEGMTO	- Get Offset from Greenwich Mean Time to Local Time
7.	CEEISEC	- Convert Integers to Seconds
8.	CEELOCT	- Get Current Local Time
9.	CEEQCEN	- Query the Century Window for a shifting window time
10.	CEESCEN	- Set the Century Window for a shifting window time
11.	CEESECI	- Convert Seconds to Integers
12.	CEESECS	- Convert Timestamp to Number of Seconds
13.	CEEUTC	- Get Coordinated Universal Time (same as CEEGMT)

72   *Date Routines*

Harold Zbiegien
American Greetings Corp.

These are several routines I have found by searching the Web, SIMTEL archives and relevant books and magazine articles. My preference was to use routines that did NOT utilize tables. All routines have been checked by me against each other and the SAS date functions in MVS SAS Release 6.08 level TS404. This level of SAS is only good for dates in the range: Jan 1, 1600< date <Feb 29, 4000. Incorrect answers result if dates outside of this range are used. The routines below have been tested by me for dates in the range: Oct 14, 1582 < date < Dec 31, 9999.

Disclaimer:

➤ I make no warranty or guarantee on the accuracy of these routines or your implementation into actual code.

➤ I speak for myself, my statements are not those of my company.

Note the Gregorian calendar, on which all these routines are based assumes the year is 365.2425 days long. This is not true. One astronomer put the figure at 365.24219879 days at the start of the 1900 epoch. ALSO the length of the year is gradually SHORTENING! Around the year 4317 we will have to drop a day, and again somewhere near the years 6000, 7500, and 9000. (reference: "The Gregorian calendar", G. Moyer, Scientific American, May 1982).

These routines should be implemented using 32 bit or 9 digit precision arithmetic in the computer language of your choice. In some cases you can get by with 16 bit precision but I'll leave that up to you, the implementor, to figure out where. All division is integer division. By this I mean you drop the remainder. i.e., 35 / 4 is 8. The routines makes use of the MOD function. This is the remainder after integer division. I.E. MOD(35,4) is 3. To make division even more clear I use the INT function, integer portion, or truncate. i.e., INT(35 / 4) is 8.

Routine A: Convert from YYYY,MM,DD to YYYY,NNN and day-of-week
Routine B: Convert from YYYY,NNN to YYYY,MM,DD and day-of-week
Routine C: Convert from YYYY,NNN to Lilian (day 1=Fri Oct 15, 1582)
Routine D: Convert from Lilian to YYYY,NNN
Routine E: Convert from Lilian to day-of-week, and notes on the use of Lilian dates and day-of-week
Routine F: Convert from YYYY,MM,DD to YYYY,NNN
Routine G: Convert from YYYY,MM,DD to day-of-week

There are other routines for converting to/from Julian dates, e.g., the Julian date that astronomers use, where day zero was Jan 1, 4713 BC. But I felt that they were not of use to me in standard business functions.

The Algorithms

Routine A: Convert from YYYY,MM,DD to YYYY,NNN and day-of-week
Reference: Algorithm 398 in the Oct 1970 Communications of the ACM
By Richard A. Stone. The day-of-week calculations were added by me.

```
Input: YYY,MM,DD
Output: NNN (1-366)
IF MOD(YYY,4) = 0 THEN LY = 1 ELSE LY = 0
IF MOD (YYYY,100) = - THEN LY = 0
IF MOD(YYYY,400) = 0 THEN LY = 1      LY is 1 if it is a leap year
NNN = INT(((MM + 2) * 3055) / 100) + DD - 91
IF NNN > (59 + LY) THEN NNN = NNN - 2 + LY
for day-of-week (0-6, 0=Sunday, 1=Monday, etc.)
T = INT(YYYY / 100) - 6 - INT(YYYY / 400)
DOW = MOD((NNN + INT((YYYY * 5) / 4) - LY - T),7)
```

EX: 1996, Nov 1 results in NNN = 306, DOW = 5

Routine B: Convert from YYYY,NNN to YYYY,MM,DD and day-of-week
Reference: This is a reversal of Routine A worked out by me.

```
Input: YYYY,NNN (1-366)
Output: MM,DD
IF MOD(YYYY,4) = 0 THEN LY = 1 ELSE LY = 0
IF MOD(YYYY,100) = 0 THEN LY = 0
IF MOD(YYYY,400) = 0 THEN LY = 1      LY is 1 if it is a leap year
WORK = NNN
IF WORK > (LY + 59) THEN WORK = WORK + 2 - LY
MM = INT(((WORK + 91) * 100) / 3055)
DD = (WORK + 91) - INT((MM * 3055) / 100)
MM = MM - 2;
for day-of-week (0-6, 0=Sunday, 1=Monday, etc.)
T = INT(YYYY / 100) - 6 - INT(YYYY / 400)
DOW = MOD((NNN + INT((YYYY * 5) / 4) - LY - T),7)
```

EX: 1996, 306 results in Nov 1, DOW = 5

Routine C: Convert from YYYY,NNN to Lilian (day 1=Fri Oct 15, 1582)
Reference: "Computer processing of dates outside the twentieth century" By B. G. Ohns, IBM Systems Journal, vol 25 no 2, 1986. This routine matches the base algorithm in IBM's CEEDAYS routine in their Language Environment implementation as best as I can figure. This routine and CEEDAYS both have the same starting date.

Input: YYYY,NNN (1-366)
Output LIL (1 = Friday Oct 15, 1582)
LIL = INT(((YYY - 1201) * 36525) / 100) -
    139444 + NNN -
    INT((YYYY - 1201) / 100)+
    INT((YYYY - 1201) / 400)

EX: 1996,306 results in LIL = 151229

EX: May 16, 1988, NNN = 137, results in LIL = 148138

Routine D: Convert from Lilian to YYYY,NNN

Reference: "Computer processing of dates outside the twentieth century" By B. G. Ohms, IBM Systems Journal, vol 25 no 2, 1986. This routine matches the base algorithm in IBM's CEEDAYS routine in their Language Environment implementation as best as I can figure. This routine and CEEDAYS both have the same starting date.

Input: LIL (1 = Friday Oct 15, 1582)
Output: YYYY,NNN (1-366)
CLD = INT(((LIL + 139444) * 100) / 3652425)
NNN = CLD + LIL + 139444 - INT(CLD / 4)
WORK = INT((NNN * 100) / 36525)
IF MOD((NNN * 100), 35625) = 0 THEN WORK = WORK - 1
(in some computer languages the 2 lines above can be implemented as divide 36525 into (NNN * 100) giving WORK remainder REM if REM = 0 then WORK = WORK - 1)
NNN = NNN - INT**WORK * 36525) / 100)
YYYY = WORK + 1201;

EX: 151229 results in YYYY = 1996, NNN = 306

Routine E: Convert from Lilian to day-of-week, and notes on the use of Lilian dates and day-of-week

Input: LIL (1 = Friday Oct 15, 1582)
Output: day-of-week (0-6, 0=Sunday, 1=Monday, etc.)
DOW = MOD((LIL + 4),7)

EX: 151229 (Nov 1, 1996, 306) results in DOW = 5

Notes on Day-of-Week

These routines are coded to return a 0 value for Sunday. If you wish to have zero represent, say Monday, just add 1 to the value inside the MOD statement. Other constant values added inside the MOD statement will equate zero to other days.

Notes on Use of Lilian Days

Once you have a Lilian day value you can easily add and subtract constant day values to answer questions like, what day will it be 30 days from now? Or how man days are between two dates? Lilian days will NOT help you in questions like, how many business days are there between 2 dates? Things like Holidays, weekends, etc. are NOT accounted for. I think that only some type of Calendar (table) and a loop through that table will be able to answer questions like this. Also they will not help in answering questions like what will the date be 15 months from now?, or what is the date on the 3rd Tuesday in September of next year?

Routine F: Convert from YYYY,MM,DD to YYYY,NNN

Reference: "The Year 2000 Computing Crisis" by J. T. Murray and M. J. Murray. Documentation on an RPG routine in their diskette that is part of their book. Most of their other code is table based.

```
IF MOD(YYYY,4) = 0 THEN LY = 1 ELSE LY = 0
IF MOD(YYYY,100) = 0 THEN LY= 0
IF MOD(YYYY,400) = 0 THEN LY = 1      LY is 1 if it is a leap year
NNN = INT(3 / (MM + 1)) * (31 * (MM - 1) + DD) +
    INT((MM + 9) / 12) * (INT(((305 * (MM - 1) - 15) +
    INT((MM + 3) / 12) * 5 * INT(18 / MM)) / 10) + DD + LY);
```

EX: Nov 1, 1996 results in NNN = 306

Routine G: Convert from YYYY,MM,DD to day-of-week

Reference: a Zeller's congruence algorithm submitted by Mike Carroll of Candle Corp to the bit.listserv.ibm-main group on May 5, 1995. (I figured out a typo in his original posting, which I hope I didn't repeat myself)

```
Input: YYYY,MM,DD
Output: day-of-week (0-6, 0=Sunday, 1=Monday, etc.)
IF MM < 3 THEN
    WMM = MM + 12
    WYYY = YYYY - 1
ELSE
    WMM = MM
    WYYYY = YYYY
    DOW = MOD((WDD + 1 + (WMM * W) + INT(((WMM + 1) * ) / 5) +
        WYYYY + INT(WYYYY / 4) -
        INT(WYYYY / 100) + INT(WYYYY / 400)),7)
```

EX: Nov 1, 1996 results in DOW = 5

73   *Extended Interval Aging*

Jerome and Marilyn Murray

From: *The Year 2000 Computing Crisis* by Jerome T. Murray and Marilyn M. Murray, copyright ©1996 by the McGraw-Hill Companies. Reprinted with permission of the McGraw-Hill Companies.

Short-interval aging produces a single parameter, say 45, 60, or even 120 days. The parameter is meaningful but relevant only as long as its range doesn't exceed the scope of comprehension. A result such as 10,220 days old would convey little information to an inquirer seeking to determine the age of an employee.

The more you become involved in activity bearing on distant dates, the more you need to age in the area of extended intervals. Extended-interval aging addresses worker's ages, unexpired time on contracts, remaining time to maturity of financial instruments such as bonds, remaining life for leases, royalty agreements, and copyrights, and the like.

Clearly, there's need for meaningful aging of extended intervals—intervals in the range of years, months, and days. This chapter, then, will produce a subroutine that can be used to age such extended intervals.

The Problem of Extended Intervals

In searching for a set of parameters that measure the age difference between two Commercial-8 dates, you're essentially asking "How many years, months, and days have elapsed between the earlier and the later date?" Implicit in the problem is the need to determine at some point the chronology of the input dates.

More important, however, is the need for a functional definition of *month*. You must deal with three units of measurement in calendar form, and of these the month is by far the most variable. Rarely do two units have equal magnitudes. Moreover, *month* is commonly referred to in one of two ways, either of which can lead to undesired consequences.

One definition of a month is the time elapsed when the relative displacement of a date to the next consecutive month has occurred. For instance, the period of time from July 18 through August 18 would count as one month. Few would fault this definition until asked "Is February 28, 1999 to March 31, 1999 one month or one month and three days?" Obviously, the argument can be settled by tearing one page from the calendar, thus demonstrating that the period is exactly one month. Of course, with such a demonstration the relative-displacement definition is often torn up also. It need not be. It simply isn't functional on month-end boundaries.

This leads to the second definition. Traditionally, one month is the period of time that allows one calendar page to be torn from the calendar, in other words, the period from the last day of a month to the last day of the next month. Attempts to use this definition will find you counting the days from a given date to the *end* of that date's month-boundary. You then count calendar pages and finally add the surplus days to those initially counted to determine the time lapse between the two dates. In practice, however, this definition, which finds the time lapse between 02/15/1999 and 04/10/1999 by adding the days elapsed between 02/15 and 02/28 to the 10 days from 04/01 to 04/10 for a total of 23 days, simply counts whole months to arrive at a solution: in this example, 1 month and 23 days. Unhappily, when given two dates such as 02/02/1999 and 04/25/1999, a distorted result is obtained: one month and 51 days. Because 51 days is certainly more than one month by any measure, relative displacement gives a more acceptable solution in this case.

Members of the business community often date contracts, leases, and the like as of the first day of the following month, with costs pro-rated if the agreement is to take effect a number of days prior to the first of the month. In this way, the aging debate is avoided and the calendar page becomes the unit of measurement. Unfortunately, businessmen have begun to throw caution to the wind in the belief that computers can count. Often, their enthusiasm springs from a conviction that you can subtract dates to find elapsed time. Insurance professionals have long subtracted the earlier date from the later to find time lapse—perhaps without realizing the false assumption inherent in this. The algorithm produces errors that might go undetected. While you can subtract in decimal arithmetic without concern, the Gregorian calendar features multiple modular arithmetics. You cannot subtract dates because the modulus in these arithmetics varies with the month and is 28, 29, 30, or 31 depending upon the month's name and whether it's a leap year.

Extended interval aging is indeed a problem. Consider Joseph Scaliger's claim that no one disputes the concept of the day. Beyond the day, all is variable and contentious in human affairs.

A Solution Strategy

In forging the solution strategy we'll proceed from the obvious to the more subtle. Clearly, if you're given two dates A and B, with A the earlier of the two, you must count calendar months (pages) if A is on its month-end boundary. For example, given 12/31/1999 (A) and 03/28/2000 (B), simply count January and February as two full months and then count 28 days to provide time-lapse parameters: PYEAR = 0, PMONTH = 2, and PDAY = 28.

You'll consistently count calendar months. Even when A is not on a month-end boundary, count the days until the next month-end boundary, count the intervening calendar months, and finally take the sum of counted days and days remaining to find your time-lapse parameters. For example, given 12/25/1999 (A) and 04/05/2001 (B), you'll find six days (31–25) until A's next month-end boundary. Calendar months separating the two dates is 15 and remaining days is 5. The parameters are then PYEAR = 1, PMONTH = 3, and PDAY = (6+5) = 11.

As you've seen, this procedure might result in a distorted PDAY value. In the last example, had B been 04/29/2001, the parameters would have been PYEAR = 1, PMONTH = 3, and PDAY = 35—hence the case for switching to relative date displacement. This strategy would displace A (12/25/1999) forward one year and four months to 04/25/2001 to produce these parameters: PYEAR = 1, PMONTH = 4, and PDAY = 4. Few would disagree with that result.

This introduces the need to define the smallest PDAY value to be considered *distorted* . The minimum PDAY value that allows a switch in strategy is the value of the maximum day limit of A's initial month (IMAX). But this criterion leads to difficulty. Given 06/29/1998 (A) and 07/30/1999 (B), witness the following logical anomaly. You first use the preferred calendar-month strategy to find PYEAR = 1, PMONTH = 0, and PDAY = 31. Since IMAX is 30 (less than PDAY), you switch to relative displacement and obtain PYEAR = 1, PMONTH = 1, and PDAY = 1. Implicit in the relative displacement is the displacement from 01/29 to 02/29, which we've counted as one month—there is in fact no 29-day February in the given interval. Obviously this criterion by itself is inadequate to assure logical consistency and freedom from error in the extended interval.

Consequently, another criterion must be invoked to determine the validity of a switch to relative date-displacement aging. Not only must PDAY be greater than IMAX, but A's initial day (ID) must be less than 29 to assure that an invalid displacement doesn't occur in a nonleap year. These restrictions to your ability to switch to relative date-displacement aging result in the possible development of a maximum PDAY parameter of 32. Consider 12/29/1997 (A) and 03/30/1998 (B). By calendar-month counting, you'll find that PYEAR = 0, PMONTH = 2, and PDAY = 32. You can't switch to relative date displacement in order to reduce PDAY, since the criterion ID < 29 cannot be met. Further, this particular interval can't be aged logically in any other manner. Relative date-displacement aging is logically impossible. Hence, by the only remaining valid definition of the month, you must accept a PDAY value as great as 32.

Your first emotional response to a PDAY value of 32 might be that some logical possibility has been overlooked. It has! If you could develop a universally acceptable numerical definition of the month for use in instances prohibiting the logical application of relative date-displacement to reduce PDAY values, you'd have a totally satisfying solution strategy. Sadly, universal acceptance is elusive. The average month's length, taken over a four-year leap-year cycle, is 30.4375 days. Hence there's a case for postulating in these instances that 31 days do constitute one month. However, many bankers will argue that 30 days constitute one month. Labor unions might insist on another value—say, 31 if PDAY = 32 and 30 if PDAY = 31. A good deal of importance might be attached to the differences.

To be sure, the occurrence of PDAY parameters of 31 or 32 in the extended interval is a function of the dates delimiting the aging interval. The A dates whose day values are less than 29 automatically switch to relative date displacement aging in the presence of PDAY ≥ IMAX, assuring a reduced PDAY value. Similarly, B dates on day 27 of the month or earlier assure an agreeable PDAY value, even if it's as large as 30—regardless of the A date's value. Hence, the solution strategy we've developed will produce an algorithm whose results meet with effortless agreement in all but a minority of cases.

The decision to convert 31-day or 32-day PDAY values to equivalent PMONTH increments can be left to the installation employing this algorithm. It might be practical to allow the programmer, acting in accord with user standards or industry fiat, to interrogate the returned PDAY parameter. If its value exceeds the convention, you can subtract to reduce PDAY, with the PMONTH parameter subsequently incremented. Alternatively, a solution that's described later in the chapter can be adopted.

Designing the Algorithm

Anticipating a straightforward and relatively simple algorithm, let's identify the several elements that will be involved. You can distinguish the two input dates, allowing M, D, and Y to represent the components of the earlier date and TM, TD, and TY representing the later date's components. Here the T indicates that in the aging activities the later date's components actually become target values that, when reached in the incrementation of the earlier date, signal termination of the procedure.

Let (Max D of M) be the maximum number of days that can occur in month M. Implicit in this definition is the dependence of (Max D of M) on the leap-year status of Y at the time of its determination. Let IMAX be the (Max D of M) for the initial M of the earliest date A, that is, M prior to the start of the aging process. Further, allow ID to be the value of the initial day of the earliest date, the D of A. Similar to IMAX, ID is the value of D prior to the start of the aging process. Allow C to be a counter.

The outputs are the three parameters PYEAR, PMONTH, and PDAY, which specify the number of years, months, and days that have elapsed between the earlier date M-D-Y and the later date TM-TD-TY. Finally, initially assume that C = 0. The calculation, then, consists of the observance of rules 1, 2, and 3:

```
   Rule 1

   If M = TM and Y = TY,
       1.1 PDAY = TD - D
       1.2 PYEAR = 0
       1.3 PMONTH = 0
       1.4 Exit

   Rule 2

   If M ≠ TM or Y ≠ TY,
       2.1 Let M = M + 1
       2.2 Let C = C + 1
       2.3 Let Y = Y + (M ÷ 13)
       2.4 Let M = M(Mod 13) + (M ÷ 13)
       2.5 Do Rule 2 until the antecedent is false

     Rule 3

Let X = TD - (Max D of M),
     3.1 If X ≥ 0,
         3.1.1 PYEAR = C ÷ 12
         3.1.2 PMONTH = C(Mod 12)
         3.1.3 PDAY = IMAX - ID + X
         3.1.4 Exit
     3.2 X < 0
         3.2.1 Let C = C - 1
         3.2.2 Let PDAY = IMAX - ID + TD
             (a) If PDAY ≥ IMAX and if ID < 29,
                 Let C = C + 1
                 PYEAR = C ÷ 12
                 PMONTH = C(Mod 12)
                 PDAY = TD - ID
                 Exit
             (b) If PDAY < IMAX or if ID ≥ 29,
                 PYEAR = C ÷ 12
```

```
PMONTH = C(Mod 12)
PDAY = IMAX - ID + TD
Exit
```

Rule 1 produces the parameters sought for equal dates or those dates differing only in their day values. If rule 1 fails to apply, rule 2 increments the unequal Y and M values until they reach the values of TY and TM, respectively. Rules 2.3 and 2.4 increment y and set M = 1 whenever M reaches 13. Otherwise, M continues to grow with each increment and Y isn't affected. When the components are equal, the iterations cease. Note that rule 2 employs the usual inclusive OR.

Rule 3 determines whether M has been excessively incremented. In Rule 3.1, the parameters are calculated directly. In Rule 3.2, X < 0, overshoot has occurred in that M has been incremented to equality with TM, but TD is less than the (Max D of M) for the incremented M. Recall that you're counting calendar pages and this implies that each increment places D on its month-end boundary—that is, D after each increment becomes equal to (Max D of M) for the newly created M.

If overshoot has occurred, you must reduce the counter by one and add the days from the initial D to the end of the month to TD, the surplus days. This is accomplished with 3.2.1 and 3.2.2.

Your final task is to adjust the PDAY value by switching to relative date displacement if the criteria permit. The adjustment is made with 3.2.2(a). Here you see that the counter is incremented. The parameters are calculated directly, with PDAY becoming the difference between TD and ID. Thus, when the criteria are met, you switch from counting calendar months to aging the relative date displacement. In place of adding beginning and ending days, calculate PDAY as a difference—the difference between the beginning-day value that was displaced to the month TM and TD, a day in TM. Thus you can avoid date subtraction, which involves _intermonth_ computation and the false assumption of a constant modulus, because you restrict your final days calculation to an _intramonth_ computation.

Rule 3.2.2(b) proceeds to calculate the parameters when the criteria fail either in whole or in part. The parameters here are the product of calendar-month counting. Note that the development of 31-day and 32-day PDAY values is directly attributable to the inconstancy of the modulus in Gregorian-calendar arithmetic. Finding it impossible to logically engage in relative date displacement, rule 3.2.2(b) calculates the PDAY parameter as the sum of days from _two_ different months. Hence, in the absence of a constant modulus, only an arbitrarily imposed standard or an authoritarian fiat can be invoked to find equivalents for values as large as 31 or 32 days.

With close inspection, it becomes clear that the 29-day criterion for the A date guarantees accuracy in an interval containing a non-leap-year February—a certainty in all intervals of 24 months or more. You can conclude that intervals of less than two years are liable to produce a debatable PDAY = 30; for instance, 04/29/1999 to 01/29/2001 renders PYEAR = 1, PMONTH = 8, and PDAY = 30. Relative date displacement aging here produces PYEAR = 1, PMONTH = 9, and PDAY = 0. Given the interval, it's the method of choice. Hence, while the example intervals were short and were chosen for illustrative purposes, an interval can be extended only at two years or more.

Defining the Algorithm's Components

Now you must define the inputs, return code, and outputs of the algorithm TUMESUB4. Two inputs are required, DATEX and DATEY. Each must be Commercial-8. CODE4, the return code, is defined as follows:

$$
CODE4 = \begin{cases}
0, \text{ if DATEX and DATEY are M/D/Y, Commercial-8} \\
2, \text{ If DATEX, M/D/Y is not valid numeric} \\
3, \text{ If DATEY, M/D/Y is not valid numberic} \\
4, \text{ If for DATEX, Y } \varepsilon \text{ \{y: } 1600 < y < 3400\} \\
5, \text{ If for DATEY, Y } \varepsilon \text{ \{y: } 1600 < y < 3400\} \\
6, \text{ If for DATEX, M } \varepsilon \text{ \{m: } 0 < m < 13\} \\
7, \text{ If for DATEY, M } \varepsilon \text{ \{m: } 0 < m < 13\} \\
8, \text{ If for DATEX, D } \varepsilon \text{ \{d\} as defined in Commercial-8} \\
9, \text{ If for DATEY, D } \varepsilon \text{ \{d\} as defined in Commercial-8}
\end{cases}
$$

In CODE4, 0 means that execution was successful, 2 or 3 identifies bad date, 4 or 5 indicates a bad year, 6 or 7 identifies a bad month, and 8 or 9 results from a bad day for DATEX or DATEY, respectively.

The outputs consist of PDAY, PMONTH, and PYEAR, representing the days, months, and years that, elapsed since the earlier DATEX and DATEY, will product the later date. Hence PYEAR is defined as:

$$
PYEAR = \begin{cases}
0, \text{ If CODE4 } \neq 0 \\
0, \text{ If CODE4 } = 0, \text{ and DATEX} = \text{DATEY} \\
N, \text{ If CODE4 } = 0, \text{ and DATEX} \neq \text{DATEY, where} \\
\quad N \varepsilon \text{ \{n: n belongs to Z, } 0 \leq n\}
\end{cases}
$$

PMONTH, however, is limited:

$$
PMONTH = \begin{cases}
0, \text{ If CODE4 } \neq 0 \\
0, \text{ If CODE4 } = 0, \text{ and DATEX} = \text{DATEY} \\
N, \text{ If CODE4 } = 0, \text{ and DATEX} \neq \text{DATEY, where} \\
\quad N \varepsilon \text{ \{n: n belongs to Z, } 0 \leq n < 12\}
\end{cases}
$$

PDAY too is limited:

$$PYEAR = \begin{cases} 0, \text{If CODE4} \neq 0 \\ 0, \text{If CODE4} = 0, \text{and DATEX} = \text{DATEY} \\ N, \text{If CODE4} = 0, \text{and DATEX} \neq \text{DATEY, where} \\ \quad N \; \varepsilon \; \{n: n \text{ belongs to } Z, 0 \leq n < 33\} \end{cases}$$

The Pseudocode for TIMESUB4

The pseudocode assumes that its input has been passed to it in two eight-byte zoned decimal fields, DATEX and DATEY. The output fields PYEAR, PMONTH, and PDAY are three-byted packed, two-bytes packed, and two-bytes packed, respectively. A counter, constants, and work fields are self-evident.

```
   * Perform general housekeeping.
 1) Let CODE4 = 0
 2) Let YRSAVX = 0
 3) Let PDAY = 0
 4) Let PMONTH = 0
 5) Let PYEAR = 0
 6) Let COUNTER = 0
   * Input-related housekeeping: DATEX.
 7) Move DATEX to WORK8
 8) Move DATEX to WORK8X in FIPS-8 format
 9) Let CONSTANT2 = 2
10) Let CONSTANT4 = 4
11) Let CONSTANT6 = 6
12) Let CONSTANT8 = 8
13) Go to 20
   * Input-related housekeeping: DATEY:
14) Move DATEY to WORK8
15) Move DATEY to WORK8Y in FIPS-8 format
16) Let CONSTANT2 = 3
17) Let CONSTANT4 = 5
18) Let CONSTANT6 = 7
19) Let CONSTANT8 = 9
   * Validate input date as numeric.
20) If WORK8 is numeric, go to 22
21) Let CODE4 = CONSTANT2, go to 88
   * Save components of WORK8 and edit Y for limit violation.
22) WORK8 → M, D, Y
23) If YRSAVX ≠ 0, go to 28
24) Move M to MOSAVX
25) Move D to DASAVX
26) Move Y to YRSAVX
27) Go to 31
28) Move M to MOSAVY
29) Move D to DASAVY
```

39) Move Y to YRSAVY
31) If Y is within limits per Commercial-8, to go 33
32) Let CODE4 = CONSTANT4, go to 88
 * Execute leap-year algorithm for y.
33) Let L = 0
34) If y is a leap year, let L = 1
 * Edit M for limit violation.
35) If M is within limits per Commercial-8, go to 37
36) Let CODE4 = CONSTANT6, go to 88
 * Edit D for limit violation.
37) If D is within limits per Commercial-8, go to 39
38) Let CODE4 = CONSTANT8, go to 88
 * Determine which date has progressed.
39) If CONSTANT8 = 9, go to 41
40) Go to 14
 * Compute elapsed time.
 * First, determine date chronology and move earliest date
 * to Y, M, and D. Then move latest date to TY, TM, and TD.
41) If WORK8X > WORK8Y, go to 49
42) Move YSAVX to Y
43) Move YRSAVY to TY
44) Move MOSAVX to M
45) Move MOSAVY to TM
46) Move DASAVX to D
47) Move DASAVY to TD
48) Go to 55
49) Move YRSAVY to Y
50) Move YRSAVX to TY
51) Move MOSAVY to M
52) Move MOSAVX to TM
53) Move DASAVY to D
54) Move DASAVX to TD
 * Second, find parameters for all M = TM, Y = TY.
55) If M ≠ TM or Y ≠ TY, go to 58
56) Let PDAY = TD - D
57) Go to 88
 * Third, store (Max D of M) in IMAX, D in ID.
58) Let L = 0
59) If Y is a leap year, Let L = 1
60) Let IMAX = (Max D of M)
61) Let ID = D
 * Fourth, begin incrementing M.
62) If Y < TY, go to 65
63) If M < TM, go to 65
64) Go to 70
65) Let M = M + 1
66) Let COUNTER = COUNTER + 1
67) Let Y = Y + (M ÷ 13)
68) Let M = M(Mod 13) + (M ÷ 13)
69) Go to 62

```
 *   Fifth, Let D = (Max D of M) for incremented Y and M.
70)  Let L = 0
71)  If Y is a leap year, let L = 1
72)  Let D = (Max D of M)
 *   Sixth, test for overshoot.
73)  Let X = TD
74)  Let X = X - D
75)  If X < 0, go to 79
 *   If no overshoot, calculate PDAY value in TD.
76)  Let TD = X
77)  Let TD = TD + (IMAX - ID)
78)  Go to 85
 *   Seventh, correct overshoot.
79)  Let COUNTER = COUNTER - 1
80)  Let TD = TD + (IMAX - ID)
81)  If TD < IMAX, go to 85
82)  If ID ≥ 29, go to 85
 *   Switch to date displacement:
 *   TD ≥ IMAX and ID < 29 . . . let TD = TD - ID
83)  Let TD = TD - IMAX
 *   Note: see Step 80, above . TD - IMAX renders TD - ID
84)  Let COUNTER = COUNTER + 1
 *   Build parameters.
85)  Let PYEAR = COUNTER ÷ 12
86)  Let PMONTH = COUNTER(Mod 12)
87)  Let PDAY = TD
88)  Exit
```

The Source Code for TIMESUB4

Figure 73.1 shows a TIMESUB4 assembly listing. TIMESUB4 was extensively tested using both short-interval and extended-interval inputs. All results were as predicted. Figure 73.2 displays a subset of the test data. TIMESUB4 was judged to be a valid algorithm.

TIMESUB4 features a loop that's executed once for each input date. It is an edit-and-save loop; no problem-solving calculations are performed until both inputs are edited and their FIPS-8 images stored in #$4WRK8X and #$4WRK8Y, respectively. In order to facilitate later manipulation, components #$4MOSVX, #$4DASVX, and #$4YRSVX (related to #$4WRK8X and DATEX) become recipients of month, day, and year values. A similar set of save fields is assigned to DATEY.

Within the edit loop, section 2 of the source code initializes the CODE4 constants and reformats each date to its #$4WRK8X or #$4WRK8Y FIPS-8 save field. In section 4, the content or absence of content in #$4YRSVX indicates the set of component save fields to be used for the input currently in process. Finally, section 8 determines which date has just completed processing by interrogating the constant, #$48.

Immediately following the edit loop, section 9 computes elapsed-time parameters and creates the output fields. The source code follows the pseudocode and earlier-discussed algorithm rules rather closely. Exceptions are purely language-dependent features.

TIMESUB4 features two embedded subroutines that facilitate executing, from multiple points in the program, the leap-year algorithm and the algorithm that accesses the address of M's day-limit for a given M. TIMESUB4 saves and restores registers 5 and 6 prior to returning control to the calling program in order to make them available for the execution of these subroutines.

The Application of TIMESUB4

It's clear from the test data displayed in Figure 73.2 that PDAY values of 31 and 32 can develop in the extended interval. A debatable PDAY of 30 can also appear in the shorter interval (less than two years). These unusual values are the result of the dates delimiting the interval.

Assume the subroutine is being used to determine the age of workers whose birthdates are retained in an employee master file. The calculations are based on the birthdate A and the current date B. If the current date is less than day 28 of the month on which the aging is being executed, nothing unusual will appear in the PDAY value, regardless of the input birthdate's values.

This is true for any aging using an interval shorter than two years. Consequently, the subroutine is invulnerable 89 percent of the time during any year when one of the dates delimiting the aging interval is the current date. The inconstant modulus of Gregorian arithmetic is neutralized.

This leads to an alternative solution that can be invoked to avoid these unusual PDAY values. It isn't necessary to interrogate the PDAY value returned in order to adjust the value using an invoked standard or fiat if you first establish a simple protocol. If the aging is being executed when the current date is later than day 27 of the month, you can write the calling program to substitute the first day of the next consecutive month. In those instances, the output results need to be identified only with the terminal date—the B date—to avoid unwarranted assumptions that the actual current date was the effective date of the aging.

```
STMT    SOURCE STATEMENT                                   DOS/VSE ASSEMBLER 16.19 99-12-31

407 *                                                                              TS400010
408 * *************************************************************** *             TS400020
409 *                                                                *             TS400030
410 * TTTTTTT   III   MM    MM   EEEEE   SSSSS   U   U   BBBBB      4  *             TS400040
411 *    T      I    M M  M M    E       S       U   U   B    B   4 4  *             TS400050
412 *    T      I    M  M  M     EEEE    SSSSS   U   U   BBB B   44444 *             TS400060
413 *    T      I    M     M     E           S   U   U   B    B     4  *             TS400070
414 *    T     III   M     M     EEEEE   SSSSS   UUUUU   BBBBB      4  *             TS400080
415 *                                                                *             TS400090
416 * *************************************************************** *             TS400100
417 * *************************************************************** *             TS400110
418 *  E L A P S E D   D A Y S ,   M O N T H S ,   Y E A R S   B E T W E E N  *      TS400120
419 *                G R E G O R I A N   D A T E S                   *             TS400130
420 * *************************************************************** *             TS400140
421 * *************************************************************** *             TS400150
422 * ***************************************************************                TS400160
423 *             THIS SUBROUTINE CALCULATES ELAPSED DAYS, MONTHS AND     *         TS400170
424 *                  YEARS BETWEEN TWO GREGORIAN DATES                 *         TS400180
425 *                                                                   *         TS400190
426 *         1.  VALID INPUT YEARS FOR THIS SUBROUTINE ARE THE YEARS    *         TS400200
427 *             1601 THROUGH 3399 A. D.                                *         TS400210
428 *                                                                   *         TS400220
429 *         2.  VALID INPUT MONTH VALUES FOR THIS SUBROUTINE ARE 01    *         TS400230
430 *             THROUGH 12.                                            *         TS400240
431 *                                                                   *         TS400250
432 *         3.  VALID INPUT DAY VALUES FOR THIS SUBROUTINE ARE 01      *         TS400260
433 *             THROUGH 31 WITH EXCEPTIONS FOR THE MONTHS LISTED:      *         TS400270
434 *                      MONTH            MAXIMUM DAY VALUE            *         TS400280
435 *                       04                    30                    *         TS400290
436 *                       06                    30                    *         TS400300
437 *                       09                    30                    *         TS400310
438 *                       11                    30                    *         TS400320
439 *                       02                    28                    *         TS400330
440 *                       02 DURING LEAP YEAR   29                    *         TS400340
441 *                                                                   *         TS400350
442 *         4.  THE DATE FORMAT MUST BE MMDDYYYY.  WHERE MM = THE TWO  *         TS400360
443 *             DIGIT MONTH VALUE, DD = THE TWO DIGIT DAY VALUE AND    *         TS400370
444 *             YYYY = THE FOUR DIGIT YEAR.                           *         TS400380
445 *                                                                   *         TS400390
446 *         5.  THE CALLING PROGRAM MUST PLACE ONE EIGHT DIGIT DATE,   *         TS400400
447 *             IN ZONED FORMAT, IN A SUBROUTINE DEFINED EIGHT BYTE    *         TS400410
448 *             FIELD, 'DATEX.'  THE CALLING PROGRAM MUST PLACE THE OTHER *      TS400420
449 *             EIGHT DIGIT DATE, IN ZONED FORMAT, IN ANOTHER SUBROUTINE *       TS400430
450 *             DEFINED EIGHT BYTE FIELD, 'DATEY,' PRIOR TO EXECUTION OF *        TS400440
451 *             THE SUBROUTINE.  NEITHER FIELD IS ALTERED BY THE SUB-  *         TS400450
452 *             ROUTINE.                                              *         TS400460
453 *             NOTE:  ***  THE ORDER OF THE DATES IS IMMATERIAL.      *         TS400470
454 *                                                                   *         TS400480
455 *         6.  A SUBROUTINE DEFINED ONE BYTE FIELD, 'CODE4,' IS RETURNED *      TS400490
456 *             TO THE CALLING PROGRAM AND CONTAINS A PACKED 0 IF THE  *         TS400500
457 *             EXECUTION WAS SUCCESSFUL.  NON-ZERO VALUES INDICATE    *         TS400510
458 *             THE FOLLOWING:                                        *         TS400520
459 *                                                                   *         TS400530
460 *             A PACKED 2 FOR DATEX (3 FOR DATEY) INDICATES UNSUCCESS- *        TS400540
461 *             FUL EXECUTION: INVALID DATA.                           *         TS400550
```

Figure 73.1 TIMESUB4 source code

```
STMT    SOURCE STATEMENT                              DOS/VSE ASSEMBLER  16.19  99-12-31

462 *                                                                      *  TS400560
463 *              INVALID DATA ARE DETERMINED IF THE LOW ORDER BYTE'S ZONE *  TS400570
464 *              CONTAINS AN INVALID SIGN, (AN INVALID SIGN IS OTHER THAN *  TS400580
465 *              X'C', X'A', X'E', OR X'F') OR IF THE PRECEDING BYTES'    *  TS400590
466 *              ZONES ARE OTHER THAN X'F', OR IF THE LOW ORDER NIBBLE    *  TS400600
467 *              OF ANY BYTE CONTAINS A VALUE GREATER THAN X'9'.          *  TS400610
468 *                                                                      *  TS400620
469 *              A PACKED 4 FOR DATEX (5 FOR DATEY) INDICATES UNSUCCESS-  *  TS400630
470 *              FUL EXECUTION: INVALID YEAR- YEAR VALUE VIOLATES LIMITS  *  TS400640
471 *              SPECIFIED IN 1., ABOVE.                                  *  TS400650
472 *                                                                      *  TS400660
473 *              A PACKED 6 FOR DATEX (7 FOR DATEY) INDICATES UNSUCCESS-  *  TS400670
474 *              FUL EXECUTION: INVALID MONTH- MONTH VALUE VIOLATES LIMITS*  TS400680
475 *              SPECIFIED IN 2., ABOVE.                                  *  TS400690
476 *                                                                      *  TS400700
477 *              A PACKED 8 FOR DATEX (9 FOR DATEY) INDICATES UNSUCCESS-  *  TS400710
478 *              FUL EXECUTION: INVALID DAY- DAY VALUE VIOLATES LIMITS    *  TS400720
479 *              SPECIFIED IN 3., ABOVE.                                  *  TS400730
480 *                                                                      *  TS400740
481 *              INSPECTION OF THE RETURN CODE IS IMPORTANT.  THE RETURN  *  TS400750
482 *              CODE, CODE4, REFLECTS THE LEVEL OF EDITING.  A RETURN    *  TS400760
483 *              CODE OF 2, FOR EXAMPLE, NOT ONLY INDICATES INVALIDITY OF *  TS400770
484 *              DATA, IT ALSO INDICATES THAT NO EDITING HAS BEEN DONE TO *  TS400780
485 *              VALIDATE THE YEAR, MONTH OR DAY VALUES.  A RETURN CODE OF*  TS400790
486 *              4 INDICATES THAT THE DATA ARE VALID BUT THAT THE YEAR WAS*  TS400800
487 *              FOUND INVALID- THE MONTH AND DAY VALUES HAVE NOT BEEN ED-*  TS400810
488 *              ITED.  A RETURN CODE OF 6 INDICATES THAT THE DATA AND    *  TS400820
489 *              YEAR ARE VALID BUT THAT THE MONTH IS INVALID- THE DAY    *  TS400830
490 *              VALUE HAS NOT BEEN EDITED.  FINALLY, A RETURN CODE OF 8  *  TS400840
491 *              INDICATES THAT THE DATA, YEAR AND MONTH ARE VALID BUT    *  TS400850
492 *              THAT THE DAY WAS FOUND INVALID FOR THE VALID MONTH GIVEN.*  TS400860
493 *              IN SHORT, THE RETURN CODE INDICATES THE LEVEL OF EDITING.*  TS400870
494 *              THE EDIT SEQUENCE IS DATEX: DATA, YEAR, MONTH AND DAY    *  TS400880
495 *              THEN DATEY: DATA, YEAR, MONTH AND DAY.                   *  TS400890
496 *                                                                      *  TS400900
497 *         7.   A SET OF SUBROUTINE DEFINED FIELDS ARE RETURNED TO THE   *  TS400910
498 *              CALLING PROGRAM:                                         *  TS400920
499 *                                                                      *  TS400930
500 *                   FIELD NAME      PACKED BYTES                        *  TS400940
501 *                   PDAY                2                               *  TS400950
502 *                   PMONTH              2                               *  TS400960
503 *                   PYEAR               3                               *  TS400970
504 *                                                                      *  TS400980
505 *              IF CODE4 CONTAINS A PACKED 0, SOME OF THESE FIELDS MAY    *  TS400990
506 *              CONTAIN POSITIVE INTEGERS.  THE INTEGERS REPRESENT THE   *  TS401000
507 *              ABSOLUTE VALUE OF YEARS, MONTHS AND DAYS THAT, WHEN ADDED*  TS401010
508 *              TO THE EARLIER OF THE TWO INPUT DATES, WILL PRODUCE THE  *  TS401020
509 *              LATER INPUT DATE.  IF THE INPUT DATES ARE EQUAL OR IF    *  TS401030
510 *              CODE4 CONTAINS A NON-ZERO RETURN CODE, THEN ALL THREE    *  TS401040
511 *              PARAMETER FIELDS; PDAY, PMONTH AND PYEAR WILL CONTAIN    *  TS401050
512 *              PACKED ZEROS.  THE PACKED ZEROS, IN THE PRESENCE OF A    *  TS401060
513 *              NON-ZERO RETURN CODE, PROTECT AGAINST THE ILLEGAL USE OF *  TS401070
514 *              A PRIOR EXECUTION'S RESULT.  THE PACKED ZEROS, IN THE    *  TS401080
515 *              PRESENCE OF A ZERO RETURN CODE, CONSTITUTE A VALID       *  TS401090
516 *              PARAMETER SET FOR EQUAL INPUT DATES.                     *  TS401100
```

Figure 73.1 *TIMESUB4 source code (Contd)*

```
STMT    SOURCE STATEMENT                           DOS/VSE ASSEMBLER 16.19 99-12-31

517 *                                                                  *  TS401110
518 *          8.   ALL OTHER SUBROUTINE DEFINED FIELDS AND LABELS ARE  *  TS401120
519 *               TRANSPARENT TO THE CALLING PROGRAM.                 *  TS401130
520 *                                                                   *  TS401140
521 *          9.   THIS SUBROUTINE IS WRITTEN TO BE ASSEMBLED WITH THE *  TS401150
522 *               CALLING PROGRAM AND SHOULD BE INSERTED IN THE CALLING  * TS401160
523 *               PROGRAM IMMEDIATELY BEFORE THE 'END' OPCODE.        *  TS401170
524 *                                                                   *  TS401180
525 *         10.   THIS SUBROUTINE USES REGISTER 6 AS THE LINK REGISTER.  * TS401190
526 *               IF REGISTER 6 IS ASSIGNED IN THE CALLING PROGRAM FOR   * TS401200
527 *               OTHER USES, IT MUST BE SAVED PRIOR TO EXECUTING THE *  TS401210
528 *               'BALR.'                                             *  TS401220
529 *                                                                   *  TS401230
530 *                                                                   *  TS401240
531 *                                         JEROME T. MURRAY          *  TS401250
532 *                                         MARILYN J. MURRAY         *  TS401260
533 * GLEN ELLYN, ILLINOIS                                              *  TS401270
534 *                                                                   *  TS401280
535 * ***************************************************************** *  TS401290
536 * ***************************************************************** *  TS401300
537 * ***************************************************************** *  TS401310
538 *                                                                      TS401320
539 *                    +++  SECTION 1- GENERAL HOUSEKEEPING  +++         TS401330
540 *                                                                      TS401340
541 *                       INITIALIZE INDICATIVE AND WORK FIELDS          TS401350
542 *                                                                      TS401360
543 TIMESUB4 ZAP    CODE4,=P'0'                                           TS401370
544      ZAP    #$4YRSVX,=P'0'                                            TS401380
545      ZAP    PDAY,=P'0'                                                TS401390
546      ZAP    PMONTH,=P'0'                                              TS401400
547      ZAP    PYEAR,=P'0'                                               TS401410
548      ZAP    #$4COUNT,=P'0'                                            TS401420
549 *                                                                      TS401430
550 *                       SAVE REGISTERS 1 THROUGH 6 IN SAVE FIELDS      TS401440
551 *                                                                      TS401450
552      STM    1,6,#$4RSAVE                                              TS401460
553 *                                                                      TS401470
554 *                    +++  SECTION 2- INPUT-RELATED HOUSEKEEPING  +++   TS401480
555 *                                                                      TS401490
556 *                       (THIS SECTION INITIALIZES FOR TWO ITERATIONS-  TS401500
557 *                       ONE FOR EACH INPUT DATE)                       TS401510
558 *                                                                      TS401520
559 *                       MOVE DATEX TO WORK FIELDS, CONVERT TO FIPS-8   TS401530
560 *                       FORMAT IN #$4WRK8X, ESTABLISH RETURN           TS401540
561 *                       CODE VALUES- BRANCH TO VALIDATE DATEX          TS401550
562 *                                                                      TS401560
563      MVC    #$4WORK8,DATEX                                            TS401570
564      MVC    #$4WRK8X(4),DATEX+4                                       TS401580
565      MVZ    #$4WRK8X+3(1),=C'0'                                       TS401590
566      MVC    #$4WRK8X+4(4),DATEX                                       TS401600
567      ZAP    #$42,=P'2'                                                TS401610
568      ZAP    #$44,=P'4'                                                TS401620
569      ZAP    #$46,=P'6'                                                TS401630
570      ZAP    #$48,=P'8'                                                TS401640
571      B      #$41DATE                                                  TS401650
```

Figure 73.1   TIMESUB4 source code (Contd)

```
STMT    SOURCE STATEMENT                              DOS/VSE ASSEMBLER 16.19 99-12-31

 572 *                                                                        TS401660
 573 *                          MOVE DATEY TO WORK FIELDS, CONVERT TO FIPS-8   TS401670
 574 *                          FORMAT IN #$4WRK8Y, ESTABLISH RETURN           TS401680
 575 *                          CODE VALUES- PROCEED TO VALIDATE DATEY         TS401690
 576 *                                                                        TS401700
 577 #$42DATE MVC   #$4WORK8,DATEY                                            TS401710
 578          MVC   #$4WRK8Y(4),DATEY+4                                       TS401720
 579          MVZ   #$4WRK8Y+3(1),=C'0'                                       TS401730
 580          MVC   #$4WRK8Y+4(4),DATEY                                       TS401740
 581          ZAP   #$42,=P'3'                                                TS401750
 582          ZAP   #$44,=P'5'                                                TS401760
 583          ZAP   #$46,=P'7'                                                TS401770
 584          ZAP   #$48,=P'9'                                                TS401780
 585 *                                                                        TS401790
 586 *                          +++  SECTION 3- NUMERIC VALIDATION   +++      TS401800
 587 *                                                                        TS401810
 588 *                          ISOLATE THE SIGN BYTE IN A WORK FIELD AND     TS401820
 589 *                          AUGMENT TABLE FOR VALID '+' SIGNS OTHER THAN  TS401830
 590 *                          X'F' FOR WHICH TABLE IS DEFINED: X'A', X'C',  TS401840
 591 *                          X'E'- EDIT FOR VALID '+' SIGN USING TRT       TS401850
 592 *                                                                        TS401860
 593 #$41DATE MVC   #$4SIGN,#$4WORK8+7                                        TS401870
 594          MVC   #$4TABL+160(10),#$4ZRO                                    TS401880
 595          MVC   #$4TABL+192(10),#$4ZRO                                    TS401890
 596          MVC   #$4TABL+224(10),#$4ZRO                                    TS401900
 597          TRT   #$4SIGN(1),#$4TABL                                        TS401910
 598          BC    8,#$4NUM                                                  TS401920
 599          B     #$4BDATA                                                  TS401930
 600 *                                                                        TS401940
 601 *                          REINITIALIZE TABLE AND EDIT FOR VALID ZONE    TS401950
 602 *                          AND DIGIT CONFIGURATIONS IN REMAINING BYTES   TS401960
 603 *                                                                        TS401970
 604 #$4NUM   MVI   #$4TABL,X'1C'                                             TS401980
 605          MVC   #$4TABL+1(239),#$4TABL                                    TS401990
 606          TRT   #$4WORK8(7),#$4TABL                                       TS402000
 607          BC    8,#$4PACK                                                 TS402010
 608 *                                                                        TS402020
 609 *                          POST 'BAD DATA' RETURN CODE AND EXIT          TS402030
 610 *                                                                        TS402040
 611 #$4BDATA ZAP   CODE4,#$42                                                TS402050
 612          B     #$4TERM                                                   TS402060
 613 *                                                                        TS402070
 614 *                          +++  SECTION 4- EDIT YEAR FOR LIMIT VIOLATIONS  +++   TS402080
 615 *                                                                        TS402090
 616 *                          PACK MONTH, DAY AND YEAR IN WORK FIELDS       TS402100
 617 *                                                                        TS402110
 618 #$4PACK  PACK  #$4M,#$4WORK8(2)                                          TS402120
 619          PACK  #$4D,#$4WORK8+2(2)                                        TS402130
 620          PACK  #$4Y,#$4WORK8+4(4)                                        TS402140
 621 *                                                                        TS402150
 622 *                          MOVE MONTH, DAY AND YEAR TO SAVE FIELDS FOR   TS402160
 623 *                          USE IN SECTION 9 WHERE THE TIME DIFFERENCE    TS402170
 624 *                          BETWEEN THE TWO DATES WILL BE ACCUMULATED     TS402180
 625 *                          AS PYEAR, PMONTH, AND PDAY-                   TS402190
 626 *                                                                        TS402200
```

Figure 73.1 TIMESUB4 source code (Contd)

```
STMT    SOURCE STATEMENT                              DOS/VSE ASSEMBLER 16.19 99-12-31

 627 *                           IF #$4YRSVX IS EMPTY, SAVE THE DATA IN          TS402210
 628 *                           #$4MOSVX, #$4DASVX AND #$4YRSVX                 TS402220
 629 *                                                                          TS402230
 630         CP      #$4YRSVX,=P'O'                                             TS402240
 631         BH      #$4SECND                                                   TS402250
 632         ZAP     #$4MOSVX,#$4M                                              TS402260
 633         ZAP     #$4DASVX,#$4D                                              TS402270
 634         ZAP     #$4YRSVX,#$4Y                                              TS402280
 635         B       #$4YRX                                                     TS402290
 636 *                                                                          TS402300
 637 *                           IF #$4YRSVX IS NOT EMPTY, THIS IS THE SECOND   TS402310
 638 *                           ITERATION AND THE SECOND DATE IS BEING         TS402320
 639 *                           PROCESSED- SAVE DATA IN #$4MOSVY, #$4DASVY     TS402330
 640 *                           AND #$4YRSVY                                   TS402340
 641 *                                                                          TS402350
 642 #$4SECND ZAP    #$4MOSVY,#$4M                                              TS402360
 643         ZAP     #$4DASVY,#$4D                                              TS402370
 644         ZAP     #$4YRSVY,#$4Y                                              TS402380
 645 *                                                                          TS402390
 646 *                           EDIT YEAR VALUE FOR LOWER LIMIT VIOLATION      TS402400
 647 *                                                                          TS402410
 648 #$4YRX   CP     #$4Y,=P'1600'                                             TS402420
 649         BH      #$4YRHI                                                    TS402430
 650 *                                                                          TS402440
 651 *                           POST 'BAD YEAR' RETURN CODE AND EXIT          TS402450
 652 *                                                                          TS402460
 653 #$4BADYR ZAP    CODE4,#$44                                                 TS402470
 654         B       #$4TERM                                                    TS402480
 655 *                                                                          TS402490
 656 *                           EDIT YEAR VALUE FOR UPPER LIMIT VIOLATION      TS402500
 657 *                                                                          TS402510
 658 #$4YRHI  CP     #$4Y,=P'3399'                                             TS402520
 659         BH      #$4BADYR                                                   TS402530
 660 *                                                                          TS402540
 661 *                       +++  SECTION 5- DETERMINE LEAP YEAR STATUS   +++   TS402550
 662 *                                                                          TS402560
 663 *                           EXECUTE LEAP YEAR ALGORITHM                    TS402570
 664 *                                                                          TS402580
 665         LA      5,#$4LEAPY                                                 TS402590
 666         BALR    6,5                                                        TS402600
 667 *                                                                          TS402610
 668 *                       +++  SECTION 6- EDIT MONTH FOR LIMIT VIOLATIONS   +++  TS402620
 669 *                                                                          TS402630
 670 *                           VERIFY THAT MONTH IS WITHIN RANGE: 1 - 12     TS402640
 671 *                             A) CONVERT MONTH TO BINARY IN REGISTER 3    TS402650
 672 *                                                                          TS402660
 673         ZAP     #$4CVB,#$4M                                                TS402670
 674         CVB     3,#$4CVB                                                   TS402680
 675 *                                                                          TS402690
 676 *                             B) STORE BINARY BYTE FROM REG 3 IN #$4FLD   TS402700
 677 *                                                                          TS402710
 678         STC     3,#$4FLD                                                   TS402720
 679 *                                                                          TS402730
 680 *                             C) INITIALIZE TABLE WITH X'00' FOR TRT      TS402740
 681 *                                                                          TS402750
```

Figure 73.1 TIMESUB4 source code (Contd)

```
STMT    SOURCE STATEMENT                        DOS/VSE ASSEMBLER 16.19 99-12-31

682              MVC   #$4TABL+1(12),#$4ZRO                    TS402760
683  *                                                         TS402770
684  *                         D) EXECUTE TRT USING #$4FLD     TS402780
685  *                                                         TS402790
686              TRT   #$4FLD(1),#$4TABL                       TS402800
687              BC    8,#$4DAEDT                              TS402810
688  *                                                         TS402820
689  *                     F) RESTORE TABLE - POST BAD MONTH RETURN CODE  TS402830
690  *                                                         TS402840
691              MVC   #$4TABL+1(12),#$4TABL                   TS402850
692              ZAP   CODE4,#$46                              TS402860
693              B     #$4TERM                                 TS402870
694  *                                                         TS402880
695  *               +++  SECTION 7- EDIT DAY FOR LIMIT VIOLATIONS  +++   TS402890
696  *                                                         TS402900
697  *                           RESTORE TABLE                 TS402910
698  *                                                         TS402920
699  #$4DAEDT MVC  #$4TABL+1(12),#$4TABL                       TS402930
700  *                                                         TS402940
701  *               EXECUTE ADDRESS OF MONTH'S DAY LIMIT ALGORITHM  TS402950
702  *                                                         TS402960
703              LA    5,#$4GETAB                              TS402970
704              BALR  6,5                                     TS402980
705  *                                                         TS402990
706  *               CONVERT SIGN OF PACKED DAY FROM X'F' TO X'C'  TS403000
707  *                                                         TS403010
708              ZAP   #$4D,#$4D                               TS403020
709  *                                                         TS403030
710  *               COMPARE DAY TABLE ENTRY (LIMIT) WITH INPUT DAY  TS403040
711  *                                                         TS403050
712              CLC   #$4D,0(4)                               TS403060
713  *                                                         TS403070
714  *               IF INPUT IS WITHIN LIMIT, EDIT DAY FOR ZERO  TS403080
715  *                                                         TS403090
716              BNH   #$4DALO                                 TS403100
717  *                                                         TS403110
718  *               ELSE POST BAD DAY RETURN CODE AND EXIT    TS403120
719  *                                                         TS403130
720  #$4BADA  ZAP   CODE4,#$48                                 TS403140
721              B     #$4TERM                                 TS403150
722  *                                                         TS403160
723  *               EDIT DAY VALUE FOR ZERO                   TS403170
724  *                                                         TS403180
725  #$4DALO  CP    #$4D,=P'00'                                TS403190
726              BE    #$4BADA                                 TS403200
727  *                                                         TS403210
728  *               +++  SECTION 8- DETERMINE WHICH DATE PROCESSED  +++  TS403220
729  *                                                         TS403230
730  *                   #$48 = 9 IF SECOND DATE HAS ALREADY PROCESSED,   TS403240
731  *                   GO TO SECTION 9 ELSE GO TO PROCESS SECOND DATE   TS403250
732  *                                                         TS403260
733              CP    #$48,=P'9'                              TS403270
734              BNE   #$42DATE                                TS403280
735  *                                                         TS403290
736  *               +++  SECTION 9- COMPUTE ELAPSED TIME  +++  TS403300
```

Figure 73.1 TIMESUB4 source code (Contd)

```
STMT   SOURCE STATEMENT                              DOS/VSE ASSEMBLER 16.19 99-12-31

737 *                                                                     TS403310
738 *                         DETERMINE WHICH INPUT DATE IS THE EARLIEST   TS403320
739 *                         (USING FIPS-8 FORMATS) AND INITIALIZE WORK   TS403330
740 *                         FIELDS ACCORDINGLY                           TS403340
741 *                                                                      TS403350
742          CLC   #$4WRK8X,#$4WRK8Y                                       TS403360
743          BH    #$4YR2                                                  TS403370
744          ZAP   #$4Y,#$4YRSVX                                           TS403380
745          ZAP   #$4TY,#$4YRSVY                                          TS403390
746          ZAP   #$4M,#$4MOSVX                                           TS403400
747          ZAP   #$4TM,#$4MOSVY                                          TS403410
748          ZAP   #$4D,#$4DASVX                                           TS403420
749          ZAP   #$4TD,#$4DASVY                                          TS403430
750          B     #$4YRMO                                                 TS403440
751 #$4YR2   ZAP   #$4Y,#$4YRSVY                                           TS403450
752          ZAP   #$4TY,#$4YRSVX                                          TS403460
753          ZAP   #$4M,#$4MOSVY                                           TS403470
754          ZAP   #$4TM,#$4MOSVX                                          TS403480
755          ZAP   #$4D,#$4DASVY                                           TS403490
756          ZAP   #$4TD,#$4DASVX                                          TS403500
757 *                                                                      TS403510
758 *                         IF M = TM AND Y = TY, LET PDAY = TD - D, EXIT TS403520
759 *                                                                      TS403530
760 #$4YRMO  CP    #$4Y,#$4TY                                              TS403540
761          BNE   #$4DALIM                                                TS403550
762          CP    #$4M,#$4TM                                              TS403560
763          BNE   #$4DALIM                                                TS403570
764          ZAP   PDAY,#$4TD                                              TS403580
765          SP    PDAY,#$4D                                               TS403590
766          B     #$4TERM                                                 TS403600
767 *                                                                      TS403610
768 *                         FIND MONTH'S MAXIMUM DAY VALUE (MAX D OF M)   TS403620
769 *                         A)   EXECUTE LEAP YEAR ALGORITHM             TS403630
770 *                                                                      TS403640
771 #$4DALIM LA    5,#$4LEAPY                                              TS403650
772          BALR  6,5                                                     TS403660
773 *                                                                      TS403670
774 *                         B)   INITIALIZE REGISTER 3 WITH BINARY MONTH TS403680
775 *                                                                      TS403690
776          ZAP   #$4CVB,#$4M                                             TS403700
777          CVB   3,#$4CVB                                                TS403710
778 *                                                                      TS403720
779 *                         C)   EXECUTE ADDRESS OF MONTH'S DAY LIMIT    TS403730
780 *                              ALGORITHM                               TS403740
781 *                                                                      TS403750
782          LA    5,#$4GETAB                                              TS403760
783          BALR  6,5                                                     TS403770
784 *                                                                      TS403780
785 *                         LET IMAX = (MAX D OF M)                      TS403790
786 *                         (SAVE (MAX D OF M) FOR INITIAL M)            TS403800
787 *                                                                      TS403810
788          ZAP   #$4IMAX,0(2,4)                                          TS403820
789 *                                                                      TS403830
790 *                         LET ID = D                                   TS403840
791 *                         (SAVE INITIAL VALUE OF D)                    TS403850
```

Figure 73.1 TIMESUB4 source code (Contd)

```
STMT   SOURCE STATEMENT                              DOS/VSE ASSEMBLER 16.19 99-12-31

 792 *                                                                      TS403860
 793            ZAP   #$4ID,#$4D                                            TS403870
 794 *                                                                      TS403880
 795 *                       INCREMENT EARLIEST YEAR AND MONTH UNTIL EQUAL  TS403890
 796 *                       TO LATEST YEAR AND MONTH WHILE COUNTING        TS403900
 797 *                       CALENDAR MONTHS                                TS403910
 798 *                                                                      TS403920
 799 #$4AGE     CP    #$4Y,#$4TY                                            TS403930
 800            BL    #$4UNDER                                              TS403940
 801            CP    #$4M,#$4TM                                            TS403950
 802            BL    #$4UNDER                                              TS403960
 803            B     #$4EVEN                                               TS403970
 804 #$4UNDER   AP    #$4M,=P'1'                                            TS403980
 805            AP    #$4COUNT,=P'1'                                        TS403990
 806            CP    #$4M,=P'13'                                           TS404000
 807            BL    #$4AGE                                                TS404010
 808            SP    #$4M,=P'12'                                           TS404020
 809            AP    #$4Y,=P'1'                                            TS404030
 810            B     #$4AGE                                                TS404040
 811 *                                                                      TS404050
 812 *                       FIND MONTH'S MAXIMUM DAY VALUE (MAX D OF M)    TS404060
 813 *                       FOR NEWLY CALCULATED M                         TS404070
 814 *                       A)   EXECUTE LEAP YEAR ALGORITHM               TS404080
 815 *                                                                      TS404090
 816 #$4EVEN    LA    5,#$4LEAPY                                            TS404100
 817            BALR  6,5                                                   TS404110
 818 *                                                                      TS404120
 819 *                       B)   INITIALIZE REGISTER 3 WITH BINARY MONTH   TS404130
 820 *                                                                      TS404140
 821            ZAP   #$4CVB,#$4M                                           TS404150
 822            CVB   3,#$4CVB                                              TS404160
 823 *                                                                      TS404170
 824 *                       C)   EXECUTE ADDRESS OF MONTH'S DAY LIMIT      TS404180
 825 *                            ALGORITHM                                 TS404190
 826 *                                                                      TS404200
 827            LA    5,#$4GETAB                                            TS404210
 828            BALR  6,5                                                   TS404220
 829 *                                                                      TS404230
 830 *                       LET D = (MAX D OF M)                           TS404240
 831 *                       (NEWLY CALCULATED M MAY HAVE DIFFERENT DAY LIMIT TS404250
 832 *                       THAN EARLIEST M DID AT START OF CALCULATIONS)  TS404260
 833 *                                                                      TS404270
 834            ZAP   #$4D,0(2,4)                                          TS404280
 835 *                                                                      TS404290
 836 *                       LET X = TD                                     TS404300
 837 *                       (PLACE TARGET DAY IN WORK FIELD)               TS404310
 838 *                                                                      TS404320
 839            ZAP   #$4X,#$4TD                                            TS404330
 840 *                                                                      TS404340
 841 *                       LET X = X - D                                  TS404350
 842 *                       (SUBTRACT NEWLY INITIALIZED D TO FIND REMAINING TS404360
 843 *                       DIFFERENCE DAYS- TO BE ADDED TO (IMAX - ID)    TS404370
 844 *                       TO PRODUCE THE DAYS PARAMETER)                 TS404380
 845 *                                                                      TS404390
 846            SP    #$4X,#$4D                                            TS404400
```

Figure 73.1   *TIMESUB4 source code (Contd)*

```
STMT    SOURCE STATEMENT                                    DOS/VSE ASSEMBLER 16.19 99-12-31

847  *                                                                      TS404410
848  *                          IF X < 0, OVERSHOOT HAS OCCURRED- BRANCH TO TS404420
849  *                          CORRECT                                     TS404430
850  *                                                                      TS404440
851          CP      #$4X,=P'0'                                             TS404450
852          BL      #$4OSHOT                                               TS404460
853  *                                                                      TS404470
854  *                          IF NOT X < 0, NO OVERSHOOT HAS OCCURRED-    TS404480
855  *                          LET TD = X + (IMAX - ID) AND BRANCH TO OUTPUT TS404490
856  *                          (TD NOW CONTAINS THE SUM OF THE DAYS COUNTED TO TS404500
857  *                          THE END OF THE EARLIEST MONTH, PLUS THE DAYS TS404510
858  *                          COUNTED TO THE TARGET DAY FROM THE END OF THE TS404520
859  *                          NEWLY CALCULATED MONTH- THIS SUM IS THE PDAY TS404530
860  *                          PARAMETER'S VALUE)                          TS404540
861  *                                                                      TS404550
862          ZAP     #$4TD,#$4X                                             TS404560
863          AP      #$4TD,#$4IMAX                                          TS404570
864          SP      #$4TD,#$4ID                                            TS404580
865          B       #$4PARAM                                              TS404590
866  *                                                                      TS404600
867  *                          THIS IS THE OVERSHOOT CORRECTION            TS404610
868  *                          LET COUNT = COUNT - 1                       TS404620
869  *                                                                      TS404630
870  #$4OSHOT SP     #$4COUNT,=P'1'                                         TS404640
871  *                                                                      TS404650
872  *                          LET TD = TD + (IMAX - ID)                   TS404660
873  *                          (OVERSHOOT IMPLIES THAT TD, PLUS THE DAYS   TS404670
874  *                          COUNTED FROM THE EARLIEST DAY TO THE END OF TS404680
875  *                          THE EARLIEST MONTH CONSTITUTE THE VALUE OF  TS404690
876  *                          THE PARAMETER, PDAY)                        TS404700
877  *                                                                      TS404710
878          AP      #$4TD,#$4IMAX                                          TS404720
879          SP      #$4TD,#$4ID                                            TS404730
880  *                                                                      TS404740
881  *                          IF TD NOT < IMAX AND INITIAL D < 29, SWITCH TO TS404750
882  *                          RELATIVE DATE DISPLACEMENT AGEING ELSE OUTPUT TS404760
883  *                                                                      TS404770
884          CP      #$4TD,#$4IMAX                                          TS404780
885          BL      #$4PARAM                                              TS404790
886          CP      #$4ID,=P'29'                                           TS404800
887          BNL     #$4PARAM                                              TS404810
888  *                                                                      TS404820
889  *                          TD NOT < IMAX AND INITIAL D < 29,          TS404830
890  *                          SWITCH TO RELATIVE DATE DISPLACEMENT AGEING- TS404840
891  *                          (SUBTRACT IMAX FROM THE CURRENT VALUE OF TD) TS404850
892  *                          PDAY PARAMETER WILL BE:                     TS404860
893  *                                      -1 < PDAY < 33                  TS404870
894  *                                                                      TS404880
895          SP      #$4TD,#$4IMAX                                          TS404890
896          AP      #$4COUNT,=P'1'                                         TS404900
897  *                                                                      TS404910
898  *                          BUILD PARAMETER FIELDS                      TS404920
899  *                                                                      TS404930
900  #$4PARAM ZAP    #$4WORK5,#$4COUNT                                      TS404940
901          DP      #$4WORK5,=P'12'                                        TS404950
```

Figure 73.1 _TIMESUB4 source code (Contd)_

```
STMT    SOURCE STATEMENT                              DOS/VSE ASSEMBLER 16.19 99-12-31

902             AP      PYEAR,#$4WORK5(3)                       TS404960
903             AP      PMONTH,#$4WORK5+3(2)                    TS404970
904             AP      PDAY,#$4TD                              TS404980
905 *                                                          TS404990
906 *                   +++  SECTION 10- TO RESTORE REGISTERS AND EXIT  +++  TS405000
907 *                                                          TS405010
908             B       #$4TERM                                TS405020
909 *                                                          TS405030
910 *                   +++  SECTION 11- SUBROUTINES  +++      TS405040
911 *                                                          TS405050
912 *             ***********************************          TS405060
913 *             * LEAP YEAR ALGORITHM SUBROUTINE  *          TS405070
914 *             ***********************************          TS405080
915 *                                                          TS405090
916 #$4LEAPY ZAP    #$4L,=P'0'                                 TS405100
917          ZAP    #$4WORK,#$4Y                               TS405110
918          DP     #$4WORK,=P'4'                              TS405120
919          CP     #$4WORK+4(1),=P'0'                         TS405130
920          BH     #$4NOLPY                                   TS405140
921          ZAP    #$4WORK,#$4Y                               TS405150
922          DP     #$4WORK,=P'100'                            TS405160
923          CP     #$4WORK+3(2),=P'0'                         TS405170
924          BH     #$4LPYR                                    TS405180
925          ZAP    #$4WORK,#$4Y                               TS405190
926          DP     #$4WORK,=P'400'                            TS405200
927          CP     #$4WORK+3(2),=P'0'                         TS405210
928          BH     #$4NOLPY                                   TS405220
929 *                                                          TS405230
930 *                        IF YEAR IS A LEAP YEAR, REINITIALIZE TO 1  TS405240
931 *                        ELSE INITIALIZED 0 REMAINS- EXIT  TS405250
932 *                                                          TS405260
933 #$4LPYR  ZAP    #$4L,=P'1'                                 TS405270
934 #$4NOLPY BR     6                                          TS405280
935 *                                                          TS405290
936 *             ******************************************   TS405300
937 *             * MONTH'S DAY LIMIT ADDRESS SUBROUTINE  *    TS405310
938 *             ******************************************   TS405320
939 *                                                          TS405330
940 #$4GETAB LA     4,#$4DATAB                                 TS405340
941 *                                                          TS405350
942 *                        AFTER LOADING ADDRESS OF DAY TABLE IN REGISTER  TS405360
943 *                        4, IF LEAP YEAR, INCREMENT TO LEAP YEAR FUNCTION TS405370
944 *                                                          TS405380
945          CP     #$4L,=P'0'                                 TS405390
946          BE     #$4NOL                                     TS405400
947          LA     4,2(4)                                     TS405410
948 *                                                          TS405420
949 *                        DIRECTLY ADDRESS TABLE DAY LIMIT FOR THIS MONTH  TS405430
950 *                          A) SUBTRACT 1 FROM BINARY MONTH VALUE IN REG 3  TS405440
951 *                                                          TS405450
952 #$4NOL   BCTR   3,0                                        TS405460
953 *                                                          TS405470
954 *                          B) MULTIPLY VALUE IN REG 3 BY 4  TS405480
955 *                                                          TS405490
956          SLL    3,2                                        TS405500
```

Figure 73.1 TIMESUB4 source code (Contd)

```
STMT    SOURCE STATEMENT                                    DOS/VSE ASSEMBLER 16.19 99-12-31

 957 *                                                                              TS405510
 958 *                              C) LOAD ADDRESS OF DAY TABLE ENTRY IN REG 4      TS405520
 959 *                                                                              TS405530
 960        LA     4,0(3,4)                                                         TS405540
 961 *                                                                              TS405550
 962 *                              EXIT                                            TS405560
 963 *                                                                              TS405570
 964        BR     6                                                                TS405580
 965 *                                                                              TS405590
 966 *                      +++  SECTION 12- DEFINE CONSTANTS AND STORAGE  +++       TS405600
 967 *                                                                              TS405610
 968 CODE4  DC     PL1'2'                                                           TS405620
 969 *                                                                              TS405630
 970 *                              THE DAY TABLE IS DEFINED WITH A PAIR OF TWO BYTE TS405640
 971 *                              ENTRIES FOR EACH OF THE 12 MONTHS- AN ENTRY FOR  TS405650
 972 *                              NON-LEAP YEAR AND AN ENTRY FOR LEAP YEAR         TS405660
 973 *                                                                              TS405670
 974 #$4DATAB DC   PL2'31',PL2'31'        JAN                                       TS405680
 975        DC     PL2'28',PL2'29'        FEB                                       TS405690
 976        DC     PL2'31',PL2'31'        MAR                                       TS405700
 977        DC     PL2'30',PL2'30'        APR                                       TS405710
 978        DC     PL2'31',PL2'31'        MAY                                       TS405720
 979        DC     PL2'30',PL2'30'        JUN                                       TS405730
 980        DC     PL2'31',PL2'31'        JUL                                       TS405740
 981        DC     PL2'31',PL2'31'        AUG                                       TS405750
 982        DC     PL2'30',PL2'30'        SEP                                       TS405760
 983        DC     PL2'31',PL2'31'        OCT                                       TS405770
 984        DC     PL2'30',PL2'30'        NOV                                       TS405780
 985        DC     PL2'31',PL2'31'        DEC                                       TS405790
 986 *                                                                              TS405800
 987 *                              TRANSLATION TABLE DEFINED FOR X'F0' - X'F9'      TS405810
 988 *                              (ALL TABLE POSITIONS EXCEPT THOSE CORRESPONDING  TS405820
 989 *                              TO X'F0' THROUGH X'F9' ARE SET TO A VALUE OTHER  TS405830
 990 *                              THAN X'00')                                      TS405840
 991 *                                                                              TS405850
 992 #$4TABL DC    240X'1C'                                                         TS405860
 993        DC     10X'00'                                                          TS405870
 994        DC     6X'1C'                                                           TS405880
 995 *                                                                              TS405890
 996 #$4ZRO  DC    12X'00'                                                          TS405900
 997 DATEX   DC    ZL8'00000000'                                                    TS405910
 998 DATEY   DC    ZL8'00000000'                                                    TS405920
 999 PMONTH  DC    PL2'0'                                                           TS405930
1000 PDAY    DC    PL2'0'                                                           TS405940
1001 PYEAR   DC    PL3'0'                                                           TS405950
1002 #$42    DS    PL1                                                              TS405960
1003 #$44    DS    PL1                                                              TS405970
1004 #$46    DS    PL1                                                              TS405980
1005 #$48    DS    PL1                                                              TS405990
1006 #$4L    DS    PL1                                                              TS406000
1007 #$4SIGN DS    ZL1                                                              TS406010
1008 #$4WORK5 DS   PL5                                                              TS406020
1009 #$4WORK8 DS   ZL8                                                              TS406030
1010 #$4WRK8X DS   ZL8                                                              TS406040
1011 #$4WRK8Y DS   ZL8                                                              TS406050
```

Figure 73.1 *TIMESUB4 source code (Contd)*

```
STMT   SOURCE STATEMENT                          DOS/VSE ASSEMBLER 16.19 99-12-31

1012 #$4COUNT DS    PL3                                        TS406060
1013 #$4M     DS    PL2                                        TS406070
1014 #$4MOSVX DS    PL2                                        TS406080
1015 #$4MOSVY DS    PL2                                        TS406090
1016 #$4D     DS    PL2                                        TS406100
1017 #$4ID    DS    PL2                                        TS406110
1018 #$4DASVX DS    PL2                                        TS406120
1019 #$4DASVY DS    PL2                                        TS406130
1020 #$4TD    DS    PL2                                        TS406140
1021 #$4X     DS    PL2                                        TS406150
1022 #$4IMAX  DS    PL2                                        TS406160
1023 #$4TM    DS    PL2                                        TS406170
1024 #$4Y     DS    PL3                                        TS406180
1025 #$4TY    DS    PL3                                        TS406190
1026 #$4YRSVX DS    PL3                                        TS406200
1027 #$4YRSVY DS    PL3                                        TS406210
1028 #$4WORK  DS    PL5                                        TS406220
1029 #$4FLD   DS    CL1                                        TS406230
1030 #$4RSAVE DS    6F                                         TS406240
1031 #$4CVB   DS    1D                                         TS406250
1032 #$4TERM  LM    1,6,#$4RSAVE                               TS406260
1033         BR    6                                           TS406270
1034         END   BEGIN
1035               =C'$$BOPEN '
1036               =C'SUBROUTINE ERROR'
1037               =C'$$BCLOSE'
1038               =A(REQUEST)
1039               =A(LIST)
1040               =C'INVALID DATA *** DATEX'
1041               =C'INVALID DATA *** DATEY'
1042               =C'INVALID YEAR *** DATEX'
1043               =C'INVALID YEAR *** DATEY'
1044               =P'00'
1045               =P'13'
1046               =P'12'
1047               =P'29'
1048               =P'100'
1049               =P'400'
1050               =P'1'
1051               =C'/'
1052               =P'0'
1053               =P'2'
1054               =C','
1055               =P'3'
1056               =P'4'
1057               =P'5'
1058               =P'6'
1059               =C'INVALID MONTH *** DATEX'
1060               =P'7'
1061               =C'INVALID MONTH *** DATEY'
1062               =P'8'
1063               =C'INVALID DAY *** DATEX'
1064               =P'9'
1065               =C'INVALID DAY *** DATEY'
1066               =C'PYEAR: YYYY, PMONTH: MM, PDAY: DD, '
```

Figure 73.1 TIMESUB4 source code (Contd)

TEST OF TIMESUB4 TO CALCULATE ELAPSED YEAR, MONTH AND DAY PARAMETERS BETWEEN DATES

DATEX	DATEY	PYEAR	PMONTH	PDAY	CODE4 CONTENTS	
08/29/1997	03/30/2000	0002	06	32	0	
06/29/1998	08/30/2203	0205	01	31	0	
04/29/1999	01/29/2001	0001	08	30	0	
06/15/1999	08/15/2121	0122	02	22	0	
12/31/1999	08/22/2408	0408	07	01	0	
12/31/1999	03/01/2711	0711	02	01	0	
12/30/2001	02/28/2009	0007	02	01	0	
03/05/2100	05/08/2483	0383	02	03	0	
12/31/2000	12/23/2004	0003	11	23	0	
03/31/2000	05/23/2085	0085	01	23	0	
12/31/1998	02/28/2003	0004	02	01	0	
12/30/1998	02/28/2115	0116	02	01	0	
12/31/1999	01/03/2042	0042	01	03	0	
11/12/1999	01/04/2057	0057	01	22	0	
08/29/1999	01/05/2091	0091	04	07	0	
04/29/1999	02/29/2051	0000	00	00	9	INVALID DAY *** DATEY
09/18/1996	10/02/2561	0565	00	14	0	
12/31/1999	03/04/2016	0016	02	04	0	
03/31/2002	02/28/2031	0028	11	00	0	
06/29/2001	02/29/2059	0000	00	00	9	INVALID DAY *** DATEY
06/29/2006	02/29/2041	0000	00	00	9	INVALID DAY *** DATEY
08/15/2003	08/15/2053	0050	00	00	0	
03/03/1988	03/03/2019	0031	00	00	0	
02/28/2000	02/28/2066	0066	01	01	0	
08/31/2003	04/09/2021	0017	07	09	0	
12/31/2001	12/23/2011	0009	11	23	0	
12/31/2009	12/27/2091	0081	11	27	0	
/ /	/ /	0000	00	00	2	INVALID DATA *** DATEX
00/31/2000	12/31/2000	0000	00	00	6	INVALID MONTH *** DATEX
12/00/2006	12/31/2009	0000	00	00	8	INVALID DAY *** DATEX
12/31/1600	12/31/1600	0000	00	00	4	INVALID YEAR *** DATEX
12/15/3400	12/02/2009	0000	00	00	4	INVALID YEAR *** DATEX
12/20/0000	12/14/2004	0000	00	00	4	INVALID YEAR *** DATEX
12/12/2100	13/31/2006	0000	00	00	7	INVALID MONTH *** DATEY
12/09/2020	12/32/2017	0000	00	00	9	INVALID DAY *** DATEY
12/31/2001	12/00/2001	0000	00	00	9	INVALID DAY *** DATEY
11/30/2006	12/31/1600	0000	00	00	5	INVALID YEAR *** DATEY
10/31/2004	12/31/3400	0000	00	00	5	INVALID YEAR *** DATEY
12/21/2001	12/31/0000	0000	00	00	5	INVALID YEAR *** DATEY
01/01/1601	12/31/3399	1798	11	30	0	
05/24/2134	05/24/2134	0000	00	00	0	
07/01/2100	09/01/2118	0018	02	17	0	
11/15/1999	01/02/2022	0022	01	01	0	
11/25/1799	12/02/1999	0200	00	07	0	

THE SUBROUTINE WAS EXECUTED   44 TIMES

Figure 73.2   A subset of test results from TEST04's execution of TIMESUB4, the extended-interval aging subroutine

74 *Reengineering Your Software for the Millennium*

William Brew
Reasoning, Inc.

This chapter is structured as follows. We first give a brief overview of the Year 2000 problem and discuss some implications of the problem. We then discuss the general nature of the solution to the problem. The remainder of the chapter discusses Reasoning/2000, Reasoning's solution.

The Problem

There are time bombs in your software that will explode sometime between now and the Year 2000. Representing and manipulating dates is central to most mission critical computer applications. Most such systems in use today are unable to correctly deal with dates that are later than December 31, 1999. The closer we get to the year 2000, the more likely it is that your applications will mishandle a date and fail. Sometimes the failure will be obvious; sometimes it will be subtle; whatever the failure mode, it represents a serious threat to your organization and cannot be ignored.

The majority of the computer applications in use today were developed years ago when the Year 2000 seemed too far in the future to worry about. These programs have historically represented the year portion of a date using only two digits. In fact, many organizations, including the United States Government, established standards that mandated that dates be represented using only two digits for the year. At the time, using only two digits to represent a year seemed like a reasonable space saving optimization. This optimization is coming back to haunt us now.

Using only two digits to represent a year in a date is really only representing years within the twentieth century. In other words, there is an implied higher order field that contains the century information "19," but this century information is not explicitly represented. A year value of "00" represents the Year 1900 and a value of "99" represents the Year 1999. Clearly this scheme breaks down in the Year 2000. The dilemma is whether the value "00" continues to represent the Year 1900 or whether it now represents the Year 2000. The ways in which the software handles this dilemma can lead to some rather strange results.

The use of only two digits to represent years leads to a number of failure modes in your software. Some of the obvious failure modes include:

> Date Calculations: Adding an interval to a date can cause the date to wrap around. For example the year 1996 would be represented using the value "96". If you are working on a 5 year forward projection and compute the year value for 5 years in the future as 96 + 05 = 01, then this year value actually represents the year 1901 instead of 2001. This will probably cause the application to fail in a rather unpredictable fashion.

> Date Comparisons: Comparing two dates that are on opposite sides of the year 2000 can lead to incorrect results. For example is the year "99" before or after the year "01"?

> Sorting: The ambiguity caused by implied century digits causes collation order problems. For example, in the year 2000, if a report is sorted by year, is the year "00" the most recent year and therefore should be at the top of the report or is it a very old year and therefore should be at the bottom of the report?

> Special Date Values: Many programs use the distinguished year values "99" or "00" to mean things like "date unknown" or "forever". This will clearly cause problems if these values are actually used to represent the years 1999 and 2000.

The Year 2000 problem cannot be ignored. The clock is ticking and the problem will cripple your organization unless you take corrective action now. The problem is unique in that

> we have advance warning—this is good

> there are time constraints that cannot be slipped—this is bad

The time constraints for this problem are not as far out as you might think. Problems will occur well before the Year 2000. Many applications need to deal with dates that are several years in the future; for example, applications used by lending institutions that deal with loan repayment schedules and cash management systems that project future returns on investments. Time is working against us; many applications are already experiencing problems.

Characteristics of the Solution

There is no silver bullet that will automatically solve your Year 2000 problem for you. The problem has a number of characteristics that will make 100 percent automated solutions impossible. However, a large portion of the solution can be automated to significantly reduce the cost over purely manual approaches.

At the highest level, the solution process for the year 2000 problem is:

Given a collection of programs, find, correct and test all the places in the programs where there are problems handling dates after the Year 2000 and make corresponding corrections to their data and associated infrastructure.

This statement is very vague and simplistic but it does hint at some of the key points in the solution to the Year 2000 problem. Let's look at these points.

We are given a "collection of programs" that need to be reworked. The important concept here is that the problem is pervasive and affects many programs. Further, a key component of an efficient and cost effective solution will be to understand interactions between programs.

We must "find" the places that will have problems. This is not easy. We need to identify the data elements that contain time-related information for which the program does not declare enough digits to accommodate dates after the Year 2000. Unfortunately, the original authors of our computer applications did not have the good sense to mark for us all of the data elements that fit the above description so that we could find them easily. Further, in most computer languages, there are insufficient semantic cues to definitively identify such data elements.

Thinking of this step as "finding" in the sense of text searching is inappropriate. A naive approach would be to pattern match the names of data elements against names that are commonly used to represent time information. The reality is that the connection between the name of a data element and its type is often very weak. Simple name pattern matching will miss many data elements that are time-related but that have unusual names (false negatives) and will also find many data elements that are not really time related but that have names that make them look time related (false positives). These errors cost time and money because they need to be corrected by human intervention. Also, failure to detect false positives before moving to the correction phase of a project can seriously damage a program and cause even more expensive rework efforts.

More sophisticated approaches use some elements of name pattern matching but back it up with heuristic data type inference techniques to identify and confirm time-related data elements. For example, if it is known that a specific data element reference contains a date, then by analyzing the data flow to and from the reference, other time-related data elements can be located and their contents characterized.

Another factor complicating identification of Year 2000 affected data elements is that time information is sometimes embedded in pseudo time-related contexts. For example, a common technique for generating invoice numbers is to make a few digits of the number be derived from the current date. This embedded time information will be essentially invisible to simple analysis tools when looking at other parts of a large system that treat the invoice number as just one number. Again, the solution is a deeper understanding of the relationships between data elements and how date type information propagates from one data element to another.

We must "correct" the problem. This can be accomplished in many ways depending on the specific applications, their use in the organization, their relation to other applications, other problems with the applications, etc. One solution to the Year 2000 problem is to not fix the problem at all but to instead retire the affected applications. Another solutions is for you to retire before the Year 2000 and pass the problem on to your successor. Assuming that neither of these solutions is practical, then the hard work begins. A number of correction techniques have been proposed: widen the data, sliding century windows, year encoding, etc. The appropriate correction technique depends on many factors, many of which may have nothing to do with technical merits.

The corrections affect both the programs and their "data". The key point here is that we must not only fix any program that mishandles its data, but in the process, we will probably need to correct the data itself. The widespread implications of this data conversion process are scary! Organizations maintain enormous amounts of data that represent a large component of the organization's value. The sheer volume of data and the interconnections and dependencies that it introduces into a Year 2000 solution process can be formidable and need to be considered carefully.

As we all know, no software project is complete until the software has been "tested" and fielded. The pervasive nature of the Year 2000 problem makes testing the corrected applications difficult. In particular, most organizations will not be able to (or want to) build complete shadow copies of all of their applications and data so that they can all be corrected and tested all at the same time. Incremental approaches that factor the problem based on isolating subsets of an organization's software portfolio for correction and testing will be necessary. Since subsystems usually cannot be completely isolated and it is logistically impractical to correct the entire portfolio simultaneously, approaches that allow corrected and uncorrected programs and data to coexist are important.

Real-life information management systems are made from more than just programs and data; there are JCL files, procedures, policies and other forms of "infrastructure" that hold things together and that are needed to make the organization run smoothly. To completely solve the Year 2000 problem will at least require examining these and perhaps updating them.

In the next section, we will bring together what we have learned about the Year 2000 problem and the general nature of the solution to the problem and present a detailed description of the major steps in solving the problem and how Reasoning Systems, Inc. is approaching each of these steps.

Solving the Problem

Overview

Now that we know the general characteristics of the solution to the Year 2000 problem, here's an outline of a process model for the solution based on Reasoning/2000.

1. Build a system model. In this step, a system model is constructed that describes all of the programs, databases, data files etc. that comprise the organization's software portfolio. The system model will play a central role throughout the project since it describes the interactions and relationships between the different pieces that are to be analyzed and corrected.

2. Isolate part of the system model for correction. Complete isolation is usually not possible but the system can usually be factored into relatively isolated subsystems.

3. Analyze the subsystem and its programs. In this step, the programs, database schema descriptions, etc. are analyzed to locate Year 2000 afflicted data elements, i.e., data elements that have insufficient width to correctly represent post Year 2000 dates. The system model is used to propagate the analysis information to other programs in the system.

4. Correct the programs. In this step, programs are modified to correct the problems that were discovered in step 2. This includes correcting data element declarations, program logic, JCL files, screen maps, report formats, etc.

5. Correct the data. In this step, the data that are manipulated by the programs in the system, both data files and databases, are modified as necessary to be compatible with the programs as modified in step 4. If the subsystem is not completely isolated from the rest of the system, this might involve adding conversion code to the programs.

6. Test the system. In this step, the modified portions of the system are tested prior to being put back into production. This includes both unit tests and integration tests.

7. Repeat steps 2 through 6 until the whole system has been corrected.

Several important steps have been omitted from the above so as to focus the discussion on the core steps in the Year 2000 solution process. Some of the omitted steps are:

> Perform portfolio assessment. Determine which applications should be retired, which should be corrected, which should be rewritten, which should be replaced by Commercial Off the Shelf (COTS) applications, etc. This step would typically precede or be combined with step 1 above.

> Achieve maintainable state. Put the system into a well maintained state, e.g., all source code is available, all programs compile, all test cases still pass, etc. This step would typically precede or be combined with step 1 above.

> Integrate vendor supplied software. Integrate with new Year 2000 compliant versions of software that you purchase from software vendors, e.g., libraries, database systems, report generators, etc.

> Rewrite or replace portions of the portfolio: Rewrite or replace subsystems identified during the portfolio assessment.

These steps should not be ignored since failure in any of them can lead to difficulties in or failure of other parts of a Year 2000 correction project. These steps are difficult to discuss in a generic sense and a more thorough discussion of them is outside the scope of this paper.

The remainder of this chapter is structured to roughly parallel the above process model and to discuss its implementation in detail.

Background on Language Modeling

At the core of Reasoning/2000 is an object-oriented Code-base Management System (CBMS) used to model software. The software model contains two types of information: a basic model of your software in the form of an Abstract Syntax Tree (AST) that is constructed by parsing code, and a set of derived semantic models that are constructed by analyzing the basic model.

The AST model is constructed by parsing COBOL programs, database query extensions, JCL files, etc. For purposes of this chapter, it is not necessary to understand the details of abstract syntax trees; all you really need to know is that they are a very detailed, object oriented, internal representation for source code and that they are applicable to any formal language. ASTs capture the structure of source code and are a very convenient and flexible representation that allows other programs to treat source code as data for purposes of analyzing and modifying it. Variations on abstract syntax trees are at the heart of most sophisticated compilers.

After an internal AST representation of your source code has been constructed, various analysis tools can be invoked to create the derived semantics portions of the software model. One way to think of the derived semantic models is as different abstractions or different views of your software. The abstractions explicate higher-level characteristics of the software so that it is easier to write tools that can analyze and modify the software. For example, one derived semantic model or abstraction that Reasoning/2000 can create is a control flow graph for a program. Once the control flow graph has been constructed, writing a tool such as a dead code analyzer is easy. As with ASTs it is not necessary for you to understand the details of derived semantic models; the key point is that Reasoning/2000 automatically builds a very rich and flexible model of COBOL systems that forms the basis for its analysis and reengineering capabilities.

Within Reasoning/2000, there is also a rule-based transformation system that can be customized to do complex transformations to your programs. The preconditions of the rules used by this system can make use of all aspects of the software model; this includes the basic AST model, as well as the derived semantic models.

Analysis

The goal of the analysis phase is to determine sufficient type information about the data elements in a system so that the subset of the data elements that actually need Year 2000 correction can then be identified. The analysis phase can be viewed as a data-flow-directed inference process that starts with a set of type clues about time-related data elements, and then effectively propagates the clues through program logic to determine a more complete set of time-related data elements and their characteristics. Based on the characterization of the data elements, it is then possible to further classify some of them as needing Year 2000 correction.

In the following discussion, the initial type clues will be referred to as *seeds*. A seed is a reference to a data element where the type signature of the data element is known with some level of confidence based on information outside of the analysis process. The actual way that seeds are created, the meaning of type signature and the meaning of confidence levels will be explained in later paragraphs. For now an intuitive way to understand a seed is from the following example.

> *In the statement CALL CD-DATE USING ANV-DD, we know that CD-DATE finds the current date and therefore we know that ANV-DD probably contains a date in the format .... Therefore the reference to ANV-DD is a seed.*

Starting with seeds, the analysis system uses a set of inference rules that propagate date type information from data element references to other data element references based on the procedure division operations in which the data elements participate. The simplest example of a type inference rule is that the source and target of a MOVE statement have similar type signatures. The inference process effectively propagates date type information through the program's logic until all time-related data elements have been determined and a type signature associated with them. The type signature on each reference to a data element will ultimately help decide if it can handle dates after the Year 2000 and whether it needs to be corrected. Note that part of the inference process is detecting the boundary between time-related and non-time-related data elements.

The most interesting property of seeds and of data elements discovered during the analysis process is their date type signature. A date type signature is a collection of properties that characterizes the values that can be stored in a data element. For purposes of Year 2000 analysis this includes semantic-oriented properties of the data element in addition to the structure-oriented properties that can be determined from the declaration of the data element. Some examples of the extra type information include:

- the units of the data element, i.e., years, quarters, months, days etc.,
- whether the data element is an absolute date or a time interval,
- related data elements that serve as higher-order or lower-order digits.

As mentioned earlier, a seed has an associated _confidence level_ that describes how reliable it is believed to be. Confidence levels affect the inference process when data elements have ambiguous type signatures, i.e., when the inference process determines that a particular data element has several allowable type signatures. Type decisions are weighted to prefer type information derived from reliable sources over type information derived from less reliable sources. Maintaining confidence levels for seeds is useful because it allows utilizing more diverse sources of information, with varying levels of quality, than would otherwise be possible.

Seeds can come from a number of different sources. The most reliable seeds come from noting uses of known date manipulation or calendar routines; for example, calls to functions to get the current date. The analysis system contains a built in library describing such routines and you can edit the library to add knowledge of site-specific date and time routines.

A less reliable source of seeds is pattern matching the names of data elements against a library of names that are commonly used for the names of time-related data elements, e.g., TIMESTAMP, ANNIVERSARY, DDMMYY, etc. The analysis system contains a site-editable library of such name patterns. This type of seed information is unreliable and over-dependence on it can lead to numerous errors such as missed time-related data elements and incorrect type signatures on other data elements. Accordingly, by default, a rather low confidence level is assigned to this type of seed.

Analysis really takes place at two different levels: intra-module and inter-module. The above paragraphs describe the essence of the intra-module analysis process. Inter-module analysis performs an abbreviated form of type inferencing between modules and will be described in the following paragraphs.

Modules typically read and write data files or databases using different aliases or names for the same data elements. The inter-module analysis system analyzes the schema used by different modules to access data files and databases to determine alias correspondences. When an intra-module analysis is complete on a particular module, type information about externalized time-related data elements is communicated to the inter-module analysis system. The inter-module analysis system then propagates knowledge of the time-related data elements to other modules that read or write the same data elements, possibly using aliases.

During the overall analysis phase, intra-module and inter-module analyses are alternated until all type information has been propagated. Inter-module analysis provides a significant benefit because it means that time-related data elements that are found in one module can assist the analysis of other modules.

The final result of the analysis phase is a set of type annotations with corresponding confidence levels on various data elements in various modules. The product presents this information in interactive textual and/or tabular reports. In the textual reports, portions of program text are displayed with the inferred type of data elements highlighted using different colors. In the tabular reports, the rows represent data elements and the columns display various properties of each data element. The reports allow you to interactively navigate to the Year 2000 trouble spots in your programs to view context, verify the analysis, make manual corrections, etc.

Program Correction

The goal of the program correction phase is to fix the program code so that the system can handle dates after the Year 2000. A number of correc-

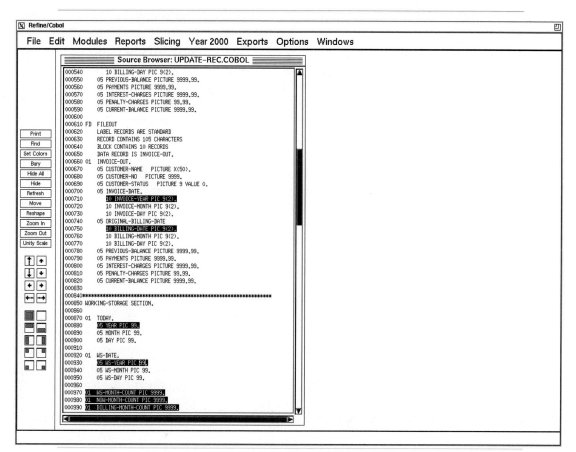

Figure 74.1   Sample report

tion techniques have been proposed in the literature, such as widening the data, sliding century windows, year encoding, etc. Reasoning's tools are designed to accommodate different correction techniques. The remainder of this chapter focuses on the *widen-the-data* solution.

The widen-the-data correction technique is probably the most straightforward of the correction approaches that have been suggested in the Year 2000 literature. As discussed earlier, the core of the Year 2000 problem is that some time-related data elements are declared with too few digits to unambiguously represent dates after the Year 2000. The obvious solution is to correct the declarations of the data elements by adding more digits. For example if the data element YEAR has been declared with only two digits in its picture clause and it now needs to include explicit century digits, change the picture clause to declare four digits. This is the essence of the widen-the-data approach, and as you can see, the actual correction is fairly easy; the trick is knowing exactly which data elements to widen, how much to widen each one, what implicit

☒ Refine/Cobol					⌐

File   Edit   Modules   Reports   Slicing   Year 2000   Exports   Options   Windows

Data Elements: UPDATE-RECEIVABLES

Data Element	Defined In	Picture	Parents / Offsets	Set/Use Info
Billing-Date	update-rec line 66	9(2)	Invoice-Out [61] Original-Billing-Date [0]	Set by Read-Invoice 134: MOVE to parent Used by Compute-Penalties 163: reference to parent Used by Write-Invoice 184: reference to parent
Billing-Month-Count	update-rec line 90	9999		Set by Compute-Penalties 165: MOVE Used by Compute-Penalties 166: reference
Invoice-Year	update-rec line 62	9(2)	Invoice-Out [55] Invoice-Date [0]	Set by Read-Invoice 134: MOVE to parent Used by Write-Invoice 184: reference to parent
Now-Month-Count	update-rec line 89	9999		Set by Setup-System 113: MOVE Used by Compute-Interest 152: reference Used by Compute-Penalties 166: reference
Ws-Month-Count	update-rec line 88	9999		Set by Compute-Ws-Month-Count 195: MOVE 196: MULTIPLY 197: ADD Used by Setup-System 113: reference Used by Compute-Interest 152: reference Used by Compute-Penalties 165: reference Used by Compute-Ws-Month-Count 196: reference 197: reference
Ws-Year	update-rec line 84	99	Ws-Date [0]	Set by Setup-System 111: MOVE to parent Set by Compute-Interest 150: MOVE to parent Set by Compute-Penalties 163: MOVE to parent Used by Compute-Ws-Month-Count 195: reference
Year	update-rec line 79	99	Today [0]	Used by Setup-System 111: reference to parent Used by Read-Invoice

Print
Find
Set Colors
Bury
Hide All
Hide
Refresh
Move
Reshape
Zoom In
Zoom Out
Unity Scale

Figure 74.2   *Data element table*

assumptions were made about the width of the data element elsewhere in the program or system, etc.

During the analysis phase, the internal representations of the data elements in your programs that deal with date and time calculations are annotated with additional semantic type information. This type information includes the units of the data element (years, months, etc.) and whether the data element is a date (as opposed to an interval). Based on this information, the correction phase first filters the time-related data elements based on their type and PICTURE clause to determine which ones cannot represent dates after the Year 2000. In most cases, it is not necessary to widen time-related data elements that strictly represent time intervals.

Program correction within a COBOL program occurs in two phases: correcting the data division and correcting the procedure division.

Once the data elements that need to be widened have been determined, correcting the DATA DIVISION proceeds fairly straightforwardly. Due to the several different ways that aliases can be introduced into COBOL programs (RENAMES, REDEFINES), a number of expert system rules are employed during the correction process and in some cases, the system may solicit interaction with the user.

In the widen-the-data correction approach, procedure division correction is primarily confined to handling various special case situations. These include:

> Use of constants that are time-valued and that need to be adjusted. For example, in YY < 95, if YY is widened to 4 digits to include explicit century information, then the 95 should be widened to 1995.

> Use of time-valued data elements in non-time-valued contexts. For example, embedding a date in an invoice number.

> Implicit dates in screens and reports.

The program correction system includes rules to detect situations similar to the above. In some cases, you might need to intervene either by manually correcting portions of the PROCEDURE DIVISION or by adding additional PROCEDURE DIVISION correction rules.

Another important type of source that needs to be corrected is screen maps. As with widening data elements in the data division, the actual process of correcting a screen map is the easy part; the hard part is deciding how to correct the screen map. Screen maps impose an additional set of constraints that are difficult to deal with in a completely automatic way. For example, adding two more digits to a year field might cause the field to bump into another field on the same line or cause some columns to no longer be aligned. The correction system can detect when a screen map might need to be corrected, but does not automatically attempt to correct it unless instructed.

Another ramification of the widen-the-data approach is that the JCL that runs a module may need to be modified. For example, if the width of a field within an I/O record is increased, the blocking factor specified in the JCL may need to be corrected.

Summary

The Year 2000 problem is a serious problem for all organizations that rely on computerized information systems. Fortunately, we have advance warning of the problem and can start to take corrective actions.

References

1. "Program Slicing," Mark Weiser, *IEEE Transactions on Software Engineering*, SE-10(4), July 1984, pp. 352-357.

2. "The Use of Program Dependence Graphs in Software Engineering," Susan Horwitz and Thomas Reps, *Proceedings of the Fourteenth International Conference on Software Engineering (ACM)*, May 1992, pp. 392-411.

3. "Application of Program Slicing and Program Transformation to Solving the Year 2000 Problem." William Brew, Karl Schimpf and Lawrence Markosian, *Proceedings of the 5th Reengineering Forum and Year 2000 Summit Meeting*, June 1996.

4. "Using an Enabling Technology to Reengineer Legacy Systems," Philip Newcomb and Lawrence Markosian, *Communications of the ACM*, May 1994.

5. *The Year 2000 and 2-Digit Dates: A Guide for Planning and Implementation*, IBM, available via anonymous ftp from ftp://lscftp.kng.ibm.com/pub/year2000/y2kpaper.ps.Z.

9 Expert: Early Testing

part

Through December of 1998, the Editor personally offers a $50,000 standing **cash reward** to **anyone** who can disprove this scheduling rule:

$$W < \frac{M}{3} - 2$$

> *Your 18-month Y2K project **must** start working on its test environment by the fourth month. 15 months? Start environment before the third month. M months? Wait less than M/3 – 2, even if all other work stops!*

Have your kids do the algebra from these three assumptions:

➤ It takes up to two months to establish a test environment.

➤ Everyone agrees testing will cost 55 percent – 75 percent of Y2K overall.

➤ Constant overall monthly effort; testing never > 100 percent of effort.

Before beginning this chapter, please review the brief chapters 23, 24, 33, and 34 on testing. Miro Medek, Dick Lefkon, ProTerm Technologies and Judy Brand give short, clear explanations of baseline testing, unit testing, integration testing, stress testing, regression testing, acceptance testing, bilateral testing, forum testing (pre-) production testing, and test case validation.

IBM's leadoff article here, "Testing Techniques," uniquely presents three other testing considerations: Recovery/Restart testing, Error Handling testing, and Manual Support testing. Most of the article covers what you'd want IBM to treat: How to change the system date, and the eight objects you endanger most when you do! IBM reminds you to isolate your Y2K environment, e.g., via a VM guest or MVS LPAR (analogous to a PC 'D' drive).

IBM's closing paragraphs on PCs lead directly to Micro Focus's Implementation Checklist. The PC COBOL vendor pointedly asks some capacity questions, which probably guide prospects a bit towards their products.

Next, Bryce Ragland gives an understandable treatment of PC platform testing. "Rags" assumes you're not a PC expert yourself. He teaches you some of the commands needed for inventory assessment, and says not to worry about Y2K for files ending .BMP, .PCX, .GIF, .TMP, .ICO, .CNI and .WAV. He criticizes some of Microsoft's Y2K plans and gives a few hints about hiring a Y2K PC consultant if you have to.

Now, two other non-mainframes are discussed for Y2K. Novell's Tom Hartmann gives a straightforward description of Netware, etc., good and bad points. For UNIX, Richard Painter makes it short and sweet: You're safe to 2038!

Sanford Feld returns us to mainframe testing, providing a detailed fill-in capacity survey. Feld prefers using an IBM "pygmy" mainframe over an LPAR or VM guest. He offers a list of skull-and-crossbones LPAR exposures, vs. a separate mainframe with a machine clock that can safely be changed. See, too, Judy Brand's "pygmy cluster" diagram in Chapter 34 where an inexpensive group of task-dedicated S/390s keeps major test groups from crashing each other's CPUs or even getting on each other's nerves!

Whatever your 390 Y2K hardware, you'll probably want to buy a date simulator to run more than one of the IBM-listed tests at a time. Of several vendors, three have furnished segments from their manuals.

Isogon's TICTOC/CICS can set EIBDATE/EIBTIME for each user, transaction or entire CICS region. Xpediter/Xchange, like TICTOC, has both batch and online capabilities. MainWare claims its Hourglass 2000 does the same SVC 11 coverage but also responds to a wide range of STCK clock inquiries. There are other date-simulators, alone or as part of other Y2K products.

Now that your environment is in place, Part 10 tells about ways to automate and speed up the two-thirds of your effort (for financial companies) which is testing.

However, please remember W < M/3–2: If your Y2K Test Environment setup plans gather any dust, the odds are you will fail.

75 *Testing Techniques*

IBM

Reprinted by permission from GC28-1251 *The Year 2000 and 2-Digit Dates: A Guide for Planning and Implementation* copyright 1995, 1996 by International Business Machines Corporation

Testing can be formalized into a 4-phase process, as follows:

Test Type	*Used To Test*
Unit Testing	A single program module
Integration Testing	A related group of program modules
System Testing	The entire software program
Acceptance Testing	The entire software program with live data for production readiness

Ideally, these phases should be completed sequentially. However, when development work is done in parallel, module coding, unit testing, integration testing are commonly integrated, followed by system testing and acceptance testing.

During the process of testing, apply a combination of verification and validation techniques. Unit and integration testing are primarily used for program verification. These two forms of testing comprise structural testing, which is used to uncover errors injected during program coding. System and acceptance testing are used for program validation, and these two forms of testing comprise functional testing, which is used to uncover errors that occurred when implementing requirements or design specifications. The following sections will cover some useful testing techniques and scenarios for Year2000 testing. There are other testing techniques. You should choose whatever techniques are best for your situation.

Structural Testing Techniques

Structural testing enables sufficient testing of a function's implementation and helps to determine that all structures of the system are integrated to form a cohesive unit. Structural testing techniques include:

Operations Testing

Apply operations testing to determine whether the system is ready for normal system (production) operations. In contrast, recovery processing (discussed below) is intended for abnormal system operations. Considering the potential scope and magnitude of your Year2000 transition, every aspect of the normal operation might be impacted to some extent as you revise programs and/or data for Year 2000 readiness. Operations testing enables, prior to production, your IS staff to properly administer the applications using the new support mechanisms, documentation, procedures, and training as you complete your Year 2000 transition.

Stress Testing

Apply stress testing to determine if the system can function when transaction volumes are larger than normally expected. The typical areas that are stressed include disk space, transaction speeds, output generation, computer capacity, and interaction with people. When testing Year 2000 changes, it is essential to verify that the existing resources can handle the normal and abnormal volumes of transactions after the restructuring of the code and the possible expansion of the data fields. For example, apply stress tests to determine:

> if existing CPU capacity is sufficient to meet expected user turn-around time when date encoding (refer to "Solution #3: A 2-Digit Encoding/Compression Scheme" Chapter 59) is applied and uses more CPU cycles and processing time for code conversion.

> if existing disk capacity is sufficient to accommodate the additional disk space and provide acceptable disk access time when full (refer to "Solution #1: Conversion to Full 4-Digit-Year Format" is applied and expands the year data field from two to four digits.

Recovery Testing

Apply recovery testing to enable the system to restart processing after losing system integrity. This is essential for systems in which the continuity of operation is critical to end users. Recovery processing normally involves the ability to go back to the last checkpoint, then reprocess up to the point of failure. The success of the recovery depends heavily on complete backup data and checkpointing. Any data integrity or unresolved exposures that lead to inconsistent data or code after you have implemented appropriate Year 2000 solutions will affect the completeness of backup data. On the other hand, checkpointing is very time oriented and sensitive. Any mishandling of the time-related data might invalidate system checkpointing. The recovery testing is thus critical in a Year 2000 testing environment. It can also involve manual functions (such as hardware or operating system failure), loss of data base integrity, operator error, or loss of input capability. Recovery testing should include all aspects of the recovery processing.

Functional Testing Techniques

Functional testing is designed to confirm that the system and end-user requirements and specifications are achieved. Functional testing focuses on the results of processing rather than how processing is implemented. To accomplish this, create test cases to evaluate the functional correctness of the system and programs. Functional testing techniques include:

Requirements Testing

Apply requirements testing to verify that the system performs its function correctly and that it remains functional over a continuous period of time. Functional checklists such as user requirements, design specifications, compliance of organization's polices and procedures are used to create test cases to enable these requirements to be satisfied following your Year 2000 transition. Note that if the Year 2000 solutions are merely restructuring code and reformatting data without major redesign of the applications or systems, most requirements testing can be covered by another method, regression testing.

Regression Testing

Apply regression testing to confirm that all aspects of a system remain functionally correct after changes have been made to a program in the system. Because the potential exists for a tremendous amount of data and programs to be involved in your Year 2000 transition, any change to an existing program in the system can have a snowballing or cascading effect on other areas in the system. A change that introduces new data or parameters, or an incorrectly implemented change can cause a problem in previously tested parts of the system, simply because of the way data can be shared between software entities.

Regardless of how an error was introduced or propagated, regression testing needs to be conducted to retest even unchanged parts or programs of the system. Normally, tests that have been previously run are reused to verify that the same results are achieved. In most cases, regression testing is automated because the test cases and the results are already known.

[Editor: Read that paragraph again:

1. You must regression-test *everything* because even the unchanged might change.
2. Per Miro Medek's Chapter 23, first you need to baseline-test.
3. Automation is an acceptable way to repeat something.]

Error Handling Testing

A normal error-handling cycle is an iterative process that either prevents errors from occurring, or recognizes and corrects errors that have occurred. Error-handling testing is necessary to determine the ability of the system to properly process incorrect transactions that can be reasonably expected as types of error conditions. For example, programs that accept only 4-digit-year-data-entry format need to provide error messages for data entry in 2-digit-year format, and vice versa for programs that accept only 2-digit-year-data-entry format. When changing from 2-digit-year format to 4-digit-year format, you need to apply error-handling testing to verify the appropriate error-handling functions.

Manual Support Testing

Apply manual support testing to evaluate the adequacy of the processes used by people (end users) who must handle the new data generated from the automated applications with Year 2000 support. Types of data from these applications include data entry and report generation. Any new data format should be easy to understand and not ambiguous. This method includes testing the interfaces (for example screens, procedures, operation manuals, and online HELP panels) between end users and the application program. End users should be trained and use procedures provided by the system personnel. Testing should be conducted without any other assistance.

Intersystem Testing

Applications are frequently connected with other applications to provide a higher or deeper level of functionality. Data may be shared between applications or systems. Multiple applications or systems may be involved in such an environment. This is the typical environment for Year 2000 projects. Intersystem testing is required to confirm that the connection functions properly between the applications. This test determines that the proper parameters and data are correctly passed between applications, and proper coordination and timing of each function exists between applications.

Parallel Testing

Parallel testing is used to determine whether the processing and results of a new version of an application are consistent with the processing and results of the previous version of the application. It should be applied when the old and new versions of the application are similar. For Year 2000 solutions without any major function redesign, this is the ideal technique. Parallel testing requires that the same input data be run through the two versions of the application. However, if the new application changes data formats, such as reformatting the year-date notation to 4-digit format, you must modify test input data before testing.

The efficiency and effectiveness of parallel processing is highly dependent on the degree of difficulty encountered in verifying output results and preparing common input. It may be difficult to automatically verify the results of processing by comparing the results on a tape or disk file. Some automated test tools or customized solutions can be used to prepare input and verify output more quickly.

How to Change Date and Time for Testing

By their very nature, Year 2000 exposures are time-sensitive and time-driven. Basic Year 2000 testing requires that you set the system date and time to a point where Year2000 exposures can be detected, then removed.

Be *extremely careful* before resetting the system timer. Some system resources and functions are time-sensitive and may be activated or de-activated when you reset the system clock. Such effects can occur when you either set the system clock forward or backward. Without careful planning, you could cause the loss of these system resources and/or functions, some of which might prove very difficult and time-consuming to recover.

Attention: The Most Vulnerable Include:

- user IDs

- passwords

- data files and databases

- authorization/protection

- licences/services

- network access

- automation functions (as well as unexpected activation)

- hierarchical storage management

Figure 75.1   Resources/functions subject to expiration

Security products (such as RACF) and other date-dependent functions require particular attention. Setting the system clock ahead can cause immediate loss of system programmer or end-user access and data expiration. Further, to maintain security in this environment, consider implementing an installation exit (available in RACF) to disable expiration date processing.

Ensure that you do not contaminate your production system or production databases when running various test scenarios. Be sure that data is not unexpectedly deleted from the system. For example, if your system is set up to scratch all files that are 1-year old, all files that are created prior to 1999/01/01 will be scratched when the system clock is change to 2000/01/01 or later. Because time stamps are saved when new data is created, be sure to remove data created before moving the system clock back to an earlier time. Unpredictable results might occur because programming might not be in place to handle normally improbable conditions, such as when the creation date of a data set is later than the current time.

System Requirements When Changing the Test System Clock

- Provide a separate, isolated test system (such as a separate logical partition (LPAR) for large operating systems)

- Provide a separate set of test data

- Turn off RACF or other date-dependent functions.

Figure 75.2   Requirements for testing on Systems/390 platforms

If resources allow, you can also provide separate storage devices (DASD) as a further measure to protect your production system and data.

Each LPAR or VM guest has its own logical clock which is separate and distinct from both the hardware TOD clocks and from the clocks of all other LPARs or guests running on the same physical machine. Any program, application, or system running in the image gets the same future date.

Any of the S/390 operating systems with a clock set to a future date can be run in a Processor Resource/Systems Manager (PR/SM) LPAR, as a VM guest, or on a dedicated machine. This is also true for images in LPARs, guests on VM, or when running a native OS/390 or MVS system. Refer to the individual operating systems below for details.

Note: Non-IBM systems that have features similar to PR/SM might not function in the same way as an IBM PR/SM LPAR.

You can change the system date through either of the following methods:

1. Set the system timer on a test system image. **However, never share data or data sets between such a test system and any other system unless all clocks are synchronized to that same date**. For example,

   ➤ **On OS/390 or MVS:**

   You can set the clock in an MVS image to a future date. To set the clock, reply to the TOD clock prompt message IEA888A [GMT DATE=...,CLOCK=...] LOCAL DATE=...,CLOCK=... REPLY U, OR GMT/LOCAL TIME in the test LPAR image. You must include ",GMT" on your response to ensure that the clock is set correctly; issue: "CLOCK=hh.mm.ss,DATE=yyyy.ddd,GMT". (Do not set the time of day (TOD) using the Sysplex Timer.)

   Note: Testing your system using the following test techniques is seldom required; you need to do this testing only for those applications that you consider truly multisystem (that is, those applications which you cannot test under a single-system sysplex image).

   A multi-system sysplex, Year2000-test environment requires that you dedicate at least an entire physical machine to the test system. **The Year2000 test machine cannot include LPARS which contain members of a different sysplex with a different date**. This is because it is not possible to set manually different dates (and times) in the several LPARs which are accurate enough to allow the sysplex to function correctly.

   There are two ways you can set a future date for the test sysplex.

   a. Using a sysplex timer

   Set the date ahead on a dedicated (to the test sysplex) Sysplex Timer and then IPL your sysplex images. The images, which are part of the Year2000 test sysplex, can be on a single physical machine or on multiple physical machines, but you cannot include sysplex images on these machines which are not in the Year2000 test sysplex. Be sure to set the ETR network ID on this Sysplex Timer to a value different from the ETR network ID used by other sysplexes.

   b. Without using a sysplex timer

   • Bi-polar machines:

   If the sysplex images all reside on a single physical machine, you can set the Process Controller clock to the future date using the SYSDEF frame.

   • CMOS machines:

Set the service element clock to the future date using the "Service Element Option" menu on the hardware master console.

Then Power_On_Reset the machine, activate PR/SM, and IPL your sysplex images with CLOCKxx parmlib members which specify SIMETRID=xx.

Note: Be certain that the SIMETRID is different from the ETR network ID used by other sysplexes.

➤ **On VM/ESA:** systems will IPL correctly with a year of 2000 or later. For VM/ESA Version 1 Releases 2.1 and 2.2, you must apply APAR VM57927. Beginning with VM/ESA Version 2 Release 1, this capability is included in the base VM system.

In order to change the date of your VM/ESA system, reply 'Yes' to the "Change TOD clock (Yes|No)" prompt during IPL, and change the date and time to the desired date and time. To specify a year of 2000, simply enter "00" as the year ("01" for 2001, "02" for 2002, and so forth).

If you change the system date, unless you have applied APAR VM60324 (this APAR is available for Version 1 Release 2.2 and Version 2 Release 1), issue a SHUTDOWN REIPL command immediately after completion of the system IPL as indicated in message HCPITM1161I (this message is displayed only on Version 2 systems). This is required because by the time VM issues the "Change TOD clock (Yes|No)" prompt, components of the control program (CP) have already developed sensitivities to the actual value of the TOD (time of day) clock. These sensitivities might cause irregular scheduling and dispatching behavior if the value of the TOD clock is changed by more than several minutes.

➤ **On VSE/ESA:** use command "SET DATE=, CLOCK=, ZONE=" to initialize the system timer during IPL time. The DATE parameter is specified in the format mm/dd/yy, whereby yy is interpreted as 20yy, when yy < 50, and as 19yy otherwise.

➤ **On TPF:** use the ZATIM (alter time) functional message to change the system time-of-day (TOD) clock, change the subsystem local standard time (LST) clock, and synchronize the TOD clock to a Sysplex Timer. Do so as follows:

• Issue the ZDTIM functional message to determine the time base before you issue this functional message.

• If you issue this functional message when the TPF system is above 1052 state, you must cycle the TPF system to 1052 state to complete the time adjustments.

- You can issue this functional message with the TOD parameter only in 1052 state.
- In a loosely coupled system, all other active processors must be in 1052 state in order to change the TOD clock without the BP option.
- The ZATIM functional message does not adjust time-initiated functions (that is, functions that were started by using the CRETC macro).

2. Intercept the call to date and time routines or system timer services. Change the date and time value returned from the routines/services to a specific value that will cause exposures. For example,

  ➣ On OS/390 or MVS, trap the MVS TIME macro (SVC 11) and the STCKSYNC macro.

  Notes:

  a. There are Solution Developer tools available that provide the function of time simulation. [Editor: Refer to Chapters 81-83.] For any time simulation tool, the change of time should be on application-level programs and should not affect the system functions and operations. The tool should allow the users to specify the scope of the applications with time change. Once the scope is specified, the change of time should be within that pre-defined scope and transparent to others applications.

  b. When you request full coverage of time references, you must ensure that all forms of time references are intercepted. For example, some date/time service routines use hardware instructions to reference time. Such tools will not intercept the STCK on OS/390 or MVS and control block references.

Testing on AS/400 Platforms

Use the CL command CHGSYSVAL (change system value) with the QDATE parameter. For example, CHGSYSVAL QDATE('101300') changes the system date to October 13, 2000 on a system using MMDDYY date formats (QDATFMT). To make sure all jobs on the AS/400 are using this new date, you should then power down the AS/400 (PWRDWNSYS) and conduct your testing after the subsequent IPL.

Testing on PCs

Use the configuration utility that sets the time and date or execute the DATE command in DOS Version 3 Release 3 or later.

Basic Testing Scenarios

The scenarios for Year 2000 testing depend heavily on the system environment and applications. Some basic Year 2000 testing scenarios that are common for most installations are suggested here:

> Set the clock to test process cycles and automatic functions that are activated on a regular basis. These scenarios can be used to identify Year 2000 exposures that need to be fixed as well as to validate programs after applying Year 2000 solutions.

- Daily
- Weekly
- Semi-monthly
- Monthly
- Bi-monthly
- Quarterly
- Semi-annually
- Annual
- Automatic archiving
- Automatic restart/restore
- On demand

> Test the setting and display of special dates, including:

- 1900/2/29—should fail—the year 1900 is not a leap year
- 1996/2/29—should succeed—the year 1996 is a leap year
- 2000/2/29—should succeed—the year 2000 is a leap year
- 00/01/01—should display an unambiguous 4-digit-year date, the value of which depends on the application. For example, 1900/01/01, 2000/01/01, and so on
- 1999/12/31—should be able to distinguish between a regular end-of-year 1999 date and a special meaning date. For example, a never-expiring date indicator.

> Test the processing of time-sensitive data with different combinations of data and time

a. Use the current system clock and then test data with dates:
- before 2000/01/01
- after 2000/01/01

b. Set system clock before the year 2000, for example 1999/12/31, and then test data with dates:
- before 2000/01/01
- after 2000/01/01

    c. Set the system clock after 2000/01/01 and then test data with dates:
- before 2000/01/01
- after 2000/01/01

Basic Scenarios to Test Your PC System Clock

[Editor: "Take a backup" is putting it mildly. Be very thorough in your preparation or you'll risk losing your data and your access to much of your PC software.]

    Some older models of the PC may not have the capability to set or roll over the system clock beyond the year 2000 because the Basic Input/Output System (BIOS) is unaware of the century digits.

    [Editor again: For general approaches to COTS and GOTS external validation, see Part 11. Standard BIOS chips made since 1997 are OK, but either confirm there were no substitutions, or test as described here.

    Some free or expensive software will perform PC tests for you; others will inventory and list what's on your PC locally or LAN-wide. If you buy one of the "professional" analyzers, shop around to avoid paying $50+ many times for a feature that lists which of your COTS packages were Y2K-conformant the day you bought the analyzer.

    If the BIOS doesn't conform and you want to keep the PC, you have at least three alternatives. If the BIOS is programmable, free replacement software is probably available over the Internet. If not, you can pull and replace the motherboard BIOS chip for about $50 plus labor. You may even find an "idiot proof" insert board which will bypass the older motherboard BIOS chip for its own Y2K-conformant BIOS.]

    Some suggested scenarios for testing for Year2000-readiness of your PC system clock follow:

Test if the system clock can be set beyond the year 2000.

1. Set the system clock to 2000/01/01, 00:01:00.
2. Check the date.
3. If the date is set correctly, power off, power on, and then re-check the date.

Test the system clock automatic update function.

1. Test the system clock automatic update function when the power is on.
   - a. Set the system clock to 1999/12/31, 23:58:00.
   - b. Keep power on.
   - c. Wait until the clock reaches the year 2000.
   - d. Check the date.
   - e. If it is set correctly, power off, and re-check the date.

2. Test the system clock automatic update function when the power is off.
    a. Set the system clock to 1999/12/31, 23:58:00.
    b. Power off.
    c. Wait until the clock reaches the year 2000.
    d. Power on.
    e. Check the date.

Test the time update by the operating system.

1. Test the time update after suspension of a time-sensitive program.
    a. Set the system clock to 1999/12/31, 23:58:00.
    b. Suspend a time-display program without a 'wake-up' timer.
    c. Keep the power on.
    d. Wait until the clock reaches the year 2000.
    e. Resume time-display program and check the date.
2. Test time update after suspension and 'wake-up' of time-sensitive program.
    a. Set system clock to 1999/12/31, 23:58:00.
    b. Suspend a time-display program with the 'wake up' timer set at 2000/01/01, 00:01:00.
    c. Keep the power on.
    d. Wait until the time display program 'wakes up.'
    e. Check the date.

76 *Implementation Issues Checklist*

Micro Focus Limited

What implementation issues might you face?

> ➤ Do you have enough human resources to handle all the necessary modifications (source code, copy books, data, etc.)?
> ➤ Do you have enough mainframe CPU cycles to handle all the necessary modifications?
> ➤ Do you have enough disk space for larger databases & files?
> ➤ Do you have enough disk space for unit/system test (source code, copy books, test data, etc.)
> ➤ How will you do a system test when a large percentage of your programs have been modified?

> How will you do a system test across multiple divisions within a company?
> How will you test/implement the new data which is used as input in PC programs (database, spreadsheets, project management, etc.)?
> How will you test/implement the data which is used as input to end user tools on the mainframe like SAS, FOCUS, etc.?
> Who is going to help end users modify their data and programs on PCs and end user mainframe tools?
> How will you handle performance issues when an expanded record no longer fits in one buffer?

77   *What Can You Do for Microcomputers?*

Bryce Ragland
USAF

From: *The Year 2000 Problem Solver* by Bryce Ragland, copyright ©1997 by the McGraw-Hill Companies. Reprinted with permission of the McGraw-Hill Companies.

In this chapter you will learn several things to do to help protect yourself from the Year 2000 problem and where to go for help.

Inventory Your Systems

This chapter is primarily addressing PC based programs. I don't currently have access to a Macintosh to identify what file types or directory structures that you would be dealing with in that environment. I think a lot of the files are the same, but I am not sure. If this section does not prove to be helpful for the Macintosh users, I apologize.

The first thing that you want to do to prepare for the Year 2000 problem, is to do a complete inventory of your systems. Make sure you know exactly what executable files that you have on your computers. Executable files are files where the extension of the file name is .EXE. Also, make sure that you know which data base and data storage files you have on your systems. Database files generally have a file name extension of .DBF. Some related files may have a .DB* extension, where the * indicates any other letter. There are also .DAT files that contain data, these files are similar to the .DBF files. The .DBF files are generally created by a database program, where the .DAT files are generally created by a non-database program. Which ones are Commercial Off the Shelf (COTS) such as Microsoft, Corel, WordPerfect, etc.? Which ones did you have someone develop for you? All of your COTS software should have manuals to go wit them, unless you bought a discount version, such as a student edition. If you have the manuals that came with the software that you have purchased, take off the shrink-wrap and start reading to see what types of files that particular piece of software generates, or needs to run. Another way to determine which file types that you may need to be concerned about, is to do a directory listing of your system, including sub-directories, for the .EXE and .CB*, then list what sub-directory they are in. The DOS command for listing a directory with sub-directories is:

DIR *.EXE /S/W | More

This will list all the .EXE files from whatever directory you are in, and all sub-directories. If you are in the top level directory on your C: drive, it will give you a listing of all the .EXE files on that drive. The /W is the wide flag, which causes the files to be displayed on the screen with 4-5 files across the screen. Without the /W parameter, the computer will display only one file per line, and in large directories, this may fill more than one screen. You would then have a hard time reviewing all the files in that sub-directory and determining their relationships. The '| More' switch causes the listing to stop at the end of a screen and wait for you to press the enter key to go on to the next screen full. This way if you are looking at all the sub-directories on the disk, it will only show you one screen at a time.

Once you have identified which directories that you have executable files (programs) in, change directories to each of those directories and do a directory listing of the entire directory. This is done by typing:

DIR | MORE

Now you start looking for files that have the same filename as the .EXE files. For instance:

If you go into an MSOFFICE and the WINWORD sub-directory, this is the directory that contains the files that are used by the Windows version of Microsoft Word. Most of the programs that you have on your computer are contained in their own directories. This will make it easier for you to do an inventory on what programs that you have.

There are some shared files that different programs use, but they are usually provided by MS WINDOWS. These files are contained in either the WINDOWS directory or the SYSTEM sub-directory of WINDOWS.

A lot of programs have set up special default directories for your applications to be stored in if you don't specify a directory for storing them. For instance, in WordPerfect 6.0, there is a sub-directory to WPWIN called WPDOCS that the program defaults to when storing your documents that you make when using WordPerfect. This is good because it allows you to store all of your WordPerfect documents in one place. WINDOWS 95 has a directory called MY DOCUMENTS that is the default directory whenever you do an open, this is even better, because it allows the user to keep all of their documents, spreadsheets, database files, etc., in the same directory. You can make sub-directories of your choice to store related items in.

Depending on the format of the computer that you are using will depend on where you will find your personal/business files, and where you will find your application files (programs). Both need to be of concern with the Year 2000 problem. The programs because they are what creates and manipulates the information in your personal/business files, and the personal/business files themselves, because you don't know what the programs have done to them. If there is any date related information in your personal/business files, chances are they will become corrupt on or before the Year 2000 because of how the programs handle the date fields.

File Types You Don't Have to Worry About

There are several types of files that you needn't worry about. These are files that are on your system that either don't contain any date information, or are used by the programs and will be upgraded when you receive a Year 2000 compliant software package.

Graphics (.BMP,. PCX,. GIF, etc.) are files that contain pictures. You will find many graphics files in your windows directories that are used for changing the wallpaper on the background of your desktop or for inserting pictures into documents. The graphics are not impacted by the system clock, or any other date related entity.

Temporary files (.TMP) created by a program are only used by that program at the time the program is running. These .TMP files are deleted whenever you get out of the program normally. If for some reason you get out of the program in an abnormal manner, say the program crashes or hangs, there will be a .TMP file created that will not be deleted when the program ends. These programs can be deleted at any time. If you are attempting to delete a .TMP file, and the system says it can't delete it, that is because there is an application running that is using that file. Don't worry about it, it will be deleted when the program ends, assuming the program ends normally. It is a good idea to occasionally go in and delete any .TMP files to clean up your disk space.

Also, backup files (.BAK) are files that some applications create when you update one of your files. They are actually the last version of that file. They can be useful at times if you are working on something, mess it up, and then save it by mistake instead of canceling it. You can go back to the .BAK file and rename it to the current file name. For the Year 2000 Problem, backup files won't help much. If your program or data gets messed up because of the clock changing, being able to go to a .BAK file of the program won't work. Going to a backup file of the data will at least get you back to an uncorrupted version of your data.

Using .BAK files for backing up your data is not how the system is designed. The system creates .BAK files for only certain items, not for everything that you do. It is just like when you are working with a word processor, it is a good idea to stop every 10-15 minutes and save your work.

Most word processors have automatic save features these days, but how many times have you spent two or more hours in the word processor developing a document, and have the system crash on you and you lose everything? This is why I recommend that you back your files up to tape or floppy disk prior to the Year 2000 date change. In fact, it is a good idea to back your system up at least once a week, just in case: If something happens to your system, you have only lost, at the most, a week's worth of work, instead of maybe a year or more. If you do a high volume of data entry or data changing, you may want to consider backing your system up on a nightly basis instead of weekly.

Generally speaking, any files with the extension .DLL is an application extension. These are files that are required by the different .EXE files. They may or may not have date fields in them, but you don't have to worry about the individual .DLL files. They will be tested with the program, not as a stand alone file. If the program as a single entity works in the Year 2000, then the .DLL files are okay.

There are several other files that you need not be concerned about. Some of the file extension are .ICO, .INI, .WAV, etc. They are files that are used by the system, but are nothing that you can have any effect over, other than getting your programs upgraded. Or they are files that are not date related at all.

Four Digit Year, but Not Compliant

Here is an interesting little twist to the Year 2000 Compliant strategy. A program that you purchase could be using four digit year fields and not be Year 2000 Compliant. An article in the July 15, 1995 issue of the Government Computer News talks about Microsoft planning to update their programs to have a date format of mm/dd/yyyy. The government and most foreign countries are concerned because the date standard both within the U. S. and internationally is yyyy/mm/dd. Therefore, if Microsoft follows through with their publicized plan, their programs will not be compatible with programs that do conform to the standards. So if you want to pass data from a non-Microsoft program to a Microsoft program, or vice-versa, you will have to have a parser routine that will separate the days, months, and years of the date, and reorder them to work with the other program. This could be both cumbersome and slow. If you are dealing with an application that is time sensitive i.e. needs to run at near real time, any additional routines that have to be executed to allow the programs to function properly will slow the system down. Plus the more superfluous routines that are contained in the programs, the greater the chance for error. It is better to have all the programs that you are using to use the same date format.

Where to Go for Help

There are many places that you can go for help with your Year 2000 Problem. Unfortunately, because of the magnitude of this problem, the majority of the consultants that are really addressing the Year 2000 Problem are focusing on major corporations. There is not enough people or time for these organizations to be able to assist every small business that is out there. However, in basically every large city, and even not so large of cities these days there are consultants available that are very computer literate. They may not be immediately involved in the Year 2000 Problem, but they can at least assist you in some of the common day problems with your system, such as: taking an inventory of your system, helping you to get more familiar with how your system works and what programs are on it

Most of the consultants will have an understanding of what the Year 2000 Problem is, and will be able to at least help get you started with contacting your vendors to determine when you can expect Year 2000 Compliant programs.

When you contact one of these local consultants ask him a few questions about the Year 2000 to see if he knows what he is talking about. After reading this book, you should have a pretty good understanding of the problem, that you could ask questions and know if they are a viable option or not. One question that you would want them to answer is whether 2000 is a Leap Year or not, and if they answer yes, have them tell you why it is a Leap Year. Don't ask just yes or no questions, but ask open ended questions that are going to require some knowledge about the Year 2000 problem to answer.

78   *Novell Products and the Year 2000*

Tom Hartman
Novell

[Editor: By the time you read this chapter, most of the defects listed will be cured. Discuss them with your Novell representative. And remember that Novell was among the *first* to give an honest, complete summary.]

Novell is committed to protecting our customers' investments in our products, and our interest in the long-term viability of the computer industry in general. With the network being a focal point for most computers, the network operating system will play a key role in the proper interaction and operation of a myriad of software products. Novell is taking the necessary steps to insure that all of our products meet year 2000 requirements and that our processes and standards will provide a path to avoid future date related problems.

A Year 2000 Compliant software product is one which will not fail specifically due to the change of year from 1999 to 2000. However, Novell feels that there is much more to correct date and time support than this. Novell uses the following standards to test if our products provide the correct date and time support.

> The range of dates and time that the programs and data supports should be made known.

> Each type of date (for example, a built-in clock, the date of a financial transaction, a date stored within a file system, an appointment date, the date of a mail message) should only be able to store valid dates.

> For a clock, once it is correctly set, the stored date and time should remain correct within the accuracy of the mechanism used to advance it.

> Where necessary, the product should correctly convert any of its supported date types between ordinal day number and date. In particular, the calculations should correctly handle leap years (2000 is a leap year, 2100 and 1900 are not, etc.).

> Ensure that calculations of Julian day number and day-of-the-week work once correctly seeded.

> All other calculations and comparisons on dates should be performed correctly.

> For all components of a date or time to be entered the component should be correctly stored as entered. It should be made clear

whether day or month should be entered first if both are numerical.

➤ If year is to be entered, the product should accept a four-digit value and correctly store it. Years outside the supported range should be rejected.

➤ If a two-digit year is entered, the corresponding full year value should be stated. For example: "80-99 are treated as 1980-1999; 00-79 are treated as 2000-2079".

➤ It should not be possible to enter an invalid or out-of-range date.

➤ If a year value is displayed, it should ideally be correctly displayed with four digits. If it must be displayed with two digits, there should be some way to determine what the full year number is.

Novell has tested their products. Listed below is a detailed description of problems or issues with correct date time handling.

NetWare All Versions

➤ NetWare supported dates are 1980 to 2155.

➤ Two-digit years 80-99 are treated as 1980-1999, 00-79 as 2000-2079. If a four-digit year is entered, the first two digits are ignored. Thus it is currently only possible to set the date to values from 1980 to 2079. NetWare displays its current date with a four-digit year. NetWare does not determine the display format for file dates, since they are displayed by workstations.

➤ The filesystem dates are compatible with those of the DOS FAT filesystem, so support from 1980 to 2107.

➤ NetWare correctly calculates the day of the week, and correctly converts from the internal clock date to a filesystem date (provided the year is in the filesystem's date range).

➤ NetWare correctly treats 2000 as a leap year, so the clock will advance from 28 February 2000 to 29 February.

NetWare 3.11, 3.12:

➤ NetWare 3.1x versions have a problem reading and writing the PC real-time clock after 1999. Patches will be released for these versions by the end of 1996. A preliminary patch is available in 312PT9.EXE. Novell patches can be downloaded off of Novell's Web site at: www.novell.com

➤ NetWare 3.1x incorrectly appears to treat the year 2100 as a leap year, it advances from 28 February 2100 to 29 February.

> NetWare 3.x will never count 29 February when calculating password expiration dates. Thus, with a 30-day password expiration time, if a user changes the password in February of a leap year, the password will expire in 31 days. If the password was changed in February of a non-leap year, the new password would correctly expire in 30 days. While this is a security violation, most people would not consider it serious.

NetWare 4.x/IntranetWare

> All version of NetWare 4 and IntranetWare correctly treat the year 2100 as not being a leap year

NetWare 4.01, 4.02 and 4.10:

> As shipped NetWare 4.0x and 4.10 versions have a problem reading and writing the PC real-time clock after 1999. A patch will be released for these versions by the end of 1996. A preliminary patch is available in 410PT6.EXE. Novell patches can be downloaded off of Novell's Web site at: www.novell.com

NetWare 4.11/IntranetWare:

> There are no known problems with NetWare 4.11 or IntranetWare concerning date time handling. It will correctly advance from 31 December 1999 to 1 January 2000 and supports dates from 1980 to 2155.

GroupWise 4.1 and 5.0

> GroupWise stores all dates internally as a four-byte number of seconds since 1 January 1970. This gives it a date range from 1970 to 2106.
> The current date and time is read from the host operating system using native calls, which of course vary according to the platform.
> All date calculations to and from this format (mainly for entry and display) correctly treat 2000 as a leap year and 2100 as not a leap year. The only operation necessary to convert to an ordinal year number is division.
> GroupWise 4.1 for Windows allows the use of dates from 1970 to 2106. GroupWise 4.1 for DOS restricts the user to 1970 to 2100.
> For date entry, the current country setting is used to determine whether day or month should be entered first. If a four-digit year number is entered, that is used as the year value. If a two-digit

year number is entered, 70 to 99 is treated as 1979 to 1999, 00 to 69 as 2000 to 2069. Dates outside the 1970 to 2106 range are not accepted, and it is not possible to move past 2106 in the calendar.

➤ GroupWise displays dates with a four-digit year number, so there is no ambiguity.

79   *UNIX Time*

Richard Painter
Painter Engineering, Inc.

This brief and program is in response to issues of the Year 2000 computer problems and one aspect of date and time for UNIX[1] systems.

The UNIX time will run out in 2039. Once the magic time arrives the time may revert to 13 December 1901 or reset to the UNIX birth date of 1 January 1970 depending on the underlying hardware and implementation.

All UNIX systems (I know of no exceptions at this time) rely on a basic system call function called *time()* to obtain the time. This function returns a (signed) long integer (4 bytes) of seconds since the EPOCH. The EPOCH is defined as the birth of UNIX, that is 1 January 1970. The internal structure *time_t* (signed long integer) is used throughout many time-related functions and data structures, including the file systems.

Without vendor support it is unlikely a feasible solution could be developed to work around this limit. There are many, many UNIX systems deployed and still in use even though the vendors don't exist or don't support them anymore. There are so many references to the *time_t* structure in the UNIX operating system, commands and applications (UNIX utilities) source code that it would not be portable without changing most versions from most vendors. For those without UNIX source there is no chance to modify the required structures, functions, and utilities.

The attached program demonstrates the limitations of the UNIX time functions and internal time representations.

The arithmetic for determining the last date and time for this *time_t* structure follows:

---

1. UNIX is a trademark of AT&T.

max seconds in a long   = 2147483647 seconds
= 35791394 minutes, 7 seconds
= 596523 hours, 14 minutes, 7 seconds
= 24855 days, 3 hours, 14 minutes, 7 seconds
= 68 years, 18 days, 3 hours, 14 minutes, 7 seconds

Therefore, 68 years plus 1970 yields 2038. The point in time that this will happen is Tue 19 Jan 2038 at 03:14 and 7 sec. AM GMT. Please note that this accounts for leap year days too.

This C program demonstrates the boundaries and effects of the start and end dates used in UNIX with the *time_t* structure. The program output sample is included at the end of the program.

```
*/
#include <stdio.h>
#include <limits.h>
#include <time.h>

main{}
{
    time_t maxt;

    maxt = 0L;
    printf("Start of UNIX GMT time (%ld, 0x%08X) is %s",
            maxt, maxt, asctime(gmtime(&maxt)));

    maxt = LONG_MAX;    /* 2147483647L */
    printf("End of UNIX GMT time is (%ld, 0x%08X) is %s",
            maxt, maxt, asctime(gmtime(&maxt)));

    maxt++;
    printf("End of UNIX GMT time plus 1 sec. (%ld, 0x%08X) is %s",
            maxt, maxt, asctime(gmtime(&maxt)));

    maxt = 0L;
    maxt--:
    printf("Start of UNIX GMT time minus 1 sec. (%ld, 0x%08X) is %s",
            maxt, maxt, asctime (gmtime(&maxt)));
}
/*
cc -O -o maxtime maxtime.c
cc -O -o maxtime maxtime.c
*/

/*          the output on a Data General AViioN is
Start of UNIX GMT time (0, 0x00000000) is Thu Jan 1 00:00:00 1970
End of UNIX GMT time is (2147483647, 0x7FFFFFFF) is Tue Jan 19
03:14:07 2038
End of UNIX GMT time plus 1 sec. (-2147483648, 0x80000000) is
Fri Dec 13 20:45:52 1901
Start of UNIX GMT time minus 1 sec. (-1, 0xFFFFFFFF) is Wed Dec 31
23:59:59 1969
*/
```

80 *TICTOC/CICS*

Isogon

TICTOC/CICS is the unique software product for CICS that lets different terminals, transactions, users or any combination of these, run under different "virtual" (fictitious) dates and times.

CICS resources (terminals, transactions and users) defined to TICTOC/CICS will be returned a virtual date when executing programs associated with these resources request the date and time through the CICS Command Level ASKTIME command.

This lets you test how CICS applications will run, for example, on or after January 1, 2000, without requiring every transaction running concurrently in the same CICS region to receive the virtual date.

This allows you to perform date simulation testing without dedicating separate CICS regions solely for this purpose.

Since only those CICS resources explicitly defined to TICTOC/CICS are affected, TICTOC/CICS can safely be used for date simulation processing even in production environments. This makes TICTOC/CICS the perfect solution for simulating midnight rollover, period end (end of day, month, year, etc.) and time zone transaction processing.

TICTOC/CICS has both a convenient full-screen menu-driven online interface and a single-line command interface to easily define which terminals, transactions and users are eligible to run under a virtual date. TICTOC/CICS requires no changes to your application programs whatsoever.

CICS Resources

Throughout TICTOC/CICS documentation, the term "CICS resources" refers to any combination of terminal, transaction and user names as defined to CICS. Terminal, transaction and user names are also referred to as TERMIDs, TRANSIDs and USERIDs respectively.

Virtual Dates and Virtual Clocks

When a transaction that is eligible for TICTOC/CICS timing services asks for the date and time by issuing the CICS Command Level ASKTIME command, it gets a "virtual date" based on TICTOC/CICS "virtual clock" definition, instead of the real date and time settings of the operating system's clock.

The term "virtual date" used throughout TICTOC/CICS documentation refers to the date, time or both values when set by TICTOC/CICS. These values are placed in fields EIBDATE and EIBTIME in the transaction's EIB control block.

The term "virtual clock" used throughout TICTOC/CICS documentation refers to a TICTOC/CICS definition consisting of CICS resource names and the virtual date to be used when a transaction, whose resource names match those of the definition, issues a CICS ASKTIME command.

TICTOC/CICS documentation describes a transaction that is eligible for TICTOC/CICS timing services as running "using" a virtual date or running "under" a virtual date. These expressions are synonymous.

When an eligible transaction issues a CICS ASKTIME command for the first time, TICTOC/CICS starts running the virtual clock, beginning at the date and time specified in the virtual clock definition. The clock will continue to run for the life span of the transaction, i.e., until the transaction terminates. When a new eligible transaction starts, the clock is reset and begins running again from the date and time specified in the virtual clock of definition.

Independent Time-Of-Day Clocks (ITCs)

You may need to perform date simulation that requires a virtual clock to continue running, without ever being reset, over the life span of more than one transaction or even for the entire duration of the CICS region's execution.

For this purpose, there is a special type of virtual clock definition known as an independent time-of-day clock definition or ITC for short. Each ITC definition consists of a unique name the ITC can be referenced by and a virtual date that the clock is to start at. No CICS resource names are specified in an ITC definition. Once defined, the ITC's clock begins running.

To use an ITC, simply define a standard virtual clock definition with the date field containing the name of the ITC to be used instead of a virtual date value.

Specifying CICS Resource Names in Virtual Clock Definitions

CICS resource names defined in virtual clock definitions can include wildcard and generic pattern characters. A question mark ("?") matches any single character in the corresponding position. An asterisk ("*") matches zero or more characters from the location of the asterisk to the end of the resource name.

For example, a USERID specified as "ACCT*" in a virtual clock definition will match any user name beginning with "ACCT". A USERID specified as A??T* will match any user name beginning with an "A" in the first position and a "T" in the fourth position.

81   *XPEDITER/Xchange*

Gary Deneszczuk
Compuware Corp.

You must provide information for the request variable, which has the following syntax:

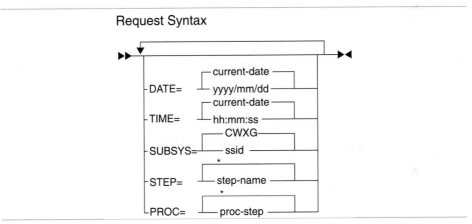

Request Syntax

Figure 81.1   Request Syntax

> **DATE:** The year, month, and day that you want Xchange to simulate. If the PREVDATE configuration parameter is set to NO (XGGCNFIG macro), dates prior to today's date are not allowed. Valid entries are as follows:

YYYY	1973 to 2039
MM	01 to 12
DD	01 to 28 (Feb.)
	01 to 29 (Feb. during a leap year)
	01 to 30 (Apr., June, Sept., and Nov.)
	01 to 31 (Jan., Mar., May, July, Aug., Oct., and Dec.)

This parameter defaults to the current year, month, and date.

> **TIME**: The hour, minute, and second that you want Xchange to simulate for the specified date. The following entries are valid:

HH	00 to 23
MM	00 to 59
SS	00 to 59

This parameter defaults to the current hour, minute, and second.

> **SUBSYS**: The subsystem ID specified in the Xchange configuration macro, XGGCNFIG. This name was specified by the product installer and is discussed on page 2-5. This parameter defaults to CWXG.

> **STEP**: The name of a specific step or set of steps within a job request. To specify a single step, enter the exact step name in this field. More than one step can be specified by substituting the wildcard character, an asterisk (*), anywhere in the step name. Specifying only an asterisk for this parameter requests all steps in the job. An asterisk is the default.

> **PROC**: The name of a procedure step or steps within a job request. You can specify a single procedure step by entering the exact procedure name, or multiple procedure steps by replacing any part of the procedure step with an asterisk (*).

Simulation Activity Report

The XPEDITER/Xchange Simulation Activity Report has the format shown in Figure 81.2.

```
MAR 3 1995                              COMPUWARE CORPORATION
13:17:08                        XPEDITER/SCHANGE SIMULATION ACTIVITY REPORT


                                                DATE       TIME
RECORD JOB        STEPNAME PROCSTEP PROGRAM  MODNAME  YYY  MM DD HH MN SS OFFSET    JOB#     USERID
     1 DFHTSTOT   STEP1             TESTPGM1 TESTPGM1 2000 01 05 13 27 36 00016CDA JOB06688 DFHTSTO
     2 DFHTSTOD   ABC               PURCHORD PURCHORD 1999 12 31 23 59 55 00030AFO JOB06688 DFHTSTO
     3 RTMNTPEB   APLO5    TSTPROC  ACCTRECV ACCTRECV 2025 09 01 01 00 00 0002F912 JOB00311 CWX0291
     4 XYZ00413   STEP4             HMNRESRC HMNRESRC 1999 12 31 23 59 55 00027BC4 JOB00682 CWXABC1
     5 JBR05055   XYZ01    ABRPROC  TEXTPGM3 TESTPGM3 2001 02 14 00 00 00 000318D8 JOB04321 JBR0505
     6 JBR05055   XYZ01    ABRPROC  TEXTPGM3 TESTPGM3 2001 02 14 00 00 10 000A36FE JOB04321 JBR0505
     7 JBR05055   XYZ01    ABRPROC  TEXTPGM3 TESTPGM3 2001 02 14 00 00 32 00036A12 JOB04321 JBR0505
     8 RTMNTPEB   APL05             ACCTINVT ACCTINVT 2025 09 01 01 00 00 00092FCC JOB00311 CWX0291
```

Figure 81.2   XPEDITER/Xchange Simulation Activity Report

Fields

> **RECORD**: The record number of the request.

➤ *JOB*: The MVS job for which the system date and time has been simulated.

➤ *STEPNAME*: The name of a specific step within the job request.

➤ *PROCSTEP*: The name of the procedure step within the job request.

➤ *PROGRAM*: The name of the program as specified on the EXEC PGM= JCL statement.

➤ *MODNAME*: The program that issues the request. If this program is different from the program in the PROGRAM field, it is a program called by the program in the PROGRAM field.

➤ *DATE*: The simulated date in year, month, and day format.

➤ *TIME*: The simulated time in hour, minute, and second format.

➤ *OFFSET*: The number of bytes, in hex, from the start of the MODNAME name to the time request (the SVC11). You can use the OFFSET figure with a link-edit map to locate the CSECT that begins immediately before the OFFSET. Subtract the address of the beginning of the CSECT from the OFFSET to determine the relative offset. The relative offset is the number of bytes, in hex, from the beginning of the CSECT to the time request.

➤ *JOB#*: The number of the MVS job.

➤ *USERID*: The ID of the user who made the request.

Using Xchange with IMS

Xchange can be used with IMS 1.3 and above. You can simulate dates and times for the following types of programs running in IMS dependent regions:

➤ Message Processing Programs (MPPs)

➤ Batch Message Processing (BMP) programs

➤ DL/I batch.

> *Caution: Do not exchange dates and times for the IMS control region, DLISAS, DBRC, or IRLM. Doing so could compromise database integrity. Compuware recommends that exchanges of dates and times for IMS only be performed in test regions.*

> *Because Xchange works for any program that issues SVC11s, IMS programs that use the ACCEPT verb or MOVE CURRENT-DATE can have their dates and times exchanged. The only exception to this is programs loaded by IMS from the Preload List, which cannot be exchanged.*

82   *HourGlass 2000*

Jerry Nelson
Mainware

HourGlass 2000 is a utility product that can provide a great amount of assistance in preparing early for the pending disaster. It can simulate any date past, present, or future that MVS is capable of returning. In addition, it has the ability to alter the time of day which can be used for time sensitive applications.

Once activated, HG2000 intercepts all requests for the date and time made via SVC 11 or via the TIME LINKAGE=SYSTEM macro. HourGlass 2000 is unique in that it also has the ability to intercept STCK requests for many products which use it, such as COBOL/370, C/370, PLI/370, NATURAL, IDEAL, IEF, and DB2. It then determines if this application is requesting an altered date/time. If not, the current date/time is returned immediately. Otherwise, the altered date/time is returned. It is that simple!

The system date can be retrieved in numerous ways externally via utilities or programming languages. Most programming languages provide a reserved word or function that returns the system date in a usable format (such as COBOL's CURRENT-DATE). Internally though, there are only three ways to retrieve this date. The first and by far the most common is via an SVC 11 call. Another less common method that is used mostly by operating system level code is the STCK instruction which returns the number of microseconds since January 1, 1900. Lastly, a special format of the TIME macro (LINKAGE=SYSTEM) which issues a PC instruction can be used. This is rarely used since it wasn't available until MVS ESA Version 4.1.

Installation and Usage of HourGlass 2000

Installing HG2000 is a snap and can generally be done in under 1 hour. The load library and sample JCL library are downloaded from the install tape using IEBCOPY. A customization job is then run which sets some defaults and instructs HourGlass as to which jobs are to be eligible for altered dates. Finally, HG2000 is activated by running an install job step. This one step requires the use of an APF authorized library. Once activated, HG2000 waits for a job step to request an altered date and/or time.

During installation, screening criteria can be specified to limit the use of HG2000 to certain jobs. This specification can be by job class and/or job name. If job name screening is used, a list of job name prefixes (e.g.

TEST meaning all jobs whose jobname begins with TEST) is specified. If job class screening is used, a list of valid job classes is specified. This eligibility screening is optional.

Once a job has passed the HourGlass eligibility test, it will only receive the altered date or time if one of the following are present: 1) a special date/time DDcard which indicates the desired date/time, 2) the jobname prefix matches an installation specified prefix where the date/time is hard-coded (usually used for time zone issues), or 3) the jobname/userid match criteria input via an ISPF dialog which allows the dynamic setting of the date/time without any JCL changes.

The DDcard technique, if used must be of the form:

//HGcyyddd DD DUMMY

where:

c is '0' for the twentieth century (1900-1999) or a '1' for twenty-first century dates (2000-2099).

yy is the two digit year.

ddd is the julian day relative from January 1. A TSO clist is provided to generate this DD statement.

To alter the time, a step must contain a DD statement of the form:

//HGdhhmm DD DUMMY

where:

d is the direction to alter the time. Time is altered by HourGlass relative to current time. It can be altered plus or minus (east or west). Valid values are 'P' or 'E' for plus/east and 'M' or 'W' for minus/west.

hh is the number of hours to adjust.

mm is the number of minutes to adjust.

The maximum time adjustment is 23 hours, 59 minutes.

No other JCL changes are required. HourGlass can be activated and deactivated on a system by running the HGON or HGOFF job steps provided.

How Does HourGlass Support My Online Applications?

In the CICS environment, an HourGlass transaction is provided which allows specification of an altered date and/or time to be set in the EIB-DATE/EIBTIME and received by all transactions issuing any format of the EXEC CICS ASKTIME command. If desired, the altered date/time can be limited to specific userids, terminals, or transactions. In fact, individual users can each be using different date/time combinations.

In an IMS DC environment, a DDcard is added to the JCL for all message regions wishing to participate in altered date/times. Then, a transaction is supplied which allows each user to individually set their own unique date/time. This date/time can be changed as often as desired.

Can HourGlass 2000 Intercept STCK Date/Time Requests?

For in-house written code that makes use of the STCK instruction, Hour-Glass 2000 provides support for this to also receive altered dates even though it is an instruction. Through a simple reassembly, these programs can now receive altered dates/times too.

If source code is not available, often times MainWare can provide a small patch to a load module which will enable HourGlass to intercept the STCK instruction. Examples of this are COBOL/370, C/370, PLI/370, NATURAL, IDEAL, IEF, and DB2 (when using the SQL special registers CURRENT DATE/TIME/TIMESTAMP of the SELECT and UPDATE statements and default values for the INSERT statement). No other product works with so may STCK products.

Other Uses For HourGlass 2000

The uses for HG2000 are numerous. Testing for twenty-first century compatibility is the obvious use. Once an application program has been shown to have date problems, it must be repaired. HG2000 should then be used again to test the changes. HourGlass can be used as a Quality Assurance tool to verify that a program change has not affected the ability for that application to work properly into the twenty-first century.

Another use for HG2000 is to provide an improved testing environment. Most shops extract or generate test databases for use by programmers. These test databases are generally not refreshed daily and therefore do not contain current data. By running all test jobs with dates near the date of the database extract, test jobs simulate the production environment in a more realistic manner.

Yet another use for HG2000 is to test date or time sensitive applications. For instance, some applications may perform different tasks at month end, quarter end, year end than they perform on other days. Hour-Glass can be used to test these special dates anytime.

Some shops have a data center that resides in another time zone from some of the end users. All reports run for that user currently reflect the time zone of the data center, not the end user, which can be confusing. By using HG2000 to alter the time, all reports may now reflect the time zone of the user who requested the report. HourGlass 2000 provides the ability for all jobs in this scenario to receive altered times without JCL changes.

After a production abend on a weekend, a fix may not be available until the next week. For date sensitive jobs, using HourGlass to alter the date back to the original run date may prevent application complications, particularly those that deal with money such as calculating interest payments.

The HourGlass 2000 Audit Facility

Included in the HourGlass 2000 software is an optional audit trail facility which can be used to report on: 1) All applications requesting the system date or time; 2) All applications requesting an altered date or time; or 3) Both.

These reports are extremely useful by initially identifying the potential scope of the twenty-first century problem and later by reporting to auditors any jobs requesting altered dates or times. Included in the audit trail are job name, job number, step name, frequency of date/time requests, and the date and time requested.

10 part

Expert: Test Tools

before proceeding, glance back to Chapter 24, Miro Medek's "How Do You Know Without Testing?" Basic common sense dictates that testing results after a Y2K code change, must be compared against "baseline" outcomes of the same tests performed before the programs are touched.

Since you'll have to use the exact same user data repeatedly anyway, you can save time and boredom by using a capture-replay package like these:

Automator, Autotester, CA-Traps, CPR, Carbon Copy, Design Recovery, Hiperstation, Playback, ProTerm, SmartTest, Vermont, etc. Help is even available in composing the test data, via CA-Datamacs, CICS McKinney, File Aid, Grayboxx, Magec, McCabe, Sleuth, STGF/IBM, XDC, etc.

"Don't Need No Stinking Test Tools," is the understandable response of folks who'd like to keep their computer testing "all natural." With this title, Randall Rice begins the chapter by recounting the keying errors, ignored malfunctions, and other mishaps due to boredom and fatigue of humans who test hard—not smart—by ignoring test tools they probably already own.

A counterexample is the one page "Script Language" title by ProTerm, showing how your planned test can be repeated indefinitely without human intervention. Your organization probably already has a scripting/capture/playback package collecting dust somewhere—ProTerm's or another. Why not find it, run off 20 copies of the manual for distribution, and welcome whoever comes back eager to use that tool! Good testers don't have to be rocket scientists.

It's almost certain that you own and use Compuware's File-Aid. What you may not realize is that it can assemble relevant live-data records for testing, tailoring them to produce just the values and logic choices your test needs. After you see the two manuals' excerpts, think how tools can reduce that 65 percent of Y2K projects earmarked for testing!

[Editor: For a quick two-page summary of the Year 2000 testing context, see figure 25.1 for a side-by-side depiction of the major Y2K test phases, and see Figure 91.1 for a test-case construction form.]

IBM's "Tool Categories" include testing simulation, analysis, managers, and data producers. (Examples of these and other Y2K related tools are listed in the named IBM reference, free on the net or inexpensive in printed form.)

The U.S. Air Force's "Test Technologies" discusses software modification in general, then lists more than thirty distinct categories of test tool. Not published here—but available free—is the 600-item test tool evaluation from which the two product lists above were gleaned.

Want Y2K-specific tools? Eighty good ones are detailed in Marilyn Frankel and Carl Gehr's Edge/GUIDE report. Most entries are categorized in dozens of ways (tool type, relevant operating systems/languages, special features, etc.). GUIDE Members can obtain the latest revision through that IBM user group and others should contact the Edge authors.

It's a good idea to get all three tool lists. More are available via the websites referenced in the Editor's Preface. Even better is to search your dusty shelves and discover some excellent test tools you already own. Once you have automated that 55–75 percent of Y2K which is testing, you stand a much better chance of reaching all your NON-testing Y2K project goals, too!

83   _Don't Need No Stinking Test Tools!_

Randall Rice
Rice Consulting Services, Inc.

This article is adapted from William E. Perry and Randall W. Rice's _Surviving the Top Ten Challenges of Software Testing_, Chapter 5, "Challenge #8: Testing Without Tools" (pp. 57-74), by permission of Dorset House Publishing, Co., Inc., 353 West 12th Street, New York, NY 10014. Copyright © 1997 by William E. Perry and Randall W. Rice. All rights reserved.

Overview

As a result of interviewing and surveying over one thousand software testers during the past three years, we have identified many common testing problems. The major finding in this study is that most testing problems are not technical, but human in nature.

In testing, as in other areas of software development and maintenance, success depends on finding the right balance of people, processes and tools. When any one of these areas are out of balance, the testing effort will take longer and cost more than necessary. Most importantly is the fact that defects can easily be missed by the lack of process, tool, or people. In Year 2000 projects, the ability to perform optimized, efficient testing will make the difference between success and failure.

Why Are Test Tools Important?

Let's face it—testing takes a lot of time and is very tedious to perform. In addition, the tester must take great care to perform the test precisely or defects can be passed along to the customer and/or user of the software. So, how can we test software to the degree that we are confident in a high level of quality?

One approach which is common but not recommended by the author is to hire more testers. Besides following Brook's Law (adding more people to a project that is already late will make it even later), humans are error-prone and will soon run out of patience to continue to perform the enormous manner of tests required for most projects, especially Year 2000 projects.

The best solution is to develop a testing process that combines effective test methods, tools that fit your testing needs, and people who are trained and motivated to perform testing using the process and tools. The solution is much harder to implement than it sounds.

First of all, tools cost money (large amounts of money in some cases) and the funding must come from senior management. In some organizations this is not a problem. In these organizations management recognizes the need for test tools and is willing to make an investment to make sure testing is done efficiently. In other organizations, testers are expected to leverage the volume of testing with sheer manual effort. In these organizations, management would rather pay people overtime than purchase a test tool. A major problem with the manual approach is burn-out as people try to perform thousands of tests. [Editor: True. Pretools, the most tenacious fatigued testers sometimes racked up twice the income for one third the productivity.] The challenge is to make a persuasive case to management for the tools you need for testing.

Most of us are quick to recognize that tools alone do not solve problems. The old maxim holds true that "a fool with a tool is still a fool." Another saying goes, "When the only tool you have is a hammer, every problem looks like a nail." This leads to the second major testing concern of making test tools part of an overall test process. This chapter explains the basics of test tools, how to pick the right tools, what happens in manual testing, and how to make sure the tool is actually used in day-to-day testing activities in your organization.

The Testing Challenge

The year 2000 project at the Big Insurance Company is not going well. With less than six months to go before December 31, 1999 the project is behind schedule and the three independent testers are working 12 hours a day to try to test the work of 25 programmers. Testing was scheduled to start two months ago, but now the testers will be lucky to have six months to test the thousands of test cases through thousands of programs that have been changed.

During the planning phase of the project, the need for an automated test tool was seen and several tools for different tasks, such as regression testing and test case generation were selected, but the purchase decision was never made because other project needs took a higher priority. The result of not securing test tools is now evident as the testers are executing manual test scripts every time a defect is fixed and returned to the test team.

As the project deadline approaches, the test team is working excessive hours to keep up with the programmers. In fact, everyone on the project is working long hours. Overtime is taking a toll on everyone, including the testers, who need to be alert to find any new defects that are introduced as a result of fixing a defect. Because of the fatigue factor combined with the boredom of testing the same program over and over, defects are missed in testing. Testing is becoming less and less effective and the testers are being blamed for not finding the defects. The testing effort is in a downward spiral—the harder the test team works, the worse things get.

The project team's problems doesn't last long. Because of excessive defects and the company's dependence on information systems, the board of directors of The Big Insurance Company decides that the business will not survive after the year 2000 and sells the company to a larger competitor. As a result, everyone on the project is looking for a new job.

Did the lack of a test tool cause the project to fail? No, but major defects were a contributing factor for the project's failure. An automated test tool, combined with an effective testing process would have found many of the defects.

In this case, the job was too much for the test team to handle. However, with an imminent deadline there was not enough time to hire more testers and it was too late to buy a test tool. If the purchase of an automated test tool had been perceived to be as important as buying a Year 2000 software converter, much time and money could have been saved by the automation of repetitive testing tasks.

Impact on Testing

Test tools, or the lack thereof, can have a great impact on the failure or success of a testing effort. In testing software, testers perform much repetitive work in executing test cases. One of the problems in testing is that there are often billions of possible test cases, yet there is not enough time to perform even a fraction of the test cases, not to mention performing them twice. Tests can and should be performed multiple times if defects are found and changes are made. Capture/playback and script execution tools are very helpful in performing regression testing of software changes. Test case generators and test data generators can help testers reduce the number of test cases needed while increasing the coverage of testing.

When selecting and using automated test tools, there are some keys to keep in mind. First, let's examine why you should consider using automated testing tools.

➢ Manual testing is random and error-prone

The best case scenario for testing is executing test scripts and well-planned test cases. The worst case scenario is where testing is ad-hoc or haphazard with no way to repeat a test. When following a written script, the tester must rely on his or her skills to follow the script exactly while observing every aspect of the software's performance. In addition, the tester must be able to document the test results completely and accurately. An automated capture/playback tool does all of this work automatically, behind the scenes.

When testing manually, there is sometimes doubt that the test was performed exactly as planned. There is also no way to duplicate a test to verify the exact actions performed. Many people say they perform regression testing, but true regression testing requires that a test be performed and compared to the previous test results. Any error in executing the text can invalidate it, resulting in defects.

➢ Manual testing is human resource intensive

There is only so much time for testing on a typical project. In many cases, there is not enough time in the schedule to perform minimal testing, much less the rigorous testing that is required for regression testing. A test that takes an hour to perform manually can be performed in a minute or less with an automated test tool. If you multiply the manual testing time by hundreds of tests, the impact on the testing workload becomes very apparent.

➢ Manual testing is slow

If it takes a person an hour to perform a given test script, an automated tool can perform the same test in a matter of minutes, document the results, and compare the results to a previous test. The impact of increased testing speed can be seen especially if the software is changing rapidly. This is the case with projects that have trouble in locking down code versions. Testers often complain that the targets keep moving. If a test suite takes four weeks to perform and the tester is getting a new version of the system to test every week, there is a problem (Figure 83.1). Sooner or later, the testers will give up trying to perform complete testing and will test only the software changes, which exposes a huge risk, that of software changes causing unintended defects. This is sometimes called the "But I just changed one line of code…" syndrome.

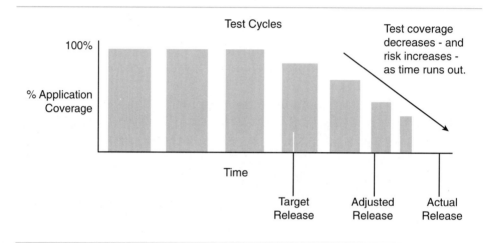

Figure 83.1   Manual testing

Automated test tools help testers keep up with rapid change by compressing the testing time as shown in Figure 83.2. In automated testing there is a significant up-front investment in capturing or writing test scripts, but the payback comes later in faster, more complete testing of future software releases.

➢ Manual testing is boring

Not that anyone ever promised that testing would ever be the most exciting job in the world, but the boredom of testing is one reason defects go undetected by testers. Automated tools not only remove the boredom of testing, but can catch small differences in the results from previous tests. Any difference in test results can indicate a defect.

Which test tools are right for you?

Choosing the right test tool can be a tricky job. The tool you select will depend on your technical environment (mainframe, client/server, etc.),

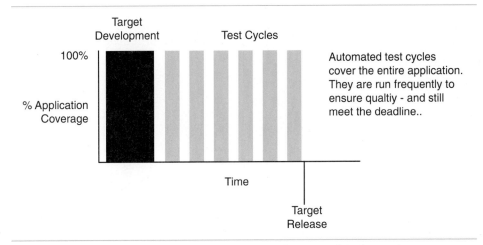

Figure 83.2   Automated testing (Courtesy of Rational Software)

the kinds of testing to be performed (unit, system, user acceptance, regression, etc.), and the people using the test tools (programmers, testers, users, etc.). Table 83.1 shows a representative listing of test tool categories and relates them to the phases of testing. Not all of the tools shown in the table are automated— some are manual. This is because a test tool is defined as any vehicle that assists in testing. Since some tools are better suited to a particular test phase than others, the degree of fitness is scored as: 1=Good Fit, 2=Limited Use, 3=Not Recommended.

Some types of testing are not suited for automated testing. For example, user acceptance testing validates the system will meet user needs by simulating the system's operation in the real world. This requires that users conduct hands-on testing of the system. A capture/playback tool helps record user test sessions for documentation purposes, but script playback defeats the goal of hands-on testing.

Test Tool Categories

Capture/Playback

Capture/Playback tools capture or record a test session to a file in a format that can played back on the system later. These tools also can compare test results to a previous test. This is one major reason capture/playback tools are required for true regression testing—they can perform comparisons with prior tests without human error.

Most capture/playback tools permit the tester to modify the test scripts or procedures to add logic such as loops and IF statements and even I/O calls to process external test data.

Table 83.1   **Test Tools by Test Phase**

Test Tool Categories	Relative Cost	Manual/Automated	Unit Testing	Integration/System Testing	User Acceptance Testing	Regression Testing
Capture/Playback	H	A	1	1	2	1
Automated Script Execution	H	A	1	1	3	1
Test Coverage Analyzer	M	A	1	2	3	2
Test Case Generator	M	A	1	1	2	1
Test Data Generator	M	A	1	1	1	1
Logic/Complexity Analyzer	H	A	1	2	3	3
Defect Tracker	L-M	A	1	1	1	1
Test Manager	M	A	1	1	1	1
Checklist	L	M	1	1	1	1
Flowchart	L	M	1	1	1	3
Test Script	M-H	A,M	1	1	1	1

Benefit: Capture/playback tools can execute and compare tests faster and more accurately than manual testing, they can record exactly which actions were performed during a test to assist in debugging, and they can perform tests in an unattended mode and document results, allowing testers to sleep at night and have a weekend off every once in a while, at least. Capture/playback tools have their greatest benefit in regression and performance testing.

Automated Test Execution

Some automated testing tools require the tester to write test scripts or procedures as opposed to recording the test session in a script. These tools have many of the same features and benefits of the playback part of capture/playback tools. As with capture/playback, these tools will perform unattended tests and automatically record and compare the results to previous tests.

Benefit: Automated test execution tools can perform and analyze tests faster and more accurately than manual testing. Like capture/playback tools, these tools can perform tests in an unattended mode and document the test results. As with capture/playback tools, these tools have the best application and payoff in regression and performance testing.

Test Coverage Analyzer

A test coverage analyzer measures how much of a module or system was covered during a test. Test coverage may be measured by lines of code tested, decisions tested, paths tested, or system paths tested, among others.

Benefit: Test coverage tools identify areas of the system or the software that have not been touched by the test. This information allows the tester accurately to measure the degree of test completeness and add test cases where necessary to increase the test coverage.

Test Case Generator

A test case generator is an intelligent tool that takes system information such as software requirements, data models, object models, and other system deliverables and turns it into meaningful test cases. Test cases created by a test case generator are also analyzed to reduce redundancy and increase test coverage.

Benefit: Test case generators save much time in automatically generating test cases that might otherwise take much time to build manually. Test case generators help eliminate redundancy by creating test cases that cover a high percentage of the software or system with a minimal number of test conditions.

Test Data Generator

Test data generators are sometimes confused with test case generators, but a test data generator is primarily used to populate test files and databases with data. Test data created by test data generators is often random, but newer tools are becoming more sophisticated and can meet specific test criteria input to the tool. The test data can be used to supplement test data created from specific test cases. Another popular use of test data generators is to populate test files or tables with large volumes of data for stress and performance testing.

Benefit: Test data generators save testers and test designers time by building test files that would otherwise be created through manual data entry.

Logic/Complexity Analyzer

Logic and complexity analyzers measure the complexity of a software module or system by analyzing the condition logic such as IF statements and loops. This is very important information to a tester since complexity is often a contributor to software defects. Many of the logic/complexity analyzer tools can also print or display a graphical picture of the logical paths in a software module or system.

Benefit: Logic and complexity analyzers help identify complex logic for designing test cases that will exercise specific, complex processing routines in the software. These tools also allow testers to perform a risk analysis and to assess software maintainability. Another benefit of logic and complexity analyzers is to measure complex logic to determine test coverage of a software module or section of code.

Defect Tracker

A defect tracker allows defect information to be recorded and routed to the correct people for resolution. Many defect trackers can be installed on a Local Area Network, with the defect information passed from one person to the next like e-mail. Defect trackers also allow testers or a defect administrator to create summary reports and graph defect trends. There are several good defect tracking tools on the market, but some organizations have chosen to invest in developing their defect tracking tools using PC databases. The issue then becomes one of determining if it costs more to build the tool yourself or to buy it.

Benefit: The most valuable information you will get from the test is not the test results themselves. Although this information is very important and has the most immediate value to you, more valuable information can be gained through studying defect trends. The information you learn from studying defect trends can be used to improve the software development and/or maintenance processes in your organization.

Another benefit of defect trackers is that paperless defect reports are not lost or misplaced. The status of any given defect can be obtained, summarized, and reported quickly and easily.

Test Manager

A test management tool helps testers plan, organize and track test products such as test scripts and test cases. Many client/server automated test tool suites have built-in test management and defect tracking features.

Few, if any, of the mainframe capture/playback tools have built-in test management. For that reason, there are several good PC-based test management tools.

Benefit: Test management tools help control and manage the test. In addition, these tools help determine test status. Test management tools can help promote the continuous improvement process by pinpointing the sources of defects.

Checklist

A checklist is an often overlooked manual test tools that prompts the tester for things to include during a test or test-related activities.

Benefit: Checklists are inexpensive, but have a high payback in providing a quality control for testing itself. Checklists help the tester remember things that are difficult to recall in the heat of the testing battle. Checklists are a low-cost way to add completeness and consistency to testing. In addition, checklists can be reused from one test to the next. You can even swap them with your other testing friends!

Flowchart

A flowchart shows an order of events to be followed when performing a process. As with checklists, flowcharts are manual tools with a big payback. To fully understand a process for testing, it helps to have the process graphically depicted. From the graphical pictures, the test designed can then ensure that all paths of the process (or the paths that are deemed most important) are tested. There are many good flowcharting tools on the shrink-wrapped market. If all else fails, you can resort to the good 'ol template, but when you make a mistake, it's difficult to make changes.

Benefit: Flowcharting is a low-cost way to document system or business processes to be tested. Documenting processes graphically lets you identify all logical paths through a process and design a test that covers the process.

Test Script

A test script describes the events to be performed during a test session. Test scripts can be created manually using tools such as word processors or they can be automated by using the capture/playback tools described earlier. [Editor: Most capture/playback tools are packaged with a scripting language so you can automate your manually-prepared scripts.]

Benefit: The primary benefit in using test scripts is that you know in advance what will be tested and the results are supposed to be. In addition, test scripts allow a test to be performed by someone unfamiliar with the process or the software to be tested. Test scripts also allow the test to be repeated to the extent of the accuracy of the scripts. Automated test scripts will be more accurate that manual scripts, simply due to the nature of humans to make mistakes in following a script.

If you would like more information about these or other categories of test tools, refer to William E. Perry's book *Effective Methods of Systems Testing*.

Solutions to the Testing Challenge

So now that you see the kinds of test tools available and how they can help you, perhaps you would like to investigate the tools further and perhaps secure some of them for your testing efforts. How do you get the right tools and make them part of your testing organization? The following suggestions have worked for other organizations and are worth trying.

Perform a tool inventory

Before rushing headlong into a tool search, you need to find out which, if any, tools your organization currently owns. You might be surprised at the results. A starting point for a tool inventory is with your systems administrator. You can also survey people to see which tools are currently being used and which tools would be of most help.

Define your requirements for a test tool

Like anything else in life, you need to know your needs before you start shopping. Defining requirements should be a team activity involving each group that will be using the tool(s). You should consider things such as:

- Hardware
- Operating systems
- Kinds of testing
- Phases of testing (Unit, integration, system, acceptance, etc.)
- People using the tool (Developers, independent testers, end-users, etc.)
- Software to be tested (Character-based, GUI, Object-oriented)
- Type of project (Traditional waterfall approach, Rapid Application Development (RAD), prototyping, etc.)
- Budget
- Training availability
- Technical support

Perform a cost/benefit analysis

How can you make the point for a test tool in terms of dollars? One of the best ways is to perform a cost benefit analysis. You can consider the following benefits:

- Reduced time to delivery
- Reduced re-work due to defects
- Using the tool(s) in all phases of testing
- Multiple people using the tool
- Defect prevention
- Test process improvement
- Test documentation
- Defect analysis and reproduction
- Increased test effectiveness
- Test management
- Test case reduction with increased test coverage

Investigate tools available

There are several good sources for test tool information:

- The World Wide Web—perform a search on test tools and stand back!
- The Quality Assurance Institute in Orlando, Florida distributes a test tool and vendor database each year. You can contact QAI at 407-363-1111.
- The Software Technology Support Center at Hill AFB has published a directory of test tools and vendors. You can get more information at 801-775-5555.

A word of advice

Narrow your list to about three to five tools that are a good fit for your requirements. You are then better prepared to communicate with a smaller number of tool vendors.

Integrate test tools with an effective testing process

Watts Humphrey has written,

> *"Automation might make an effective software process more effective, but a chaotic one even worse— often at considerable expense. Many managers who are not familiar with software issues thus emphasize tools and ignore the critical need for better manage-*

ment and technical methods. Tools are important—unquestionably so—but they should not distract us from the greater need for appropriate process management methods."[1]

Plan of Action

➤ Form a team to perform a tool inventory and to select new tools.

➤ Identify your tool requirements and prioritize or rank your needs.

➤ Determine how you will judge or score the tools to be evaluated.

➤ Perform the tool search.

➤ Contact tool vendors for further information.

➤ Evaluate the finalists based on the evaluation criteria in step 7.

➤ Select the tool.

➤ Develop the tool implementation plan, which includes integrating the tool and the testing process.

➤ Train the staff in the new testing process and how to use the test tool to support the process.

➤ Continue to improve the test process.

➤ Continue training as new people are hired and as refresher training is needed.

1. Watts Humphrey, "Software and the Factory Paradigm," *Software Engineering Productivity Handbook*, ed, Jessica Keyes, (New York: McGraw-Hill, 1992) p. 32.

84   *Capture End User Sessions*

Platinum Technology, Inc.

TransCentury Enterprise Tester is an example of capture/replay/scripting products. It provides a mechanism for invoking the online system with the RECORD and/or TRACE feature already automatically activated. That allows the capture of end user sessions without the need to train a user in the use of TSO/ISPF.

[Editor: Typically, such products provide a table to specify activation by time, region, user, transaction, or terminal.]

The captured script can be used for unit, concurrency, automation, and stress testing of online applications. The RECORD facility can be paused at any point during testing, allowing users to interact with the online system before resuming. This feature allows users to select only those pieces of an application needed for testing purposes.

```
SET&count
ALLOCATE edifile
      DATASET 'edi.test.pds'
      MEMBER 'edidate'
      SHR
OPEN edifile INPUT
      ENDFILE end-of-file
LINK    cicslogn
TYPE    <1,1>          'cust add'
                       ENTER
read-nex-record
      READ    edifile      INTO&record
      SET     &count       UP1
      SET     &customer    TO&record(,1,20)
      SET     &bill-type   TO&record(,21,6)
      TYPE    <4, 10>      &customer
              <6. 10>      &bill-type
                           ENTER
      GOTO    read-next-record
end-of-file
      CLOSE edifile
      LINK    cicslogf
      LOG 'Total Records Added='&count
      END
```

Figure 84.1   A simple TransCentury Enterprise Tester script can load an entire database through existing application transactions.

Play

The PLAY facility executes recorded or user-written scripts allowing testing of applications without the need to rekey input. Stress testing the system can be accomplished by playing many scripts at the same time instead of having many people enter transactions. Scripts can be played to accomplish many types of online system testing or to enhance productivity by automating repetitive tasks.

Interactive Control of Stress Testing

Online system tests can be performed by concurrently playing an unlimited number of scripts on multiple interactive system virtual terminal ports. To an online system, concurrent sessions appear to be multiple end users entering transactions onto 3270 terminals.

When conducting a stress test interactively, users can set the initial speed of the test before starting and increase or decrease speed while the test is running. If an individual session encounters a problem, users can select the session and review the screens leading up to the problem to see what went wrong. Additional scripts can even be played while a test is in progress.

Trace

A TRACE facility monitors activity on a TransCentury Enterprise Tester session and captures session events in the form of screen images that reflect terminal input and online system responses. The captured screen images can be used as input to the ANALYZE facility for subsequent regression testing or strictly for documentation purposes.

Batch Testing

Batch testing is made easy with the script capabilities. Distributed scripts can submit batch jobs, text completion codes and compare printed output with previous output.

Figure 84.2 uses a LINK verb to run a sequence of existing scripts for testing—or, after Y2K, for automation.

Scripting

Figure 84.1 shows how a simple script can exercise a loop to load an entire database through existing application transactions.

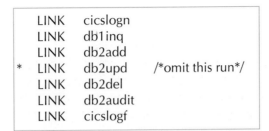

```
      LINK    cicslogn
      LINK    db1inq
      LINK    db2add
  *   LINK    db2upd      /*omit this run*/
      LINK    db2del
      LINK    db2audit
      LINK    cicslogf
```

Figure 84.2   *This script uses the LINK verb to include scripts that perform various functions for testing or automation.*

Analyze

The ANALYZE facility is used to automate regression testing of online applications. A session analyzer rekeys terminal input and compares live system responses with previously captured responses, identifying any changes since the previous run. Using a masking feature, differences such as date and time can be ignored automatically.

85   *File-AID/MVS*

Compuware Corp.

Specifying Quick Selection Criteria

Because you specified selection criteria usage code Q (Quick), the next screen displayed is the Unformatted Selection Criteria screen as shown in Figure 85.1. You use this screen to specify what data condition(s) you are looking for in a record in order for the member containing that record to be included on your member list.

In this example, you are looking for a JCL statement containing the string PGM=FILEAID.

You use the CO (Contains) relational operator (RO) to specify a scan of each statement starting at Position 1. No length is specified because File-AID defaults the length of a scan to: "end of the record".

Steps:

1. On the first line type **1** in the Position column.
2. Type **CO** in the RO column.
3. Type **PGM=FILEAID** in the Data Value area.

```
File-Aid ------------- Unformatted Selection Criteria --- ROW 1 TO 16 OF 25
COMMAND ===> END                                          SCROLL ===> CSR

Use END command to continue, use CANCEL command to return to main screen.

      AND
Cmd /OR Position Length RO                    Data Value
--- --- -------- ------ -- -------------------------------------------------
___        1               CO PGM=FILEAID                                  _
___ AND  _____ _____   EQ _____
___ AND  _____ _____   EQ _____
___ AND  _____ _____   EQ _____
___ AND  _____ _____   EQ _____
___ AND  _____ _____   EQ _____
___ AND  _____ _____   EQ _____
___ AND  _____ _____   EQ _____
___ AND  _____ _____   EQ _____
___ AND  _____ _____   EQ _____
___ AND  _____ _____   EQ _____
___ AND  _____ _____   EQ _____
___ AND  _____ _____   EQ _____
___ AND  _____ _____   EQ _____
___ AND  _____ _____   EQ _____
___ AND  _____ _____   EQ _____
```

Figure 85.1   Search/Update Utility—Unformatted filed selection criteria screen

4. Use the END command or PF key (default PF3) to proceed with PDS scanning and member list generation.

Using the CHANGE Command Prompt Screen

The CHANGE command prompt screen in the PDS Find/Change utility is similar to the File-AID Edit CHANGE command screen. Basically, you specify the "From string" and the "To string", set any other optional parameters you want and press <Enter>.

Usually you use the CO (Contains) relational operator and leave the "Start column" and "End column" fields blank to search from the beginning to the end of each record.

Steps:

1. Type **????????.FA.VRRMM.LOAD** in the "From string"
2. Type **SYS9.FA.V8R0M0.LOAD** in the "To string"
3. Type **CO** in the "Relational operator" field
4. Type **Y** in the "Confirm changes" field
5. Type **N** in the "Condense member list" field

```
File-AID -------------------- PDS Change Command -------------------------
COMMAND ===>

 From string             ===> ????????.FA.VVRRMM.LOAD
 To strint               ===> SYS9.FA.V8R0M0.LOAD

 Stard column            ===>        End column ===>

 Relational operator   ===> CO     (CO, EQ, NE, LT, LE, GE, GT)

 Confrim changes       ===> Y      (Y = Yes; N = No)
 Condense member list ===> N      (Y = Yes; N = No)
 PDS statistics        ===> Y      (Y = Yes; N = No; A = Add)

 Maximum changes       ===> ALL    (ALL or number of changes)

You may bypass this screen by entering the CHANGE command with operands:

C(HANGE) string-1 string-2 ((NO)CONFirm) ((NO)CONDense) (col-1 (col-2)) Max(n)

EXAMPLES:   c abc xyz        change abc (upper or lowr case) to XYZ
            c c'Abc' c'xyz;  change Abc (exactly as entered) to xyz
            c a, b, c xyz    change a or b or c (upper or lower case) to XYZ
            c "a,b,c" xyz    change a, b, c (upper or lower coae) to XYZ
```

Figure 85.2   Search/Update Utility—Specify CHANGE parameters

6. Type **Y** in the "PDS Statistics" field
7. Type **ALL** in the "Maximum changes" field
8. Press <Enter>.

86   *Tool Categories*

IBM

Reprinted by permission from GC28-1251 *The Year 2000 and 2-Digit Dates: A Guide for Planning and Implementation* copyright © 1995, 1996 by International Business Machines Corporation

With the critical time constraint of the Year 2000 challenge there is an immediate need for Year-2000-ready applications. In addition, there is a demand for Year2000-ready applications of high quality at a reasonable cost. It would not be possible to achieve this without the use of powerful and productive tools. There are a variety of tools available from Solution Developers that can help you confront the Year 2000 challenge.

To be effective and efficient in providing the ability to rapidly change programs and data to properly handle the year 2000, the tools must have certain characteristics. Some important tool characteristics and tool types that are necessary to make these changes are summarized in this chapter.

Tool Characteristics

The tools should provide necessary features such as:

- interactive environment
- batch processing capability
- graphic user interface
- ease of use
- rapid prototyping
- speedy and easy editing/updating
- stepwise refinement
- backward recovery

In addition, consider both the software **development** and **deployment/target** environment of the tools such as:

- Platform
  - Host only
  - Workstation only
  - PC only
  - Client/Server-based
  - Cooperative processing with host
  - LAN based
- Prerequisite hardware (both minimum required and recommended for PC specification, if necessary) such as:
  - memory/storage required
  - DASD needed for tool installation
  - DASD needed for tool usage
- Prerequisite software that is required and supported such as:
  - Host operating system(s)—for example: OS/390, MVS, VM/ESA, VSE/ESA, OS/400, Windows NT, OpenVMS, AIX
  - PC/Workstation operating system(s)—for example: DOS, Windows, OS/2, Unix, MacOS
  - Network operating system(s)—for example: Netware, Banyan, Windows NT

- Communication protocols—for example: TCP/IP, SNA, IPX, NetBios
- Languages supported or generated such as: COBOL, C, C++, PL/I, FORTRAN, RPG, PASCAL, Smalltalk, Assembler
- Client/server models supported such as:
  - Transactional—for example: CICS, Encina, Tuxedo, Remote Procedure Call (RPC)
  - Conversational—for example: APPC/CPI-C, NetBios, IPX, TCP/IP, SNA
  - Database server—for example: DB2 family, Sybase, Oracle, EDA/SQL, SQL Server

Once you run the appropriate tools against your operating system to reformat Year 2000 exposures, be certain that the 'newly created' system maintains its ability to:

- Achieve good machine performance
- Process a reasonably large number of users
- Process reasonably large databases
- Process high-traffic volumes
- Provide networking access
- Provide recovery from failures
- Provide security
- Provide audibility or accounting
- Provide ease of maintenance.

That is, your system performs essentially as it did before running the tools.

Tool Categories

The following sections highlight some useful tool types for handling the Year2000 challenge. A brief description is provided for each of the types. Most of these tools are used in normal prototyping and application development. Tool types can be categorized as follows:

Impact Analysis

To analyze the impact to your programs, you can use tools to:

- *Analyze complexity*

  Determines the complexity of a software design or code using a metric such as 'fan-in/fan-out,' degree of nesting, or other characteristics. These tools provide complexity analysis to allow you to estimate the effort required to change the date/time-related items in your source code.

> *Analyze impact*

Analyzes the program modules and related data to determine what is impacted and related. These tools are very time-efficient but do not always guarantee the accuracy of their analysis because they tend to over-estimate what is affected. When an impact analysis tool indicates that some data is affected, it does not always mean that the data will need to be changed (such as to reformat the date-related data and programs for Year 2000 readiness).

> *Analyze metrics*

Collects, analyzes, and reports the results of metrics quantification and analysis activities. These tools can analyze and predict how much work, in quantification, will be needed to reformat the date related data and programs for the year 2000, based on a metrics or cost model. You must validate the accuracy of the metrics you intend to use; that is, its predictions against actual human performance in real-life situations.

> *Analyze database*

Investigates the structure and flow within a database to observe the characteristics of the database and determine if certain measurements/requirements can be realized; for example, analyze the year fields of the databases for any use and cross reference of 2-digit years.

Project Management

To help manage the project, you can use tools to:

> *Inventory software*

Determines all code, JCL, databases, and other programs that constitute your system to provide a complete list for impact analysis. The list can be further divided into lists of subsystems when partitioning and prioritization of the project is necessary.

> *Track changes*

Tracks and logs all requests for code and/or data changes. Requests are tracked through completion or resolution. Any inconsistent/missing changes of data or programs due to date format changes will then be minimized.

Program Level Analysis

To analyze programs and data, at a program level, you can use tools to:

➤ *Analyze data flow*

Shows the flow of data among modules in procedures or programs. Determines if a data-flow diagram is complete, consistent, and adheres to those rules established that govern flow. This provides both high- and low-level views of data flow within the system, and can be used to verify completeness of the program and data changes.

➤ *Diagram logic structure*

Diagrams how program modules call sub-modules, and what data and control information these program modules share. These tools display multiple program views.

➤ *Diagram data structure*

Diagrams the representation of appropriate parts of a data model as the structure is used by a database management systems structure and relational structures.

➤ *Diagram relationships*

Illustrates multiple relationships of a program module or data element at the same time. This is useful to understand how data is shared among the programs that have access to it.

➤ *Diagram decomposition*

Allows a high-level overview specification, for a design or data model, to be successfully decomposed into smaller entities for further observation and analysis. It facilitates the partitioning of a project that is too large to tackle all at once.

➤ *Slice programs*

Allows you to view all the code affecting a given variable or statement. Forward slicing starts with a name or statement, and indicates what that name or statement affects. Backward slicing starts with a name or statement, and indicates all the parts of the program that could affect it.

➤ *Analyze logic*

Inspects the use of control logic within a program, determines if it is proper, and mechanizes the specified design. It is useful for verification and validation of the correct manipulation of time when windowing techniques are used.

Code Editing and Restructuring

To help edit and restructure code for your programs, you can use tools to:

> ➤ *Power browse*

Allows you to scan and inspect code. Scanning can be switched between program (data) structure charts and code. These tools are more powerful than regular text editors. They can provide, for example, syntax checking, sophisticated capability to find data or information, or the ability to edit multiple programs. These types of tools can also include reverse engineering tools or maintenance workbench tools.

> ➤ *Find dates*

Locates date-oriented data, variables, declarations, comments, or other information in code for investigation of potential reformatting.

> ➤ *Comparison*

Compares two software programs, files or data sets to identify commonalities and/or differences. It is extremely useful for verification of program changes when date reformatting is done by simple field expansion.

> ➤ *Cross reference*

Lists where variables, procedures, or other items are located in the code. These tools speed up browsing and provide a limited form of impact analysis.

> ➤ *Expand fields*

Automatically expands 2-digit-year fields into 4-digit-year fields. It saves editing time tremendously and provides complete coverage of field expansion.

> ➤ *Analyze interfaces*

Determines if a range of variables in the programming interfaces is correct, as the variables are referenced across the reference boundaries. It can designate 4-digit-year format as a standard interface and enforce the standard in the programming interfaces.

> ➤ *Analyze standard/consistency*

Determines whether prescribed development standards have been followed. Identifies inconsistency in conventions used in requirements, designs, or programs. These tools can help you introduce standard or more uniform names to date-oriented fields or keywords, and improve the consistency and accuracy of data. These tools enforce consistent indentation and alignment.

> *Trace requirements*

Traces how the requirements are realized in the design and code.

> *Modularize code*

Generates modular code and top-down control flow. Reduces the scope of complex programs by creating separate modules. Identifies routines that are frequently referenced or changed, for example date/time services routines, and creates re-usable code libraries.

> *Standard date subroutine*

Creates reusable program modules that have correctly implemented date handling. These date subroutines can replace individually developed date subroutines to standardize the use of a date routine. These tools also reduce the chance of error and the cost of development, maintenance, and testing.

Code Generation

To generate code for your programs, you can use tools to:

> *Generate database code*

Generates database code directly from the data structure diagram.

> *Paint screen*

Generates code for the screens of a computer-user dialog or data entry when the screens need update for reformatting of date.

> *Generate dialog*

Generates dialogs that conform to specified standards, for example, 4-digit-year input/output standard in any dialog.

> *Generate reports*

Generates code for the structure and layout of a report, along with calculations of derived fields in the report.

> *Generate code*

Automate Testing

To automate testing for your programs, you can use tools to:

> *Simulate*

Represents certain features or functions of the behavior of a physical or abstract system. One example of such a tool is a clock simulator that can change your system clock, while being transparent to your programs. Tools such as these provide an easy way to quickly expose your programs to Year2000 scenarios.

> *Analyze tests*

Determines the test case coverage on a set of programs being tested (whether a segment of code had been tested by other testing).

> *Generate test data*

Generates test data directly from a specification and facilitates a sequence of testing steps.

> *Test data libraries*

Organizes test data for use. These libraries are most useful in regression tests.

> *Test drivers*

Automates testing by triggering test cases during testing. These tools often provide test input, execute the test cases, compare actual test output with expected results, and report test results.

87   *Software Testing Technologies*

Gregory T. Daich, Gordon Price, Bryce Ragland and Mark Daewood
United States Air Force

The STSC's Test Technologies Group has been researching software testing technologies including practices and tools. The tools include government-owned tools as well as commercial-off-the-shelf (COTS) tools. This report identifies a number of tools that support software testing in typical development and maintenance organizations of the government. The section on "Testing Terminology" defines important testing terms. Section "Software Testing: Current Practices" characterizes current practices in software testing. Section "Software Test Tool Classification" provides a test tool classification scheme.

Testing Terminology

Definitions of some commonly used testing terms will help introduce state-of-the-practice software testing technologies. To start with, Bill Hetzel's definition of testing is provided as follows:

> *"Testing is any activity aimed at evaluating an attribute or capability of a program or system and determining that it meets its required results."*

This definition advances the concept of testing as a process of executing a program or system with the intent of finding errors. Hetzel suggests that there are many ways to evaluate (or test) a system without executing it. For example, you can test a requirements specification or design document by building test cases based on those specifications or documents. This activity involves testers early on the project and helps correct requirements and design problems before they are coded when they are more expensive to fix. Another point that Hetzel makes is that our intuitive understanding of testing is built on the notion of "measuring" or "evaluating," not trying to find errors. He says, for example, that we don't test students to find out what they don't know, but rather to allow them to demonstrate an acceptable understanding and grasp of the subject matter.

Both views of testing (any evaluation activity and executing code to find errors) are important. In this document, testing refers to the act of detecting the presence of faults in code or supporting documentation, or demonstrating their absence by confirming that requirements are met, and is distinguished from debugging where faults are isolated and corrected. This definition of testing, and the following five paragraphs, define several important testing terms and were adapted from a paper entitled, "An Examination of Selected Commercial Software Testing Tools."

An *error* is a mistake made by a software developer. Its manifestation may be a textual problem in the code or documentation called a *fault* or *defect*. A failure occurs when an encountered fault prevents software from performing a required function within specified limits.

Four test execution stages are commonly recognized: *unit testing*, *integration testing*, *system testing*, and *acceptance testing*. In unit testing, each program module is tested in isolation, often by the developer. In integration testing, these modules are combined so that successively larger groups of integrated software and hardware modules can be tested. System testing examines an integrated hardware and software system to verify that the system meets its specified requirements. Acceptance testing is generally a select subset of system test cases that formally demonstrates key functionality for final approval and is usually performed after the system is installed at the user's site.

In *bottom-up* testing, the modules at the bottom of the invocation hierarchy are tested independently using *test drivers*, then modules at the next higher level that call these modules are integrated and tested, and so on. *Top-down* testing starts at the highest-level module, with stubs replacing the modules it invokes. These stubs are then replaced by the next lower-level modules, with new stubs being provided for the modules that these call, and so on.

Dynamic analysis approaches rely on executing a piece of software to determine if the software functions as expected. This can involve running the software in a special test environment with stubs, drivers, simulators, test data, and other special conditions or running the software in an actual operating environment with real data and real operating conditions. The effectiveness of any dynamic analysis technique is directly related to the test data used. Current tools attempt to detect faults rather than demonstrate the absence of faults. Additionally, most of these tools can only detect faults whose effects propagate to software outputs, unless the software has been specially instrumented to monitor internal data elements (*intrusive*) or special hardware monitors have been attached to the system (*nonintrusive*).

Static analysis refers to the evaluation of software without executing it using automated (tool assisted) and manual mechanisms such as desk-checking, inspections, reviews, and walkthroughs. Static analyzer tools can demonstrate the absence of certain types of defects such as variable typing errors. Static analysis alone cannot detect faults that depend on the underlying operating environment. Consequently, effective testing requires a combination of static and dynamic analysis approaches.

In support of dynamic analysis, different strategies or heuristics can be used to drive test data generation. Commercial automated support is currently available for both *functional* and *structural* strategies. Functional (*black box*) tests are derived from system-level, interface, and unit-level specifications. Structural (*white box*) tests require knowledge of the source code including program structure, variables, or both. With functional strategies, test data is derived from the program's requirements with no regard to program structure. Functional approaches are language-independent. In structural strategies, test data is derived from the program's structure.

Functional strategies can be applied at all testing levels. System tests can be defined at the requirements analysis phase to test overall software requirements. During the design phase, integration tests can be defined to test design requirements. During the coding phase, unit tests can be defined to test coding requirements.

Figure 87.1 illustrates the software development lifecycle with test development and execution activities. The left side of the figure identifies the specification, design, and coding activities for developing software. It also indicates when the test specification and test design activities can start. For example, the system/acceptance tests can be specified and designed as soon as software requirements are known. The integration tests can be specified and designed as soon as the software design structures are known. And the unit tests can be specified and designed as soon as the code units are prepared.

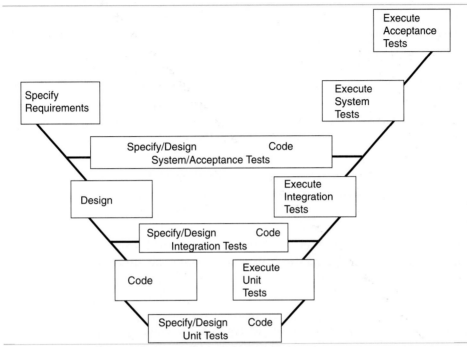

Figure 87.1   Software Development Lifecycle—Modified V Model

Building tests may be the most objective type of testing for requirements and design specifications before code is available to execute. This may also be some of the least expensive testing that we can do. The right side of the figure identifies when the evaluation activities occur that are involved with executing and testing the code at its various stages of evolution.

Requirements-based test case generators create functional test cases by *random, algorithmic* , or *heuristic* means that can be applied at all functional test levels. Superior quality test case generators will use all three means. In random or statistical test case generation, the tool chooses input structures and values to form a statistically random distribution. In algorithmic test case generation, the tool follows a set of rules or procedures. Several popular algorithms or methods employed by test case generators include *equivalence class partitioning, boundary value analysis* , and *cause-effect graphing*. When generating test cases by *heuristic* or *failure-directed* means, the tool uses information from the tester. Failures that the tester discovered in the past are entered into the tool. The tool uses that history of failures to generate test cases.

Equivalence class partitioning involves identifying a finite set of representative input values that invoke as many different input conditions as possible. Test cases that exercise boundary conditions usually have a higher payoff than other types of test cases. Building test cases to exercise specific functions supports demonstration of requirements. Regarding cause-effect graphing, causes relate to distinct input conditions, and effects relate to the resulting output conditions or system transformations. Test data is derived from a combinational logic network that represents the logical relationships between causes and effects.

The structural strategies at the unit testing level include *statement coverage, branch coverage*, and *path coverage* testing. Statement coverage only detects which statements have been executed and is not considered adequate for structural testing. Branch coverage testing requires each conditional branch statement and the code segment whose execution is controlled by this conditional to be executed at least once. A variation of branch coverage involves exercising all feasible true and false outcomes of each logical component of compounded conditional statements. Path coverage testing requires execution of every path including loops. Path testing is the more stringent strategy but can incur unacceptable computational costs. There are variations of path coverage testing that require basis paths be executed or that require at least one loop iteration be executed for all loops in addition to all conditionals. A *structural coverage* strategy at the integration level requires that each pair of module invocations be executed at least once.

Prototyping is becoming more widely accepted and implemented as an iterative development activity on many projects. The use of this technique is being accelerated by the availability of more automated tools that enable quicker and easier prototyping of system components. Prototyping evaluates (tests) requirements specifications at the conceptualization phase or the requirements analysis phase and can save a considerable amount of development time when properly managed.

Verification is defined by the MIL-STD-2167A as "the process of evaluating the products of a given software development activity to determine correctness and consistency with respect to the products and standards provided as input to that activity" [216788]. Verification is a testing activity that occurs at all lifecycle phases using the inputs of a phase to evaluate the products of that phase. *Validation* is defined by the MIL-STD-2167A as: "the process of evaluating software to determine compliance with specified requirements" [216788]. Validation ensures that software meets the requirements as specified at all requirements definition phases, i.e., phases that define system requirements, software requirements, design requirements, and coding requirements.

Software Testing: Current Practices

Many organizations approach software testing with the same practices and tools they used 10 or more years ago. This was evident in a survey conducted by Software Quality Engineering, Inc., of leading software organizations. While many recommended testing practices are more than 10 years old, there is more tool support available for testing software in today's market. Organizations should regularly review their testing practices and industry practices for potential opportunities for improvement.

Test development, execution, and analysis is still labor-intensive like most development activities. Testing can consumer over 50 percent of software development costs (note that testing costs should not include debugging and rework costs). In one particular case, NASA's Apollo program, 80 percent of the total software development effort was incurred by testing.

[Editor: 80 percent of NASA's Apollo software development effort was incurred by testing. Only 55 to 75 percent of your Y2K effort will be testing. But your enterprise's objective also is to avoid crash-and-burn.]

In general, schedule pressure limits the amount of testing that can be performed. Furthermore, defects frequently lead to failure of operational software. Barry Boehm tells us that 3 to 10 failures per thousand lines of code (KLOC) are typical for commercial software, and 1 to 3 failures per KLOC are typical for industrial software. With a rate of 0.01 failures per KLOC for its shuttle code, however, NASA has demonstrated that lower defect counts can be achieved. The cost of correcting defects increases as software development progresses for example, the cost of fixing a requirements fault during operation can be 60 to 100 times the cost of fixing that same fault during early development stages. Consequently, timely defect detection is important.

Improved practices and automated tools can reduce testing costs. In addition to eliminating some repetitive manual tasks, tools can promote effective dynamic analysis by guiding the selection of test data and monitoring test executions. Through capturing and reporting data gathered during the performance of testing activities, tools also support quantitative process measurement that is necessary for controlling the testing process. Benefits claimed by some of the tools discussed later include:

> A coverage analyzer tool that has saved a developer $15,000 or more per KLOC.

> A requirements-based test case generator that has given clients 8:1 reduction in test development effort, and one client has achieved a reduction from 1.3 to 0.072 failures per KLOC.

Of course, testing tools are not the only mechanism for improving software quality, reliability, and productivity. Software inspections, for example, have been reported to find 60 to 90 percent of software defects, while reducing total development costs by as much as 25 percent.

Software Test Tool Classification

1. *Configuration managers*   monitor and control the effects of changes throughout development and maintenance and preserve the integrity of released and developed versions. Change control of software and test documentation (including test plans, test requirements, test procedures, and test cases) must be carefully managed. Configuration managers can be some of your most powerful testing tools. Code version retrieval, defect tracking, change request management, and code change monitoring capabilities are typical features of configuration management systems. Configuration management technologies are analyzed and published in the *Configuration Management Technologies Report*   .

2. *Project managers* help managers plan and track the development and maintenance of systems. These tools document the estimates, schedules, resource requirements, and progress of all project activities. Test planning activities are often neglected, delayed, or impacted by delays in early lifecycle phases. Project managers can elevate the role of testing in a project with management's documented commitment. Project management technologies are analyzed in the *Project Management Technologies Report*.

Requirements and Design Test Support Tools

It is widely acknowledged that testing must be considered at both the requirements analysis and design phases. Software requirements and design information provide primary input to define test requirements and prepare the test plans. CASE tools that support the requirements analysis and design phases are often called Upper-CASE tools. The following paragraphs describe several requirements and design test support tools:

1. *Analyzers for software plans, requirements, and designs* evaluate the specifications for consistency, completeness, and conformance to established specification standards. These tools are reviewed in the *Requirements Analysis and Design Technologies Report*.

2. *System/Prototype simulators* merge analysis and design activities with testing. Requirements are refined while obtaining rapid feedback of analysis and design decisions. Requirements can be initially validated,

Test Resource Management Tools
    Configuration Managers
    Project Managers

Requirements and Design Test Support Tools
    Analyzers for Software Plans, Requirements, and Designs
    Systems/Prototype Simulators
    Requirements Tracers
    Requirements-Based Test Case Generators
    Test Planners

Implementation and Maintenance Test Support Tools
    Compilers

    Source Code Static Analyzers
        Auditors
        Complexity Measurers
        Cross Referencing Tools
        Size Measurers
        Structure Checkers
        Syntax and Semantics Analyzers

    Test Preparation Tools
        Data Extractors
        Requirements-Based Test Case Generators
        Test Data Generators
        Test Planners

    Test Execution Tools (Dynamic Analyzers)
        Assertion Analyzers
        Capture-Replay Tools
        Coverage/Frequency Analyzers
        Debuggers
        Emulators
        Network Analyzers
        Performance/Timing Analyzers
        Run-Time Error Checkers
        Simulators
        Status Displayer/Session Documenters
        Test Execution Managers
        Validation Suites

    Test Evaluators
        Comparators
        Data Reducers and Analyzers
        Defect/Change Trackers

Figure 87.2   **STSC Test Tool Classification Scheme**

altered, or canceled by demonstrating critical system functions much quicker than is possible under normal full-scale development.

Prototyping tools allow more efficient consideration of design alternatives, evaluation of user interfaces, and feasibility testing of complex algorithms. Prototyping must be carefully monitored and controlled to ensure that appropriate full-scale-development objectives are considered. Otherwise, prototyping can result in ad hoc development with no documentation. It is anticipated that prototype simulators will be reviewed, and a report will be written as STSC customer interest prescribes.

3. *Requirements tracers* can significantly reduce the work effort of tracing requirements to associated design information, source code, and test cases for large projects. The tools provide links between requirements and design, code, and test cases. What has normally been a lengthy, manual process can be significantly automated using these tools. Requirements tracers are reviewed in the *Requirements Analysis and Design Technologies Report*.

4. *Requirements-based test case generators* can help developers evaluate requirements and design information during the requirements analysis, design, and code phases. Early consideration of the types of test cases that a tool builds encourages developers to improve requirements and designs to pass those kinds of tests.

5. *Test planners* assist developers in planning and defining acceptance, system, integration, and unit-level tests. Test cases (including test inputs, expected results, and test procedures) should be defined and assigned early in the development of lifecycle to help prevent errors.

Implementation and Maintenance Test Support Tools

Some CASE tool vendors advertise full lifecycle support because they provide consistency and completeness checking of the requirements and design specifications, some of which offer no testing support at the implementation and maintenance phases. This has increased development time because unit, integration, and system-level testing needs were not properly considered at the requirements analysis and design phases. Note that some of these types of tools are built in-house and then discarded (or adapted for other projects) after use. The following paragraphs describe implementation and maintenance test support tools:

1. *Compilers* are not generally considered testing tools, even though testing source code is a major function of these tools. It is anticipated that compilers (particularly Ada compilers) will be reviewed, and a report will be written as STSC customer interest prescribes.

2. *Source code static analyzers* examine source code without executing it. Static analyzers extend the analysis performed by compilers. Various kinds of static analysis tools are available.

   a. *Auditors* analyze code to ensure conformance to established rules and standards. Typical rules and practices include adherence to structured design and coding constructs, use of portable language subsets, or use of a standard coding format.

   b. *Complexity measurers* compute metrics from the source code to determine various complexity attributes associated with the source code or designs written in a program design language (PLD). This is accomplished by evaluating program characteristics such as control flow, operands/operators, data, and system structure.

   c. *Cross referencing tools* provide referencing between various entities. Some of these tools provide a comprehensive on-line cross-referencing capability. Some of the types of data that cross referencing tools provide include cross indexes of statement label, data name, literal usage, and intersubroutine calls.

   d. *Size measures* count source lines of code (SLOC). SLOC counting tools typically provide counts for comments, executable lines, semicolons, declarations, total lines, etc. Some of these tools automatically collect code information and provide historical databases that track code growth, changes, and trends.

   e. *Structure checkers* identify some structure anomalies and portray the structure of the source code through graphics or text. Examples of typical charts that are produced are di-graphs (directed graphs), structure charts, data flow diagrams, flowcharts, and call trees. Note that the static data flow and static path flow analyzer tool types identified in and have been included with structure checkers to simplify the classification scheme in this report.

   f. *Syntax and semantics analyzers* have been traditionally called static analyzers. Compilers perform these functions but usually with limited scope. FORTRAN syntax and semantic analyzers are often needed to identify type conflicts in calling arguments of separately compiled subroutines. Ada compilers do not have this problem due to the characteristics of the Ada language. Other syntax and semantic analyzers (such as UNIX lint) identify unused variables.

3. *Test preparation tools* include tools that prepare test data or test case information that may require various levels of follow-on formatting. Also included with the test preparation tools are the test planners.

   a. *Data extractors* build test data from existing databases or test sets. Call the STSC for a current list of data extractors.

    b. *Requirements-based test case generators* help developers evaluate code requirements by building test cases from requirements following the rules of the tool's formal specification language.

    c. *Test data generators* build test inputs that are formatted (or can be readily formatted) in the required files. Some test data generators build statistically random distributed test data sets.

    d. *Test planners* assist developers in planning and defining tests.

4. *Test execution tools* dynamically analyze the software to be tested.

    a. *Assertion analyzers* instrument the code with logical expressions that specify conditions or relations among the program variables.

    b. *Capture-replay tools* automatically record test inputs (capture scripts) and replay those test inputs (playback scripts) in subsequent tests after code changes. These tools can dramatically improve tester productivity. Some of these tools can fully automate regression testing when combine with the capability to automatically compare previous results with current outputs. Many communications programs (e.g., PROCOMM PLUS) provide scripting capabilities that could support some testing activities such as capture of test sequences. (These tools were not included because testing was not an advertised function.)

    c. *Coverage/frequency analyzers* assess the coverage of test cases with respect to executed statements, branches, paths or modules. These tools generally require instrumentation of the code to be able to monitor coverage; that is, special code is added to monitor the execution paths.

    d. *Debuggers* often directly support the testing effort even though their prime intent is to locate errors resulting from testing. Some debuggers have coverage analysis capabilities that directly support testing. Debuggers can be used to perform various low-level testing functions and are the only test execution tools that some organizations have. Contact the STSC for a current list of debuggers.

    e. *Emulators* may be used in place of missing or unavailable system components. Emulators are generally hardware simulations of various system components that usually operate at the real-time speed of the components being emulated. Terminal emulation is a capability commonly found in communications tools, some of which may be used for testing software. Emulation is usually done for economic or safety reasons. Either the emulated components are not yet available or they are too expensive to waste by permitting some destructive functions to be tested.

    f. *Network analyzers* are a special class of testing tools that draw upon the technologies of several other types of tools. These tools have the capability to analyze the traffic on the network to identify problem areas and conditions. These analyzers often allow you to simulate the activities of multiple terminals.

g. *Performance/timing analyzers* monitor timing characteristics of software components or entire systems.

h. *Run-time error checkers* monitor programs for memory referencing, memory leaking (using memory outside program space), or memory allocation errors. These tools may also automatically monitor the use of stacks and queues.

i. *Simulators* are used in place of missing or unavailable system components. Simulators are generally software implementations of hardware components in which only the necessary characteristics are simulated in software. Example types of simulators include environmental, functional, and instruction simulators. Like emulation, simulation is also done for economic or safety reasons.

j. *Status displayers/session documenters* provide test status information and record selected information about a test run. Call the STSC for a current list of status displayers/session documenters.

k. *Test execution managers* are a general classification of test tools that automate various functions of setting up test runs, performing a variety of tests, and cleaning up after a test to reset the system. Test execution managers perform many of the same functions as capture-replay tools by automatically executing test cases using scripts and sets of input files. Test execution managers additionally maintain a test results history. This category includes tools that have been termed *test drivers*, *test harnesses*, and *test executives*.

l. *Validation suites* validate software against a well-defined standard such as the Ada coding standard ANSI/MIL-STD-1815A, 12 Jan 83, and are often used with compilers and operating systems.

5. *Test evaluators* include a variety of off-the-shelf and system specific tools that perform time-consuming, error-prone, and boring functions.

a. *Comparators* compare entities with each other after a software test and note the differences. Capture-replay tools often provide a dynamic comparison capability, which compares entities while the software is under test.

b. *Data reducers and analyzers* convert data to a form that can be more readily interpreted and can sometimes perform various statistical analyzes on the data. Key information can be extracted from execution logs to determine correctness or appropriateness of system behavior.

c. *Defect/Change Trackers* keep track of error information and generate error reports. Accounting for requirements and design errors should be considered in these tools. Defect/change trackers are often part of configuration management systems. Also, they can be integrated in Software Engineering Environments to automatically keep track of error information, saving engineers and managers considerable error reporting time. Refer to the *Software Engineering Environments Report* for more information about integrating defect tracking into an SEE.

88   *Relational Test Data*

Joseph Allegra
Princeton Softech, Inc.

Application testing is considered to be the single largest effort of the Year 2000 upgrade, consuming 50–60 percent of the total time. The cost of application outages due to insufficient testing is even more expensive.

Creating high quality test data has always been a difficult process. Creating high quality *relational* test data is particularly difficult, because flat files have been replaced by complex normalized relational data bases. Creating test data bases and verifying application results can prove to be so difficult that many applications are simply not tested. Many bugs are found and fixed at the most expensive point of the application life-cycle— in production.

With a good set of relational test tools, you can:

> *Build* relationally-intact test data bases with only a few minutes of effort.

> *Transform* production data as you copy it to a test data base. This facility is especially useful for generating test data that includes future dates and for Year 2000 changes that include data base modifications.

> *Inspect and edit* related data, adding special test cases to your test data base.

> *Verify* the accuracy of your applications by comparing "before" and "after" images of your test data base.

> *Refresh* your test data base to ensure that your iterative tests access stable test data.

> ➤ *Port* relational subsets of data from DB2/MVS to Oracle, Sybase, DB2 for OS2 and AIX, and XDB to enable testing in client/server environments.

The worst possible result of a company's effort to resolve all Year 2000 date problems would be to introduce production crippling problems during the upgrade.

With the unique capabilities of the Relational Tools to help you to build relational test data and verify test results, you can assure that your DB2 applications are fully tested.

89   *Selecting Your Automated Test Tools*

Dick Lefkon
Millennium Associates

The time has come to try your hand at automated test tool selection. Without looking to external resources, try a preliminary fill-in of Figure 90.1's automated tools planning table, based on your knowledge of

> ➤ your enterprise's known platforms
> ➤ the tools you already own
> ➤ a first-guess entry of missing tools based on firsthand experiences of a local business neighbor you trust.

If your "first cut" of this worksheet is nearly done and missing only one to three entries, you are invited to telephone the author at (212) 539-3072 for suggestions. He has been selecting/recommending/using such tools for decades—before and since Y2K became noticed—and will know (or locate) tool(s) most closely fitting your need and budget.

Piped Testing

You already see two residual Y2K benefits: Knowing your inventory (and cropping the deadwood), and knowing what will be affected if you modify a particular module. Y2K testing brings two more benefits; a comprehensive testbed of cases, and permanent automation of the testing process.

Automating the testing process is the one case where a large dollar outlay brings *immediate* payback of whatever cash you had to spend. Reducing critical path testing duration from 65 to 40 percent of project, may eventually mean the difference between Y2K failure and survival for the enterprise.

Platform: Category	MVS/ VSE	AS400	(O)VMS	AIX	SOLARIS	HP-US	WIN/ LAN
Capture & Playback							
Transaction Scripting							
Batch Comparison							
Test Case Generation							
Test/Case Management							
Date Simulation							
Time Machine/ Firewall							
Version Control/Merge							
Bridges YY<>YYYY							

Figure 89.1   **Year 2000 test tools worksheet** *(Copyright © 1997 Dick Lefkon)*

One other benefit is this: Suppose you are responsible for UAT testing of incompletely perfect module clumps arriving from the remediation/coding group. When you catch a flawed program, your schedule won't get shredded on time-consuming retesting when it comes back cured. Because of automated capture-replay tools, etc., re-running 997 good modules and three fixed ones just costs some electricity, not the patience and sleep of a manual testing staff.

UNIX utility users are already familiar with the concept of pushing one item at a time through a sequence of programs, rather than a batch at a time. They call the process Piping. And so, we'll use the phrase Piped Testing to indicate a thorough UAT treatment of just one or two modified modules arriving for validation.

Thus, not only does automation enable you to resurrect early testing scripts in later testing phases; it also lets you repeat the full test cycle with minimal human effort.

part

11 Manager: User Successes

The User Y2K Successes in this chapter are sequenced by completion date.

Dick Lefkon's "Two Y2K Factories" recounts the Risk Analysis and other steps required 13 years ago when bond trading reports at a large securities firm were seen exchanging profits for losses. He describes homespun scanner/parsers from the first effort and more sophisticated means of the second. Lefkon cautions that to cut a normally five-year effort by more than two thirds, you'll have to change and intensify management style, plus win top leadership's backing: There will always be opposition to your Y2K effort, although not necessarily for the reasons these business users had.

Chronologically second comes Christos Andritsoyiannis's account of BIAMAX's '95-6 Y2K rollover. The auto dealer's success was eased by coding rules, single language, standardized features, and much handwritten documentation. Assume "any untested code does not work," they had to decide, and urge you!

After writing up checklists on 4000 programs and 2500 files, BIAMAX reduced 92 percent disk usage to 56 percent by scrubbing and flushing the libraries. During a four month freeze they duplicated the environment, rewrote date routines and modified business functions one by one. After reworking whole-firm conversion so it would fit into one weekend, they took the plunge late in May of '96. The pivot year 1995 is used as necessary in EDI, but internally all is YYYY.

University of Florida in Gainesville targets completion for late 1998. Robin Marin writes that they're pursuing the steps of Awareness, Assessment (completed), Planning (current), Conversion/Testing (begun), and Implementation. UFG's approach is opposite BIAMAX's: "Because most systems are being implemented in a 'piecemeal' fashion, we hope to avoid any system-wide failures."

The Social Security Administration understandably was an early Y2K starter. SSA leads the Federal agencies with at least 30 percent completion entering '97. Its lay discussion involves databases, tools, awareness, missing code, online screens, scheduling, coordination, forms, and certification of purchased software. This SSA article can be a low-pain handout to show business users some of their Y2K problems and the fact it isn't your fault.

Brenda McKelvey's Agriculture Canada Project Plan Outline likewise is a good introduction to the 8-phase process, with extra emphasis on documentation along the way. At three pages plus diagram, try showing it to junior IS staff so they get a solid idea of what Y2K involves and the fact that yours isn't the only organization faced with it!

"How have different organizations structured their year 2000 projects?" asks Bill Wachel. "What are the advantages and disadvantages of each method?" His user groups article extols the monthly meeting where local Y2K-involved companies, may appear in panels and answer questions.

In "You Don't Have to Face It Alone," Stan Price gets into the mechanisms of setting up a user group. Arizona Millennium Group lets vendors present but excludes them as members in the interest of free discussion. One outcome: Company A's Y2K person visits Company B's decisionmakers meeting.

Now it's time for *your* user success. Dick Lefkon returns with some practical tips for Your First Three Steps.

Unpleasant P.S. Never shrink from upending the nay sayers, or others might begin to believe them. Lefkon's Chapter 91 contains a key Y2K example dating back to Quayle's first term: Not everyone's agenda is overt. Take the case of a certain PC software company that insists there's no Year 2000 problem. If your main control device is a game port not a keyboard, they're right. Otherwise, it's a matter of profits, not prophets: The day you push past their "unprejudiced superior insights" and start to rescue your organization, is the day some of your dollars move to your core systems, away from PC-Co.'s published annual earnings.

90   *The First Two Year 2000 Factories*

Dick Lefkon
Year 2000 Committee of AITP SIG-Mainframe

This chapter describes the implementation of two time-constrained, highly coordinated Y2K projects, utilizing a conveyor-belt model of shipping application clusters from team to team for phased refinement.

Project Management Office

In 1984 the author set up and ran the Project Management Office of a large investment company. Among other duties we managed quality assurance, budgets, and distribution of new work to application managers. We supported business users who daily traded securities worth about a tenth of a trillion dollars.

Several thousand modules were present, primarily in FORTRAN and COBOL, along with some DG Assembler. On arrival it was apparent that upper management could use some control over its own systems, which had been instituted eight years earlier by a tight-lipped consulting group. In response I'd set aside a workweek making a scanner to isolate and interrelate the code's copybooks, program calls/interfaces, and file/TP accesses. With modification, the scanners could later help Y2K.

Any major corporation will have some long-standing errors in its systems, and ours were no exception. One persistent error brought to my attention was a bond profit-loss calculation involving time.

Most bonds traded on major exchanges carry a time series of payouts, or coupons. In the early 1980s, brokerage firms got the bright idea to separate off and sell each of these coupons (and the body of the bond) as its own single-payment "Zero Coupon Bond."

To keep ahead of the competition, our firm had to find a quick means to fit these new Zero Coupon Bonds into an existing security type on the automated applications. The math calculations for regular bonds wouldn't do at all; but the mathematics of Treasury Bills was an exact match.

There was one qualitative difference that didn't show up in the equation: T-Bills typically mature in about a year, whereas ZCB's can last as long as your mortgage! After awhile, ZCB's shook hands with the Year 2000.

This company- and industry-wide problem spurred what was likely the first Y2K awareness paper at a refereed symposium, NIST/NSA's 14th National Computer Security Conference, where the author chaired a session on destructive software outcomes. His paper, "Nuclear Disaster and the Millennium Trojan Horse," begins on page 693 of the 1991 Proceedings and is excerpted here in Chapter 21.

One of the programming managers presented a bad printout which his business users seemed to like "as is." He couldn't schedule labor for the fix because our protocol (see Figure 90.1 and 106.7) required all system changes to be initiated by the bill-paying users, and his user wasn't initiating. We figured out why.

You'll remember that ZCB trades were being booked as T-Bills having a glandular condition. This was fine for short-lived bonds. But since T-Bill calculations hadn't been programmed to carry a four-digit year, the subtraction "2004—1984" equalled "04—84." The time factor of a 20-year bond was therefore calculated as "–80" instead of "20."

The reason why Dave's two bond traders refused to request the fix was that they were losing money on the trade, but the minus sign was generating reports that showed them instead as winners—and by four times as much! Each autumn this report became a basis for trader bonuses, providing incentive for the failed attempt to stall the fix.

Seven Code Change Methods

As noted in Chapter 7, there are seven main options in changing programs to make them Y2K conformant:
1. Prune the business—we couldn't and stay competitive.
2. Wait until things cure themselves—for sixteen years?
3. Purchase or New build—bettering functionality.
4. Expand YY Fields to YYYY—straightforward but lengthy.
5. Date encoding—often more work than option 4.
6. Date window(s).
7. Date-shift code or data.

Our company chose a combination of options 3 and 4. As Phase II we'd replace the main trading system with a more modular one so that new business products could be implemented directly and not through workarounds. For the near term, we would expand the year digits.

Development and testing already possessed a segregated pair of processing/TP midrange computers with separate diskpacks, and since all development was Y2K we had our "time machine."

We also were fortunate to have these benefits in place for a YYYY expansion: Fewer than fifteen million lines of code; an experienced programming staff familiar with the systems; existing in-house scanner/parser already described.

Control No: 98073
Originator: A. Welles
Description: Sort report 102 on region and volume. Page break for region: skip line between offices.

Testing contact name: _____   Phone: _____

List departments potentially involved: _____

Check only the boxes that apply:

☐ On-line: Please enter the product or account, etc., for each transaction type.

Transaction No.	Transaction Type	Prod/Acc/ Ticket #	Other Parameters	Expected Results
_____	_____	_____	_____	_____
_____	_____	_____	_____	_____
_____	_____	_____	_____	_____

☐ On-line day II: Next day or follow-up inputs if appropriate

Transaction No.	Transaction Type	Prod/Acc/ Ticket #	Other Parameters	Expected Results
_____	_____	_____	_____	_____
_____	_____	_____	_____	_____

☐ "Weekend" processing?   _____

☐ Reports: Recipient and phone:

_____   _____
_____   _____
_____   _____

☐ Special considerations:

_____

Signatures: User _____   ___/___/___   Technical:_____   ___/___/___

For systems use only: Initials:____ Target date:___/___/___ Mtg date:___/___

Dates of: DB____/___/___ On-line I____/___/___ On-line II___/___/___
Batch ___/___/___

Figure 90.1   User test plan

We froze maintenance/enhancements except for production emergencies, then doled system segments out to various teams. With an existing book of test cases (see Figure 90.1), each programmer was able to code and verify the highlighted changes for his/her set of programs.

File conversions were minimized by the dual application constraints of required external file layouts plus frequent existing use of floating point numbers and integers (COMP-2 and COMP-4). This also meant that our Common Calcs module had sufficient digits internally in most cases, albeit the DISPLAY and COMP-3 interfaces had to be changed.

In less than a quarter our sixteen consultant programmers had completed the code changes, and QA plus user trials had verified them for business validity and regression versus the tested baseline.

After the live parallel runs, cutover could be accomplished during one Thursday night, because the systems dealt with billions of dollars per account, not millions of accounts. Happily, the changes held and there was no need for Recovery Weekend.

Build or Buy

The business users knew the main trading system still had to be modularized to keep up with the flow of new products. Steps for the coming buy-or-build were identical to those for Choice 3 or Y2K code upgrades.

IS proposed a migration path to replacement software, but a key business user liked the report formats of an existing package, so we assigned resources and did a systematic look at it. As PMO head, I advised the regular meetings. A patch of quicksand was avoided, one which might tomorrow capture the unsuspecting IS Director bent on New-Buy to solve the Y2K problem. Before discussing New-Buy, think a moment about Upgrade.

When planning to achieve Y2K conformance by upgrading purchased packages to their current versions, enterprise systems heads sometimes forget that their prior customizations must be re-implemented and the entire new configuration re-tested in parallel with the production system. Thus the perceived "free ride" of a COTS version upgrade may prove as costly as the various code-modification alternatives.

Back in the 1980s, the weekly New-Buy analysis meetings began to make it clear that the package customization necessary to encompass our most profitable products, would grow and surpass the costs of installing the "package" itself: Like some self-described Silver-Bulletteers in Y2K today, these folks were really selling a project, not a product.

Finally one Wednesday I emptied the meeting room and sent the user representatives back to their departments by drawing a large cauldron on the markerboard. I explained the analogy to the children's story of Stone Soup, a myth in which three soldiers arrive and tell the townspeople they can produce a plentiful, magical stew from just three round stones. IS managers are cautioned against playing the part of the townspeople, who expended great resources to make the vendor's promise come true.

Now authorized to discard "Buy" and take the "Build" alternative, we set up a time-condensed factory approach.

We built "right," having no reason to truncate dates within the new systems. From a technical standpoint, the Common Edit module, which interpreted and enforced formats and applied reasonableness checks, was a coding precursor of today's windowing modules.

A Second Y2K Factory

The New Build Factory involved dividing the software into functional clusters. Each function group went through a business design phase equivalent to Y2K Code Analysis and Costing. As it left that process for Coding, a different function group rode a virtual conveyor belt into the Analysis unit (in 1980s, people; today, software).

Overall, the flow of function groups proceeded down and across the abbreviated diagram shown as Figure 90.2:

The optimal clusters of business functions were determined at the time by human designers. Today this function—and several other unobvious ones—can be automated for a price by using the offerings of several vendors. There is a tradeoff, though, in finding and learning the appropriate tool so that it can be used in time for that project phase.

Even now, more than a decade later, I speak on Y2K and have frequent consultancies to help companies select among today's Y2K tools, primary conversion strategies and testing approaches. Organizations can buy such information at a fair price; but project leadership must be bred.

Y2K Time Compression And Management

The two Y2K FACTORY efforts described in this article required a lot more "management" than is uniformly present in most smoothly-functioning IS departments. Using traditional programmer-initiative methods, the hundreds of work-years expended in the New Build should have taken five years: We did it in a third that time.

Time compression was not without cost. Programmers who had formerly functioned as "artisans" had to surrender some of their independence

Project Phase of Function Group	Calendar Time				
	Period A	*Period B*	*Period C*	*Period D*	*Period E*
Impact Analysis thru Planning	Group I	Group II	Group III	Group IV	Group V
Coding & Unit Testing		Group I	Group II	Group III	Group IV
Integration thru Assurance Testing			Group I	Group II	Group III
Parallel, Stress, Implementation				Group I	Group II
Documentation and Retraining					Group I

Figure 90.2   *Function groups flow*

and slip into the yoke. Those who wouldn't weren't discarded—their supervisors had to work a little harder than ordinarily.

Long dates for unit deliveries—usually pretty dependable based on the trusted staffer—nonetheless had to be shortened drastically so that large deliverables could be coordinated and trouble spots identified in a day or two, not after weeks, so that resources could address them. We used inchstones, not milestones.

Managers had to manage. The author kept PMO duties (including QA) but in the other hand took on three team managers responsible for transaction entry, inventory, and programs that performed what in manufacturing systems would be referred to as assembly building. If you think it was a picnic to get technicians who "understand it better than you" to think through and granularize their coding/testing steps onto "paper"— think again! Yet this had to be done. In ALL cases. [Editor: See also Chapter 23.

Fully 22 percent of project costs had to go into management and coordination, possibly more. This was not the biweekly happy-meeting where subordinates tell success stories. It was grueling milestone-by-milestone coordination via telephone, visit, and common report repository. There were long daily meetings for general progress, task exchange, exception follow-up, method/methodology update, staff allocation, etcetera. The half-inch-thick task list was republished at least weekly, with each work unit showing days-cost, original dates, slip dates, test dates, remarks, and—ALWAYS—the pride-or-shame initials of the smallest player.

Face it, this does not sound like your old 1996 department. It WILL BE your department in 1998–1999. And if you choose to outsource some or all of your Y2K to somebody else's organization, you will need some continuing way to verify that the lucky sitemeister has both the experience and the willingness to run things on a factory basis—not professional-initiative basis—and also has the track record of getting numerous under-managers to do so as well.

In order for a Y2K Factory to succeed, it needs enunciated support from the top. Treasurer, Chief User, IS Director—or anyone else your Y2K team leaders routinely encounter at least once per month—must be primed to describe the necessity and ultimate benefits of your factory lockstep to these significant managers and their respective reports; who in turn dependably retransmit that message to their own constituencies.

Maintaining Factory Focus

Authority is one of those things that flow downhill. Your Y2K effort has no recent precedent, diverts other people's imagined resources, and is a big nuisance in other ways, too. Without recurring public boosts by those at the helm, success becomes more vulnerable. Even with it, remain prepared to handle stumbling blocks contributed by colleagues. Turf envy won't disappear, nor will cantankerous business users, nor even some people's belief that they'll be promoted if all others fail—even Y2K!

Pay attention to individuality and morale, and occasionally rearrange the chairs to forestall burnout. But avoid being swayed by nostalgia for times when you managed less and your individual IS professionals took most of the planning initiative.

One thing is certain: You *will* see relaxed times again—beginning either at your job-well-done parties in 1999, or when your company folds.

91   *The Y2K Project at BIAMAX S.A.*

Christos Andritsoyiannis
BIAMAX, S. A.

Introduction

BIAMAX S.A is a national dealer of passenger cars, trucks and special vehicles in Greece. Its main businesses of vehicle importation and distribution, spare parts management and distribution and service-warranty management as well as its human resource, financial and accounting management require the processing and storage of a large number of date information.

The first applications were first built in the early 80s, on an IBM midrange system that is still being used today. All software since then has been produced in-house. The early applications, some of which survive today, suffered from bad design, lack of documentation and inadequate testing. These early mistakes and the involvement of people with organizational skills in the MIS team resulted in the formulation of a software engineering methodology that is being used since for the development of all software. This methodology has been critical in the success of the Y2k project.

One central point to the above methodology is the detailed documentation of each program. The documentation is produced at the design stage and updated during the life of the program. The above documentation describes the fields/files used and updated, the screens, the validations, the program logic and anything else relevant to the program. It is very close to the programming language but in a way independent of it. Although the above documentation is handwritten and not produced and maintained by any automated software as a CASE tool it has proved simple and very successful in quickly identifying software problems and impact points.

Another point in our methodology calls for keeping the features used in our programs standardized. Also all applications have been written in the same programming language (RPG III) and there has been an effort to use certain standards during coding. These last two facts vastly simplified the work of the programmers and allowed them to adopt a methodology of working with all programs in a standard way that speeded their work considerably.

The Y2k problem was first identified in 1989, during the development of a major application (module). Because of the high level of integration among applications it was decided that design and implementation would become too complicated in order for the new module to use 4-digit year fields and the rest of the modules to use 2-digit year fields. Only files used for storing statistical data were built with 4-digit year fields.

It was decided to go ahead and build the critical applications that were needed by the company at that time and leave the Y2k project for a later date. Finally in 1995, during the redesign of our legacy payroll application into a human-resource management module it was decided that it was the time to go ahead with the Y2k project.

Along with fixing the Y2k problem we decided to fix another problem, similar in scope, that we had identified in earlier years. We have always built our applications to be able to handle multiple companies on the same computer system which is a feature not yet used and never really tested. During the study of the Y2k problem we discovered that the multiple company feature did not work properly in a large number of programs. This only came to prove that it is a safe bet to assume that any untested code does not work. Fixing this "bug" would be a second Y2k project so we planned to fix it now along with the date problem.

Personnel Involved

The people involved in the project comprise the entire MIS department of the company:

1. Two consultants: They are responsible for designing and applying the software engineering methodology used and have designed, managed and tested all the programs built with the above methodology.
2. Three programmers: One of the programmers has been with the company since the early 90's and is the most experienced. The other two programmers were hired one year ago with very little experience and were trained in-house.
3. Two general support personnel: They were partly involved in the project while attending to their usual everyday duties.

First Stage—Preparation

During the summer of 1995 one of the consultants spent 2 Months planning the project. The documentation of the database and all programs was gathered and studied. The work started with the database and all date fields where identified and recorded by database file. These notes would be used later to guide the programmers in changing the database. Then all programs where studied, module by module, for impact points. For each program needing changes notes where written outlining the impact points and the way to fix them. Handwritten lists where produced indicating what programs needed changes. These lists would be used as one of the checklists used later in the project. They also gave us a first glimpse of the size of the task that lay ahead. It consisted of 830 database files (171 physical and 659 logical files) and five modules consisting of 3,773 programs (1,201 RPG programs, 1,276 display files and 381 CL programs). It was a huge task and it was clear from the beginning that it would be the quality of the project management that would be the critical factor in the outcome of the project.

Second Stage—Inventorying—System Cleaning

The second stage of the project involved inventorying and cleaning of our computer system of old and unused software so as to start our main Y2k project with a clean, tidy system. This was necessary so as to have better control and make sure we would not leave out anything important later in the project. Like many other companies around the world we were faced with the unpleasant surprise of finding out that our system was not as tidy as we thought it was. Our software libraries where badly organized and a large number of forgotten files (old versions of source, object and data files) just lay there tying up a lot of disk space. At that point our disk usage had reached 92 percent and we where considering buying more disk space. Now, after the project has been completed, the disk usage has fallen to 56 percent (!) even though we are now using four digits, instead of two, for the storage of the year throughout our database.

We also found out that a few programs where not fully documented (usually old programs) and had to take time to document them.

The process of cleaning up our system took three months during which one programmer and one consultant worked on the task exclusively. Apart from cleaning our system we introduced new guidelines so as to prevent such a situation to emerge again in the future. So the cleaning part of the project was a prerequisite for starting the main Y2K project but the results will also have a positive impact in building and maintaining future applications.

During the cleanup stage we produced lists of all the remaining software in our system. Using these lists we would later check the progress of the main Y2K project (assignment of programs, compilation, testing). These lists also gave us an even better estimation of the project size. The database accounted of 350,000 LOC and the programs accounted for 1,350,000 LOC, totaling 1,700,000 LOC.

Main Project

We decided that we would build and test the new software in a parallel system of software libraries on the same computer. When all data files and programs where ready we would replace our existing software with the new software. Then we would restore the company data in the new database files and the whole system would be ready to work. The problem was that restoring the company data in the new database files would have to be done by special programs that would also translate the 2-digit year to a 4-digit year (by adding "19" or "20" in the first two digits). Our first estimates told us that these translation-restoring programs would have to run for five days nonstop in order to move the three Gbytes of company data into the new database file. Because of the high integration among our modules it was crucial that the whole roll out would be made in one stroke. Initially it looked impossible to fit the whole task in one weekend but during the end of the project we finally found a software solution that speeded our system enough to complete the data transfer in 48 hours.

We also decided to freeze all other development work. So we "solved" the parallel change management problem by trying to avoid it as much as possible. We decided to commit the whole MIS team in the project in order to minimize the total risk. Before starting we made an effort to complete all the changes that were requested at the time but after that our sole consideration became the Y2K project. On this we had to get the full commitment of the management first. Without it we could have been pressured to interrupt our work for something that the management might consider more urgent and this would be disastrous for our project. Nevertheless a few bugs that needed immediate fix did surface and we did have to do a little parallel change management.

We tracked the programs involved closely and did extra testing on the features fixed so as to insure that the Y2K compliant releases of our programs included all the changes. I believe that parallel change management cannot be avoided completely during projects that drag for months.

Having built the parallel system of software libraries we then transferred all the source code from the old software libraries to the new ones and where ready to start. First we fixed our reference files (database field directories used in IBM midrange systems) and then worked on the database files themselves. We compiled them with the new date fields and also took the chance to standardize any nonstandard source code. The above changes where checked by both the programmers and the consultants through printouts produced by the system. This was the easy part. Next we worked on the CL code (Control Language of the IBM operating system). We use CL code mainly for building our application menus. This was also fairly easy since our menus rarely contain date fields. We took the chance to check them for other problems identified in earlier years (such as the proper use of commitment control commands during the call of programs). After finishing with the CL programs we where ready to move into the RPG programs.

We started by fixing all the routines, and rewrote all the date routines. Then we started with the programs themselves. We worked by module (vehicles, spare parts, service-warranties, e.t.a.), completing one module before starting another one. The first few programs that we attempted to fix gave as a clue as to the kind of work that was needed. The programmers made a list of standard things to watch for and fix.

Using this list as a checklist, the program documentation and the notes written for each program during the summer of 1995 the programmers worked their way through each program they where assigned.

Testing

Normally when we build or change a program the programmer has to test the program first. Then one of the consultants has to do a second complete test on the program before it is released. This two tier testing method has proved to be very reliable because it is made by two people that have a different set of mind. However the situation now was different. The programmers had to make few changes in a large number of programs rather than build a whole new program. The time needed to fix each program was too little to allow for the programmer to comprehend each program in the context of the application. As a result it would take the programmer too much time to build the correct test data for testing the program. On the other hand the consultants who have designed all the programs have a much better understanding of each program and where able to test the programs almost as fast as the programmers got them ready. It was decided that testing would not be conducted by the programmers at all. All programs would be tested once by the consultants. A key to quick testing was the sequence by which the programs where tested. First we worked by module and secondly we prepared the programs in the sequence by which information is produced in the company. For example in the vehicle module we first prepared and tested the programs that create the vehicle orders. By running and testing these programs we created a number of orders in our database that would be used as test data for the next bunch of programs that process orders into arrivals. By running and testing the programs that create the arrivals we created test data for the next programs to be tested and so on. By that way we avoided to manually enter test data for every program and improved both the reliability and time of testing.

The fact that the programmers did not test the programs resulted in more bugs being found during testing and programs being sent back more often than usual. It also resulted in the three programmers producing more programs than the two consultants could test. As a result the programmers worked 8-10 hour days while the consultants worked 14 to even 18 hour days in order to complete testing in time and attend to the general organizational tasks of the project.

The part of fixing and testing the software took 4 months. During the last weekend of May 1996 the software was ready and the personnel involved in the project worked around the clock to replace the old software with the new and convert-restore the company data into the new database files. It was a well-prepared task that took a lot of discipline but updated the whole system in one stroke rather than piece by piece that would be much more complicated and prone to problems.

Aftermath

During the next two weeks of operation we watched for any bugs that would be missed during testing. The whole company was notified to look for any irregularities and report them. A few bugs did surface in the first few days and where fixed.

We changed all the date fields to a 8-digit format in all our display and print files as well as in our database files. Of course there were cases (certain subfiles) where there was not enough room to accommodate a 4-digit year at which cases we used the 2-digit year format. But all input dates are now 8-digit. This approach looked simpler with regard to programming and testing. From the point of view of the users it took them a maximum of two days to get used to inputting the 4-digit year. In all date input fields we use a common validation that does not allow the input of a date before year 1900. Of course most of the people did show some dissatisfaction at the beginning but it did not last long. On the contrary I now believe that just looking at the 8-digit dates has provided enough proof to all non-technical people (from secretaries to upper management) that our Y2K project has been successfully completed. I found no other proof as convincing as this. Maybe because one believes what one sees with his own eyes.

We also have external interfaces with supplier factories abroad. We import their EDI files in our midrange and special programs update our database files. All our EDI partners use the 2-digit year format so we use a certain routine to translate it into a 4-digit format by using the threshold of 85 to distinguish between the centuries. This threshold will not cause any problems for the kind of data we exchange. But this is not the real problem. What if one of our EDI partner does not become Y2K compliant.

Then there is no way that we can predict how his systems will react. The dates in his EDI files could be erroneous and our systems will have accepted a large number of wrong dates before anyone notices. And even if we notice in time we will have to interrupt EDI communications until the problem is solved. We can not afford that to happen. Therefore we are now in the process of getting in touch with our EDI partners on the Y2K compliance issue.

This project has covered 171 physical files, 659 logical (index) files, 1,201 RPG programs, 1,276 display files and 381 CL programs, accounting for 1,700,000 LOC but it did not include certain legacy applications built in the early 80s that do not comply with the software engineering methodology presently used. These legacy applications are the payroll, bills receivable and fixed assets and fortunately consist of a few programs each. From these the accounts receivable are being fixed now by the programmer that coded it in the first place. The other two applications are due for replacement before they start having any Y2K problems.

I have estimated the cost of our Y2K project by using the current Greek market prices asked for the programming and consulting work-hours consumed. In dollar terms it turns out to be $0.30/LOC. But since the per capita income of the US is 3.5 to 4 times that of Greece the same project in the US would cost $1.05 to $1.20/LOC. From this cost up to 30% accounted for testing of changes unrelated to dates. Only 20% of the total cost accounted for actual programming work. The largest cost item was testing time. Of course the above costs must be judged in the light of the method used to complete the project.

Conclusions

It seems that the level of organization in a information technology department is very critical in the success of a project entailing small changes in a huge number of programs and database files, such as the year 2000 project. In trying to make estimations of the resources needed for such a project (in $/LOC or people terms) the organizational foundation is the prime factor.

92 *University of Florida*

Robin Marrin
Information Systems, University of Florida

The Information Systems department at the University of Florida designs, develops and maintains computerized administrative business systems for various campus entities. Executive awareness of potential cross-century processing problems in these systems was first addressed last year. Since that time, year 2000 awareness has remained a management consideration for planning and budgeting.

A project leader was assigned in March 1996 to estimate impact, establish a viable project plan, and organize a team. During this initial period, six separate project phases were identified: Awareness, Assessment, Research & Planning, Conversion & Testing, Implementation, and

Monitoring. These phases, and our experiences with each through January 1997, are described below. Our overall target completion date for all phases has been set to December 31, 1998.

Awareness: To raise the awareness of executive management and certain user groups as to the risks and impact of the year 2000 on critical operations. This was accomplished via presentations to campus-wide computing groups, the distribution of a "white paper" to selected department directors, and the establishment of a "University of Florida Year2000 Information Center" on the Web. This Web page is an ongoing effort to share information related to the project status and strategies of various IT departments of campus (http://www.is.ufl.edu/bawb015h.htm).

Assessment: To make an initial determination of the potential exposure and scope. 13,000 possible source "objects" were identified in our source management libraries, consisting of 4.4 million lines of code. An additional two thousand permanent datasets were identified. A project tracking database was designed and loaded with information about the compliancy status and event triggering of each source object. System surveys were distributed to our internal system coordinators. These surveys helped us establish priorities and schedules. An estimate of resources was made, including personnel, software, hardware and storage capacity. A core team of research analysts was assigned and four research pilot projects were completed. Several impact analysis tools were evaluated and two were purchased: Intersolv's Maintenance Workbench (MWB) and Microfocus' Revolve.

Research & Planning: To establish date representation and testing standards and to further set sub-project priorities and conversion schedules . A pilot conversion project was completed successfully. This pilot demonstrated the need for additional testing tools. A separate CICS region was established and software to exchange the system date is currently under evaluation. To aid in source control management, we are migrating to Intersolv's PVCS version manager. MWB has proved to be our primary analysis tool; we have loaded a "global" view of all our source interrelationships and dependencies. For a more intimate, graphical view of specific systems, we are using Revolve. Each system is currently undergoing detailed analysis to determine the preferred conversion approach. In older, isolated systems, a sliding window approach is usually chosen. Otherwise, we are changing the data files. Where there is enough space on the record, we are duplicating the old date with an 8-byte (YYYYMMDD) compliant date. This allows both converted and original problems to access the same file. If there is insufficient space, we are adding a single-byte century indicator for each date (using '1' for the 1900s and '2' for the 2000s). As a last resort, we are expanding and reformatting the file.

Conversion & Testing: *To convert and test all identified systems. The first regular conversion project was completed successfully.* This project involved carrying both old and new format dates on the files; a record length expansion was not necessary. Average productivity statistics were computed from this project and have been used to set target completion dates for upcoming projects. Six other systems in our high-priority payroll area are currently in the research and conversion phases. To assist in these efforts, several team members have been added, bringing the year 2000 staff to six full-time members and two half-time members. It is anticipated that the team will eventually consist of twelve full-time members. Team members are currently sharing the following roles: research, construction of test data, conversion/unit test, construction of bridging or verification subroutines, system test, and quality assurance.

Implementation: *To implement all modified objects and files into the production environment.* This includes consideration of critical timing issues: some portions of a system may need to be implemented prior to others. We have been converting the files and update modules first and then allowing the system to run while we monitor the verification routines for date integrity. Only after several successful cycles are additional objects moved to production. Other considerations include notification of the system users and possible training, coordination with external users of the data files, and the establishment of contingency plans.

Monitoring: *To monitor, identify and correct any data corruption or system failure as a result of the year 2000 effort*   . This includes possible disaster procedures and recovery. We have installed date integrity verification procedures which will be left in place for several years as quality assurance. The users have been notified of the possible types of data corruption which could occur. In the event of catastrophic system failure or corruption, the users have been asked to develop short-term manual emergency procedures. Because most system conversions are being implemented in a series of small phases, we hope to avoid any system-wide failures.

In conclusion, although this is a large, complex project, through aggressive management and interdepartmental cooperation, we will achieve a fully compliant campus well before the clock strikes midnight on December 31, 1999.

93   *White Paper—SSA*

Social Security Administration

Background

The Year 2000 problem is easy enough to describe. Most computer systems represent dates in the format MMDDYY, where 12/31/95
represents December 31, 1995. The century is not represented in the date
and we simply assume that 12/31/95 refers to a date in the twentieth century. Most computer programs that perform arithmetic and logic
operations on these date fields use only the last two digits of the year
when they make their calculations. As long as all the dates in question
are in the same century this works fine. Problems arise however when
the century changes. Subtracting 12/31/95 from 12/31/05 to determine
someone's age for example, does not produce the correct answer of 10. It
actually produces a result of -90.

Magnitude of Problem

Although the problem is easy to describe it is very difficult to solve for a
number of reasons, and can be likened to looking for a needle in a hay-
stack. The visual image of looking through hay is not difficult to conjure
up but the painstaking execution of the solution is awesome. The sheer
size of the problem is the first of these. Dates are everywhere, which
means that all program code must be examined to determine if a change
is necessary. Most large corporations and government agencies have
thousands of programs containing millions of lines of code. The Social
Security Administration has approximately 25 million lines of code in
production at any given time. There is usually another 25 million under
development. A programmer will have to examine every one of those
lines and make a decision as to whether or not it has to be changed for
the Year 2000. There is no automated way to do this. A date field can be
called date, or it can be called ballgame.Many people in the data processing industry, when confronted with the Year 2000 issue, refuse to believe
the size or scope of the problem. Many of them argue that changing dates
to include a century should be a relatively easy process. This fails to take
into account the large number of changes that must be made and the
coordination and testing of those changes. There are also many data processing professionals who have indicated that they do not view this
problem as "theirs" because they will be retiring before 2000. Ownership
of the problem is critical to its solution.

Changes to Databases

The SSA formed a workgroup to address this issue in 1989. The group initially focused on the way dates were represented on major master files and databases. It was obvious that we needed a place to store the new dates before we changed the programs to create the new dates. A plan was established and we began to change dates to include a century indicator on these files. That phase of the Year 2000 effort will conclude in August of 1995.

Tool Procurement

As that work effort began to wind down we shifted our focus to the other areas that needed attention. We searched the marketplace to try to find an automated way to make the source code changes. We determined that Year 2000 tools fall into two major categories. The first category contains those products that change the system date for a particular program, allowing you to see how that program will react when confronted with a date after 12/31/99. The other major category contains the products that help identify date fields in code and trace the flow of dates through a system as they are moved from field to field. We decided that a tool from this second category would be most helpful to us and began the procurement process in August, 1994. The tool we selected was awarded in July, 1995. We are very fortunate to have all of our program code in a single repository, so we will be able to use the recently procured tool and the scan capabilities of the repository tool, ENDEVOR, to help us focus on those areas in the code that are most likely to contain date fields. None of these tools do away with the absolute necessity of manually looking at every line of code, but they should make that process quicker and easier.

Awareness

We conducted division level meetings throughout the systems organization in order to raise the awareness level. As part of this we ran pilots, where representative programs were selected, and all time used to modify them for date changes was logged and accounted for. From our actual experience, individual divisions could then extrapolate from the pilot code to what they would need to allocate and only then did the magnitude of the problem begin to surface. At a time of downsizing and streamlining, and trying to do more with less, came a project with "no perceived benefit" to our user community. For the hundreds of workyears we must expend there is no added functionality.The divisions are currently examining their software and establishing schedules and resource estimates for making the coding changes. Those people that were unaware of the problem or skeptical of the effort that will be required were gradually converted to a different viewpoint when they were presented with the long list of activities that must be undertaken to solve this problem. A key piece of our strategy was to create a "sense of urgency."

Missing Source Code

No data processing installation wants to admit to this but it is almost a certainty that no installation is free of it unless they have already made their Year 2000 changes. The problem is that modules continue to run in production, but cannot be modified because the source code used to create them has been lost. In a normal environment these modules can run for years if they don't need changing and don't stop working. But because of the Year 2000 issue they must be "disassembled" and examined to see if they contain code which operates on dates. There is no easy way to do this.The first step is to identify programs with missing source code. Even this effort is painstaking and time consuming but is well underway at SSA and we are happy to say has netted a very tiny inventory so far. We will then re-create these programs to determine if any changes are needed to handle century processing.

Online Screens

The representation of dates online was also an issue that had to be resolved. The online screens which our users see only contain two digit dates. The screens themselves were so full that to increase the representation to four digit dates would involve overflowing to a second screen and changing all the path logic behind them. As a result we decided to continue to show two digit years on the screens except for those dates such as date of birth where a century could not be determined through the application of an algorithm.

Scheduling

The most difficult aspect of this project is scheduling when the century changes will be made for each system. The SSA is planning to have completed its work by December, 1998. This will give us an entire year to run our millennium changes in a production environment, thus ensuring that current functionality is unaffected and that the Year 2000 changes also function as designed. In anticipation of this date each major system: Title 2, Title 16, Earnings and Enumeration must also develop schedules which allow them to completely code, test and validate their changes. And, of course, all other work must remain on schedule.

Timing

The passing of data from one program to another, one system to another, and from one agency to another is one of the factors which gives the Year 2000 such complexity. Timing considerations become very important because either the sending or receiving entity will need to convert the files from one format to another unless both are ready to make their Year 2000 changes at the same time. For example, every employer in the United States with 250 or more employees must report earnings data to the SSA in some form of magnetic media. It is unlikely that they will all be converted by the same time. What is more likely is that they will run their output through a filtering program to place it in a date format we are expecting. We have initiated contacts with all other government agencies with whom we share data.

Forms

We have also begun to look into the issue of forms. Many forms currently in use have a 19__ representation of date fields. These must be changed to handle Year 2000 dates. Since preprinted forms require such a long lead time we wanted to address this issue early on.

Vendor Software

All vendors who provide us with software, whether in the LAN or mainframe arena, have been contacted about the readiness of their software to handle the Year 2000. We have asked them if their code handles the century correctly now or in which release it will. At a Year 2000 seminar we were informed that certain vendors will probably be going out of business in 1998 or 1999 instead of upgrading their products because their customer base is too small to support such a costly process.

Conclusion

One final point to keep in mind is that this is probably the only project we will work on that has an end date that can't be changed. January 1, 2000 is looming on the horizon. It is now only 50 months away and that is not a long time in the world of data processing.

94   *Project Plan Outline*

Brenda McKelvey
Agriculture and Agri-Food Canada

Recommended steps for preparing an organization for Year 2000 are shown in Figure 94.1. The arrows stretching the length of the phases: Project Management, Communicate Awareness, Document, and Validate and Verify/Quality Assurance, indicate that these are ongoing tasks for the duration of the project. The arrows that loop back to previous phases, indicate the iterative nature of this project. New information coming into the project may change decisions already made and care must be taken to address the impact of this on project plans. Phases 4 to 7 are concluded on a system by system basis. Different systems will be in different phases depending on their event horizon and critical time line. Estimates will be revised to reflect real data as the project proceeds, keeping in mind that the final deadline cannot be changed.

Phase 1: Project Initiation

This phase involves researching the issues associated with Year 2000, developing a project plan and beginning an awareness campaign to prepare managers and support staff for the pervasiveness and magnitude of the problem. In a large organization, this phase can take 6-9 months. The Project Plan is produced as part of this phase, and a steering committee should be established with representation from the business lines.

Phase 2: Establish Baseline Inventory

Essential to the next phase of this project is the establishment of a comprehensive inventory of assets that will allow assessment of the extent of the problem. This first inventory collection is a manual process to identify systems. Surveys should be designed to provide information that can be supplied without extensive review of the systems, but will still allow initial high-level estimates to be prepared. In a mainframe world, the numbers of lines of code may be easily available. In a midrange environment, the number of programs will likely be more realistic. This inventory will facilitate credible high level estimates, and provide baseline information for planning strategies to deal with this problem in your organization.

This company-wide inventory will be one of the major benefits of a Year 2000 project, and plans should be made to ensure that it lives beyond the life of the project.

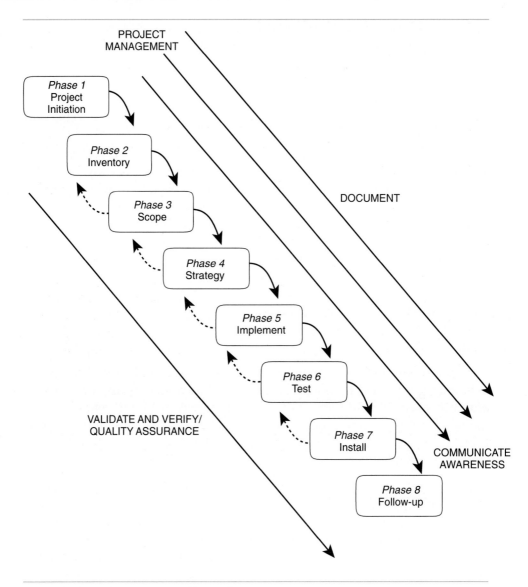

Figure 94.1   Year 2000 project phases

Phase 3: Scope

This phase will assess the size of the effort to make systems Year 2000 compliant. It will provide ballpark estimates showing the magnitude of the problem in dealing with Year 2000 and outline the risks and implications for the organization. It will also identify critical systems, event horizons and reconcile the time with the cost. Critical systems should serve as the drivers for setting scope and priority. When and if outside vendors are used, it will be important to establish how they are scoping and estimating, so that their techniques can be reconciled with those used in this phase.

Phase 4: Strategy

Once a clear picture of the Year 2000 problem has been established, you will need to review the options for each system and select the correct mix. This may mean:

- replacing some systems with off the shelf [Editor: "COTS"] software,
- redeveloping some systems,
- fixing existing systems, or
- shutting a system down.

If a system is to be fixed, a decision must be made on the type of fix. If a system is to be replaced, care must be taken to ensure the replacement system is Year 2000 compliant. Some tasks will be best performed by existing support staff and others by outside contractors. A project team of experts may be established to address changes. This phase will establish the mix of solutions that ensures Year 2000 compliancy is reached in the most efficient way possible.

Phase 5: Implementation

This phase puts in place the strategies developed, in the priority and on the time line set in the previous phase. It will involve changes to i) application programs, ii) system executable programs, iii) communication tools, iv) data files and databases, and will require v) ensuring vendor compliance, vi) reconciling import and export files with bridge programs, vii) hardware changes, viii) revisions to user interfaces for collecting and reporting on data, and ix) the coordination of all the changes—to name a few. It will be important to have standardized change control procedures in place. Those sections wishing to make changes not in the standard procedures for developing Year 2000 compliancy should submit their change and reasons for approval.

Phase 6: Test

Besides module testing to ensure that functionality has not changed once date logic has been modified, there will have to be systems integration testing, and date simulation testing—not only for the Year 2000, but for other critical dates that have been identified as potential problems (1999, 2001, 2002, 2003). Coordinating testing of systems as changes are implemented a piece at a time will be a major challenge. Some systems may also require regression testing to validate data. Test suites will have to be developed to test applications.

Phase 7: Install

Installation will also be a challenge. It will not be possible to implement all application corrections, and operating system and hardware fixes at the same time. What happens to production systems while new procedures are being installed? How long can systems be down for installation? How do we bridge between systems that are four digit year dates and systems that are still running with two digit years? The output of this phase will be operational systems that will continue to work through the new millennium date change.

Phase 8: Post Project Follow up

Follow up procedures will have to be put in place to cross check systems as "real date and time" arrive. Data should be checked on a regular basis to ensure expected output is being received. Any changes to the system before Year 2000 arrives must be retested. A functioning process to metre the project's success should be produced.

95   *Leveraging the Experience of Others*

Bill Wachel
The Greentree Group

Introduction

The year 2000 will impact many information technology applications and processing environments. This paper introduces the reader to potential impacts from the change in century, overviews the phases of a year 2000 project, and explains how user groups can help organizations avoid repeating lessons previously learned by others. It also addresses the role of user groups in gathering input on tool and service provider performance and in assembling information regarding the actions of others in an industry segment as the organizations prepare for impacts from the year 2000.

What Is the Problem?

The Millennium 2000 problem is simple but complex. Simple in that it can be solved by expanding the number of digits in the year field in computer programs and data from 2 to 4. Simple in that it is easy to understand. Today the year 1995 is expressed as 95 in computer programs, but when the year 2000 arrives that 95 could be interpreted as 1995 or 2095 making the two-digit year worthless. Complex in that virtually all mainframe legacy systems developed in the 1960s, 1970s and 1980s used a two-digit field for the year to save storage space. These two-digit dates exist on millions of data files used as input to millions of applications. Complex in that these two-digit dates affect data manipulation, primarily subtractions and comparisons that can occur in mainframe applications, client/server systems that pull down corrupted data from mainframes, third-party data feeds and electronic commerce transactions with other companies. The following generic examples of the Millennium 2000 problem are provided to help the reader comprehend the subtleties of the problem:

1. *Time span.* If you were born in 1942 and wanted to calculate your age in the year 2000, the computer application would subtract 42 from 00 and state that you were -42 years old instead of 58 years old. This may result in incorrect billing amounts for insurance companies, driving and professional licenses being issued to minors, etc.

2. *Sort problem.* You have data records and you want to sort them by date e.g. 1965, 1905, 1967, 2016. The computer application that only reads the last two digits would sort them incorrectly (05, 16, 65, 67). Many traditional master file and transaction file mergers will be in error from incorrect sorts. Data records may be deleted as being outside the parameters for the file merge (e.g. the application will believe the processing date has already passed).

3. *Effective date precedes the current date.* In 1999, an employee is granted a pay raise effective January 1, 2000. The computer application grants the pay raise immediately because the effective date precedes the current date.

Almost every organization, whether public or private, will have information technology applications and environments impacted by the forthcoming year 2000.

Year 2000 Project Structure

Corporations across America and around the world are forming project teams to identify and remediate impacts from the year 2000. Many vendors are involved, providing tools, methodologies, and labor to address impacts from the year 2000. Although each organization and vendor may name them differently, the typical year 2000 project consists of six major project phases (each vendor or organization may group the phases differently):

> *Inventory or Blueprint*—comprehends the identification of all current and planned information technology assets within the organization. Each application and processing environment must be inventoried, capturing information such as languages used, platforms executed on, business functions and organizations supported, criticality to the business, etc.

> *Assessment*—based on the high-level information assembled in the Inventory Phase, applications and processing environments are prioritized for impact assessment. Several tools are available within the marketplace to scan, parse, and analyze application code and provide metrics on number of date fields, number of potentially impacted date fields, complexity of the code, interfaces with other applications and data files, etc.

> *Detailed Planning*—armed with the impact analysis data from the assessment phase, upgrade units are identified. The driving factor is that one wants to minimize the number of bridges and interface points that must be created and coordinated by grouping together applications that share common data into one upgrade unit. Fewer interface points reduces the overall complexity of the remediation projects and allows for smoother implementations.

> *Remediation*—this phase comprehends the actual modifications of code and operating environments to remediate the year 2000 impacts. Remediation may take many different forms including modifying the existing application, rewriting the application, replacing the application with commercial-off-the- shelf software, installing new versions of an operating system or compiler, etc.

> *Testing*—While many changes can be tested individually during the remediation phase, overall system testing must occur across multiple upgrade units.

> *Implementation*—Most organizations only implement major application and processing environment changes on weekends. Many future weekends are already committed to planned changes and improvements. And yet, there are less than 160 weekends left before January 1, 2000. Each of the remediated upgrade units must be implemented into the production environment on a coordinated and scheduled basis.

Each organization structures their year 2000 project according to their individual business requirements, available resources, and culture. Because of the short time remaining before the year 2000, many corporations are conducting multiple year 2000 projects building from a common inventory and prioritized impact list at the corporate or divisional level.

With a common understanding of some of the potential impacts from the year 2000 and a common framework for what a year 2000 project looks like, one can address year 2000 user groups.

What Are Year 2000 User Groups?

Year 2000 user groups take many different forms and shapes. Several large national and international vendors are sponsoring user groups. In addition, several existing organizations such as the Data Processing Management Association (DPMA) and the Data Administration and Management Association (DAMA) are creating year 2000 user groups or dedicated special interest groups (SIGs) for the year 2000 issues.

A year 2000 user group is a collection of individuals willing to work together to share information about identifying, analyzing, and remediating potential impacts from the year 2000. Organizational structure may vary from formal and highly structured to informal with little structure. Different user groups may migrate towards different areas of concentration. Vendor sponsored groups often concentrate on the strengths and weaknesses of a vendor's product or service. Other groups concentrate on broader, non-vendor topics.

D-FW Prep 2000, is a year 2000 user group located in the Dallas-Fort Worth metropolitan area of Northeast Texas. This group has been meeting since May, 1996, and has had 60+ individuals representing 45+ different corporations attend various meetings. In example of some of the topics addressed by a year 2000 user group, D-FW Prep 2000, a D-FW DAMA special interest group, adopted the following mission statement:
"The mission of D-FW Prep 2000 is:

> To educate local organizations and individuals about the year 2000 crisis

> To provide a forum for organizations and individuals to share their experiences in identifying, assessing, and resolving the impact of the year 2000

> To provide information on different methods of identifying, assessing, and resolving the year 2000 impacts, including briefings and demonstrations of vendor supplied products and services

It is the intent of D-FW Prep 2000 to form a vendor-independent group, composed of individuals actively working to address the year 2000, that share and learn together."

Most year 2000 user groups meet at least monthly and provide a formal program with a speaker on a year 2000 related topic at each meeting. Speakers may be from a corporation currently progressing a year 2000 project or may be from a vendor providing tools or services to assist on year 2000 projects. Some of the most worthwhile user group programs are when the group provides a panel of local corporations with active year 2000 projects and allows the audience to ask questions to the panel members.

Avoiding the Negative: Learning from Others

Participating in a local year 2000 user group will enable the reader to obtain valuable information from others who are ahead of them in addressing the year 2000. Through formal programs and talking with fellow user group participants, one should be able to gather information on the following:

> How did others convince senior management, especially outside of the IS department, that the year 2000 is a real potential problem for the organization that should be addressed now?

> How have different organizations structured their year 2000 projects? What are the advantages and disadvantages of each method?

> Are other organizations having more success with one common inventory and assessment for the corporation or structuring the project at a lower level such as division or directorate?

> Where does one obtain qualified people to work on the year 2000 project? What types of individuals and professional skills are needed?

This information will allow the reader to begin to organize and structure the year 2000 project internally within their own organization while leveraging the experiences of many other corporations who have year 2000 projects underway and have had such for one to two years, allowing the other corporation time to learn from and adjust to errors in the organizational structure.

Information on Year 2000 Tools and Services

Once one has learned about the many alternative ways of communicating the year 2000 problem to management and initiating the initial project team, they can move towards gathering information year 2000 tool and service providers. Many individuals actively participate in year 2000 user groups primarily for this reason.

Many different types of year 2000 tools exist. There are tools for scanning application code looking for date variables on a key-word or pattern basis (e.g. all fields with "DT" in the name or all fields 6 characters in length). Other tools parse the code and use intelligent logic to detect actual usage of date fields thus identifying fields that may contain dates but are not named such (e.g. the programmer who named the data fields after the women he was dating at the time). Experience has shown that most members of a user group will share informally any information or experiences they may have regarding which vendors' software tools perform well and which do not. They also share first-hand experiences regarding which products are easy to use and which are more difficult. In addition, members will share how to make the use of successful tools even more successful.

Within the marketplace, year 2000 vendors are also providing methodologies for completing a year 2000 project and personnel to assist in leading and completing year 2000 projects. User groups also provide a mechanism for soliciting informal and non-biased feedback on how well different methodologies work and what level of service different staffing organizations provide.

Industry and Competitive Analysis

A seldom mentioned and yet important benefit of active participation in a year 2000 user group is the ability to collect information on the actions and preparedness of others within an industry segment related to the year 2000. Every organization, independent of the industry, is interested in what other organizations involved in that industry are doing, year 2000 related or otherwise.

Year 2000 user groups provide a forum for talking with other companies to see how they are approaching the year 2000 challenge. By effectively networking with corporations and vendors present, one can assemble a picture of where other organizations are in addressing the year 2000. Simple questions such as:

➤ Have you started a year 2000 project yet?

➤ How are you approaching the analysis phase?

➤ Do you really believe this year 2000 problem is real?

➤ What is "corporation A" doing about the problem?

will provide great insight into what others in an industry segment are doing about the year 2000.

Incidentally, do not forget to gather information about any corporations or organizations that one may be an investor in. As a shareholder, one should be very concerned about the corporation's plan for identifying and remediating any potential impacts from the year 2000. User groups provide a solid forum for gathering this information as well given many large corporations are not issuing a public statement regarding their readiness for the year 2000.

Next Step: Joining a Local User Group

There are over 20 local year 2000 user groups currently active across the United States. New groups are being formed every month. The best resources for identifying a local group to join are the user group list on the Year 2000 Information Page, located at www.year2000.com on the World-Wide Web, and the list of active user groups and those looking for a group sponsored by the Tick, Tick, Tick newsletter, a quarterly newsletter dedicated to year 2000 issues (www.henterprises.com/tick3).

Active participation in a year 2000 user group offers many benefits. Typically, active participation can be achieved through attending one to two meetings a month and paying dues of $75 -150 annually. This level of participation allows one to leverage the experiences of others to build a more effective response to the year 2000 challenge within their own organization. This, in turn, saves the organization time and money and enables them to be more competitive and to expend greater resources in the organizations "core" business such as retailing, transportation, banking, etc., rather than expending the resources to address the year 2000. And, achieving greater success in the "core" businesses results in greater individual and corporate success, raising the quality of life for all involved.

96   *You Don't Have to Face It Alone!*

Stan Price
Arizona Millennium Group

As an information systems professional working to solve the year 2000 problems for your company or government organization, you are faced with several challenges. The first is that your own management may not believe that a problem truly exists. Or maybe there's awareness of the problem but for reasons of perceived competitive disadvantages, the company will not publicly admit that a problem exists. Or perhaps you're evaluating vendors' solutions to the problem but it's difficult to independently verify their claims. Or you may have completed an assessment, but you're having difficulty convincing your management that the projected scope and cost are reasonable. What resources are available to provide help and assistance with these and other Year 2000 issues?

Users groups offer an excellent forum for the exchange of information and experiences. They provide sources of information on the availability and efficiency of solution tools and services. They provide the networking vehicle for the exchange of statistics and data for addressing and planning the solution. An organized group also can serve to focus attention on the issue and provide increased credibility among IS professionals, corporate management and the general public.

If there is a Year 2000 users group in your area, I encourage you to investigate membership and participation requirements. The support, exchange of information and experiences, and the chance to make a contribution to a significant effort can be rewarding, both for your company and you personally. If there is not already a Year 2000 users group your area, then you have a rare opportunity to really do something unique for yourself and your company. Go organize one!!!

The idea may at first be a little intimidating but a few ideas an help make it simpler and easier than you think. The Arizona Millennium Group was formed as a result of a conversation between a colleague and me in the parking lot after attending a Year 2000 vendor presentation. We were commenting on the fact that we seemed to learn as much or more from discussions among the attendees in the audience as we did from the formal vendor presentations. My colleague, who is actively engaged with an SAS users group, suggested that what we possibly needed to do was form a local Year 2000 users group. I "volunteered" to lead the effort. This raises the issue of the first essential ingredient for starting a users group. We've found that it takes someone willing to make the commitment to put in the time and work to get the group organized and then to keep pushing to keep it functioning. You are likely to find that many people are willing to attend and participate at a meeting once a month, but do not wish to get involved in the details of keeping minutes, serving on program committees, preparing flyers about the meetings, and so on. Someone has to be the catalyst get it going, then hopefully pull in enough attendees/members who are sincerely interested and will actively contribute to the effort.

Start-Up Activities

The first major effort is to contact other people who are interested in the Year 2000 issue. One place to start is to solicit mailing lists from your vendor representatives. Tell them you want a name and mailing address for

in any of their accounts who are information systems users or developers. If they are hesitant about providing that information, ask them to distribute flyers as they call on their clients. Solicit specific names of people who are likely to be interested in the subject. In your flyer, request that if that person is not the individual in the organization addressing the Year 2000 problem, then to please forward the information to the person who is likely to have that responsibility.

Another good method is to work through existing IS organizations such as SIM, AITP and local vendor specific user groups. Try sending notices of organizational meetings to your local newspapers. Most will at least post the notice in their "Activities" column. Don't miss your area's business newspapers. Most metropolitan areas have one or more of these types of publications.

And don't forget to post a notice on the Year 2000 list. You'll be surprised at how many people in your area are "lurking," waiting for someone to take the initiative to get a group started. Be that someone!

Organizational Structure

Keep it simple!!! We chose not to have a formal organizational charter. In fact, we wanted to keep the structure of the Arizona Millennium Group as simple as possible. We wanted to keep the focus on the Year 2000 issues and not on running an organization. Remember, this is one organization that will have a built-in "sunset" date. That is, it automatically has a date on which the need for it will cease to exist (well, it might be functional for a couple of years beyond the Year 2000!).

With that of the guiding principle, we established a set of rules as follows. (1) The only officers initially are the Chairman and Cochairman. Others will be added when the group determines the necessity. Since I had taken the initiative to organize the group, I was elected to be Chairman, and my cofounder, the cochairman. There are no dues, thereby eliminating the need for a treasurer.

Anyone except vendors of Year 2000 solutions can be a member of the group. We invite vendors to the meetings to present product overviews, but we want to keep the environment open to freely discuss people's experience with specific vendors and their products. Another good reason for this rule is that there is a segment of the media and general public that perceives the Year 2000 problems as a creation of software companies for their monetary gain. The elimination of vendors as members establishes our credibility as a group untainted by those allegations.

Our group is individual oriented rather than company oriented. Although all individuals have the tacit permission and support of their company, it is not the company who is a member. We do not restrict the number of representatives from any one company. Any one who is interested may participate. One of the reasons for focusing on the individual is that a number of people wanted to join the group to get help convincing their management that they had a problem at their company. Also, while their management allowed their participation, they would not pay dues to join as a company.

Our meeting locations are rotated among and hosted by the membership. The meeting host is responsible for compiling the notes (minutes) of the meeting. We do not require extensive or detailed minutes. We originally agreed that we would have bimonthly meetings, but the high level of interest quickly forced us to change to a monthly schedule. At each meeting we solicit topics of interest for the program and discussion for the next meeting. As previously mentioned, we have a vendor at each meeting to provide a product presentation. After their presentation, we ask them to excuse themselves for the remainder of the meeting. At this time, we have a waiting list of vendors who have requested to do presentations to the group.

Interaction with the Press

Although one of the goals of the group is to promote awareness through publicity, this must be accomplished very carefully. Many companies simply will not want any publicity about the fact that they may have a concern with the Year 2000 issue. However, most of the media are willing (reluctantly, perhaps) to work within this limitation if you can provide other organization statistics, such as numbers of companies and organizations participating. Suitably vague descriptions of the type industries involved, etc. also work. But most of all, you need to have an understanding with the members as to which of their companies are willing to face at least some publicity on the subject. Fortunately, an increasing number are willing to do so.

Sharing of Information

The Arizona Millennium Group provides a forum for year 2000 information exchange and discussion. We do not attempt to document specific practices, as we have found an extremely wide variation in interest and topics. What does frequently occur is that when one member raises a particular topic, other members will arrange one-on-one in-depth discussions of that issue with those who have the experience or interest.

We have also experienced situations where one member invites another member from a different company to have a discussion with their management or other members of the company. It is an easy, inexpensive method of bringing in an outsider's perspective without the cost or formality of a consulting contract. Also, often the most effective input is from someone who has the actual experience and who has no vested interest in the material presented or discussed.

Users groups should not be viewed as the only viable resource for the Year 2000 issue, but they do represent a quick way of bringing together the experience and knowledge of a large group of IS professionals facing a common problem. Getting started requires some work. Continued care and nourishment will be required to remain productive. The investment of time and effort will provide an effective, readily accessible source of experience and information. It will also provide a return in another way: having the knowledge and assurance that there are people who are successfully addressing the century date change problem who are available as resources.

97   *User: Your First Three Steps*

Dick Lefkon
Year 2000 Committee of AITP SIG-Mainframe

Copyright © 1997 Dick Lefkon

By now you're keenly aware that your successful Y2K predecessors have begun their projects by taking three preliminary steps: Awareness, Inventory, and Risk Assessment and Scheduling.

Awareness

Powerpoint and an overhead transparency projector are good ingredients for starting a good awareness campaign. No matter how many times you repeat the same basic presentation, always remember that your stone in the water is supposed to cause successively wider circles of realization that those two simple bytes can force your organization out of business.

Even when addressing just the CEO, let the room's darkness express the seriousness—and public nature—of the Y2K emergency. When you speak of insurance cancellation and officer liability, let your auditorium-ready visuals drive in the fact that these are publicly known—and publicly defensible—conclusions, not just oracular insights of a prophet on the hill.

The single best product for generating positive awareness, is this compendium. SEC repercussions? Try Ernst & Young's Chapter 4. Death from Brutus-like trading partners? Miech's Chapter 28. Physical plant threats? Carruther's 13. Proof they're unprepared? Paragon's Chapter 112 survey—or any Assessment process—or, if you're with the government, Congressman Horn's frontispiece to the book, backed by his survey in Chapter 20. And if you want to generate some time-urgency due to disappearing resources, throw a dart at any page of Jones' widely quoted Chapter 41. As a tension breaker, consider Doc Farmer's Top Ten List on page 3; just remember to allow for the rebuilding of concentration after presenting this or similar lists appearing elsewhere in this volume.

Finally, if you're clutched for ideas and nearing a presentation deadline, flip slowly through all the chapters. Then take one last look at Casey and Fisher's Part 5.

Always remember that organizational authority flows from money. Your preliminary study ought to be apportioned its very own small budget. Otherwise people might accord your results the same degree of attention they bestow on other charity cases—and you'll also have indicated you're overstaffed!

After basic awareness gets you your first, small budget, you'll need to take out your tin cup two more times. Planning steps sometimes grouped as Assessment, will themselves need to be written down by those paid from your first money; then actually carried under a second, larger helping of funds. Finally, once you've scoped and budgeted the full conversion and follow-up, you'll request a third, yet larger dollar amount.

As your project moves along, small awareness gimmicks like a boring Y2K newsletter/website, boring weekly e-mail broadcast, or boring division-wide Y2K meetings all serve to reinforce awareness of Y2K and acceptance of the general premise that those snubbing Y2K are out-of-step.

Inventory

Why does a food store package contain eight hot dog rolls but 12 hot dogs? That's easier to answer than: How much time and money does it take to fix the date problem in an unspecified number of programs?

There are many good inventory products, both Y2K-designated and not. The best one is the one you already own and use. It costs less and requires less training. You need not automate this process if (1) you recently did it for a Data Center move or a COBOL version migration, or (2) your Application Manager surveys—and those people's honesty/thoroughness—are sufficiently fine tuned to elicit reliable data.

The Inventory process should also match source to load modules and deduce which are not being used and which (about 7 percent) are missing the correct source. Biamax (Chapter 91) had the resources to do this manually and saved nearly half their disk storage by eliminating unused programs. If you can drop half your inventory before planning the fix, you'll drastically lower Y2K conversion costs.

Assessment

The Risk Analysis/Assessment phase takes a month or two and results in a full project plan with projected costs. Once you have developed a reliable program count, there's nothing wrong with manually inspecting a representative sampling of programs, then calculating a program change ratio and the overall cost of inspection, fix and unit test for your mix of different program types.

In the absence of pilot conversion for some representative programs, the half-day inspect and half-day code with unit test, is a good (and generous) costing rule. Remember that the actual changes are rote once you decide what you do to which type of date problem. Don't forget to allow for bridges, more rigorous testing, and database reworking wherever you don't just window.

Project Workbench, MS Project, Primavera, even Exel, are fine aids to project planning if you've lost your felt-tip pens and oversize paper.

The code inspection products work pretty much alike: You enter a "seed" list of name fragments and numerical formats. You also list exclusions, so that MOMMY doesn't qualify as MM. You run the tool, which also recognizes fields that feed or consume the stated date variables. And since the printout is too thick to use at first, you repeat these steps.

After three iterations, there should be a usable list of date occurrences in the code, and then human eyes or product feature will determine whether those code lines mean trouble.

There are some analyzers that work not primarily on code but on data. Datastores themselves are inspected to find fields with dates as contents. Then again, perhaps a strictly manual code-remediation effort may be better for your enterprise in terms of quality, speed, and/or dollar cost.

Let's face it: The puzzle of analyzing the programs and laying out the right course of action, is very interesting: The 110 pages of technical Parts 7 and 8, are testimony to that! But the remediation phase will occupy only one sixth of your Y2K project time and resources, whereas two thirds will be taken up by boring old testing.

Considering testing's relative importance, you might decide to turn back to the 80 pages of testing Parts 9 and 10, and read them five times each! These shorter sections do, after all, represent four times as much Y2K expenditure as the larger chapters on fixing the code.

12

part

Manager: Compleat Y2K Manager

*Y*OU CAN DO THIS. Once you've chosen among the Seven Methods of Part 7, further technical details are without mystery. Remember that your competitors—and the consulting house team managers—also are learners since at the start of 1997 fewer than two dozen project managers (your Editor among them) ever had actually COMPLETED SUCCESSFULLY Y2K conversions.

Beginning this chapter are three distinct author views of Y2K. All agree you should start NOW and have active commitment at the highest levels.

Gerhard Adam discusses project structure, plus strategies such as spreading this low-status work over the most possible staff. The eight Y2K project steps he details are component analysis (including triage), modeling, parsing study, change strategies, testing/implementation, and formal certification.

IBM lists nine major project phases, beginning with an explicit listing of a score of high-level players whose cooperation you'll need to gain. Have a pen, pad and organization phone directory handy as you read this fourth general introduction to Year 2000 Project management.

Before going deeper into management strategies, browse through the USAF Compliance Checklist for a real document logging real results.

Dick Lefkon's "Concurrent Phasing: Heart of the Y2K Factory" illustrates an excellent method for rapid completion of Year 2000 work. If you haven't personally run a massively parallel software development or conversion project, at least study carefully the visuals here and in Chapter 91. These project management techniques may be new to some; but they have been proven on the firing line and will help bring your Y2K project in on time.

Next there are three distinct views of the Project Management Office (PMO). Rita Tragesser describes one of the earliest PMOs, which GTE set up to ramrod its unprecedented GTEIS brokerage terminal to market. As with today's Y2K, it was mission-critical to knock Humpty Quotron off the wall—so much so that those joining the GTEIS PMO were required to sever ties to their old units. Jumping forward 20 years, Cesar Gonzalez shows us the structure of USAA insurance company's Y2K PMO, explaining what it does and how it's doing.

Going back to the 1980s, Dick Lefkon shows us various forms and procedures he constructed to implement a PMO function and get the process audit folks off his division's back. This chapter [plus Figure 91.1] has a dozen forms and reports to help you set up a PMO. Either the business users write-in test cases and scenarios, or you make/buy a capture tool. Regularly publish goal lists showing names, dates, slippage, etc.

Now Bill Goodwin revisits Y2K conformance. "Century Date Compliance" reprints most of his Tick-Tick-Tick article analyzing GTE's popular specification: General Integrity, Data Integrity, Explicit Century and Implicit Century. Among other benefits, writing your own organization's spec can make workplans more sensible—and helps all parties agree when you've succeeded.

Manager Lefkon's standards article next provides 39 good starting points to help your Y2K effort boost maintainability.

Nearing the end of Year 2000 Road, IBM's "Migration Weekend," focuses on the final pre-production event: Conversion Weekend. IBM gives nine task clusters for planning your migration to the new/fixed software, and a collection of 30 bullet points for performing it. Including the dress rehearsal(s), you'll be performing these 30 steps at least two or three times, so it's a good idea to word-process equivalent steps and publish them periodically with dates and assignees' names and phone numbers.

As an exercise, stop here and handwrite an 18-month, 40-milestone plan based on these chapters. Make sure you take the five or ten minutes required to complete it, as an "open book" test. In a moment, you'll be told where to find a "grading sheet" containing correct answers, but first complete your 40-milestone list.

After you finish the exercise above, please return to "Conversion Methodology," by Twig Terwilliger and N. T. Shivkumar.

Finally, the U.S. General Accounting Office (GAO) has printed approximately fifty key steps for Year 2000 projects. "Assessment Guide" is condensed from the complete report on the GAO website, which also includes a preparedness survey.

98   *Project Planning*

Gerhard Adam
Syspro, Inc.

This chapter addresses the process of establishing and launching a Year 2000 project. Section 1 of this paper will discuss some of the preliminary activities and provide background for understanding the nature of the Year 2000 effort. Section 2 provides the information necessary for structuring the Year 2000 project. While section 3 addresses the specific steps to be followed for the initiation and implementation of the Year 2000 solution. Realizing that there are numerous variations within companies and project management approaches, this paper seeks to provide a general review of activities which will need to be performed.

Section 1: Preliminary Activities

The Year 2000 project is not a typical undertaking within the IT organization. It is a problem which has enterprise-wide implications, touching nearly every platform and application within the organization. In some companies the changes required will be more extensive than in others, but nearly all will be impacted.

Problem Recognition

The first step in addressing the Year 2000 is recognizing that the problem exists. While this may seem obvious, it is more complicated than it first appears. Part of Year 2000 problem recognition is accepting the fact that it cannot be solved within the IT organization alone. There are too many business units which will also have to participate in the conversion, directly and indirectly. As an example, data may originate at desktops, be incorporated in secondary applications such as spreadsheets and reports, or be downloaded from central databases, none of which can be addressed without specific end-user involvement.

Keep in mind that the Year 2000 problem is not one of programming, but rather data integrity. Regardless of the reasons for expressing
years in two digit formats, the result is that the year is being expressed
incorrectly since it is properly a four digit value. This indicates that it is
the data itself and not the programs which are in error.

The Year 2000 effort is time consuming and resource intensive. This
may result in existing mission-critical projects, new applications and/or
technologies being deferred when conflicts arise with meeting the Year
2000 objectives. The difficulty arises because the resources required to
meet the requirements of the Year 2000 project will be unavailable to perform other activities.

Corporate Commitment

Corporate commitment is an aspect of problem recognition whereby the
enterprise recognizes the risk and is prepared to devote its resources to
resolving the Year 2000 problem thereby ensuring its continued viability
as an organization. This issue of continued business viability is not an
exaggeration as is sometimes implied. For a businesses using dates with
compromised integrity, it may become impossible to track the most basic
corporate functions and therefore, the business itself may no longer be
able to operate.

Another element of corporate commitment is budgeting and
resource allocation. As an enterprise problem, it must be funded and
managed on behalf of the entire organization. Many IT managers hope to
address the Year 2000 problem with minimal budgetary disruptions or
corporate involvement, however this will prove to be nearly impossible
in all but the smallest organizations. While IT will certainly be the driving force for the Year 2000 effort, it is erroneous to assume that IT can
perform this task in isolation.

Year 2000 Coordinator

Once these preliminary steps have been taken, the assignment of a corporate Year 2000 coordinator is necessary to act as liaison between the
parties (internal or external) working on the project and all the business
units that will be impacted by their activities. It is this individual that will
ensure that all the necessary components are being brought together to
achieve successful implementation of the Year 2000 project. It is important
that this individual have sufficient political influence and management
access to facilitate the necessary decisions when conflicts arise.

In summary, the Year 2000 project must be recognized as an enterprise-wide activity whose purpose is to preserve the viability of the

organization into the next century. It is a project will cannot tolerate "slippage" and should be given the highest priority for completion.

Section 2: Structuring the Project

Project Elements

The structure of the Year 2000 project consists of three (3) basic elements; Applications Programming, Data Center Operations, and End-user Computing. These represent three distinct projects areas which will run concurrently and require continued coordination to achieve the desired results.

The applications development area tends to be the primary focus when discussing the Year 2000 activities in most organizations. This involves locating, correcting, and implementing changes to all date references within the applications systems driving the enterprise. This element of the project is usually host-centric and the focal point for most IT efforts.

Data center operations consists basically of two efforts; ensuring that the basic systems and software necessary for continued operations are in place (as well as support for the year 2000 activities required by applications), and ensuring that adequate capacity and resources are available for the conversion (changes and testing). Many organizations don't consider the data center elements of the Year 2000 project, although the adequate planning of required resources is a critical step in determining the pace at which changes can occur. For example, capacity planning should occur to ensure that the resources are available for file conversions, parsing, and testing. Failure to do this could result in impacts to normal operations, or in some cases the project itself may grind to a halt.

The end-user computing environment includes most of the distributed platforms and their applications. This involves educating the enterprise regarding the year 2000 exposure as well as providing assistance for end-users who may have applications which need to be changed. In addition, this group must coordinate changes which occur in applications which have "down-stream" ramifications to the end-user community (i.e., file transfers, etc.). This element of the Year 2000 project should be driven by the end-user since much of the exposure will be undetectable until end-users indicate the functions being performed.

Within these three project areas, the sizing or assessment activity will obtain the preliminary data necessary for budgeting and resource allocation. In particular program inventory needs to be taken, vendor products identified, and the overall volume of change activity needs to be assessed.

Staffing

Additional consideration involves planning the staffing requirements for the year 2000 project. While there is certainly a temptation to assign a "task force" it should be recognized that the Year 2000 project is ultimately an arduous unrewarding task. The personnel assigned to the project may well view it as a career "dead-end," so care should be taken to ensure that the responsibility for implementing the year 2000 changes is spread as evenly as possible among all the groups.

In addition, it is important to ensure that all groups within the enterprise have a vested interest in seeing the year 2000 project succeed. It is fruitless to have groups competing for resources because their criteria of success is different than the rest of the enterprise. It is for this reason, that many organizations will turn to outside expertise for assistance. In the area of project management, this approach has many advantages by reducing the learning curve of internal staff to become expert in Year 2000 methodologies, while still maximizing the control maintained by in-house staff.

It may be necessary to supplement in-house personnel with additional help depending on the volume of change activity and projects which may have to be worked on. It is tempting to consider simply outsourcing the entire project, however, this may introduce more complications than it solves, and is generally the lease desirable approach to the problem.[1]

Section 3: Year 2000 Project Steps

The year 2000 project consists of eight specific steps ranging from analysis to final implementation and certification. While there may be many ways to view the divisions between these tasks, the activities identified must be performed for a successful project.

Analysis

Analysis consists of identifying all the related components (IE: programs, files, JCL, parms) within a given system for changes. Documentation should be reviewed as well as identifying elements (IE: program source code) which may be missing for the systems affected. It is during this phase that an assessment should be made regarding the impact of future projects on targeted systems.

---

1. The most obvious complication is the conflict of interest generated by internal staff working on competing projects while external staff is changing existing programs. The ability to "freeze" changes for indeterminate periods may be unworkable.

A very common argument against correcting year 2000 problems is the notion that these systems will be replaced anyway. During this phase, a realistic assessment of this must be made. If a system is to be replaced, then that IS THE YEAR 2000 PLAN for that system. Target dates and responsibilities (as well as resources should be assigned). If this doesn't occur, then the system cannot be realistically considered a candidate for replacement.[2] The output of the analysis process should consist of clear identification of all components which will need to be addressed.

Modeling

Modeling consists of defining the relationships of all components to establish the conversion unit. A conversion unit is that grouping of programs, files, and support elements (IE: parms) which will be converted together. The difficulty in this is to establish a size for a conversion unit which is realistic enough to avoid continually returning to make changes.

It should also be understood that some applications may overlap sufficiently with other conversion units that they may in fact be part of an interactive conversion. In other words, the application may need to be converted several times as files and support elements change for other systems. While this sounds unappealing to most programmers the issue here is project management and not technical requirements.

During this phase, the priority of a system should also be determined so that the proper ordering of systems based on the risk they present to the business is established. In many cases, the question is raised about systems which may not be modified in time. NOTE: ANY SYSTEM WHICH IS NOT READY must be considered UNUSABLE.

Parsing/Data Collection

The parsing/data collection phase involves the use of tools and utilities intended to allow mass scrutiny of date references and the building of a database to begin managing the process of changes. An important consideration in assessing the value of tools, is to not become so enthralled with them that they begin to dictate the direction of the project. The purpose of the tool should be to expedite the collection of information so that the proper evaluation of the date exposure can be determined. Anything else

---

2. If a system is to be replaced, then that becomes the Year 2000 change strategy and responsibilities, target dates, and budget should be assigned so that it is clear that the solution being proposed is system replacement. This will tend to avoid the more speculative projects which can surface during the early stages of Year 2000 assessments.

should be suspect as potentially adding more uncertainty or shifting focus into other areas which are not necessary.

Another point regarding parsing is that the project should be based on the implicit assumption that things will be missed. This should be accompanied so that anything which was undetected can be corrected during the later phases. Claims of 95 percent accuracy are grossly misleading. In an environment with 30,000 programs, even assuming only one date reference per program, would result in 1500 references which went undetected. Needless to say, anything less than 100 percent accuracy indicates potential failure.

Change Strategies

The selection of a change strategy should occur after all of the preliminary analysis and data gathering have been completed. This should include the information provided by vendors indicating how purchased systems have achieved compliance. The selection of a strategy should specifically focus on the objective to be achieved.

Correcting the problem requires changing the files. Anything else is simply a simulation of date correction. In some cases, accommodation through "bridges" or subroutines may be necessary to provide compatibility between different techniques (especially as they may relate to purchased systems).

The selection of a change strategy will have profound ramifications in the requirements for testing later. There is a considerable difference in the testing requirements of a file conversion versus those of a programmed simulation. Any choices made at this stage should clearly evaluate any anticipated savings against the costs incurred later during the more difficult phases of the project.

Coordinating Changes

Coordinating the changes is going to involve the selection of the conversion unit, writing any file conversion programs, building the test environment, making modifications to programs and JCL, and coordination with the technical support and end-user environments for assessing the ramifications of these changes.

Changes to files will require coordination of backup/recovery procedures to ensure that backups are replaced. Decisions involving the use of archived data sets and/or tape data sets will have to be made. Data transferred by end-users and employed in second tier applications will have to be coordinated. For example, if data is being transferred between host and PC-based applications, like spreadsheets, the entire effort must coordinated to ensure continued operation for these processes.

Testing

Testing the systems will follow several approaches depending on the change strategy chosen earlier. If the data is changed, then the testing need focus only on the impact of the data within existing applications.

If date simulation was chosen, then more significant testing must occur to validate the logic added to applications as well as ensuring that the dates used to populate the files represent likely occurrences to be tested.

While it may be desirable to parallel test systems, this may not be feasible for exceptionally large or long-running systems. The criteria regarding successful testing should be established so that concurrence is reached regarding the implementation of a system.

In addition, second tier, or "down-stream" systems must also be tested for success before implementation can proceed.

It is important to remember, that most testing is going to involve the use of, or introduction of year 2000 based dates into files. The simplistic testing based only on setting the CPU date will tend to confirm very little and may have little or no impact on most systems, since most applications operate based on dates within files, rather than the external dates obtained from the system.

Implementation

Once testing has been successfully completed, the final cutover should be planned. This will involve repopulating files with current data where date fields have been converted. Bridges and/or subroutines which have been temporarily placed will need to be removed and applications retested. Any second-tier applications (i.e.: spreadsheets, PC databases) which may be impacted by central changes will have to be validated to ensure that the change is implemented uniformly.

In addition, coordination for system management purposes should proceed at this stage to ensure that the issues of file recovery, backups, disaster recovery, performance, etc. have been addressed and that these processes are aware of and capable of responding to the new files.

Certification

Certification is the formal recognition that the way dates are represented electronically is a corporate-wide standard. This becomes the means by which systems will be evaluated for future changes as well as ensuring that problems are not introduced inadvertently years later.

This becomes extremely important if simulation mechanisms have been employed. If data windowing exists, then the standard to be used must be understood by all parties as long as that system is run. It is entirely possible that changes occurring in other systems may render current implementations impractical and require further modification. In short, it is not that any particular solution is not working, but rather that any solution may have ramifications later unless they are identified and recognized as a pre-existing condition for all future changes.

In addition, the certification process is one which can be employed to validate claims of Year 2000 compliance especially from vendors and business units. By establishing a basic criteria of testing and confirmation, the ability to assess claims ensures that systems are not simply accepted as compliant without review.

Summary

As can be seen, the year 2000 project contains many complexities and subtleties which will have to be managed for successful implementation. While the technical difficulties are not particularly complex, the logistic difficulties can rapidly become nightmarish. There is very little time remaining to travel down blind alleys and to experiment. This is no "slip date" for this project. We must get it right the first time.

99   *Planning to Resolve Your Year 2000 Exposures*

IBM

Reprinted by permission from GC28-1251 *The Year 2000 and 2-Digit Dates: A Guide for Planning and Implementation* Copyright © 1995, 1996 by International Business Machines Corporation.

To successfully address the challenges present within your computer system, you need to obtain your management's understanding, support, and an uncompromising commitment to provide resources to meet your needs. Expect the need for a knowledgeable executive sponsor to address budgetary, personnel and hardware resource requirements, cross-department and cross-divisional requirements, and overall scheduling and project management. It is imperative that this effort begin with and be managed through a central focal point responsible for critical project aspects such as overall scheduling, coordinating, and setting a consistent methodology through all project phases.

This chapter focuses on Year 2000 project phases: planning, exposure identification, exposure elimination, testing, migration, and the selection of available tools. The larger your computing environment, the more diverse its software, the more decentralized its physical environment, the greater control you must exercise, and the greater the communication that must exist across the individual projects.

The time to begin both planning and your Year 2000 transition is now. Consider the following:

> Getting requirements and design changes into the development cycle takes time. The review and modification of the application takes time. Securing resources and skills takes time. (If you have not kept current with the latest technology, your challenge might be greater and your options fewer.) Handling the problem in real time will disrupt your customer services, and the business impact might be significant.

> Most organizations are already short-handed when addressing their current workload and the challenges they face. Therefore, with this additional effort, perform a risk assessment and identify what is critical to the success of your business and determine and prioritize those work items.

> A significant amount of code rework might be required to complete your Year 2000 transition. It is not merely a problem that can be fixed by expanding the data fields. You must make changes to your data dictionary, data bases, files, programs, and so on.

> Within some institutions, programs are already producing incorrect output, and many organizations that aren't experiencing problems today, can reasonably expect problems in the future. For example, insurance companies in 1998, when calculating rates for persons born in '97, might find themselves assessing 101-year-old rates on a new-born scale, or potentially assessing a new-born at the same rate as a centenarian.

For some organizations, it might not be mandatory to act now, but it could save code redesign, especially data rework. Each day that passes prior to your Year 2000 transition allows more data to be added to your databases and the potential for additional routines and programs that are not Year-2000-ready to be added to your system. Also, expertise that is present today might not be available later. Finally, there have been projections that the availability of consulting and outsourcing services to meet Year 2000 transition needs will become increasingly limited as we approach the year 2000. For organizations with applications that handle future dates or those with thousands of application programs, the consequence of delaying the resolution of the problem could seriously impact their continued future success.

Planning Considerations

You need to plan for changes across all aspects of your IS environment. The following task categories might prove useful when approaching this task:

1. Identify and communicate the organization goal:

   The goal is to have the function and operation of an organization Year2000-ready before any disruption caused by 2-digit-year data occurs. IBM defines YEAR-2000-READY as follows: The capability of a Product, when used in accordance with its associated documentation, to correctly process, provide and/or receive date data within and between the 20th and 21st centuries, provided that all other products (for example, hardware, software, and firmware) used with the Product, properly exchange accurate date data with it.

2. Identify the deliverables and associated schedules for the following:

   ➤ Hardware

   ➤ Software

   ➤ Documentation

   ➤ Training

   ➤ Maintenance

   ➤ Operations

   ➤ Administration

   ➤ Acceptance criteria for all deliverables

3. Analyze job assignments

   For each task,

   ➤ Identify the responsible person or organization, for example

   • Customers

   • Management
       – Chief Executive Officer
       – Chief Financial Officer
       – Chief Information Officer
       – Software Development Managers
       – Operation/Administration Managers
       – Budget/Finance Managers
       – others

   • Computer vendors

   • Solution Developers

   • IT outsourcing vendors

   • Consulting/Integration services providers

- System analysts
- System designers
- System/Application Programmers
- Operations personnel
- End Users
- Auditors, quality assurance people
➤ Measure the estimated completion time
➤ Identify precedences/dependencies
➤ Identify resources and skills
➤ Identify critical path schedule
➤ Measure efforts
➤ Measure costs
➤ Identify technical factors
➤ Analyze potential benefits
  - Return on investment
  - Achievement of business goals
  - Potential quality and acceptance of the approach
  - Your business keeps running
➤ Analyze risk factors:
  - Complexity of the task
  - Resource/time constraints
  - Length of project
  - Critical development skills

4. Measure the criticality of each task and prioritize:

   Evaluate and determine how critical the functions of each entity are to the business success of the organization, and prioritize the sequence of providing Year-2000-ready solutions. An entity could be an individual, a department, a division, a business unit, customers, vendors, and so on, that are involved in the operations of the organization. The factors contributing to how critical you consider a task to be might include pressure of demand from end users for Year-2000-ready systems, legal issues, financial issues, or political issues.

Impact to Business

To determine the impact to your business, consider including these tasks:

➤ Critical to the operation of the business (such as legal compliance)
➤ Critical to the uninterrupted operation of the business (such as payroll)

> ➤ Required to support the business (such as management and financial reports)
> ➤ Required to support the business; however, the importance and timetable for the activity is lower than an item above (such as regular scheduled reports)
> ➤ Desirable, but not absolutely required to support the business.

Impact to Operations

Once classified by task, then determine impact severity. For example, you could use categories such as:

Fatal   Operations will ABEND or terminate

Critical   Operations will produce an incorrect result. (For example, expiration dates for food or pharmaceutical products are calculated as over 100 years old, not one or several days old.)

Marginal   Minor inconvenience, annoyance, or irritation. (For example, inventory reports collate dates of 00 prior to 99.)

Based on the impact to a particular process, evaluate the desirability of reworking a particular piece of code. Here is an opportunity for your IS management and your business strategists to improve overall business efficiency by taking inventory, accessing your IT strategy, and making more efficient use of your IT infrastructure. Together these groups should consider possibilities such as:

> ➤ Abandoning the business process
> ➤ Combining the process with other processes
> ➤ Replacing the process with a new state-of-the-art process.

5. Establish a 'critical event horizon:'

   Business environments are unique. The initial date your institution will begin experiencing Year 2000 problems is also unique. If you prepare business forecasts of a 3-year cycle, the fourth quarter of 1996 might be your critical event horizon. If you deal in automobile loans, 1995 might be your critical event horizon. It is likely to be a very rare institution that will not experience some form of Year 2000 difficulty until 1999 or 2000.

6. Provide data administration:

   > ➤ Identify the scope and responsibility of migrating the affected data
   >   • Exclusive. The affected data object is created and processed exclusively by this business area and is independent of any other business area. This could be at an individual, depart-

ment, or the business area level with further decomposition and analysis.

- Primary responsibility. The business area defines the affected data object and other business areas should use that definition or negotiate for its redefinition.
- Secondary responsibility. The affected data object is defined and created by a different business area in the enterprise, and is distributed only within the scope of the enterprise. Each business area defines its own use of the object which is provided by the business area with the primary responsibility.
- External exposures
- The affected data object is defined and created by either this or a different business area in the enterprise, and is distributed beyond the scope of the enterprise.
- Data is created outside your enterprise and then imported and used within it.

➤ Determine formats of the data dictionary

➤ Determine procedures for changing and entering data elements

➤ Determine procedures for collaborative data sharing and use

7. Decide project technical and management approaches:

➤ Programming standards, conventions, and guidelines

➤ Platform for application development

➤ Hardware/software

➤ Development methodology

➤ Development and test procedures

➤ Prototyping and parallel development

- Commonly used in software development projects and should be applied wherever appropriate.
- Apply a divide-and-conquer approach to partition the Year2000 project into smaller projects so that development and testing can proceed in parallel.
- Parallel development can shorten the development cycle. This is extremely critical when dealing with time-sensitive projects such as this Year2000 project.

➤ Process/data modeling

➤ Data dictionary

➤ Documentation structure, layout, and standards

➤ Reviews and walk-throughs

➤ Quality assurance procedures

➤ Testing methodology
➤ Automated tools
➤ Migrations of and bridgings to existing Year2000-ready systems
➤ Estimated future costs of maintenance

8. Identify project constraints, interfaces, and dependencies:
   ➤ End users/customers
     • Availability of test and other data
     • Availability of facilities and services
     • Responsibility for reviews
     • Responsibility for end user tests
     • Other actions.
   ➤ Special contract negotiations
   ➤ Outsourcing and consulting services
   ➤ Interfaces and dependencies with other projects
   ➤ Supporting services and facilities required
   ➤ Hardware and software to be used
   ➤ Solution-Developer-automated tools to be used
   ➤ Risks and alternative solutions
   ➤ Other assumptions.

9. Provide standards, guidelines, quality assurance, and review procedures:
   ➤ Year-2000-ready standards for purchasing of hardware/software vendor products.
   ➤ Year-2000-ready system requirements on request for proposal for outsourcing and integration services providers.
   ➤ Organizational Year-2000-ready standard/guidelines/process for specification, design, development, and testing of new and existing software.
   ➤ Year-2000-ready checklists for potential exposures.
   ➤ Standard for machine-human interface
   ➤ Procedures for submitting and processing proposed changes. The procedures should evaluate why change is needed, consequence of not making the change, and its effect on product, cost, and schedule
   ➤ Procedures for sign-offs and approvals. The procedures should solicit comments from knowledgeable and affected people about likely effects on product, documents, schedule, and costs.
   ➤ Procedures for future follow-up.

Inventory Your Software Portfolio

Once you have put your Year 2000 plan in place, you can then begin the task of converting your software programs for Year 2000 readiness.

The first step requires that you thoroughly understand your computing environment and compile an inventory of all the software programs within that environment. Such an inventory allows you to:

> ➤ analyze your portfolio for definition and movement of date-related data elements and the use of date-related calculations and manipulation

> ➤ identify and remove Year 2000 exposures

> ➤ track and control changes to your portfolio to more easily monitor and prevent injecting new Year 2000 exposures into your inventory while your Year 2000 resolution work progresses

> ➤ test the new (Year-2000-ready) version of the software programs in your portfolio.

Once you have completed the above activities, you are ready to migrate from your current computing environment to your Year2000-ready environment. The following chapters discuss these activities in detail and provide options and suggestions for your consideration.

Inventory Your Hardware Systems

Contact hardware manufacturers regarding the Year 2000 readiness of hardware components of your system.

To identify the potential exposures caused by using 2-digit-year representations of dates, you first need to locate references to all date-related data.

100   *USAF Compliance Checklist*

U.S. Air Force

The purpose of this checklist is to aid system managers in ensuring their systems are compliant for the Year 2000. Make sure the following items are included in your Year 2000 testing and certification process for all of the developed, gratis, licensed, and purchased software, hardware, and firmware used in your systems operation, development/maintenance, support, and testing activities.

Please respond to each question with the appropriate answer.

System Identification
(An asterisk indicates an optional question)

1. Please provide system information.

   a. Name of system:

   b. Defense Integration Support Tools (DIST)
       Number of system:

   c. Operational date of system
       (current or a future date)*:

   d. Planned or actual replacement date of
       system (retirement or discontinuation
       qualifies as replacement)*:

   e. For planned replacement what is
       the contingency plan and under what
       conditions will it be invoked?*:

   f. What are the safety critical portions
       of the system, if any?*:

2. Each system has its own window of time, before and after the present date, in which it functions. Planning and scheduling systems work with dates that are weeks, months, and sometimes years in the future. Likewise, trend analysis systems and billing systems regularly reference dates in the past. For your system, and its window of time, please verify its ability to successfully process data containing dates with no adverse effect on the applications functionality and with no impact on the customer or end user beyond adjustment to approved changes in procedures and data formats.

	Verified	No	N/A
a. Dates in 20th century (1900s)	_____	_____	_____
b. Dates in 21st century (2000s)	_____	_____	_____
c. Dates across century boundary (mix 1900s and 2000s)	_____	_____	_____
d. Crosses 1999 to 2000 successfully	_____	_____	_____

Other/Indirect Date Usage

3. Have you verified performance (and corrected if necessary):

	Verified	No	N/A
a. Dates embedded as parts of other fields	_____	_____	_____
b. Dates used as part of a sort key	_____	_____	_____
c. Usage of values in date fields for special purposes that are not dates (e.g. using 9999 or 99 to mean "never expire")	_____	_____	_____
d. Date dependent activation/deactivation of: passwords, accounts, commercial licenses	_____	_____	_____
e. Date representation in the operating systems file system (creation dates and modification dates of files and directories)	_____	_____	_____
f. Date dependent audit information	_____	_____	_____
g. Date dependencies in encryption/ decryption algorithms	_____	_____	_____
h. Date dependent random number generators	_____	_____	_____

  i. Date dependencies in firmware

  j. Personal Computer BIOS and RTC does not reset the year to 1980 or 1984 on reboots after 31 December 1999 *(corrections by operating system utilities allowed)*

Leap Year

	Verified	No	N/A

4. System accurately recognizes and processes Year 2000 as a leap year.

  a. February 29, 2000 is recognized as a valid date

  b. Julian date 00060 is recognized as February 29, 2000

  c. Julian date 00366 is recognized as December 31, 2000

  d. Arithmetic operations recognize Year 2000 has 366 days

Usage of Dates Internally

5. Internal application usage of dates and date fields must be clear and unambiguous in the context of the systems which use them.

	Verified	No	N/A

  a. Display of dates is clear and unambiguous (the ability to correctly determine to which century a date belongs either by explicit display, i.e. 4-digit year, or system or user inference)

  b. Printing of dates is clear and unambiguous

  c. Input of dates is clear and unambiguous

  d. Storage of dates is clear and unambiguous

External System Interfaces

6. External interactions are identified and validated to correctly function for all dates.

	Verified	No	N/A

a. Interaction between this system and any other external time source, if existing, has been verified for correct operation.

	_____	_____	_____

For example, the GPS system is sometimes used as a time source. Many GPS receivers cannot correctly deal with the rollover of the GPS 10-bit epoch counter that will occur at midnight, 21 August 1999. GPS receivers also deal with an 8-bit Almanac Week counter which has a 256 week roll-over span.

b. You and the responsible organization for each interface have negotiated an agreement dealing with Year 2000 issues.

	_____	_____	_____

For example, is the interface currently Y2K compliant, is it being worked on, does it have an unknown fix date, or will it be fixed by a future date you have mutually agreed on.

For each interface that exchanges date data, you and the responsible organizations have discussed and verified that you have implemented consistent Year 2000 corrections that will correctly work for date data passed between your systems.

Date Field Type

7. Describe the type of date fields used by the system, in either software or data bases.

	Verified	No	N/A

a. Does the system use 4 digit year data fields?

	_____	_____	_____

b. Does the system use 2 digit year data fields?

	_____	_____	_____

c. If 2 digit, does the system use a century logic technique to correctly infer the century?

	_____	_____	_____

d. At what date will the century logic fix
    fail?

e. Are there any internal data types for
    dates?

    If yes to e, what is the range of dates that the date field can represent?
    Minimum Date _____   *Maximum Date* _____

Year 2000 Testing Information

8. Optional: Please provide the following information with regard to testing the
    application for Year 2000 compliance:

                                                      Narrative Answer

a. Testing Organization

b. Name of Test Team Chief

c. Date that Year 2000 compliance testing
    was completed

d. How was Year 2000 compliance
    determined? (certified by vendor or
    contractor, tested in-house, in-inspected
    but not tested, etc.)

                                                      Yes   **No**

e. Are the test data sets available for
    regression testing on the next version
    release for questions 2, 3, 4, 5, 6, 7d, and
    7e?

f. Are the detailed test results and reports
    available for review and audit for
    questions 2, 3, 4, 5, 6, 7d, and 7e?

g. Do you follow a defined process for
    tracking the status of all Year 2000
    problems reported, changes made,
    testing, compliance, and return to
    production?

COTS/GOTS Components

9. Optional: Please provide the following information with regard to COTS/GOTS components.

	Yes	No	N/A
a. Does the system use COTS/GOTS application packages and/or infrastructure components?	_____	_____	_____
b. If yes, have those items been verified to be Year 2000 compliant?	_____	_____	_____

Narrative Answer

c. How was Year 2000 compliance determined? (certified by vendor or contractor, tested in-house, etc.)

Certification Levels

Certification levels are defined below. Yes, verified, and N/A are considered positive responses. No is considered a negative response.

Level

0 System retired or replaced

1a Full independent testing completed with either:

  - *All questions have positive responses except possibly 7b and e*

1b Full independent testing completed with either:

  - *All questions have positive responses except possibly 7a and e*

2a Independent audit of system and existing testing completed with either:

  - *All questions have positive responses except possibly 7b and e*

2b Independent audit of system and existing testing completed with either:

  - *All questions have positive responses except possibly 7a and e*

3 Self-certification
CAUTION: Self-certification assumes a higher risk level of potential failures

3a Self-certification with full use of 4 digit century date fields

- *All questions have positive responses except possibly 7b and e*

3b   Self-certification indicates risk due to use of 2 digit century fields

- *All questions have positive responses except possibly 7a and e*

3c   Self-certification indicates risk due to ambiguous usage of dates

- *Question 5-a,b,c or d have negative responses.*

3d   Self-certification indicates potential problems (System needs additional work before Year 2000 processing can be assured with any level of reliability)

- *Question 2-a,b,c or d have negative responses, or*

- *Question 3-a,b,c,d,e,f,g,h,i or j have negative responses, or*

- *Question 4-a,b,c or d have negative responses, or*

- *Question 5-a,b,c or d have negative responses, or*

- *Question 6-a or b have negative responses, or*

- *Question 9-b has a negative response.*

4   Not certified or not certified yet.

It would be advisable but not required for the system/program/project manager to have the responsible programmer(s) fill out a similar checklist covering the software they are responsible for before completing this checklist for the overall application.

LEVEL OF CERTIFICATION FOR THIS DATA SYSTEM: (Circle only one)

0   1a   1b   2a   2b   3a   3b   3c   3d   4

I certify that the information provided above is true and correct to the best of my knowledge and belief:

Additional Comments:

_____

_____

_____

_____

System Manager   _____   Date _____

I certify that the information provided above is true and correct to the best of my knowledge and belief.

Additional Comments:

_____

_____

_____

_____

System Customer   _____   Date   _____

101   *Concurrent Phasing: Heart of the Y2K Factory*

Dick Lefkon
Year 2000 Committee of AITP SIG-Mainframe

One problem with Year 2000 remediation efforts is that by the time the system is finished, the business it serves may have evolved into something distinctly different. Users will not stand by quietly without good cause if their key systems are frozen for a lengthy period to accommodate the programming department.

When time means money—or in Y2K's case, survival!—time frame acceleration can make a large-scale project more costly, but the extra expense may be justified by return on investment and other considerations.

Traditionally, a typical small system plan might call for four professionals to spend four years each to put in the new system or enhancement. But Y2K won't permit your business to wait for more than 18 months to receive the working functions. Using a number of simple DP management practices—grouped under the strategy of concurrent phasing—can speed the process to meet the schedule, although at a higher cost.

The 16 person-years, originally spread over four years among four people, might appear at first glance to be covered easily in 1 1/2 years by 11 or fewer people (since 1 1/2 x 11 = 16 1/2 person-years). In reality, management and interfacing costs would probably raise the required staffing to 13, 14 or even 15 people to get the job done in the shorter time.

In general, bringing the remediated system live significantly earlier means that the resulting benefits in savings, profit increment or marketplace leadership are cumulatively in effect for that much longer. Business users pay attention to this return on investment. For Y2K efforts, add "enterprise survival" to the benefits list.

There also are operational benefits from speed:

> Employee salaries and consultant costs will be billed at today's rates rather than increase over coming months.

> The new system can use state-of-the-art software rather than, for instance, a data base package that has aged several additional years upon system delivery.

> The necessary freezing of present procedures will be shorter and cause correspondingly less disruption to the conduct of business.

Once upper management decides to pay for accelerating the project, the recommended strategy to accomplish this acceleration is concurrent phasing. This umbrella approach unites the concepts of subtasking; ganging, or grouping, and reordering tasks; team separation; data base definition; and modeling. The first three of these are best explained in terms of frequent milestones, ganged labor, checkerboard technique, documented interfaces and the phasing concept itself.

Inchstones

Progress should be measured as a count of successive milestones, not as an estimated percentage of work completed. Basic to the other practices discussed here is the need for dividing tasks finely enough. Avoiding any overly long tasks is especially important at project start-up, where it often happens that at least some tasks are inadvertently grossly underestimated.

For instance, consider two similar tasks: X, which is expected to take a week, and Y, which is scheduled for two months. Task X is inherently easier to manage than the longer Task Y. If Task X is running late, management will know by the end of that week and will be able to take action.

Even with the most competent and trusted programmer, no large task such as Y should be allowed to stand as is without negotiating a subdivision into one-week-or-less verifiable milestones. If this practice is new to the programming unit, a staff member may experience discomfort in the first such negotiation. It is up to the manager to persist in getting the programmer to identify and commit to each subtask. [Editor: see Chapter 23, "Ignore the 'New' Y2K Project Management at Your Peril."]

Show Some Character—Frequent, Trackable Milestones

> ➤ "Trust me, this will take six weeks"

> ➤ "It can't be broken down more finely"

> ➤ "Nobody ever required this before"

> ➤ "I can't work until Joe finishes"

> ➤ "These milestones are targets, right?"

> ➤ "It's 80 percent finished"

> ➤ "It's coded by the delivery date"

> ➤ "Testing wasn't in the original plan"

Figure 101.1   Good managers learn to respond

A manager does well to offer supplementary staffing or reasonable added time for subtasks that, once isolated, are discovered to be more complex than was originally assumed. This combination of firmness and helpfulness makes the subordinate's next set of estimates more reliable and quickly conveys to all programmer/analysts the key role their own reporting plays in project control. (During the Risk Analysis through Scheduling phases, you *will* need to distribute a second survey to application "owners" containing additional questions to probe blind spots evidenced in the returns to your initial questionnaire.)

The manager does not have to inspect all the milestone evidence—or even understand clearly what all the bite-size subtasks entail. Because the potential for management inspection is always there, it is often sufficient to accept the word of the staff member that the subtask has been completed and verified in the standard way.

The practice of making small, trackable milestones has not been developed explicitly for Y2K projects, but: Violate it at your peril.

Ganged Labor

The time frame of a large Y2K task can be compressed, even though it appears to lie along one irreducible path. But you cannot readily achieve this by behaving as though perhaps it cannot be done. After subdividing the task into many pieces, its underlying structure—or lack of it—shows clearly where parallel programming can make use of ganged labor.

If there are two, three or four mostly independent processes, these can be transformed into the same number of "clumps" that are remediated and tested simultaneously. A 15–30 percent programming overhead may be necessary to separate and reunite the function. Putting the dollar and resource cost aside, this means that splitting one application in half might reduce the number of days until delivery by 40 percent; in thirds, by 60 percent, and in quarters, by 70 percent.

Brian O'Shea recounts his pre-Y2K experience as a member of a coding gang at Citicorp, NA in New York. They were assigned to subdivide a single large program for follow-up processing of complicated orders on a multi-million-dollar real-time system.

The program specification ran 79 pages in length, and O'Shea's coding group had established a rule of thumb of one coding day for any page of specifications received from that particular author. At 22 workdays per month, this one program would have spanned the entire time period allotted for coding all order entry and follow-up programs.

"This would have been a four-month effort if assigned to one person," O'Shea observes, "and the probability of failure would have been appreciably higher" than with a ganged effort.

The specification was divided into eight distinct programs. Please refer to Figure 101.2. O'Shea still smiles when thinking about the results: "Four-fifths of the original composite whole was up and running in Systems in four to five weeks, and the remaining functions were implemented within two weeks after that."

The Checkerboard Method for Y2K Factories

Sometimes, a programmer is justified in insisting that the components of a large program (or clump) are too interrelated for a clean separation. Even in this case, a complicated task can still be sliced up and done in parallel, using the perpendicular sense of a two-dimensional, or checkerboard, scheduling method. This is illustrated by a case study of the teleprocessing controller program in a sales processing system—again, pre-Y2K. (This is an excellent method for completing Year 2000 work.)

By Period 4 in Figure 101.2, the controller program had originally been specified and tested successfully for Subsystems A and B. Now was the time to add functionality for Subsystem C, restructure the controller so that common functions fell in a fourth section, and modify all the pre-existing programs for Subsystems A and B.

One programmer would have needed two months to finish the modification, and even more time to change the programs that used it—sound similar to your Y2K effort?—yet the deadline given was five weeks away.

	Period 1	Period 2	Period 3	Period 4	Period 5
Programmer 1	Place common routines in one section	Place Subsystem A routines in one section	Place Subsystem B routines in one section	Produce a new Subsystem C routines section	Unit test the new Subsystem C controller section
Programmer 2		Unit test the common subroutines controller section	Unit test the Subsystem A controller section	Unit test the Subsystem B controller section	Write the first Subsystem C screen program
Programmers 3–8				Modify the old Subsystem A screen programs	Modify the old Subsystem B screen programs

Figure 101.2   Checkerboard method of subtasks for rewriting programs

In several negotiations during a two-day period, the author-manager got the lead programmer to subdivide the effort into nine tasks, each lasting approximately five days, plus the subsequent modification of old programs. Figure 101.2 shows the checkerboard solution reached. The downward diagonals of the checkerboard show how each subsystem component passed from programmer to programmer.

Programmer 1 did only coding. As soon as he finished a piece of controller code, other people would unit test it. As soon as the revised functions A, B and C emerged from testing, still other programmers modified the pre-existing programs and tested their own results.

In the typical programming maintenance department, a programmer/analyst takes her clipboard to the business user's office to investigate a new business need and writes and obtains signoff on functional specifications. Then she writes, discusses, and obtains approval on a programming design and codes and unit-tests. Finally, she helps support subsequent testing.

Concurrent Phasing differs. At each stage, a written hand-off takes place. It is in each author's personal interest to make that product as complete and self-explanatory as possible; otherwise the originator will have to spend valuable time in face-to-face explanation and eventual rewriting for clarification.

In principle, each successive team should be able to receive a document thrown over a high wall by an anonymous author and to send its own product past the next wall to an equally anonymous recipient. The point is not that project members should not be sociable, only that no real turnover has taken place if sender and recipient must both be present to interpret the product delivered.

Concurrent—Not Sequential—Phases

The traditional large software development project schedule has fixed sequential phases for creating functional specification, programming design, coding, unit-testing, integration-testing and user-testing. It parallels the behavior of an individual maintenance programmer constrained to making small enhancements on a system that is already stable and settled.

Not only does this new development approach (Concurrent Phasing) provide the freedom to vary traditional scheduling, but common sense and courtesy to the user community may also demand it.[3]

In Y2K Concurrent Phasing, fixed teams are built around remediation plans and programs to be passed downstream, business linkage specifications, change specifications, and phased testing. For typical systems maintenance, the programmer/analyst/tester moves through these steps for each program or clump. For Concurrent Phasing, it is the Y2K business function, not the person, that moves. And that's what enables Y2K Factories to work!

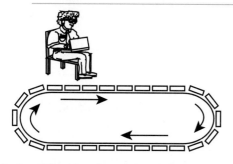

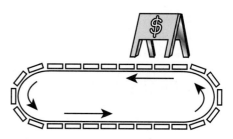

In traditional software maintenance, the programmer/analyst moves through several main steps for each business function.

When you run your Y2K Factory using concurrent phasing, it is the business function, not the person that moves.

Figure 101.3 *In Y2K Concurrent Phasing, it's the Y2K business function, not the person, that moves.*

3. ...well, new anyway when the author's original "Speeding Software Delivery" predecessor article was published in the May 12, 1986 *Computerworld*.

The concurrent phasing of a subsystem enables staff members to concentrate on doing only what they do well and supports real teamwork in which other staff members are made available as resources if a promise date starts to slip. [Editor: See, too, Chapter 23.]

In the traditional approach, where all change specifications are written at one stage and so on, the business users suddenly appear in the last time period and are expected to validate and approve, in a brief interval, an entire application system on which their livelihoods may depend.

That normal scheduling strategy is no better for the coders and testers, especially consultants hired to implement the project. If taken seriously, traditional project phasing might require that all new programmers be screened (but not working) while Y2K functional specifications were written, be paid to learn the environment while system designers write the coding specifications, work during the official programming phase and move on to other employment at the outset of integration-testing.

To say the least, the training time before the programming phase—and the missing expertise immediately after it—are respectively costly and extremely risky. Also, having all these programmers sitting at their desks does not guarantee the desired manpower in case of an emergency. This is because their slack times happen all at once and do not make any of them available to help during each other's busy times.

The use of a specialized Y2K coding and testing teams is assumed if the project size requires temporary staff expansion. But the constraint on staff members helping each other would be just as true for a slower project in which each subsystem was produced in sequence by programmers who all participated in writing functional specifications, designing programs and coding. Moreover, each programmer would tend to bog down at his weakest skill, while spending less time than planned where the greatest proficiency lay.

In the concurrent phasing approach, each Y2K program clump rides a conveyor belt past the fixed teams. It receives a well-documented remediation design from the business analysts; next, the system specialists place an unambiguous change specification on the conveyor belt. Then, the programmers remove the specification and replace it with unit-tested programs.

The system testers either accept each program or have it improved, then place it back on the belt with a set of successful test cases that fit the business and probe behavior on and near the critical dates. Finally, the functioning program drops into the testers' and users' laps for further validation. (Please see right side of Figure 101.3.)

These steps may sound similar to those of the traditional approach, but there are three striking differences: The conveyor belt is in a steady state; the project teams represent fixed stations at which each distinct program clump must stop; and business functions or subsystems are phased in, not done all at once or done in spurts.

In the initial time period, while Business Component A is being analyzed, programmers are brought up to speed technically, and systems analysts can busy themselves analyzing the data elements and logic of the pre-existing automated systems. In the second time period, Business Component B is analyzed, the Component A change specifications are transformed into a coding design for Subsystem A, and programmers experiment with a model system.

By the third period in Figure 101.4, programmers are working full-time implementing Subsystem A, while Business Components B and C are proceeding though remediation analysis and design. In the fourth time period, Subsystem A is integration-tested, while business analysts begin to look at Business Component D.

Note that Subsystem A reaches the users at the start of the fifth period, before Y2K analysis of Business Component E has taken place. Each Y2K phase is being done concurrently but for different subsystems.

Representatives of Business Department A, who worked with the business functional analysts at the beginning, return in the fifth time period to critique a subsystem that has been demonstrated to hold together during system integration testing.

If the Department A end users pinpoint an urgent Year 2000 fix requiring business analysts, system designers, programmers or testing personnel, these specialists can be assigned to this task because the time period imposes no particular stress on any of the specialized teams.

In Concurrent Phasing, end users thus become a dependable, regular component of the process, gradually increasing their skills and understanding of the automated system. They encounter no overwhelming surprise when, at the end of intensive automated and manual testing, they are asked to authorize a move to the production environment.

Database Comes First

Bad programming is not irreversible. Bad data planning may be.

For instance, two functioning batch COBOL programs can be combined for controllability by concatenating their respective divisions, recompiling to eliminate redundancies and retesting. One real-time COBOL program can be subdivided for paging efficiency, partial rewrite and so on by dissecting the procedure division, reproducing the other divisions in both places, recompiling to eliminate unused fields and program retesting.

If produced carefully, the combined (or bifurcated) program cannot be distinguished from one originally designed to exist in that final form.

This is definitely not the case with a database or any systemwide data store, including one or more flat sequential files, especially if expansion via century bytes is to take place. Whether the major subcomponents of a system are remediated in sequence or in parallel, an extensive database should be produced initially, tentatively populated, and used uniformly by all system components.

From the traditional design development viewpoint, early implementation of a comprehensive data base has four advantages:

> It facilitates modeling.
> It forces major functional components to communicate properly with each other.
> It prevents data redundancy, which is practically impossible to eliminate when combining two or more sub-databases later in a project.
> It forces the early planning effort to concentrate on and understand the meaning and use of the actual business data fields.

In a Year 2000 project, any expansion to the database (to accommodate CC digits) ought to be done at the outset. Let bridges connect the *final* database to incompletely fixed programs; but give "final" programs immediate access to the new, *real* data.

Skeleton Activity: Pilot, Shakedown, and Baseline

Critical as specifications are, it is a mistake to conclude that the programmers' hands must be idle while the first coding specifications are being produced.

All the new hires know the programming software, and each of the old-timers assigned to coding has expertise in the business, automated interfaces or data fields. Based on their collective expertise, the programmers can shake down the new Y2K testing environment, perform early baseline tests on everything in sight, and perform soup-to-nuts coding through testing on a select number of "pilot" programs to validate initial cost estimates.

"Many people think of models as something to be reused," says John LeKashman, vice-president of operations services for the Stauffer Chemical subsidiary of Chesebrough-Pond's, Inc. in Westport, Conn. "But in modeling you rarely intend to run those original programs over and over forever. They are simply there to confirm, or refute, the logic or proce-dures on which you want to test feasibility or tuning characteristics."

In practical terms, the pilot exercise of a programming effort can uncover where supporting software and coding/testing aids do not work. Also, other limitations of the environment and staff can be learned and acted upon before important deadlines appear on the horizon.

Year 2000 Concurrent Phasing

Subtasking, ganging and tightly documented handoffs, along with the concepts of database definition and modeling, can be synthesized into the overall scheduling strategy for larger tasks known as Concurrent Phasing. Concurrent Phasing is designed to keep all participants produc-tively busy, permit resource shifts when problems arise and maintain a delivery schedule of highly visible subsystems that the business user can test, critique and ultimately approve for production. This integrated project management approach is now at least 21 years old, having been proposed and reported by this author/manager in a 1975 National Sci-ence Foundation study.

Concurrent Phasing is successful in Y2K Factories because of this: It is un-necessary to complete remediation specifications for a given subsystem in the second project month if coding will not begin until the sixth project month. This fact is largely ignored in traditional development scheduling.

Represented schematically, a Concurrent Phasing diagram looks very much like Figure 101.2, except that Programmer 1 becomes Func-tionals Team, Programmer 2 becomes Design Team, Programmer 3 becomes Programming Team and a line is added for QA and Testers and for Business users, as in Figure 101.4.

The contexts of each box in the Figure 101.4 Concurrent Phasing scheme would, of course, be a magnitude larger than that of Figure 101.2. The entire process currently illustrated in Figure 101.2 is summarized as Code Subsystem C and occupies only the white box on the right side of the third row in Figure 101.4.

The first column of such a schematic diagram for Concurrent Phas-ing lists Plan changes for A (for the analysts), Data Flow and Change, Run a Pilot Effort, Set Up Testing Environment, and Business A Func-tions (for the end user).

This kind of two-dimensional checkerboard would be inappropriate to represent the more traditional scheme of software modification, since the main business needs there are all to be analyzed at the same time, specified for programming at one subsequent time, coded simulta-neously, integration-tested all at once and UAT-tested at the very end.

Responsible Individual or Group:	Period I:	Period II:	Period III:	Period IV:	Period V:	Period VI:	Period VII:	Period VIII:	Period IX:
Business Analyst:	A change plan	B change plan	C change plan	D change plan	E change plan	train operators and clerical staff	....		
Systems Analyst:	Data flow and change	A Y2K fix specifications	B Y2K fix specifications	C Y2K fix specifications	D Y2K fix specifications	E Y2K fix specifications	perform maintenance and small upgrades		
Programmer/ Analyst:	Run pilot effort	Load the Database	A coding and unit testing	B coding and unit testing	C coding and unit testing	D coding and unit testing	E coding and unit testing	Perform maintenance	
QA and Testers:	Testing Environment	Document	Ensure Database	A integration testing	B integration testing	C integration testing	D integration testing	E integration testing	Maintenance
Business User:	A cases	B cases	C cases	D, E cases	A acceptance UAT testing	B acceptance UAT testing	C acceptance UAT testing	D acceptance UAT testing	E acceptance UAT testing

Figure 101.4   Five subsystems with phasing and balanced loading

Y2K Factory: An Active Management Team

The additional dimension of a Concurrent Phasing diagram illustrates the need for an active project management team.

Once they understand the rudiments of Concurrent Phasing, task supervisors should be willing to carry these out, since they have already benefited from them.

The typical 60 percent decrease in project delivery time has necessitated a tripling of their staff size and may have precipitated their own hiring in the first place.

However, many IS managers may be unfamiliar with Concurrent Phasing and at first may have difficulty conceptualizing this management-intensive method. It is important that this accelerated approach be presold to those with systems influence in either the data processing or end-user departments and explained carefully as new individuals enter the management chain. Otherwise, Y2K factories can falter.

Limitations

Except for subtasking, the synthesis of techniques discussed here have not produced the projected acceleration with efforts of less than four to six person-years. Projects of that duration have insufficient resources present to facilitate ganging; in addition, the complexity of the task is probably not great enough to reap a net time gain from pilot efforts. Also, the project management team must take an active role, meeting at least weekly to discuss problems and alternative solutions. Fortunately—or not, depending on your viewpoint—most Y2K efforts expend dozens or hundreds of times that effort!

Because it runs counter to the traditional linear schedule, Concurrent Phasing should periodically be discussed with those to whom it has already been explained. A loud "This method will never work!" can decelerate progress if left unanswered enough.

On the other hand, common sense should be applied: Coders should be discouraged from breaking up a program in circumstances where the time lost for component linkage coding and testing is comparable to the time gained by coding in parallel. Subordinates must understand that the deadlines are real and that 80 percent completion is not good enough.

Finally, if a new software technology is used as the Year 2000 remedy, veteran practitioners of only the old technology should be kept off the program design team. Otherwise, their knowledge of the business, seniority and self-confidence may converge so strongly that they lead the real software experts to come up with the wrong system architecture.

Y2K Factory: Concurrent Phasing

Concurrent Phasing is a two-dimensional approach that integrates the management practices of task subdivision, subtask ganging, checkerboard scheduling, functionally distinct remediation teams, early completion of the common database, and the use of pilot efforts to improve cost estimates and shake down procedures and the environment.

The chief benefit of Concurrent Phasing is that it smooths and reduces the staff load required to complete the Y2K software remediation project in a greatly accelerated time frame. The final software products delivered by your Y2K Factory are not necessarily any better than those produced with other approaches; and completing a project in 1 1/2 years with this strategy will cost significantly more than permitting the same project to take five years to go live. But when the time means money or business survival, this more expensive project management strategy can be just the right one. After all, five years may be an overlong interval between now and 2000!

102   *Commitment Counts*

Rita Tragesser
Germaine Industries

Will every company address the year 2000 issue? Eventually.

Has your company designated a year 2000 program manager?

How did you choose this person?

The director of planning of a major firm responded to that question. He stated, hopefully tongue in cheek, that while hiring a software engineer, he asked if the young technician was familiar with the Y2K issue. When the new hire said he had read an article on the subject, he was dubbed the company expert. What a frightening thought. The drop dead dates will come and go but for some they won't be recorded and those people will remain in the not so gay nineties. One line from a recent best seller stands out "The funeral will be well attended."

Will your company be left behind with the casualties? It's a management decision. Management avoids that fate, not by paying lip service to the concept of a Y2K expert but by committing its best resources to participate in the Y2K certification process.

Conversion efforts are expensive to plan, manage, develop, test and integrate. They're costly in terms of funding, system inconvenience, interruption of daily processes, increased workloads and diversion of talent. In the past there's been an upside to a large scale effort: faster processing, better turnaround, and improved services. The Y2K investment promises only survival and business as usual; not much of an incentive. It becomes a task of the well managed project team to identify and develop its own rewards. It is left to management to underwrite the effort knowing that survival may be the only reward. **Only management can make the difference**.

In the 1970s GTE/IS, the IT standard bearer of the financial community, introduced an intelligent desktop quotation system with mailbox and message switching capabilities. Our engineering department was responsible for the innovative design; our management commitment was in great part responsible for its success. We converted a major brokerage firm with more than a hundred offices in the US, a switching system in London and offices from Rome to Japan. Every talent in GTE/IS supported the effort. Some software was contracted out, but managed in-house. When one of the technicians assigned to a London system had a family problem, management signed him up for a flight on the SST. Maintaining morale is part of the management commitment. The Financial Services System was a real Wall Street phenomenon. More than one brokerage firm had the occasion to say "Thank you GTE."

Management brought together the most talented and experienced PMO of any company at the time. Management temporarily reassigned, and in some cases transferred: a division VP, Director of Planning, Director of Software Development, Manager of Quotations Systems, and a Senior Design Engineer. They each brought with them ten to twenty years experience with the company, averaged two degrees, 15 years computer design and programming, and seven years of brokerage experience—and the group included a CPA. One member of this group directed every Brokerage House proposal presented by GTE/IS, and program managed every proposal that was accepted. The GTE/IS terminal and system had an unprecedented success record. We had a knowledgeable software department, a talented engineering group, a dynamic sales force, support personnel who cared and management willing to commit the resources to reach its goal.

Have you decided to do it? Good.

1. Appoint your Program Manager.
   > Allocate resources
   - Preliminary funding
   - Personnel (Program management team/project management teams)
2. Step back and let the Teams perform.

- ➤ Scoping /Sizing
  - Operating systems
  - Number of programs   used/unused
  - Languages   one/more
  - Occurrences of date- impact- critical/slight/none
  - Date formats
  - Data files   current/archived, used/unused
  - Data fields   date occurrence/form/impact
- ➤ Defining /Scheduling
  - Method of change   digits/window/marker
  - Programs   purged/changed/rewritten
  - Files   purged/changed/rewritten
  - Changes   in-house/out-sourced
  - Operating System   modify/replace
- ➤ Funding
- ➤ Certification
  - Program testing
  - System testing
  - Contingency plan
  - Acceptance
- ➤ Integration
- ➤ Communication

You may find that you not only stepped successfully into the 21st century but managed to achieve faster processing, better turnaround, increased capacity and improved services.

103   *Project Management Office, USAA*

Cesar Gonzalez, PMP
USAA

Business Need: Century conversion and certification of business applications to ensure correct processing of Year 2000 data.

Program Description: The change of century PMO provides
- ➤ Project management
- ➤ Outsourcing acquisition

➤ Timemachine/certification assistance
➤ Repository support
➤ Disaster recovery planning
➤ Communication

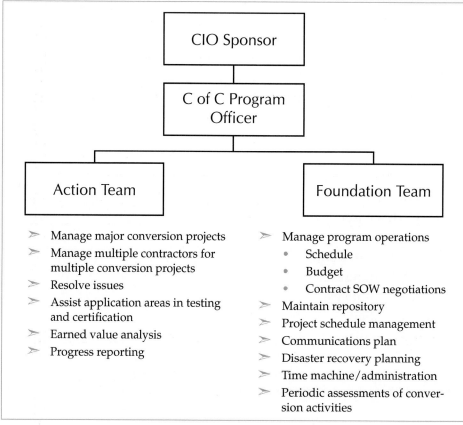

CIO Sponsor

C of C Program Officer

Action Team

➤ Manage major conversion projects
➤ Manage multiple contractors for multiple conversion projects
➤ Resolve issues
➤ Assist application areas in testing and certification
➤ Earned value analysis
➤ Progress reporting

Foundation Team

➤ Manage program operations
  • Schedule
  • Budget
  • Contract SOW negotiations
➤ Maintain repository
➤ Project schedule management
➤ Communications plan
➤ Disaster recovery planning
➤ Time machine/administration
➤ Periodic assessments of conversion activities

Figure 103.1   Change of century program office

The Challenge: Not a technical challenge as much as a management challenge

- Sizing
- Scheduling
- Funding
- Communications

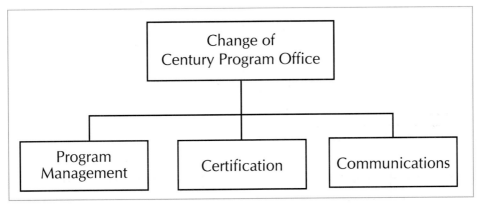

Figure 103.2 *Change of century program process*

Program Management Office

Business Need: Century conversion and certification of business applications to ensure correct processing of Year 2000 data

Program Description: The change of century PMO provides

- Project management
- Outsourcing acquisition
- Time machine/certification assistance
- Repository support
- Disaster recovery planning
- Communication

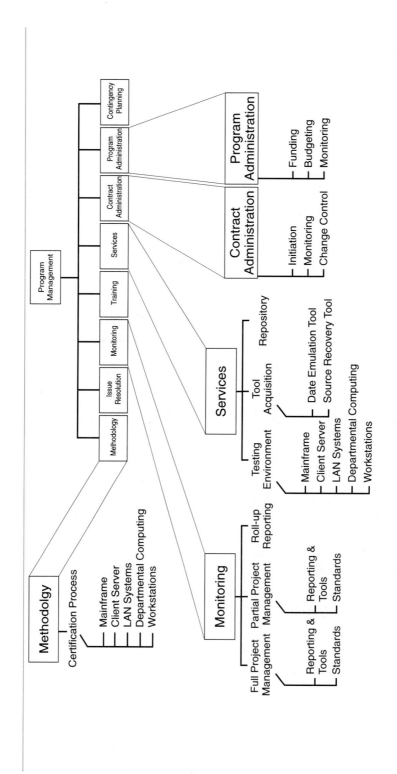

Figure 103.3   Program management process

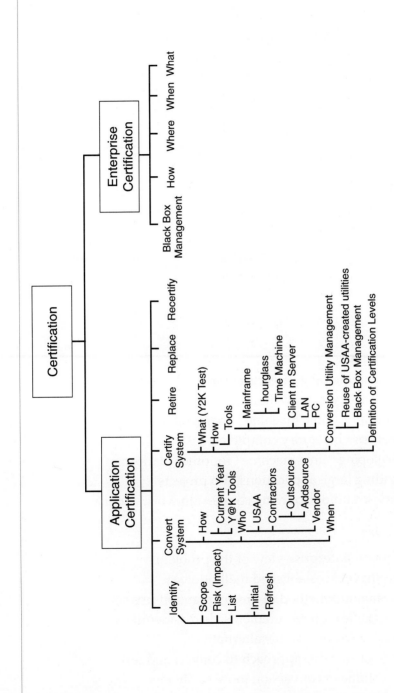

Figure 103.4 Certification process

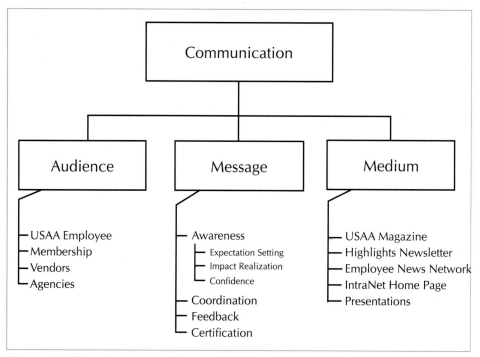

Figure 103.5   Communication process

Progress

- ➤ Outsourcing pilot projects completed
- ➤ Dependency analysis finalized
- ➤ Mainframe "time machine" operational
- ➤ Enterprise inventory completed
- ➤ Developing "time machine" for other platforms
- ➤ Dividing large applications into projects
- ➤ Inhouse and outsourcing conversion work underway

Lessons Learned

- ➤ Required enterprise view of the problem
- ➤ Must have an established methodology
  - Standard method of project plan roll-ups
  - Certification requirements clearly identified
- ➤ Outsourcing as a viable alternative
  - Cost effective approach to convert and test
  - Volume of conversion more easily met
  - Minimizes impact on other IS projects

➤ Requires consistent staffing to maintain continuity
  • Centralize project management staff
  • Avoid rotation of experienced members
➤ Communications is critical to success
  • Management
  • Business customers
  • Vendors
➤ Document future opportunities

Recommendations

➤ Market PMO concept with senior management
➤ Develop PMO organizational roles and responsibilities
➤ Pursue pilot outsourcing initiatives
➤ Establish communications plan
➤ Get started now!!!

104 *Program Management Office in Action*

Dick Lefkon
Year 2000 Committee of AITP SIG-Mainframe

Copyright © 1997 Dick Lefkon.
Adapted from author's August 9, 1987 *Computerworld* feature article.

[Editor: The general principles presented here should be followed in all projects, but they are especially needed for Year 2000 projects.]

Bill's first call after being made systems maintenance manager for catalog sales came from Frank, the vice-president handling cost containment. "Could Bill switch the weekly goods pricing tape by the end of the quarter, which was in six weeks?" he asked. It would save the firm at least a thousand dollars a month.

"Sure," Bill replied, "a tape's a tape."

Later it was discovered that while the new tape gave quantities in dozens, the old one used quantities in scores [twenties]. Said Hank, one of the old-timers, "I did notice that—I'm just not big on volunteering information."

This story, a composite based on the real experiences of several companies, raises a number of questions which the Year 2000 project head should consider. Did this manager do any of the following:

➤ Define his tasks before committing resources?

➤ Make sure the service agreements were final?

➤ Perform cost/benefit analyses?

➤ Get the users to rank their priorities?

➤ Require adequate testing and allow for regression testing?

➤ Get user validation of results?

➤ Coordinate testing by different user areas?

➤ Guarantee adequate technical input?

➤ Provide for staff continuity?

Nobody likes to hear the alarm clock in the morning. But we make sure it is on every night because we know it somehow benefits us. Similarly, reasonable controls on programming efforts may constrain the freedom of analysts, programmers and users, but they come to accept these controls because they realize the wisdom of implementing some safeguards, both on the work itself and on work flow emanating from the users.

An inexpensive on-line tracking and management database provides documentation of these controls while holding down the required signed documents to less than one loose-leaf binder per year.

True, many status reports will be distributed, but only signatures need be preserved on paper—the detailed data can be hidden away on disk.

Coping with the Real World

Year 2000 management—unlike new development—must cope with a world that already exists, inhabited by users, resources, code and personalities, none of which the manager has created and none of which is 100 percent dependable.

The difference between the two worlds is a study in contrasts in four areas: task definition, scheduling, standards and continuity.

➤ Task definition

  In new development, the objective can be determined in isolation; for Year 2000, the base applications are already in place.

➤ Scheduling

  In development, project components may have some flexibility, and completion date is the only deadline carved in stone; your Y2K remediation goal is fix *everything* early enough to be tested and adjusted before an ironclad deadline.

➤ Standards

Development teams are selected in part because they will do things in the way the project mandates.

By contrast, at least some captured staff members may not cooperate fully, feeling their own ways are more beneficial to themselves or the organization than the Y2K manager's.

➤ Continuity

Personnel with similar skills tend to behave as equals when a development effort gets rolling; however, in Y2K, the routine nature of the work may lead to people problems.

These four areas are ones in which the newly ordained Y2K manager may be greatly challenged.

The responsibilities of this unglamorous position can be held to reasonable proportions by setting up a firm structure to make most procedures routine. This practice is preferable to treating each software event as unique or, as in development, trying to mesh all tasks into a single, patterned whole. Crucial to the establishment of this structure are the forms used to explain, control and expedite the tasks.

A Clear Understanding

In many ways, the definition of a task is more urgent than its subsequent management. If the work agreed upon is not clearly understood—by user, technician or manager—even a well-structured control system will leak like a well-structured sieve.

Perhaps the move valuable advice managers can gather from this article is to *request* from users, *write down* and *publish* the most detailed paragraph possible concerning the task. Figure 104.1 provides an example.

The more the planned change is defined in user—not programmer—terms, the more likely users will be to approve completed work. This way, they can see that nothing less, more or different was requested initially.

The first defense for scarce systems resources is the service request form, on which the user first asks that a specific task be done.

Next, a user test plan (e.g., Figure 91.1) is completed up front; users who know what needs to be done define their topics objectively.

Finally, while most shops differ on the subject of formal programming specifications, maintaining a standard required form such as Figure 106.4 ensures that at least minimal investigation and planning take place. [Editor: for more detail, see Chapter 112.]

Planned Testing and Production Moves Date of this Report: 12/11/97			
Move to Production	Department	Title of Change	Description of Change
12/12/97	Accounting	Prevent Dual Logon	Same user ID entered second time should log off both
		Convert report 211 to online	Load report contents to disk file accessible to report retrieval package. Allow browsing only by depts 18-41 or sales managers
	etc.		
	Sales	Require manager approve online commission	Place Y N field on order entry screen 73 to permit manual override of std commission. Manager must match employee record.
	etc.		
12/26/97	etc.		
	Sales	Sort report 101 on region and volume	Page break for region. Skip lines between offices.
01/09/98	etc.		

Figure 104.1   **Planned Implementations Report**

Service Request Form

Basic to any successful maintenance and enhancement effort is the initial service request form.

This form should identify the relevant system, category of change, dates submitted and received, name and telephone number of user contact and authorizer, other departments potentially affected, a sequential tracking number, a brief title and a longer description and business justification for the change.

On the form's reverse side, a second page might be printed, consisting of two large columns for each of a dozen or so categories.

For each major category affected by the request, users describe the present function or data on the left and the desired outcome on the right. Any unaffected categories are marked "OK" in the right columns, thus permanently eliminating them from the scope of the request.

After all, users may not understand a data base structure, but they know better than programmers whether, for instance, the sales contest rewards deduced from the orders file are simply to be stored somewhere in payroll or are to be printed on checks right away.

And when priorities must be debated, the additional recorded detail means that business users can vie with each other over the value of a task, leaving the programming manager out of the debate.

The sequential tracking number is the keystone of honest and orderly task management. Just the fact that the brief title and its number are displayed regularly on a pending requests report makes users feel good, eliciting such responses as, "I haven't been ignored," and "The whole world knows I've asked the systems people to do this."

Pending Requests for Sales Department				11/26/97
Control Number	Work Status	Contact & Phone	Descriptive Title	Work Days
97078	Submitted	A. Welles 668-2315	Sort report 103 on region & volume	3
97135	Coding	D. Azier 558-5429	Require mgr approve online commission	12
etc.				

Figure 104.2   **Pending request report: overall or by unit**

This number may also prove helpful to users jockeying for priority among other requests.

Service requests that are not well formed should be sent back to the user.

This does not really require all that much backbone on management's part. If the user complains, "Why are you sending this back to me?" the software manager can simply explain why the request was returned and will, in general, receive a more concise submission containing such items as sample screens, reports and so on. [Editor: for a complete flowchart of the process of request and fulfillment, please refer to Figure 91.1.]

The fact that the users themselves scope out much of the task helps to distinguish maintenance programming from new development. So, sometimes, does the urgent nature of things, such as Y2K.

User Test Plan

Those who have children in school may recognize the phrase, "teach to the test." In the classroom, it is not always desirable to focus all efforts on what will be tested. But in programming, this restriction works well.

Formalizing the user test plan validates the outcome or fix. Once programming is complete, one of two things will happen during acceptance testing: Either the system will work as described, or it won't. If it does work, users approve it because they can see it is correct—from the user test plan form—as well as complete—from the initial service request form.

User Name	Date ___/___/___	Time :
User Phone	Department	User ID
Contact By ☐ Us ☐ Other	Contact ☐ Phone ☐ Visit ☐ Written	
The Problem ☐ Delivery ☐ Nonfile-Abend ☐ Files ☐ Other		
User Description of Problem		
User Description of Setup		
How We Helped		
Follow Up		Staff Initials

Figure 104.3   *User MIS Contact Form*

Specifying details on the user test plan also means that during coding the programmers can simulate the kinds of results for which users will be looking.

If business users complete the test plan before any coding specifications are written, they will still recall clearly what system features failed, under what conditions they failed, how the requested change will better the situation and exactly what would have happened had the fix or enhancement been in place.

This clear truth has 100 percent applicability to Year 2000 conversion efforts. A well-known Y2K-testing firm advised by the author, pulls aside and trains roomfuls of client non-technicians, in test case recognition, and has the *business*-side employees construct the test manuals which the technicians will use.

The process of thinking things through may bring to light either limitations or other related tasks that can be noted easily and publicly documented as a service request modification.

Although scheduling "changes to changes" as the second phase of the project is generally the best practice, sometimes users' test planning uncovers an urgently needed realignment.

Specification

After users describe the business use and desired test results of a requested change, it is generally up to a systems analyst to translate the business need into a programming specification. A checklist or fill-in form is a good place to start (see Figure 104.4). Listing items such as files that will be affected is worthwhile, even for small or quick jobs. Such a form is very easy to fill out for the simplest tasks, essentially by writing "NA" (not applicable) in almost every category. This helps the programmer by clarifying which system or code components can safely be bypassed.

Whatever format is used, coding specifications should stand on their own; a coder should not have to consult the specifications' author. Also, the specifications should be updated and reissued if the functional need changes.

At the discretion of systems management, users may be given a copy of the completed programming specifications form. They may not understand all its contents, but it provides documentary support, both for the labor estimate it contains and because of its relevance to user requests.

Straightforwardness also helps when describing resources. Showing three real available days per programmer per week rather than five padded ones offers two benefits: It is, and appears to be, honest, and it prevents cutting into the bone if and when the day arrives that new enhancements are drastically curtailed.

Scheduling: A Definite Work Flow

In situations in which high-level users compete for scarce programming resources, the maintenance manager must be a tactician—regularly saying no, saying nothing or saying yes but stalling any action.

Control No: 87135
Originator: D. Azzaire
Description: Require manager to approve on-line commission: place y/n field on order entry screen (#73) to permit manual override of standard commission. Subsidiary screen format attached. Manager must match employee record.

Report(s): _____

_____

Screen(s): _____

Function(s):_____

_____

Program(s): _____

Subroutine(s): _____

_____

Copy member(s): _____

Command file(s): _____

Logic added or changed: _____

_____

_____

_____

_____

Test case(s):_____

_____

No. of specimens for new reports attached: Mgr.: _____

No. of specimens for new file layouts attached: Pgmr.: _____

Time estimate: _____ workdays   Check here if continued: _____

Signatures: Mgr: _____   ___/___/___   Technical:_____   ___/___/___

*Figure 104.4   **Programming specifications form***

All of these tactics are made less uncomfortable and more credible by having a definite flow of stages through which every work request must pass.

Initial Service Request and Establishment of Priority

The first stage starts with the initial service request. If a report is needed, the user furnishes a sample of the desired format. If a new federal regulation must be implemented, it, too, should be attached, with appropriate user markup. Once the user submits the service request, the PMO head, or designee, decides whether the documented request is feasible. Nothing is wrong with a calm assertion that something is impossible, if it is.

Fair treatment of all users requires that, aside from production emergencies, no service requests be initiated formally over the telephone.

The sequential tracking number provides measures of currency and date priority. Regular public documentation of the descriptive title, extended detail and allocated workdays, including testing, helps focus attention on the agreed task and its cost.

Priority screening can be done within the systems department. Even if a request goes on the back burner, users will not feel totally ignored because the sequential number and title are distributed to all users every week.

Design and Time Estimate

After preliminary setting of priorities, a functional design and estimated time frame for the request is established. Ballpark figures for completion—for example, six to 18 months—are recommended for large projects. Such a project could itself require at least a day or two to estimate. This time should not be expended if users do not confirm that the request warrants immediate estimation. The time is better spent producing a one-time report of moderate importance rather than a cost estimate for an unsponsored project.

Through a weekly meeting or a central coordinator, users now establish the priority of their requests, listing which should start next. It is important that the attendant systems manager concentrate on giving honest technical advice and not intrude on lively discussions of priorities among the users.

"I make sure not to be the bad guy when I attend the steering committee meeting," notes James Ripplinger, director of MIS for Grenada Mailrite Services, Inc. in Richmond, B.C.

"I go in there carrying my list of proposed work items with their anticipated costs and benefits to the company," he explains. "Representatives of the various divisions then decide collectively what is best for the company. Nobody feels there is any favoritism because—whether or not they like it—they understand why efforts are being directed toward those specific tasks."

Detailed Design and User Test Plan

Next, the detailed design and the user test plan for each user-approved project are developed hand in hand.

After programming and unit/integration testing, users meet to work to improve upon the original user test plan. Whether in an ad hoc or regular meeting, representatives of departments that affect each other consider the change. Accounting, computer operations, programming and various other functional departments of the business pick through and upgrade the test plan.

Collectively, this group may well enhance the plan by raising issues that the person making the original request had not thought about. The group's varied viewpoints can help reveal different dangers and benefits.

Helpful Standards

The user work requests and scheduling discussed so far require interaction with external departments. But within the systems department itself, steps must be taken to ensure quality and maintainability of the software produced. Chapter 109 discusses coding standards.

Standards for coding and internal program documentation are important for maintainability. The aim is not to force programmers into a lockstep but rather to make each programmer's products look and perform in a manner sufficiently routine that they can be maintained by another trained technician.

This task is a bit more difficult to do in maintenance than in development. In the latter, the bulk of the application software has already been written. It may be undocumented, styled poorly or tailored to yesteryear's machine limitations and technology. And even if the logic flow were clear originally, it may have become concealed by years of successive patching.

Requiring the placement of a four-column modification log—date, programmer, change, purpose—at the top of each old program that has been modified, means that the next programmer or other investigator knows something about the least seasoned parts of the code.

Another documentation standard—requiring an average of one comment line per procedure lines, not rigidly interleaved—encourages coders to leave blank comment lines that guide the eye and to write boxed descriptions at the start of major processes.

A good practice is to hold one or more sessions in which the programming staff consider a set of proposed standards in a meeting chaired by the systems manager. The staff is given the opportunity to modify, reword, add or deleted standards subject to the manager's approval.

Such a process gets the programmers working as a group under management supervision, demonstrates to junior staff that certain good practices are industry-wide and avoids having the staff members perceive the standards as something meaningless that management has thrust upon them.

Testing

In the simplest installations, enhancements are programmed in a development environment or system and are subsequently migrated to the production environment. Placing an additional two or three distinct environments along this migration path may be preferable. Each successive library—or complete environment, including data and logon IDs—presumably maintains tighter control than the one preceding. Once a program is found to be satisfactory at a certain level of security, moving it onward protects it from inadvertent harm at that or a looser level of protection.

Once the programmer has unit-tested the code in development, an independent systems testing function can perform integration testing to ensure that individual transactions track properly through pre-existing programs. This subclass of testing need not involve users directly.

In the next physically distinct environment, the assurance testing function performs individual transaction testing from the user's viewpoint, concentrating not so much on program flow as on confirming the correct integration of those transactions through the broader system. Systems testing staff may assist here, but the program's authors are strictly excluded.

Finally, acceptance (UAT) testing involves users alone, possibly enhancing the assurance testing data but closely paralleling the real business situation in which systems assistance routinely does not take place. Simulation packages exist for building canned stress-testing data files, as detailed in Part 10. Lacking automation, one uses the usual data entry operators to perform a live parallel test if network volume is an issue.

The Human Element

Keeping coders and the on-line system at peak availability involves human relations at least as much as technical effort. In negotiations with other departments, the official confirming memo can be just as important as the initial deal struck, for without it, a good agreement can evaporate.

Within and outside the systems department, issues meetings ascertain status and identify open issues. No deal or resolution is expected in these meetings, and the manager has to control the urge to reach such conclusions.

In fact, unbiased observation and controlled communication are just as relevant as a resolution in dealing with staff supervision and system crises.

A standard requirement made by the corporate auditing department is that a proven backup site and disaster plan be established for physical plant mishaps. This idea may also be valid for staff members: Individuals who are reputed to be indispensable should be made replaceable as soon as soon as possible.

Noticing this, one new maintenance manager designated an enthusiastic trainee as resident JCL expert. With some coaching, this trainee absorbed the material and within two weeks truly was the corporate JCL leader. Eventually all employees learned JCL, and the supposedly key consultant, who subsequently failed a concealed examination in his area of expertise, was released from his job.

Sometimes, a manager may hesitate to elevate—or demote—a staff member because of the person's current image. But staff perceptions of each other can be changed, even reversed, as a result of visible management support and the showcasing of the individual's capabilities.

For Package:
  • Subleg Function Breakdown
  • Program Checklist
  • Overall System Flow

For Each Program:
  • General Description/Pseudocode
  • Functional Hierarchy Chart
  • Layouts/Copybooks/Specimens
  • Explained Formulas
  • Sensitive Logic
  • Edits
  • Errors/Responses
  • Planned Avorts
  • Test Data Description

Figure 104.5   Structured walkthrough document checklist

Function	Main	Infiles/Screens (by user)	Outfiles/Screens/Rpts (by user)
etc.			

Figure 104.6   Functional breakdown of system leg

Testing Real-Time Systems

User testing on a volatile real-time system requires tighter user coordination than on batch or even on a more stable real-time system.

A batch system—or the testing of distinct batch changes—could conceivably be done anytime the machine was available, as long as users were provided with comparison reports generated by the old programs against equivalent data.

Even a fairly static real-time system is easier to test because changes may be limited to one or two types of processing.

Testing Y2K changes may involve such interaction issues as whether to implement one change on schedule when others tested in interaction with that change have failed.

Volatile real-time systems present unique scheduling problems in testing modifications and enhancements.

A planning roundtable of users is necessary because the system intermingles the effects of service requests from unrelated departments.

Rewards and Crises

Maintenance/enhancement efforts depend on good upward communication. This is encouraged by showing that rewards go to those staff members who give high priority to the unit's announced needs and policies, even for small things like hand delivering the new report to a user so a human collects the "thank you" in person.

Otherwise, some individuals may opt for different rewards, such as the feeling of importance that they may derive from a departmental crisis.

A challenge to management is to detect that staff member who is eager to announce both inside and outside the systems department that a crisis exists and whom fellow workers consider to be "always calm during an emergency and knows just what to do."

The manager must resist the temptation to buckle before what may be an invented emergency: Some crises aren't.

Handling the Crisis

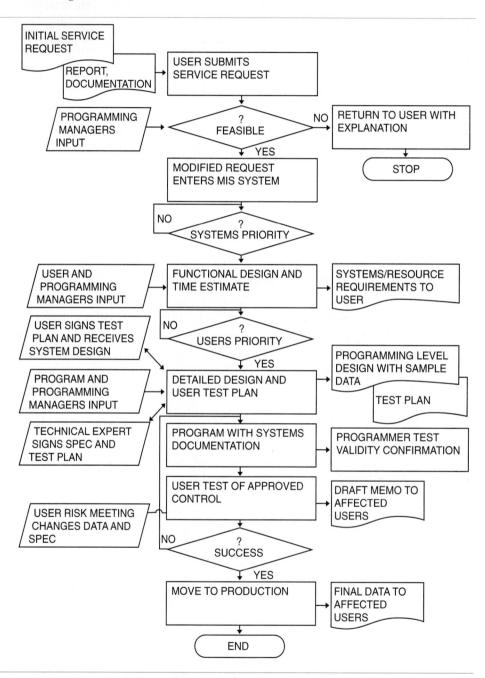

Figure 104.7   Workflow of user requests

Of course, crises do occur. The real-time system crashes; a key player on the team is hospitalized; the month-end profit-and-loss statement is found to be drastically wrong only two days after its electronic handoff; a routine mishap in the batch cycle cascades into round-the-clock data entry and the concomitant need for staff coverage.

After preliminary symptoms are gathered, the management team and relevant experts convene until all conceivable causes and actions have been listed and that list is reduced to a manageable size.

Specific staff members are made responsible for resolving the crisis, and the rest are sent back to their regular tasks but remain available to that crisis team.

A single contact point for business users should be established, but all systems staff should be kept abreast of the problem's current status: When can the staff resume regular operations? How late will the reports be? Which reports will initially be corrupt? What cleanup work will the user have to do? The important point here is to satisfy the user's need to know.

Minimize Disappointments

Maintenance and enhancement programming is a greater challenge to manage than new development.

Clearly, administered procedures minimize the disappointments in task definition, scheduling, standards and continuity. The familiar service request form can evolve within a simple automated MIS system to produce a variety of helpful reports: Next-to-Program, Recently Completed, Soon-to-Go-Live, Overall Requests, Requests by Department.

Where sufficient detail is available, the appearance of each item becomes an unambiguous, documented service contract.

Good instructions guide users in preparing a more definitive initial request, and an automatically produced test plan form gets users to supply an additional level of task definition before any systems resources are committed.

Automated programming specification forms deter serious omissions and help both users and the software manager to understand the extent of the task. Accurate costing is essential in establishing priorities for tasks that are competing for limited systems staff man hours.

Software documentation begins with placing a modification log in old programs as they are changed. In addition, new programs should implement full standard documentation and techniques.

Testing is standardized by securing the source code as it succeeds in progressively more realistic environments.

The scheduling of new programming is done primarily at a weekly users meeting, at which the maintenance manager serves primarily as a technical and feasibility advisor.

Continuity of system accessibility is increased by Help screens, on-line run books, automated source-code scanners/modifiers, and a definite approach to crisis management.

Continuity of collective staff expertise rests on cross-training, regular meetings, a clear chain of command and the elevation of those who help the organization.

The controls established by an automated management system encourage analysts, programmers and users alike to deal with the turbulence of urgent projects such as Year 2000.

Good controls also help these professionals think things through in a more organized fashion than they might otherwise.

Finally, a well-managed project engenders mutual respect between staff members and users—a necessity for its successful completion.

105   *Century Date Compliance*

Bill Goodwin
TickTickTick

At one end of the scale we have a definition of century date compliance from a consulting company: "Year 2000-compliant application systems are capable of correct identification, manipulation, and calculation using dates outside of the 1900-1999 year range and have been tested as such." Somehow, I get the feeling it was run off over a lunch hour.

At the other end of the scale, we have a man from GTE who gave a presentation on how his company created a Y2K program to make their own shop CDC. GTE has very generously been willing to release their findings. Their generosity may have been prompted by the realization that we're all in the same boat. You can't be selfish. If we don't help each other, we could all fail.

This program is so good, the man in charge of Y2K for the State of Texas copied it verbatim and put it on the Internet (without attribution) as their approach to defining CDC.

We are restating the GTE material, which should not be relied upon or used without consulting the source. It needs to be pointed out that this material was not intended for external use. We use it here only for exposition.

General Integrity

No value for current date will cause interruptions in desired operations.

> Nothing should break because of defects in how software handles system dates.

> Operating systems should maintain correct current date and provide correct current date to applications.

> Current date is accurate in other contexts. This covers:

- Some operating systems limit for system date (2038-01-19)
- Ignoring the century in an O/S Call
- Some earlier versions of PCs
- Problems with disk-archive products.

This also means your system date for the day after 12/31/1999 is not 01/01/1900 or April 1, 1980, and that Feb. 29, 2000 is a valid date. In other words, the current date will always be accurate.

Data Integrity

All manipulations of time-related data (dates, durations, days of week, etc.) will produce desired results for all valid date values within the application domain.

Manipulations include:

> Calculating durations, days of week, dates after duration, converting between representations and formats, converting between calendars

> Storing, retrieving, sorting, searching, indexing

> Any operations using dates will work as expected for all reasonable values

> "Reasonable" is application-specific.

This covers:

- Negative ages for people
- Invoices
- Depreciation
- 366 days and February 29 in 2000
- 99 in year field interpreted as forever
- 00 in year field treated as an interrupt or no data
- Screen edits rejecting valid dates in 2000.

(The Social Security Administration uses an algorithm to convert the two-digit year field to four digits internally.)

Explicit Century

Date elements in interfaces and data storage permit specifying century to eliminate date ambiguity.

- ➤ Ability to accept and accurately retain century designations in date elements
- ➤ You don't have to use it, but the capability must be available.
- ➤ Applies to any representation of date (e.g., ISO 6801, base and off-set, military, etc.)

This covers:

- Any example of century ambiguity
- Storing and retaining the century accurately
- Default century in application
- Third-party product is 19xx.

Automated disk archiving lost three months of data in 1995 because the system added five years to the year field, got "00" and compared it to the current date.

Implicit Century

For any date element represented without century, the correct century is unambiguous for all manipulations involving that element.

- ➤ "Century ambiguity" can't *always* be resolved with the *available data*.
- ➤ The goal is to eliminate century ambiguity rather than force a representation of date.
- ➤ Allow for applications that must use two-digit year in specific cases, can resolve century on-the-fly rather than reformat massive, archived data to contain explicit century and have limited real estate on screens and reports and have no ambiguity.

This covers:

- Date-of-birth field versus invoice-due-date field
- Expiration date encoded on credit card
- Dates in electronic commerce.

In essence, GTE did not use a "one-size-fits-all" method. They took a hybrid approach—a little of this and a little of that.

How Does this Spec Help You?

Or, "How does writing the spec help you?" You are expected to do the work yourself. This doesn't mean you can't use their findings, but it does mean you have to rewrite the spec to address your own situation. You can use writing the spec to help you focus as you go through the various stages:

> Design your inventory program
> Drive your impact analysis—if a there is a two-digit year field in a program, is it a critical, serious or cosmetic problem?
> Guide conversion decisions—will you expand the fields in this program and not that one?
> Develop test plans/procedures. This is the most important reason for writing the spec—you will need it to write your test plan
> Update design standards—they can use this spec when designing new systems. This will ensure CDC
> Select third-party products—are the products you're looking at compliant with your spec?
> Select outsourced services—can they, and will they, guide their work by your spec?

*Don't forget that **you** are ultimately responsible* for the project, no matter how many outsiders you hire.

106 *Standards*

Dick Lefkon
Year 2000 Committee of AITP SIG-Mainframe

Copyright © 1997 Dick Lefkon

Coding standards, especially when they are set with the enthusiastic help of programmers, work. Such standards are usually self-enforced with little need to inspect each line of code.

If such shared decision making is in place, there may even be times when a staff member will suggest removing some rules. A manager's sense of the ideal (your ego?) may suffer slightly; yet the programs will be better and more maintainable.

The 40 standards contained here may not be a perfect fit for every manager's needs. The process used to develop them may be the best path to take, however.

How Rules Were Developed

Employee and consultant programmers alike were invited to attend two major meetings during regular business hours. The coders and designers on every relevant application team—not just representatives form one manager—participated in at least one session. Stressed was that these meetings are not an extracurricular activity but rather a regular part of the assigned workload.

Before each meeting convened, a preliminary set of standards was written on the markerboard.

Then staff was invited to brainstorm, giving reasons and negotiating additions, modifications or striking particular standards. As one participant put it, "The only way to get people to stick to standards is by consensus that they're good. Because of the brainstorming, we felt the standards were our own."

Match with Skills, Common Practice

Another side effect of such input—standards are not at variance with the skills of existing staff.

If even a single experienced programmer cannot accept a particular rule—and peer pressure by other staff hasn't taken over where the discussion leader's persuasion has failed—the standard is dropped immediately. It's erased in plain view of everyone.

Aware or not, that objector has just bought into support of the full set of rules eventually produced by this meeting. Others also present evidence that standards will not be imposed arbitrarily, yet must be observed once finalized.

This author used this step with a senior technician who was reluctant even to enter the room and join the others who were shaping the new rules. Her objection from outside the doorway was immediately acted upon. Subsequently, she did support the full set of standards, and years later remarked (concerning Rule 37 in this article), "I hate the numbers, but I follow it."

The senior staff with broad experience will help to ensure that the final set of rules is consistent with practice elsewhere. The junior staff sees their technical leaders support standards that are reasonable and positive. They also observe and participate in the discussion of why the various practices are desirable.

Tell What the Program Does

Rule 1: The most basic documentation improvement for any program is a modification log near the top of that program. Its columns are titled DATE, NAME, CHANGE and REASON. This identifies the programmer to be consulted in case of failure; contains a description of the

Tell What It Does

1. Modification Log

2. Retro-Document: Files, Calls, JCL

3. Hyphenate Fields

4. Hyphenate Fields

Control the Flow

5. GO TO Same Thought

6. GOGACK, Don't STOP

7. SECTIONS or THROUGH

Structure

8. Keep Main Stem General

9. Segregate READ, WRITE, HSKP, Exceptional, Occasional

10. Indent Subordinates Only

11. Use Parentheses

12. Avoid NOT

13. Nest up to Six

Code Efficiently

14. Frequent Logic Early

15. Realtime Messages Inline

16. COPY, Don't CALL

17. WRITE large TP Handoffs

Document the Dump

18. "XX WORKING STORAGE STARTS HERE.X"

19. Fullword Flags & Counters

20. INTO and FROM

Plan for Change

21. Library DB Code

22. Avoid Table Values

23. Softcode Limits

Update Status

24. Use 88s

25. Close with Statistics

26. Save Process Name

27. Crash with Hints

28. BLLSELF and RELOAD

TP Screens

29. Initially ERASE

30. Subsequent DATAONLY

31. Explain First Error

32. Use Stop Bytes

Eliminate Clutter

33. FILLER Unreferenced

34. No ALTER, DEPEND, CORR

35. Don't Continue VALUEs

Document

36. Prefix Field Names

37. Number Paragraphs

38. Don't MULTIPLY

39. No Special Characters

40. No NOTE

Figure 106.1   **Summary of standards** *(Courtesy of* Data Management *Magazine)*

present change for comparison with the work request and test results; and provides an indication of which prior changes may still be recent enough to result in bugs related to circumstances infrequently occurring.

Rule 2: Document retroactively. No matter the quality of a system's program, it will most likely need ongoing maintenance. This will become adequately documented over time if insertion of the documentation is required prior to any testing of program fixes and enhancements. The REMARKS section at the top of the program should include a minimum function description, a list of files and called programs with purposes and a modification log. Batch programs also might include a representative job control language (JCL) to assist others in using the code.

Enforcement of this retro-documentation requirement may be uncomfortable at first. Once some programmers conform, the rest will follow.

Rule 3: No unhyphenated data names. COBOL was first created, in part, to be self-documenting, allowing management to peek into and understand the program's workings so that slick consultants could not hand in the same symbol-laden code again and again and charge high fees repeatedly for work they hadn't really done.

The purpose of COBOL's 30-character naming is defeated if the variables are named C1 (as in BASIC) or YTDSAL (as in FORTRAN). Demanding at least one hyphen per field name encourages coders to write meaningful names such as TOTAL-COST-AFTER-TAXES. This takes up only slightly more storage for the source code—but no extra core storage at all when the program has been compiled and actually runs!

Moreover, programmers don't have to keep typing the longer name repeatedly because they generally use online editors when composing or inputting their source code.

Rule 4: Average one "Starline" per PROCEDURE line. Every major programming language provides the facility for inserting comment lines: COBOL and BAL (*), PLI and JCL (/*), BASIC (REM), FORTRAN (C), etc. One way to get programmers to write good advice for later maintenance is to require that on average there be one comment line for each procedural line of code.

One-comment-line-per-statement emphatically does not mean that alternating lines must interleave. Whenever programmers rigorously do that (usually as a joke), the code is in fact less clear than before. "MOVE SALARY TO REPORT" only distracts from the basic readability of the original COBOL, "MOVE MST-ANNUAL-SALARY TO RPT-ANNUAL SALARY." Similar to inclusion of print-oriented compiler commands like SKIP2, such clutter can actually increase the number of coding errors (hiding the absence of a period in a long string of conditional statements, for example).

Instead, most programmers will comfortably summarize each paragraph or section in a box at its top, interspersing blank starlines within the code to emphasize important groupings visually, yet saving between-the-lines comments for especially confusing procedures. Some good programmers write a complete set of comments under the main paragraph and section headings before filling in the detailed code. One recently recalled that it "tells me this is the business reason for doing that. Besides guiding my initial coding, the comments help me later on to refresh my understanding."

To repeat—comment lines can be valuable even if they contain only spaces. They emphasize graphically the inherent structure of the logic.

Other visual formatting that enhances readability includes underlining the names of paragraphs and called programs, and indentation of levels. One of the properties of COBOL and other high-level languages is that they are written free-form without the need to enter commands in certain columns. Thus, if there is a hierarchy of logic or data, this can be displayed visually. It helps the reader avoid having to guess which is the more important or governing aspect of the logic or data storage.

Where Do We Go Next?

Rule 5: GO TO within the same thought. Many people have the mistaken impression that "GO TO" is a dirty word. It isn't—as long as the eye can still see where to GO TO.

If the GO TO is used to loop back to the top of the paragraph, or jump to its concluding exit, no confusion will result. It is only when program control is transferred to an entirely different program location that its return must be guaranteed by the preferential use of PERFORM over GO TO.

If a single pencil line, drawn through the "GO TO" control points and back, starts to look like a tangle of spaghetti, then the code should be made more modular. Just place each function unit in its own performed paragraph or SECTION. A PERFORM verb in the controlling paragraph provides the benefit of grabbing control back immediately after the end of the invoked paragraphs(s). This eliminates the need to pencil in traffic lines all over the program.

Rule 6: GOBACK, don't STOP RUN. Another control issue involves the ending of a called program. "GOBACK" or "EXEC CICS RETURN" hands control back to the immediate invoker of this program. But "STOP RUN" abruptly surrenders control to the operating system itself. This means that if a called date-conversion program ended in "STOP RUN," its invokers would never finish their work. That's because, when the called program was over, it would pass control directly to the system, washing out the calling program in the process!

Rule 7: Use SECTIONS throughout, or place at end. When the word SECTION is added to a paragraph label, everything under it (up until the next SECTION heading) will be executed as a unit when that label is PER-FORMed. If SECTIONs are only allowed for the SORT verb, place them at the end or else they will swallow the rest of the program as well.

Without SECTIONs, always use THROUGH to dictate an exact ending point of a PERFORM sequence.

Be Structured and Clear

Rule 8: Keep the main stem general. It is amazing how many people think that "TOP-Down Programming" is a code that starts at the top of the page and proceeds straight down the page, ending at the bottom of the page.

This, in fact, is better termed "In-Line" or "Straight-Line" coding. It is often quite desirable for teleprocessing, where a GO TO or PERFORM might result in thrashing and delays due to losing the storage for that piece of code while the computer was occupied elsewhere.

"Top-Down" coding refers to an approach that starts with a high bird's eye view and gradually focuses on smaller and more limited processes. Through the use of the PERFORM verb, a main stem—which simply names the broad business functions—gives way to high-level paragraphs that describe these in business terms. It eventually leads to yet more subordinate layer(s) of paragraphs that contain a nuts-and-bolts code.

The main stem is left purposely vague.

In fact, a properly planned program can be started by coding all the main paragraph names and their interconnecting PERFORM statements. Thus, programming is truly built around the program's structure. An original purpose of the COBOL language is achieved: Lay managers can read and understand a good deal of what is happening in the code.

Rule 9: In Batch, Segregate and PERFORM all READ, WRITE, Page turns, Housekeeping, Exception and Occasional Processing, as long as straight-line coding is not required. Segregating business or coding processes has three main benefits. Each process can be written and tested independently and legitimately validated. Isolation means that a procedure can be changed without searching for its side effects all over the code. When time is critical, coding gangs can attack all the lowest level paragraphs at once.

Rule 10: No indentations for nonsubordinates. Indentation of subordinate conditions in "IF" logic helps reinforce visually the condition structure and the actual number of tests being performed at the same time.

Yet when a series of ELSE/IF tests really reflects a classification or "case structure" analysis, no true subordination is taking place and the series of clauses should line up flush, not diagonally across the page.

As a matter of fact, rather than being indented, these parallel ELSE/IFs are best arranged in a particular sequence—descending order of frequency of occurrence in the real business world.

While not as neat looking as a lineup on ascending transaction code, this sequencing will insert business knowledge into the code. It also makes the program run slightly faster through elimination of value comparisons that almost always fail to match.

Rule 11: Use Parentheses for Complicated Logic. (Self-explanatory.)

Rule 12: Avoid "NOT." With minimal effort, most conditions based on a negative can be rephrased in a positive way specifying a new outcome opposite to the original. Not only does this enhance readability, it also avoids the bug in some COBOL compilers which cannot interpret the word "NOT" properly when the logic becomes even slightly complicated.

Rule 13: Maximum "IF" nesting is six. "IF CITY-IS-DETROIT, THEN IF TODAY-IS-FRIDAY, THEN IF SALARY-IS-BIWEEKLY" is an example of nested "IF" logic. Assuming each subordinate level is indented four spaces for reading clarity, such logic can eliminate the mind-boggling quantity of GO TOs that used to make readers of FORTRAN and Assembler cross-eyed.

The cutoff of six levels is greater than the usually prescribed three or five, for this reason: In general there will be either "a few" or "very many" nested conditions. If there are very many, obviously the logic must be subdivided, probably spreading it over more than one paragraph. If there are only a few, giving a wide boundary means that the rule can be obeyed in more cases without the programmer having to get permission to violate it.

Rule 14: Place frequent logic early. Placing all the most commonly used procedural logic near Working Storage mans it is less likely to be "paged out" of storage. One-time codes such as sorts and housekeeping tasks should be placed at the end, since they will be paged out once at worst.

Rule 15: Place Realtime Messages in the code. Every CICS teleprocessing program receives its own new copy of Working Storage. Fixed literal data placed there will use up its own storage footprint over and over for as many users as are running that program. But all users share only a single copy of the Procedure Division. So that's where fixed literals should be placed. Also all lengths (except for RECEIVE INTO) should be numbers in the code, not symbols.

Rule 16: COPY inline any teleprocessing calls less than one page. To avoid the delays associated with loss of control, teleprocessing programs should redundantly contain code for small routines that might constitute called programs in a batch environment.

Rule 17: Consider WRITE/WRITEQ to pass more than 4k. When a very large amount of data must be passed to another teleprocessing program, limited core storage may be monopolized unnecessarily while that program is getting started. Sending the data temporarily elsewhere will free up some of the storage associated with that terminal. [Editor: This rule dates back to 1985; in ESA systems it can be ignored.]

Document the hexadecimal dump, too!

Rule 18: Working storage starts here. This works especially well in the IBM world. When a program crashes, it produces a formatted hexadecimal dump of core memory. A special translation column, occupying 32 characters on the right side of the page, displays an English language version of any hexadecimal data that can be translated (with periods holding the place of whatever cannot). Thus, as a programmer gazes down the right column of the dump, the eye is caught by a 32-byte roadblock that says "XX.PGMNAME STORAGE STARTS HERE.X."

This eye-catcher runs the full width of that column, either as a wraparound or straight across it. Assuming that program flags, counters and other diagnostic aids have been placed at the top of storage, they can be picked out immediately from the dump without requiring the most recent compile listing for that program.

This is important because the correctly dated listing is usually not available at 2 am (or even 3 pm) when the debugging takes place—if at all.

Rule 19: Use word flags and signed packed numbers. Usually no harm is done (see Rule 15) if a "file flag" is large enough to have values "OPEN", "DONE", "CLOS" instead of 1, 9 or 2. When viewed at the top of the dump this makes the file's status immediately clear. Each four-letter word neatly fills one hexadecimal column of the formatted dump, which makes tracking easy.

Similarly, a seven-digit packed (COMP-3) number occupies its own column and is easy to spot because it begins with zeros and ends with a letter representing the sign. Insisting on packed, rather than binary (COMP), numbers also means that garbage data is detected immediately as nonnumeric and is not left unnoticed until somebody receives a multi-million dollar weekly paycheck.

By embedding a four- or eight-byte value (such as "COUNTERS") in a FILLER field preceding diagnostic data, they are referenced even more clearly, at minimal storage cost.

Flags and counters should be detail fields (level 05) in one or two high-level records set aside for this purpose. An archaic use as individual items (level 77) confuses and is not necessary.

Rule 20: In batch, READ INTO and WRITE FROM. You will always have a full copy of the record in Working Storage next to all the important diagnostic data.

Rule 21: Use library code for databases. External records and other common formats should be copy-members, so they can be changed consistently in all programs. This also applies to definition and binding of files and segregated I/O procedures. Within a few years your installation will be using a different access method, and the conversion should not require inspecting every paragraph of every program.

Rule 22: Leave tables in the database. You may have an office bet on which territory will become the 51st state, but the code should not have to be changed (and storage realigned) when it happens. The only justifiable hard-coded table values are those in a table of hexadecimal test bytes or screen attribute bytes. Such code, of course, should be stored centrally and COPYed. Also, any table handling should use indexes (required by SEARCH) and not add the excess baggage of subscripts.

Rule 23: Softcode all limits. Counter stops should be given values in Working Storage whether a date cutoff or the number or print lines per page. When your customer statements expand you will change one value, not several comparison statements where a thumb might slip and harm the code.

Constantly Update Status

Rule 24: Use conditions instead of logical comparisons. The COBOL data level 88 permits easy testing for "CUSTOMER-IS-RETAIL" instead of "CUSTOMER-CLASS = 1 OR 3 OR 7 OR 26 OR 42."

Rule 25: Close with statistics. All significant events should be counted and displayed at the finish.

Rule 26: Update location in program. Especially in teleprocessing, set aside an 8-byte area on top of Working Storage to receive the name of each procedure as it begins. Then the dump tells immediately what was happening when the program crashed. This rule, combined with Rules 19 and 20, makes up for any CEDF or TRACE/EXHIBIT statements eliminated when the program goes live.

Rule 27: When crashing, tell why. Especially in teleprocessing, use a handling paragraph to display messages and key helpful data, or to write these to a trouble file. Better still, invoke a common routine which does this.

Rule 28: Update BLLSELF and SERVICE RELOAD. At the start of a teleprocessing program, move a base-locator pointer to a binary full-word WS-BLL-SELF-POINTER preceded by an embedded filler marked "BLLSELF" to help find it.

"SERVICE RELOAD" should also be used at program startup and every time a pointer is SET to make sure the addressing field is updated.

Screens Should Communicate

Rule 29: Use ERASE with the initial SEND. If no variable data is sent to start with, also use MAPONLY to save time.

Rule 30: Use DATAONLY with subsequent SENDs. The map is already there, so only refresh the modified data.

Rule 31: The first screen error gets the message. Multiple error messages are not a common practice. The operator expects to correct the first mistake first.

Rule 32: Use stop bytes after enterable fields. Why make the operator keep hitting the key until the end of the screen line when only eight characters can possibly be entered?

Eliminate Clutter

Rule 33: All unreferenced variables are FILLER. Compiled program listings generally contain orderly reference tables of paragraph headings and field names. If the code does not PERFORM (or GO TO) a paragraph label, it should be starred into a comment or eliminated altogether. That way, only real headings will appear in the reference listing.

Because variable fields vastly outnumber paragraph names, the situation is much more critical for field names. The cross-reference listing shows the exact number of the line where each field was defined and of every line that references it. This key diagnostic aid may be the only way to find out how a key variable came to contain a wrong value. The listing size can be halved and the clutter removed by using "FILLER" instead of a meaningful name where a field must be defined so that adjoining ones are spaced apart properly. "FILLER" fields contain the same data as otherwise, but they don't show up on the cross-reference.

Rule 34: Don't ALTER, DEPEND or CORRespond. "ALTER" is an archaic verb which actually changes the load module as it is running.

When the run crashes, the truly "current" state of the code will not be reflected by any listing in your possession.

"GO TO DEPENDING ON" may save a bit of space over a well-documented case structure using ELSE/IFs. But it is unmaintainable because some day a line of code will be erased or added and the target paragraphs will become mysteriously out of sequence.

"MOVE CORRESPONDING" is another archaic form that once was used to save a few source code keystrokes when moving many fields. Unfortunately it only provides one statement number for the total operation and hides the identity of the particular MOVE which resulted in the bad data field.

Rule 35: Don't continue VALUEs. Instead of requiring column placement to continue a long value, break up the item into several FILLER fields, each short enough to hold its value on one line of code. The result is the same but the program is easier to read and maintain.

More on Documentation

Rule 36: Prefix the data names. Fields belonging to the same record should have the same two- or three-letter prefix. General fields in working storage might begin WS-.

Rule 37: Number and underline paragraph labels. Ideally, paragraph labels should be up to 25 characters long, including a 3- or 4-digit prefix. The paragraph exit consists of the same name, plus -EXIT. These will be printed next to each other on the procedure cross-reference listing. Left-most digits describe processes or program subdivisions, with subordinate numbers corresponding to detail steps. Common prefixes are 0000- for housekeeping and 9000- for exceptions. Whichever is used, it will also help locate paragraphs during debugging.

Rule 38: Don't MULTIPLY or DIVIDE. The COBOL "COMPUTE" verb (or BASIC "LET") permits calculations to proceed using standard elementary algebra formulas. The "MULTIPLY" verb is misleading because it actually places the result in the opposite variable to what most people expect. Long ago, business users may not have been able to use "/" for division, etc. They surely can today. Ambiguity is eliminated if one standard for computations is followed. Additions and subtractions should follow this format, too, except in the common usage of incrementing or decrementing a counter by one.

Rule 39: No special characters besides COMPUTE's *, (), =, −, /. Printers have different character sets. Not every printer has an exclamation point or even the sideways "< >" that represent "LESS THAN" and "GREATER THAN." "IF ANNUAL-SALARY IS GREATER THAN

SOCIAL-SECURITY-CUTOFF THEN PERFORM 3010-BYPASS-SOC-SEC-DEDUCTION" is easily understood. It wouldn't be if it began, "IF ANNUAL-SALARY   SOCIAL-SECURITY-CUTOFF" due to the absence of the mathematical symbol on that print chain.

Rule 40: No "NOTE." An archaic form of the starline (*), "NOTE" used to be employed in procedures to place comments on the same line as the code itself. Once "NOTE" is encountered, all other text until the next period is considered a comment. Not only would this clutter the code if used, it contains an unexpected danger: "NOTE" at the top of a paragraph (or section) will change that entire unit of code into one big comment. In fact, this "danger" gives rise to the only helpful use of "NOTE". During testing it can be used to shut off all paragraphs other than the one(s) being investigated.

Applying the Standards

The large-scale teleprocessing and database coding standards given here are unfortunately not ordinarily catalogued and explained in writing.

Thoughtful steps, such as those described here, should be taken to adapt to these or other standards in the installation and the sensibilities of the programmers who must use them.

However, even if the reader did not go through the implementation steps suggested, and instead promulgated rules which were much less inclusive than these, such standards would still boost the quality and maintainability of programs in an installation that previously had no required coding rules.

It is better to have almost any set of common standards than to have none.

Programmers must not be forced repeatedly to write in such a way that they feel is ridiculous.

Whatever standards are required, it should be understood that they are to be observed "if at all possible." There should be written justification supplied where the technician feels a particular rule cannot or should not be carried out.

By requiring a specific reason for not applying a standard in a specific situation, management shows respect for the programmer's intelligence and initiative. This does not undermine the validity and enforceability of the overall set of rules by permitting wholesale violation of one or more of them.

Avoid Common Management Pitfalls

The author recalls two unwelcome remarks concerning the implementation of the standards described, one from a subordinate manager and one from a colleague in a technical support area.

When the work group was first charged with developing standards, the under-manager said, "I am glad we got the standards task so early. I have heard of some interesting methods used at Company X, and if you agree with the writeup we can make sure the programmers do things our way."

After the first brainstorming session, but before the second, the colleague challenged, "I think you are going about this all wrong. How can your people respect you as a manager if you let them set their own standards? It is management who should discuss and decide on the rules, then hand them to the staff as policy to be followed."

It was fairly easy to explain to this junior manager about asking favors too often. From time to time a truly urgent and unpleasant task simply must be done. A staff member is asked to go out of his or her way to do it. This cheerful willingness can be used up too quickly if daily every staff member must grudgingly follow a set of procedures that is perceived as both remote and flawed. Answering the colleague required some cleverness but was really no more difficult.

A person so fixed on rigid lines of authority could be answered pleasantly if not altogether comfortably. When the logic of buy-ins failed to sway, the colleague was simply reminded that the manager charged with the task should be accorded the same free hand as anyone else. Only time would tell whether the more participatory mode of creating and enforcing standards would succeed. Some may have yet another reservation about the standards development process described here: "What about dropping a rule when only one person objects? Isn't that a bit extreme?"

The programmer who objected from outside the room was emphatic about the wrongness of the rule. The discussion leader could not even get a "Well, okay" out of her. And, most important, no other programmer rose to defend the standard in a peer-to-peer dialogue.

The fact that nobody pressed for the rule proposed constituted no glowing enthusiasm for it. The objector probably voiced what others were thinking. And the removal of that rule helped prevent halfheartedness among the other staff.

Having a supportive programmer at the adjacent desk is the best way to see that each staff member observes teleprocessing and database standards.

107 *Migration Weekend*

IBM

Reprinted by permission from GC28-1251 *The Year 2000 and 2-Digit Dates: A Guide for Planning and Implementation* Copyright © 1995, 1996 by International Business Machines Corporation.

To accomplish a successful migration and eliminate your current Year 2000 exposures, you will need to follow a well-architected migration plan and prepare to execute that plan prior to actually performing the migration. This section provides an outline that you can use as a checklist of those steps that will help you plan, prepare, and execute your migration. Note that some steps might not be necessary for your specific environment, and your environment might require steps other than those listed here.

[Editor's Note: Most people reading this book have already survived a Migration Weekend. But this one will be bigger than you've ever seen! Besides, you've forgotten most of the prep steps you took then, and should probably circulate "Migration Weekend" to everyone on that team.

Every smart enterprise has an annual walkthrough of its Business Recovery looseleaf book. And you'll need more than one rehearsal to perfect a Y2K migration weekend of *any* size. For example, Christos Andritsoyiannis' IS staff could all fit into a large 'rec' vehicle, but in Chapter 92 you saw that his dress rehearsals ran too long and sent the BIAMAX team back to the drawing board!]

An Example Plan for Migration

1. Plan for Migration
   - Determine the sequence of steps needed for migration
   - Review the migration procedures with your system administration staff and your end-user community
   - Determine the resources/time required for migration
   - Assign individuals/organizations to each migration step
   - Document the migration sequence and responsibilities
   - Develop a schedule for migration of the new system to reach production mode
2. Examine all changed data that use new/changed date format
   - Determine the source of the new data in the existing systems
   - Determine the data that can be converted automatically
   - Determine the data that must be converted manually

3. Design bridges/interfaces among packages and reusable modules to maintain compatibility, if needed
   - Design bridges/interfaces to application packages, if needed
   - Design bridges/interfaces to reusable application systems, if needed
   - Design bridges/interfaces to old systems that will coexist with the new systems, if needed
   - Design tests for the verification and validation of these bridge facilities, if needed
4. Design procedures for manual data conversion
   - Update documents/procedures that will be used for manual data entry
   - Determine checking mechanism for the accuracy and completeness of manually entered data
   - Design the new screens with new date format for manual entry of new data and review with your end-user community
   - Design/update the software to load the manually prepared data into the new system
   - Run a rehearsal of the manual data entry and estimate the impact of the new data format on data entry time
5. Design procedures for automated data conversion
   - Design new software or use automated tools for automated data conversion
   - Determine a checking mechanism for the accuracy and completeness of automatically converted data
   - Design recovery procedures for conversion of data errors caused by missing data
   - Estimate the resources and time for automated data conversion
6. Develop the data conversion systems
   - Develop subsystems to convert existing data
   - Develop subsystems for the entry of new data
   - Develop bridges/interfaces to old systems which will remain in production
   - Develop bridges/interfaces to application packages and reusable modules
   - Verify and validate the accuracy of the data conversion systems
7. Plan the hardware installation for new system, if needed.

This might include upgrading your operating system to a machine capable of running Year-2000-ready software as well as other system components such as storage resources. Additional storage (DASD or tape) that could double your current needs might be required to provide:

➤ Backup of the original source code prior to your Year 2000 conversion

➤ Space to store the new source libraries following your Year 2000 conversion

➤ Space for the new versions of the system software while it is being installed and tested, while the old versions are still in production

➤ Backup of the original data bases prior to your Year 2000 conversion

➤ Space for the new versions of the data bases (which will require additional space due to expanded date fields) while the old versions are still in production

➤ Test file space

➤ New JCL (and PROC) libraries to handle situations such as: sort problems, system parameter changes, program name changes, data set name changes, while the old JCL (and PROCs) are still in production

➤ Backup of your current load libraries

➤ Space for the new load libraries while the old versions are still in production.

8. Plan for final system testing

➤ Determine the testing strategy

➤ Develop the detailed test plan and schedule

➤ Determine the types of tests to be conducted on the new system

➤ Plan the testing environment

  • Design the migration tests for the systems and applications

  • Determine what testing software or tool(s) will be used for each type of testing

  • Determine what testing libraries will be used for each specific set of programs and data

  • Install needed testing software. For example, test data generator, test utilities, debugging utilities, and so on.

  • Build test libraries, and test data

  • Coordinate the testing with your development team and your system administration staff

9. Documentation and training
   - Update your 'corporate standard guideline'
   - Update your technical documentation. For example, development guidelines and testing handbooks
   - Update the production procedures
   - Update the user documentation
     - Update the on-line documentation, including HELP screens, on-line manuals, computer-aided training, and so on.
     - Test the on-line HELP and training aids with your end users to evaluate the acceptance of the new on-line information
     - Update all hard-copy documentations to reflect changes and review those documentation with your end users
     - Plan and conduct training program to smooth the migration process

Perform Migration

1. Update production procedures, if necessary
2. Install the Year-2000-ready production system environment
   - Coordinate with vendors for the hardware installation, if needed
   - Install the hardware of the new production system, if needed
   - Coordinate with system programmers/operators for installation of the Year-2000-ready software
   - Install the Year-2000-ready system/vendor/application software on the new production system
3. Perform data conversion process
   - Load existing data into the new system's databases
   - Execute the data conversion programs or automated tools for data conversion
   - Load manually-prepared data through data entry
   - Integrate the existing and converted data
   - Test the integrated data to verify data integrity
4. Perform final system/migration testing
   - Plan the sequence in which separately developed subsystems will be tested and verified in reasonable combinations.
   - Verify that the portions of the system that have no changes still run properly as changes are made to other portions of the system
   - Verify that the program handles all its transactions correctly and remain stable for a defined period of time

> Verify that the system can accept input from, and provide output to, other systems with which it interfaces as interfaces change
> Verify end-user acceptance of the new system to certify the system as acceptable for production.

5. Activate the new system in production
> Switch the new system to production mode
> Run the new system in parallel with the old system
> Phase out the old system as the new system becomes stable

6. Migration review
> Monitor and evaluate system performance, throughput, and reliability
> Determine what system tuning is needed based on system status records
> Track and evaluate user acceptance of the new system
> Determine and document what system and application function enhancements are needed
> Plan and schedule the system and application function enhancements
> Coordinate system function enhancements with vendors
> Design and develop required in-house application-function enhancements
> Determine when the system and/or application enhancements will be applied
> Apply the enhancements, once available, to the new system.

108   *Conversion Methodology*

N.T. Shivkumar
Curt Terwilliger
HCL America, Inc.

[Editor's note: There are many trans-border conversion houses besides HCL America, and many software alternatives to C-MILL. But of all papers submitted to the SIG-Mainframe competition, this one laid out in greatest detail the specific technical steps your Y2K remediation should try to pursue—even if yours is *all* manual and *all* in-house!]

This section describes in detail the conversion process:

> A. Survey
>   • Generation of reports defining the existing software.
>   • Identification of software which will require data conversion
>   • Location of problematic modules in the early stages of the process
>   • Creation of data base files which define the relationship between all programs at the site
>   • Definition of conversion Clusters (logical groups)
>   • Development of a detailed work plan for conversion of the site
> B. Enhancement
>   Enhancement of the databases created during Step A, to ensure their validity as input into the automated conversion process.
> C. Generation
>   Generation of all required control parameters for the conversion routines for the source code, copies, JCL, data files, etc.
> D. Conversion
>   Execution of the actual conversion of all relevant components at the site, including programs, data files, JCL, copies, etc.
> E. Test
>   Automatic creation of the test environment and execution of the tests at unit and system levels.
> F. Implementation
>   Controlled transfer of the converted system into production environment.

Phase A - Survey

The Survey phase is critical to the efficiency and reliability of the conversion process. This phase results in a number of essential products including:

> Detailed reports regarding date fields, software items, etc.
> Summary reports and statistics regarding date fields, software items, etc.
> Division of the software into conversion Clusters (logical groups), to support a prioritized phased conversion approach
> Creation of a database showing all program relationships and usage of date fields

The database files (Date database) which are created during the Survey phase serve as input to the subsequent phases of the conversion. Therefore, this phase is vital prior to proceeding with the conversion.

There are various inputs to the Survey and analysis phase, and for each site the inputs are defined in order to generate the appropriate output to support the conversion process.

The product reads and merges all of the input data which is defined for this phase and generates files and reports from this data. The inputs required include:

➤ Naming Conventions Used at the Site

After we understand the naming conventions used for all programs, files, and job names, we will need to set-up the utilities for reading system files. We will also use the naming conventions in the process of defining the conversion Clusters.

➤ Procedure Libraries and JCL

Analysis of these libraries result in the definition of the relationships between procedures, main programs, DD names, and Data Set names.

➤ Transaction and Program Control (Telecommunications Tables)

From the telecommunications tables we will be able to define the relationships between the transactions and main programs.

➤ Source/Copy/Load Libraries

In general we utilize the Source and Copy libraries in addition to control tables during this phase and only use the Load library in instances in which the Source or Copy libraries are incomplete. The data which is derived from the Source library includes date fields, relationships between programs and routines, copies, and data regarding relationships between programs and special file types (e.g., IMS segments).

➤ SMF Files

SMF files are scanned to identify the main programs which were active during this period. Some of these programs may not need to be converted.

➤ Additional Files

Additional data, such as file sizes, may be needed and will be generated as needed to support this process. These files may include: CA7, CA1, DMS, RACF, etc.

The Survey phase is an iterative phase which includes multiple simulations and adjustments

The major products of the Survey phase include:

➤ List of Programs Without Source Code [Editor: generally 7 percent in a sleepy IS shop]

As part of the Survey process, we will identify all programs which do not have available source code. For each program which does not have source code, a customized approach will have to be developed for undertaking the conversion where a reverse engineering approach would be likely.

➤ List of "Problem" Programs

Programs for which we may encounter conversion problems will be identified during the Survey process. Conversion problems may result from a number of factors: Programs which will require manual intervention (e.g., Assembler routines); Programs which have already been partially converted. These represent exceptions which an automatic conversion process will not be able to recognize and handle properly.

➤ Conversion Clusters [Editor: also called "clumps"]

A task as extensive and complex as Year-2000 program conversion must be undertaken in phases. One of the important requirements of the conversion process is to prioritize the applications based on different parameters. Therefore, it is necessary to perform the conversion in a phased fashion using convention Clusters.

A conversion Cluster includes one or more projects that share programs and/or data files, and have relatively little interface with other conversion Clusters.

This process will use as input the naming conventions of the projects and the logical relationships, to the extent to which they exist, between the projects. The process will result in a suggested optimized conversion approach for the conversion Cluster.

A conversion Cluster may be, in some instances, one project plus a number of programs from different projects.

With the formation of the conversion Clusters, an approach will also be developed regarding programs/data files which are shared between conversion Clusters. This issue will be an important factor in determining the work plan and timetable for the conversion. There are, however, a number of approaches to handling shared programs/data files, some of which are:

- Converted programs and routines may be placed in the STEPLIB library
- Data files may be duplicated
- A central I/O module may be created for handling data files
- Data files may be converted temporarily using SYSDA, while running a certain job

- Additional solutions are available for shared programs/files and will be selected during the Survey phase.

➤ Program Relationships at the Site

Program relationships do not refer to the field level, such as date fields, but rather at higher levels. During the Survey phase we will generate data base files and reports which will show such Relationships as:

- Programs - Routines (Programs tree)
- Program - Copies
- Transaction/Jobs - Programs and Files

For each file, input and output programs will be identified. Both files and segments are included in this process.

➤ Raw Data in Date Fields

In programs and in data files, the method for identifying date fields is as follows:

Understanding of naming conventions and review of essential file structures at the site in order to specify field names which are used for date fields

Completion of internal tables to search for dates, such as:

- INCLUDE LIST - strings which may include dates such as DAT, YY, YEAR, and other appropriate names. The INCLUDE LIST is divided into a list of fields which indicate the year and list of fields which indicate the date, in general (not only the year)
- EXCLUDE LIST - Sections of titles which, if they exist, do not include dates. For example, appearance of the word UPDATE, which includes DAT, would be reason for exclusion from the list of candidate fields.

A proprietary recursive algorithm derives all affected fields from all identified date fields.

The product receives the above lists as inputs and checks all source libraries and Relationship files as follows:

- Extracts all date fields that meet the INCLUDE LIST-EXCLUDE LIST criteria
- Extracts data fields

In addition to the existing field names in all programs / copy, we will retrieve their characteristics: offset of the year from the beginning of the field, and the instructions which are executed on the above date fields.

As an output of this process we will receive:

- Detailed reports listing date/year fields
- Summary reports showing the number of programs/data files which we identified, as requiring special treatment: change of file layout or change of application code.
- Data base files which include the data at a date field level to be used during the remainder of the conversion process.

Summary of the Survey Phase

For the purpose of performing the Survey phase, which comprises an initial and important phase of the conversion process, we will perform several activities, after consultations with Client personnel and study of work flows and Client's naming conventions. We will perform multiple iterations of some of these activities until the desired results are achieved.

For certain aspects of the survey, we will need to work together with Client personnel, while for other aspects we will work independently on our own dedicated computer equipment, or at Client site.

After completion of the Survey phase we will be able to submit a detailed work plan regarding each conversion Cluster which has been identified as targeted for conversion.

Phase B. Enhancement and Enrichment

The Enhancement phase is intended to complete the data in the Date fields database that was created during the prior phase.

There are some pieces of information which are not possible to collect automatically and thus define their characteristics. After review and correction of several data items it will be possible to conclude and correct additional date information (connected fields identified at the Survey phase). The data which may be missing includes:

- Offset of the year from the beginning of the date field
- Size of the year element in the date field
- Characteristics of the field after conversion

Work Method for the Enhancement Phase

Through ISPF screens we will adjust, with Clients assistance, the data in the Date and Relationship databases. After a set of adjustments have been entered, we will execute a Job to read the adjustments that were made in the Date field database and data from additional Relationship database and decide upon automatic changes of certain fields.

Enhancement

Specific elements of the Enhancement process may be executed completely automatically. Should Client determine that a date field in certain reports and inquiries can stay in two-digit year format, C-MILL will prepare the programs and Relationship database to indicate that these fields should remain with their current structure.

The Need for the Enhancement Phase

We are not able to determine automatically that all date fields will be expanded by two positions. Some existing files at the site are received from or sent to external computer centers, and some of the files are used by clients such as screens, reports, update screens, etc. In these cases it may be reasonable that these fields will not be expanded and it will be necessary to provide an application solution within the software itself.

These fields will be flagged for further processing through the next steps.

Phase C—Automatic Generation of Conversion

[Editor: If you're 100 percent in-house and 100 percent manual, *keep reading* anyway! Surely the authors wouldn't automate what follows if it weren't worth doing in the first place.]

After the completion of the Enhancement Phase and as of this phase, all remaining phases of the conversion project will be automatic. Programs without source-code and "problem programs," identified during the Survey Phase, will be handled manually. (Manual handling means in most of the cases the manual generation of parameters to be processed automatically in further phases).

The Input to this phase includes all data-bases created by previous phases. These databases will be used to generate control cards (commands). These control cards will function as routines for the software conversion, used as parameters for the conversion process.

Automatic conversion routines will be generated for the following components:

> ➤ Sequential and VSAM files

For each file, specific parameters for the conversion routine will be generated, based on data retrieved from the conversion databases.

➤ Backup files

It may not be necessary for all backup files to be converted to the new file format as some will use bridge routines, depending on expected usage.

➤ Parameters

For input parameters for utilities, such as SORT IDCAMS, etc., a routine will be generated for each member. The routine will update the SORT fields and the VSAM definition cards.

Members that include input files (as parameters for a program) that specify a date field will be dealt with as a standard file for conversion.

➤ Databases

Databases will automatically have an appropriate utility installed for them, which will implement the files UNLOAD and will convert the required records. (An example of file conversion would be the conversion of all the lists in a given segment.)

After conversion completion, a sort of records will take place, if necessary, as will the reLOADing of the file.

At the time of conversion, the DBD structure is changed and assembled.

➤ JCL Libraries/Procedures

Control cards for JCL conversions will be generated. The main subjects to be included in these libraries will be as follows:

- The addition of STEPLIB in some cases.
- Changes in file space sizes.
- Changes in the DCB of files (LRECL and BLKSIZE).

Documentation cards for JCL changes will be generated together with procedures for the Test Phase.

➤ Program Libraries and Copies

Source code libraries can be converted automatically, in a number of ways, according to the information recorded in the Date database.

There are several alternatives:

Should the year field size grow from two positions to four, control cards will be developed which will change the field definition in the Working Storage only. Data strings located in the Working Storage or in the Procedure Division will be altered as needed.

Should the date remain within a two digit structure, the application program will have to be revised. Application changes may deal with the following issues:

- The addition of interim fields to the program in the Working Storage
- The performance of a general routine within the system, which will identify the year beyond which it would be necessary to add 1900 and before which it would be necessary to add 2000.
- The establishment of fixed sections responsible for the computations and logical tasks for adding the century to the interim fields.
- Before each manipulative command on the date field (a manipulative command is a command which includes a comparison between date fields and/or a calculation with date fields) the following steps must be taken:
  - Transfer the date fields to the interim fields
  - Move to the special section created for the notation of the century
  - Leave the IF command with the interim variables defined

In cases where within a given program it is deemed necessary to make both conversions mentioned, both solutions will be utilized.

➤ Manual Revisions

In spite of all that has been said above, if at some point we are faced with a program that has been impossible to convert automatically, it will be dealt with individually.

Phase D - Physical Conversion of the System

All conversions will be made on a separate set of libraries, files and databases. There are a number of types of parameters which will be input:

➤ Global revisions of any kind of converted program, e.g. the addition of STEPLIB to every Step or the addition of comment cards to all programs converted

➤ Program conversion revisions concerning each program will be subject to conversion parameters

➤ Manual revisions will be subject to conversion parameters unique to each program when possible.

The physical conversion of a system will take place according to the order and priority decided upon in earlier phases concerning each Cluster of conversions (prioritization).

During the conversion of a Cluster, all the components of the program will be converted.

During conversion of a given Cluster, problematic areas may transpire, which means that in certain cases it will be necessary to apply changes to parallel files / jobs or due to shared resources. The conversion process will not be perfect, until these problematic areas are cleaned.

After completion of the conversion process, a final clean-up will be performed in which all STEPS created because of shared resources will have to be discarded.

Current Date Issue

We recommend the global conversion of the entire system for the reception of a date from the computer clock from one central routine, for the following reasons:

> Some programs are written in COBOL OS/VS and some in COBOL II. Assuming Client is in the process of converting to COBOL II, this will save the trouble of conversion from structure to structure later on.

> All the dates will be represented in a single structure for MMD-DYY/DDMMYY or MMDDYYYY/DDMMYYYY, depending on the routine parameters.

> This routine will be able to check the existence of "DD Dummy" and accordingly, will facilitate the decision whether to accept a real date from the computer clock or, alternatively, a date from the DD card. This subject is important for tests and is useful for tele-communication and batch programs.

Performing Compilations

Subsequent to the conversion of programs and Copies, it is necessary to compile and link the programs to separate Load libraries, so as to facilitate the tests.

C-MILL will automatically produce JCL cards for compilation and afterwards the SYSLOG will be read for the results of Compile and Link. For runs completed with RC=00, JES commands will be issued, canceling the SYSOUT. Jobs completed unsuccessfully will be analyzed manually to check for the problems and correct accordingly.

At this stage we may require the assistance of Client's technical staff in resolving compilation errors that are due to outdated copies or programs. Such fixes will be documented for future program refreshes.

Freezing and Refreshing Programs

There could be a time lapse between the time the program is first taken up and converted to the time it is moved into production. During this period of time, versions existing in the libraries could be changed and be different from to that stored in the converted library set.

As all stages of the conversion are made by automated tools, there is no reason not to make changes in the program up to the System Test Phase.

Any changes in the program will be discovered in automatic routine control checks and the program installed after conversion, will be refreshed automatically. In cases where the changes in the program did not involve the date fields, then the conversion program can simply be run through from the beginning. If date fields or new programs have been added, it will be necessary to refresh the Date Fields Database and then run through an updated conversion program.

[Editor: One strictly manual process you may want to investigate by survey, is the sharing/sending/receiving of files with external applications—or at least apps not accessible to the methods herein. What once was an innocent paper report or screen display may today take an electronic form that is "scraped" for data which are input to some unnoticed automated system.]

109   *Assessment Guide*

General Accounting Office

Every federal agency is at risk of widespread system failures. Because converting systems to a 4-digit year will be a massive undertaking for large systems, agencies must start now to address this problem. They need to identify their inventories of mission-critical computer systems, develop conversion strategies and plans, and dedicate sufficient resources to converting and adequately testing their computer systems and programs before January 1, 2000. The condensed guide is divided into five phases supported by program and project management activities: Awareness, Assessment, Renovation, Validation, Implementation. A full electronic version is available from http://www.gao.gov. Plan and manage the Year 2000 program as a single large information system development effort. Promulgate and enforce good management practices on the program and project levels.

Awareness

Assess the Year 2000 impact on the enterprise. Identify core business areas and processes, inventory and analyze systems supporting the core business areas, and prioritize their conversion or replacement. Develop contingency plans to handle data exchange issues, lack of data, and bad data. Identify and secure the necessary resources.

1. Define the Year 2000 problem and its potential impact on the enterprise.

   Provide executive management and staff with a high-level overview of the potential impact.

2. Conduct a Year 2000 awareness campaign.

   An important first step.

3. Assess the adequacy of the agency's program management capabilities, including policies, guidelines, and processes for program and project management, configuration management, quality assurance, and risk management staffing levels and skill mix.

   Success depends on the agency's system development and program management practices and its experience in managing large-scale software conversion or system development efforts.

4. Develop and document a high-level Year 2000 strategy.

   A roadmap for achieving compliance, it should discuss such key issues as the program's management structure, program metrics and reporting requirements, the mix of enterprise-wide solutions, and provide initial cost and schedule estimates.

5. Obtain and formalize executive management support through issuance of a Year 2000 policy directive/Year 2000 program charter.

   Formalize by the issuing a Year 2000 policy directive, and/or program charter. Without such support, information resource managers may not be able to mobilize adequate resources.

6. Establish a Year 2000 executive management council.

   Continually coordinate, and quickly resolve conflicts on priorities between programmatic and functional areas.

7. Appoint a Year 2000 program manager and establish an agency-level program office.

   Solutions extend beyond simple software conversion, hardware upgrades, and database restructuring; high dependencies among information systems; conversion and validation standards; inspection, conversion and testing tools; the need to coordinate the conversion of cross-boundary information systems and their components; establishment of priorities; and reallocation resources as needed.

8. Identify technical and management points of contact in core business areas.

   A Year 2000 program should not be viewed as a system development or maintenance effort. Technical and management staff of the core business areas must work closely with the year 2000 project teams in the assessment and testing process.

Assessment

Determine which systems are mission-critical and must be converted or replaced, which support important functions and should be replaced, and which support marginal functions, and may be handled later. The process must include assessments of the impact of systems' failures on core business areas and processes. It also must include non-IS, such as building infrastructure systems and telephone switching equipment.

1. Define Year 2000 compliance.
2. Focus on and develop a Year 2000 assessment document based on core business areas and processes.

   Information systems are not created equal. Establish priorities for the Year 2000 program.

3. Assess the severity of an impact of potential year 2000-induced failures.

   Failure assessment needs to be done for each core business area and associated processes.

4. Conduct an enterprise-wide inventory of information systems for each business area.

   Ensure that all systems are identified and linked to a specific business area or process, and that all enterprise-wide, cross-boundary systems are considered.

5. Use inventory data to develop a comprehensive automated system portfolio.

   Each system should identify links to core business areas or processes platforms, languages, and database management systems; operating system software and utilities; telecommunications; internal and external interface owners; the availability and adequacy of source code; and associated documentation.

6. Analyze the portfolio.

   Each system should identify non-repairable items (lack of source code or documentation) conversion or replacement resources required for each platform, application, database management systems, archive, utility, or interface.

7. Prioritize system conversions and replacements.

   Rank by key factors, such as business impact and the anticipated failure date. Also identify applications, databases, archives, and interfaces that cannot be converted because of resource and time constraints.

8. Establish multi-disciplinary project teams for business areas and major systems.

   Teams should contain domain experts in relevant functional areas, system and software specialists, operational analysis specialists, and contract specialists. Access to legal advice is also needed.

9. Develop a Year 2000 program plan.

   Include schedules for all tasks and phases of the master conversion and replacement schedule: identification of system components, assessment, selection of outsourcing options, assignment of conversion or replacement projects teams, risk assessment contingency plans for all systems.

10. Identify, prioritize, and mobilize needed resources—money and people.

    Make informed choices about IT priorities by assessing the costs, benefits, and risks of competing projects. In some instances, agencies may have to defer or cancel new system development efforts and reprogram the freed resources to achieve compliance. [Editor: See Figure 20.2]

11. Develop validation strategies and testing plans for all converted or replaced systems and their components. Identify and acquire automated test tools and develop test scripts.

    Regardless of the selected validation and testing strategy, the scope of the testing and validation effort will require careful planning and use of automated tools, including test case analyzers and test data libraries. [Editor: See Chapters 83 and 89.]

12. Define requirements for Year 2000 test facility.

    Agencies may have to acquire one to provide an adequate testing environment and avoid potential contamination or interference with the operation of production systems.

13. Identify and acquire Year 2000 tools.

    They facilitate the conversion and testing processes.

14. Address implementation schedule issues.

    Include the identification and selection of conversion facilities, time needed to put converted systems into production, and conversion of backup and archival data.

15. Address interface and data exchange issues.

    Include the development of a model showing the internal and external dependency links between enterprise core business areas, processes, and information systems; notification of all outside data exchange entities; data bridges and filters; contingency plans if no data are received from an external source; and validation process for incoming external data contingency plans for invalid data. [Editor: See Figure 25.2]

16. Develop contingency plans for critical systems and activities.

    Develop realistic contingency plans—including the development and activation of manual or contract procedures—to ensure the continuity of core business processes.

17. Identify vulnerable systems and processes outside the IS area.

    Develop a separate plan renovating telephone and network switching equipment, and building infrastructure systems. [Editor: clinical devices, too.]

Renovation

The renovation phase—conversion, replacement, or retirement—involves making and documenting software and hardware changes, developing replacement systems, and decommissioning eliminated systems. In all three cases, the process must also consider the complex interdependencies among applications, hardware platforms, databases, and the internal and external interfaces.

Make all changes to the information systems and their components under configuration management to ensure that changes are adequately documented and coordinated. Assess dependencies and communicate all changes to the information systems to internal and external users.

1. Convert selected applications, databases, archives, and related system components.

   Consider changes in operating systems, compilers, utilities, domain-specific program products, and commercial database management systems. [Editor: Minimize these due to complication and time cost.]

2. Develop data bridges and filters.

   Ensure that all internal and external data sources meet the year 2000 date standards. Develop bridges or filters to convert non-conforming data.

3. Replace selected applications, platforms, database management systems, operating systems, compilers, utilities, and other commercial off-the-shelf (COTS) software.

   Ensure that replacement products are compliant, including handling the leap year. Direct contract specialist and legal staff to review contracts and warranties.

4. Document code and system changes.

   Use configuration management procedures to ensure all changes to systems and components are properly documented and managed.

5. Schedule unit, integration, and system tests.

   Coordinate with other project teams to ensure that all components—including data bridges or filters—are available for testing.

6. Eliminate selected applications, platforms, database management systems, operating systems, utilities, and COTS software.

   Prepare to eliminate them upon the successful completion of acceptance testing.

7. Communicate changes to information systems to all internal and external users.

   Communicate specifically all changes to date formats for data exchanged with other systems or external organizations. Document changes through the configuration management process.

8. Track the conversion and replacement process and collect project metrics.

   Use project metrics to manage cost and schedule.

9. Share information among Year 2000 projects and disseminate lessons learned and best practices.

   Ensure that project staffs understand this need. Develop dissemination strategy and tools, such as intranet web sites and newsletters.

Validation

Agencies may need over a year to adequately test and validate, and this process may consume over half of the year 2000 program resources and budget. The length and cost are driven by the complexity inherent in the Year 2000 problem. Agencies must not only test compliance of individual applications, but also the complex interactions between scores of converted or replaced computer platforms, operating systems, utilities, applications, databases, and interfaces. Moreover, in some instances, agencies may not be able to shut down their production systems for testing, and may thus have to operate parallel systems implemented on a Year 2000 test facility. [Editor: See Chapters 25, 34, 40, 83, and 89.]

All converted or replaced system components must be thoroughly validated and tested to (1) uncover errors introduced during the renovation phase, (2) validate Year 2000 compliance, and (3) verify operational readiness. The testing should take place in a realistic test environment. A Year 2000 test facility may be required to ensure adequate testing of licensed software and converted applications while preventing the contamination or the corruption of operational information systems and related databases.

1. For each converted or replaced application or system component, develop and document test and compliance plans and schedules.

   Most suppliers of COTS software do not disclose their source code or the internal logic of their products, therefore, testing should be complemented by a careful review of warranties and/or guarantees.

2. Develop a strategy for managing the testing of contractor-converted systems.

   Any contract conversion must be adequately tested and closely managed to ensure that the contractor follows Year 2000 conversion standards.

3. Implement Year 2000 test facility.

   Testing the converted or replaced systems and their components for Year 2000 compliance will likely require an isolated test facility capable of simulating Year 2000 requirements. It should provide sufficient disk storage for large test databases and multiple versions of the application software.

4. Implement automated test tools and test scripts.

   They have the potential to significantly reduce the testing and validation burden. Test management tools may prepare and manage test data, automate comparison of test results, schedule, track incidents, and manage test documentation.

5. Perform unit, integration, and system testing.

   Include regression, performance, stress, and forward and backward time testing. [Editor: See Figure 25.1.]

6. Define, collect, and use test metrics to manage the testing and validation process.

7. Initiate acceptance testing on the Year 2000 test facility with duplicate databases to avoid risk to the production systems and the potential contamination of data.

   In this final stage, the entire information system—including data interfaces—is tested with operational data.

Implementation

Because of the scope and complexity of the conversion changes, integration, acceptance, and implementation will likely be a lengthy and costly process.

Since not all system components will be converted or replaced simultaneously, expect to operate in a heterogeneous computing environment comprised of a mix of Year 2000 compliant and non-compliant applications and system components. The reintegration of the Year 2000 compliant applications and components into production must be carefully coordinated to account for system interdependencies. Parallel processing—where the old and the converted systems are run concurrently—may be needed to reduce risk. [Editor: See Chapters 59 and 60.]

1. Define transition environment and procedures

   The transition will be difficult and complex. Some key components of the agency systems—Year 2000 compliant databases, operating systems, utilities, and other COTS products—may not be available until late 1998 or early 1999. External data suppliers may not plan to complete their conversion and testing until 1999. Third, the testing, validation, and correction processes may take much of 1999. Fourth, replacement systems may not be ready for testing until late 1999. As a result, agencies may be forced to operate—at least for a time—parallel systems and databases.

2. Develop an implementation schedule.

   The implementation schedule should indicate all major milestones and the critical path for the completion of the Year 2000 program.

3. Resolve data exchange issues and interagency concerns, including: ensuring that all outside data exchange entities are notified, data bridges and filters are ready to handle non-conforming data, contingency plans and procedures are in place if data are not received from an external source, contingency plans and procedures are in place if invalid data are received from an external source, the validation process is in place for incoming external data.

   All data issues and interagency concerns must be resolved prior to acceptance testing and implementation. Bridges and filters should be in place, as should contingency plans and procedures.

4. Deal with database and archive conversion.

   Because the conversion of large databases from 2-digit to 4-digit year fields is a time consuming effort, agencies may consider off-site conversion alternatives.

5. Complete acceptance testing.

   In general, formal testing uncovers about 80-90 percent of software errors, with the remaining 10-20 percent of errors discovered during operations. Complete acceptance testing no later than Fall of 1999, to allow sufficient timeforthecorrectionofsoftwareerrorsdiscoveredfollowingimplementation.

6. Develop contingency plans.

7. Unlike routine system development or maintenance efforts where schedule slippages are non-fatal—and common—the Year 2000 program must be completed on time. Develop realistic contingency plans—including the development and activation of manual or contract procedures—to ensure continuity of core business processes. Update or develop disaster recovery plans.

   All compliant systems—including the converted and replaced systems and related databases—should have disaster recovery plans in case of extended outage, sabotage, or natural disaster.

8. Implement converted and replaced systems.

   Reintegrate into the production environment.

part

Manager: Outsourcing

Now that you've finished this book, you UNDERSTAND MORE about Year 2000 Computing than typical vendor salespeople with whom you'll be negotiating. Hooray! That's exactly what SIG-Mainframe intended when we sent out the original Call for Papers (reprinted inside rear cover), then subsidized this book and the series of free conferences for major corporate and agency Y2K heads!

If you were to negotiate a Y2K outsourcing without this knowledge—many do!—you'd be buying a pig-in-a-poke. You'd be led to negotiate the wrong things in the wrong way and be left with inadequate controls, subject to nonperformance and/or ballooning costs. Gregory Cirillo's kickoff article is entitled, "Negotiating Your Y2K Assessment/Remediation Contract." The barrister is on-point in separating the survey-feasibility-estimate-plan phase from the later "do" phase. The former used to take half a year but today typically is finished in a month or two. Probably priced at less than a half million dollars even for large corporations, outsourcing this find-the-truth phase can be a bargain if you're the only one on your management team well-versed in Y2K—or the others don't possess the planning and interpersonal skills to obtain and organize really embarrassing findings without getting thrown down an elevator shaft.

The much larger "do" phase can often be handled with mostly in-house consultants and employees—as long as their project leaders are willing to program no-brainers and test more than they ever thought possible! However, if there are business reasons to leave your own coders alone, you'll need to use a separate "factory," either internal or outsourced.

Cirillo points out that your Y2K deliverables cannot be extended, almost-right or made up as you go along. You and everyone else will have to "triage:" Fix, replace, or ignore/toss. His and the next paper urge you to get a substantial company "on the hook" as guarantor of outsourced work.

Your editor *disagrees* with this last point because a college friend once got a disastrous result when she was operated on by a building. Maria could readily identify the prestige logo (Mayo Clinic) but none of the three consecutive individuals who made her nose what it is today! Don't swoon before vendor size or status! Human cloning won't produce adults before 2000, so the big outsourcers must use the same labor pool as the smaller ones. Therefore, either choose proven outsiders you have reason to trust, or at least satisfy yourself that the presented "expert(s)" actually ran a successful Y2K project at a referenceable customer. You'll be losing more than the cost of their on-the-job training, if they recommend an automated code analyzer and then prove too dumb or lazy to run it repeatedly with successive re-seedings. Whatever their prestige, why would you ever entrust such people with millions of dollars, not to mention the life or death of your organization?

Don't forget to re-read Cirillo before attending vendor presentations. For more on the law, see Part 6—especially Jeff Jinnett's Chapter 52.

Next, John Rovito expresses these and other issues in nine brief questionnaires: Management Commitment & Awareness, Technical Environment, Potential Legal Liabilities, Assessment & Conversion Tools, Project Methodology, Performing the Work In-House, Selecting an Outside Service Provider, Service Provider Project Management and Project Costs. (See also the Micro Focus Assessment Metrics Checklist in Part 3, Chapter 30.)

Paragon follows these with a set of open-ended questions on service provider background. (Ed: Like Cap Gemini's list in Chapter 32, they urge you away from smaller vendors. Don't automatically discard a trusted provider that has already done pressured conversions for you before.)

Finally, Gerhard Adam furnishes a questionnaire to be filled in for each software package you use. Is it compliant? If not, when will they make it so, and by what method? What support commitments will the vendor make?

[Editor: Don't be embarrassed out of requesting a full *component list* for each PC or other hardware product, requiring there be *no substitutions*, and getting the Y2K compliance status of *every* component. If they make fun of you because you inadvertently asked whether a cable was compliant, shrug it off and continue taking the steps necessary for enterprise survival.]

Novell's compliance description is included as an example of honesty. For enterprises with no mainframe platforms, "3Q98" (October) may be an acceptable conformance promise. Not so for mainframe-linked testing.

110 *Negotiating Your Remediation Contract*

Gregory Cirillo
Williams, Mullen, Christian & Dobbins

If you have succeeded in getting the attention of senior management, and you have been given the go-ahead to contract for assessment and assurance of your firm's system preparedness for the Year 2000 date change, then your next challenge will be negotiating with outside vendors offering analytical and remedial services.

The Y2K Remediation Industry

Where there is opportunity, you will find opportunists. The Y2K assessment/remediation industry is currently defining itself from a few different directions is evolving around the four principal talents required to assess and problem:

1. technical capabilities (including systems testing and code crunching),
2. project management capabilities (including project management, personnel management),
3. financial analysis—including tax-effects planning and accounting, and
4. legal assessment and negotiation capabilities.

Firms active in one or more of these industries are racing into the marketplace, and each contestant puts its own specialty in the forefront. As a consumer of these services, you should make certain that all four elements are represented and balanced in order to achieve an optimum result at lowest cost.

Contracting Concerns—Technical Capabilities

The technical aspects of the contract should cover systems testing, and an analysis of systems options ranging from system remediation to system replacement.

The remediation contract should include diagnostic testing to determine the scope of the problem and the required or recommended fixes. Specialists now estimate that 40–60 percent of the time and cost of remediation will be devoted to testing in the periods before, during and after remediation. If all problems are not identified in testing, the remediation process could be severely undermined. Testing results should result in the generation of an analysis of options and outcomes, including remediation time and resource commitment. Be cognizant of the inherent outcome bias that may creep into a remediation recommendation (with software resellers leaning toward system replacement, "code crunching" shops leaning toward system remediation, and lawyers recommending class action law suits against the developers of your systems). The recommendation should be a balanced result, considering all technical, financial, legal and timing factors. The recommendation should also be presented as a series of options so that your management response is not limited to merely the first option that has been formulated.

Defining Deliverables

> Y2K Remediation Contracts Should Integrate with your In-House Capabilities including:
> > Technical staff
> > Project management capabilities

> The Service Contract(s) Should Include:
> > Assessment
> > Remediation
> > Testing

> Services should be segmented/independent.

To be "fixed" a system must:

> Address, process, calculate and otherwise use dates from, on and past the Year 2000 without error.

> Maintain, without modification, an accurate date on all applicable software and hardware through the Year 20XX.

> Permit the full processing and other use of all data previously generated.

> Interoperate with specified, existing systems at all times through 20XX.

Contracting Concerns—Project Management

There is an immutable deadline in any Y2K remediation project. You cannot postpone the Year 2000.[1]Therefore, the remediation process must conform to a strict time line, with the understanding that slippage is unacceptable. This raises the issue of whether the project management can be entrusted to the same firm undertaking the technical testing and remediation. In any event, the remediation contract should provide for hard deadlines and incentives to meet or beat deadlines, as well as status reports that will identify time line slippage as soon as it occurs.

The contract should also describe the information systems ("IS") personnel needs and the manner in which personnel needs will be satisfied. The Y2K problem may create a personnel crunch, leaving remediation contractors with a demand far exceeding supply. To an extent, you may be required to devote a portion of your IS staff to the project. Keep in mind that this is not going to be glamorous or challenging work, and your IS staff may not be lining up for the assignment. Also consider your legal relationship with the individuals retained to undertake remediation. If a remediation contractor employs them, you may risk losing them if and when the contract relationship sours. A direct contractual relationship may provide leverage and security through completion of the project, and the ability to replace a weak link in the project chain without starting over. The downside of direct retention of Y2K programmers is the short-term, dead-end nature of their jobs. Costly employment disputes are like airliner crashes; they are the most likely to occur at the very beginning and the very end of the process. Y2K programmers are going to be hired and terminated en masse.

Contracting Concerns—Financial/Accounting Advice

Fix, replace, or ignore? Recommendations will all fall within one of these three categories. To make the correct decision, you must know: (1) the cost of each option, including likelihood of cost overrun; (2) the efficiencies achieved or lost by each option (e.g., efficiencies gained by system replacement or lost by ignoring the problem); (3) the likely actions to be taken by competitors and the resulting competitive advantages/disadvantages associated with matching their actions; and (4) the effect of each

---

1. Keep in mind that the Y2K problem will arise whenever your systems are required to address the Year 2000. This may occur much sooner than the Year 2000 if your system is prospective in function (e.g., a loan amortization or financial projections). Many financial organizations and municipalities are facing the issue now.

option on your financial statements (including ongoing compliance with lenders' financial covenants and regulatory requirements).[2]

Systems contracts typically:

➤   Flaunt designated deadlines
➤   Fudge or gloss over the details on deliverables (because we all know what we want—or we'll figure it out)
➤   Fudge or gloss over the breach and remedies procedures (because we all trust each other)

The Y2K contract will be different:

➤ The Deadline	➤ No extensions. ➤ No compromises. ➤ No such thing as "good enough."
➤ The Deliverable	➤ There is not time to "figure it out as you go."
➤ Delivery, Breach and Remedies	➤ Typical treatments of liability ($$$) are of limited value if your business is not ready.

Contracting Concerns—Legal Analysis

For any system that requires remediation or replacement, there may be a warranty breach entitling your company to replacement, upgrade or remediation. Even where no remedy is available, you may need source code access and other rights from the program developer in order to accomplish complete remediation through legal means.

The assessment process in any Y2K contract should consider potential legal remedies, and the various remediation options should consider and place a value and a cost on legal remedies and legal expenses.

> *The assessment phase should, upon completion, define the scope of work for remediation (including timelines), as well as the remediation alternatives and their estimated costs. The assessment report should be capable of transition to another vendor.*

---

2. As of the date of submission, FASB advises that the cost of system replacement can be capitalized, whereas system remediation costs must be expensed as incurred. Depending on your position, one accounting outcome may be preferable.

The Nuts and Bolts of the Contract

If the Y2K personnel crunch that is being predicted actually occurs, there may be many remediation firms left with contracts they cannot fulfill. There may be selective breaches, last-minute renegotiations, or bankruptcies. You cannot stop any of these events from occurring; however, you must make every conceivable effort to ensure that your contract is the last one breached. That is easy to say; in practice, it will depend on your bargaining power. Due to the nature of the problem (the "immutable deadline"), a breach can create an irreversible situation. In fact, the risk of breach should be factored into the remediation decision (e.g., system replacement may prove more reliable than remediation because breach is less likely to occur).

Take Me to Your Parents

It appears that many substantial firms are setting up special-purpose ventures or subsidiaries to enter into Y2K remediation contracts. A contract is only as strong as the party standing behind it. If a substantial parent will not sign, it should be asked nonetheless to guarantee performance. You are not necessarily looking for a deep pocket for a breach; rather, you are looking to make a breach as painful as possible.

What? Me? Breach!?!

> ➤ Even the best vendor may find itself over-committed, understaffed and under priced.

> ➤ Do not apply the "good guy" or the "valuable long-term business relationship" standard when negotiating the remedies sections of the Y2K remediation contract.

Easier said than done...

> ➤ Get a substantial company "on the hook" as contractor or guarantor.

> ➤ Lock-up (by direct contract) the personnel and subcontractors hired to do the job.

> ➤ Require prepaid errors and omissions insurance or a performance bond to protect you directly from the effects of a breach.

Time Lines and Progress Reports

Remediation within such a rigid time frame will require firms to produce realistic Time Lines and progress reports at each step in the process. You cannot be assured of remediation unless you are prepared to monitor carefully the work of these firms and to have qualified individuals to rely on in assessing performance. You can use Time Lines and progress reports not only as a management tool but also for information on how well the firm is complying with the remediation agreement.

Dealing with Deadlines in the Y2K Contract

> ➤   Agree to Clear Timelines.
>
> ➤   Mandate Status Reports.
>   Consider separating responsibility for project management from responsibility for project performance.
>
> ➤   Anticipate Slippage.
>
> ➤   Specify Staffing and Work Parameters.

Insurance Preparedness

You can use insurance to bolster the security of your Y2K remediation contracts. Any firm responsible for remediation of your Y2K problem should have errors and omissions ("E&O") insurance coverage to protect you against nonperformance by that company, including nonperformance that results in a complete or partial failure in completing the remediation contract successfully.

E&O insurance is generally a "claims made" insurance product, meaning that coverage will apply if the company is insured at the time that the claim for coverage is made (not when the error or omission occurs). Therefore, it is important that the insurance run through the last date on which any such failure could occur, which is certainly a date even after the Year 2000. Your agreement with any such firm should make E&O insurance mandatory throughout period, possibly with a requirement to prepay the policy; and it should also prohibit any cancellation or any alteration in the scope of coverage without notice to you. In time, we may see insurance companies limit the ability to buy this sort of protection, so it pays to move quickly.

Your insurance may not help you (Part I). Business interruption insurance will likely not protect you from losses arising from your Y2K problems because the cause of the loss is due to human errors or negligence and not natural forces.

Your insurance may not help you (Part II). Exclusions will begin to appear in insurance policies and addenda to policies specifically addressing the Y2K issue. In the late 1980s it was impossible for a savings and loan association to obtain director and officer liability insurance at reasonable rates. The probability and potential size of insurance claims were so high that insurance companies backed away from that market. It is possible that the same thing will happen in the Y2K arena. D&O coverage for lawsuits based on director/officer negligence in failing to address the Y2K issue may be excluded from coverage unless the insurance company (i) is made comfortable that your company is ready, and/or (ii) is compensated for the risk through higher premiums.

When the breach occurs...

> Traditionally, a breach triggers a stop in the contract, with nothing left to do but assess the damage.

> In Y2K contracts, every effort should be made to keep the project alive and moving unless the breach is "fatal."
> Maintain incentives to cure a breach and keep the project moving.
> Establish a fast-track remediation or arbitration process to address interpretive disputes.

Using Alternative Dispute Resolution

Disputes in the course of performance a Y2K remediation will be a disaster unless they are resolved quickly. Instead of engaging in costly and time-consuming litigation to obtain a remedy against a Y2K remediation firm, it may be advisable in most instances to seek alternative dispute resolution ("ADR"). That may achieve a more immediate result in making certain that you are protected in the event that the firm doesn't complete the job successfully. Therefore, it may be desirable for an agreement between you and the remediation firm to include a binding ADR provision. To accelerate the ADR process, you should agree to procedural rules (number and identity of arbitrators, length of proceedings) in advance.

111   _Questionnaires_

John Rovito
Paragon

Management Commitment & Awareness

	Yes	No	Not Applicable	Don't Know
Management does not think this is an urgent problem				
No one has been appointed to research problem				
No budget has been set for the current or following year				
Other companies in your industry have initiatives underway				
Other companies in your industry are Year 2000 ready				
Your industry is highly date sensitive				
Your industry has already experienced century date problems				
Your company's has already experienced century date problems				
Your company's fiduciary responsibility is high				
Management thinks this is a technical problem, not a business risk				
Management is not aware of the possible legal implications				
Management thinks this is a "turnkey solution"				
Management continually lowers the priority of the project				

Technical Environment

	Yes	No	Not Applicable	Don't Know
Environment is large and diverse				
There are many obscure or specialized languages				
There are numerous interfaces to internal systems				
There are numerous interfaces to external data sources				
There are numerous vendor packages				
Vendors have historically had poor performance on upgrades				
Vendor packages are not at the current release level				
Technical documentation is poor				
There are many user-developed programs				
Vendor packages have been modified by users				
Organization does not have up-to-date inventory of portfolio				
Some of your systems will potentially fail before Year 2000				
Systems with "Failure Potential" would have critical business impact				
Some vendor packages are no longer under maintenance contract				
Regression test bed does not exist				
More than 1 percent of code may be missing				

Potential Legal Liabilities

	Yes	No	Not Applicable	Don't Know
You have not fully documented your entire inventory				
A legal audit has not been performed				
Outside data enters your systems unfiltered				
New software is not warranted for Y2K compliance				
Licensed software prohibits 3rd-party modification				
Export encrypted software is being utilized				
Acquisitions are planned without Y2K due diligence				
Y2K project is not fully documented				
Y2K initiative is projected as being behind schedule				
You don't have adequate business disruption insurance				
You don't have adequate Directors & Officers insurance				
Your company won't disclose Y2K status on financial statements				

Assessment & Conversion Tools

	Yes	No	Not Applicable	Don't Know
Work will be performed manually				
Tool is not fully automated				
Tool is not expert-based				
Tool does not provide high level of accuracy				
Tool cannot be used for both assessment and conversions				
Tool has not been used successfully on previous projects				
References are not available				
Tool does not generate user-friendly reports				
Tool does not automatically generate bridges				
Tool does not automatically generate cost estimates				
Tool can only be used by tool vendor				

Project Methodology

	Yes	No	Not Applicable	Don't Know
Methodology does not address all activities critical to success				
Methodology is not modular and task-specific				
Methodology cannot be customized to your needs				
No fully documented milestones, reviews, sign-offs and deliverables				
There are no detailed tracking and reporting processes				
There is no documented vendor/ customer communications process				
There is no documented process for monitoring and controlling quality				
Methodology has not been used in similar types of projects				
Risk management is not documented				

Performing the Work In-House

	Yes	No	Not Applicable	Don't Know
Company has little experience with projects of similar size				
Company has little experience with projects of similar complexity				
Company has not delivered at least 90% of its project on time				
Company has not delivered at least 90%+ of its projects within budget				
Company has limited in-house resources to perform work				
Senior management is not visibly driving project				
Internal people are not enthused about the project				
Numerous development projects are scheduled or underway				
New development is typically done by external partners				
An inexperienced project manager would head project				
There is talk of "adding value" to the project				

Selecting an Outside Service Provider

	Yes	No	Not Applicable	Don't Know
Service provider has no Year 2000 experience				
Service provider has not managed similar conversion-type projects				
Service provider has no experience managing complex projects				
Service provider does not have a relationship with your company				
Service provider does not have a diversified "tool box"				
Service provider tools do not address a variety of languages				
Service provider has no testing tools				
Service provider does not offer any off-site options				
Service provider has less than a 15% annual growth rate				
Service provider has been in business for less than five years				
Service provider is financially suspect				

Service Provider Project Management

	Yes	No	Not Applicable	Don't Know
Provider does not have experience managing complex projects				
Provider has no documentation for projects delivered on schedule				
Provider has no documentation for projects delivered within budget				
Provider does not provide a senior subject matter expert for your project				
Provider does not provide a senior liaison officer for your project				
Project managers have not been employed by provider for at least 6 months				
Project managers do not have a minimum of ten years experience				
Provider does not have a documented quality system				
Provider does not have a documented Y2K risk management program				
Project managers do not have good interpersonal skills				

Project Costs

	Yes	No	Not Applicable	Don't Know
Service provider's price is 50% or more below average bid				
Service provider's price is 50% or more above average bid				
Service provider's price is not itemized for each phases of the project				
Management approaches cost on a per diem staffing basis				

Service Provider Background

> *What is your experience with Year 2000 projects?*

Companies that have extensive Year 2000 experience provide the lowest risk. The next level of acceptance should be firms who have experience with similar projects, preferable conversions and platform migrations. If a firm does not have experience with either of the above, the red flags should go up.

> *What level of service do you provide?*

A service provider may have Year 2000 experience, but unless they can take you straight through to conversion and implementation, they may not be the most efficient solution. For example, if a company only does assessments of the date occurrences, their assessment may not be usable to by other service providers who may need to either re-run the code through their own tools or, at a minimum, validate the first company's findings which will add to the cost.

> *What is your project management experience?*

The most critical factor in a successful Year 2000 initiative is project management. A service provider should have a range of experience with engagements of similar size and complexity. They should utilize experienced managers who receive in-depth training on the tools and methodologies utilized in your initiative. They should deliver a minimum of 90%+ of their projects on time, within budget, and with all requirements met.

> *Are you willing to perform a pilot of your solution?*

A pilot program (either assessment and/or conversion) reduces your risk by requiring the service provider to prove the viability of their methodology and tools. A good pilot should be small and inexpensive, yet representative of the overall portfolio in terms of application size and complexity.

> *What makes your company different?*

Everyone seems to have a story to tell. Unfortunately, for most it's the same old story. Look for differentiators that add value and reduce risk—things like expert-based tools, flexible methodologies, service delivery options, risk management processes, quality assurance systems, etc.

Assessment Services

> *Which languages will your tool(s) support?*

Most technical environments utilize more than one language. It's important that a service provider not be limited by one tool, but possess a variety of automated tools that can address many of these languages. Automated conversion tools will lower your costs, improve the accuracy of your conversion, and shorten your project's lifecycle. Equally important, they will help minimize manual intervention which research shows will introduce new, non-Year 2000 defects due to human error.

> *What kinds of output does your assessment tool(s) provide?*

It's important that you can use a tool's output to help you move on to the next phase of your project. The results should be categorized (example: data vs. code). Complexity of conversion effort should also be indicated. Tools should provide detail line of code, files affected, copybooks affected, date occurrences by program, level of complexity for manual conversion, etc.

> *is the output stored in a proprietary of a standard database?*

For a larger organization, using more than one service provider can diversify your portfolio and lower your risk. For such a strategy to be successful, it's necessary for all providers to share information. Proprietary databases and tools make this difficult.

> *Does your tool show interdependencies among programs, data stores, etc?*

After the initial assessment identifies date occurrences, the next step is to decide (a) what to change (b) how to change it (c) and in what order to make the revisions. You therefore need to know the ramifications of each potential change. Understanding which programs use what data, copybooks and files is essential. Tools should trace date effects across programs and jobs.

> *On what hardware & operating systems will your tool run?*

A Year 2000 conversion should not be a drain on the CPU or require the purchase of additional hardware. A tool should therefore be able to run in a stand-alone environment.

Assessment Services

> *Can the tool be run at your site? The company location? Is this optional?*

By offering the option of performing the work off-site, the service provider eliminates potential strains on your physical space requirements. The option of off-shore delivery can significantly reduce your costs — but only if the provider can provide documented quality-driven tracking and reporting processes that enable you to monitor and control risk.

> *What resources do you expect the client to provide during analysis?*

Many service providers perform only the assessment phase of the process, leaving analysis and the final business decisions to the client. Unless you have complete confidence in your ability to understand the potential impact of all date occurrences as well as the most efficient solution for addressing each type, an assessment-only arrangement can increase your risk. If, however, you choose to leverage a service provider's Year 2000 expertise, make sure that the firm has the necessary business application knowledge. If they do not, you again increase your risk.

> *Describe your project methodology.*

Year 2000 methodologies should be comprehensive, yet flexible enough to be customized to the requirements of your individual technical environment. The methodology should be proven successful on projects of similar size and complexity. Comprehensive means everything — JCL, screens, databases, control cards, source code, copybooks, etc.

> *How do you deal with missing components?*

The best tools are able to identify missing source code, copybooks, etc.

Conversion Services

> ➤ *Does your tool create bridge programs to convert data to be received?*
>
> Data bridge programs are often required to convert date with dissimilar formats. Bridges will also need to be created between converted and not-yet-converted programs and systems. To do so manually would not only add time and cost, but may introduce additional defects due to human error.
>
> ➤ *How does your tool deal with data keys which need to be modified?*
>
> The service provider's tool(s) should be able to identify which sorts and databases need to be changed based upon the date correction technique selected.
>
> ➤ *What other conversion methods do you provide?*
>
> For some environments, it may be advantageous to utilize a variety of date conversion methods across the portfolio. These may include field expansion, packing, time windows, and century indicators. Tools should possess this flexibility.
>
> ➤ *How do you address version merging?*
>
> If the Year 2000 methodology and tools do not support version merging, then each system must be "frozen" from maintenance activity during the conversion process.

Testing Services

> *What assistance do you provide for testing converted programs and dates?*

Testing is the largest portion of your Year 2000 initiative, accounting in many instances for up to 40–60% of the entire project. If you do not have the in-house expertise to take on the testing, it's important to know if the vendor has a proven and documented methodology and tools to support Year 2000 testing. Does the service provider have the subject-matter expertise needed during testing? What references can they provide? Can the provider perform validation and intersystem testing? Can the provider create the test data and test cases?

> *Can you simulate event horizon dates for testing?*

Applications containing date logic are usually driven in two ways (1) by the system date (2) by the dates contained in the data. The service provider should be able to simulate the event horizon in order to test the dates for Year 2000 readiness.

> *Does your testing include those programs addressed by bridges?*

Many bridges may be required in a large, segmented portfolio. Each bridge may need to operate efficiently for several months during the conversion process. The testing process should therefore address the "application/bridge" combination to ensure data integrity between programs and systems.

Training & Support

> Does Your Company Perform All Critical Tasks or Use Subcontractors?

The lowest risk is attached to those service providers who have experienced and trained in-house resources. If the service provider utilizes subcontractors, you need to understand the depth of their training as well as the control processes employed to ensure the quality of their performance.

> Do You Provide Training in Your Tools & Methodology?

If you are performing the conversion jointly with the vendor, how will they train your in-house staff in the tools and methodologies utilized in the initiative? If the service provider is assuming full responsibility, you need to know the depth of the training provided to their staff. The last thing you want is "experts" who engage in on-the-job training.

Miscellaneous

> *What is your experience in Year 2000 and other conversions?*

- Number of customers under contract

- Number of customers in our industry

- Number of conversions completed

- Total client conversions

- Applications completed

- Lines of code or programs in largest application completed

- Languages of completed applications

> *What are your licensing options?*

- Per program

- Per line of code

- Fixed fee

- Per diem

> *Do you have a quality management system?*

A Quality Management System should address all areas of a Year 2000 initiative. It can serve as an excellent form of risk management, especially in the strategic assessment of tools, resources and methodologies. It will also provide a control over the progress and integrity of the actual project. A service provider's system should be documented, understood, and practiced by all members of their team. Third-party certified systems such as ISO 9000 are a definite plus.

> *What is your Year 2000 risk management methodology?*

A Quality Management System is an excellent means for assessing and minimizing risk. In the absence of such a system, the service provider should have a documented process or methodology to identify and control all areas of risk attendant to a Year 2000 initiative.

112 *Product Questionnaire*

Gerhard Adam
Syspro, Inc.

The purpose of this questionnaire is to provide the guidance necessary to estab-lish the level of readiness in vendor products for year 2000 support. Where applicable a brief explanation of the question's intent has been provided for clarification.

1. Product name: _____

2. Vendor: _____

3. Is *installed* release of product year 2000 compliant?   Yes ☐   No ☐

   If **NO**, proceed directly to question 6.

The next two questions are intended to determine whether there is a vendor pro-vided mechanism for validating year 2000 compliance, or whether this is something which must be addressed as a separate project.

4. Is there a testing/validation method available from the vendor?

   Yes ☐   No ☐

5. Is there a specific testing/validation method recommended by the ven-

   dor? If so, specify _____

   _____

Proceed to technical strategy questions.

6. Is there a current release of product which is compliant?

   Yes ☐   No ☐

   If **YES**, proceed directly to technical strategy questions.

7. When is product scheduled for a compliant release?

8. Is the current year 2000 strategy known?   Yes ☐   No ☐

   If **NO**, then vendor is not ready, and product should be carefully reviewed.

Technical Strategy

The next set of questions focuses on the specific technique used to achieve year 2000 compliance. Since different techniques will have different ramifications it is important to get as specific an answer as possible to these questions.

9. What technique was used to achieve compliance?

   ☐ Two-digit to four-digit conversion
   ☐ Windowing techniques
   ☐ Date encoding techniques

Proceed to appropriate section (all that are checked).

Two-digit to four-digit conversion

This technique requires that all date references in data files be expanded to the full four-digits. A conversion is necessary to provide the century indicators (i.e.: "19") for all existing records. In addition, it will be necessary to convert files and programs simultaneously so a migration plan is essential.

10. Is there a conversion tool available for all data files affected?

   Yes ☐   No ☐

11. Does the product documentation provide a migration plan?

   Yes ☐   No ☐

Proceed to evaluation section.

Windowing

Windowing techniques (static or sliding) do not require file conversions, however it is impossible to determine the century outside the program logic employing the technique. In other words if the window consists of the range from 1950 to 2049, the program would check for two-digits greater than or equal to fifty (50) and use "19" for the century. If the two-digits were less than fifty (50) the century would be "20." While this technique can work within an application, it would be impossible for a user to download this file into a spreadsheet and determine the proper century without knowing the precise window used within the application program.

12. Does the product documentation provide information on how the technique was used?

   Yes ☐   No ☐

13. Is there a recommended testing procedure to validate year 2000 compliance?   Yes ☐   No ☐

Testing of windowing techniques is extremely difficult since an error would be virtually undetectable unless actual year 2000 dates were used for testing.

14. Will test databases and/or data be provided?   Yes ☐   No ☐

15. Will documentation be provided for handling data which may be transferred to other systems (i.e. PC file transfers)?   Yes ☐   No ☐

Proceed to evaluation section.

Date encoding

This technique attempts to set "bits" or provide a binary representation of the date to avoid expanding the date fields in files. This approach has numerous caveats which need to be carefully reviewed. File transfers may be impossible because of imbedded binary data in files. If special binary codes are used to represent the date, then file conversions would have to be performed to make all current data compatible with this technique. Testing is equally difficult because of need to use year 2000 data to validate that the program's logic is operating as intended.

16. Does the product documentation provide information on how the technique was used?   Yes ☐   No ☐

17. Is there a conversion tool for all data files affected?   Yes ☐   No ☐

18. Is there a recommended testing procedure to validate year 2000 compliance?   Yes ☐   No ☐

19. Will test databases and/or data be provided?   Yes ☐   No ☐

20. Will file transfer utilities be provided for movement to other systems?   Yes ☐   No ☐

Proceed to evaluation section.

Evaluation Section

21. What options are available in the event problems are discovered with the strategy chosen by the vendor?

_____

_____

_____

22. What commitments is the vendor prepared to make regarding year 2000 support?

_____

_____

_____

Upon completion of this questionnaire, a better understanding of the vendor's product and/or intentions should be achieved. It is not the intent of this questionnaire to place pressure on a vendor, but rather to promote an understanding of the exposures and migration considerations when addressing year 2000 compliance in purchased products.

Note: There are numerous ways in which technical solutions may be employed, and this questionnaire is not exhaustive. While this document can assist in improving the process of planning for the year 2000 conversion, it is not intended to replace more formal project planning and technical reviews.

Biographies

About the Editor

Dick Lefkon

A speaker on the coming Year 2000 crisis since 1970, Dick Lefkon was an Editorial Board co-founder of *Year 2000 Journal* and was then selected by Auerbach Publishers to run its prestigious monthly, *The Year 2000 Practitioner.* Manager Lefkon ran the first pair of Year 2000 Factories (1984–86), presented the first Y2K awareness paper at a refereed symposium (1991 NCSC), and originated NYU's trailblazing course, Year 2000 Best Computing Practices. He's managed or advised technically at Citibank, Dean Witter, BONY and Equitable. Invited as expert witness before the U.S. House of Representatives Technology Committee, Dick's spoken on four continents and earned BYTE's readers' best-of-year award, for networks analysis. The American Management Association has distributed Y2K consultant Lefkon's eighty topic hardware/software assessment kit, to AMA's 25,000 IT members.

Mr. Lefkon's recent Year 2000 related consulting assignments include:

- PMO. Strategic Planning of Y2K Projects. Contract/RFQ Writing, Screening.
- Assembling Y2K-Expert Teams: CIO/CEO-Advice, Evaluation, Defect Cure.
- Designing, running Automated Testing for Y2K Compliance Certification.
- Direct management of Project Staff or Project Leaders; and their training.
- Tool Selection. Large-Scale Project Planning, Hiring and Scheduling.
- Technical Troubleshooting of elusive mainframe and network glitches.
- Client-site delivery of 2-day conference contents as NYU course X53.9807.

Professor Lefkon holds the AB in mathematics from Columbia and MS (ABD) in General Relativity from the University of Pittsburgh. He has taught (and coded) platforms such as MVS, UNIX, VMS, AS400 and DOS/NT; software including C/C++, COBOL, FORTRAN, PL1; CICS, IDMS, IMS, DB2; Oracle and Sybase. Matching his NYU and AMA courses in Cost Accounting and Project Management, are over 30 articles on "Speeding Software Delivery" and similar topics. Among college and trade textbooks are *Understanding CICS Internals, Selecting a Local Area Network, Safe Computing,* and *Statistics for Management and the Helping Sciences.*

About the Presidents

Kathryn D. Jennings
SIG-Mainframe President

Kate Jennings was a cofounder of SIG-Mainframe in 1988. A leader in education, she organized our track at the 1996 Council of CIOs, Denver. Fluent in computer languages, Braille, and Spanish, Ms. Jennings leads technical retainers at the University of Phoenix. A recognized Year 2000 keynoter, she is also a co-author of this book.

Patrick J. Hagan
Chapter 368 President

Patrick Hagan has nearly 20 years of COBOL/BAL/BASIC programming experience. Currently consulting at Chase Manhattan Bank, he is an experienced system programmer as well as financial applications specialist. Pat's previous clients include National Railway, Metropolitan Life, and the New York Federal Reserve. Mr. Hagan is co-editor and a co-author.

Directory

Contacting the Co-Authors

Gerhard Adam	(248) 657-2826	Dick Lefkon	(212) 539-3072
Joseph Allegra	(800(457-7076	Mike Lips	(800) 234-1528
Christos Andritsoyiannis	+301 813-6358	Robert Louton	(610) 277-3535
Tom Backman	(617) 271-2725	Robin Marrin	(352) 392-1285
Courtney Bailey	(202) 408-4000	Brenda McKelvey	(613) 759-6912
Larry Baltezore	(916) 322-1148	Miro Medek	(703) 610-1835
Richard Bergeon	(425) 688-1000	Micro Focus	(650) 938-3700
Judy Brand	(800) 543-2606	Daniel Miech	(800) 837-2797
William Brew	(415) 494-6201	Jerome Murray	(212) 337-6013
Cap Gemini	(732) 906-0400	Marilyn Murray	(212) 337-6013
James Cappel	(517) 774-3554	Jerry Nelson	(612) 475-8495
Harold Carruthers	(314) 515-7322	NIST	(703) 487-4650
Chris Casey	(404) 523-0205	Ken Orr	(913) 228-1200
Greg Cirillo	(202) 371-0472	Richard Painter	(607) 757-9778
Compuware	(248) 737-7300	Bill Payne	(972) 530-4790
Gregory Daich	(801) 777-8057	Platinum Technology	(630) 620-5000
Andrew Eldridge	(610) 277-3535	Stan Price	(205) 345-1841
Ernst & Young	(212) 773-3000	Bryce Ragland	(801) 546-2597
Don Estes	(781) 860-5277	John Reda	(201) 930-8260
Doc Farmer	(+44) (171) 711-3120	Warren Reid	(818) 986-8842
Timothy Feathers	(816) 221-0355	Randall Rice	(405) 692-7331
Sanford Feld	(888) 588-1999	John Rovito	(908) 709-6767
Ted Fisher	(404) 586-2304	Phil Scott	(972) 488-8401
Michael Gerner	(+44) (123) 256-1000	N. T. Shivkumar	(203) 326-3004
Cesar Gonzalez	(210) 913-2993	SyncSort	(201) 930-8260
Bill Goodwin	(800) 643-8425	Curt Terwilliger	(408) 523-8319
Milt Habeck	(414) 681-3111	Rita Tragesser	(609) 654-8070
Patrick Hagan	(212) 818-9092	John Trewolla	(913) 648-5522
Tom Hartman	(972) 448-3627	Yngvar Tronstad	(408) 943-0630
Isogon	(212) 376-3200	Viasoft	(602) 667-2827
ITAA	(703) 522-5055	Bill Wachel	(214) 333-6221
Kathryn Jennings	(760) 665-8124	John Westergard	(212) 947-3853
Jeff Jinnett	(212) 424-8000	Harold Zbiegien	(216) 252-7300
Capers Jones	(617) 273-0140	Jim Zetwick	(614) 841-0640
Ira Kasdan	(202) 342-5200		

1996 Original Announcement of Best Practices Competition and Book

Kathryn Jennings
AITP SIG-Mainframe

(adapted from summer/fall 1996 issues of *Information Executive* and other publications, including Internet lists)

Every major data center in the world is now—or will soon be—running a large-scale "Year 2000" programming project. For most companies and governments, it will be the first time a dangerous bug lurking in potentially every line of code must be found and fixed in older "legacy" systems. Here's why.

Anyone who will graduate in the "Class of 98" knows it's unnecessary to say "nineteen" before the class date because the millennium and century are obvious from the context. In computing's first few decades it was not only obvious but often necessary to drop the extra two digits due to physical constraints on memory and storage.

As the Year 2000 draws near, such economies aren't just unnecessary, they're downright dangerous! For instance, some product deliveries made on New Year's Eve of 1999 will print out the next day as having reached the loading dock 99 years earlier. To see this, just drop the first two digits of "2000" and then subtract 99 from it! Similarly, ten years of bank interest gains might suddenly become 90 years' worth of losses. *A real problem.*

This fall, DPMA/AITP's Special Interest Group (SIG) for Mainframe Computing will construct a compendium of position papers and approaches to solving this critical problem. Complimentary copies will be sent to each contributor, to SIG-Mainframe members, and to key technical leaders of government agencies and members of the U.S. Senate and House Committees on technology.

All readers are invited to contribute, as are their organizations. From official policies/procedures to pinpoint analyses and recommendation, substantive submissions between two and forty pages will be accepted and published in the "Year 2000" book. *Please note, previously published materials are also acceptable.*

Association of *Information Technology Professionals* Membership Application

Please complete all sections of the application *(PRINT LEGIBLY OR TYPE)*	☐ CDP ☐ CCP ☐ CNA	☐ CSP ☐ ASP ☐ CNE

☐ Former Member

Name: First   Last   Initial

Employer Name: Your Title   Dept./Div.

Employer Address: City   State/Prov.   Zip+4/Postal

Home Address: City   State/Prov.   Zip+4/Postal

Send Mail To: ☐ Home   ☐ Company

Business Phone: Home Phone:

FAX (if any):   E-Mail Address (if any):

Association Dues: $80.00

Chapter Dues Waived: $0.00 for Financial Industries Chap
Processing Fee Waived: $0.00 for Financial Industries Chap
Total: $80.00 ($96 Canadian)

Payment by: ☐ VISA   ☐ MC   ☐ Check   ☐ Money Order

Card Number   Expiration

I hereby make application for membership in AITP. I agree to comply with the requirements of the Bylaws and Code of Ethics and all regulations adopted by the Association.

Applicant's Signature   Date   Sponsor's Name

AITP, Box 885 Wall Street Station, New York, NY 1005
(800) 224-9371   FAX: (212) 734-4431

AITP Code of Ethics

I acknowledge:

That I have an obligation to management, therefore, I shall promote the understanding of information processing methods and procedures to management using every resource at my command.

That I have an obligation to my fellow members, therefore, I shall uphold the high ideals of AITP as outlined in Association Bylaws. Further, I shall cooperate with my fellow members and shall treat them with honesty and respect at all times.

That I have an obligation to society and will participate to the best of my ability in the dissemination of knowledge pertaining to the general development and understanding of information processing. Further, I shall not use knowledge of a confidential nature to further my personal interest, nor shall I violate the privacy and confidentiality of information entrusted to me or to which I may gain access.

That I have an obligation to my employer whose trust I hold, therefore, I shall endeavor to discharge this obligation to the best of my ability, to guard my employer's interests, and to advise him or her wisely and honestly.

That I have an obligation to my college or university, therefore, I shall uphold its ethical and moral principles.

That I have an obligation to my country, therefore, in my personal, business, and social contacts, I shall uphold my nation and shall honor the chosen way of life of my fellow citizens.

I accept these obligations as a personal responsibility and as a member of this Association, I shall actively discharge these obligations and I dedicate myself to that end.